The ency
reli
ritu als

The Routledge encyclopedia of religious rites, rituals, and festivals

Frank A. Salamone, Editor

Religion & Society
A Berkshire Reference Work

Routledge
Taylor & Francis Group
NEW YORK AND LONDON

First published as *Encyclopedia of Religious Rites, Rituals, and Festivals* 2004 by Routledge

This edition published in paperback as *The Routledge Encyclopedia of Religious Rites, Rituals, and Festivals* 2010 by Routledge
270 Madison Ave, New York, NY 10016

Simultaneously published in the UK and ROW by Routledge
2 Park Square, Milton Park, Abingdon, OX14 4RN

Routledge is an imprint of the Taylor & Francis Group, an informa business

Printed and bound in Great Britain by CPI Antony Rowe, Chippenham, Wiltshire

British Library Cataloguing in Publication Data
A catalogue record for this book is available from the British Library

Library of Congress Cataloging in Publication Data
Encyclopedia of the religious rites, rituals, and festivals/ Frank A. Salamone, editor.
p. cm – (Routledge encyclopedias of religion and society)
"A Berkshire Reference work"
Includes bibliographical references and index.
1. Religions - Encyclopedias. 2. Rites and ceremonies – Encyclopedias. I. Salamone, Frank A. II. Series.
BL31.E47 2004
2039.8903-dc22
2003020389

ISBN13: 978-0-415-94180-8 (hbk)
ISBN13: 978-0-415-88091-6 (pbk)

Contents

Editorial Advisory Board

List of Entries

Introduction

Scholars of religion have yet to agree on just what ritual is. They also have yet to agree on the boundary (if such a boundary exists) between religious ritual and secular ritual. To some extent ritual is one of those phenomena that falls under the heading of "you know it when you see it." Despite the absence of a definition—or perhaps because of the absence—ritual has drawn much attention from religious studies scholars, anthropologists, historians, sociologists, psychologists, and other experts. Perhaps this is because ritual is often the most visible manifestation of religion and the one that first comes to the attention of outside observers.

Ritual is an enormously large and complex topic. Ritual is not static; it has varied enormously over the course of human history and across cultures. The anthropological literature is filled with detailed descriptions and analyses of rituals of several thousand cultures around the world. This means that no reference work on rituals can be truly encyclopedic because there is simply too much to cover. Nonetheless, we have chosen to be broad and inclusive in our coverage in this encyclopedia, not only covering a broad range of topics but also providing summaries of the knowledge on rituals developed by scholars from a broad range of disciplines. These scholars include anthropologists, sociologists, theologians, religious studies specialists, historians, folklorists, popular culture experts, and philosophers. This inclusiveness provides a number of perspectives that enable the reader to profit from diverse views on religion and ritual. The encyclopedia examines the relationship between secular ritual and religious ritual, between rituals and beliefs, and the manner in which rituals are used to attain practical goals. Authors provide insight into world and local religions and examine the major theories that help explain religion and ritual.

Anthropology and the Study of Religion and Rituals

Although many scholarly approaches contribute to this encyclopedia, anthropology is in the forefront because it has had a profound influence on the manner in which other scholars view religion and ritual. Anthropology has its roots deep in the field of religion, its rituals, and its performances. Its earliest scholars, such as E. B. Tylor, Sir Henry Maine, Fustel de Colanges, and Lewis Henry Morgan, sought the origins of religion and along the way discovered a great deal about religion and its relationship to culture. E. B. Tylor (1832–1917) is generally regarded as the father of the anthropology of religion. Tylor is best known for his evolutionary theory of religion, proposing stages of religious development that correspond to stages of material development. Other scholars proposed other evolutionary theories, and along the way these scholars also left their marks on the field of the anthropology of religion and religious studies in general. Sir James Frazer's (1854–1941) comparative mythologies still inspire work today, as does the stimulating work of R. R. Marett (1866–1943).

Although these scholars inspired a formidable body of work, the general foundation of the modern study of ritual in anthropology, history, sociology, religious studies, and related fields rests on the work of the grand thinkers of the nineteenth century—the French sociologist Emile Durkheim, the German sociologist Max Weber, the German political philosopher Karl Marx, and the Austrian neurologist Sigmund Freud. Durkheim (1858–1917) stressed the importance of understanding religion as being comprised of "social facts" that support the maintenance of social solidarity; that is, they hold society together. His nephew and successor, Marcel Mauss, and his student Lucien Levy-Bruhl added important concepts to the study of religion. Mauss put forward the idea of gift giving, an important component of many rituals, and its role in building reciprocal relationships in society. Levy-Bruhl focused on so-called primitive religion and what he termed "pre-logical" thought. The French sociologist Arnold Van Gennep (1873–1957) wrote the influential *Rites de Passage* looking at rituals of transformation.

German scholars made major contributions to the study of religion and religious rituals and performance. Max Weber (1864–1920) noted relationships between the social sphere and the economic sphere of human activity. Karl Marx (1818–1883) centered his studies on spiritual alienation resulting from unequal distribution of economic resources and the role of religion in perpetuating this inequality. The Austrian Sigmund Freud (1856–1839) provided insight into the world of rituals, including religious rituals. He also examined the ties between religious experience and biological and social instincts and drives.

Each of these scholars demonstrated the ties between religion and ritual and other realms of life. In doing so they helped develop ways to study religion and integrated those ways into other fields, making religion more comprehensible to students.

The German diffusionist school has had a major impact on the U.S. field of religious studies. That school, originated by anthropologist Father Wilhelm Schmidt (1868–1954), opposed the basic premises of the English and French evolutionary schools. The diffusionists argued that cultural similarities usually result from diffusion from the original place of invention to other places. Franz Boas, often seen as the father of U.S. anthropology, insisted on the primacy of culture over other factors in his work. Along the way he influenced and inspired generations of U.S. anthropologists down to the present.

In England, Bronislaw Malinowski (1884–1942) carried on the fight against cultural evolutionists, insisting on the importance of solid ethnography (cultural study) over abstract theory. Malinowski tried to establish the validity of Frazer's distinction among magic, science, and religion. The British social anthropologist A. A. Radcliffe-Brown (1881–1955) added to the work of his time in understanding the role of religion in society by establishing the connection between myth and the maintenance of the natural order of things. In a direct line with Boas, Malinowski, and Radcliffe-Brown, the British anthropologist E. E. Evans-Pritchard (1902–1973) struggled against the dichotomy between "primitive" and modern religions. The old distinctions between concepts such as monogamy and promiscuity, white and brown, and animists and monotheists made no sense in light of the data coming from fieldwork.

Current studies in the anthropology of religion have many trends. The works of scholars such as Claude Levi-Strauss, Mary Douglas, Clifford Geertz, Melford Spiro, and Victor Turner put a greater stress on the understanding of ritual. The role of psychoanalysis has remained strong, and the works of Freud and the French psychoanalyst Jacques Lacan (1901–1981) are important in contemporary arguments. At the same time studies using the insights of Durkheim and Weber have continued.

Recent work has also centered attention on shamanism and states of consciousness. Much of the work has strong psychoanalytical and psychological roots. The emphasis is on the states of consciousness of people undergoing religious experiences and rituals. Other studies focus around the use of literary criticism and the tradition of colonial criticism. These studies focus on the manner in which religions are discussed and on possible inherent biases in viewing the religions of the less powerful.

Scholars have done a great deal of soul searching in the social sciences in general and in anthropology in particular over the last fifty or so years. That soul searching has led to a greater sensitivity in the field of religious studies. There is, for example, resurgence in the study of religions of the so-called developing world, seeing the strange in the familiar and seeing the familiar in what had once been strange in the studies of the religion and rituals of traditional societies.

Salient Points

This encyclopedia contains 130 articles, 60 sidebars of mainly primary text, and 60 photos that together are meant to provide broad and representative coverage of rituals in human history and across cultures. As with other volumes in the *Religion & Society* series, attention is given to the non-Western world. The articles fall into four general categories.

- The first category provides context and understanding of rituals in general by focusing on key concepts or topics that have applicability across all or most forms of ritual. This category includes articles on asceticism, *communitas*, magic, and taboo.
- The second category focuses on specific types of religion and their diversity and similarities across cultures and religions and includes articles on agricultural rituals, identity rituals, rituals of rebellion, and naming rituals.
- The third category provides overviews of the major rituals of major world religions, cultural regions, and specific cultures.
- The fourth category covers specific rituals such as Christmas, Kwanzaa, and *Star Trek* conventions.

This encyclopedia draws on the work of scholars from a number of disciplines—anthropology, sociology, religious studies, history, cultural geography, and philosophy. It also draws on the work of outstanding international scholars. There are contributors from Asia, North America, South America, Europe, and Africa. There are representative scholars from all the world's major religions as well as scholars who profess no religion at all. These scholars provide perspectives from the cutting edge of their disciplines without neglecting prior scholarship.

Acknowledgments

I want to thank these scholars for their contributions to this encyclopedia and for their skill in presenting often-complex topics in clear and readable manner. I also want to thank David Levinson at Berkshire Publishing for inviting me to edit this volume and Elizabeth Eno for providing careful and diligent management of the process.

Frank A. Salamone

A

Academic Rituals

Because the very nature of the university is one of transition and initiation, the majority of academic rituals deal with rites of passage, as students are indoctrinated into, move through, and ultimately complete the educational process. Within this transitional state, rituals practiced in higher education range from familiar and formal graduation ceremonies to a wide variety of discrete rituals of individual institutions and student bodies. Most academic rituals serve both to accentuate and assuage the anxiety of the educational process, to impress upon participants the necessity of commitment to the ideals of the institution, and to remind the community, year after year, of the unique nature of the university and its relationship to the rest of the world.

Medieval Beginnings

Almost every distinguishing element of academic rituals today dates back to twelfth- and thirteenth-century Europe at the time when universities were first forming. Early universities constituted self-governing communities of scholars with the authority to confer degrees and with the jurisdiction to provide a protected environment for scholars. University governance had to deal with a rebellious and youthful student population, with an independent faculty of diverse interests, and with a local community often at odds with university values and goals. In such an atmosphere, demonstrations of authority and impressive emblems of office were often necessary to fend off challenges to the rights and powers of the university. Dramatic collective rituals imposed periodic order and served to remind participants and the community at large of the nature and purpose of a university.

The ritual dress for modern American academic ceremonies—the robes, hoods, and headwear of the faculty and graduates—represent what was once standard dress for scholars in northern Europe. Most medieval scholars were required to make at least minor vows to the church, so their dress was determined by the regulations of their clerical order and usually consisted of a black robe with cowl or hood. During the sixteenth century, scholars adopted the Tudor robe, worn over ordinary clothing, and the biretta hat, from which the mortarboard evolved. The specific look of the modern gown, hood, mortarboard, and even the tassel derive from those worn at Cambridge and Oxford since the sixteenth century. The variably colored hood, originally the clerical cowl, is now used to identify the individual's degree, field of study, and academic institution.

Emblems of office—charters, gavels, seals, medallions, chains, banners, and ceremonial maces—were originally granted to universities by secular and church authorities to demonstrate official approval. They remain an invariable part of the symbols used in academic ritual today, as do other survivals of the medieval past—the parchment diploma, the titles of office, the dramatis personae, and the college system. Even the ritual setting is often medieval, since many modern universities replicate Gothic architecture. The need to bring the university world into focus and to state its mission in a dramatic way continues to exist, and even after centuries of radical change, the legacies of early universities are part of the pageantry of academic life.

THE TRADITIONAL EXAMINATION SYSTEM AND RITUALS IN KOREA

In traditional East Asian societies such as China, Korea, and Japan those who sought prestigious employment in government were required to take a rigorous examination that determined their fate after many years of study. The following example describes the exam setting and rituals that awaited those who succeeded in Korea.

The aspirants to higher honors, armed with their diplomas, set out to Seoul to attend at the proper time the national examination. The journey of these lads, full of the exultation and lively spirit born of success, moving in hilarious revelry over the high roads, form one of the picturesque features of out-door life in Corea. The young men living in the same district or town go together. They go afoot, taking their servants with them. Pluming themselves upon the fact that they are summoned to the capital at the royal behest, they often make a roystering, noisy, and insolent gang, and conduct themselves very much as they please. The rustics and villagers gladly speed their parting. At the capital they scatter, putting up wherever accommodations in inns or at the houses of relatives permit.

Though young bachelors form the majority at these examinations, the married and middle-aged are by no means absent. Gray-headed men try and may be rejected for the twentieth time, and grandfather, father, and son occasionally apply together.

On the appointed day, the several thousand or more competitors assemble at the appointed place, with the provisions which are to stay the inner man during the ordeal. The hour preparatory to the assignment of themes is a noisy and smoky one, devoted to study, review, declamation, or to eating, drinking, chatting or sleeping according to the inclination or habit of each. The examination consists of essays, and oral and written answers to questions. During the silent part of his work, each candidate occupies a stall or cell. The copious, minute, and complex vocabulary of terms in the language relating to the work, success and failure, the contingencies, honest and dishonest shifts to secure success, and what may be called the student's slang and folk-lore of the subject, make not only an interesting study to the foreigner, but show that these contests subtend a large angle of the Corean gentleman's vision during much of his lifetime.

Examination over, the disappointed ones wend their way home with what resignation or philosophy they may summon to their aid. The successful candidates, on horseback, with bands of musicians, visit their patrons, relatives, the examiners and high dignitaries, receiving congratulations and returning thanks. Then follows the inevitable initiation, which none can escape — corresponding to the French "baptism of the line," the German "introduction to the fox," the English "fagging," and the American "hazing."

One of the parents or friends of the new graduate, an "alumnus," or one who has taken a degree himself, one also of the same political party, acts as godfather, and presides at the ceremony. The graduate presents himself, makes his salute and takes his seat several feet behind the president of the party. With all gravity the latter proceeds, after rubbing up some ink on an ink-stone, to smear the face of the victim with the black mess, which while wet he powders thickly over with flour. Happy would the new graduate be could he escape with one layer of ink and flour, but the roughness of the joke lies in this, that every one present has his daub; and when the victim thinks the ordeal is over new persons drop in to ply the ink-brush and handful of flour. Meanwhile a carnival of fun is going on at the expense, moral and pecuniary, of the graduate. Eating, drinking, smoking, and jesting are the order of the day. It is impossible to avoid this trial of purse and patience, for unless the victim is generous and good-natured, other tricks and jokes as savage and cruel as those sometimes in vogue in American and British colleges follow.

Source: Griffis, William E. (1992).
Corea: The Hermit Nation.
New York: Charles Scribner's Sons, pp. 340–42.

Rites of Passage

Because of the deliberately transcendent purpose of the university—turning raw youth into learned and responsible adults—the study of academic rituals has focused on rites of passage, those rituals marking the passage of a person from one stage of life to another. In a process first described by Arnold van Gennp (1873–1957), participants in rites of passage undergo three phases: separation of participants from the group, a transitional or "liminal" phase, and incorporation back into the group. Victor Turner (1920–1983) extended van Gennup's theory, developing the concept that the liminal phase was often more than just an intermediate, neither-here-nor-there state. Societies use the liminal phase both to instill values and lore in participants and to evoke self-doubt and reflection. Liminality, therefore, is often fraught with anxiety and uncertainty and could even constitute a permanent category of people who are marginal within their societies. At the same time, the liminal state produces a feeling of group warmth, solidarity and unity, or "communitas," among its participants.

The typical university experience reflects the universal elements of the liminal state. On the threshold of adulthood, incoming freshmen are detached from normal life as they enter the university. Even the physical setting is strange, often consisting of ancient-looking buildings and parklike grounds that deliberately set off the university world from the ordinary. Customary procedures are different; the best-reasoned argument outweighs majority rule and personal freedom is a given. Even the hours of the day no longer correspond to the past: class time and personal time are jumbled, meals are taken at random, and no one bothers to order the night. In this setting, students pass from youth to adulthood, from ignorance to knowledge, and from dependence to independence. Graduation ultimately reincorporates them into the ordinary world.

The principal types of academic rituals represent all or part of the many facets of the liminal state. The most well-known and impressive rituals are convocations, formal ceremonies that assemble the entire university community—faculty, students, officials, and supporters—for a special occasion, such as graduation, a presidential inauguration, a special anniversary, or to mark the beginning of a new term. The full panoply of academic symbols and performances are usually brought into play as the university uses convocation to intensify commitment to the institution, arouse self-reflection among participants, and reinforce the university's role in the community. Ritual reunions of former students represent attempts to reestablish commmunitas, as former students make pilgrimages to the campus for annual reunions or homecoming events that bring them under the authority of the university once again, reinforce cohesion with other former students, and impress upon current students the advantages of extended loyalty to the school. Other common academic rituals are the initiation rites regularly conducted by scholarly, social, and service societies to induct new student members. These rites can range from the reverent to the outlandish to hazing activities. In addition to these commonly known rituals, academic life contains a multitude of informal and small-scale rituals related to the everyday activities of the university, such as the ritual involved in a faculty member applying for tenure or the preparations a student makes to study for an exam.

Commencement

The most widely observed and familiar American academic ritual is undoubtedly commencement, the conferring of degrees on graduating students. Employing all of the formal ritual elements found in academe, the typical, modern-day commencement ritual is considered archaic and inefficient, fundamental characteristics that serve to accentuate the contrast between the academic world and the ordinary world. Traditionally held at the end of the spring semester, the ritual action begins with the processional, the

People gather, wearing traditional colors, for a reunion at Mount Holyoke College, in Holyoke, Massachusetts. COURTESY OF STEPHEN G. DONALDSON PHOTOGRAPHY.

march into the staging area by university officials, special guests, and faculty—all ordered by rank, dressed in academic regalia, and carrying the emblems of office—followed by the graduating students arranged by college. The liturgy consists of short speeches from officials, honored faculty, honored alumni, and special guests—all of which serve to remind the participants of the role of the university and to link its purpose to the concerns of the world at large. Outstanding students give short speeches, and honorary degrees are bestowed on notable persons.

The commencement address is delivered by a person of distinction, and the message usually dramatizes the new responsibilities and opportunities to be faced. Thus, as students leave the liminal state, fear and hope and the past, present, and future are all evoked at the same time. The liturgy orders all of these elements and ultimately confirms that these graduates have worked hard and now possess the training and knowledge to face the challenges of the world they are entering. The central ritual action is the conferring of degrees on the graduates. Students traditionally walk across the stage, are handed their diplomas, receive handshakes, and return to their seats, students no longer. The concluding remarks adjust the graduates to their new status, affirm the solidarity of the group with the school, and reiterate the sacredness of their common values. The participants then march out in the recessional, the final ritual act of reincorporation into the ordinary world.

Inversion and Paradox

Rites of passage contain within them distinct antistructural and chaotic elements. The feelings of equality, humility, and oneness that arise during communitas oppose the structure of the traditional social order, which tends to emphasize rank and distinction. Levi-Strauss (b. 1908) points out that, since all human beings belong to both nature and culture, rites of passage serve to mediate our biological destiny with our cultural experiences. At such times, rituals of rebellion, antistructural play, role reversals, and paradoxes become part of the ritual process.

Thus, the university "civilizes" and educates a student, but the nature of the student as a human being with biological instincts and urges is not destroyed. Ritual exposes this paradox and even exaggerates it in order to affirm reconciliation despite conflict. For example, most college campuses hold periodic inversion rituals where, amid festivity, playful fighting, and hijinks, participants are permitted to do that which is normally forbidden. Students may ridicule the solemnity of academe with their own ritualistic performances, such as a fake commencement ceremony.

One classic example of the antistructural, nature-versus-culture elements in a rite of passage is the Italian *festa di laurea*, the graduation party. Upon receiving word that a student will successfully graduate from an Italian university, close friends make a *papiro*, a long, poster-sized paper scroll containing ribald and mocking accounts and images of the graduate's life. Often in poetic form and emphasizing sexual activity and supposed vices, the *papiro* is then posted in a public place. On graduation day, the *laureata* reads her *papiro* aloud to a gathering of friends and family. Every time she makes a mistake in the reading, she must chug from a bottle of wine. Finally, the graduate is paraded around the city, singing along with her friends and family in celebration. Thus, the *festa di laurea* counterbalances the solemn ritual of a commencement ceremony, which celebrates the intellect, by both glorifying and ridiculing the noncerebral, sexual instincts of the graduate. The sensuality and debauchery of the *festa di laurea* ritual draw attention to the chaos that would result were order not to be imposed. The juxtaposition of the two rituals heightens and preserves the dignity and solemnity of the formal ritual while acknowledging the inherent conflict in every rite of passage.

Changes over Time

Looking from the broad perspective begun in medieval times, academic rituals have changed little over the centuries. One recent exception occurred in the United States in the 1960s, when schools ceased holding the baccalaureate, a special religious service for a graduating class, in response to increased concern over the separation of church and state. As the student population has increased in size, commencement exercises are now held at the end of every semester in many schools. The 1960s and early 1970s also ushered in increased informality and individuality among graduates at the commencement ceremony, which has continued into the twenty-first century. While faculty and school officials maintain strict protocol in regalia and ritual action, students often bend the rules slightly by writing messages or pasting objects on their mortarboards, adding a small accessory to their robes such as a political button, or wearing outlandish shoes. Some schools began allowing individual groups, such as ethnic or gay groups, to hold separate commencement ceremonies. Music, which was traditionally slow and dignified, has also been loosened up. Many graduates now march not to "Pomp and Circumstance" but to popular music.

Jaclyn L. Jeffrey

See also Communitas; Liminoid

Further Reading

Babcock, B. (1996). Arrange me into disorder: Fragments and reflections on ritual clowning. In R. Grimes (Ed.), *Readings in ritual studies* (pp. 1–21). Upper Saddle River, NJ: Prentice Hall.

Bell, C. (1997). *Ritual: Perspectives and dimensions.* New York: Oxford University Press.

Eliade, M. (1958). *Rites and symbols of initiation: The mysteries of birth and rebirth* (W. R. Trask, Trans.). Dallas, TX: Spring Publications.

Gunn, M. K (1969). *A guide to academic protocol.* New York: Columbia University Press.

Hargreaves-Mawdsley, W. N. (1978). *A history of academical dress in Europe until the end of the eighteenth century.* Westport, CT: Greenwood Press.

Levi-Strauss, C. (1964). *Introduction to a science of mythology*, Vol. 1, *The raw and the cooked* (J. & D. Weightman, Trans.). New York: Harper & Row.

Moore, S., & Myerhoff, B. (1977). *Secular ritual.* Amsterdam: Van Gorcum.

Sullivan, E. (1977). Academic costume code and an academic ceremony guide. In *American Universities and Colleges* (15th ed.). New York: American Council on Education & Walter de Gruyter, Inc.

Turner, V. (1969). *The ritual process: Structure and anti-structure.* Ithaca, NY: Cornell University Press.

Van Gennup, A. (1960). *The rites of passage* (M. B. Vizedom & G. L. Caffee, Trans.). Chicago: University of Chicago Press.

Africa, Central

In the central African worldview ancestors are important and have to be honoured through rituals. Central Africa comprises Congo, Rwanda, Burundi, Zambia, and Malawi. Rituals are also performed to ask the protection of the spirits, usually ancestral spirits, to ward off danger, misfortune, tensions, and problems. Rituals are also performed to initiate people into a new stage of life or a new status; these are called "rites of passage."

Rituals can be performed at certain occasions, for example, when a couple gets married, when a girl reaches puberty, or when a person dies, but rituals can also be performed when there are tensions in the community: when people are quarrelling, when they are worried because the rains have not come, when someone unexpectedly dies, or when there is illness and danger, such as the fear of or accusation of witchcraft (the use of sorcery or magic). In these cases a ritual can be performed to ask the spirits for the protection, fortune, and health of the entire community.

Rituals can be performed before a person begins a difficult or dangerous undertaking, for example, going hunting or fishing. Hunting rituals and fishing rituals are performed to ask the spirits for a good and safe trip and a good hunt or catch.

Also, rituals can be performed in a personal situation, for example, for someone who is in danger or who needs protection. For instance, during a wedding one needs protection because marriage involves the first sexual act of the couple, and in the central African worldview, this is dangerous and therefore has to be surrounded by a ritual.

Rituals serve the person involved as well as the community; they have sociocultural, religious, and symbolic meaning, and involve power. All rituals are events with a social meaning and symbolic actions.

The function of rituals is to confirm the structure of society. Rituals perpetuate and clarify norms and values in a society. Through rituals conflicts within society are made clear and may be solved. A ritual is a comment on society.

Rituals re-establish and confirm social relationships within a community. On the social level, rituals bind the community, eliminate tension between people, and provide them with the belief that the ancestors will support them and restore peace in the community.

Rituals are symbolic acts and have a religious connotation because they are related to spirits and the supernatural world. A rite is a series of rituals, for example, an initiation rite, which consists of several rituals and can last for months. A ceremony is similar to a rite but has no religious connotation.

When a group of people honour spirits, this is called a "cult." Central Africa has many regional cults, which are related to the land, and shrine cults, which are related to a divinity.

THE IMPORTANCE OF ANCESTORS IN THE RELIGION OF THE BEMBA OF NORTHERN ZIMBABWE

Veneration of and rituals to appeal to ancestors are a key element of many African religions. The following ethnographic account shows their importance to the Bemba.

... The form of the prayers is interesting. There is no fixed formula laid down, but it is absolutely essential that the spirits should each be mentioned by name. By this means their help is invoked. At a tribal ceremony I noticed that Citimukulu always prayed with one of his senior *bakabilo* at his elbow to prompt him if he forgot one ancestral title out of the twenty to thirty dead chiefs to be called upon, and for a chief even to mention the names of his ancestors when walking to a ceremony was described to me as a form of prayer (*ukulumbula*). Headmen also call their ancestors by name when invoking them. Then again it is important that the dead should be named as having taught the particular activity upon which the living are about to engage, and this is especially the case at the tribal ceremonies. In fact one of the chief functions of this type of prayer, is, I think, to give traditional sanction to the gardening methods now praised and to confirm the people's belief in them by tracing their origin to the past. The words of one or two such prayers will illustrate what I mean. For instance, Mwamba, when invoking the *imipaski* at the beginning of his tree-cutting ceremony, prayed: "We have come to you Great Mwambas. It was you who left us the land. We beg for the power to work in it in the way you showed us you worked in the place from which you came (i.e. Lubaland). And we ourselves began to learn (i.e. how to cut trees) when we were still children, until at last we found we had learnt the way. We followed (lit. fell into) your words."

Source: Richards, Audrey I. (1939).
Land, Labour, and Diet in Northern Rhodesia: An Economic Study of the Bemba Tribe.
Oxford, UK: Oxford University Press, p. 363.

Rituals are an intrinsic part of life and of society and are related to the cosmic view. In this view spirits take care of the life of the living and therefore have to be placated and honoured. Spirits are classified as ancestral spirits or as natural spirits, such as waterfalls, trees, and rocks.

Shrines

At many places where natural spirits are thought to linger, shrines are built to honour the spirits and to perform rituals to honour them, to make offerings to them, and to ask their advice, health, and assistance. This is done by a traditional priest, who has inherited the profession from his or her grandparent.

Ancestral spirits are honoured in homes. In case of danger or misfortune, prayers are said and objects are offered to the ancestors, and they are asked for assistance. This can be done by the eldest man or woman in the home. Usually women are said to have more contact with spirits. Therefore, rituals to honour the spirits or seek their help are usually performed by women.

Rites connote power. Power is ascribed to sacrificed objects and to the people performing the rites. Rituals exist to confirm the power of certain people. Knowledge is often related to power. The legitimacy of ritual teachers is that of traditional knowledge and often includes experience and a high social position. This power can be with the performer, the healer, or the ritual leader, who is usually considered to be guided by one or more spirits. In female initiation rites power is with the ritual leader but also with the elderly women. The one who performs a rite is usually a healer as well. He or she is thought to have contacts with spirits that guide him or her through the rite.

A ritual is a special type of action, and its performance requires the cooperation of individuals directed by a leader or leaders. Rules indicate which persons should participate and on what occasions;

often the rules excluding certain categories of people are just as significant as those that permit or require other categories of people to take part.

The theoretical viewpoint of functionalist anthropologists was common during the period of 1950–1980. The most famous of these anthropologists was Victor Turner. He followed the viewpoints of the French sociologist Arnold Van Gennep (1909) and elaborated them. From the functionalist viewpoint rituals serve the community. For example, they provide the community with unity and strength, establish and reconfirm social ties, eliminate tensions, and pass on norms and values.

Rituals have religious aspects as well because people use them to seek assistance of the ancestral spirits, both in performing the rituals in a proper way and in acquiring what the people wish, for example, rain, health, good crops, or a new status as an adult.

Another viewpoint of rituals is that of structuralist anthropologists, of which the French anthropologist Claude Levi-Strauss was the main scholar. He considered the world to be divided into binary oppositions, for example, black-white, high-low, men-women, human-animal, and so forth. Together the oppositions articulate a structure of transformation (structural way of changing). Rituals clarify oppositions and point to crossing the boundaries between oppositions to remove the contradictions between them.

There is also a symbolic viewpoint of rituals. This viewpoint emphasizes that in rites, such as that of initiation rites, the novice passes from a passive to an active state. Also, in this view the human body is important, since by experiencing a rite, the body incorporates social norms. Furthermore, this viewpoint stresses productive relations with others. The viewpoint has become more common since the 1990s. Scientists who study rituals from this viewpoint include Moore. However, the functionalist viewpoint is still dominant.

Rites of Passage

Rites of passage are similar to initiation rites and are rites of transition. They are performed to transform a person and guide him or her to another stage in life. Rites of passage comprise a variety of rituals accompanying the crossing of boundaries and changes in time and social status. The most common are initiation rites, in which a boy or a girl is transformed into an adult; but such rites are also performed at a wedding, at a widow's release from mourning, at a person's death to transform his or her spirit into a good ancestor, and at changes in life and function, such as when a chief is installed.

Van Gennep (1909) has shown that all rites of passage consist of three stages. The first stage is separation, in which the novice (the person being transformed) is separated from the community. This separation can be done by taking the novice to the bush or another space where no other people are. The second stage is seclusion, in which the novice is brought back to the community but is still separated from others. During the seclusion stage the novice is considered a nonperson. She or he is considered an unborn child who knows nothing, who is ignorant of the world. During the rite of passage she or he will gain knowledge about how to behave as an adult, about fertility, female or male duties, and the spiritual world.

The third stage is integration, in which the novice is reincorporated into the community. During these stages rituals are performed. Rites of passage may also require that the notice be nearly naked, be humbled, and be shaved and anointed with white chalk. At the coming-out ritual the novice is dressed in new clothes.

Female initiation rites usually are performed individually for girls and coincide with puberty. Therefore these rites are usually performed at the onset of menstruation or when a girl's breasts begin to grow. These rites emphasize womanhood because the girl has become a woman and therefore has to know what womanhood is about and how she should behave as a good woman. Female initiation rites emphasize the girl's responsibility for her future marriage, her future husband and children, food taboos, domestic duties, agricultural duties, and duty to others in the community. They also emphasize showing respect, in particular to elderly people.

Male initiation rites prepare boys for adulthood and manhood and emphasize male duties such as hunting. Because such duties are mainly community duties that can be done together, boys are initiated as a group. Male initiation rites usually include circumcision and the filing of teeth. The age of the boys can vary.

Symbolic Death

The initiation rite is a preparation for adult life and the hardships that one may encounter as an adult. Therefore, the initiation rite is a difficult period when the novice has to experience hardship. After the initiation rite the novice is considered an adult and is reincorporated into society but with a different status. In initiation the novice symbolically dies in order to be reborn as an adult.

These stages can be seen in rites of passage all over the world, whether they are initiation rites for passage into adulthood or for the installation of a chief or priest.

Healing

Another type of ritual is that of healing. Healing rituals are performed when a person is ill or experiences misfortune. A priest asks the ancestral spirits to reveal the cause of the illness or misfortune, then a ritual is performed to cleanse the person of the illness or misfortune. Usually the person has to offer something to the spirits, often a chicken or goat, money, or other goods.

A ritual also is performed in cases of infertility. In the case of a woman who fails to deliver a child, her husband and relatives are involved, showing that a ritual is not only for the person involved, but also for the community.

There are also agricultural rituals, such as the first fruit rituals performed at harvest (March and April). These are performed to honour the spirits that have been willing to provide the people with a new harvest. In these rituals the first fruit is offered to the chief.

Another agricultural ritual involves setting a bush area on fire. This is done at the beginning of the annual agricultural cycle (August and September) to burn the old and dead branches of the plants and to fertilize the soil with the ashes. The chief gives the sign to set the bush on fire after he and a traditional priest have said prayers for the ancestors.

Many rituals are centuries old. An example is the Nyau ritual in Malawi. The Nyau ritual is a mask dance ritual and is related to initiation rites for boys but also to rain-making rituals.

Only a few rituals are held for a large audience. An example is the Kazanga festival, which takes place in Lusaka, Zambia's capital, and is organized by and celebrated for the Nkoya, a small ethnic group. Other ethnic groups in Zambia also have their rituals, such as the Ngoni, the Lozi, and recently the Bemba with their Ngweena festival. These rituals developed in the 1970s or later. They serve to establish unity among members of an ethnic group as well as to distinguish that group from other ethnic groups. These rituals are not authentic but rather came into being as a result of ethnic mingling in towns, migration and urbanization, and globalization.

In general, rituals are performed to provide unity to a community, to emphasize norms and values, and to honour the spirits, which are an intrinsic part of daily life in central Africa.

Thera Rasing

See also Africa, West

Further Reading

Bell, C. (1992). *Ritual theory, ritual practice*. Oxford, UK: Oxford University Press.

Beattie, J. H. M. (1970). On understanding ritual. In B. Wilson (Ed.), *Rationality* (pp. 240–268). Oxford, UK: Basil Blackwell.

Beidelman, T. O. (1997). *The cool knife: Imagery of gender, sexuality, and moral education in Kaguru initiation ritual*. Washington, DC: Smithsonian Institution Press.

Bloch, M. (1986). *From blessing to violence: History and ideology in the circumcision ritual of the Merina of Madagascar*. Cambridge, UK: Cambridge University Press.

Devisch, R. (1993). *Weaving the threads of life: The Khita gyn-eco-logical healing cult among the Yaka*. Chicago: University of Chicago Press.

Douglas, M. (1975). *Implicit meanings: Essays in anthropology*. Boston: Routledge & Kegan Paul.

Droogers, A. (1980). *The dangerous journey: Symbolic aspects of boys' initiation among the Wagenia of Kisangani, Zaire*. New York: Mouton.

Grimes, R. L. (2000). *Deeply into the bone*. Berkeley and Los Angeles: University of California Press.

La Fontaine, J. S. (1986). *Initiation*. Manchester, UK: Manchester University Press.

Levi-Strauss, C. (1966). *The savage mind*. Chicago: University of Chicago Press. (Original work published 1962)

Linden, I. (1975). Chewa initiation rites and Nyau societies: The use of religious institutions in local politics at Mua. In T. O. Ranger & J. Weller (Eds.), *Themes in the Christian history of central Africa* (pp. 30–44). London: Heinemann.

Lutkehaus, N. C., & Roscoe, P. B. (1995). *Gender rituals: Female initiation in Melanesia*. New York: Routledge.

Mauss, M. (1974). *The gift: Forms and functions of exchange in archaic societies*. London: Routledge & Kegan Paul. (Original work published 1954)

Moore, H. L. (1999). Gender, symbolism and praxis: Theoretical approaches. In H. L. Moore, T. Sanders, & B. Kaare (Eds.), *Those who play with fire: Gender, fertility and transformation in east and southern Africa* (pp. 3–38). New Brunswick, NJ: Athlone Press.

Rasing, T. S. A. (1995). Passing on the rites of passage: Girls' initiation rites in the context of an urban Roman Catholic community (Research Series No. 6). London: Avebury/Africa Studies Centre.

Rasing, T. S. A. (2001). *The bush burnt, the stones remain: Female initiation rites in urban Zambia*. Leiden, Netherlands: African Studies Centre.

Richards, A. I. (1982). *Chisungu: A girl's initiation ceremony among the Bemba of Zambia*. London: Tavistock. (Original work published 1956)

Schoffeleers, J. M. (1979). *Guardians of the land: Essays on central African territorial cults*. Gwelo, Zimbabwe: Mambo Press.

Turner, V. W. (1967). *The forest of symbols*. New York: Cornell University Press.

Turner, V. W. (1969). *The ritual process*. New York: Cornell University Press.

Turner, V. W. (1981). Encounter with Freud: The making of a comparative symbolist. In G. D. Spindler (Ed.), *The making of psychological anthropology* (pp. 558–583). Berkeley and Los Angeles: University of California Press.

Van Binsbergen, W. M. J. (1981). *Religious change in Zambia: Exploratory studies*. London: Kegan Paul International.

Werbner, R. P. (1977). *Regional cults*. New York: Academic Press.

Werbner, R. P. (1989). Umeda maskerade: Renewing identity and power in the cosmos. In R. P. Werbner (Ed.), *Ritual passage, sacred journey: The process and organization of religious movement* (pp. 149–184). Washington, DC: Smithsonian Institution Press.

Africa, West

Although a number of belief systems and ethnic groups exist in west Africa, many of the region's religions and religious rituals have a number of traits in common. This commonality is one of the reasons why the region's rituals influenced the development of rituals and practices in many other regions, including the United States, Latin America, and the Caribbean. A significant feature of west African religious rituals is the blending or absorption of diverse religions into contemporary practices so that even among modern Christian or Islamic churches, many older traditions and rituals continue to be practiced.

The region is comprised of the modern nations of: Benin, Burkina Faso, Cameron, Chad, Cote d'Ivoire, Gabon, Gambia, Ghana, Guinea, Guinea Bissau, Liberia, Mauritania, Mail, Nigeria, Niger, Senegal, Sierra Leone, and Togo.

Religious Commonalities

Among west African nations are three broad categories of religion: indigenous religions, Christianity, and, Islam. Among the indigenous, or traditional religions, are a number of similarities and common practices that are manifested through the rituals and ceremonies of different groups. For instance, most indigenous religions are animistic in that they believe that all or most objects, whether alive or inanimate, contain spirits. Many religious rituals are thus performed in order to maintain or curry favor with animals, crops, the seasons, and so forth because spirits may live in mountains, streams, or forests. In order to maintain the favor of deities, spirits, and ancestors, most tribal groups utilize a variety of everyday rituals.

West African tribal groups usually do not make much distinction between religious rituals and social rituals. Usually the two kinds of rituals are blended so that religion reinforces the cultural and traditional mores of a tribal group. For instance, tribal initiation rites use religion to reinforce notions of duty and obligation to the group. Furthermore, increase rituals—designed to improve crop or livestock yields—serve both a religious purpose and a social purpose.

The majority of religious groups do not have a formal hierarchy of priests. Instead, religious rituals are overseen by one of two groups. The first are tribal elders, who within many cultures serve as the main religious figures and determine the time, nature, and intricacies of rituals. The second are shamans (priests or priestesses who use magic to cure the sick, divine the hidden, and control events). Shamans are believed to have special insights or an ability to communicate with the spirit world beyond that of most individuals. The elders or the shamans have special roles in religious rituals and retain their power based on the perceived success or failure of rituals.

ISLAM AND INDIGENOUS RELIGION WEST AFRICA

A marked feature of religion and rituals in west Africa is the merging of indigenous religion with Islam and Christianity. The following example indicated how rural Hausa combine a belief in Allah with their indigenous beliefs in spirits.

As might be expected from the long period during which, as we have seen, the bush Maguzawa have been in contact with the Mohammedanized life of the cities, many Islamic elements have become thoroughly incorporated into Maguzawa culture. One of these elements is the belief in Allah as a supreme being.

The Maguzawa freely admit that Allah is the ultimate control of the universe. Yet He does not occupy the central role in their beliefs and practices that is so characteristic of the Moslem Hausa. Among the Maguzawa there are no rites connected with the belief in Allah, and all supernatural response to worship, whether good or bad, is attributed to spirits called *'iskoki* (singular, *'iska*). The 'iskoki only perform their work with the permission of Allah, but the Maguzawa in their traffic with the supernatural consider it sufficient to deal with the *'iskoki*, and ignore Allah as being remote and uninterested in the affairs of men. Although the pagan Hausa have no formal cult of Allah, it should be noted that Allah is particularly implored for rain and that formerly, in times of drought, the women donned men's clothes and, carrying implements characteristic of men's occupations, went into the bush crying, "Allah, give us rain."

It must be understood that the concept of Allah as the Supreme Being is only elicited by direct questioning. Ordinarily the Maguzawa pay no attention to Allah, and His name is only heard in the oaths and common expressions involving God's name which these folk share with their Moslem neighbors, but which, unlike them, they use less frequently.

Source: Greenberg, Joseph H. (1946).
The Influence of Islam on a Sudanese Religion.
Monographs of the American Ethnological Society, Vol. 10. New York: J.J. Augustin, p. 27.

In addition, most religions are polytheistic, having a large number of gods and other deities. Some groups, such as the Yoruba of Nigeria, believe in a high god, Olorun, and a number of lesser deities. One result of this belief is that there are usually elaborate rituals to honor the higher deities, whereas lesser gods may be acknowledged through simple rituals such as pouring a libation onto the ground. These common traits result in a great degree of similarity among religious rituals.

Ancestor Worship

One specific feature common across west African religions is ancestor worship. Most African religions accord the dead great reverence, although distinctions are made between the dead who are honored and the dead who are dishonored because of the circumstances of their death or actions during their lives. Honored or remembered ancestors are often perceived to be intermediaries between the living world and the dead. Long after the death of honored ancestors rituals are performed whereby descendants of the dead "feed" them by placing their favorite foods near their graves or offering some tokens of esteem. Once every sixty years the Dogon people of west Africa perform a community-wide collective ritual to honor the dead. Meanwhile, the dishonored dead, often referred to as the "undead" or "living dead," often create problems or cause pain and disease among people. Some societies believe that if a person is not buried according to a specific ritual, that person will return as the living dead.

Many burial rituals can be elaborate. For instance, when a chief dies among the Ijaw and Ibo peoples, the formal burial ritual occurs over an entire year. Such rituals are marked by extensive protocols, and any deviation from custom is considered a harbinger of bad times for the village or tribe because the breach of protocol will anger the gods and prevent the spirit of the chief from entering the spirit world. Among the Kalabari people a chief's burial involves three rituals over a year. Each ritual features funeral plays, known as "Kala Ekkpe Siaba," ritual body painting, dancing, and often sacrifices. These rituals are culminated when a specially carved image of the chief is placed in a shrine *(arua)*, which also contains the images of the chief's ancestors.

Great care is usually taken of the deceased's body. Almost all tribes utilize some form of ritual cleansing of the body. For some tribes this may involve a ritual washing of the body by family members, whereas other tribes use special solutions that may not be allowed to drip and touch the ground. During the actual burial, dancing may be used to ritually pack the earth as the dancers perform over the grave. The LoDagaa people of Ghana believe that a river conveys the dead from this world to the next, so the deceased would be buried with the items necessary for a river journey.

Burial rituals are less elaborate for the common people. For example, among the Ijaw people, if an old woman or man dies, that person is given a single burial ritual with feasting and dancing. Younger members of the tribe are given less elaborate burial rituals. In general, among many tribes ritual masks are used only in the funeral rituals of males. In addition, when people die a dishonorable death, such as when women die during childbirth or people commit suicide or outlive their children, their bodies are disposed of without ritual, often being thrown into a river or secretly buried.

Sacrifice

Many burial rituals involved sacrifice, which played a part in many other religious rituals. Sacrifices were offered to appease or gain favor with earthly spirits, ancestors, and deities. Most sacrificial rituals involved animals. For example, after someone's death, a cat might be sacrificed in order to transfer its night vision to the deceased so that the deceased could see in the underworld. Similarly, a parrot might be sacrificed in order to provide the deceased with a clear voice. Many tribes would sacrifice a dog during times of trouble in the hope that the dog's ability to detect danger would protect the tribe. Some animals, such as eagles, were sacrificed as a means to bestow honor on someone living or to acknowledge the importance of some who died.

Animal blood was also commonly used to appease the gods during a time of famine or drought. During the many agricultural ceremonies and rituals, animal sacrifices were perceived as a means to improve the harvest or the hunt. Finally, animal sacrifices were common before a battle. Warriors would be offered the blood of "strong" or "brave" animals in order to bolster their courage and ferocity.

Although most sacrificial rituals involved animals, some tribes did practice a limited amount of human sacrifice. However, this practice often took place only during extraordinary circumstances, such as the death of a monarch. For example, among tribes in Nigeria the death of a king would be followed by the sacrifice of his slaves. Among the Ibo the death of a king resulted in the ritual murder of his favorite slave wife, known as the "Aho'm," whose body was then thrown into a large grave. Her sacrifice was followed by a ritual in which the strongest and bravest warriors of the tribe would break the arms and legs of the king's other female slaves and bury them alive. Other tribes would sacrifice people by cutting their throats and hanging them upside down from a tree so that their blood could fertilize the ground and appease the gods.

Dance

Dance also was often an integral part of religious rituals. Dance was usually a communal rather than an individual act. The high point of most religious festivals usually involved some form of dance. Unlike most Western dance, African religious dance was highly participatory and involved interaction between the dancers, the audience, and the musicians through a "call and response" system, which was spread by the African diaspora, the movement of Africans to the Western Hemisphere as a result of the slave trade, and emulated in the Western Hemisphere in religious art forms such as gospel music.

Often dance was symbolic. For example, during their annual agricultural festival, the Irigwe men of Nigeria would jump at heights that mimicked their crop yields. Dance also was an important aspect of therapeutic rituals. At the core of the west African religious practice of *bori* or *ajun* was a three-month-long ceremony in which women who had mental or emotional problems were isolated from the rest of the tribe at a shrine where they learned special dances designed to exorcise their problems.

Although there was wide latitude for improvisation, most ritual dancing had precise components and rhythms that were performed by people according to their status within the tribe. For instance, among the Yoruba, during the *igbin* dance each tribal member had a specific part according to his or her rank and status. The dances of the Asante people of Ghana were usually begun by their king, whose royal authority was either enhanced or undermined by his ability to dance.

Dances were marked by the use of masks and other ceremonial customs. Masks varied in size from 15 centimeters to 4 meters. They may have covered only the eyes or the face or the entire body. Masks and costumes allowed dancers to masquerade as deities or ancestors. The masked dancers served to mediate between the gods and the people and between the living and the dead. Dances also allowed elders to pass on knowledge about religious beliefs. By imitating birds, the Ewe people of Togo had a dance that presented the migratory history of their people, who, the Ewe believed, followed a bird to their present lands.

Christian missionaries originally tried to suppress the indigenous dances of west Africa. In some colonies such dances were officially banned. However, decolonization and the development of churches that blended Christianity and traditional, indigenous, religious practices lifted most of the official constraints on dance. Nonetheless, by the late 1900s traditional dances had lost most of their religious connotations and increasingly integrated U.S. and European influences.

Initiation Rituals

Initiation rituals were the main vehicles through which religious knowledge was passed down to successive generations. These rituals often included both sacrifice and dance. At a minimum, most west Africa tribes had at least one initiation ritual designed to transition the young of the tribe to full membership. Many tribes had multiple rituals. For instance, the Asanti had a naming ritual one week after the birth of a child (the high infant mortality rate was the reason for having it in one week). A child of the Ifa people underwent an *ikose w'aye* or "stepping into the world" ritual, which was performed by a priest in order to determine the probable future of the child. This ritual was followed three months later by the "knowing the head" ritual, which was designed to divine the *ori inu* (spirit or personality) of the child.

Usually the most important initiation ritual occurs around puberty or soon after. Such a ritual involves the segregation of men and women and is designed to prepare the young for full membership in the tribe, including marriage. Among many tribes the initiates' heads are shaved as a symbol of their new life after the ritual. Some tribes, such as the Dagara, force young males to go through a ritual death that actually can be fatal because of the deprivation of food and sleep.

Often initiation rituals involve both male and female circumcision and some form of isolation from the rest of the community (there are also usually periods of fasting and silence). The impact of Christianity and Islam has altered many rites of passage in contemporary times. For instance, many male infants are now circumcised at birth, and among Muslim communities cattle have replaced pigs as sacrificial animals.

Among most groups these rituals occur annually, although some groups have extended periods between initiation rituals. For example, the Jola people of Senegal hold their male initiation rituals only once every twenty to twenty-five years (about once for each generation). These mass rites of passage are known as *bukut*s. Males between the ages of twelve and thirty-five undergo a mass initiation ritual that culminates in a period of seclusion in the forest, after which the men emerge as full adults. Part of the reason for the length of time between rituals is their elaborateness; villages often begin preparing years in advance so that people can learn the intricate dances and other rituals involved.

Ritual Calendar

Because most traditional west African societies are agrarian, their religious rituals are based on the changing of the seasons. The main exception occurs when funeral rituals or battle rituals take place. Among the Yoruba the main festival is Bere in January of each year. The ritual marks the end of the harvest season and is celebrated with a ritual burning of the fields, which symbolizes the start of a new season of growth. Other Yoruba festivals include a celebration for the god of divination in July and a series of ceremonies to honor Olorun Orun, the god of fate, every September (and in preparation for the harvest season). Meanwhile, the Bambara people end their harvest season with a celebration of the tribe's mythical ancestor Thy Wara, who is believed to have taught people how to grow crops and raise livestock. Many tribes also perform rain ceremonies at the start of the rainy season in order to ensure that there is enough precipitation for the crops.

Many west African tribes have a New Year's celebration in March. The celebration usually involves both individual and community-wide purification rituals. For the individual these rituals may mean confessions, whereas for the community they may mean sacrifices and special cleansing rituals. In Benin there are annual whipping festivals in which the young men of different villages literally beat each other in an effort to prove toughness and to cleanse impurities. The Dogon people of Mali celebrate the dead each year in a festival that begins in April and lasts through May. Usually initiation rituals occur well before the harvest season and often begin in June or July in order to allow the men to heal from any ritual wounds, including circumcision, in time for harvest.

Tom Lansford

See also Africa, Central

Further Reading

Awolalu, J. (1979). *Yoruba beliefs and sacrificial rites.* New York: Oxford University Press.

Baeta, C. (1962). *Prophetism in Ghana.* London: SCM Press.

Bascom, W. (1969). *Ifa divination: Communication between gods and men in west Africa.* Bloomington, Indiana University Press.

Booth, N. (Ed.). (1977). *African religions.* New York: Nok.

Buckley, A. (1985). *Yoruba medicine.* New York: Oxford University Press.

Fardon, R. (1990). *Between God, the dead and the wild: Chamba interpretations of religion and ritual.* Washington, DC: Smithsonian Institution Press.

Horton, R. (1993). *Patterns of thought in Africa and the West: Essays on magic, religion and science.* New York: Cambridge University Press.

Isichei, E. (1977). *Igbo worlds.* London: Macmillan.

Levtzion, N. (1973). *Ancient Ghana and Mali.* London: Methuen.

Matthews, D. H. (1998). *Honoring the ancestors: An African cultural interpretation of black religion and literature.* New York: Oxford University Press.

Mbiti, J. (1969). *African religions and philosophy.* London: SPCK.

Parrinder, G. (1954). *African traditional religion.* London: Sheldon Press.

Parrinder, G. (1975). *West African religion: A study of the beliefs and practices of Akan, Ewe, Yoruba, Ibo, and kindred peoples.* London: Epworth Press.

Van Binsbergen, W., & Schoffeleers, M. (Eds.). (1985). *Theoretical explorations in African religion.* London: Kegan Paul International.

Zuesse, E. M. (1979). *Ritual cosmos: The sanctification of life in African religion.* Athens: Ohio University Press.

African-American Churches

African-American churches have been the cornerstone of the African-American community since their founding in the eighteenth century. They are a combination of faiths and denominations within faiths. Although there is evidence of religious practice and the praise house, a specific designated place for worship, dating back to the early days of the slave community in the United States, the first organized black denomination may have been founded as early as 1750. The first black or African-American churches were Baptist. The first institutionalized, independent black churches were Methodist.

Denominations and Distinctions

The majority of African-American churches are Christian. Eighty percent of African-Americans belong to seven major Protestant denominations: African Methodist Episcopal (A.M.E.), African Methodist Episcopal Zion (A.M.E.Z.), Christian Methodist Episcopal (C.M.E.), National Baptist Convention of America, Unincorporated (N.B.C.A.), National Baptist Convention, USA, Incorporated (N.B.C.), Progressive National Baptist Convention (P.N.B.C), and Church of God in Christ (C.O.G.I.C.). All but the Church of God in Christ are black outgrowths of related Euro-American denominations. Approximately 10 percent of African-Americans are Catholic.

African-American churches differ in terms of style of worship, hermeneutics (the study of the methodological principles of interpretation) and homiletics (the art of preaching), and music and hymnody. With respect to style of service, some churches are sermon centered, whereas others are liturgy (rites prescribed for public worship) centered. Some allow active and spontaneous participation of the congregation, whereas others engage the congregation in relatively limited and specified ways. The minister's activities in some churches are shared with other members (e.g., deacons, ministers, or lay assistants).

Scholars have categorized African-American churches as ecstatic, emotional, escapist, or liturgical, with a few churches being a combination. The ecstatic and emotional churches are highly demonstrative with respect to the role of the clergy and their assistants and that of the congregation, often having a dialogue-and-assent form of interaction between the celebrant and the congregation and spontaneous eruptions of dancing, shouting, and testifying. Emotionality varies by intensity from church to church. The content of services is centered on other-worldliness as well as on contemporary issues. The structure of services of these churches is relatively informal.

By contrast, liturgical churches have a more formal structure of services. The more central the liturgy is to the service, the more structured the service. These churches allow less opportunity for emotional demonstrativeness—especially by an individual—on the part of the congregation and the clergy.

African-American affiliation and type of church are largely based on socioeconomic status. The upper class is more likely to attend liturgical churches of denominations such as Episcopal, Congregational, and Presbyterian. The sociologist V. E. Daniel (1942) identified these churches as the churches of the black elite. The lower and working classes are more likely to attend Baptist and Pentecostal churches. The social lives of the lower class are more church centered. The black church functions to build morale within this class. The social lives of the upper class are not particularly church centered, and the rate of attendance falls as socioeconomic status rises, as it does among white Christians.

Black Theology

Influenced mostly by Protestants versus Catholics, black theology grew out of black clergy from both faiths speaking out against racism. The civil rights and Black Power movements gave rise to vocalizing discontent within black churches. The concept of a black theology emerged in the late 1960s through ministers who began to, according to theologian James Cone, "theologize from within the black experience" (Cone 1984, 5), as opposed to adopting or continuing a Eurocentric theology of Christianity. These ministers tried to respond to the question of what it means to be both black and Christian. They attempted to explain how the God of all of humankind allows those of color to be categorically oppressed—by society and even by the Christian Church. They asked how the teachings of Christ can coincide with white prejudice and discrimination. They also asked how one understands the Christian God in this context. Black Catholics, in addition, sought to gain greater individual church community control. Black Catholics had established caucuses focused on their issues within the Catholic Church as early as the 1880s. In the 1960s and 1970s caucuses were established anew and were similar to such caucuses in the black Protestant church community. Black theology is important to church ritual because it has a significant impact on homiletics (the art of preaching), hermeneutics (interpretation of scriptural texts), and hymnody (singing or composing hymns). The emergence of black theology reflected the need among black Americans to Africanize Christianity as they attempted to make it relevant to their struggles and experience and their social location in the United States. They lent their own interpretations to the Bible, church music, sermons, and style of worship.

Rituals, Rites, and Ceremonies

In African tradition rituals in religious practice were an important element of behavior. When Africans came to the New World, some continued to practice their African religions. Others converted to Christianity. All continued some of the African rituals in their religious activities, with Christians combining the traditions of African religions with those of Christianity. African-American Christianity was a blend of religious social experience. The blended rituals were integrated with a hermeneutics of hope in a god of the oppressed. Today the structures and expressions of many African rituals continue.

Rituals in African-American churches vary, determined by factors such as denomination, category of church—for example, liturgical versus ecstatic—social class, and geographic location. Ceremonies, systems of formal public rites, also vary and include baptism, general blessings, induction and invitation to membership, healing, preparation for death and/or burial, Eucharist and Holy Communion, confession, profession of faith, "sainting,"(the ritual of making a saint, whereby a believer receives the Holy Ghost and is moved to a state of ecstasy) marriage, ordination, and the blessing of sacred objects. Rituals and rites in the main service or mass in the Catholic Church—including black Catholic churches, which are liturgical and formally structured—include the introductory rites of entrance, greeting, and praise; liturgy, including the gospel readings and homily; eucharistic offering, liturgy, and prayer; communion rite; and the concluding rite, including the blessing of the congregation. Ecstatic churches have fewer rituals and rites compared to the more formal, liturgical churches.

Offerings and Prayers

Monetary offerings are a part of most African-American worship services. Sometimes offerings are given and collected in a perfunctory way. At other times they are given and collected after the minister implores the congregation to be generous and sometimes requests that the plate be passed around again. Special collections are frequently taken up for a specific cause or group, such as the poor, flowers for the altar, or educational programs.

Prayers are a regular part of some but not all churches' services. Some churches use several formal prayers, whereas others use none. Some use only the Lord's Prayer. Prayer themes include comfort, confession, contrition, praise, thanksgiving, expression of hope for a better life, divine aid/intervention/assistance, forgiveness and repentance, repose of the souls of the departed, and special intentions.

Churches vary greatly in the nature of their religious symbols and the extent of use of such symbols. These symbols include candles, the crucifix, prayer books, Bibles, hymnals, ministers' vestments or robes, hymn boards, collection plates and baskets, bread, wine, water, uniforms for attendants, choir robes (sometimes more than one change), flowers, and incense. More secular items such as musical instruments—including pianos, organs, drums, and horns— are often part of religious services. Seating ranges from pews to benches to folding chairs.

Water is frequently used as a symbol in baptism rituals. The symbolic use of water is as much a part of indigenous African religions as it is of European Christian religions. In Africa water was viewed as significant to the creation process, linking God and humankind. Rituals of thanksgiving for rain were not uncommon. Water was used in rites of passage similar to the ways in which it is used in Christian baptism—to purify, to symbolize a death of the old and a birth of the new. Community sharing of such rites was an important reification (the process of regarding something as a material thing) of the possibilities of new life. Africans' view of water was incorporated into the significance and symbolism of baptism in African-American churches.

Baptism takes different forms in the different types of churches and denominations. The use of water ranges from a light sprinkling in liturgical churches to a full body dunking in some of the more ecstatic churches. The person to be baptized, and sometimes other participants, is usually dressed in white, ranges in age from newborn to adult, and sometimes is in an altered state of consciousness. There is typically preparation for baptism, especially for adult initiates.

Invitation to Membership

During the worship service of many churches an acknowledgment and a greeting of visitors are given. An invitation to membership is typically extended during the service in most Protestant churches; in Baptist churches such an invitation is extended after the sermon. Many churches provide some sort of preparation for membership.

Preaching Style and Sermons

The preaching of the sermon is the first draw to African-American church services. The minister's style may be theatrical, as is typically the case in the emotional and ecstatic churches, or solemn, as in the liturgically centered churches. In emotional and ecstatic churches the minister's style is often characterized by a great deal of bodily motion, including expansive hand and arm gestures and rapid, jerking, and rhythmic movements, and by dramatic changes in voice inflection, tone, pitch, and volume. The minister sometimes incites so much emotion in the congregation that the atmosphere of the church nearly resembles bedlam. The minister's sermon may take the form of a dialogue and assent with the congregation. Common responses to the minister's words include "Yes, Lord!" and "Thank you, Jesus!" and "Praise the Lord!" Responses may be specific to the minister's queries. The congregation may be incited to swooning, running, dancing, jumping, shouting, "fervent praying," (ardent, intense with feeling) receiving the Holy Spirit (ecstasy), raising one or both arms and hands, praying loudly, clapping hands, shuffling feet, and speaking in tongues—including talking rapidly, sometimes saying only one word, which may resemble gibberish. In contrast, the minister in liturgical churches may incite only the most controlled and conservative displays of emotion.

Dance

Dance was a traditional part of African religious ceremony and ritual and was carried over into religious practices of slaves in the New World. The African ring shout or ring dance enabled slaves to perform spirituals of African and African-American origin. Performers walk and then shuffle in a ring and gradually gain momentum and sing with those persons outside of the ring, who sing in support and dialogue. One group (either those inside or outside of the ring) sings melody, the other the supportive bass or chorus.

The inclusion of dance in religious practices comes out of the African tradition of prayer in combination with song and movement, the ring signifying unity. Contemporary worshipers continue this tradition when they shout and testify, especially in ecstatic churches. Running, swooning, shuffling, toe tapping, and hand raising are also a part of this tradition.

Music

Music is the second draw to African-American church services. Two of the leading contemporary scholars of the African American Church, C. Eric Lincoln and Lawrence Mamiya refer to church music as "the performed word."(1990, 346) The musical expressions of African-American people are perhaps the most informative and enlightening expressions of their culture.

African-American music in general grew from spirituals. Some people say spirituals were created out of traditional African songs with which first-generation slaves were familiar. Spirituals were often sung as slaves worked on plantations. Because of the circumstances in which spirituals were created—with spontaneity and the lack of literacy in those times—they had to be relatively short, using a repetition of lines so that they could be remembered. Although the words and melodies of spirituals are simple, they are often embellished upon. In spirituals as well as in gospel songs, harmonies can be multiple and complex. Rhythm, as is the case in secular African-American music, is a prominent characteristic. Spirituals and gospel songs are typically sung in one of two tempos: slow (sorrow) or brisk (jubilee). Singers and musicians may improvise and stylize a piece in a spontaneous fashion, especially in more fundamentalist churches. There is no requisite instrument for accompaniment. Although piano (or organ) is the most popular instrument for spirituals and gospel music, gospel music may also employ bass guitar, drums, and horns. Body movements (clapping hands, stomping feet, tapping toes) also provide accompaniment, accentuating a beat and adding to the flow. These are not contrived movements but rather movements that flow naturally from members of the congregation.

Spirituals include the themes of hope for salvation despite seemingly insurmountable odds and people's worth as expressed in God's willingness to grant salvation (e.g., "Jesus loves me and will carry me home"). They also include themes of suffering. Black theology and social ethics Theodore Walker describes African-American music and the cultural art form of spirituals as "the emotional articulation of pain and suffering." He further asserts that "traditionally African American music has been an indigenous folk articulation of our social circumstances" (Walker 1991, 75). A latent function of such songs written in the past is that they teach cultural and historical lessons of black suffering and oppression to the generations who followed their composers.

Gospel music was created about 1930, with the Church of God in Christ and holiness churches (outgrowth of a religious movement in the late nineteenth century) contributing largely to its birth and growth. Its themes have a broader range than that of spirituals. Both are important African-American musical forms and contributions to African-American culture and U.S. church music.

A Blending of Traditions

African-American church music includes forms other than spirituals and gospel music. Spirituals began the black church musical tradition. Some of these were created within specific denominations. They were followed by an African-Americanized version of Dr. Isaac Watt's English hymns. There was also an African-Americanizing of Anglo-American hymns. Finally, the early era of gospel music was followed by the contemporary gospel era, which began in the 1960s.

Music also varies by type of church. In liturgical churches African and African-American musical traditions blended and combined with music of the European and Anglo-American traditions. In the more conservative liturgical churches blacks did not include spirituals in their services until after the civil rights movement era. For them there was a separation between black music and church music, with church music being more Anglo-American. African-American music was private, social, and apart from worship. Today, because of increased multicultural awareness, even churches such as mainstream Episcopal churches contain some music in the African-American tradition. Furthermore, European hymns are often modified and infused with African-American flavor.

During the last decades of the twentieth century hymn projects in liturgical and other churches and denominations were undertaken, systematically incorporating African-American music into hymnals. According to the Anglican Church, African-American church music ideally "affords free expression; promotes congregational participation and a sense of community; captures the essence of the liturgy; enhances spiritual growth and understanding; and develops the parish's musical productivity and potential" (Church Hymnal Corporation 1993, xxv). According to black Catholics, "black sacred song is soulful song" (*Lead Me, Guide Me* 1987, iv). It is holistic, participatory, reality based, spirit filled, and life giving.

African-American church music is ecumenical (general). Its roots predate the formation of the denominational structures and black churches. Although the type of African-American church music varies, it is an important part of the services in all African-American churches as congregations "make a joyful noise unto the Lord." (Psalm 100)

Susan D. Toliver

Further Reading

Carpenter, D. (Ed.). (2001). *African-American heritage hymnbook.* Chicago: GIA Publications.

Church Hymnal Corporation. (1993). *Lift every voice and sing II.* New York: Church Pension Fund.

Cone, J. H. (1984). *For my people: Black theology and the black church.* Maryknoll, NY: Orbis Books.

Costen, M. W. (1993). *African-American Christian worship.* Nashville, TN: Abingdon Press.

Daniel, V. E. (1942, June). Ritual and stratification in Chicago Negro churches. *American Sociological Review,* 7(3), 352–361.

Douglas, K. B. (1994). *The black Christ.* Maryknoll, NY: Orbis Books.

Felder, C. H. (Ed.). (1991). *Stony the road we trod: African-American biblical interpretation.* Minneapolis, MN: Fortress Press.

Herskovits, M. J. (1941). Africanisms in religious life. In M.J. Herskovits (Ed.), *The myth of the Negro past* (pp. 232–235). New York: Harper & Row.

Johnson, J. W., & Johnson, J. R. (1942). *The books of American Negro spirituals.* New York: Viking Press.

Johnson, J. W., & Johnson, J. R. (1987). *Lead me, guide me: The African-American Catholic hymnal.* Chicago: GIA Publications.

Lincoln, C. E., & Mamiya, L. H. (1990). *The black church in the African-American experience.* Durham, NC: Duke University Press.

Massey, F., Jr., & McKinney, S. B. (1976). *Church administration in the black perspective.* Valley Forge, PA: Judson Press.

National Advisory Task Force on the Hymnbook Project. (1981). *Songs of Zion.* Nashville, TN: Abingdon Press.

Nelsen, H. M., Yokley, R. L., & Nelsen, A. K. (Eds.). (1971). *The black church in America.* New York: Basic Books.

Paris, P. J. (1995). *The spirituality of African peoples: The search for a common moral discourse.* Minneapolis, MN: Fortress Press.

Rabateau, A. J. (1978). *Slave religion: The "invisible institution" in the antebellum South.* New York: Oxford University Press.

Sernett, M. C. (Ed.). (1985). *Afro-American religious history: A documentary witness.* Durham, NC: Duke University Press.

Shannon, D. T., & Wilmore, G. S. (Eds.). (1985). *Black witness to the apostolic faith.* Grand Rapids, MI: William B. Eerdmans.

Walker, T. (1991). *Empower the people: Social ethics for the African-American church.* Maryknoll, NY: Orbis Books.

Afro-Brazilian

Afro-Brazilian is a term used to describe sociocultural behavior, traits, ideology, and so forth that are perceived to be at least somewhat derivative of African culture. Brazil's long history of slavery—beginning in the sixteenth century and abolished (the last New World colony to do so) in 1888—and the fact that Brazilian slaves were drawn from many different regions in Africa, facilitated the development of a much larger range of African-derived religions than generally found in other areas of the New World. A general African cultural presence in the religious life of Brazil is evident in the language of liturgy (rites prescribed for public worship), names of gods, ritual practices, and general philosophy regarding such issues as the relationship between the spirit and physical worlds, the nature of the supreme god, and humankind's place in the universe are similar if not identical to their sub-Saharan African counterparts. Thus, the focus here is on culture and sociocultural behavior rather than on "racial" types. That many adherents of Afro-Brazilian religions are phenotypically African is obvious, but it is also accidental. That is, in the study of Afro-Brazilian religions—indeed, in the study of all African-derived religions in the New World—when considering the proper subject of study, the presence of Africanized culture and ideology is necessary and sufficient, whereas the presence of an Africanized phenotype is merely incidental. This issue is especially germane given the fact that Afro-Brazilian religions are comprised of a number of disparate religio-cultural traditions and practiced by a population that consists of peoples drawn primarily from three continents: Africa, Europe, and South America.

Afro-Brazilian Religions

During the eighteenth and nineteenth centuries—the period that included the development of many of the African-derived religions of the New World—a large majority of the Africans shipped across the Atlantic to the Americas hailed from the Bight of Benin (the coastal area extending roughly from eastern Ghana to western Nigeria), the Bight of Biafra (the coastal area extending roughly from central Nigeria to western Cameroon), and west-central Africa. Thus, not surprisingly, the three cultural groups whose religious beliefs and practices are the most salient in Brazil—the Yoruba, the Ewe/Fon, and the Bantu/Kongolese—are all located in or near these areas.

Although Salvador, Bahia, on the east coast of Brazil, with its long history as an entry point for native Africans, no doubt is the area of strongest African cultural influence and perhaps home to the greatest number of highly Africanized religious groups, Afro-Brazilian religions can be found as far north as Belem in the northern state of Para and Porto Alegre in the extreme southern state of Rio Grande do Sul. It is important to bear in mind that the middle passage (the transportation of Africans to the New World) and the slave trade in general were not conducive to the smooth and comprehensive transfer of cultural traits from the Old World to the New World, hence the liberal usage here of the adjective *Africanized*.

In addition to the more commonly recognized or mainstream religions or religious groups such as Roman Catholicism and Protestantism, a number of traditional/folk religions are practiced in Brazil today, and a number of terms have been used to refer to them directly or to some aspect of their worship, including *Umbanda, Catimbo, Macumba, Batuque, Candomble, Kardecism* (spiritism), and *Xango*. This list of terms is by no means exhaustive, but those groups noted here are certainly the most widespread of the traditional/folk religions in Brazil. Those religious groups that could be described as "Afro-Brazilian," that is, that engage in practices and recognize ideologies that are Africanized to a significant degree, would include Candomble, Umbanda, Batuque, Macumba, and Xango. In regard to symbols, beliefs, and practices, there is actually a considerable overlap between what is meant by the terms *Candomble, Macumba,* and *Xango,* so here the term *Candomble* will be used in a general sense to refer to all three of these groups.

Candomble is a member of a family of African-derived religions in the New World that also includes Vodou (recognized in the southern United States as voodoo), Santeria, Xango, Orisha, and others. It is the most Africanized of Brazilian religions and originated during the eighteenth century in the state of Bahia. Perhaps the most salient characteristic of Candomble (and the other groups noted earlier) is the syncretism (combining different forms) of African gods (*orixas*) and Catholic saints. This practice, aided considerably by the perceived similarities between the two "pantheons," was certainly a by-product of the difficulties encountered by Old World Africans as they attempted to make the transition to the colonial plantation system of the New World. Spirit possession is by far the most significant event in Candomble and is an integral part of virtually all rites and ceremonies.

AN ACCOUNT OF CANDOMBLE POSSESSION FROM BAHIA BRAZIL

Once I had a party at my house for some friends. But Xango [the god of lightning and thunder] sent me a message that I should go to the candomble. I said that I was not going because I was having a party. A little while later, while I was dancing with my friends. I suddenly got a stiffness in my legs. But I didn't pay much attention to it. Then I suddenly felt an "opening of the body" [*aperto no corpoa* "trembling of the body," signifying that the orixa [god] wished to enter and to "manifest himself" in human form.] and I didn't know anything more. When I came to, I was dancing in the candomble. When the candomble was over, I went running clear to the top of Boeiros do Inferno ["Funnels of Hell"] without knowing anything about what I was doing. These are two hills called by that name because they are so high. I didn't feel anything. Afterward, Xango beat me on the hands, and my hands swelled. When he "arrived" again, he said that I should pay more attention to him, or he would beat me some more. Once he struck me. On that day I was very tired, but I went to the candomble and danced anyway.

I dance when there is a big ceremony; I dance for hours at a time without getting tired. The spell seizes me, and sometimes I dance more than three days without feeling the least bit tired. When the orixa "arrives in my head," I spend a week or more "sleeping" [That is, moving about, but unconscious of what is happening.] I don't feel anything. I don't see anything. People talk to me, but I don't know anything about what is going on.

If one drinks water, the orixa doesn't "arrive." For instance, one feels cold. That cold is in the body. The orixa wants "to arrive." Then one drinks water. He who is of the preceito [the control of the deity over one] does not drink water. And whoever drinks, breaks the preceito. It is prayed ten times [One must at the same time pray ten words and tap the ground ten times.]

***Source*: Pierson, Donald. *Negroes in Brazil: A Study of Race Contact at Bahia.* (1967). Carbondale and Edwardsville: Southern Illinois University Press, p. 267.**

Umbanda is a religion that is much more derivative of the New World, Brazilian cultural context than is Candomble for two reasons. First, this religion did not begin to take hold until the early twentieth century, and, in fact, it appears as though spiritists (people, such as adherents of Kardecism, who believe that spirits of the dead communicate with the living) played an important role in this process. Second, many of the spirits recognized in Umbanda are native to Brazil, for example, *caboclos* (Native American spirits). Not surprisingly, Umbanda is markedly less Africanized than is Candomble and tends to be characterized more by its Catholic, Native American, and, of course, spiritist influences than is Candomble. Again, however, the ideology and practice of spirit possession and mediumship are significant.

Batuque is an important Afro-Brazilian religion that originated during the early part of the twentieth century in and around the city of Belem in northern Brazil. It, too, like Umbanda but unlike Candomble, is a religion that is almost exclusively Brazilian for the same reasons noted earlier, although it should be noted that spiritism is not an important component of Batuque beliefs and practices. The pantheon is generally conceived of as being comprised of two tiers of spirits: Catholic saints and *encantados* (highly anthropomorphic [having human traits] spirits, many of Brazilian origin, who inhabit the tangible world). Spirit possession and mediumship are, again, integral to Batuque worship.

Rituals

The French anthropologist Michel Agier observed Candomble initiation ceremonies in Salvador, Bahia, in 1992. Eight young women were initiated into a *terreiro* (a religious compound or worship center) under the direction of the *mae-de-santo* (priestess of the saints/*orixas*). A crowd of two hundred "spectators," including tourists, black political activists, friends, neighbors, and visitors from other *terreiros*, was present for the ceremonies; another two dozen people were actually involved in the ceremonies. Given the setting, the ceremonies were apparently quite crowded, and many people had to watch through the windows of the main building. The priestess and her assistant directed the proceedings, but the eight young initiates were personally assisted by other initiated adherents.

A total of nine ceremonies lasted for several hours during alternating nights over seventeen days. The nine ceremonies included seven rites for the individual initiates (two initiated under the same *orixa*), a rite for Xango, the spirit recognized as the "patron" saint or *orixa* of the *terreiro,* and, finally, a final rite for Oxala, the spirit who, according to the priestess, "comes last" and completes the ceremonial cycle. The order in which the *orixas* were honored and celebrated, one each night over the nine nights, followed precisely the ritual calendar of the *terreiro*. Although each night was dedicated to one *orixa,* the nine separate nightly rites also involved the recognition of the *orixas* in an order following the ritual calendar as well. At this particular *terreiro* the order was Xango, the principle *orixa,* followed by three masculine *orixas*, then Oxumare, considered half-male/half-female, followed by three female *orixas*, and, finally, Oxala.

Each night the priestess presented each initiate to drummers and then, accompanied by the drummers and those in attendance, sang a song to invoke the initiate's "patron" *orixa*. Agier notes that the various *orixas* would manifest and identify themselves. The *orixas* also manifested themselves on several audience members as well. The seventeen-day ritual was highly organized and, in the opinion of those present, carefully orchestrated to closely adhere to the Yoruba tradition embraced by that particular *terreiro*.

In their ethnography (cultural study) on Umbanda in Sao Paulo in southern Brazil, the sociologists Fernando Brumana and Elda Martinez describe the opening ceremony of a longer ritual. Those people in attendance included three drummers, the *pai-de-santo* (highest ranking male of the *terreiro*), the *mae pequena* (female assistant), and two lines of men and women dressed in white (the mediums). Accompanied by the drummers, the *pai-de-santo* sang the opening ritual song. Everyone then kneeled as he recited the "Our Father" and the "Hail Mary." The *pai-de-santo* then prompted everyone to stand, and he began to sing a number of songs for the various *orixas* (in this context this term means "spirits" in a general sense). They first sang for Exu, an *orixa* referred to as "the spirit of the shadows" (Brumana & Martinez 1989, 63), an apt description for a spirit generally known throughout sub-Saharan west Africa and the New World as a trickster. A medium then fumigated the area with a censer while the others sang a song for Ogum (also commonly known as "Ogun"). After completion of this song, first the *pai-de-santo* and then the others threw themselves down in front of the altar and hit the ground with their foreheads while singing another song that recognizes the *caboclo* (Native American spirit). Brumana and Martinez note that the spiritual forces recognized and invoked at ceremonies such as these are so powerful that the assistance of the spirits sung for in this opening part of the ceremony is crucial.

Stage Is Set

The preliminaries were now complete, and the stage set for the manifestation of the *orixas*. The drummers begin to play more deliberately, and the *pai-de-santo* summoned the *caboclos* with a song. Within minutes the Native American spirit Urubatao, the spiritual "chief" of this *terreiro,* manifested upon the *pai-de-santo*. The *pai-de-santo*'s assistant gave him the accoutrements associated with this particular spirit, including a cigar (which is smoked by the manifesting spirit) and a feather head ornament. The other mediums underwent similar dissociative states and took cigars as well.

Those in attendance mingled with the manifested spirits to receive counseling, medical advice, and so forth. The *caboclo* that manifested on the *pai-de-santo* greeted those present, welcomed them to the *terreiro,* and told them that their problems would be solved by the power of God. The *pai-de-santo* later ritually embraced everyone, one by one, kneeled in front of the altar and in front of the drummers, and sand a farewell song. At the conclusion of this song, his body collapsed as the *caboclo* left his body. After a short while, the *pai-de-santo* recovered and directed dismissal songs for the spirits that had manifested on the other mediums. A final song was sung for the *caboclos* to thank them for their participation.

Those people present then turned their attention to the *bahianos*, spirits of northeastern Brazil described by Brumana and Martinez as "merry, drunk, always with a joke on their lips" (Brumana & Martinez 1989, 65). As they manifested on the mediums, they were given hats, whips, and cigarettes. The spirits mingled with one another and the people in attendance; there was a party-type atmosphere as the spirits smoked, laughed, danced, and so forth. The spirit that manifested on the *pai-de-santo* finally informed the other spirits that it was time to go, and a farewell song was sung for this purpose.

The last spirits to manifest that night, the *eres* (infantile, childlike spirits), began to present themselves through the mediums. *Eres* will generally play, soil themselves, run, laugh, speak incoherently, demand gifts, and so on. The atmosphere is described as carnival-like. Eventually those people present began to tire of the antics of the *eres* and tried to convince them to go. This was finally achieved only with a certain amount of difficulty. After the *eres* departed, the *pai-de-santo* repeated the introductory prayers at the altar; those present saluted the altar. A final farewell song was sung, and the ceremony ended.

Batuque

Among the many rituals and ceremonies of Batuque, one of the most important is the annual rite that is carried out in honor of the "patron" *encantado* (spirit) of a medium of a particular *terreiro*. Leacock and Leacock described the ceremony as it is practiced in Belem. The *pai-de-santo* opens the ceremony with a short prayer; the *pai-de-santo* himself is solely responsible for the form and content of the prayer. This prayer is derived from the more elaborate *ladainha* (a series of prayers for the saints) of folk Catholicism. The Catholic saints having been honored, the ritual focus is redirected on the *encantados*. At this point, before continuing any further, songs for the Exus ("demon spirits" in this context) are sung in order to politely and respectfully "dismiss" them from the proceedings. It should be pointed out that the "dismissal" of Exus (or Eshus) from public ceremonies is a common practice in African-derived religions in the New World, especially those that are associated with the Yoruba cultural tradition, including Candomble and Xango in Brazil and Orisha in Trinidad.

After the Exus have been appeased, songs are then generally sung for Averekete (a Dahomean spirit associated with St. Benedict); after Averekete has been acknowledged, songs are sung for Rainha Barba (an *encantado* associated with Saint Barbara). The anthropologists Seth Leacock and Ruth Leacock note that at this point the only other *encantado* that is certain to be called or sung for is the spirit in whose honor the ceremony is being held. Other spirits are then called in a more or less random order, with the exception that the more important and prestigious *senhores* are called before the lower-ranking *caboclos*. It should be pointed out, however, that virtually any *encantado* can show up (manifest itself) at any time, although it is generally the case that the *senhores* tend to appear before the *caboclos*.

During public ceremonies such as the one described here, it is not uncommon for the proceedings to be momentarily halted to allow a person to complete a ritual act in fulfillment of some obligation owed to an *encantado*. Later, various foods or drinks are offered to the various *encantados* honored by the mediums who are present. It is not unusual for people to become possessed while participating in the food and drink ritual. The ceremony just described might last an hour.

General Comments

Clearly, the practice of spirit possession serves to both culminate and legitimize Afro-Brazilian rites and ceremonies. Spirit possession, more than any other ritual activity, provides the link—and a direct and intimate one at that—between the world of the worshipers and the world of the spirits. However, the adherents of the three groups—Candomble, Umbanda, and Batuque—interpret the phenomenon somewhat differently. Candomble is essentially a "conservative" religion in that it is viewed primarily as a New World version of an ancient African religion, and its practitioners are content, for the most part, with the status quo. Umbanda and Batuque, on the other hand, embrace a theology and a ritual program that facilitates a greater degree of individual expression, given that they are highly eclectic, relatively open belief systems that embrace and even revel in the diverse pantheons drawn from both New World and Old World religious traditions.

What is seen in the Afro-Brazilian religions is a manifestation of perhaps the most significant problem confronting all worshipers: Does one embrace a form of religion that serves the collective need to undergird a code of appropriate cultural behavior and a system of values with a static, conservative, and, hence, legitimizing belief system, or, on the other hand, does one give up the psychological "comfort" of ideological conservatism in exchange for the existential (relating to existence) desire to continually enrich one's personal ideology and one's perpetual need to adjust to the contingencies of everyday life? The rites, ceremonies, and ideology of Afro-Brazilian religions present the worshiper with any number of responses to this question.

James Houk

See also African-American Churches; Yoruba

Further Reading

Agier, M. (1998). Between affliction and politics: A case study of Bahian Candomble. In H. Kraay (Ed.), *Afro-Brazilian culture and politics: Bahia, 1790's to 1990's* (pp. 134–157). Armonk, NY: M. E. Sharpe.

Bastide, R. (1978). *The African religions of Brazil: Toward a sociology of the interpenetration of civilizations* (H. Sebba, Trans.). Baltimore: Johns Hopkins University Press.

Brumana, F. G., & Martinez, E. B. (1989). *Spirits from the margin, Umbanda in Sao Paulo: A study in popular religion and social experience*. Stockholm, Sweden: Almqvist & Wiksell International.

Ireland, R. (1991). *Kingdoms come: Religion and politics in Brazil*. Pittsburgh, PA: University of Pittsburgh Press.

Leacock, S., & Leacock, R. (1975). *Spirits of the deep: A study of an Afro-Brazilian cult*. Garden City, NY: Doubleday Natural History Press.

Voeks, R. A. (1997). *Sacred leaves of Candomble: African magic, medicine, and religion in Brazil*. Austin: University of Texas Press.

Afro-Caribbean

Afro-Caribbean ritual systems are deeply rooted in African spiritual traditions. Having also been shaped by New World slavery, they always express the wrenching experience of the African diaspora (the story of how Africans, though scattered and dispersed, managed to retain their traditions and reform their identities in a new world). During four hundred years of contact with African traditional religions and Catholicism or Protestantism, African slaves and immigrants not only retained much of their original beliefs and practices, but also modified religious rituals of the Christian faith.

The African Legacy

These processes created (1) ritual traditions in the Caribbean mainly based on African traditional religions and (2) ritual traditions that bear a strong African flavor and constitute attempts to adapt the Christian faith to suit African cultural facets.

Ritual traditions in the Caribbean mainly based on African traditional religions, being extensions of the west African Òrìsà/vodun (voodoo) cultures and ritual systems, include rituals of African-derived religions such as vodun in Haiti and the Dominican Republic; Regla de Ocha (or Lucumi or Santería), Palo Monte (or Mayombe), and Abakuá (or Nañigo) in Cuba; Santería (or Lucumi) in Puerto Rico and elsewhere in the United States; Kumina, Convince, and Myal in Jamaica; Orisha religion (or Shangó) in Trinidad and Tobago; Kélé in St. Lucia; Big Drum Dance in Carriacou/Grenada; and Maria Lionza in Venezuela.

Ritual traditions that bear a strong African flavor and constitute attempts to adapt the Christian faith to suit African cultural facets, having been heavily influenced by Christianity, include rituals of the Spiritual Baptists and Shouters in Trinidad/Tobago and Grenada; "Tie Heads" in Barbados; Shakers in Saint Vincent; and Revivalists in Jamaica.

Rastafarian rituals, partly derived from the Old Testament, constitute a rather new social-religious phenomenon that emerged in the 1930s in Jamaica in response to the need for persons of the African diaspora to maintain an attachment to the ancestral homeland of Africa.

Beyond these major Afro-Caribbean ritual traditions, a number of less-known ancestral rituals are practiced throughout the Caribbean within most families. Ancestors might, for example, appear in dreams and demand food and ritual attention. The subsequent creative communion with a variety of ritual offerings for the ancestors will then ensure their benevolent influence on the living.

During the past four centuries Afro-Caribbean ritual systems have served their followers mainly as a form of cultural resistance against slavery and colonial domination in the struggle for spiritual identity and power. Today they offer to their followers, in addition to their religious inspiration and healing potential, primarily an African model of personality building, creativity, and cosmic integration.

Heaven and Earth

African ritual systems in the Caribbean have developed a complex know-how to establish ritual contact with the protective forces of human life. The basic idea, shared by most ritual traditions in the

Caribbean, is the direct contact between human beings (horizontal plane) and energetic spiritual beings (vertical plane). The latter—*axis mundi* (ladder to heaven)—is represented, for example, by the center pillar *(poteau mitan)* of the Haitian vodun temple.

Such ritual contact and communication between heaven and Earth are essential for continued balance in the world and in human life. Afro-Caribbean religious rituals are thus means of celebrating the totality of existence in its larger dimensions. This aesthetic approach to spirituality makes use of all human senses to connect the individual with the suprasensual realities—with the larger community of material beings and spiritual beings.

According to the cultural anthropologist Joseph. Murphy, ceremonies within the African diaspora in the Caribbean and elsewhere are seen by their practitioners "as both works for the spirit and works of the spirit. The reciprocity between community and spirit is expressed in physical work as the community works through word, music, and movement to make the spirit present. The spirit in turn works through the physical work of the congregation, filling human actions with its power. Diasporan ceremonies are thus services *for* the spirit, actions of sacrifice and praise to please the spirit. Also they are services *of* the spirit, actions undertaken by the spirit to inspire the congregation. Thus, the reciprocity of diasporan spirituality is affirmed: Service to the spirit is service to the community; and service to the community is service to the spirit" (Murphy 1994, 7). Service is the central value of communal life. Service shows the spirit in ceremony and wherever one member serves another.

The power of the spirit, *ashé* (from the African language Yoruba) or *sé* (from Fõ, a west African language like Yoruba), is a vital creative force, uplifting individuals and communities. It can increase or decrease depending on the ritual practice and rigorous observance of religions duties and obligations. *Ashé* is contained in and transmitted by representative elements of vegetal, animal, and mineral offerings. *Ashé* is a power that is received, shared, and distributed through ritual practice. Symbolic concepts and elements are used as vehicles within the mystical and initiating experience.

Ritual as an Initiatory System

An important aspect of Afro-Caribbean rituals is the fact that they are initiatory systems. Ritual knowledge is acquired, transferred, and developed. In the Òrìsà/vodun ritual system initiates partake of an experience, during which they receive *ashé* or *sé.*

Initiation rituals are designed to incarnate the spirit. Such incarnations are encounters between the human being and the spirit in ritual. Spiritual growth is measured in experiences gained through ritual actions. The dynamism of the initiatory system suggests a mysticism of identity as well as the dialogic relationship of human being and *orisha* (from the west Arican Yoruba language *orisa*).

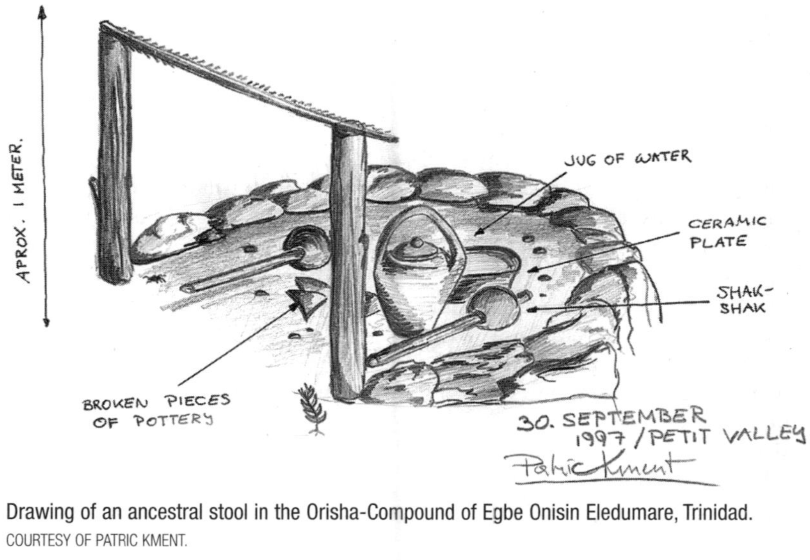

Drawing of an ancestral stool in the Orisha-Compound of Egbe Onisin Eledumare, Trinidad.
COURTESY OF PATRIC KMENT.

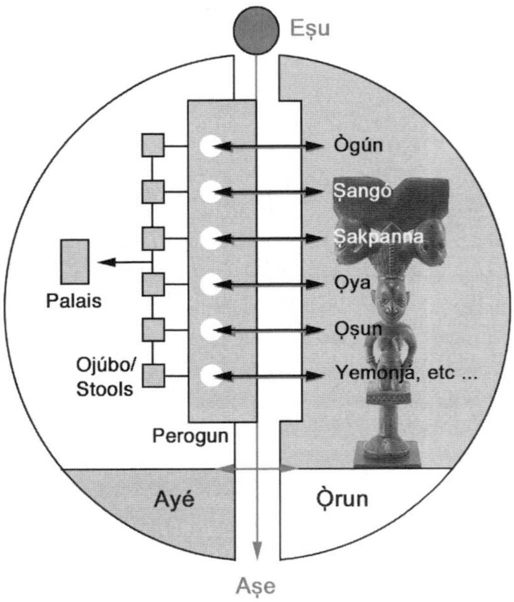

Cosmology of Orisha-Religion in Trinidad and its correlation with the Orisha-Compound. Concept and design by Patric Kment. COURTESY OF PATRIC KMENT.

The first occasion of an individual's ritual manifestation of the spirit transforms the inner nature of the individual. To be mounted, crowned, or converted by the spirit is to die in a former life and be reborn in a new one "in the spirit." When an individual receives the spirit, a part of his or her inner nature is also transformed to partake of the spirit's divinity.

In the Santería initiation ritual *kariocha* (the placing of the *orisha* on the head), for example, the initiate *iyawo* (bride of the *orisha*) not only makes a pact with the *orisha* but also has the spirit placed "upon" and "inside" her or him. This process is seen as the ritual death and rebirth of the initiate (in the *kariocha* ritual). One dies in the old life and is reborn *en santo* (in the spirit). The innermost identity of the *iyawo,* the *ori* (head, soul), becomes the "throne" or "seat" for the *orisha,* the head's "master."

Santería shares this psychology with Candomblé (the largest African-derived religion in Brazil), in which the *orisha* becomes an alternate personality, a more powerful and authentic dimension of the self. The transformation of the initiation ritual *kariocha* gives *santero*s (priests) new eyes to "see" the presence of the *orisha*s in objects and people. "The *orisha*s are manifested through a variety of symbolic media. They are both 'in' herbs and 'are' herbs, 'in' natural forces and 'are' natural forces, 'in' drum rhythms and 'are' drum rhythms, "in" human beings and 'are' human beings" (Murphy 1994, 112).

Trance and Ritual Possession

Ritual possession is the climax of Afro-Caribbean religious practice and is the most profound spiritual achievement for the individual as well as for the community. It consists essentially of the incorporation of a spirit in her or his devotee. Spirit possession is an altered state of consciousness during which a person is said to be "mounted" like a horse by a spirit. The invasion of one's body by a spirit may temporarily displace the personality of the possessed, substituting the envisaged mythological persona of the spirit.

To become possessed by a spirit is to "make the god," to capture the numinous (supernatural) flowing force *ashé* within one's body. When this happens, the face of the devotee usually freezes into a mask, a mask often held during the entire time of possession by the spirit. Not only is the spirit "made" in rituals, but also it causes a special state of mind. To be "in the spirit" is to bring the consciousness of the spirit into one's own and to share it with others. Whoever is empowered to manifest the spirit does so for the benefit of the community to allow others to share in the consciousness, either in dialogue or in identity with their own.

The entrance into the world of the spirit may be interpreted as a process of self-discovery. The importance of the spirit at work can be seen here, whereby the spirit might at once be conceived of as a divine personality, a crossing point of humanly constructed coordinates, and a level of awareness. Through initiation the spirit is made an essential "part" of the person, a dimension in a constellation of elements that comprises a person. However, the spirit is not the conscious self but rather something greater, which may subsume the self, overcome its borders, and direct the whole person. The spirit is rather the sanctified state that the self has experienced.

The Aesthetics of Ritual Healing

Relations between humans and spirits are never one sided but rather are reciprocal. People give to the spirits and expect to receive from them in turn. When the spirits are satisfied with their rituals, they bring healing power and sage advice to those who approach them.

People employ many ritual techniques to feed and please the spirits, using all the human senses and the entire body with all its expressive and communicative potential. These ritual techniques may include music, drumming, rhythmic stimulation, dancing, gestures, hyperventilation, singing, prayers, incantations, baths, emblems, clothing in bright symbolic colors, and offerings of foods, drink, and sometimes blood sacrifices—all in all, a work of art.

Vodun, for instance, has been described as a danced religion or a dance of the spirit—a system of movements, prayers, and songs in veneration of the invisible forces of life. Depending on the specific ritual tradition, the ritual may include elaborate ritual salutations, including a flag parade or twirling dances, invocation formulae, libations of rum, visual representations of the spirits along with their paraphernalia or signatures (such as the *vèvès* in voodoo), sacrificial offerings, the speaking of the sacred drums—with their rhythms corresponding to the individual spirits—and a gourd rattle directing the spirit in action. The living spirit cannot be shown except in activity, and this activity makes it present in the ritual to be shared by all "in the spirit." The actions of the spirit and their relationships with human actions express the heart of spirituality of Afro-Caribbean religions.

Priests and priestesses in Afro-Caribbean religions often derive a considerable part of their income from work as healers. They use a variety of ritual techniques to treat problems whose causes lie within the complex, densely populated invisible world of Afro-Caribbean cosmologies (branches of metaphysics that deal with the nature of the universe). Where the medical doctor or the herbalist fails, priests and priestesses expect to succeed because they understand the forces from which these problems originate, caused by spiritual entities such as ancestors or the deities whom people serve.

The Christian Legacy

Many Afro-Christian Revivalist leaders in Jamaica build their churches on reputations of healing. First the nature and causes of the ailment or problem are divined, and then prayers and charms are prescribed, or ritual baths and other efficacious acts are administered. Healing sites, once known as "balm yards," are now churches, which are sometimes erected in the leader's yard, with clients spanning a range of social classes.

Revivalist rituals have two parts. The first part is devoted to the singing of choruses to the rhythms of bass and rattler drums and to reading of the psalms. The second part is devoted to invoking the spirits and possession. In Zion possession (sky bound spirits prevail) follows trumping, a form of hyperventilation, accompanied by forward and backward steps while moving sideways, counterclockwise in circle. In Pukumina full possession (ground spirits, including ancestors, prevail), by eastbound spirits such as the Water Mother and the Indian Spirit, is sudden, without warning, and is followed by "laboring," as trumping is called (Chevannes 2001, 283–284).

By far the most important ritual in Jamaican Revivalism is the "Table," so called because a table is spread with fruits, bread, and other foods and decorated with candles, flowers, and other sacred objects, around which members dance counterclockwise and possession occurs. Tables, which last three or four days, are held periodically for thanksgiving, petition, appeasement, or other reasons. The ritual sacrifice of a goat is made on the final day.

The Spiritual Baptists or "Tie Heads" (because both men and women wrap their heads in cloth during services) of Barbados are closely tied to African religious traditions and rituals. Members do not enter their courts (temples) wearing shoes. They worship with their whole bodies—they bow, spin, and whirl before the altar. Lively music is often accompanied by hand clapping, foot stomping, and dancing. Often prayers are said in singsong, wailing, and weeping form. Sometimes all members of the church "go down in Pentecostal prayers" (pray aloud together).

White candles are burned at various sections of the church, particularly at the altar. Sweet meditative incense burns through the service as well. At given points in the worship, bells are taken from the altar and rung several times; a conch shell is blown, and a gong is banged. Members "go off in the spirit"—stamp their feet, make strong guttural sounds, and talk in other languages. The four corners of the church are specially marked and decorated by members with the *lota* (a brass vase with flowers, water, and a lit candle in the center).

The Tie Heads are also known for their Mourning Ground rituals. After accepting the faith, the members are baptized in "living water" and given instruction in the doctrine. The born-again then mourn "a godly sorrow which calls one away from the busy walks of life." The Mourning Ground is a sacred section of the church set aside for this purpose and tended by chosen members. Here, in isolation, the mind is cleansed by prayer and purification for seven to ten days.

Global Transformations

Many Afro-Caribbean ritual traditions have become more international in recent years. They are no longer practiced only in the Caribbean but increasingly in metropolitan centers of the United States, attracting many followers among middle-class African-Americans and other cultural and ethnic groups. As a consequence of the rising popularity in the African diaspora, many Caribbean governments have granted legal status to Afro-Caribbean religions.

At the beginning of the twenty-first century some priests and entrepreneurs of vodun and Santería are gaining a presence in cyberspace as their often-elaborate websites attract new clients—with the whole world being their potential public. They are thus on their way to once more transforming the already historically transformed Afro-Caribbean ritual traditions into new forms of global ritual culture. Cybertrans formations of Afro-Caribbean rituals are pioneering the advent of African digital diaspora religions of future generations.

Manfred Kremser

See also Rastafari; Santeria; Shakers; Vodun

Further Reading

Appiah, K. A., & Gates, H. L., Jr. (Eds.). (1999). *Africana: The encyclopedia of the African and African American experience*. New York: Basic Civitas Books.

Barnes, S. (Ed.). (1997). Africa's *Ogun: Old World and new*. Indianapolis: Indiana University Press.

Brandon, G. (1993). *Santería from Africa to the New World: The dead sell memories*. Bloomington: Indiana University Press.

Canizares, R. (1993). *Cuban Santería: Walking with the night*. Rochester, NY: Destiny Books.

Chevannes, B. (1994). *Rastafari: Roots and ideology*. Syracuse, NY: Syracuse University Press.

Davis, K., & Elias Farajaje-Jones, E. (Eds.). (1991). *African creative expressions of the divine*. Washington, DC: Howard University School of Divinity Press.

Deren, M. (1953). *Divine horsemen: The living gods of Haiti*. New York: Thames and Hudson.

Desmangles, L. G. (1993). *The faces of the gods: Vodou and Roman Catholicism in Haiti*. Chapel Hill: University of North Carolina Press.

Dunham, K. (1969). *Island possessed*. New York: Doubleday.

Glazier, S. D. (1991). *Marchin' the pilgrims home: A study of the Spiritual Baptists in Trinidad*. New York: Sheffield Publishing Group.

Houk, J. T. (1995). *Spirits, blood, and drums: The Orisha religion in Trinidad*. Philadelphia: Temple University Press.

Kremser, M. (1993). Visiting ancestors: St. Lucian Djiné in communion with their African kin. *Caribbean Quarterly, 39*(3–4), 82–99.

Kremser, M. (Ed.). (2000). *Ay BoBo—African-Caribbean religions* (2nd ed., 3 Vols.). Vienna, Austria: WUV-Universitätsverlag.

Kremser, M. (Ed.). (2003). *ADDR—African digital diaspora religions*. London: Lit-Verlag.

McAlister, E. A. (2002). *Rara: Vodou, power, and performance in Haiti and its diaspora*. Berkeley and Los Angeles: University of California Press.

Métraux, A. (1959). *Voodoo in Haiti*. Oxford, UK: Oxford University Press.

Murphy, J. M. (1981). *Ritual systems in Cuban Santería*. Ann Arbor, MI: University Microfilms International.

Murphy, J. M. (1994). *Working the spirit: Ceremonies of the African diaspora*. Boston: Beacon Press.

Murphy, J. M., & Mei-Mei, S. (Eds.). (2000). *Osun across the waters: A Yoruba goddess in Africa and the Americas*. Bloomington: Indiana University Press.

Olmos, M. F., & Paravisini-Gebert, L. (Eds.). (1997). *Sacred possessions: Vodou, Santería, Obeah, and the Caribbean*. New Brunswick, NJ: Rutgers University Press.

Agricultural Rituals

Agricultural rituals have traditionally been among the most common forms of religious rituals. With the exception of death rituals, agricultural rituals may be the oldest continuously practiced form of religious rituals. Throughout the world most major religions have either incorporated agricultural rituals into their ceremonies and practices or based such ceremonies and practices on agricultural rituals. This is true of both the details of agricultural rituals and, more significantly, their timing. The purpose of agricultural rituals usually is to improve crops and livestock or poor

RITUALS FOR RAIN IN INDIA

As with all farming people, an adequate and reliable supply of water is a major concern for the Garo slash and burn farmers of India. Some of the rituals they use are described below.

As the Garos are entirely dependent on agriculture for their support, it is but natural that they should regard with some anxiety either too prolonged a drought or too continuous or unseasonable rain. The spirits which rule the seasons and upon whose offices the growth of the crops depends, are, therefore, the most important in the Garo mythology, and at all stages of cultivation and harvesting some kind of sacrifice must be offered up to them.

Religious observances in this connection may be said to commence when a man first decides on the piece of ground which he wishes to clear and cultivate. Before beginning, he consults the omens in the following manner. In one corner of the plot of ground he makes a little clearance called opata, and then goes home. The next night, should he dream a bad or unlucky dream, he abandons the land which he proposed to open out, and seeks another piece where the omens are more propitious. Having cut his jungle and let it dry, he sets fire to it, and on the following day the first sacrifice to the god of the field takes place. It is called Agalmaka, and consists in the sacrifice of a fowl.

The next stage in cultivation is the sowing of the seed. To ensure the favour of the spirits, this must be preceded by the Gitchipong and the Michiltata ceremonies. The first is a personal sacrifice which each individual must offer, and the second a collective ceremony in which the whole village joins. The spirit invoked is Rokime, the "mother of rice." In this ceremony, the priest strikes the earth with the handle of a dao or chopper and reminds the spirit that certain flowers in the jungle have blossomed, which is a sign that it is time to sow the rice of which she is the mother. He implores her favour and protection that the crop may be a good one. In this connection the Garos believe that the spirit who first taught them to cultivate as they now do, was named Misi-agrang-Saljong-sang-gitang. He returns to the country every year, scatters the seeds which later spring up as weeds, and tells the people not to forget the lessons which he taught them about keeping their fields clean.

Source: Playfair, A. (1909).
The Garos. London: David Nutt, p. 93.

growing conditions such as drought or famine. This purpose is usually accomplished by appeasing or gaining the favor of deities and other spirits. Hence, many agricultural rituals form part of a reciprocal arrangement between the worshiper and the deity that must be maintained in order to ensure favorable crop and livestock production.

The Basis for Other Religious Rituals

Religious rituals are found all over the world and are practiced by both urban and rural populations. These rituals are often seen as mechanisms or forums for people to communicate with deities and other spirits. A number of the features of agricultural rituals were initially distinct from most other religious rituals but came to dramatically influence the development of later religious rituals.

First, most agricultural rituals have a long history and have even incorporated older hunting rites. For instance, many of the agricultural rituals of the ancient Greeks were based on older hunting myths in which the hero's survival is dependent upon the sacrifice of an animal. These myths are important because they established the precedent of sacrifice as a key component of the rituals and because they reinforced the relationship between humans and animals. In the story of Polyphemus and Odysseus, the hero escapes only by clinging to the stomach of a ram, which later must be sacrificed. Through the years animal sacrifice, and even human sacrifice, would become an important part of agricultural rituals.

Second, agricultural rituals are tied to the growing, hunting, or fishing seasons and therefore are usually based on the lunar calendar and not the contemporary Western solar calendar. Hence, most agricultural rituals are "cycle rituals" and tied to the passage of time and the change of seasons. By establishing accepted times of the year when communities would gather, agricultural festivals laid the foundation for the calendars of future religious activities. Although the specific dates varied, almost every agricultural society celebrated the first harvest with an elaborate religious ritual. For the ancient Greeks, this ritual was known as the "festival of flowers" and coincided with the spring equinox (in March). Among sub-Saharan African tribes, First Fruits festivals were celebrated in January.

Third, agricultural rituals established the precedent of bringing people together to either prepare for the growing season or to celebrate the harvest. Over time special areas or temples were built to serve as the focus of these rituals. For instance, among the tribes of Botswana, Africa, special kraals (villages) were built by chiefs or kings to house subjects who traveled to the royal site to take part or witness the annual rain and harvest feasts. As such, early agricultural rituals also served a social purpose because they brought people together and were often the only times of the year when whole tribes or populations came together. Among aboriginal people in Oceania (lands of the Pacific Ocean), these rituals provided a forum for marriages to be arranged and initiation rites to be undertaken.

Fourth, the hierarchy of a culture was often reinforced by agricultural rituals. Usually shamans or priests preserved the intricacies and often-elaborate steps of rituals, not only giving the shamans or priests significant status within a culture, but also often resulting in rigid hierarchies. For instance, among the Kayan people of Borneo, both priests and shamans exist, but only the priests direct the important agricultural rituals. In many religions a great deal of information is passed orally. This information often gives the priest or shaman the ability to seemingly perform miraculous feats. In previous centuries Daoist priests went through extensive training to be able to recognize when the meteorological conditions were favorable for rain. Only then would they perform rain ceremonies. On a more elemental level most primitive agricultural rituals have the feminine at their core and often revolve around female deities because of the association of nurturing, birth, and growth with the female portion of the population. For instance, among the Ashanti of Ghana, Africa, shamans are believed to derive their divine blood from their mother, who has transferred it from the goddess of the Earth.

Fifth, a variety of talismans and other religious objects was developed for use in religious rituals. These objects included altars for sacrifices, ritual masks, and small totems for personal use. For instance, the Ifugao people of the Philippines continue to prize small craved figures, known as *bulul*s, which serve as the earthly home of the spirits of the rice gods during the harvest time. In addition, some peoples of western African use elaborate masks, some as tall as three meters, to ward off evil spirits during the planting season. In addition, the Kenyah-Kayan people of Borneo in the Malay Archipelago carve intricate masks *(hudoqs)*, which are designed to frighten malevolent spirits away from the precious rice fields. The Maya of Central and South America required people to first cleanse themselves through fasting and then to ritually cleanse their idols before the idols could be used in ceremonies or festivals. In some societies precious metals or minerals were reserved for use in producing objects used in agricultural rituals. The Shang dynasty of China restricted the use of bronze for ceremonial items and royal use. Jade would also become widely used for agricultural totems in China.

Increase (or Produce) Rituals

Most agricultural rituals are increase (or produce) rituals. In other words, they are designed to improve crop or livestock yields. An agricultural ritual can be designed to appeal directly to the gods, or the components of an agricultural ritual itself can be used to improve yields. For instance, during the Celtic period in Great Britain people would light great fires known as "Beltaine fires" as part of elaborate agricultural festivals. The ashes from these fires were thought to be able to significantly improve the harvest and were spread over the fields. In Japan the sport of sumo grew out of agricultural religious festivals designed to please the gods and prompt them to provide a good harvest. Among the coastal Australian aborigines increase rituals are directly tied to the maintenance of sacred sites. Tribes or clans within the tribes are responsible for the care of specific sacred places, and if they fail to care for the places, the people believe that poor harvests or problems with livestock will occur.

Although most agricultural rituals are calendrical, some increase rituals and other rituals can take place at any time of the year. During times of trouble divination rituals are held to determine what actions have displeased the gods and what steps can be taken to appease them and improve growing conditions. This is especially true of rain ceremonies or those ceremonies designed to halt floods or famine or infestations of rodents and insects. During droughts or intense heat the Iroquois of North America performed a ritual they called the "Thunder Rite," which was thought to convince the gods to constrain the sun and prevent crops from being scorched or withered.

Agricultural rituals also played an important practical role in agricultural societies. These rituals often combined religiosity and agricultural techniques that were passed down from generation to generation. In this way agricultural rituals ensured the accurate transference of agricultural practices. For example, the Iroquois developed a complex planting system for their main staple crops: corn, squash, and beans (crops they nicknamed the "three sisters"). A tribe's women were responsible for an elaborate ritual that involved presoaking the seeds in water, blessing them, and individually planting them. Among the Paiwan, an Asiatic people, during the harvest ceremony *(masarut)*, a priest ritually divides the crops into categories for human consumption, for livestock consumption, and for seeds to plant the next year. For the Maya the corn god Yum K'aax was perceived as defenseless against the various animals and diseases that plagued corn. Therefore, the god needed humans to protect him through rituals, and, in return, Yum K'aax provided food for the community. Many Filipino tribes have developed ceremonies in which they plant seeds at night. These ceremonies have a practical component because most chicken and other village fowl are in their roosts at night and therefore less likely to dig up the seeds. These types of beliefs and rituals reinforce the need for good husbandry.

At the core of many agricultural rituals is the notion of balance (or harmony). Many rituals encourage farmers to grow enough to feed the family but not to overproduce. In early agricultural societies this notion was important because there were few markets for excess production. Instead, overproduction could significantly harm the soil or lead to insect or rodent infestations. One manifestation of this trend is the Zapotec people of Central America. If the spring rains are heavy, the Zapotec farmers plant less because they know that crop yields will be higher, and the farmer seeks to produce only enough for the family's subsistence and any ritual purposes.

As societies developed more sophisticated tools and agricultural techniques, rituals were developed to bless the tools to improve crop yield. Among some societies these rituals involved the use of fire to "purify" (or cleanse) the tools. The Bunan people of Taiwan even worshiped their tools after the harvest and then carefully put them away in anticipation for the next growing season.

Sacrifice

Sacrifice often plays an important role in agricultural rituals. In some cases people perceive the sacrifice of an animal or person, whether real or symbolic, as part of the broader cycle of life, which involves death and rebirth or sacrifice and renewal. Among the Celts there was even a belief that the sun god sacrificed his energy through marriage to the Earth goddess. The resultant transference of energy was responsible for the growth of crops. Because even the gods sacrificed themselves for agriculture, it was incumbent upon humans to practice sacrifice. In other societies sacrifices were seen simply as a means to appease or gain favor with the spiritual world or a particular deity. Peoples of the Caucasus region sacrificed animals after a period of foul weather as a means to appease the gods and protect the crops. They developed an elaborate hierarchy of animals, ranging from bulls to wild ibexes, which would be sacrificed depending upon the severity of the weather or famine.

People usually view sacrifice as an obligation between worshiper and deity—when sacrifices are made, the deity is obligated to respond. Sacrifice rituals are far more common in agricultural societies than in hunter-gatherer societies such as the Australian aborigines or the Plains tribes of North America. This is because only agricultural societies regularly have the excess livestock to undertake ritual sacrifices.

Agricultural rituals usually demand the sacrifice of the best produce or livestock. For instance, both the Old Testament of the Bible and the Hindu tradition prohibited the sacrifice of animals with deformities or exterior blemishes. Some religions used human sacrifice as part of their agricultural rituals. Among the Aztecs of Central America, two of the most important gods were Tlaloc, the god who controlled rain, and Xipe Totec, the god of the spring rebirth. Because of the importance of agriculture, people deemed that these gods should have only the most valuable sacrifices, which were young children because of their innocence and the belief that their tears symbolized rain.

The rituals surrounding the act of sacrifice could be intricate. In ancient Greece the festival of Thesmophoria was designed to honor Demeter, the goddess of agriculture, and to celebrate the annual reunion between her and her daughter Persephone (which marked the revival of the growing season). The festival was divided into three parts and involved a variety of rituals, including animal sacrifice.

Modern Effects

Many agricultural rituals continue to affect modern society in both religious and nonreligious ways. For instance, the European ritual of celebrating May Day is tied to pre-Christian agricultural rituals that celebrated the onset of spring and the growing season. The maypole itself represented the tree of life and was generally recognized as a fertility symbol. The core aspects of this ancient ritual have now been secularized and incorporated into contemporary society. In addition, both religious and secular Jews celebrate Sukkot. This was originally a harvest festival that occurred at the end of the autumn fruit season to celebrate the wanderings of the Jews through the desert after their exodus from Egypt. Also, the modern custom of planting trees as a remembrance of the deceased has its roots in older agricultural rituals.

Throughout the early period of the Christian Church people adapted pagan agricultural rituals to Christian services. The celebration of the corn king in the British region of Cornwall was adapted as the Christian ceremony of Lammas (loaf-mass) in which loaves of bread were baked from the first harvest of the year. This trend continues in the modern period. For example, the Saora people of India have translated the Bible into their language and have adapted their agricultural rituals to conform with Christian theology.

Other religions have incorporated older agricultural rituals into their contemporary theology. For instance, the Andhra and Pradesh people of India have blended Hinduism with older agricultural rituals, including the "Frog Song" *(Kappatalli pata)*, a ritual chant designed to prompt frogs to croak because the people see frogs as harbingers of the rainy season. In secular China people continue to invite Daoist monks to perform rituals in order to stop natural phenomena such as flooding or plagues of grasshoppers or other pests. In some cases the codification of ancient rituals actually formed the core of contemporary beliefs. For example, the Shinto religion of Japan developed from the Matsuri agricultural rituals, which performed held periodically to ensure a prolific rice crop.

Tom Lansford

See also Calendrical Rituals; Crisis Rituals; Iban; Sacrifice and Offerings

Further Reading

Bhattacharyya, S. (1976). *Farmers rituals and modernization: A sociological study*. Columbia, MO: South Asia Books.

Duncan, C. (1996). *The centrality of agriculture: Between humankind and the rest of nature*. Buffalo, NY: McGill-Queen's University Press.

Grim, J. (Ed.). (2001). *Indigenous traditions and ecology: The interbeing of cosmology and community*. Cambridge, MA: Harvard University Press.

Henry, D. (1989). *From foraging to agriculture: The Levant at the end of the Ice Age*. Philadelphia: University of Pennsylvania Press.

Mol, H. (1982). *The firm and the formless: Religion and identity in aboriginal Australia*. Ontario, Canada: Wilfrid Laurier University Press.

Schusky, E. (1989). *Culture and agriculture: An ecological introduction to traditional and modern farming systems*. New York: Bergin & Garvey.

Smith, B. (1992). *Rivers of change: Essays on early agriculture in eastern North America*. Washington, DC: Smithsonian Institution Press.

Spielmann, K. (Ed.). (1991). *Farmers, hunters, and colonists: Interaction between the Southwest and the southern Plains*. Tucson: University of Arizona Press.

Turner, D. (1985). *Life before Genesis, a conclusion: An understanding of the significance of Australian aboriginal culture*. New York: Peter Lang.

White, K. (1970). *Roman farming*. Ithaca, NY: Cornell University Press.

Altered States of Consciousness

"Consciousness" refers to perception of oneself and one's surroundings achieved through the ordinary workings of the five physical senses. Awareness can also be achieved through perception arising in other ways, such as in dreams, trances, hypnotic states, and episodes of mystical ecstasy—all examples of altered states of consciousness, which are often interpreted as religiously significant.

Naturally Occurring Alterations

Dreams are natural in origin and universal in occurrence, but some cultures attach particular importance to them as doors to higher levels of insight. Other naturally occurring altered states may be due to such phenomena as epilepsy or schizophrenia—medical conditions according to modern understanding, but at other times and in other cultures considered signs of spiritual connectedness. Epileptic seizures closely parallel the trance states shamans enter for curing or other public rituals. Julius Caesar was probably epileptic, and his periodically altered state was considered not a disability but a token of divine favor, as it was believed that in this state he could communicate directly with the gods. The visual and auditory hallucinations associated with schizophrenia could be interpreted as legitimate channels of spiritual communication in the case of Joan of Arc, whose mission was guided by supernatural voices. Today she would be treated as a psychiatric patient; in her own time she was considered either a witch or a saint, but in either case was taken seriously as someone in touch with spiritual beings.

Induced Alterations

Some states of consciousness are deliberately altered. Trance states may, for example, be induced through sensory deprivation—reducting outside stimuli and restricting motor activity. In some cultures, sensory deprivation is cultivated as a way to tap into supernatural guidance. The "vision quest" ritual of traditional Native American groups required a boy approaching puberty to leave the campsite to fast and undergo other physical austerities in hope of being contacted by a guardian spirit who would indicate his future course in life. Among the Ojibwa, for example, the guardian spirit usually appeared in the form of an animal said to "adopt" or "take care" of the boy. Another form of deliberate sensory deprivation occurs among working class African-descended Pentecostals (locally known as "Shakers") on St. Vincent, a West Indian island. Shakers who wish to become elders must undergo a ceremony of "mourning" for past sins. This requires that they be isolated, lying blindfolded on pallets for up to two weeks taking little or no food. In the resulting altered state they are able to put aside their sinful ways, something believed difficult to do amid everyday activities.

The opposite of sensory deprivation, sensory enhancement, may also induce trance. One form of sensory enhancement common in ritual settings is rhythmic drumming, shown in laboratory experiments to affect the central nervous system so as to produce hallucinations, involuntary muscular movements, and a distorted sense of time. In Haitian Vodun, rituals are held to summon spirits. Each spirit responds to its own particular pattern of drumbeats, so rhythmic drumming is integral to the ceremony. Drumming is already in progress as participants enter the ritual compound; it gradually increases in tempo (with documented hypnotic effects), continuing for the entire nighttime ceremony, which may last many hours. The drumming is accompanied by dancing, and the resulting physical exertion can lead to hyperventilation, increased adrenaline production, and a drop in blood sugar—physical factors that together create altered consciousness.

Spiritually desirable altered states can also be induced by mental and physical exercises. Yoga, for example, is a method of controlling "normal" physiology so as to clear the mind for higher perceptions. Moments of "inspiration" can also arise spontaneously, as well as through deliberate meditative techniques, leading to bursts of artistic or other creative activity that seem to "come out of nowhere." This is only the case, however, if the inspired person is open to the possibility that the unexpected perception of a "higher truth" is real, and not simply a fleeting fantasy.

Considerable scholarly attention has been directed at trance induced through use of hallucinogenic drugs, some of which (e.g., the ancient Indian *soma* or the *peyote* of Native North America) occur naturally and have been used since antiquity. Recent studies by the geologist Jelle Zeilinga de Boer have suggested that the oracle at the ancient Greek shrine at Delphi uttered her pronouncements (believed to be communications from the god Apollo) while inhaling ethylene gas seeping from fissures beneath the shrine. Ethylene has known anesthetic properties and also produces feelings of "aloof euphoria." The content of drug-induced hallucinations is culture-specific, as are norms of usage. For example, among the Campa of eastern Peru, the hallucinogen *ayahuasca* is ingested only by the shaman in order for him to enter into

ALTERED STATES IN AFRICA AND MEXICO

An altered state of consciousness of the leader and the participants in religious rituals is found in many religions. The following examples are of possession as experienced by Sufi mystics in Somali and of trance as experienced by Tarahumara Indians in northern Mexico.

It is evident that this ceremony has inherent susceptibility to syncretism in the services (*dhikr*) of the Sufi tariqas. Especially is this true of the most popular forms of the *dhikr*, where trance states in which 'fading' or 'death' of self, believed to result in mystical union with God, are induced by direct stimulation. The *dhikr* held by the Ahmediya at their annual pilgrimage to the tomb of Sheik Ali Maye Durogba have been described as follows. 'Thousands come to the tomb from all parts of Somalia. The festival lasts fifteen days and culminates in a great *dhikr* on the last night when the pilgrims form an immense circle and, to the accompaniment of singing, recite their formulae in raucous saw-like voices rhythmically swaying their bodies. This continues until day-break. Once they have got well worked-up, large numbers fall foaming to the ground in induced epileptic convulsions (Barile, 1935). This is neither an informed nor a sympathetic description but it serves to indicate how closely the tariqa dhikr resembles the *saar* dance and suggests a syncretism which is well established in Egypt and elsewhere.

Source: Lewis, I. M. (1955–1956). "Sufism in Somaliland: A Study in Tribal Islam, I & II." *Bulletin of the School of Oriental and African Studies (17–18)*, 33.

To give a peyote fiesta, in the cure of some sick person, tesguino [corn beer] is made, a cow sacrificed, and lots of food prepared. As in other native fiestas, the *dutuburi* is danced on a patio that has three crosses. Matachines may also be danced in front of a special cross. At some distance to one side, there is a special patio for the peyote dance (*hikuli nawikebo*). Two crosses are placed here, one beside the jar containing the peyote, and one for God. Peyote is not dedicated to the four directions but is merely put in front of the two crosses for a time. At this patio for peyote, there is a hole into which one must spit and throw old cigarette butts. One must remove his hat and cross himself on approaching the patio. And one must ask permission to leave it. A quarter of beef is placed here, with all vitals included. The *peyotero* [ritual specialist] takes this beef in the end, in payment for his services. A big fire, around which the peyote dancers move, burns all night on the patio.

After dusk, the dancing ceases and everyone present eats a bit of peyote (it is dry and served ground up and mixed with water). Then they drink a little *tesguino*. All night long they are drunk from the effects of the peyote, although they do not eat it again. If any remains, the special dancers finish it in the morning.

After the eating of the peyote, the shaman rasps with his notched stick for a while. A circle or hole marked with a cross is made, into which peyote is placed and covered with a bowl, calabash, or small olla. The end of the notched stick is then placed on the overturned container and scraped with another stick. The container gives resonance to the rasping. The rasping sticks are made from wood which grows in the peyote country. On the trips to obtain peyote, one of these sticks is made and brought back. It is considered dangerous to bring back more than one at a time. Only shamans keep them in their possession, since the layman would be in danger of death should he keep one.

Source: Wendell C. Bennett and Robert M. Zingg. *The Tarahumara: An Indian Tribe of Northern Mexico.* (Chicago: The University of Chicago Press, 1935), 293.

trance as he conducts rituals. Among the Huichol of Mexico, however, the entire group consumes *peyote* (under the guidance of the shaman) and enters into the altered state together. Some perceptions do, however, transcend culture: a very bright light in the center of the visual field, pulsations in imagery, the sensation of traveling through a tube, and the replacement of naturalistic images with geometric forms.

A person in an induced trance may receive direct communication from spiritual beings. If, however, a spirit enters into and speaks to others through the entranced person, the latter is said to be possessed. If possession is involuntary, either through the willful action of the spirit itself or the result of a sorcerer casting a spell, rituals of exorcism will be performed to drive the invading spirit away. If, however, the possession is desired, the trance state can be used for important religious purposes, insofar as the possessed person can act as a medium through whom spirits convey prophetic information or advice. Cross-cultural survey research indicates that belief in possession tends to be found in socially stratified societies, often ones with institutionalized slavery. Possession also seems to be more frequently reported among women than among men. It may be that in traditional, stratified societies, women—like slaves—ordinarily had no legitimate public voice. Only when in a possessed trance could their voices be expressed and heeded. In most cases, possession trance is a public performance. In cultures in which possession is seen as desirable, it is achieved in the presence of an audience whose participation socially validates the entranced person's claim to have entered a different and presumably higher level of consciousness.

People in altered states are hypersuggestable, meaning that there is a decrease in normal critical faculties and a diminished capacity or willingness to distinguish between subjective and objective reality. To compensate for this loss of control, people in altered states typically depend on hypnotists, psychotherapists, shamans, or spiritual guides (depending on the culturally appropriate role) to lead them and interpret their experiences. For example, spiritist healer-mediums of Brazil have successfully performed surgeries without anesthesia or antisepsis, doing so while in self-induced trances entered into during public rituals. Sidney Greenfield, who has observed and described these surgeries, contends that the patients are also in altered states, although not in any formal or even acknowledged way. Rather, their consciousnesses are altered through the force of their belief in the powers of the healer and expectations of successful surgery. The patients undergo hypnosis via autosuggestion, a more potent form of the reaction experienced in our own society when people given a placebo think they are taking a real drug and feel better anyway.

Analysis

Several major theoretical trends dominate the analysis of trance states. For example, there is a neobehaviorist psychological model exemplified by the study by Walter and Frances Mischel of the Shango cult of Trinidad in the West Indies. Shango is a syncretic religion combining beliefs deriving from the Yoruba people of West Africa with elements of Christianity. Shango devotees seek possession during group ceremonies. The possessed person is referred to as a "horse," regarded as subordinated to and in effect "ridden" by the possessing spirit. At the same time, horses can assume a dominant role vis-à-vis the other participants, insofar as they can command others to do things in the name of the spirit. Such activity illustrates the behaviorist principle of reinforcement: ordinarily powerless people frequent these ceremonies in the hope of being possessed and thus given the chance to exercise power. This especially comes into play when a woman is possessed by a male spirit, and is allowed to act in an otherwise forbidden domineering "male" manner. Her willingness to put herself through the ritual is reinforced by the benefits she receives when possessed. Possession might also reduce guilt and anxiety, since one is permitted to engage in self-abasing acts (e.g., throwing oneself to the ground, wounding oneself) otherwise considered unseemly or inappropriate. The horse is also permitted very close physical contact with other participants, allowing expression of otherwise repressed sexual and hostile impulses, or simply of a need for intimacy. While possessed, a horse may ask the spirit to resolve disputes or other problems; according to the neobehaviorist model, doing so relieves the horse of personal responsibility should the advice not work out well.

A somewhat more sociological line of analysis has been proposed by I. M. Lewis, who looks for the social-structural rather than the individual-psychological roots of possession. Lewis has characterized possession-based cults as protest movements directed against dominant social groups—most typically women against men, or lower-class people against elites. Lewis concludes that the possessing spirits must be seen as "amoral" or "peripheral" to the moral code of the society in question. This analysis probably reflects the situation in the Muslim community in Somalia where he conducted fieldwork. Women in that culture are possessed by spirits who exist outside the range of orthodox Muslim belief and probably represent an older indigenous animist tradition largely supplanted by Islam.

Anthropological students of possession have tended to resist such universal explanations, noting that such activity varies depending on the particulars of the cultures in which they are found. It has been pointed out, for example, that there can be multiple types of possession in a single culture (four among the Kalabari of West Africa studied by Robin Horton and three among the Tonga of central Africa studied by Elizabeth Colson) said to be caused by different classes of spirits. Moreover, some anthropologists have highlighted the role of possession in maintaining status, as distinct from the "protest movement" function emphasized by Lewis. Dolores Shapiro's research demonstrates how possession groups in northeastern Brazil are vehicles through which social identity is defined, negotiated, and solidified. Others have accepted the proposition that possession is a way for sub-dominant people to gain greater social importance, even if only temporarily, but they reject the characterization of the possessing spirits as necessarily peripheral. For example, Lesley Sharp's study of the Sakalava of northwest Madagascar demonstrates that some possessing spirits are those of deceased royalty; when a woman is possessed by such spirits (called *tromba*), she is said to have achieved a sacred and honorable status central to the identity of the people as a whole. The *zar* cult of the Sudan, like the cult described by Lewis in Somalia, has flourished in a Muslim context. According to Susan Kenyon, however, the *zar* has grown beyond its peripheral status and "protest" function and has become an important element in social modernization. It provides women with a strong support network apart from their families and enables participants to deal with new situations, groups, and ideas by linking people from once separate communities into a new ritual orientation with its own ideas about the nature of reality. One of the ironies of Sudanese *zar*, however, is that as it has become more acceptable as an element in the modern society, its most prominent leadership roles—once reserved for women—are being taken over by men.

Centrality of Culture

An underlying physiological condition may well be common to all people under the influence of hallucinogenic drugs or experiencing other forms of trance. Culture, however, is what indicates whether that condition is desirable or not, whether it is expected to happen frequently or is rare and miraculous, whether it is real and commendable or the product of a diseased mind, and whether it is accessible to many or the preserve of an elite.

There has been extensive discussion as to whether it is fair and accurate to claim normative status only for ordinary sensory perception, an assumption that seems to treat "altered" states as less than real. Nevertheless, the term is well established in the language of the social and behavioral sciences, and it is possible to provide descriptive analyses of perceived altered states without getting bogged down in the question of whether or not they are real. The fact is that people in many diverse cultures believe that ordinary sensory perception is not a uniquely realistic form of consciousness. They believe that altered states are also indicative of authentic consciousness, and this belief has consequences for behavior in both ritual settings and everyday life.

Michael V. Angrosino

See also Afro-Brazilian; Vodun; Yoruba

Further Reading

Bourguignon, E. (1973). *Religion, altered states of consciousness, and social change*. Columbus: Ohio State University Press.

Bourguignon, E. (1976). *Possession*. San Francisco: Chandler and Sharp.

Crapanzano, V., & Garrison, V. (Eds.). (1977). *Case studies in spirit possession*. New York: John Wiley & Sons.

Furst, P. T. (1972). *Flesh of the gods: The ritual use of hallucinogens*. New York: Praeger.

Furst, P. T. (1976). *Hallucinogens and culture*. San Francisco: Chandler and Sharp.

Goodman, F., Hardy, J. H., & Pressel, E. (1974). *Trance, healing, and hallucinations*. New York: John Wiley & Sons.

Harner, M. (1973). *Hallucinogens and shamanism*. London: Oxford University Press.

Klass, M., & Weisgrau, M. K. (Eds.). (1999). *Across the boundaries of belief: Contemporary issues in the anthropology of religion*. Boulder, CO: Westview.

Tart, C. T. (Ed.). (1972). *Altered states of consciousness*. Garden City, NY: Anchor.

Winkelman, M. (2000). *Shamanism: The neural ecology of consciousness and healing*. Westport, CT: Bergin and Garvey.

Animal Sacrifice *See* Blood Rituals

Asceticism

Asceticism is common to all of the world's major religions. Although in contemporary times asceticism is most often found in fringe sects or cults, it is also manifested in some form in many mainstream religious rituals. At its most basic level, asceticism is the conscious rejection of physical pleasure through continuous self-denial as a means to attain or improve spirituality. For many religions, asceticism serves as the principle mechanism by which a follower can obtain true enlightenment or holiness. While asceticism revolves around the notion of self-denial, some more extreme groups have incorporated self-mutilation and physical pain into their ascetic rituals. However, these extreme forms of asceticism are often regarded as taboo among more highly regulated religions.

The Basis for Ascetic Rituals

In general, there are two broad forms of asceticism in religion. One is natural asceticism and the other is spiritual asceticism. People who engage in natural ascetic rituals hope to improve their physical or mental capabilities for personal reasons. For instance, followers of the Greek philosopher Pythagoras endeavored to rid themselves of emotions and passions. However, this effort was philosophical or intellectual rather than religious. Much more common are ascetic rituals designed to enhance the spirituality of an individual through the subjugation of worldly desires and pleasures to the divine.

The origins of spiritual asceticism in various religions have different roots. For instance, in Christian theology, besides scripture, the Bible provides the example of the Rechabites, an ancient Hebrew group which practiced asceticism by foreswearing wine and permanent dwellings. The example of Jesus, who foreswore earthly worldly pleasures, including those of the senses, family ties, and personal possessions, served as the basis for many later Christian ascetics. Within Buddhism, Siddhartha Gautama (the Buddha) initially practiced extreme asceticism, but eventually espoused a middle way that emphasized harmony and balance. After attaining enlightenment, he formed a monastic community known as the Sangha. Since Buddha left no written scripture, the monks became the guardians of his teachings through an oral, and later transcribed, tradition. This feature has reinforced the monastic or collective nature of Buddhist asceticism.

In India, Brahmins engage in a lifestyle that revolves around ascetic rituals. For instance, the tenets of their belief forbid indulgences such as gluttony, drunkenness, or wealth. If the Brahmin violates these then he must engage in a variety of ascetic rituals to make atonement. Brahmin have been forced to stand on tip-toe during the day, continuously roll around on the ground, or sit in the rain and wear wet clothing. At times, the Brahmin must also engage in long-term fasting that may result in death.

In Islam, organized ascetic communities include the Sufi orders that spread Islam throughout Sub-Saharan Africa and into Asia. To belong to a Sufi order one had to become a fakir or initiate and renounce worldly goods. To become a fakir, the initiate would have to undergo a series of rituals including sleep deprivation, seclusion, and fasting. A Judaic ascetic group was the Essenes, who survived for about 400 years before their demise in the second century CE. This small religious order practiced ritual immersions and celibacy and endeavored to lead a modest lifestyle. Their practices would, in turn, influence early Christian ascetic groups. Asceticism in the form of fasting was also common in a number of indigenous religions in Africa and the Americas. Often such fasting was used to achieve a state where the individual could obtain special insight or experience visions. In India, believers in Jainism engage in extreme fasting and sometimes starve themselves to death as they seek the highest forms of spirituality and sainthood.

Solitary and Communal Asceticism

Ascetic rituals can be expressed individually or through group actions. A common manifestation of asceticism is seclusion, and one of the most common ways to undertake an ascetic lifestyle is for an individual to become a hermit, or solitary holy person. By

EXTREME FORMS OF ASCETICISM

The most extreme forms of asceticism involve behaviors that may cause the individual bodily harm. Examples from two cultures are given below, but each causes much less injury than might be expected.

The Santal of India

Before we conclude, it may be interesting for the reader to have some idea of the original Hook-swinging festival, which has been declared now a criminal act by legislation, because of danger to human lives. Man in his Sonthalia and the Sonthals, gives a description which shows how the hooks for suspending the devotee were "inserted in the muscles of his back, who was generally an inebriated oracle. He was then suspended in mid-air and swung round, apparently hanging by the hooks. I have, however, seen a good many of these revolving martyrs, and although to a casual observer it appears very dreadful to behold a man thus pendant, it is not quite so bad so as it seems, for his friends took the precaution to tie a girth of strong cloth round the victim's body, in such a manner that his weight rests upon the cloth rather than on his muscles. The perforation of the flesh may cost him a few drops of blood, but that is all."

Source: Mukherjea, Charulal. *The Santals.* (1962).
Calcutta, India: A. Mukherjee and Company, Private Ltd., p. 270.

The Blackfoot of the Plains

Inside the lodge, rawhide ropes are suspended from the centre post, and here the men fulfil the vows that they have made during the previous year. Some have been sick, Or in great danger at war, and they then vowed that if they were permitted to live, or escape, they would swing at the Medicine Lodge. Slits are cut in the skin of their breast, ropes passed through and secured by wooden skewers, and then the men swing and surge until the skin gives way and tears out. This is very painful, and some fairly shriek with agony as they do it, but they never give up, for they believe that if they should fail to fulfill the vow, they would soon die.

On the fourth day every one has been prayed for, every one has made to the Sun his or her present, which is tied to the centre post, the sacred tongues have all been consumed, and the ceremony ends, every one feeling better, assured of long life and plenty.

Source : Grinnell, George B. (1962).
Blackfoot Lodge Tales: The Story of a Prairie People.
Lincoln, University of Nebraska Press, 1962, p. 267.

renouncing or minimizing human interaction, the hermit is free to concentrate on the study of religion. Traveling solitary holy figures were common in Eastern religions, including Buddhism, and among early Christians, permanent self-imposed solitude was common and was personified by early religious figures such as St. Anthony. Often the hermit would be confined within a single room in a church as the anchorite or anchoress. Hermits would often also locate in remote areas. In the early Eastern Christian churches, the solitary religious life was seen as a higher form of monastic life only open to the most devout monks. This rejection of human interaction served as one of the highest forms of asceticism and was itself a daily ritual. In other words, the solitary lifestyle became a continuous religious ritual.

Communal asceticism emerged as the more common form among most mainstream religions. The monastery provided a forum for the ascetic life while still retaining the ability to teach and train monks. Ascetic orders such as the Franciscans renounced worldly wealth, and many orders incorporated vows of silence and abstinence. The monastic tradition remains particularly strong among Buddhists in the contemporary era. Such communal life also reinforces the ritual aspect of the ascetic life.

Key to both solitary and communal ascetic rituals is the notion of rejecting worldly pleasure and pursuing spirituality. One of the most effective means to achieve this is through isolation from the everyday or secular world. As a result, most ascetics, whatever their religion, take steps to locate themselves in remote areas. Traditionally, this meant a location in the woods or mountains or simply a life of travel. Over time, the development of monasteries provided a means to achieve isolation even within an urban setting. One result has been that the majority of the major ascetic rituals take place in areas removed from the public. However, various religions have incorporated asceticism into the theology utilized by common adherents.

Fasting

The most common ascetic ritual is fasting. Fasting is found in almost every religion and involves the deliberate self-denial of food or water. In some cases, fasting may mean the avoidance of certain foods or drink, especially foods considered to be "rich" or gluttonous, and alcohol. Often such item-specific fasting is manifested throughout religious groups on a wide level. For instance, during the holy month of Ramadan Muslims abstain from food, drink, smoking, and sex during the day. This fast is designed to reinforce the notion of submission to Allah by submitting worldly desires to spirituality. Among the Jains, the most important fast occurs in August or September and lasts eight days. This period is supplemented by two periods of semi-fasting in September or October and April or March, when the Jains eat only one meal per day.

Fasting can be both a ritual in itself and a means to access other rituals. The physical toll that prolonged fasting takes on the body can lead to altered mental states. In such states, ascetics are more open to visions or spiritual guidance. For instance, the Crow tribe of Native Americans uses fasting to achieve a mental state whereby one can more easily see visions. This is also true of a number of Asian religions, including Jainism and Taoism.

Roman Catholics engage in a forty-day long fasting period known as Lent each year, beginning on Ash Wednesday and ending on Easter. Lent initially involved extensive fasting, but now may involve abstinence or only giving up certain foods (the Catholic Church now differentiates between fasting—eating only one meal a day—and abstinence or eating nothing). Other Christian fasts include Advent, the period before Christmas. A number of evangelical Protestant sects increasingly use fasting as part of their revival rituals. The main fast of Judaism is Yom Kippur or the Day of Atonement.

Fasting may also be a spontaneous expression of religious sentiment undertaken in response to specific events instead of being part of the religious calendar. Several religions use fasting as a form of penance in response to sin. In addition, ritual fasting may form part of religious ceremonies surrounding death or other major events. The Zoroastrians engage in three days of ritual fasting as part of their funeral services.

Among many religious groups rituals accompany the practice of fasting. For instance, during fasts people may not cut their hair or bathe. These rituals are not ascetic in nature, but reinforce the ceremonial and religious nature of the process. Conversely, many religions have strict codes as to how ascetic fasting must be accomplished by the individual. A person may be required to sit upright and not lie down or must fast in silence. As a ritual, fasting has been transformed from a religious activity into a broader means of social protest. The hunger strike, which first gained global attention through the fast of Mahatma Gandhi, is now a common form of protest.

Celibacy

Another common form of ascetic ritual is celibacy. Depending upon the religion, celibacy may be short or long term. For example, during specific periods of the year people may be asked to abstain from sex. This is the case during Ramadan, when Muslims should abstain from sex during daylight hours. On the other hand, some religions require their priests or holy people to take a permanent vow of celibacy. Roman Catholic priests and nuns take lifelong vows of celibacy, as do Buddhist and Taoist monks, and Brahmins. Conversely, some religions encourage celibacy only for short periods of time. For instance, while on pilgrimage, Muslims are supposed to remain celibate. In addition, Hindus believe that celibacy serves as a means to convert sexual energy (*retas*) into spiritual energy (*tejas*), and thus those on pilgrimage or engaged in the study of religion should abstain from sex. Before most major religious ceremonies, both Hindu men and women practice celibacy. The warriors of many Native American and African tribes also engaged in celibacy as part of more complex religious rituals before battles.

Under some circumstances, the effort to maintain or ensure celibacy can take extreme forms. An early Christian leader, Origen, castrated himself to ensure celibacy. Later, castration as a means to ensure celibacy became widespread in the third century CE, but was rejected by the mainstream church.

Self-Mutilation

Castration was but one form of ascetic self-mutilation. In the Christian Church of the Middle Ages, several ascetic cults emerged which practiced ritual self-mutilation as a religious rite. The best-known of these groups was the flagellants. The early Church approved self-flogging as a form of penance, but by the fourteenth century, large, organized groups of flagellants began to arise. These groups traveled throughout Europe and engaged in public displays of flagellation. Secular authorities tried to suppress the cults, but the spread of the Bubonic Plague led to their reemergence. Pope Clement VI formally banned the practice in 1349 and flagellants were branded as heretics. Nonetheless, the practice continued and spread to Spanish colonies in North America. Ritual mutilation also occurs among a variety of Asian religious sects. For instance, during the Ngan Kin Jeh (Chinese Vegetarian Festival) in Thailand, ascetics perform self-flagellation with axes and pierce their cheeks with long poles in an effort to maintain favor with the gods.

Less painful and scarring forms of ascetic self-mutilation include the O-Kee-Pa rituals of Native Americans. During these rituals, individuals are suspended vertically through piercings in the upper chest. They then remain suspended for long periods of time to purify themselves and attain the ability to receive special visions. Other examples would include bloodletting rituals of the Australian Aborigines, wherein individuals have cuts made in their upper arms in order to produce prodigious quantities of blood. Many other indigenous religions practice ritual scarring. Fire is a central component in other ascetic rituals. The flames are seen as a cleansing agent and may be used to purify individuals through ceremonial burns. Almost all of the world's major religions and all of the Western-based religions continue to manifest some strains of asceticism. Nonetheless, in the contemporary era, extreme asceticism, especially that associated with self-mutilation or extreme denial, is most commonly associated with fringe religious movement and cults. This is especially evident as mainstream religious groups have institutionalized and most ascetic rituals so that they have taken on symbolic forms. Even in this highly regulated and symbolic manifestation, asceticism remains a principal path for believers to reach holiness or true enlightenment.

Tom Lansford

See also Altered States of Consciousness; Food and Rituals; Hinduism; Monastic Communities; Vision Quest

Further Reading

Brakke, D. (1998). *Athanasius and asceticism*. Baltimore: Johns Hopkins University Press.

Eskildsen, S. (1998). *Asceticism in early Taoist religion*. Albany, NY: State University of New York Press.

Chadwick, O. (1958). *Western asceticism*. Philadelphia: Westminister Press.

Grimm, V. E. (1996). *From feasting to fasting, the evolution of a sin: Attitudes to food in late antiquity*. New York: Routledge.

Laurie, T. (1974). *The history of corporal punishment: A survey of flagellation in its historical, anthropological, and sociological aspects*. Detroit, MI: Gale Research Co.

Oliville, P. (Trans.). (1992). *Hindu scriptures on asceticism and renunciation*. New York: Oxford University Press.

Shiels, W. (1985). *Monks, hermits and the ascetic tradition*. Oxford, UK: Blackwells.

Trimingham, J. (1971). *The Sufi orders in Islam*. Oxford, UK, Clarendon Press.

Wagtendonk, K. (1968). *Fasting in the Koran*. Leiden, Netherlands: E. J. Brill.

Wiltshire, M. G. (1990). *Ascetic figures before and in early Buddhism: The emergence of Gautama as the Buddha*. New York: Mouton de Gruyter.

Australian Aboriginal

The rituals of Australian Aboriginal religions are different from those of most other major religions. Among the Aboriginal groups there are no formal temples or churches in the traditional sense and no religious text similar to the Christian Bible or the Islamic Qur'an (the book of sacred writings accepted by Muslims as revelations made to Muhammad by Allah). Nonetheless, the Australian Aboriginal religions contain the world's oldest continuously practiced religious rituals.

Unique Features

A variety of features makes Australian Aboriginal religions and religious rituals unique. First, at the core of all Aboriginal religions is the concept of Dreamtime or the Dreaming (known in Aboriginal languages as *altjiranga, bugari, djugurba,* or *wonger*). This concept refers to a time when the ancestors of the Aborigines shaped the present world. Before the Dreamtime the world was barren and shapeless, then the ancestors emerged and traveled the world. With each step and subsequent footprint, life emerged as the ancestors sang and wove into the existence all of the different life-forms (this story has a number of minor variations). These travels created "songlines" across the Australian continent. Songlines are paths once traveled by the spirits which tell the story of the creation of people, plants, animals, and even geographic features such as mountains. Each Aborigine family or clan has its own songline and the tribespeople travel these paths to commune with the spirits. The Aborigines believe that each contemporary feature of the landscape being, whether it be human being, animal, plant life, mountain range, water hole, and so forth, is a manifestation of the seeds or spirits of these ancestors. For instance, the *guruwari* (particles or spirits) of the kangaroo were responsible for the birth of the species, and each modern kangaroo is given life from the same *guruwari*.

Another unique feature of Aboriginal rituals is their individualistic, participatory nature. Aborigines go on pilgrimages, commonly referred to as "walkabouts," in which they retrace the songlines of their ancestors, the spirit-beings. These metaphysical pilgrimages, which are taken alone, are an important component of Aboriginal rituals because they establish and reinforce the relationship between people and the spiritual realm. For instance, some tribes believe that as women walk along, the *guruwari* ascend from the ground and enter the women's wombs, thus giving life and spirit to the unborn (and even unconceived). During the pilgrimage a variety of minor rituals must be employed. For example, when approaching a watering hole, an Aborigine will throw a stone to alert the spirit-beings of the person's presence.

Throughout the year, Aborigines, either individually or in small groups, are required to travel to sacred sites within their tribal territory. As they travel the songlines, Aborigines stop at these sites to clean or purify them. This may involve touching up or adding to rock paintings or creating ground paintings as a means to please the spirit-beings. In return, it is expected that the spirit-beings will renew or help sustain the land. Hence, among the desert tribes, groups travel to different sites in the last months of the dry season, usually September and October, in order to ensure that the rains come during the later rainy season.

Large ceremonies are most often dependent upon the availability of food resources rather than a specific calendar date or season. Most Aboriginal tribes are hunter-gatherers, and until recently the people did not domesticate livestock or grow crops. Instead, during the wet or summer season—November through April—tribes gather when food is plentiful. Although Aborigines spend most of their year in small groups, for intervals of two to three weeks during the wet season, they gather to conduct religious ceremonies and socialize. These large ceremonies are arranged either by messengers who travel with special message stones, passed down through generations, or by the use of smoke signals created by intermittently holding large pieces of bark over a fire to separate puffs of smoke. Often tribes engage in hunting rituals in which they imitate animals as a means to confuse the spirits and make the animals easier to catch. Increasingly Aborigines perform these large ceremonies at specific religious centers, including Jigalong, Wiluna, Warburton, and the Central Lands.

Although Aborigines possess limited instruments, music is important to Aboriginal rituals. For instance, the didgeridoo (a long wooden tube that produces a drone) is often utilized as a means of communicating with spirit-beings. Some tribes also utilize the didgeridoo as a means to pass on oral history through the memorization of songs.

ARANDA DREAMTIME

The so-called dreamtime of the Aboriginal peoples of Australia was something unknown to the European colonizers of the continent. The following is an extract from one the first reliable accounts of the dreamtime and associated rituals.

> It was during our work amongst the Arunta in 1896, when we were able to watch and study in its entirety the long and great Engwura ceremony, that we first became acquainted with the terms Alchera and Alcheringa. For four months in succession, and without interruption, we witnessed a wonderful series of ceremonies, all connected with the doings of the far past ancestors and the mythic times in which they lived. These mythic times, and everything associated with them, were continually spoken of as Alchera. There was never any person or individual spoken of as Alchera or Altjira. The word Alchera was always, and only, used in reference to past times during which the ancestors of the different totemic groups, all endowed with powers such as their descendants do not possess, lived and wandered over the country. In the ordinary language of to-day Alchera is also used for "dream": to dream is alcherama—that is, to see a dream. As indicating a past period of a very vague and, it seemed to us, "dreamy" nature we adopted, to express as nearly as possible the meaning of the word alcheringa (alchera, a dream, and ringa, a suffix meaning "of" or "belonging to"), the term "dream times." For each individual there is an Alchera, a far past time, associated with his totemic ancestors and their doings. A man's totem and his Alchera are so closely interwoven in his thoughts that they are practically inseparable.

Source: Spencer, W. Balwin, & Gillen, Francis J. (1927).
The Arunta: A Study of a Stone Age People.
London: Macmillan and Company, p. 592.

Initiation Ceremonies

During these large gatherings some of the most important ceremonies and rituals revolve around the initiation of the young into the tribe. For young males the first stage of initiation involves a ritual circumcision prior to puberty. The initiation ceremony varies slightly from tribe to tribe. For instance, the Yoingus call the initiation "Dhapi" and circumcise youths at about age eight or nine, whereas the Walbiri wait until the boy is between eleven and thirteen. During the ceremony the males of the tribe carry the boy away from the females and form a circle. While two tribesmen hold the initiate, a third removes the foreskin in a series of cuts. The boy is then conveyed, or carried, over a fire as a means of spiritual purification.

Some tribes also use ritual scarring as a later part of the initiation process. For example, the Walbiri practice subincision (or ritual scarring of the genitals). After being circumcised at an early age, male youths are subincised in a ceremony at about age seventeen. Within the tribes who practice circumcision and subincision, failure of a boy to go through the ceremonies means that the boy cannot marry, enter an elder's lodge, or participate in other religious ceremonies. Usually initiation ceremonies begin when a bull roarer (a musical device used to produce a deep bass sound) is spun on a long string. The resultant deep rumbling is supposed to be representative of the voice of a spirit-being and serves as a warning for women and uninitiated males to stay away from the ceremonies. Women have their own ceremonies, including the *yawalyu,* which is designed to maintain the health of the land. In addition, widowed or estranged women are kept separate from the community in a camp known as a *jilimi.*

Totemism

Australian Aboriginal rituals are also marked by totemism (the belief that there is a special relationship between people and certain classes of animals or other natural objects—the totem). Hence, members of a tribe may identify with the spirit-being responsible for emus and call themselves the "Emu-men" and refrain from eating emus because doing so would be akin to eating a human member of one's own tribe. This totemism reinforces a notion of association with natural beings or objects and determines a series of rights and responsibilities. A tribe linked with a water hole has rituals designed to protect and maintain the water hole (this may mean cleaning the area around it of brush or preserving it through rain-making rituals).

One manifestation of the ritual nature of totemism involves physical markings. The Aborigines believe that the more substantial rock paintings, some over two meters tall, were, in fact, originally painted by the spirit-beings. By touching up the paintings with markings or by just caring for the paintings, the Aborigines help to re-create or restore the world. The markings are often based on geometric designs, circles, and straight or wavy lines and are an acknowledgment of the songlines of people's ancestors. For instance, circles often represented the Dreamtime, whereas lines emanating from them represented the proliferation of life from the spirit-beings. Tribal elders pass on the specifics of the markings, which must be made in a predetermined manner, often using ochre pigments. Body painting could also be used to signal that a young girl was of marriage age. Bloodletting was also common among Aboriginal rituals. Most commonly, a cut would be made on the upper arm and blood mixed with pigments to form paint. The Aborigines believed that blood helps awaken or attract the spirit elders.

Aborigines also adorned objects as part of their rituals and ceremonies. For example, a *tjurunga* (often spelled *churinga*) is a ritual object made of either wood or rock and measures from 5 centimeters to 3 meters in diameter. These objects were intricately carved with patterns and usually served as the centerpiece for ceremonies, including initiation ceremonies. Most art and many objects associated with rituals and ceremonies are temporary. Body paintings and sand sculptures dissolve quickly. In addition, even more permanent objects, such as *pukamani* poles, which are used during mortuary rituals, are left to decay naturally.

Fire

Almost every ritual of the Australian Aborigines utilizes fire at some level. Fire provides both heat and light and is used to signal other tribes about rituals and even to help heal ritual cuts. The most common colors used in rituals and painting represent fire (white, orange or red, and black). Fire figures prominently as a cleansing or purification tool. For instance, newborns are often held over a fire to seal the life spirit and to prevent evil from entering the body. Ritual cleansing through fire is also accepted as a means to get rid of an evil spirit.

Fires are also used during death ceremonies to ward off evil spirits. Such fires were also maintained by the families of recently deceased Aborigines as a means of discouraging the dead souls from coming back to their family or tribe. Some tribes would even bury special fire reeds with the dead for use in the afterlife.

Regional Differences

There is not a single, overarching Australian Aboriginal religion. Instead, variations of some core qualities are found throughout the tribes and groups. When the Europeans first encountered the Aborigines in Australia, there were four hundred to five hundred tribes with two hundred identifiable languages. These tribes could be divided into two broad categories: those who lived in the woodlands and coast and those who lived in the interior deserts.

Although there are similarities between the rituals of the two groups, the greater availability of food and other resources along the coast meant that these tribes developed a calendar for rituals that was far more regular than that of tribes in the interior deserts, who often based the timing of rituals around access to food and water. Hence, rituals are often held not according to a specific calendar, but rather according to when there are enough resources to bring together the extended tribe for several weeks.

The availability of resources has led to several other key differences between the two groups. Because of the harsh climate and limited food and water of the interior deserts, the rituals of interior tribes are usually centered around issues dealing with reproduction or increases in food production (these are known as "increase rituals"). For instance, circumcision and subincision as part of male initiation ceremonies are common among the interior groups, such as the Aranda of central Australia and the Walbiri people of the desert. However, circumcision and subincision are rare among the coastal and woodland groups. Whereas the rituals of the interior Aborigines focus on human reproduction and food production, the rituals of the coastal and woodland tribes most often focus on death and the transition of the departed. Rituals of the coastal and woodland tribes also have a more formal quality. For instance, these tribes were more likely to use sacred objects, such as necklaces of pearl shells, in their rituals.

The Impact of Europeans

When Europeans began large-scale settlement in Australia in the 1780s, Aborigines numbered between 300,000 and 1 million. However, by 1901 that number had declined to around ninety-five thousand because of disease, loss of land, and armed conflict with Europeans. In terms of religious practices, European law on private land ownership disrupted the ability of the Aborigines to walk the songlines, and European efforts to spread Christianity further eroded traditional religious rituals. By the 1990s only about 5 percent of Aborigines regularly practiced their traditional beliefs, whereas about 70 percent practiced some form of Christianity. However, even the majority of those Aborigines who profess to be Christian often continue to engage in some traditional rituals and ceremonies. In addition, Aboriginal Christian churches, which are based on Christianity but incorporate some customary rituals (the result is sometimes referred to as "rainbow spirit theology"), are widely popular in the Aboriginal community.

Tom Lansford

See also Africa, West; Micronesian; Native Americans: Arctic; Native Americans: Northeast; Native Americans: Northwest Coast; Native Americans: Plains; Native Americans: Pueblo

Further Reading

Arden, H. (1994). *Dreamkeepers.* New York: HarperCollins.

Bell, D. (1993). *Daughters of the dreaming.* Minneapolis: University of Minnesota Press.

Charlesworth, M., Morphy, H., & Bell, D. (1984). *Religion in Aboriginal Australia.* St. Lucia, Australia: University of Queensland Press.

Chatwin, B. (1987). *The songlines.* New York: Viking Penguin.

Eliade, M. (1973). *Australian religions: An introduction.* Ithaca, NY: Cornell University Press.

Flood, J. (1997). *Rock art of the Dreamtime.* Sydney, Australia: Angus & Robertson.

Mol, H. (1982). *The firm and the formless: Religion and identity in Aboriginal Australia.* Ontario, Canada: Wilfrid Laurier University Press.

Pyne, S. J. (1991). *Burning bush: A fire history of Australia.* Seattle: University of Washington Press.

Swain, T. (1993). *A place for strangers: Towards a history of Australian Aboriginal being.* New York: Cambridge University Press.

Turner, D. (1985). *Life before Genesis, a conclusion: An understanding of the significance of Australian Aboriginal culture.* New York: Peter Lang.

Azande

The Azande or Zande are located in the countries of the Sudan and the Congo, formerly Zaire. They are situated in the southern part of the Sudan in Western Equatorial and Bahr al Ghazal provinces, into which they migrated in the eighteenth and nineteenth centuries. They soon became the dominant group among the large number of small groups in the area. They constitute around 8 percent of the population.

The Azande were part of the expansion of groups of hunters, divided into aristocrats and commoners, which entered northeastern Zaire and southwestern Sudan. The aristocrats provided rulers but not a centralized state. Therefore, a son succeeded his father only through conquering any of his brothers who challenged him. The conquered brothers were free to conquer elsewhere, thus expanding the Azande territory. This pattern of expansion also accounts for the diversity within the Azande population. By the early twentieth century, however, the Azande were a poor people, who had given up hunting for cultivation. Sleeping sickness had begun to plague them and Belgian and British colonial rule set the patterns of their lives.

The Role of Evans-Pritchard in Understanding Azande Ritual

British social anthropologist E. E. Evans-Pritchard sought to understand these patterns, making major contributions to understanding of religion and ritual. He was interested in the role of diviners in resolving conflicting claims in disputes. When the process fails, then the community seeks to explain why it did not

EVANS-PRITCHARD ON AZANDE ORACLES

Social anthropologist E. E. Evans-Pritchard is well known for his field work among the Azande. Below are his descriptions of Azande Oracles.

ORACLES: techniques which are supposed to reveal what cannot be discovered at all, or cannot be discovered for certain, by experiment and logical inferences therefrom. The principal Zande oracles are:

(a) benge, poison oracle, which operates through the administration of strychnine to fowls, and formerly to human beings also.

(b) iwa, rubbing-board oracle, which operates by means of a wooden instrument.

(c) dakpa, termites oracle, which operates by the insertion of branches of two trees into runs of certain species of termites.

(d) mapingo, three sticks oracle, which operates by means of a pile of three small sticks.

***Source*: Evans-Pritchard, Edward Evan. (1937). *Witchcraft, Oracles and Magic among the Azande.* Oxford, UK: Clarendon Press, pp. 10–11.**

work. Usually, there is focus on the failure of the substance or the process. The substance might be bad or else the details of the ritual were not executed properly. Or sorcery was used to spoil the ritual.

Evans-Pritchard noted the role of the practitioner in the efficacy of the ritual. Success is dependent on performance, and the diviner's knowledge and ability, therefore, play a significant role in its success. The performance of ritual is a public event and therefore the participants are aware of an audience, including the spiritual forces invoked in the ritual, the patient-client, and the community. The goal of the ritual is to restore right relationships in Azande society. Azande religious specialists must observe the relevant taboos and purification rites. The rite must be marked off from the everyday; it must be set aside, for it is sacred.

Evans-Pritchard was quick to note that the sacred among the Azande, and by extension other non-Western peoples, is not a result of faulty reasoning. He gave the classic example of a granary, eaten by termites, falling on someone. The Azande had no problem realizing that the granary fell because the termites had destroyed it. What concerned them was why it fell on certain people who happened to be there when it fell. Coincidence was not a sufficient answer, and it is at this point that the diviner enters into the picture to seek out who might have worked witchcraft to cause the death of those involved. The diviner is aware of the many ways in which people can tear the fabric of society, and the diviner's job is to repair the damage. Thus, it is his psychological understanding of the people involved in disputes that is a key element of his work in repairing the damage.

Oracles

One of the rituals used to discern who is telling the truth in a dispute is that of taking poison. The ritualist gives poison to a chicken. If the chicken dies, then the person bringing the complaint is lying. If it lives, then the complainant is telling the truth. Sometimes the poison is given to people. In that case, the person is betting his or her life on telling the truth. The diviner, of course, is in control of the amount of the dosage. However, belief in his ability is at the heart of the system and those who may be wrong will seek reconciliation if the rituals point to them. There is a goal of restorative justice operating; the aim is to heal the breach and bring people together.

The poison oracle *(benge)* addresses serious questions or concerns in Zande life. Thus, the *benge* examines charges of adultery or sorcery. For the Azande, divination is a means for reducing uncertainty through using spirit forces to secure guidance in dealing with negative human feeling and behavior.

Since the Azande world is one that requires frequent and close interaction with kinsmen, neighboring peoples, and ancestral spirits and other spiritual powers, witchcraft is an integral part of their life. Divination is used to discover when witchcraft, often unintended or unknown to the witch, is used. Divination thus links the present with the past, for the witch is often a relative of the victim. Divination also connects the past, present, and future, looking at the possible use of witchcraft to harm someone taking a journey.

The poison oracle is used primarily to discern the use of witchcraft. It is performed in the untamed bush outside a village. A man who knows the appropriate procedures may perform the ritual. All those involved as parties or witnesses to the procedure join him outside the village. Questions are asked of the *benge* that are neither too specific nor too vague. The chicken is given the poison. If the chicken dies, the supplicant's suspicions are confirmed and another chicken is tested to check on the first one. *Benge* is expensive, and, therefore, it is employed only for the most grievous offenses, such as death of a family member, serious illness, adultery, or infertility. For less serious problems, the Azande use the termite oracle *(dakpa)*. The oracle offers termites branches from two species of tree—*dakpa* and *kpoyo*. The oracle interprets answers to questions according to which of the tree branches the termites choose to eat. If both are eaten, then the oracle must interpret the answer. If further confirmation appears needed, then the oracle will resort to the *benge* oracle.

The friction oracle, *iwa,* is the most widely used, but the least reliable. It has the advantage of being cheap and readily available. It uses a friction board. The board has a male and female part. The oracle holds the friction board still through stepping on a leg that protrudes from the bottom of the board. The board is rubbed with a hot iron and then rubbed with juices from a number of plants. Then it is buried under soil on a path for some days, where people walk over it. Once the *iwa* is carved, proper preparation is essential. The rubbing implement is dipped in water regularly. When a question is addressed to the oracle, he rubs the board. The movement, whether easy or difficult, indicates the answer to the question. A second test is always made as in other forms of divination.

The Significance of Evans-Pritchard's Work

Because Evans-Pritchard's work on the Azande was so thorough, it became, along with that of Bronislaw Malinowski's in the South Pacific reported in *Coral Gardens and Their Magic* (1935), a means for understanding ritual and magic in other cultures around the world. For example, Malinowski and Evans-Pritchard hold that those who practice medicine are able to separate the magical from the practical. Evans-Pritchard reports that the Azande were always more confident in tasks that required routine empirical procedures. Most anthropological analyses of witchcraft in Africa are based on Evans-Pritchard's *Witchcraft, Oracles, and Magic among the Azand*e (1937, reprinted 1977).

Evans-Pritchard noticed that the Azande made a distinction between witchcraft and sorcery. People are born with a substance that causes them to be witches, but sorcerers study to be able to manipulate the magic they can access. The same distinction that exists between witches and sorcerers also distinguishes witch doctors from magicians. The witch doctor, in common with the witch, has *mangu,* a witchcraft substance. But the magician, like the sorcerer, relies on outside devices. For the Azande, as for many other peoples, these practitioners are distinguished on the criteria of means and legitimacy.

Another important aspect of Evans-Pritchard's work is his arguing that Azande beliefs are intellectually rational. "Is Zande thought so different from ours that we can only describe their speech and actions without comprehending them, or is it essentially like our own though expressed in an idiom to which we are unaccustomed?" he wrote (1937, p. 21). In finding that categories of Azande thought, such as magic and witchcraft, are coherent and flexible, he was arguing that most religious beliefs of so-called primitive peoples were just as intellectually rational as our own. Azande religious and magical ideas explain the inexplicable. The Azande idea that a granary that collapsed and killed two people under it had more than one cause is a case in point. They were aware that termites had eaten away the supports. But they were more interested in what led the two people who were killed to be there at the exact moment it fell. The Azande had to turn to witchcraft to answer the second question.

The Azande system seeks social and intellectual goals. It seeks to relate unusual events to larger forces and to control these events through these forces. The system is one filled with interpretations and ritual activities that can deal with many events of different types. It is also vague enough to escape being disproved by empirical events. The Azande, like many other peoples, use both empirical (has a logical explanation when understood from the insider perspective) and magical means to get through their daily lives.

A study of Azande ritual reveals that the seemingly incongruous becomes clear when a full understanding of the people and events is present. Certainly, Evans-Pritchard's study of the Azande has served as a model for other studies of ritual and led to further expansion of our understanding of the ritual process itself.

Frank A. Salamone

Further Reading

Bell, C. (1997). *Ritual: Perspectives and dimensions*. New York: Oxford University Press.

Crawford, J. W. Foundations of African philosophy: A definitive analysis of conceptual issues in African tought. *Research in African Literatures, 28,* 165–171.

Evans-Pritchard, E. E. (1963). *Essays in social anthropology*. New York: Free Press of Glencoe.

Evans-Pritchard, E. E. (1965). *Theories of primitive religion*. Oxford, UK: Clarendon Press.

Evans-Pritchard, E. E. (1967). *The Zande trickster*. Oxford, UK: Clarendon Press.

Evans-Pritchard, E. E. (1971). *The Azande*. Oxford, UK: Clarendon Press.

Evans-Pritchard, E. E. (1973). Some notes on Azande sex habits. *American Anthropologist, 75*(1), 171–176.

Evans-Pritchard, E. E. (1977). *Witchcraft, oracles, and magic among the Azande*. London: Oxford University Press. (Original work published 1937).

Glazier, S. D. (Ed.). (1999). *Anthropology of religion: A handbook*. Westport, CT: Praeger.

Heinze, R. (Ed.). (2000). *The nature and function of rituals: Fire from heaven*. Westport, CT: Bergin & Garvey.

Karp, I., & Bird, C. S. (Eds.). (1980). *Explorations in African systems of thought*. Bloomington: Indiana University Press.

Malinowski, B. (1935). *Coral gardens and their magic*. New York: American Book Company.

Middleton, J., & Winter, E. H. (Eds.). (1963). *Witchcraft and sorcery in East Africa*. London: Routledge & Paul.

Reining, C. (1966). *The Zande scheme: An anthropological case study of economic development in Africa*. Evanston, IL: Northwestern University Press.

Sachs, K. (1979). Causality and chance on the upper Nile. *American Ethnologist, 6*(3), 437–448.

Winthrop, R. H. (1991). *Dictionary of concepts in cultural anthropology* (R. G. McInnis, Ed.). New York: Greenwood Press.

B

Baha'i

The Baha'i faith has believers in virtually every country. The ordinances and rituals of the faith are based upon the teachings of its two prophet-founders: Mirza 'Ali Muhammad (1819–1850), who assumed the title of the Bab (Gate), and Mirza Husayn 'Ali (1817–1892), known to Baha'is as "Baha'u'llah" (Glory of God). Although the Baha'i faith emerged within the context of the Islamic traditions of nineteenth-century Shi'ite Persia (modern Iran), its basic teachings make a particular claim to universality and modernity by embracing all of the world's major religions and upholding the standards of reason and science. The essential principles of the Baha'i faith are expressed most succinctly in its formula of the "Three Onenesses": the oneness of God, the oneness of religion, and the oneness of humanity.

In general, the Baha'i faith renounces the emphasis on rituals characteristic of many other religious traditions, seeing them as inessential historical accumulations that obscure the core principles of true religious faith. The rituals and ceremonies of Baha'is, therefore, tend to be relatively simple and nonliturgical (not having rites prescribed for public worship). Indeed, the absence of a clergy in the Baha'i faith places a natural limit on ritualistic forms of religious practice. The Baha'i community is led by a democratically elected "spiritual assembly" of nine representatives who serve in a purely administrative, rather than sacerdotal (priestly), capacity. The only rituals practiced by Baha'is are those specifically ordained in their sacred scriptures, particularly in the *Kitab-i-Aqdas* (Most Holy Book) revealed by Baha'u'llah in 1873. There are also some traditions and ceremonies that commemorate important events in the history of the faith or the lives of its founders.

Baha'is have their own calendar, which consists of nineteen months of nineteen days each (361 days), with either four or five intercalary days between the eighteenth and nineteenth months to adjust the calendar to the solar year. The first day of the year falls on 21 March (vernal equinox) of the Gregorian calendar, and the beginning of the Baha'i era corresponds to the year 1844, when the Bab was said to have declared his mission as a prophet of God. The Baha'i New Year *(Naw-Ruz)* and the "Declaration of the Bab" (23 May) are regarded as holy days by the Baha'is and are normally celebrated by festive gatherings in private homes or the local house of worship *(Mashriqu'l-Adhkar)*, where members of the community recite Baha'i prayers or read aloud from the Baha'i sacred scriptures. Afterward the community shares food and engages in informal social activities. Other holy days, which are celebrated similarly, include the birthdays and ascensions (deaths) of the Bab and Baha'u'llah and other events relating to the lives of these central figures. The most important occasion of the year is the Festival of Ridvan (21 April–2 May), which commemorates Baha'u'llah's declaration of his prophethood during a twelve-day sojourn in the Garden of Ridvan outside of Baghdad in 1863. The Festival of Ridvan is celebrated by recitations of Baha'i prayers and scriptures by selected members of the community, followed by refreshments and social activities.

Feasts

Regular gatherings of the Baha'i community are called "feasts" and occur every nineteen days on the first day of each Baha'i month. Like other Baha'i gatherings, this Nineteen-Day Feast is not characterized by what would normally be considered ritual. During the "spiritual" portion of the feast, the community simply listens to prayers and selected passages from the Baha'i scriptures recited by members of the local community. This may be accompanied by some brief musical performances or melodic chanting, depending upon the talents and culture of the individual community. Afterward, during the "business" portion of the feast, the officers of the Local Spiritual Assembly inform the community of news and information of both regional and international significance to the Baha'i community. Finally, during the "social" portion of the feast, the community shares refreshments and engages in informal conversation or casual entertainment.

Baha'i rituals pertaining to such events as marriages and funerals are also relatively simple compared to those of many other religions. The Baha'i marriage ceremony requires only that the bride and groom, in the presence of two witnesses, recite the phrase "We will all, verily, abide by the Will of God." Other portions of the marriage ceremony vary from region to region and normally incorporate elements from the diverse cultural traditions of the regions where they are held. Baha'i rules require that the body be interred within twenty-four hours after death and within an hour's journey from the place of death. These rules are intended to prevent the community from attaching excessive significance to the physical remains of the individual after the spirit has departed. For the same reason, the coffin of the departed remains closed during the funeral. Baha'is are not, however, permitted to cremate the deceased, and several ordinances govern the washing and wrapping of the body prior to burial. The funeral itself consists of solemn recitations of Baha'i prayers or selections from the Baha'i scriptures, including an obligatory "Prayer for the Dead" that represents the only occasion during which Baha'is engage in a specifically prescribed congregational prayer.

Rituals

In addition to their communal activities, all Baha'is are obliged to practice several devotional rituals that pertain to their individual spiritual development. All Baha'is, for example, are enjoined to recite one daily obligatory prayer. The believer can choose from three such prayers. Each of these prayers is to be recited at a specified time of the day and is to be accompanied by certain bodily movements, such as the raising or washing of the hands, that symbolize obeisance or purification. During the nineteenth month of each Baha'i year a believer is also required to observe a fast by abstaining from food and drink from sunrise to sundown. This yearly fast is intended to purify the believer from worldly desires and to sever the believer from all except God. Like the rituals practiced communally, Baha'i rituals pertaining to the individual are not regarded as imbued with any magical or spiritual potency of their own, but rather serve primarily as a symbolic expression of devotion to the religious principles and central figures of the faith.

Michael C. Lazich

See also Catholicism; Islam; Jainism; Judaism

Further Reading

Baha'u'llah. (1993). *The Kitab-i-Aqdas* [The most holy book]. Wilmette, IL: Baha'i Publishing Trust.

Cole, J. R. (1998). *Modernity and the millennium.* New York: Columbia University Press.

Esslemont, J. E. (1980). *Baha'u'llah and the new era.* Wilmette, IL: Baha'i Publishing Trust.

Hartz, P. R. (2002). *Baha'i faith (world religions).* New York: Facts on File.

Hatcher, W. S., & Martin, J. D. (2002). *The Baha'i faith: The emerging global religion.* Wilmette, IL: Baha'i Publishing Trust.

National Spiritual Assembly of the Baha'is of the United States (Ed.). (1982). *Baha'i prayers, a selection of prayers revealed by Baha'u'llah, the Bab, and 'Abdu'l-Baha.* Wilmette, IL: Baha'i Publishing Trust.

Birth Rituals

Birth is a Janus-faced (relating to the Roman god with two faces) human experience because it is at once the most private and the most public event. Mother and child share the moment in a most secluded time and space with rituals of undisclosed details, and society takes note of it. The community into which the baby

VIETNAMESE BIRTH DEITIES

Rituals associated with birth are usually meant to win the favor of supernatural forces. The following list is of deities commonly invoked by Vietnamese women to reduce the uncertainty and danger associated with birth.

Doai Cung Thanh Mau. Or "holy Mother of the western Palace," regarded as the patron of mothers; her alter traditionally has been a carved niche to the right of the entrance of the Vietnamese home.

Ba Chua Thai Sanh (also known as Ba Chua Vai and Ba Mu Thien), who is the goddess of procreation and birth.

Ba Ba Mat (also known as Ba Luc Cung Thuy Trieu), or the "Three-faced Lady," believed to be the patron of wet nurses. Her assistance can be obtained both before birth to determine the sex of the child and after delivery to assure the baby's continued good health.

Ba Ba Muoi Hai Mu, or the "Three Ladies and Twelve Celestial Midwives," who not only guide the mother safely through childbirth but continue to care for the newborn, teaching him to suck, to smile, and to take his first steps.

Ca Cuu Thien Huyen Nu, a goddess considered to be the protectress of women and newborn infants, whose statue is found in village Buddhist temples.

In addition to these deities, special attention is also given during pregnancy and childbirth to Ong Dia or "God of the Earth," regarded as being the guardian spirit of a certain locality, as well as to the beneficent spirits of powerful men of the past—emperors, generals, and sages. Non-Christians impressed by the efficacy of their neighbors' beliefs, may also direct their prayers to Christ and to Catholic saints. Furthermore, there are certain evil spirits which must be avoided or appeased, principal among these being the spirits of women who have died in childbirth or the spirits or stillborn infants.

***Source*: Couglin, Richard J. (1965). "Pregnancy and Birth in Vietnam." In *Southeast Asian birth customs: three studies in human reproduction*, by Donn V. Hart, Phya Anuman Rajadhon, and Richard J. Coughlin. New Haven, CT: Human Relations Area Fules Press, p. 214.**

is born joins the process with its own rituals, with which it pledges its care for the newest member and claims the baby as one of its own. Birth rituals, both private and public, facilitate the welcoming of the baby into the world, both spiritually and socially, and in the intense and intricate unfolding of childbirth, religion, superstition, and magic vie for recognition as mediators of the well-being of the mother and the baby.

Obstacles for Researchers

Some legendary figures, such as Enoch and Elijah of the Hebrew Bible and Utnapishtim of the Gilgamesh epic, may have evaded death, and enlightened Buddhist beings may have overcome the chain of rebirths; however, no human ever came into being without a birth. Birth is the most common human experience, for which religion and science have formulated the most meaningful ways to welcome the baby into the world.

On the one hand, birth is like clockwork, which cannot be amended without drastic implications. On the other hand, with all the high level of predictability of the duration of gestation, birth is capable of taking the world by surprise, and various cultures have developed rituals to assist the mother and the rest of the expecting community to deal with the event. The invasive nature of birth (which preempts everything else in the life of the baby's significant others) forces rituals (such as circumcision or baptism) to give way to unfettered expressions of pain and hope. Superstitions and sympathetic magic, which are otherwise shunned, seep into the birthing room because the pressing moment of birth leaves little room for the leisure of conceived orthodoxy.

The irretrievable ritual moments that require no priest conceal their scanty details in their aftermath because birth rituals surrounded by the immediacy of birthing take place in a space reserved for only a handful of women. Until the introduction of modern obstetrics, prospective fathers were not usually allowed in the birthing room. The presence of the father in the delivery room still seems odd to many non-Westerners.

The Mother

Most of the details of rituals of birthing are focused on the mother. Along with the baby, who is less vocal (or much too vocal) about the significance of the event, the mother is present during all phases of birth rituals surrounding the delivery from labor to the cutting of the umbilical cord, the washing of the baby, the bonding, and the naming.

Labor itself is part of the birth rituals that the mother goes through. She can verbalize her analysis of the cause of pain in her own way. As the mother seeks an answer to why so much pain has to be involved, she is not exactly searching for religious discourse, even though that is often the only reply established religion offers. In a rare historical record of travail, a woman in the seventeenth century, having been told about Eve's transgression as the cause of the birth pang, responded, "I wish the apple had choked her" (Cressy 1997, 20–21).

The mother's labor tends to suspend common religious requirements. The Talmud (the authoritative body of Jewish tradition) declares the primacy of the need of a woman in labor over other requirements of Torah (the body of wisdom and law contained in Jewish Scripture and other sacred literature and oral tradition), for which Sephardic (relating to the occidental branch of European Jews settling in Spain and Portugal) tradition cites Genesis 21 or 1 Samuel 1. Judaism entertains an idea of women being exempt from the demands of Torah learning and associates and associates the exemption with their role as mothers.

Midwives

In antiquity, as childbirth was recognized as a painful process, the mother often received the service of midwives. In the Hebrew Bible the excuse that Shiphrah and Puah offer to Pharaoh, who questions why they let the Hebrew boys live, is that the Hebrew women do not need assistance in childbirth (Exodus 1). Among Native American tribes it is not uncommon for women to give birth without the assistance of midwives.

Midwives carried out part of the birth rituals. They received no formal training; their know-how came from their experience and a type of apprenticeship, which included lessons on birth rituals.

Midwives were an important part of the community. They knew the local customs and ethos (distinguishing character, sentiment, moral nature, or guiding beliefs), even though the introduction of modern medical care has left their position precarious and the modern medical profession disapproves of some of their practices. Where medical service was unaffordable, however, midwives stepped in to assist women in labor. Because their service was rendered in the context of communal support, their fee took the form of a gift. Often midwives considered their job a divine calling, and the mystic experience was not uncommon in midwives' sense of vocation.

Protection

Whether the birth is assisted or unassisted, the protection of the mother and the baby is a primary concern in birthing and birth rituals. Although maternal mortality is often exaggerated, women do die while giving birth. Also, although babies are not as fragile as they may appear, infant mortality remains a medical concern.

To protect the mother and the baby, prayers, sympathetic magic, and other apotropaic (designed to avert evil) measures commonly fill the room. Because birth is part of the process that begins at conception, protective measures are introduced during pregnancy. In some cultures sweets are placed under the table to keep evil spirits occupied with their sweet dreams. One custom in British Columbia has pregnant women wear an object that can slide to the ground; as the object drops, the pregnancy is anticipated to lead to an uneventful birth.

A northwestern tribe of Kwakiutl Native Americans keeps pregnant women from touching injured animals. Jewish customs include amulets in a menorah shape, and a prayer is said to protect the baby and the mother from Lilith the she-demon. In places where shamans are engaged, they say blessings to ease pain and to ward off evil spirits.

Purification

Birthing is surrounded by images of battle against the forces of contamination, and thus postnatal rituals take the form of purification. The notion of uncleanness in birth is commonly based on the woman's discharge after delivery. Where birth is regarded as pollution either by itself or as an outcome of sexual intercourse, birth invariably requires purification. The Hebrew Bible stipulates that the period of uncleanness ends with a burnt offering and a sin offering (Leviticus 12). The Talmud warns that a breach of purity law could result in infant mortality.

The duration of purification is often set with clear perimeters but seldom comes with any clear basis. Biblical law regards the mother as unclean for seven days after the birth of a boy and fourteen days after a girl. In China birth renders a mother unclean for three days.

These ancient rituals of purification play an important role in helping communities come to terms with the life-changing event of birth and should be construed in the context of their culture and not in the context of the modern definition of hygiene. Anthropologically, these rituals function as an acknowledgment that the mother has been separated from the community for a period of time required for birth and through purification finds her way back into the community.

Celebration of Life

The pain and fear of birth are welcomed in birth rituals because they anticipate the arrival of a new life. More ceremonious forms of celebration take place after the immediate jubilation upon birth, and the delay allows the mother and child to recover and reduces the possibility of premature celebration. In Korea the celebration of childbirth is delayed as long as one hundred days (which, incidentally, marks an anniversary of the conception of the baby). In China the feast of *manyei* (full moon) marks one full month of the baby's life. Jewish tradition also considers a child who reaches the first full month of life to be viable.

In the West each birthday becomes an extended birth ritual, but some cultures place more emphasis on certain birthdays than on others. In Korea the celebration of *dol,* the first birthday of the child, is a major communal celebration that features prayers and wishes for the health and success for the child. The feast table is set with objects that have symbolic meaning, including the brush representing the career of a scholar (which was coveted under Confucianism), threads suggesting long life, and coins symbolizing wealth and abundance. Any choice by the child triggers festivities over the auspicious beginning of the new life.

Welcoming the Baby into the World

A birth affects every member of the community as new relationships are created. With the birth of a baby the whole community is reconfigured. As a baby is born, a girl is made a mother, and possibly another woman a grandmother, and a boy a granduncle.

Most of all, a birth affects the status of a mother in the community. In a profound way a mother becomes the mother of the community. One gets a glimpse at the communal jubilation in the story of Ruth in the Hebrew Bible, in which the women of the town congratulate Naomi, the mother-in-law of Ruth, who had just given birth to a son. The women say to Naomi, "Blessed be the LORD, who has not left you this day without next-of-kin; and may his name be renowned in Israel! He shall be to you a restorer of life and a nourisher of your old age; for your daughter-in-law who loves you, who is more to you than seven sons, has borne him" (Ruth 4:14–15, NRSV).

In the midst of the jubilation that turns a biological event into a communal event, the arrival of the child obliges the community to redefine itself. The ritualized moments give society an opportunity to recognize that the birth has added to the community and has ensured its future. In some Asian cultures adulthood is defined by having a child because the new parents then participate in the care of the future of the community. In time the young one will grow up to take care of the community. Ancient Hittites and many others believed that the child would continue to provide for the parents even after they died.

With all the changes that the baby brings about, birth rituals give expression to a society's claim on the child and its caring for the child. The Jewish practice of circumcision on the eighth day after birth declares the child as a member of the community of Abrahamic covenant. Christening in Anglo-Catholic traditions, infant baptism in most Protestant traditions, and dedication in Baptist traditions also function as the communal claim on the child.

These rituals are at once religious and secular because they seek the blessings of the deity and integrate the baby into the community. Anglican tradition has the custom of churching the mother, in which the new mother makes a pilgrimage to the church with the child. The church recognizes the labor of the woman and welcomes her and the baby into its fold. Catholic tradition has a custom of godparents, who function as the religious community's pledge of care for the child. Protestant traditions that have discontinued the custom of godparents include in their liturgy (rites prescribed for public worship) a covenant that invites the congregation to assume the role that had been fulfilled by godparents traditionally.

Birth rituals reemerge later in the child's life because birth continues to offer profound metaphors for rites of passage. In Christian traditions the profession of faith and the sacrament of baptism are couched in the images of rebirth. Marriage is a birth of a new union. In many religions and cultures death does not terminate life but rather functions as a pathway through which one is born into a new mode of existence. The widely attested practice of burial in the fetal position seems to have been based on a belief that in death one is given birth into the afterlife.

Reconfiguring Birth Rituals

The advent of modern medicine has moved the place of birth from a secluded home or hut built for that purpose to a hospital. Birth has become a medical procedure, and the first life experience of a baby is that of a patient.

Although the new arrangement ensures adequate medical care for the mother and child during a potentially life-threatening procedure, the new arrangement tends to dissociate birth from the communal context by reducing the need for the community's attention to it. Maternity wards of modern hospitals have made concessions to the fact that birth is not merely a medical procedure but also an occasion of welcoming the baby into society. They feature homey wallpapers and large glass windows, which facilitate visits by family and friends while keeping out bacterial and viral visitors. Nurses join the jubilation of the newly revised family, and physicians offer a form of ancient birth rituals, such as circumcision, even though Judaism would not consider a circumcision valid if performed by a physician and not by a trained *mohel,* the professional circumciser certified to perform the procedure in accordance with the Jewish religion. However, in spite of these concessions, modern medicine can create the notion of pregnancy as illness and of children as primarily liability.

Birth rituals of past times and cultures can offer resources that could help humanity to claim the moments of life that are worthy of care and celebration. In past times and cultures the care for the mother and the child was not regarded as a medical procedure for which one could assign a monetary price. Instead, the whole community welcomed the child, and established religion and orthodoxy respectfully kept a distance from the mother in labor as well as from the few other women in the birthing room.

Drawing upon the communal resources in birth rituals of past cultures may require that people reinterpret them for modern times. As an example of the appropriation of an ancient custom, purification rituals can be reconstrued not so much as occasions for having women purified as contexts in which the world is being purified to receive the baby. Physically, infants may not have had an opportunity to express their opinion on the matter of birthing, and they may indeed be in need of professional medical care, but birth rituals can represent babies not as patients but rather as precious new members whom the community is happy to receive. After all, the future of the community is dependent on the babies who are born and welcomed into the community through birth rituals.

Jin Hee Han

See also Body and Rituals; Crisis Rituals; Haircutting Rituals; Identity Rituals; Naming Rituals; Passage, Rites of

Further Reading

Beckman, G. M. (1983). *Hittite birth rituals* (2nd ed.). Wiesbaden, Germany: Otto Harrassowitz.

Best, E. (1976). *Maori religion and mythology.* Wellington, New Zealand: A. R. Shearer.

Bradshaw, P. F. (1996). Christian rites related to birth. In P. F. Bradshaw & L. A. Hoffman (Eds.), *Life cycles in Jewish and Christian worship* (pp. 13–31). Notre Dame, IN: University of Notre Dame Press.

Cressy, D. (1997). *Birth, marriage, and death: Ritual, religion, and the life-cycle in Tudor and Stuart England.* Oxford, UK: Oxford University Press.

de Veries, R. G. (1981). Birth and death: Social constructions at the poles of existence. *Social Forces, 59*(4), 1074–1093.

Demand, N. (1994). *Birth, death, and motherhood in classical Greece.* Baltimore: Johns Hopkins University Press.

Dougherty, M. C. (1978). Southern lay midwives as ritual specialists. In J. Hoch-Smith & A. Spring (Eds.), *Women in ritual and symbolic roles* (pp. 151–164). New York: Plenum Press.

Geffen, R. M. (Ed.). (1993). *Celebration & renewal: Rites of passage in Judaism*. Philadelphia: Jewish Publication Society.

Hoffman, L. A. (1996). Rituals of birth in Judaism. In P. F. Bradshaw & L. A. Hoffman (Eds.), *Life cycles in Jewish and Christian worship* (pp. 32–54). Notre Dame, IN: University of Notre Dame Press.

Hunt, N. R. (1999). *Colonial lexicon of birth ritual, medicalization, and mobility in the Congo*. Durham, NC: Duke University Press.

Krohn, P. J. (Ed.). (1985). *Bris milah: Circumcision, the covenant of Abraham—a compendium of laws, rituals, and customs from birth to bris, anthologized from the Talmudic and traditional sources*. New York: Mesoah.

McLaren, A. (1984). *Reproductive rituals: The perception of fertility in England from the sixteenth to the nineteenth century*. New York: Methuen.

Nourse, J. W. (1999). *Conceiving spirits: Birth rituals and contested identities among Laujé of Indonesia*. Washington, DC: Smithsonian Institution Press.

Paige, K. E., & Paige, J. M. (1973). The politics of birth practices: A strategic analysis. *American Sociological Review, 38*(6), 663–676.

Robertson, N. (1983). Greek ritual begging in aid of women's fertility and childbirth. *Transactions of the American Philological Association, 113*, 143–169.

Wales, H. G. Q. (1933, July–December). Siamese theory and ritual connected with pregnancy, birth and infancy. *Journal of the Royal Anthropological Institute of Great Britain and Ireland, 63*, 441–451.

Wolf, A. P. (1978). *Studies in Chinese society*. Stanford, CA: Stanford University Press.

Blood Rituals

Groups perform blood rituals in several forms: animal sacrifice, human sacrifice, cutting or bloodletting rituals, rituals associated with menstrual blood, and rituals using symbolic blood. Additionally, blood rituals are rumored to exist in the realm of public imagination. Most blood rituals contain spiritual significance, often reenacting or articulating a cultural myth. Blood rituals can be offerings to a higher power. Some mark the movement from one social status into another: rites of passage. Usually blood rituals, like other rituals, demand repetitive and similar performances without deviation from a script. According to the French sociologist Emile Durkheim (1947), rituals reinforce group bonds, a sense of identity, and feelings of security through the ceremonial display of collective symbolism. Blood contains an almost universal imagery of the life force throughout various magical and religious metaphors. Blood symbolizes supernatural power in most contexts. From the standpoint of theorists such as Rene Girard (1977), the controlled violence of blood-spilling rituals directed against designated victims channels the potential violence of the group so that the violence does not become directed toward other individuals.

Blood-spilling sports, such as the gladiatorial matches and the animal fights of ancient Rome, are somewhat related to blood rituals, although they hold more entertainment value than religious significance. Likewise, contemporary vampire imitators of the Goth subculture drink real or fake blood as part of a fad rather than as part of a true ritual experience. Furthermore, a public execution, which can involve considerable amounts of blood, is not viewed as a blood ritual unless it is a religiously based human sacrifice that follows a ritual script.

Animal Sacrifice

Animal sacrifice is an ancient custom that is even recorded in the Bible. The Book of Genesis speaks of the sacrifice offered by Adam and Eve's son, Abel. Animal sacrifice occurs frequently in many sacred practices, although modernized religions have done away with the custom. In the United States the Afro-Caribbean derivative belief called "Santeria" still uses animal sacrifice, as do some imported religions from southeastern Asia, such as Laotian Mien shamanism.

The cult of Mithras, popularized in ancient Rome around the second century CE, practiced the sacrifice of bulls whose blood was used for baptisms. The cult's creed promised immortality and a spiritual ally against the dark forces afoot in the world. Followers were male, and countless Roman soldiers joined the cult.

Many hunting and warrior societies drank the blood of prey, sometimes reciting prayers in conjunction as part of a ritual. The pre-Columbian Zuni hunters covered their bodies with animal blood and also buried blood to appease ghosts. The headhunters of the central Celebes (Sulawesi) in Indonesia drank the blood and ate the brains of their human prey in order to receive their strength and bravery through

A WEST AFRICAN ANIMAL SACRIFICE

The sacrifice of an animal to win the favor of the supernatural is a very common blood ritual around the world. This example is from the Hausa people of Nigeria.

This would seem to point their principal orientation toward the attainment of agricultural prosperity. The natives, however, couch such explanations [for making a sacrifice] as they offer in very general terms, giving such reasons as "that everything should be well," or "that we may prosper." The primary sacrifice to each spirit is a sheep or goat, but a chicken may be substituted if a man finds the larger offering too burdensome.

In making the sacrifice, the throat of the animal is slit with an iron knife so that the jugular vein is severed. When the blood spurts forth the operator addresses the spirit to whom the offering is being made with the words, "So-and-so, here is blood. Drink it!" The blood flows into one of two previously prepared holes, each about one foot in diameter. The one which receives the blood is immediately covered with a stone "so that the dogs won't get at it," a happening which would anger the spirits. The other hole receives the entrails. If the sacrifice is a chicken, a feather is inserted in the ground "as a witness" for "all blood looks the same." The carcass is roasted or boiled, according to the spirit that is the recipient of the offering. It is then eaten by members of the household; some of it, however, is reserved for distribution as a *sadaka* [alms].

Source: Greenberg, Joseph H. (1946).
The Influence of Islam on a Sudanese Religion.
Monographs of the American Ethnological Society, Vol. 10. New York: J.J. Augustin, p. 45.

magical means. Ancient Norwegian hunters drank bear's blood. In East Africa the Masai hunters drank lion's blood to receive the lion's legendary prowess. In contrast, some societies developed taboos against drinking the blood of animals; thus developed Hebrew kosher laws, as well as restrictions among some Native American groups.

Human Sacrifice

Mythology dictates which deities require blood sacrifice. Devotees and priests of the Indian goddess Kali have maintained temples for centuries where animal and human sacrifices took place. The British Raj (rule over India) of the nineteenth century banned human sacrifices, although today in isolated instances individuals still make sacrifices to Kali in order to improve their fortunes. According to legend, Kali, who wears skulls around her neck, manipulates death and destruction as part of the cycles of the universe. Kali once fought a demon called "Raktabija" (Blood Seed). When Raktabija was attacked, new demons would emerge from its blood-spouting wounds. In order to defeat the demon, Kali devoured it and its offspring, thereby acquiring a taste for blood.

The Vikings, who terrorized northern Europe from the ninth century to the eleventh century, saw the spilling of blood in combat as a tribute to their warrior gods. They blessed their long ships by driving the keels across the bodies of prisoners in an early version of ship "christening." Although some experts say this is fictional, the Vikings were said to practice the blood eagle sacrifice, in which a man's rib cage was split open to form a shape like an eagle's wings. In ancient Norse tradition the act of sacrifice meant to redden with blood.

Some pre-Columbian societies of Central and South America supported human sacrifice as part of the normal affairs of state. The Aztecs cut out the hearts of thousands atop their pyramids in public spectacles that were held to ensure that the cosmos held its order. The Aztecs displayed the heads of victims on enormous skull racks. Like the Aztecs, the Maya executed thousands of prisoners of war as tribute to their gods in torturous, prolonged ceremonies. In Peru the precolonial Moche made similar offerings to their decapitator god in temple rites aimed at promoting agricultural fertility.

Priests and the occasional priestess drank the blood of their victims.

Bearing some similarities to Santeria, voodoo, which is practiced in Africa, the Caribbean, and in the Americas, sometimes sacrifices animals depending on the group involved. Nigerian traditional healer, Isiah Oke gives a chilling first-hand account of the related African sect of Ju-Ju, which drank chicken blood and tortured and sacrificed humans.

Bloodletting

Bloodletting rituals take numerous forms. Using blood to forge agreements or to make a blood covenant is probably one of the oldest practices of humans. The idea of making a blood brother or creating a social bond through co-mingling blood comes from antiquity. Some bloodletting involved self-sacrifice, as in the example of the Japanese suicide ritual hara-kiri *(seppuku).* If a samurai suffered dishonor, he made two crossed incisions in the abdomen followed by a twist. The practice of committing suicide because of dishonor has not completely vanished in modern Japan.

During the Middle Ages, Christian zealots, some of whom became saints, engaged in mortification of the flesh, which could involve self-flagellation until the flesh bled. In contemporary Bali in Indonesia the ceremonial temple cockfights are called *"tabuh rah"* (blood spilling). Cocks wear razors tied to their legs. The purpose of the cockfights is to placate demons through this form of purification.

Aztec priests would extract their own blood in auto-sacrifice rituals in which they pierced and cut their bodies. They skewered their tongues in some cases or slashed their ears while also allowing blood to flow from other wounds in rites that placated the lord of the underworld, Mictlantecuhtli. Aztec blood-offering rituals are well illustrated in Aztec artwork, although only a portion of it survived colonial times. Their blood rituals supposedly satisfied any number of fearsome deities.

Among the Mesoamerican Maya, elites performed essential bloodletting rituals. Through these rituals, the elites contacted their ancestors and spirits, reporting their visions as a means of guidance for the state. Important political or social events demanded bloodletting rituals, which were performed with ceremonial tools, such as stingray spines or obsidian lancets. Blood fed the gods and facilitated spiritual communication. Sculptured depictions of these rituals from around 770 CE show royal women pulling thorny ropes through their tongues, while male rulers pierced their foreskins as blood dripped onto parchment. Out of their pain came visions from the gods.

Rites of Passage

Many groups used blood rituals as part of a rite of passage. The Chinese secret society dedicated to martial arts, called the "Triad," had blood-drinking initiations. Members pricked their fingers to remember that if they betrayed the organization their blood would flow. Among the Poro, the male secret societies of western Africa, historic accounts tell of human sacrifices and rarer cannibal rituals as part of initiation. Boys endured ill treatment, including scarification and frightening ceremonies, so that they would become hardened, as adult men were expected to be.

Scarification is practiced in many cultures. In the Nuer society of East Africa older boys receive the marks of Gar to symbolize their passage into manhood. The marks of Gar consist of six horizontal cuts on the forehead. A boy lies motionless as an elder digs into his skin, and the blood flows profusely. If a boy flinches, he is disgraced. Elders later sacrifice an animal in his honor.

Some traditional aborigines of central and western Australia took blood from the older men and smeared it on the younger men during initiation into adult status. Tribal groups in many parts of the world, particularly in Africa and Australia, cut off the foreskin of young men during puberty rituals.

Traditionally, Jewish male infants are circumcised in a ritual called the "bris" or *bris milah.* The man who performs the ritual (the *mohel*) places his mouth on the wound to suck up the blood. In recent times this part of the ritual has begun to change to accommodate concerns about modern etiquette and disease transmission.

A contemporary cult in Japan called "Aum Supreme Truth" follows the odd charismatic leader Shoko Asahara. In 1995 a few members of this cult filled a Japanese commuter train with poisonous gas, killing twelve people. Rumors from the cult said some members paid seven thousand dollars for initiation ceremonies at which they could drink a small bit of the leader's blood.

Menstrual Blood

Many societies view menstrual blood as polluting, and some have taboos that separate women from society during the monthly cycle. Traditional Jewish women use a purification bath called a *"mikvah."* As part of a newer feminist consciousness, many women seek to overthrow any negative connotations from the past. Feminist spirituality groups have evolved new rituals celebrating the "moon time." In addition, they have rewritten old legends about goddesses and female spirits in order to change the status of women in mythology. Feminists and others concerned with human rights have called for an end to the procedure of clitorectomy (removing the clitoris and sewing up the vulva), sometimes called "female genital mutilation." Girls in certain parts of Africa undergo the procedure from older women as a rite of passage. Done without sterile instruments, the crude procedure can lead to infection and sexual dysfunction.

Despite the mixed messages about menstrual blood, numerous cultures celebrate a first period (menarche) with initiation ceremonies or rites of passage. For example, the Apache conduct the Changing Woman Ceremony, in which a young woman receives gifts from the community. Many cultures maintained menstrual huts where women retreated during menstruation. Although women did segregate themselves at that time and although that can be seen as an indication of stigma, time in a menstrual hut could also be seen as an experience of relaxation and renewal.

Symbolic Blood

As do some other religions, Christianity uses symbolic blood. The Christian practice of taking communion entails the symbolic ingestion of the body and blood of Christ. Christ is often referred to as the "Lamb of God," meaning that the Crucifixion was the ultimate sacrifice to replace all others. Some folk magic practices use artificial substitutes such as dove's blood or dragon's blood ink to write spells and incantations. Bloodstone (a type of quartz) supposedly wards off evil. Such items can be purchased on the Internet or in shops that sell magical supplies. Because real blood is perishable and involves cost, pain, and potential illegality, substitutes are often found. Traditions explain any use of symbolic blood.

Rumors of Blood

Many rumors of blood ritual emerged from medieval Europe. Allegedly, witches signed pacts with the devil in their blood and conducted ceremonies with the blood of unbaptized babies. Witches were said to nurse their familiars (magical animal companions) with their own blood. People believed that burning witches killed their power, which lived in their blood. Similarly, European Jews suffered periodic witch hunts in which they were falsely accused of using the blood of Christian infants in rituals. In recent decades Satanists have been blamed for animal mutilations, as have space aliens. But isolated incidents of animal mutilations are probably more related to the work of juvenile delinquents and mentally ill individuals than they are to any real Satanist practice. In certain regions of the United States Santeria activity is mistaken for Satanism.

The Future of Blood Ritual

Many formerly accepted religious practices are being examined today. Human rights groups alert the public to any incidents of human sacrifice. The painful alteration of genitalia during puberty rites also has been called into question through international awareness campaigns. Animal sacrifice seems odd in the electronic age. Nevertheless, primal religions outside the established Western traditions continue to use blood rituals. The philosophical task ahead is the balancing of religious tolerance with modern ideas, such as human rights and animal rights.

In this era of technology and medicalization of blood products, blood as a life-force symbol will probably lose its significance. In the industrialized world the displacement of animal slaughter from the public to mechanized slaughterhouses shields people from animal blood spillage. By the close of the twentieth century modern medicine had linked blood to the deadly AIDS virus and the stigma of HIV infection. In some parts of the world, the majority of blood symbolism has shifted from watching spectacles of sacrifice to watching television and playing video games. Warfare and hand-to-hand combat are also more likely to be enacted electronically, potentially giving rise to the new symbolism of virtual blood rather than physical blood. As societies change, symbols change, and so, too, will blood rituals.

Diana Tumminia

See also Body and Rituals; Cannibalism; Clothing and Rituals; Healing and Rituals; Hunting Rituals; Oaths and Ordeals; Sacrifice and Offerings; Santeria; Sport and Ritual; Vision Quest

Further Reading

Bawden, G. (1996). *The Moche*. Cambridge, MA: Blackwell Publishers.

Benson, E. P., & Cook, A. G. (Eds.). (2001). *Ritual sacrifice in ancient Peru*. Austin: University of Texas Press.

Campbell, J. (1988). *The power of myth*. New York: Doubleday.

Cavendish, R. (Ed.). (1970). *Man, myth, and magic: An illustrated encyclopedia of the supernatural*. New York: Marshall Cavendish.

Davies, N. (1981). *Human sacrifice: In history and today*. New York: William Morrow.

Durkheim, E. (1947). *The elementary forms of religious life*. Boston: Free Press.

Geertz, C. (1973). *The interpretation of cultures*. New York: Basic Books.

Girard, R. (1977). *Violence and the sacred*. Baltimore: Johns Hopkins University Press.

Hsia, R. P. (1988). *The myth of ritual murder: Jews and magic in reformation Germany*. New Haven, CT: Yale University Press.

Josephy, A. M. (1961). *The American Heritage book of Indians*. New York: American Heritage Publishing.

MacKenzie, N. (Ed.). (1967). *Secret societies*. New York: Collier Books.

Murphy, J. M. (1988). *Santeria: An African religion in America*. Boston: Beacon Press.

Oke, I. (1989). *Blood secrets: The true story of demon worship and ceremonial murder*. Buffalo, NY: Prometheus.

Pritchard, E. E. (1940). *The Nuer*. Oxford, UK: Clarendon Press.

Richardson, J. T., Best, J., & Bromley, D. G. (Eds.). (1991). *The Satanism scare*. New York: Walter de Gruyter.

Schele, L., & Miller, M. E. (1986). *The blood of kings: Dynasty and ritual in Maya art*. New York: George Braziller.

Townsend, R. F. (2000). *The Aztecs*. London: Thames & Hudson.

Vermaseren, M. J. (1963). *Mithras, the secret god*. New York: Barnes & Noble.

Walker, A. (1992). *Possessing the secret of joy*. New York: Harcourt Brace Jovanovich.

Walker, B. G. (1983). *The woman's encyclopedia of myths and secrets*. San Francisco: Harper & Row.

Body and Rituals

The body has long been a subject of studies of ritual, but in the past few decades it has become an increasingly visible, often central focus for the development of theory on ritual. Regarding the role of the body in ritual theory more specifically, two themes stand out as particularly influential. The first is body symbolism, which focuses on representations of the body, and on the body and its parts as represented in ritual. The second, more recently developed theme is practice theory. Here, interest has mainly focused on bodily practice, i.e., the physical action carried out during ritual. Bodily practice and body symbolism are two dimensions often intertwined in the ritual itself, not just in contemporary ritual theory; but since they rest, at least partially, on different theoretical bases, they will be treated separately in this presentation.

Body Symbolism in Ritual

In many analyses of ritual, the body is seen as providing a symbolic system of representation. The work of Mary Douglas stands out as influential in this area, and books such as *Purity and Danger: An analysis of concepts of pollution and taboo* ([1966] 2000), and *Natural*

Initiation rituals in New Guinea are marked by the piercing of the nasal septa or earlobes to accommodate ornaments.
COURTESY OF PAUL SILLITOE.

Symbols: Explorations in cosmology ([1970] 1996), put forward the body, its components, functions, wastes, and so on, as a basic scheme for all symbolism in human societies and as having a significant role in ritual settings. The body becomes an ultimate symbol of thinking society, order, and disorder: "Just as it is true that everything symbolizes the body, so it is equally true (and all the more so for that reason) that the body symbolizes everything else" (Douglas [1966] 2000, 123). Systems of body symbolism may vary greatly between cultures. In some instances, the body is represented in ritual mainly as a vehicle of life; in others, the body and its products are viewed as dangerous and polluting (Douglas [1970] 1996, xxxvi). In her view on the significance of ritual to a community, Douglas follows the early work of the French sociologist Emile Durkeim (Durkeim [1915] 1965), who gave ritual a fundamental role in defining society (Douglas [1966] 2000, 63).

In her ethnographic analyses, Douglas focuses mainly on how ritual symbolically incorporates a culture's basic attitudes about bodily control in social settings. In general, body symbolism can be found throughout ritual practices on many more levels. Bodily change in itself can (at least partially) constitute a catalyst for ritual: disease, maturing, senescence, death, etc., are all potential reasons for a ritual response that may define, confirm, or deny the changes. One of the most striking examples of this is provided by the ritual response to death. At death the body and the physical changes it undergoes often become a system of references that symbolize society as a whole. Also, stages of change in the dead body (due to natural decay or artificial intervention) can symbolize a change in the state of the dead individual. Thus, a society's ritual response to the changes in the dead body are often linked to myths about death and the afterlife.

The first to put forward the relationship between mortuary ritual, attitudes to the dead body, and beliefs about the afterlife was the French sociologist Robert Hertz. He noted ([1907] 1960) that the double obsequies in South East Asian funerary rituals relate the physical state of the corpse with the fate of the soul. More recently, anthropologists have built substantially on this pioneering work. The contributions in *Death and the Regeneration of Life* focus on "the significance of symbols of fertility and rebirth in funeral rituals" (Bloch & Parry 1996, 1). The changes in the body are shown to provide symbols for death and the afterlife, and the rituals surrounding death are intimately linked to these symbols in myths. However, a rejection of the force of death can motivate ritual attempt to control it. This relationship between the symbolic impact of the dead body and how it is handled in ritual can be studied in contemporary Western society, where the denial of the physical changes at death are expressed, for example, in the common North American phenomenon of the open casket burial ritual (see Huntington & Metcalf 1979, Mitford 1963).

The body may also constitute a physical medium on which symbols of change are made. Following the ideas initially formulated by Arnold van Gennep (1909) concerning so-called rites of passage, these ritual actions literally redefine the social identity of the individual who participates in them. The mark on the body both expresses and embodies this social change. An example of transformations through bodily change and marking can be seen in the circumcision among the Merina in Madagascar, as described by Maurice Bloch (1986). He relates the symbolic meanings in the various elements of the ritual to the entire Merina social structure. Through the removal of the foreskin the male child is symbolically removed from the world of women (associated with house, dirt, natural fertility, division, etc.) and becomes part of the male collective (associated with purity, tomb, ancestors, "real" fertility, unity, etc.). Bloch also describes how the circumcision ritual has changed over time in recent history, underscoring the basic connection between ritual and society. In his work on male circumcision in Morocco, Vincent Crapanzano (1980) nuances how bodily marking embodies a broader symbolic meaning in what may be considered a classic rite of passage ritual. Crapanzano points out that the circumcision symbolically *changes* nothing; the child himself is not aware of any social change, nor does he take on a different social identity in the eyes of others. Instead the circumcision is simply a procedure that has to be done. This bodily change, as well as the permanent marking and the physical and emotional pain it entails for the participants, symbolizes loyalty to God through submission to His commandments, rather than a clear transition into manhood.

These examples show the great variety in the roles that the body can play in symbolic representation in ritual. However, body-symbolic approaches to ritual tend to presuppose a shared mental view, by all of the participants, of the meaning of the symbolic system interpreted by the ethnologist.

Bodily Practice of Ritual

In fact, since the 1970s, the idea of shared symbolic meaning in ritual has been challenged by the practice-theoretical perspective, which focuses more on the ritual action than on what it may mean. In practice-theoretical approaches, the body remains a central concept, but instead of being a passive medium for symbolic meaning, the active participation and social interaction in the ritual is seen generating meaning, which may in fact vary from participant to participant.

Practice theory may very basically be described as combining structuralism and Marxism. It theorizes the relationships between social and cultural structures, on the one hand, and individual agency and human action, on the other, viewing them as mutually interdependent. The consequence for ritual studies emerges in two steps. First, while structuralism suggests that symbolism in ritual may be reduced to a linguistic formulation of meaning, practice theory sees language as one practice among others. Thus, practical bodily competence and experience per se is considered as important as meaningful mental representation in structuring social phenomena, from rituals to social values (see for example Bourdieu 1977, Parkin 1992, 11). Catherine Bell (1992) deconstructs the category "ritual," focusing instead on "ritualization," which distantiates certain acts from everyday life, giving ritual its identity and ultimately contributing to its transcendent effects. As with all practical action, ritualized acts are at once structured and are themselves structuring. Through the structured and structuring production of ritualized actions, the participants develop a chain of complex associations, forming a logical system of embodied experience, with clear, hierarchically organized order that tends to be experienced as natural and desirable. The ritualized action—physically carried out—creates a structure that can draw in and generate a whole coherent world of social and cultural values and rules. Similar ideas can, for example, be found in the work of David Kertzer (1988).

Second, since the ritual is generated through embodied experience displayed as practical bodily action, practice theory rejects the idea of ritual as primarily referential. There is no underlying, culturally shared meaning to which the ritual refers. Individuals might not be familiar with the meanings that others give to the ritual, yet all can execute it with competence. The meaning attached to the ritual is, and can only be, generated through the practical experience of it. The kernel of this concept is already present in the works of Emile Durkeim ([1915] 1965) and Marcel Mauss ([1936] 1973). These ideas have been central to the work of Talal Asad. In his book *Genealogies of Religion* (1993), he emphasizes the importance of analyzing the body (in ritual) as "an assemblage of embodied aptitudes, not as systems of symbolic meaning" (Asad 1997, 47). Asad wants to develop an anthropology of practical reason; ritual practices train the body, and in turn, these bodily practices actively shape the mind.

David Parkin (1992) emphasizes keeping social context at the forefront theoretically in order to understand how ritual as embodied practice in "social space" structures cultural phenomena. Ritual is "fundamentally made up of physical action, with words, often only optional or arbitrarily replaceable, that it can be regarded as having a distinctive potential for performative imagination that is not reducible to verbal assertions" (Parkin 1992, 11–12). While the participants might not completely share ideas about its meaning, the physical features of ritual (actions, bodies, etc.) may have important symbolic relationships that structure not only the individual's embodied memory but also the relations of power that influence social interactions before, during, and after the ritual. Parkin points out that the body remains a focus of symbolic structuration of ritual practice. As one example, he refers to a mortuary ritual that involves the participants physically dividing the dead into parts and spatially relocating the body. The symbolic relationships between the dead body, the spatial locations in which its parts are interred, and the social positions of the participants define a coherent political order that effects control over the participants. Thus, practice theory can show how individual experience and action, the symbolic form of ritual, and wider political structures are interrelated social phenomena (see also Bloch 1986).

Practice theory still allows analysis that focuses on linguistic representation, but it emphasizes that the semantic content of thought and uttered speech cannot be isolated from embodied experience and action in ritual. Filip De Boeck (1995) examines how individuals can activate ritual knowledge into mind through physical performance of ritual. In his work with the aLuund in Southwestern Zaire, De Boeck argues that in the space and time of ritual practice, semantic memory—that is, representations of the ritual and its meaning—is generated and experienced through the bodies of the participants. For the participants, after the ritual is over, this knowledge slips back into forgetfulness. De Boeck points out that the ritualized practical re-creation of memory nevertheless affects, and is affected by, everyday life. This approach stresses how the practice of ritual can use non-linguistic embodied experiences to bring forward personal and cultural knowledge (see also Grimes 2000, 5, Humphrey & Laidlaw 1994).

Future Developments

Despite some of the differences between the body-symbolism and embodied-practice perspectives, they could indeed be successfully combined. Practice theory clearly integrates aspects of structuralism so important to body-symbolism approaches. Also, many body-symbolism studies refer to the importance of action in ritual. As Douglas ([1966] 2000, 64) observes, ritual action focuses our attention, framing its symbolic features. In the future the links between these perspectives could be investigated and expanded. Indeed, the symbolism of the body and bodily practice are both likely to remain central in ritual studies. Yet, within body theory more generally—crossing disciplines from religious studies, gender studies, and anthropology to art criticism—the concept of the body as such will continue to be discussed and specified. This will certainly have implications for how to approach the body in ritual theory.

Liv Nilsson Stutz

See also Cannibalism; Clothing and Rituals; Gender Rituals; Healing and Rituals; Oaths and Ordeals; Passage, Rites of Sacrifice and Offerings

Further Reading

Asad, T. (1997). *Genealogies of religion: Discipline and reasons of power in Christianity and Islam.* Baltimore, MD: The Johns Hopkins University Press.

Bell, C. (1992). *Ritual theory, ritual practice.* New York: Oxford University Press.

Bloch, M. (1986). *From blessing to violence.* Cambridge Studies in Social Anthropology. Cambridge, UK: Cambridge University Press.

Bloch, M., & Parry, J. (1982). *Death and the regeneration of life.* Cambridge, UK: Cambridge University Press.

Bourdieu, P. (1977). *Outline of a theory of practice.* Cambridge Studies in Social and Cultural Anthropology. Cambridge, UK: Cambridge University Press.

Coakley, S. (1997). *Religion and the body.* Cambridge, UK: Cambridge University Press.

Crapanzano, V. (1980). Rite of return: Circumcision in Morocco. In V. Muensterberger & L. Bryce Boyer (Eds.), *The psychoanalytic Study of Society 9*: 15–36. New York: Psychohistory Press.

De Boek, F. (1995). Bodies of remembrance: Knowledge, experience and the growing of memory in Luunda ritual performance. In G. Thinès & L. de Heusch (Eds.), *Rites et ritualisation.* Paris: Librairie Philosophique J. Vrin.

Douglas, M. (2000 [1966]). *Purity and danger: An analysis of concepts of pollution and taboo.* New York: Routledge.

Douglas, M. (1996 [1970]). *Natural symbols: Explorations in cosmology.* New York: Routledge.

Durkeim, E. (1965). *The elementary forms of religious life.* New York: The Free Press, Macmillan Publishing Co. (Original work published 1915)

Gennep, A. van (1909). *The rites of passage.* London: Routledge and Kegan Paul.

Grimes, R. (2000) *Deeply into the bone: Re-inventing rites of passage.* Berkeley and Los Angeles: University of California Press.

Hertz, R. (1960). A contribution to the study of the collective representation of death. *In Death and the right hand.* Glenoce, IL: The Free Press. (Originally published in *L'Année Sociologique 1907*, 1907, Paris: Presses Universitaires de France)

Humphrey, C., & Laidlaw, J. (1994). *The archetypal actions of ritual. A theory of ritual illustrated by the Jain rite of worship.* Oxford, UK: Oxford Studies in Social and Cultural Anthropology, Claredon Press.

Huntington, P., & Metcalf, R. (1979). *Celebrations of death: The anthropology of mortuary ritual.* Cambridge, UK: Cambridge University Press.

Kertzer, D. L. (1988). *Ritual, politics and power.* New Haven, CT: Yale University Press.

Mauss, M. (1973). Techniques of the body. *Economy and Society* 2, 70–88.

Mitford, J. (1963). *The American way of death.* New York: Simon and Scuster.

Parkin, D. (1992). Ritual as spatial direction and bodily division. In de Coppet, D. (Ed.), *Understanding Rituals.* New York: Routledge.

Buddhism

Buddhism is a world religious tradition defined by the diverse philosophies, practices, communities, and beliefs that center around the historical, legendary, and archetypal figure known as the "the awakened one" or Buddha. A major religion with approximately 500 million adherents worldwide, Buddhism stretches back over 2,500 years to the lifetime of the historical Buddha, Siddhartha Gautama (c. 563–c. 483 BCE), and his disciples in India. From the the fifth century BCE, Buddhism spread to Sri Lanka, Thailand, Cambodia, Burma, Laos, and Vietnam, as well as to China, Japan, Korea, and Tibet. Over the last two centuries, Buddhist beliefs and practices have further spread to Western countries, becoming an essential feature of the religious pluralism now characteristic of the Western world.

The Buddha

Buddhism in India began during the life of the historical Buddha, who was born along the modern Indo-Nepalese border into a noble family around 563 BCE as Siddhartha Gautama. Realizing that he could not escape the inevitabilities of aging, sickness, and death, at the age of twenty-nine he abruptly renounced all worldly pursuits in order to attain spiritual liberation. After almost six years of rigourous asceticism and meditation, Siddhartha sat under a banyan tree in Bodh Gaya, India, and resolved not to stir until he attained enlightenment. Shortly after, he attained his goal and became the Buddha.

The details of the Buddha's life embody the universal story of all buddhas in the past and the future who achieved ultimate freedom from suffering, and who subsequently assisted others to attain spiritual liberation. Buddhas are actually a rare and exceptional class of sentient beings who appear throughout time and who know and see the world "just as it is" (Sanskrit, *yatha-bhata*). Out of their sympathy *(anukampa)* and because of their altruistic aspirations for the liberation of suffering of all sentient beings *(bodhicitta)*, buddhas teach manifold methods throughout the universe by which sentient beings can attain release from the suffering of existence. In a sense, the Buddhas' teachings and the ritual practices undertaken by followers of the historical Buddha the world over are the many means to achieve spiritual awakening and release from suffering, just as the historical Buddha did more than two thousand years ago.

The Buddhist World View

Buddhism asserts that all beings experience rebirth *(bhava* or *punarbhava)*, migrating from one subsequent life to the next. Buddhist metaphysical texts divide the cosmos into three realms: the form realms of the gods; the formless realms inhabited by gods without form who blissfully exist in a state of pure consciousness; and the desire realms, inhabited by humans, demigods, animals, ghosts, and hell beings all wandering within the beginningless cycle of birth and death *(samsara)*. The experiences of the desire realm are contingent upon their inhabitants' virtuous and nonvirtuous mental, verbal, and physical actions and the pleasurable or painful effects (karma) such actions generate. Thus, innumerable Buddhist rituals focus on creating a foundation of merit to ensure a long, healthy life; to purify negative karma for one's own benefit and that of all sentient beings; and, above all, to ensure an existence conducive to the practice of dharma and eventual liberation.

Theravada (see below) Buddhists, for example, recite or listen to *paritta*s (Pali, meaning "protective runes") from the Pali canon to create such extraordinary effects. When carefully recited or listened to, a *paritta* calms the mind, radiates auspiciousness, wards off numerous evils, pleases gods who are devotees of the Buddha, stimulates past positive merit to fruition, or simply generates more merit. The impetus of recitation in Shinran's (1173–1262 CE) Japanese Pure Land School (Jodo-Shinshu) of Buddhism contrasts with the function of the Theravada *paritta*. Pure Land Buddhist salvation comes from gratefully accepting the Buddha Amida's saving grace and not by generating merit through ritual or engaging in virtuous deeds. According to Shinran, rather than endlessly repeating the *nembutsu* (Japanese, a short formula calling upon the Buddha Amida) as traditionally done in other Chinese and Japanese movements related to the Pure Land School, merely one sincere recitation of the *nembutsu* is sufficient for salvation.

The Four Noble Truths

The first teaching of the Buddha, known as the Four Noble Truths, is of paramount importance. The first truth is that all existence is suffering. The second truth holds that all suffering is caused by the afflictions of craving, aversion, and ignorance. Ignorance itself is caused by an incorrect understanding of the nature of reality, which is described as an erroneous belief in an

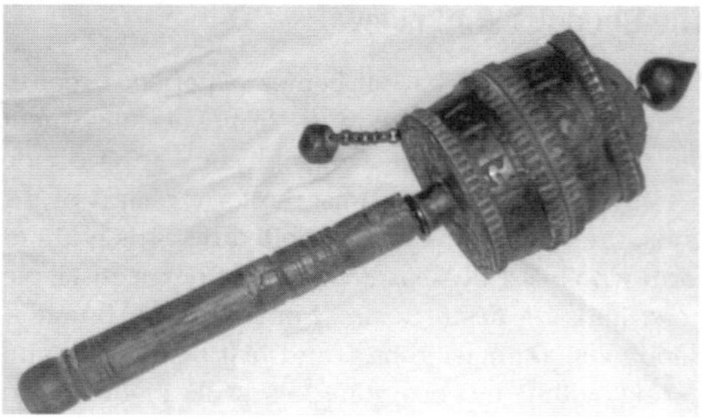

A Buddhist prayer wheel used by monks in Northern Thailand.
COURTESY OF KAREN CHRISTENSEN.

Although Buddhism began as an Asian religion and remained as such for two thousand years, it is now a world religion with many adherents in Western nations. Here, a homeless man in London, England expresses his devotion to Buddha and attracts donations by drawing the Buddha with colored chalks on the Sidharth. COURTESY OF KAREN CHRISTENSEN.

independent, permanent self or soul *(atman)*. The third truth affirms that the suffering of existence can cease in a state described as "passing away" (nirvana). Finally, the fourth truth is the actual path comprised of techniques for achieving the cessation of suffering and supreme enlightenment. Traditionally, meditation or the development of concentration *(dhyana)*, ethics *(shila)* restraint from the nonvirtues of body, speech, and mind, and the cultivation of wisdom *(prajna)* in order to correct erroneous views of reality compose the fourth noble truth. However, Buddhist ritual practices and rites all either directly or indirectly contribute to the cessation of suffering, and as such are also a fundamental aspect of this final noble truth.

Followers of the Buddha

Buddhists are those who "take refuge" in three categories considered treasures of the greatest spiritual worth, known as the Three Jewels *(triratna)*. These are (1) the community of buddhas, or followers of Buddha; (2) the path, knowable phenomena, regulation, or doctrinal tradition (dharma); and the community of the Buddha's lay and monastic followers *(sangha)*. In this context, refuge is not a hiding place; rather, refuge is found within the Three Jewels, which are capable of protecting and ultimately liberating all beings from the sufferings of the cycle of rebirth *(samsara)*. The act of taking refuge solidifies one's resolve to engender virtuous spiritual qualities inherent within oneself as represented in the Three Jewels and to aspire toward spiritual liberation (nirvana) and well-being. Hence, the most fundamental and all-pervasive ritual for both monastic and lay Buddhists throughout the world is to take refuge. Upon becoming a Buddhist, a refuge ceremony is performed to mark the practitioner's entry into the Buddhist tradition. By reciting the formula "I take refuge in the Buddha [meaning the community of all buddhas], dharma, and *sangha*" three times, one's commitment is affirmed within one's body, speech, and mind. Concurrent with taking daily refuge, Buddhists may further show reverence to the Three Jewels by pressing the hands together at the heart *(anjali mudra)* or by prostrating the whole body to the ground at least three times before a representation of one or many buddhas.

Buddhist Communities

The Buddhist community *(sangha)* consists of monks, nuns, laymen, and laywomen. While entry into the Buddhist stream for lay followers involves taking refuge and adhering to precepts of right ethics, meditative cultivation, and the cultivation of wisdom, Buddhist monks and nuns are ritually ordained in two stages: first as a novice, and then as a fully ordained bhikshu or bhikshuni (literally, "almsman" or "almswoman"), although in most Buddhist countries women still cannot receive full ordination. At the time of ordination, head hair is shaved off, representing the renunciation of vanity, and monastic robes, an alms bowl, and a new ordination name is taken. For the most part, monks and nuns do take a vow of celibacy and agree to numerous precepts prohibiting intoxicants and entertainments. However, the adherence to all these precepts is not a pan-Buddhist phenomenon. Newar Buddhists of Nepal for instance, have done away with a celibate *sangha* due to their interactions with Hinduism. For Japanese Tendai monks, there is no strong lay-monastic distinction, as monks leave their robes and eat meat when interacting with the laity. Overall, the Buddhist monastic order can be regarded as a body of ritual specialists who transmit the knowledge of Buddhist scriptures. Moreover, they are a "field of merit" to whom the laity may endow gifts. In Theravada Buddhism, giving to one's community and primarily to the monastic community items of food, robes, lodging, and medicine is a way of generating merit, which increases as a donor's intentions become more pure. Thus, ritualized almsgiving or the act of generosity *(dana)* is an integral ethical activity for spiritual development in Buddhism. The continual practice of giving is also considered an auspicious practice that gradually reduces the donor's attachments and possessiveness. In turn, monks and nuns reciprocate *dana* by giving an even greater gift of the Buddhist teachings, considered a gift to excel all gifts, to lay practitioners.

Theravada Buddhism

Buddhism today is divided into three main branches, known as Theravada (Pali, "Way of the Elders"), Mahayana (Pali, "Great Vehicle") and Vajrayana (Pali, "Diamond Vehicle"). While each branch represents a series of religious movements originating in India, they do not represent strict historical phases, ideological shifts, distinct ritual and ethical systems, or even progressions in ritual efficacy. Thus, no one branch can be perceived as a uniform, monolithic whole.

Theravada Buddhism finds it roots in the early Buddhist community that flourished in India during the Mauryan dynasty (324–187 BCE) and spread throughout Southeast Asia up to the present day. Theravada Buddhism claims to be the oldest and most authentic form of Buddhism and possesses a wealth of ritual and devotional practices. In Sri Lanka for example, where Theravada Buddhism is influenced by folk religions and other pre-Buddhist movements, ritual healing ceremonies known in Sinhalese as *bali* are performed to propitiate planetary deities and to pay homage to the Buddha. As well, Sinhalese Buddhists perform the *tovil,* an exorcism ceremony, in which uttering the name of the Buddha alone is sufficient to drive away any demons invading the body of the possessed individual.

From the time of early Buddhism, the veneration of hemispherical reliquaries (stupas) containing the relics of the Buddha or revered masters has been an important form of Buddhist ritual worship. Considered to bestow blessings, devotion at a stupa is performed by making pilgrimages to it, by making offerings at its base, and by circumambulating it in a clockwise manner. The commissioning, building, and ritual consecration of Buddha images is said to accrue great merit and are activities that continue up to the present day. The ritual bathing of Buddha statues is another popular practice present in Southeast and East Asia. Pilgrimage is also common form of devotional worship and merit generation throughout the Buddhist world. Aside from stupas in India, other pilgrimage sites are the Buddha's tooth relics and the places of his birth, his first teachings, his enlightenment, his passing into nirvana *(parinirvana),* and his footprints, found in modern Nepal, north India, and Sri Lanka.

Mahayana Buddhism

Mahayana Buddhism expresses an ideological shift in soteriology from that of Theravada Buddhism, rather than a dramatic change in Buddhist ritual practice. Theravada Buddhism emphasizes the destruction of one's own cognitive afflictions through the constant practice of analytical meditation (Sanskrit, *vipashyana;* Pali, *vipassana).* In some schools of Burmese Buddhism, the primary practice of lay and monastic practitioners is to meditate on the transient nature of human existence, by observing the subtle and coarse physical sensations that arise and dissipate throughout the physical body. One who breaks through the illusion of the immutable self is an arhat ("worthy one"). In contrast, Mahayana Buddhism emphasizes the practices of the bodhisattva, an exceptional being who generates the altruistic attention to attain enlightenment *(bodhicitta),* dedicating all his or her actions to the welfare and liberation of all beings. In Mahayana Buddhism, formal rituals are enacted for practitioners wishing to take the bodhisattva vow in order to liberate beings from cyclic existence (samsara). At such ceremonies the officiant, speaking on behalf of the Buddha, declares that the disciples present will become buddhas in the distant future.

Vajrayana Buddhism

Vajrayana Buddhism or Tantric Buddhism first evolved as a heterogeneous body of esoteric practices in India from the eighth century CE, spreading across

Asia and more recently into the Western world. Vajrayana ritual or *sadhana* ("means of achievement") involves the Tantric practitioner invoking the Buddha and an assemblage of celestial deities through a complex process of visualization, the performance of ritual hand gestures *(mudra)*, and the speaking of sacred syllables and words of power *(mantra)*. There are two kinds or tantric *sadhana*. In the first kind, the practitioner invokes the deity with the aspiration to receive blessings. The other kind involves a practitioner imagining him- or herself as a fully enlightened buddha in body, speech, and mind. Highly skilled practitioners are said to have the ability to appear in the form of the enlightened deity in order to assuage the suffering of sentient beings. The most well-known Tantric Buddhism tradition thrives amongst Tibetan Buddhists scattered throughout the world.

The Buddhist Calendar

As most Buddhist countries follow divergent calendars, which often revolve around agricultural cycles and local traditions, there is no universal Buddhist calendar; however, there are several festivals that Buddhist countries share in common. Theravadins sometimes follow the Buddhist Era, which commences in 543 BCE, the date Theravadins assign to the death of Gautama Buddha. Tibetan and Chinese Buddhists adhere to a hexagenary cycle, during which twelve animals and five elements are combined each lunar year, repeating this combination of patterns every sixty years. All Buddhist traditions harmonize solar and lunar calendars. Typically, calendars must intercalate an extra month into the twelve-month year. Hence, as the Buddhist year follows the solar calendar, holidays and festivals will always fall during the same season; however, actual festival days will usually fall on specific days of annual lunar cycles. Thus for Tibetan and Chinese Buddhists, the new year begins in either January or February on the day of a new moon. Days in the Buddhist calendar generally unfold from midnight to midnight; however, in Buddhist Sri Lanka days run from dawn to dawn.

Buddhist Festivals

Buddhist festivals are opportunities for reaffirming devotion, making merit, purifying one's misdeeds, strengthening community ties, and entertainment. (See table 1.) Some communities do celebrate major

TABLE 1. BUDDHIST FESTIVALS

Festival	Description	Date
Uposatha	Purification and confession for monastics and laity	New and full moons of every lunar cycle
New Year	Purification of past misdeeds; focus on worldly welfare	Varies
Magha Puja	All-Saints Day or Dharma Day, Laos and Thailand	February
Monlam	Prayer festival celebrating Buddha's victory over evil	February
Vesakha	Buddha's birth, death, and parinirvana	May–June
Wan Atthami	Buddha's cremation, Thailand	May–June
Dzamling Chisang	Day of purification; offering to protector spirits, Tibet	June
Poson	Establishment of Buddhism; Sri Lanka	June–July
Tavatimsa	Buddha's secret return from Tavatimsa heaven	July
Vessa	Beginning of the Rains Retreat	July
Asalha	Buddha's First Sermon	July–August
Asalha Perahara	Procession of Buddha's Tooth Relic, Sri Lanka	July–August
Ullambana; O-bon	Festival of Hungry Ghosts; China and Japan	August
End of Vessa	Ritual conclusion of Rains Retreat	October
Kathina/Post-vessa	Laity ritually endow monks with robes	October–November
Nagcho Chenmo	Death anniversary of Tsongkhapa; Tibet	October–November
Gutor	Two-day festival marking the year end; Tibet	December

***Source*: Gombrich (1986).**

festivals that may not be wholly Buddhist, but pertain as well to agricultural cycles, national heroes and deities, or local religious cults. Major days for purification and meditation occur on *uposatha* days, during a new or full moon. On the full moon of the lunar month of Vesakha (in the month of May), the Buddha's birth, enlightenment, and passing into nirvana *(parinirvana)* is celebrated. Another important festival is the annual three-month period of Vessa (Rains). During Vessa, monks and nuns retreat to their home monasteries, focusing on study and meditation, while the laity perform fasts and confession, and take on additional precepts to deepen their religious commitment, during the new and full moon regular uposathas (i.e. the first, eighth, fifteenth and twenty-third days of the monthly lunar cycle).

Outlook in the Twenty-First Century

In the last two centuries, diasporic Asian Buddhist communities have migrated to the West, where there has been a steady increase in non-Asian peoples converting to Buddhism. While Asian Buddhist communities generally experience ritual and devotion as commensurate with spiritual and cultural identity, many modern first-generation Buddhists in the West have embraced Buddhist rituals and festivals, primarily viewing them as an integral part of Buddhist practice with genuine therapeutic and salvific import. Hence, even while prayer festivals like Vesakha and *uposatha*s are now typically performed in urban Buddhist communities in Europe and North America, some Western Buddhists continue to grapple with issues of the efficacy and necessity of Buddhist ritual objects and praxis altogether. Hence, one of the more complex undertakings for the future of Buddhism in the Western religious tradition will be to establish the appropriate and meaningful placement of old and new rituals within the framework of the modern, global Buddhist community and its sustaining soteriology and doctrine.

Sujata Ghosh

Further Reading

Akira, H. (1990). A history of Indian Buddhism: From Sakyamuni to early Mahayana. Honolulu: University of Hawaii Press.

Beyer, S. (1978). The cult of Tara: Magic and ritual in Tibet. Berkeley: University of California Press.

Cannon, D. W. (1996). Six ways of being religious: A framework for comparative studies of Religion. Belmont, CA: Wadsworth.

Eckel, M. D. (1990). The power of the Buddha's absence: On the foundations of Mahayana Buddhist ritual. Journal of Ritual Studies 4, 61–95.

Gethin, R. (1998). The foundations of Buddhism. Oxford, UK: Oxford University Press.

Gombrich, R. (1986). Buddhist Festivals. In A. Brown (Ed.), Festivals in world religions (pp. 31–59). New York: Longman.

Harvey, P. (1990). An introduction to Buddhism: Teachings, history, and practices. Cambridge, UK: Cambridge University Press.

Kitagawa, J. M., & Cummings, M. D. (1989). Buddhism and Asian history. New York: Macmillan.

Lopez, D. (1995). Buddhism in practice. Princeton, NJ: Princeton University Press.

Prebish, C. S. (1999). Luminous passage: The practice and study of Buddhism in America. Berkeley: University of California Press.

Reynolds, F. E. (1995). Image and ritual in Buddhism. History of religions 34, 201–280.

Santideva. (1999). Siksa-Samuccaya: A compendium of Buddhist doctrine. Delhi, India: Motilal Banarsidass.

Snellgrove, D. (1987). Indo-Tibetan Buddhism: Indian Buddhists and their Tibetan successors. Boston: Shambhala Publications.

Strong, J. S. (2002). The experience of Buddhism: Sources and interpretations. Stanford, CT: Wadsworth.

Williams, D. R., & Queen, C. S. (1999). American Buddhism: Methods and findings in recent scholarship. London: Curzon Press.

C

Calendrical Rituals

Calendrical rituals are celebrations that occur on an annual cycle, usually to mark a particular date or season, and are linked to a repetitive notion of time and the regular commemoration of seasonal changes. Calendrical rituals are most developed in agricultural societies, where the annual rhythm of time is associated with the harvesting of particular crops, and often with ideas of the renewal of the earth and the rebirth of particular plants. They also occur in societies with printed calendars and a formal cycle of annual events, even highly industrialized ones. They are least common among peoples who live as hunters and gatherers in tropical regions, where seasonal oscillations in daylight and rainfall are less important than other markers of change in the natural world. Some societies seem almost totally without calendrical celebrations—like the Huaulu of Seram, Indonesia, or the Iraqw of Tanzania—while others, like the Balinese have an almost endless succession of such festivals.

The Balinese celebrate temple festivals *(odalan)* on a 210-day cycle, but they also commemorate a number of other events on 3-day cycles of named days, a 5-day market week, as well as a 7-day week labeled with Hindu names for celestial bodies. Each is defined in relation to its position within nine different cycles, and the intersections of these cycles provide the most propitious days for marrying, building houses, cremating the dead, or planting and harvesting crops. Geertz argued that there were so many confusing linkages between cycles (which also included systems of personal names and status titles) that time itself appeared to be immobilized into a "motionless present" (1973, 404). He asked the intriguing question of whether an almost excessively complicated calendar would have the paradoxical effect of banishing a notion of the passing of time.

Calendars themselves are complex creations, and do not always coordinate events in relation to the annual solar year. Many smaller-scale societies use lunar cycles rather than seasonal oscillations, and both the Chinese calendar and the Islamic one emphasize phases of the moon, so that a key festival (like the Muslim month of Ramadan) may migrate around the seasons of the Roman calendar. The ritual calendars of smaller societies use a variety of different seasonal cues for intercalation, including the seasonal swarming of sea worms in the Pacific, astronomical markers, the growth cycles of various plants, and even the migration patterns of animals. Human ritual activities have the practical purpose of gathering together and mobilizing labor for the clearing of fields and planting of new crops, so the priest of calendrical rituals is often also the person who bears primary responsibility for agricultural productivity.

Calendrical rituals occur in both stratified and nonstratified societies, and they can emphasize the shared experience of seasonality or stress instead hierarchical differences in access to specialized knowledge of the calendar. They are generally contrasted with rituals of the human life cycle (held in relation to individual stages of development or accomplishment) and rites of affliction.

THE HOPI AGRICULTURAL CALENDAR

Month	Primary Ceremony	Purpose	Sequent Agricultural or Climatic Event
February	Powa'mu	germination	planting of vegetables and early corn
March	Un'kwa-ti	germination	planting on main corn crop
April May June	Katchina dances of spring and early summer	rain	period of drought followed by onset of summer rains
July	Niman katchina		corn knee-high
August	Snake-Antelope flute	rain and ripening of early crops	vegetables and early corn ripen
September	Marau, Lako'n	ripening of main corn	main corn crop ripens
October	Oa'qol	harvest	main corn crop harvested

***Source*: Adapted from: Bradfield, Richard M. (1973). *A Natural History of Associations.* New York: International Universities Press, Inc., p. 185**

Calendrical Rituals and Temporality

A key controversy concerning calendrical rituals is exactly how widely shared their values and expression are, and how these are related to the practical experience of time. Bourdieu has argued that indigenous calendars perpetuate a "synoptic illusion" (1977, 164), which is divorced from the "real" time of work, leisure, and exchange in everyday life—substituting a "linear, homogeneous, continuous time" for "incommensurable islands of duration of practical activity" (1977, 105–6). But he has also detailed how the Algerian peasant "lives his life at a rhythm determined by the divisions of the ritual calendar which exhibit a whole mythical system" (Bourdieu 1968, 57). The technical acts of planting and harvesting are coordinated with "liturgical acts" to commemorate calendrical moments to produce a system that he calls "mythology-in-action," in which the peasant does violence to the nourishing earth in order to fecundate her and wrest her riches from her.

Agricultural societies have the most elaborately developed calendrical rituals because the regulation of time is crucial for practical activities such as planting and harvesting. For this very reason, it is necessary to coordinate all members of the society and some sort of authority structure is needed for this coordination. The guardian of the calendar, sometimes referred to as "priest of the months" (Hoskins 1994, 94; Geirnaert-Martin 1992, 12), therefore holds an important position within indigenous systems of knowledge as someone who not only "counts out the months" and determines the time for festivals, but also someone who determines the best moment in an agricultural cycle for particular activities to take place. His function is both ritual and practical, since he is both a "Father Time" figure with great symbolic importance (and often a heavy burden of personal taboos) and the leader of the most significant forms of labor cooperation.

Calendrical rituals can also become occasions for commemorating historical events, so they are not always concerned with simple ideas of repetition and cycles. After the bombing of a tourist nightclub on Bali in 2002 that claimed almost 200 lives, plans were made to hold a massive ritual sacrifice *(pecaruan)* on the site of the bombing in Kuta, timed to coincide with Sugian Bali—a day when all commoner Balinese pray to their ancestors in family ancestral shrines to prepare for Galungan. Galungan is a calendrical rite held every 210 days to commemorate the defeat of a fourteenth-century tyrant, and it is a time when each family gathers for purification and celebration. The intersection of a historical commemoration and a sacrificial ceremony to satiate the demons attracted by the blood and grief caused by the bombing is not a coincidence. Instead, these two rites demonstrate a belief that the cosmos is a suprahuman reflection of the internal cosmos of the body, so the purification of the individual body must also be accompanied by a purification of the social body.

The body is an important presence in calendrical rituals because so many of them involve temporary periods of ritual reversals or transgressions. As Edmund Leach first noted in his seminal essay "Time and False Noses" (1961), the end of a ritual cycle is often a period of license, silliness, and masquerade. He associates this with a temporal structure in which there is a passage from the profane to the sacred, at the opening of a calendrical feast, and then from the sacred to the profane, at the close. The celebration of Mardi Gras or Carnival before the beginning of Lent is a prototypical example of this oscillation of temporal modes, and it is indeed a time when men dress up like women, people walk backwards, and authority figures may be teased, parodied, or even burned in effigy. Leach stresses the fact that these behaviors occur within a temporal pendulum, but in many cases the events do not occur in the order he postulates.

Calendrical Rituals and Transgression

Bakhtin has emphasized the disruptive, trangressive element of feasting in his argument that "carnival does not know footlights" (1984, 7): its performances are not framed by distinctions between actors and outsiders, performers and spectators. This is the difference between a spectacle and a calendrical rite like carnival, which is full of people making fun of each other and of the official actors. The subversive force of laughter—and especially a particularly graphic, bodily humor—is said to confront the boundary between spectacle and spectator and dissolve it into general participation by all around: "As opposed to the official feast, one might say that carnival celebrated temporary liberation from the prevailing truth and from the established order; it marked the suspension of all hierarchical rank, privileges, norms and prohibitions. Carnival was the true feast of time, the feast of becoming, change and renewal. It was hostile to all that was immortalized and completed" (Bakhtin 1984, 9–10).

Certain calendrical feasts emphasize ritual discipline, respect, and hierarchy, and serve to enshrine a sacred memory that is important for the collectivity. Others—the more ribald and disrespectful ones that Bakhtin speaks about—are designed to explore and celebrate the regenerative powers of difference: between men and women, juniors and seniors, past and present. If, as Bakhtin says, "laughter is the enemy of hierarchy" (1984, 10), then ribaldry can be interpreted as asserting the heterogeneity of ritual participants and their resistance to official authority, The Rabelaisian flavor of the European Carnival is also found in *nale* rice festivities of the Kodi people of Sumba, eastern Indonesia, the *milamala* yam festivals of the Trobriand Islanders of Papua New Guinea, and many celebrations of the harvest in other places. Unmarried young men and women are allowed to dance sexually suggestive dances, tease each other, imitate the behavior of the opposite sex, and sometimes even escape for private liaisons without suffering social sanctions. Transgression and the legitimate violation of all the usual forms is a characteristic of the period following the death of a king in both Africa and Polynesia, but it is not accompanied by joyfulness and is not in any way festive.

Trangression in itself cannot be taken to define calendrical festivals, but it also seems inappropriate to assume that transgression is simply liminality, a moment of antistructure in a dialectical process of structure making, as does Turner (1969). Rather, it would seem that calendrical festivals allow for the expression of divergent political sentiments in order to bring opposing forces into contact to affirm their power to generate a new whole. They represent the fact that diverse societies contain many marginalized groups that have to be included within a yearly cycle of renewed unity. The goal of a calendrical feast is to create a transparent totality of relations. As Valeri argues: "If in the feast separations fall away and chaos seems to infiltrate its way into the cosmos, it is not because the feast is the negation of order, but because it represents order as totality. It is therefore necessary that what is set apart as dangerous and rejected as disorder in daily life should be part of feasting" (2001, 11).

Calendrical Rituals and the Human Life Cycle

Calendrical rituals mark moments in the life of the collectivity that are distinct from the "rites of passage" of biographical time and its idiosyncratic events. Rites that occur on a yearly cycle form an important part of the cultural heritage of a great many societies, and are articulated through origin narratives, ideas of precedence and authority, spatial maps, and the ritual functions of objects, according to Hoskins (1998). The birth or death dates of particular individuals are commemorated as calendrical rituals (Christmas, President's Day, the Queen's Birthday, Martin Luther King Day, etc.) only when historical events give particular prominence to that person's biography.

Calendars and their celebrations create a social sense of time that is larger than the human life span and more enduring. Whether these feasts are commemorating historical events or natural processes, they are important because they provide a collective ordering of past, present, and future, and they direct human activities toward locally valorized ends. Most calendrical rites are presented as texts without authors—a narrative of the past that was generated in some long distant age, created by "founding ancestors" who prescribed the forms and procedures to be followed. But since ritual cycles are often also disrupted by contingent events, these rites also require new authors and interpreters to continue or become revitalized in new circumstances. The crisis of modernity has intensified the "biographical content" of many calendrical rituals, and tied them more closely to famous persons and their recent accomplishments, as these rituals are reinvented by each new generation that performs them.

Janet Hoskins

See also Agricultural Rituals; Iban

Further Reading

Austen, L. (1939). The seasonal gardening calendar of Kiriwina, Trobriand Islands. *Oceania, 10,* 30–53.

Bakhtin, M. (1984). *Rabelais and his world.* Bloomington: Indiana University Press.

Bourdieu, P. (1968). The attitude of the Algerian peasant toward time. In J. Pitt-Rivers (Ed.), *Mediterranean countrymen: Essays on the social anthropology of the Mediterranean* (pp. 221–249). Paris: Mouton.

Bourdieu, P. (1977). *Outline of a theory of practice.* Cambridge, UK: Cambridge University Press.

Geertz, C. (1973). Person, time, and conduct in Bali. In *The interpretation of cultures.* New York: Basic Books.

Leach, E. (1950). Primitive calendars. *Oceania, 20*(4), 245–66.

(1964). Primitive time reckoning. In C. Singer, E. Holmyard, & A. Hall (Eds.), *History of technology* (pp. 142–154). Oxford: Clarendon Press.

Leach, E. (1961). Time and false noses: Two essays concerning the symbolic representation of time. In *Rethinking anthropology* (pp. 123–139). London: Athlone Press.

Geirnaert-Martin, D. (1992). *The woven land of laboya: Socio-cosmic ideas and values in West Sumba, Eastern Indonesia.* Leiden, Netherlands: Centre of Non-Western Studies.

Hoskins, J. (1994). *The play of time: Kodi perspectives on calendars, history, and exchange.* Berkeley: University of California Press.

Hoskins, J. (1998). *Biographical objects: How things tell the stories of people's lives.* Routledge: New York.

Lansing, J. S. (1991). *Priests and programmers: Technologies of power in the engineered landscape of Bali.* Princeton, NJ: Princeton University Press.

Malinowski, B. (1927). Lunar and seasonal calendars in the Trobriand Islands. *Journal of the Royal Anthropological Institute, 157,* 203–15.

Malinowski, B. (1935). *Coral gardens and their magic.* Bloomington: Indian University Press.

Thornton, R. (1981). *Space, time, and culture among the Iraqw of Tanzania.* New York: Academic Press.

Turner, V. (1969). *The ritual process: Structure and anti-structure.* Chicago: Aldine.

Valeri, V. (2000). *The forest of taboos: Morality, hunting, and identity among the Huaulu of the Moluccas.* Madison: University of Wisconsin Press.

Valeri, V. (2000). *Fragments from forests and libraries.* Durham, NC: Carolina Academic Press.

Camp Meetings

Camp meetings were fervent Protestant Christian religious and social gatherings that originated out of nineteenth-century frontier life in the American South. The meetings were highly emotional, demonstrative, and devoted to converting sinners to repentance and spiritual rebirth through faith in Jesus Christ. Camp meetings helped integrate and affirm sparsely scattered and diverse congregations through intense collective experience. The name itself derives from the tradition of rural families setting up tents or makeshift shelters, camping out around a central meeting area, and attending services over a period of several days. Camp meetings are also known as tent, arbor, or brush-arbor meetings, all of which reflect their temporal and out-of-the-ordinary nature. In addition to the predominant evangelistic theme, a camp meeting offered one of the few large-scale social events on the American frontier in the early 1800s, providing an opportunity for people to come together for reunions and lengthy visits with family and friends. In the latter half of the twentieth century, as churches sought more family-centered activities, camp meetings enjoyed a revival by emphasizing the social aspects of the tradition, with religion taking a secondary role.

The outdoor chapel at the Methodist Camp Quinipet at Shelter Island, New York. COURTESY OF BECCI SEARLE-SCHRADER.

History

Historically, camp meetings are considered to be a distinct phenomenon of the American frontier, but they have a number of precedents, specifically European holy fairs. In the United States, they are associated with the Second Great Awakening and revivalism movements during the early 1800s, where churches addressed the crisis of declining membership in an increasingly diverse and widespread frontier population. Presbyterians in Cane Ridge, Kentucky, probably held the first camp meetings around 1800. The idea was soon embraced by Methodists and then Baptists, and early camp meetings were often interdenominational, although always Protestant. The early gatherings were highly dramatic and extremely emotional, with attendance occasionally numbering in the thousands. By the 1840s, however, meetings were dying down, due in part to discord engendered by the slavery debate. They vigorously reemerged after the Civil War, followed by the Chautauqua and Bible Conference Movements, probable outgrowths of the original camp meeting concept. More permanent compounds were built, and recreational activities were added to the intensely religious fare. Many church retreat centers operating today originated as camp meetings during this era.

The typical camp meeting was organized by local, ordained clergy, who scheduled the event after the harvest, usually in late summer, and located it in an area with sufficient water, shade, pastureland, and accessibility to accommodate large numbers of families from the surrounding countryside. Meetings were usually held for four days to a week, with services lasting from early morning to late night. Since services allowed little free time, most socializing and renewing of friendships occurred at the beginning or end of the camp. Lay preachers—men *and* women—assisted the clergy during the services, moving about among the congregation encouraging sinners to repent, praying, and giving testimonies. The audience consisted of women as well as men, sometimes seated in separate sections, and whites as well as blacks, *always* seated in separate sections.

Structure of Services

Structurally, the services at camp meetings of the early 1800s do not differ radically from revivals held today among evangelical groups. The services were highly structured and designed for the primary purpose of generating emotional turmoil in the unconverted and the lapsed Christian, which would lead to their submission to the will of God and ultimate spiritual transformation. A secondary goal, generating a sense of commonality among the saved and affirming their faith and righteousness, was desired but not required. The success or failure of each meeting was determined by the number of converts tallied up at the conclusion of the camp.

The structure of the services was designed to propel potential targets toward conversion and was, therefore, intentionally disturbing to those of uncertain faith. Through a combination of fire-and-brimstone preaching, praying, audience response, singing, and testimonials, the emotional state of the unsaved was manipulated to accept the simple religious message. Preaching, by local and occasional guest clergy, took the form of passionate exhortations against sin and dire warnings of the fate that awaited the sinner. Prayer—individual, communal, and responsive—reinforced the admonishments with more passion, desperate calls to the sinners, and pleas to Jesus. Audience response included shouting, weeping, and pleading, spreading and growing louder as the tempo of the service increased. Nearly everyone in the audience participated in exhorting the converts and delivering testimonials. After potential converts acknowledged submission, they would be taken to sit with other converts to think through their decision as the service continued. Music consisted of easy-to-learn gospel songs or shape-note singing, and choruses were often repeated over and over to give sinners time to make up their minds. Testimonies, personal histories of the previous sinful lives of converts and how they came to be saved, were integral to the services. Great value was placed on testimonies, and the most dramatic were highly sought after. At the end of a service or during membership induction at the last service, converts would be expected to give their testimonies.

The ritual structure and meaning of the camp meeting operated at several levels. Locating the gatherings in the wilderness defined the ritual, encouraged a sense of liminality, and served as a reminder of the function of religion as a civilizing agent to tame the wildness of the human spirit. For the participants, leaving their homes for a week of spiritual renewal represented a break from the ordinary and the opportunity for transformation, after which to return to their everyday lives on a higher spiritual plane. The exceedingly emotional activities increased the likelihood of inculcation, and the structure of the camp promoted *communitas*, that feeling of great solidarity and equality characteristic of people who have undergone an intense group experience, such as a rite of passage. Finally, the juxtaposition of opposites reinforced the ritual message of security amidst danger. The nature of the services emphasized the tension between the wretchedness of the worldly life and the serenity and confidence of the saved. The camplike, communal, and temporal setting of the gathering was set dramatically against the urgent message being delivered, which was intense, individualized, and ultimately focused on the eternal.

Jaclyn L. Jeffrey

Further Reading

Brown, K. (1992). *Holy ground: A study of the American camp meeting*. New York: Garland Publishing.

Bruce, D. D. (1974). *And they all sang hallelujah: Plain-folk camp-meeting religion, 1800–1845*. Knoxville: University of Tennessee Press.

Eslinger, E. (1999). *Citizens of Zion: The social origins of camp meeting revivalism*. Knoxville: University of Tennessee Press.

Johnson, C. A. (1985). *The frontier camp meeting: Religion's harvest time*. Dallas, TX: Southern Methodist University Press.

Cannibalism

The earliest known reference to cannibalism was provided by the Greek historian Herodotus in the fifth century BCE. He wrote of the "Anthropophagi" (Man-Eaters) who lived on the frontier of Greek civilization. Two thousand years later Christopher Columbus would coin the term *cannibal,* based on a mistaken Spanish translation of the term *Carib,* referring to a supposedly (literally) bloodthirsty aboriginal group found in the New World. Even though Columbus never actually witnessed the alleged human flesh-eating himself, he nonetheless spread the lurid details of this most repulsive and "savage" behavior, a cultural trait that, unfortunately, would become virtually a standard characteristic of indigenous peoples the world over, at least from the perspective of "civilized" Europeans. Of course, such notions went a long way toward assuaging or eliminating whatever guilt and apprehension Europeans felt as a result of colonizing and enslaving native peoples around the globe.

It should be noted that even in early reports of anthropophagy (cannibalism) one sees, perhaps, more evidence for xenophobia (fear of strangers) than cannibalism; the anthropologist William Arens, in fact, was much more impressed by the former than the latter. In his controversial *The Man-Eating Myth: Anthropology and Anthropophagy*, Arens argues that although it is likely that "survival cannibalism" has occurred on many occasions (and, in fact, has been well documented), there are virtually no reliable data to support the contention that instances of routine, cultural, and ritualistic cannibalism have ever occurred. Arens's understandable lack of confidence in the validity of reports from missionaries, travelers, traders, and adventurers notwithstanding, a review of the literature on the subject reveals quite convincingly that he is mistaken. The hundreds of reports from eyewitnesses and cultural anthropologists, the archeological data, and the ubiquity of cannibalism lore, legends, and mythology provide a database of sorts that cannot be ignored, and, in fact, few cultural anthropologists today deny the reality of cannibalism, ritualistic, survivalistic, or otherwise.

One might argue, however, as the anthropologist Peggy Reeves Sanday does in *Divine Hunger,* a symbolic analysis of cannibalism in the context of cultural mythology, that given the cross-cultural presence of the notion in every continent around the globe, whether or not cannibalism actually occurred is somewhat moot. Clearly, the sheer ubiquity of the idea itself (if not the actual practice) cries out for explanation.

TALES OF CANNIBALISM

Tales about cannibals and cannibalism are found in many folklore traditions around the world. The following two are short examples from the Amhara of Ethiopia and Iroquois of New York State.

> **Once there was a cannibal. He lived among many people. He had no food in his house; he was poor. But even if he had not been poor, he just liked to eat the flesh of man. In his house was a big hole which he covered with a carpet. He would invite somebody into his house and tell him to sit down on the chair over the hole. When the person sat down and fell into the hole, he would climb down by a ladder and eat him. In this way he ate all the people in his village one by one—about a hundred people. When he had eaten all the people in his village he returned to live in the forest, because there was nobody left to eat.**

***Source*: Levine, Donald N. (1965). *Wax and Gold; Tradition and Innovation in Ethiopian Culture.* Chicago, University of Chicago Press, p. 229.**

Direct confrontation with the child was avoided, but when things got seriously out of hand, parents sometimes turned older children over to the gods for punishment. A troublesome child might be sent out into the dusk to meet Longnose, the legendary Seneca bogeyman. Longnose might even be impersonated in the flesh by a distraught parent. Longnose was a hungry cannibal who chased bad children when their parents were sleeping. He mimicked the child, crying loudly as he ran, but the parents would not wake up because Longnose had bewitched them. A child might be chased all night until he submitted and promised to behave. Theoretically, if a child remained stubborn, Longnose finally caught him and took him away in a huge pack-basket for a leisurely meal. And—although parents were not supposed to do this—an unusually stubborn infant could be threatened with punishment by the great False Faces themselves, who, when invoked for this purpose, might "poison" a child or "spoil his face."

***Source*: Wallace, Anthony F. C. (1972).**
The Death and Rebirth of the Seneca.
***New York*: Vintage Books, p. 37.**

Categories

Cannibalism has been categorized using various schemes based on the function of the practice (ritualistic, nutritional, or gustatory) and whether or not the victim is an "outsider" or an "insider" (exocannibalism and endocannibalism, respectively). In some cases, it is necessary to combine categories. For example, many experts have noted that the Aztecs considered human sacrifice essential for the appeasement of gods and the general flow of time in an orderly, predictable manner. Other experts, such as Marvin Harris and Michael Harner, have argued that the Aztecs were simply motivated by protein deficiency to consume human flesh. Not only have Harris and Harner's cultural materialistic treatments of Aztec cannibalism and sacrifice been effectively refuted, but also it seems clear from the many ethnographies (cultural studies) and monographs on the subject that cannibalism is simply too "traumatic" emotionally and intellectually to involve simply consumptive activities stripped of any ideological or cultural significance whatsoever.

One of the more popular forms of ritual cannibalism involves the consumption of the dead, referred to as "mortuary endocannibalism" or simply "necrophagy." In this case, the deceased is simply consumed after his or her death—no sacrifice is involved.

The Fore people of New Guinea provide, perhaps, the most famous case of necrophagy. This case came to light only after the degenerative disease *kuru* began to appear in a large number of women and children; given the ritual roles of women and residence patterns, a link to cannibalism soon became evident.

Vital Life Essence

Many anthropological interpretations of necrophagy focus on the unbroken perpetuation of the vital life essence of the group by "incorporating" the deceased individual into the bodies of the living. In some cases—for example, the Gimi-speaking peoples of New Guinea—the practice is "genderized" because only women engage in consumption of the dead. Explanations of this practice often focus on the women's attempt to manipulate culturally accepted gender roles to fuse conceptions of "masculine" and "feminine."

Whereas endocannibalism tends to be practiced to enhance the bond between members of a local group, exocannibalism seems to accomplish just the opposite. Often hostile peoples will be consumed in order to strike fear into the enemy in an attempt to demoralize them and take away their willingness to fight. It is interesting to note that when the "others" are eaten, they are eaten as everyday "food" in a context that is bereft of the obligatory solemnity of religious ritual. This is completely harmonious with the age-old custom among all peoples to equate the "outsiders" or the "other" with animals (or "savages") and to consider only themselves worthy of the label of "people" or "human beings."

James Houk

See also Blood Rituals; Body and Rituals; Food and Rituals

Further Reading

Arens, W. (1979). *The man-eating myth: Anthropology and anthropophagy*. New York: Oxford University Press.

Brown, P., & Tuzin, D. (1983). *The ethnography of cannibalism*. Washington, DC: Society for Psychological Anthropology.

de Montellano, B. R. O. (1978) Aztec cannibalism: An ecological necessity? *Science, 200*(4342), 611–617.

Fernandez-Jalvo, Y., Diez, J. C., Cáceres, I., & Rosell, J. (1999). Human cannibalism in the early Pleistocene of Europe (Gran Dolina, Sierra de Atapuerca, Burgos, Spain). *Journal of Human Evolution, 37*(3–4), 591–622.

Harner, M. (1977). The ecological basis for Aztec sacrifice. *American Ethnologist, 4*(1),117–135.

Harris, M. (1977). *Cannibals and kings: The origins of cultures*. New York: Random House.

Petrinovich, L. (2000). *The cannibal within*. New York: Aldine de Gruyter.

Rhodes, R. (1997). *Deadly feasts*. New York: Simon & Schuster.

Sanday, P. R. (1986) *Divine hunger: Cannibalism as a cultural system*. Cambridge, UK: Cambridge University Press.

Turner, C. G., & Turner, J. A. (1999). *Man corn: Cannibalism and violence in the prehistoric American Southwest*. Salt Lake City: University of Utah Press.

White, T. (1992). *Prehistoric cannibalism at Mancos*. Princeton, NJ: Princeton University Press.

Carnival

See Mardi Gras; Rituals of Rebellion

Catholicism

Catholicism includes all those Christian denominations that base their claim to the authority of their priesthood in the claim of "Apostolic Succession," a line of ordination that stretches from their contemporary bishops back to the Apostle Peter. The three major groups of Catholic denominations include the Roman Catholic church, the Eastern Orthodox churches, and (by this definition) the Anglican churches. The major rituals of Catholicism are the seven sacraments (from the Latin *sacramentum*, meaning "oath"). The sacraments are baptism, confirmation, the Eucharist (Holy Communion), reconciliation (penance), anointing the sick (extreme unction), marriage, and Holy Orders. There are also rituals called "sacramentals" that may be performed as adjuncts within the celebration of any of the sacraments or by individuals alone.

The Sacraments

Baptism for the forgiveness of sins and for membership in the Church may be by immersing the candidate or, more commonly, by pouring water on the

ITALIAN CATHOLIC FESTIVALS IN NEW YORK CITY

Public festivals in honor of particular saints are an important rituals in Italian-American communities. The account below describes three such festivals held each year in New York City. The festivals express religious devotion, maintain ties in the local community, and also maintain symbolic ties to the home community in Italy.

The great Neapolitan festa, held in Mulberry Street on September 19, honors San Gennaro, who was martyred by the Romans at Pozzuoli in A.D. 306. Unlike the celebration in Naples, where the patron's day is observed as a public holiday, the merrymaking here is generally confined (save for the women) to the evening. The narrow street is arched with electric lights of varied colors, and a procession of worshipers follows the effigy of the saint up and down the roadway between booths laden with candies, candles, votive offerings and the like. There are fireworks to top off the festivities.

On Sant' Agata's Day, February 5, her effigy is borne up and down Baxter Street, with several thousand Sicilians following in procession. This saint, the legend has it, performed an unparalleled miracle when, nearly 250 years ago, she deflected with her veil the flow of molten lava from Etna on the very edge of the city of Catania, saving the population from certain death.

Western Sicilians on September 4 turn out on Fourteenth Avenue, between Sixty-second and Sixty-fifth Streets (in Brooklyn) to pay homage to Santa Rosalia, who nearly 300 years ago saved the city of Palermo from a pestilence. It was her bones, her followers believe, that accomplished this miracle, for at the time she herself had been dead for more than four centuries.

Source: Federal Writers Project (New York, New York). (1969).
The Italians of New York. New York: Arno Press;
The New York Times, p. 90. Originally published in 1938.

head of the candidate while the officiator says, "I baptize you in the name of the Father, and of the Son, and of the Holy Spirit" (Catholic Church 1995, 348). Baptisms are normally performed by a bishop, priest, or deacon, but in situations of necessity, anyone who has the right intent may baptize. (Thus, baptisms performed in some other Christian denominations are accepted as valid.) Although only water and the appropriate prayer are necessary, the ritual normally also includes other symbols, such as a baptismal candle that symbolizes Christ as the light of the world; blessed oil and chrism (a mixture of oil and balsam), which represent the power and comfort of the Holy Spirit; and white baptismal clothing, which signifies being clothed in Christ.

Those persons born to Catholic families are baptized as infants. The parents and godparents of the infants must promise to rear them in the faith. Adults who join the Church go through the Rite of Christian Initiation of Adults (RCIA), which was approved by Pope Paul VI in 1972. RCIA has four stages: (1) a period in which the candidate's questions about the teachings of the church are answered, (2) a period of more intense instruction into the doctrines, the liturgy (rites prescribed for public worship) of the Church, and the obligations of members, (3) the season of Lent, when the candidate learns about the liturgies of Lent and undergoes the sacraments of baptism (if he or she has not previously received a valid baptism), confirmation, and the Eucharist during the Easter Vigil, which ends the season, and (4) the time from Easter to Pentecost, during which new members are taught about the mysteries of Christ's death and resurrection.

Confirmation is the sacrament through which a baptized person becomes a more fully participating member of the Church by the bestowal of the Holy Spirit. It is normally performed by a bishop.

A Roman Catholic priest blesses the taxis in Copacabana, Bolivia in June 1997. COURTESY OF STEPHEN G. DONALDSON PHOTOGRAPHY.

A girl kisses the toes of the statue of St. Francis in Caceres, Spain. COURTESY OF BECCI SEARLE-SCHRADER.

In confirmation the bishop lays his hands on the baptized member and anoints the member with chrism while he addresses the member by name and says, "be sealed with the Gift of the Holy Spirit" (Catholic Church 1995, 363, 367). When undergoing confirmation, a candidate may choose as a "confirmation name" the name of a favorite saint who will serve both as a role model and as an intercessor with God. Each candidate also has a sponsor who is committed to helping the candidate through prayer and support.

The Eucharist, or Holy Communion, is based on the final meal during which Jesus shared bread and wine with his disciples during the Jewish celebration of the Passover. Roman and Eastern Orthodox Catholics believe that the "substance" (as opposed to the outward appearance) of the bread and wine becomes the body and blood Jesus through the miracle of transubstantiation. The Anglican communion speaks, instead, of the "real spiritual presence" of Christ in the bread and wine. The central words spoken by the priest in the sacrament of Holy Communion are

> The day before he suffered he took bread in his sacred hands and looking up to heaven, to you, his almighty father, he gave you thanks and praise. He broke the bread, gave it to his disciples, and said: Take this, all of you, and eat it: This is my body which will be given up for you. When supper was ended, he took the cup. Again he gave you thanks and praise, gave the cup to his disciples, and said: Take this, all of you, and drink from it: This is the cup of my blood, the blood of the new and everlasting covenant. It will be shed for you and for all so that sin may be forgiven. Do this in memory of me. (Catholic Church 1985, 544–545).

Reconciliation (penance) begins with contrition, the experience of sorrow for one's sins and conversion, a change of heart and intent not to sin again. This is followed by confession of sins to a priest. After confessing the penitent expresses sorrow for his or her sins through short prayer, such as "Jesus, I am sorry for all my sins. Have mercy on me" or "My God, I am sorry for my sins with all my heart. In choosing to do wrong and failing to do good, I have sinned against you whom I should love above all things. I firmly intend, with your help, to do penance, to sin no more, and to avoid whatever leads me to sin. Our Savior Jesus Christ suffered and died for us. In his name, my God, have mercy" (Catholic Church 1995, 382). After this the priest recites the prayer of absolution (a declaration of forgiveness), "God the Father of mercies, through the death and Resurrection of his Son, has reconciled the world to himself and sent the Holy Spirit among us for the forgiveness of sins. Through the ministry of the Church, may God give you pardon and peace, and I absolve you from your sins in the name of the Father, and of the Son, and of the Holy Spirit" (Catholic Church 1995, 382–383, 404). After contrition and confession comes satisfaction (doing penance for one's sins and making up for harm that has resulted from those sins).

In the Anglican communion a ritual of penance is performed only in a group setting as part of the preparation for the Eucharist. In this preparation the priest prays, "Almighty God, our heavenly Father, who of his great mercy hath promised forgiveness of sins to all those who with hearty repentance and true faith turn to him; have mercy upon you; pardon and deliver you from all your sins; confirm and strengthen you in all goodness; and bring you to everlasting life; through Jesus Christ our Lord. Amen" (Church of England 1928, 236), to which the penitents say, "Amen."

The sacrament of anointing the sick (extreme unction) can be received by any baptized person who has reached the age of reason and is on account of sickness or age in danger of death. Its effect is the strengthening of the soul, often of the body as well, and, in the necessary conditions, remission of sins. In so doing, it can ease the transition from this life to the next. This sacrament can be performed only by a priest. The priest lays hands on the head of the sick person, anoints the forehead with blessed oil, and prays, "Through this holy anointing may the Lord in his love and mercy help you with the grace of the Holy Spirit." The priest then anoints the hands and prays, "May the Lord who frees you from sin save you and raise you up" (Catholic Church 1995, 421).

In Catholicism marriage is a contract between two persons raised by Christ to the dignity of a sacrament. Its two defining elements are unity and indissolubility. The unity of matrimony includes the requirement of sexual fidelity, and the purposes of this sacrament are to aid the mutual support of the spouses and to increase the number of the people of God. The sacrament of marriage is a human act by which two persons freely give themselves to one another through the expression of consent: "I take you to be my husband" and "I take you to be my wife" (Catholic Church 1995, 453). After receiving the consent of the couple in the name of the Church, a priest blesses the couple.

Holy Orders is the ordination of priests to the dedicated labor of service to God by offering sacrifice and leading the formal worship of the Church. For instance, the sacraments of the celebration of the Eucharist and of anointing the sick can be validly performed only by one who has undergone the sacrament of Holy Orders. Holy Orders includes three ordained offices: deacon, priest, and bishop.

The rituals of ordination differ somewhat for the offices of deacon, priest, and bishop because the obligations of these three offices differ. In the rituals of ordination for all three offices, the necessary acts involve the laying on of hands and the recitation of a prayer of consecration by the bishop. "Laying on (or imposition of) hands" refers to the act of the bishop's placing his hands on the head of the candidate for ordination. In the ordination of a priest, the prayer of consecration includes the words "Almighty Father, grant to this servant of yours the dignity of the priesthood" (Catholic Church 1985, 66–67), whereas in the consecration of a bishop (who is a successor to the Twelve Apostles), the prayer includes the words "So now pour out upon this chosen one that power which is from you, the governing Spirit whom you gave to your beloved Son, Jesus Christ, the Spirit given by him to the holy apostles, who founded the Church in every place to be your temple for the increasing glory and praise of your name" (Catholic Church 1985, 94–96).

The Sacramentals

In addition to the seven sacraments, Catholics practice a number of sacramentals, such as using holy water in various nonsacramental ceremonies, making the sign of the cross, giving alms, blessing people and things such as ashes, palm branches, or candles, and praying the rosary. These are rites that resemble the sacraments in being sacred rituals and using symbols that call the sacraments to mind. As symbols of the spiritual effects of the sacraments, the actions, words, and objects used in sacramentals help Catholics to be receptive to God's grace. For instance, holy water is water that has been blessed by a priest and is reminiscent of the sacrament of baptism when it is used in various settings, and making the sign of the cross—a sacramental in which a Catholic touches his or her forehead, heart, and shoulders, tracing a cross by the hand—is a reminder that Christ was crucified to give new life.

The rosary is an aid for individual prayer and contemplation of the mysteries of Christ's incarnation, his ministry, his suffering and death, and his resurrection as if through the eyes of Christ's mother, Mary, in her role as mother of Christ. In the form used by nuns and monks, the rosary consists of a circular cord with 150 beads in fifteen groups or "decades" of ten. The smaller, more common form of the rosary used by laity in general has only fifty beads arranged in five decades. Each of these beads represents an individual prayer to be spoken. Attached to the circular cord is a shorter cord or "pendant" with five beads and a crucifix.

The Liturgies

The Liturgies, from the Latin word for "works," consist of official worship of the Church. One of the most important of the Liturgies is the mass. Mass consists of two parts: the Liturgy of the Word and the Liturgy of the Eucharist.

The Liturgy of the Word begins with the sign of the cross, after which the priest and the people greet one another. This is followed by a brief silence during which each member of the congregation remembers his or her sins and an act of sorrow. On Sundays and certain other special days this is followed by the congregation praying the Glory, a hymn of praise. The priest then offers a prayer, and there is a Scripture reading, followed by a responsorial psalm, a second Scripture reading, an acclamation verse, and a reading from one of the Gospels, followed by a recitation of the creed, a concise statement of the essential beliefs of Catholicism.

In the Liturgy of the Eucharist a collection is made, and the priest places the offerings of the congregation next to the altar, places bread and wine on the altar, and presents them to God. The priest washes his hands as a symbol of the need for purification. The priest and congregation pray, asking God to accept the sacrifice. Then comes one of nine eucharistic prayers, which all include the words spoken by Jesus during the Last Supper. These words, called the "words of consecration," affect the transubstantiation of the bread and wine so that they become the body and blood of Christ. This is followed by a recitation of Our Father, the prayer that Jesus taught his disciples to pray, then a prayer for deliverance from evil and a prayer for peace. After this, members of the congregation receive the consecrated bread or bread and wine. A period of quiet reflection and thanksgiving followed by a prayer and blessing by the priest ends the mass.

Liturgy of the Hours

The Liturgy of the Hours, also called the "divine office," is an extension of Christ's command to "pray without ceasing." It consists of individual prayers, psalms, and meditations at seven times during the day: (1) a morning prayer (Lauds), (2) a prayer before noon (Terce), (3) a prayer for midday (Sext), (4) an afternoon prayer (None), (5) an evening prayer (Vespers), (6) an "Office of Readings," and (7) a night prayer (Compline). As liturgical practices, these seven ceremonies follow variants of this pattern: (1) an entrance procession accompanied by organ or choir, (2) an introduction or invitatory with all present standing, (3) a hymn sung by all standing, (4) a reading of psalms with the congregation standing or seated, (5) a Scripture reading, a short homily (sermon), a period of silence, and an optional responsorial (a spoken or sung anthem) with the congregation seated, (6) a Gospel canticle by the choir with all standing, and (7) a concluding canticle consisting of prayers, a blessing, a dismissal, and a procession.

The Ritual Calendar

The ritual calendar of Catholicism is referred to as the "liturgical year." The celebrations of the liturgical calendar recall the great events of salvation. The liturgical year begins with Advent, four weeks of preparation for Christmas. Christmas, celebrated on 25 December, is a remembrance of the birth of Christ. The Sunday after Christmas is Holy Family Sunday, which emphasizes the family of Jesus. This is followed by the Solemnity of Mary, Mother of God (celebrated on New Year's Day). Next are Epiphany (celebrated on the first Sunday after 1 January to commemorate the coming of the Magi in the Roman communion and the inclusion of the Gentiles in the plan of salvation) and the Baptism of the Lord (usually the Sunday after 6 January). Next comes Lent, a forty-day period of penance, reform, and preparation for Easter.

Lent begins on Ash Wednesday, when Catholics are marked with ashes on their foreheads as a reminder of their mortality and a need for repentance. Lent is followed by the Triduum, the three days beginning with the Mass of the Last Supper on the evening of Holy Thursday, Good Friday (commemorating the crucifixion and death of Jesus), the Easter Vigil in the evening Holy Saturday (which celebrates the history of God's dealings with humankind and includes the initiation of new adult members into the church), and the Easter Masses of Easter Sunday (which usually falls in April and celebrates Jesus's resurrection). Easter season continues through Ascension Thursday (or, in some countries, Sunday) forty days after Easter when Jesus ascended into heaven and ends on Pentecost Sunday (ten days later, in celebration of the coming of the Holy Spirit to the members of church). The first Sunday after Pentecost celebrates the Trinity, and the next Sunday celebrates the Body and Blood of Christ (in emphasis of the real presence of Christ in the bread and wine of Holy Communion). Five weeks before Christmas the Solemnity of Christ the King celebrates the lordship of Christ.

Variation within Catholicism

In terms of liturgy there are three major "communions" within the Catholic tradition: Roman Catholic, Eastern Orthodox, and Anglican. Their shared characteristics include a sacrament of Holy Orders in which priesthood is vested in bishops, priests, and a deaconate. Catholic denominations also assert that their priesthood authority in matters of faith, morals, and the valid administration of the sacraments is based on apostolic succession, an unbroken chain of bishops to the Apostles of Jesus. Although the Anglican communion may be classified as Catholic in terms of the shared liturgical tradition, including the sacrament of Holy Orders and its attendant concept of apostolic succession of bishops, many Anglicans classify their denomination as Protestant, based primarily on a doctrinal difference in their conceptualization of the Eucharist, because they share the Protestant concept of the "real spiritual presence" of Christ in the Eucharist as opposed to the doctrine of transubstantiation of the Eucharist into the real substance of Christ, which is shared by Roman and Eastern Orthodox Catholics.

Although all Catholic denominations view the office of bishop as being based on apostolic succession, the Roman Catholic communion holds that the bishop of Rome has a special role of leadership among all bishops because the succession of bishops of Rome traces its authority directly back to the apostle Peter, who was the leading apostle and also served as the first bishop of Rome. The Eastern Orthodox communion, which looks to Constantinople rather than to Rome as the seat of its most prestigious bishopric, consists especially of the Catholic churches of Russia, eastern Europe, and Asia that separated from the Roman Church in 1054 CE, largely over issues of papal authority. The Anglican communion arose with the emergence of the Church of England in 1534 CE through separation from the Roman Church. The separation was preceded by a shift from Latin to the local spoken language in the Anglican liturgy and culminated in the Anglican communion's rejection of the authority of Rome over the Anglican churches. Today Anglican churches are found throughout the world under denominational names such as the "Anglican Church of Canada" or the "Anglican Church of Australia." Anglican liturgy is guided by one version or another of the *Book of Common Prayer*, which was written by the English prelate Thomas Cranmer and published in 1549 CE.

Changes over Time

The Second Vatican Council (Vatican II), a gathering of Roman Catholic bishops from 1962 to 1965, instituted many changes in the forms of worship. For instance, prior to Vatican II, Latin had been the lingua franca (common language) for conducting the mass and other sacraments in all parts of the world, but the council authorized the use of native-language vernacular translations for use in parts of the mass and in all other sacraments as well as in sacramentals. The council also instituted other changes in the performance of the mass. Chief among these was a change in the orientation of the altar so that the priest would face the congregation when he offers the mass. Prior to Vatican II the sacrament of anointing the sick was commonly reserved for those near the point of death. Vatican II emphasized that anointing may be used for anyone who is seriously ill.

Richley H. Crapo

See also Baha'i; Buddhism; Eucharistic Rituals; Hinduism; Islam; Jainism; Judaism

Further Reading

Ball, A. (1991). *Handbook of Catholic sacramentals.* Huntington, IN: Our Sunday Visitor.

Barry, J. F. (1996). Our Catholic faith/*Nuestra fe Catholica.* New York: William H. Sadlier.
Catholic Church. (1976). *The rites of the Catholic Church as revised by the Second Vatican Ecumenical Council.* New York: Pueblo.
Catholic Church. (1985). *The Roman missal: The sacramentary.* New York: Catholic Book Publishing.
Catholic Church. (1995). *Catechism of the Catholic Church.* New York: Doubleday.
Church of England. (1928). *Book of common prayer with additions and deviations proposed in 1928.* Oxford, UK: University of Oxford Press.
Elliott, P. J. (1995). *Ceremonies of the modern Roman rite: The Eucharist and the Liturgy of the Hours: A manual for clergy and all involved in liturgical ministries.* San Francisco: Ignatius Press.
Sokolof, D. (1975). *A manual of the orthodox church's divine services.* Jordanville, NY: Holy Trinity Monastery.

China: Popular Religion

Most religious practices in China originated in Daoism, Buddhism, and native folk beliefs. These practices may have been first performed thousands of years ago by primitive people to, for example, pacify the gods or to pray for good harvests. Today, although these practices are still performed, many Chinese perform them only for the sake of tradition. The dates of festivals and religious practices explained in this article all refer to the lunar calendar.

The Third Month

The Qing Ming (Bright and Clear Festival) falls on the third day of the Third Month, or about 106 days after the winter solstice. Three days prior to the Qing Ming is the Cold Food Festival (Hanshiri), during which people eat cold food to commemorate the statesman Jie Zitui, who lived in the state of Jin during the Spring and Autumn period (770–481 BCE). The Jin ruler, Duke Wen, forbade the use of fire after Jie sacrificed himself in a fire. On the day of Qing Ming people take their family to visit their ancestors' graves *(saomu).* Offerings of food such as chicken, vegetables, and fruits are brought to the gravesites, and children are taught to put their palms together in a prayer gesture. Sometimes paper money is burned and firecrackers used.

Another popular festival during the Third Month is the Festival of Mazu (Tianhou), the Heavenly Queen. It is held on the twenty-third day and is an important festival for patrons in Taiwan and Fujian Province, China. Mazu, the youngest daughter of the Lin family in Fujian, was born on this day in 960 CE. During the centuries fishermen along the coast of Fujian claimed that Mazu appeared to them in the midst of storms and carried them to safety. Mazu is the guardian spirit of fishermen and those who make a living at sea. Her shrine is in every junk cabin, and her temples line the seashore.

The Fourth Month

The eighth day of the Fourth Month is Buddha's birthday, which is widely celebrated in Thailand, Cambodia, China, Vietnam, Japan, and Korea. This day is also called the "Festival of Buddha's Bath"

Woman and children with incense and prayer candles at Louhan Temple, Changqing, China in 1996. COURTESY OF STEPHEN G. DONALDSON PHOTOGRAPHY.

COMMUNITY PARTICIPATION IN RITUALS AND FESTIVALS

Because rituals have social and psychological functions as well as religious ones, non-believers often participate, as shown in this account from a village on Taiwan.

The social compulsion to participate in such festivities was brought out in an interview with a 35 year-old Taiwanese woman married to a mainland Chinese. She was a non-believer, but she and her husband nevertheless participated, like everyone else, in community celebrations and in required private rituals of ancestor worship. She told me that this had not always been so: when they were first married, her husband was an army sargent, and they lived in the town of Ying-ko. Living primarily among mainlanders, they had no ancestral tablets in their house and had never participated in any aspect of the folk religion. When they first bought a house in Ploughshare, they had not participated either. But a few holidays on which they were the only people in the community who did not prepare special foods and offer them to gods and ancestors left them acutely embarrassed, and now they are full participants in all required religious observances.

Even old Ong Chhiu-tik, the most intellectual of Ploughshare believers, was forced by group pressure to engage in rituals he thought worthless. In keeping with his moral view of the supernatural, he was certain that no merit-making ritual could possibly improve the position of the deceased in the spirit world, nor could burning paper money to a god bring aid to a supplicant. Nevertheless, he told me he had hired priests to perform the *kong-tik* after the deaths of both his parents. His reason for doing this was simple: if he had not, people would have talked. It was better to go through the ceremony to satisfy the neighbors, even if its overt purpose was so preposterous as to make it otherwise a waste of time and money. Similarly, he always burned the minimum amount of paper money at each festival, if only to show people that he, too, was a member of the community.

***Source*: Harrell, C. Stevan.**
***Belief and Unbelief in a Taiwan Village.* (1975).**
Ann Arbor, MI: Xerox University Microfilms, pp. 146–147.

(Yufojie) because the Buddha statue is symbolically bathed. Patrons carry containers for water known for its healing power when drunk. Sometimes sugar is added to enhance the taste. Another ritual performed on this day is the Life-Releasing Ritual (Fangsheng). As patrons pay for the sacred water from Buddha's bath, they purchase a bird, fish, or tortoise and then release it back to the wild. This is an act of good karma (the force generated by a person's actions and held to perpetuate transmigration and to determine the nature of a person's next existence), serving as a prayer for longevity.

The Fifth Month

Duanwujie (Dragon Boat Festival) is held on the fifth day of the Fifth Month to honor a patriotic statesman, Qu Yuan, who lived in Chu State during the Warring States period (403–221 BCE). Libeled by his colleagues, Qu fell from the ruler's favor and was exiled to Mi-Lo (Changsha, Hubei Province). On the fifth day of the Fifth Month, he jumped into the Mi-Lo River and died. Local supporters rowed boats up and down the river to drive away fish that might devour his body. To suppress the fishes' appetite, sweet rice and meat wrapped in bamboo leaves called *"zong"* were dropped into the river. Today dragon boat races are held annually all over the world where Chinese people reside, and the *zong* remains a popular festival food in countries influenced by China: Vietnam, Thailand, Korea, and Japan. A sulfuric wine called *"xionghuang"* is drunk by adults who believe that it will keep them safe from diseases. Portraits of Zhongkui, a Daoist god with an exceptionally ugly face, are hung at doors to protect the household from devils and disaster.

Chinese women participate in the highly ritualized "sport dancing" at the Temple of Heaven in Beijing in 2002.
COURTESY OF KAREN CHRISTENSEN.

The Sixth Month

Guanyindan, held on the nineteenth day of the Sixth Month, celebrates the enlightenment of Guanyin, the goddess of mercy (Avalokitesuare in Sanskrit). Guanyindan and Guanyin's birthday on the nineteenth of the Second Month are the most popular Buddhist festivals besides the birthday of Buddha.

A statue of Guanyin is found in almost all Buddhist temples. It is usually clad in white, a water bottle in one hand and a willow twig on the other. The water is a symbol of life and the willow, peace. She is portrayed with rows of hands arranged in the shape of a halo behind her back. Thus, she is also referred to as the "Thousand-Hands Bodhisattva (Deity)," saving thousands of lives by reaching out to people. Women call her "the son-giving Guanyin"*(songzi Guanyin)* as they pray for sons after marriage. The goddess of mercy also is effective in curing diseases, helping women during childbirth, and delivering men from crisis. Those whose prayers are answered must return to the temple on this day to give thanks. Bound with wooden handcuffs, these people are usually dressed in red or blue prison uniforms. They knock their heads on the ground with every step they make toward the temple. These symbolic rituals are performed to show their sincerity to the goddess for her release of their suffering.

The Seventh Month

Two festivals are held during the warm Seventh Month: Qiqiaojie on the seventh day and Yulanhui on the fifteenth day.

Qiqiaojie (Festivals of Seven Talents) is Chinese Valentine's Day. According to legend, this is the only day of the year when the loving couple, the Cowherd and the Weaving Maid, are allowed to meet on the Milky Way. The Heavenly King, the Weaving Maid's father, angered by their heterogeneous relationship but touched by their devotion to one another, transforms them into the stars Altair and Vega, which come together once a year. Celebrations of Qiqiaojie began during the Han dynasty (206 BCE–220 CE). Young women would gather to pray to the heavenly princess for a loving husband and for talents in weaving and embroidering. To obtain these talents, women vied to thread needles in the dark. These needles could be as intricate as having seven holes, which took seven colorful threads. Sometimes young females would keep spiders in a box and check for webs in the morning; more webs meant more talents in weaving.

Celebrations of Yulanhui or Yulanpen (Ghost Festival) on the fifteenth day actually cover the entire Seventh Month. On the Buddhist calendar this is the time for the salvation of wandering spirits and hungry ghosts. "The Great Maudgalyayana Rescues His Mother from Hell," a story from the Yulanpen Sutra, tells the salvation of Maudgalyayana's mother, a selfish woman who hides her son's donation to the temple and hence suffers in hell as a hungry ghost. Maudgalyayana pleads with Buddha, who descends from heaven to open the gate of hell and announces that every year on the fifteenth day of the Seventh Month, all hungry ghosts will be able to eat their fill. This is the origin of Yulanhui Festival in China, the Bon Festival in Japan, and the Avalamba Festival in India.

In the twenty-first century different rites are carried out in different regions of China. Incantations, prayers, and masses are said by all Buddhist organizations. Along the coastal areas of China and Taiwan, for the entire Seventh Month lights are installed in uninhabited areas to guide wandering spirits. Small lanterns are seen floating down rivers to lead the water spirits onto land. All weapons are put away so that the spirits will not be frightened. Throughout the month foods are placed outside for the consumption of spirit guests. However, most people prepare a sumptuous meal with poultry, fish, vegetables, rice, and even alcohol on the evening of the fifteenth day. Some Buddhists stay vegetarian for the entire month to commemorate their deceased relatives.

The Eighth Month

On the fifteenth day of the Eighth Month the Chinese celebrate the Mid-Autumn Festival (Zhongqiujie), sometimes called the "Moon Festival." This is the day for family reunions because the full moon signifies completeness. Ethnic foods eaten are mooncakes *(yuebing)* made with grounded lotus seeds and egg yokes, which symbolize the moon, as well as seasonal produce such as taro and persimmons.

Children are told the story of the moon goddess Chang E, who, in order to attain immortality, swallows the entire amount of elixir given to her husband for the two of them by the Queen Mother of the West. The elixir causes her body to float, and she ends up in the moon, separated from her husband, accompanied only by a rabbit, which is busy pounding herbs on a grinder. Her immortality comes with a price—eternal loneliness.

According to legend, a man named "Wu Gang" is also trapped in the moon. A lazy man, Wu is left there by his Daoist mentor, who tells him that the only way for him to leave the moon is to hack at a cassia tree five hundred strokes continuously. Wu never manages to reach this number before he needs to rest.

The Ninth Month

On the ninth day of the Ninth Month, Chongyangjie (the Double Nine Festival) is held. During the Han dynasty (206 BCE–220 CE) a man was told by his mentor to wear the *zhuyu* herb, carry chrysanthemum wine, and go up a hill with his entire family. Returning at the end of the day, they found that their livestock and other animals had died. The mentor told the man that these animals had died in lieu of his family members. This is the origin of the custom *denggao* (ascending to the high). Chinese people today practice *denggao* by taking members of the family to visit their ancestral graves in the hills, similar to what they do during the Qing Ming Festival.

The Eleventh Month

Dongzhi (Coming of Winter) falls on either 22 or 23 December of the Western calendar. To many Chinese, Dongzhi is as important as the Chinese New Year, if not more important. This is when family members gather and businesses close. Pastries and dumplings are prepared, the most popular being *tangyuan,* a tiny ball made of glutenous rice, cooked with vegetables and meat in soup. The word *tangyuan* is phonetically similar to the word *tuanyuan* (reunion). The whole family, sitting around the dinner table and enjoying hot *tangyuan* soup, is a familiar scene during Dongzhi.

The Twelfth Month

The Twelfth Month is called "Layue" (Month of Offerings). In traditional agricultural society, after a good harvest people make offerings to the gods and the ancestors. Hunters make use of the dry, cold weather to cure surplus meat from their catch. A ceremonial dance called *"nuo"* is performed in order to keep devils of pestilence away. In this dance strong young men are dressed as gods playing the drums. When Buddhism became popular (c. 600 CE), all of these activities combined with other Buddhist rites to be carried out on the eighth day of the twelfth month. Hence the term *laba,* the eighth day of Layue, and the festive food *labazhou,* a rice soup with meat.

On the twenty-third or twenty-fourth day, seeing Zaojun (the kitchen god) off calls for special food offerings such as fish, pork, and sweet bean paste. As the kitchen god ascends to heaven to make an annual report on the family's deeds during the past year, desserts become important in order to sweeten his lips. The god is due to return on New Year's Eve, when a new poster of the god will be placed in the kitchen.

Other Common Practices

Other practices pertain to special occasions. Following are some current practices that are performed regardless of one's religious affiliation. Overall, red is the color of luck, whereas white is the color of death.

Newborns

Today the traditional phrase printed on an invitation for a banquet celebrating a birth is still used to indicate the gender of a newborn. *Nongwa zhixi* (happiness in playing with tiles) denotes the birth of a girl; *nongzhang zhixi* (happiness in playing with jade) denotes the birth of a boy. A banquet *(manyuejiu)* is given when the infant is one month old. All those attending receive a boiled egg dyed red—the symbol of a new life that is lucky.

When a boy reaches the age of one year, some families perform a rite to predict his future. A writing brush, an abacus, and other related objects are placed in front of the boy, who reaches out for them. If he grabs a brush, an academic future will be his lot; an abacus, a mercantile future.

Birthdays

After the *manyuejiu* children are given a boiled egg on their birthdays. For men the most important birthday celebration is at age sixty, a *jiazi* (one astrological cycle), then seventy, and so on. Consequentially, women opt for age sixty-one, seventy-one, and so on. Birthdays are celebrated on that day or before, never after. Prebirthday celebrations *(nuanshou)* are popular with celebrities and older people.

Noodles and peach buns are the ritual food at a birthday banquet. Peaches symbolize immortality, whereas uncut noodles symbolize longevity.

Funerals

It is not surprising that a traditional Chinese male makes plans for his own funeral needs before his death. A feng shui (the ancient science of balancing the elements within the environment) expert or a geomancer (a person who divines by means of figures or lines or geographic features) chooses an auspicious gravesite for the whole family. The site is of importance because the location has critical effects on the family's future prosperity. At a person's death masses are said to ensure the deceased's entry into heaven.

On the eve of the burial, paper effigies made in the images of a mansion, servants with names attached, cars, and cash are burned for the dead. Traditional funeral processions require the attendees to walk for at least some distance, sometimes up a hillside of the graveyard. Behind the coffin is the deceased's eldest son or the closest male relative. Immediately after are the wife and daughters. Coffin bearers always appear in multiples of eight. Throughout the ceremony from procession to interment, a band plays dirges to set the mood and to cover the mourners' wails. At the grave more offerings are burned for the dead. Funerals for those who die at an old age are concluded with a banquet celebrating his or her longevity.

Weddings

In traditional Chinese marriages the groom is required to pay for all expenses covering the banquet, the future residence, and the *lijin* (ritual money) to the bride's parents. The amount of the *lijin* has no limit. In return the bride's family usually provides furniture and household items for the couple's home.

On the morning of the wedding day the bride pays her last respects to her parents and ancestors. A propitious hour is chosen for the groom to come to the bride's door. Flanked by his best men, the groom has to answer to the bridesmaids' wishes before the door is opened. This usually concludes with the groom paying "ransom money" *(kaimen lishi).* Again, the amount of this "ransom" varies, and often the bridesmaids use it to buy a gift for the couple.

The groom then takes the bride to his parents' home to pay their respects and greet the close relatives of the family. At the ceremony the bride offers each guest a cup of tea with a respectful bow, and the recipients of this rite usually give a present of jewelry or cash. The highlight of the wedding banquet is dessert, which is usually *hongdou lianzi tang,* a sweet soup made with red beans and lotus seeds. Red symbolizes the lucky occasion, and *lianz*i is a homophone (having the same sound) for the word meaning "a son yearly."

The bride pays a visit to her prenatal family on the third morning after the wedding. This rite is called *"huimen"* (returning to the door), and presents are given again. However, the bride does not stay but rather goes home with her husband.

Grand Openings

Most Chinese people start their businesses by consulting a geomancer in the matters of location and decoration. Both the exterior and interior designs of a restaurant or shop must be compatible with the astrology of the owner in order to ensure success. Details such as the direction the main entrance faces might be crucial because the entrance is where business and profit enter. Interior arrangements such as the location of the owner's office, the fish tank, and so on are just as important. A design with too many corners might be unlucky because the god of fortune may get lost or distracted. Angular forms might be too "sharp" or "edgy" for those who work in the office.

On the day of the grand opening most owners hire a lion dance group to perform at the door. Firecrackers will also be popped to attract attention and to scare away evil spirits. Inside the restaurant or shop, two altars are lit. The first, with the image of Guan Gong (d. 220 CE), a valiant general from the Han dynasty, sits above head level in the front of the shop. The second altar is for Tu Di Gong, the local Earth god, whose name is written on a tablet placed on the altar on the ground. These two Daoist gods are the most popular patron saints of Chinese businesspeople.

Issues to Consider

China is a country with a variety of ethnic groups, cultures, and dialects spread over a massive area. Changes through the centuries and international, especially Western, influence have given a new face to many rites. Readers and researchers must be wary when information is required about rites by a particular ethnic or native group. Similarly, more research is needed to trace the development of rites from the classical period to modern times.

Fatima Wu

Further Reading

Bodde, D. (1975). *Festivals in classical China.* Princeton, NJ: Princeton University Press.

Burnkhardt, V. R. (1976). *Chinese creeds and customs.* Taipei, Taiwan: Fan Mei Tushu Youxian Gougsu.

Bush, R. C. (1977). *Religion in China.* Niles, IL: Argus Communications.

Chen, P. (n.d.). *Zhongguo Gudai Jieiri De Youlai yu Xisu* (The origins and customs of ancient Chinese festivals). Taipei, Taiwan: Mingming Chubanshe.

DeBarry, W. (Ed.). (1999). *Sources of Chinese tradition.* Volume 1, 2nd edition, New York: Columbia University Press.

Eberhard, S. (1952). *Chinese festivals.* New York: H. Wolff.

Li, J. (1976). *Zhongguo wenhua gushi* (Stories of Chinese culture) (Vol. 3., Miscellaneous Monthly Series No. 12). Taipei, Taiwan: Zonghe Yuekan She.

Ma, Y. W., & Lau, J. (Eds.). (1978). *Traditional Chinese stories.* Bloomington: Indiana University Press.

Morgan, H. T. (1942). *Chinese symbols and superstition.* South Pasadena, CA: P. D. and I. Perkins.

Pastva, L., Sr. (1986). *Great religions of the world.* Winona, MN: St. Mary's Press.

Shi, W. (2000). *Taiwan de Mazu xinyang* (The belief in Mazu in Taiwan). Taipei, Taiwan: Taiyuan Chubanshe.

Smart, N. (1993). *Religions of Asia.* Princeton, NJ: Prentice Hall.

Thompson, L. G. (1979). *Chinese religions* (3rd ed.). Belmont, CA: Wadsworth.

Walls, J., & Walls, Y. (Eds. and Trans.). (1984). *Classical Chinese myths.* Hong Kong: Joint Publishing.

Wang, S. (1988). *Zhongguo jeiling xisu* (Chinese festivals and customs) (5th ed.). Taipei, Taiwan: Xingguang Chubanshe.

Williams, C. A. S. (1976). *Outlines of Chinese symbolism and art motifs.* New York: Dover.

Christianity *See* African-American Churches; Camp Meetings; Catholicism; Christmas; Easter; Epiphany; Eucharistic Rituals; Exorcism; Greco-Roman; Mardi Gras; Monastic Communities; Mormons; Orthodoxy; Pentecostalism; Protestantism; Shakers; Television and Ritual

Christmas

The word *Christmas* comes from the Old English words *Cristes maesse,* meaning "Christ's mass." It is a Christian holiday commemorating the birth of Christ that has come to be celebrated on 25 December. Like Easter, it is celebrated as a secular holiday and a religious holiday.

The exact date of Christ's birth is not known. Many people believe that Christ was born in the spring. Others believe that he was born in late summer or early autumn. Regardless, by the first third of the fourth century Christmas was celebrated in both the eastern and western parts of the Roman Empire. The western part of the empire celebrated the holiday on 25 December. However, the eastern part of the empire marked both the birth of Christ and his baptism on 6 January. In Jerusalem 6 January marked the birth of Christ but not his baptism. By the end of the fourth century most churches of Christianity accepted the 25 December date.

Jerusalem took a bit longer to accept the 25 December date; the Armenian Church never did. That church still celebrates Christmas on 6 January. The baptism of Christ came to be celebrated by the Armenians on Epiphany, 6 January. In the Western world, however, 6 January marks the visit of the Magi to Christ in Nazareth.

The most likely explanation for celebrating Christmas on 25 December is that early Roman Christians wanted their celebration to occur when

THE BIBLICAL ACCOUNT OF THE BIRTH OF JESUS

The Biblical account of the birth of Christ is found in the synoptic Gospels. That of Luke (2:1-11 NKJV) is frequently quoted since tradition has it that Luke received it directly from Mary, the mother of Jesus, herself.

> **And it came to pass in those days that a decree went out from Caesar Augustus that all the world should be registered. This census first took place while Quirinius was governing Syria. So all went to be registered, everyone to his own city. Joseph also went up from Galilee, out of the city of Nazareth, into Judea, to the city of David, which is called Bethlehem, because he was of the house and lineage of David, to be registered with Mary, his betrothed wife, who was with child. So it was, that while they were there, the days were completed for her to be delivered. And she brought forth her firstborn Son, and wrapped Him in swaddling cloths, and laid Him in a manger, because there was no room for them in the inn. Now there were in the same country shepherds living out in the fields, keeping watch over their flock by night. And behold, an angel of the Lord stood before them, and the glory of the Lord shone around them, and they were greatly afraid. Then the angel said to them, "Do not be afraid, for behold, I bring you good tidings of great joy which will be to all people. For there is born to you this day in the city of David a Savior, who is Christ the Lord.**

other Romans were celebrating so that the Christians could fade into the background and protect themselves from persecution. The 25 December date coincides with the Roman festival marking the winter solstice, the feast of the unconquered sun. The days begin to grow longer, and the sun climbs higher into the winter sky. December was also the time of the Saturnalia (festival of Saturn) and the birthday of Mithras, the Persian (Iranian) god whose mysteries have influenced Christian expression. Moreover, 1 January, New Year's Day for the Romans, was a time of decorations of greenery and lights. Gift giving, celebrations, and agricultural rites marked the time.

Through the years other peoples brought their customs into the celebration of Christmas. The Germans and Celts added foods, Yule logs, Yule cakes, fir trees, and other touches. Christmas has always been a time for family and family feasts, traditions, and celebrations.

Controversies

Many Christians object to the syncretic (combining different forms) nature of Christmas. They believe that the absorption of pre-Christian customs concerning Roman and Persian sun gods distorts the simplicity that should be Christmas. The further additions through the years, including the secularization of the holiday, further offend many Christians.

On the other hand, many Christians note that the love and joy associated with the holiday often transcend a person's religion. Many non-Christians take joy in the holiday, even accepting many Christian or Christianized customs, such as Christmas trees and Christmas songs.

The wave of Protestant reform in the sixteenth and seventeenth centuries brought strong opposition to the manner in which Christmas had come to be celebrated in Catholic tradition. English statesman Oliver Cromwell and his Puritans took control of English government (1649–1660). As part of their promise to end corruption, they cancelled Christmas celebrations. In 1660 King Charles II regained the throne of England and reinstituted the celebration of Christmas. In North America the American Revolution marked a reaction against English customs, including Christmas. However, in North America there were exceptions in both prerevolutionary and postrevolutionary times. The Jamestown settlement, for example, celebrated Christmas with great enthusiasm without interruption.

Christmas was unpopular in parts of the Puritan colonies of North America. In 1659 Boston authorities banned it until 1681. They fined people for celebrating Christmas. The Puritans increased their penalties for celebrating Christmas when they found people ignoring them and celebrating Christmas in a hearty fashion. Writers such as Charles Dickens and Washington Irving did much to restore Christmas traditions in the United States. Dickens's popular Christmas stories, especially *A Christmas Carol,* transcended national differences. Irving brought many English customs back to the United States and wrote movingly about an old English Christmas.

Recent Changes

Christmas had regained its earlier popularity by 1870, when it became a U.S. national holiday. Like other peoples, Americans had grown to love the celebration of peace, love, and goodwill. Americans began to reinvent Christmas in a way that is copied in many other parts of the world. Christmas became a family-oriented day of fun rather than a festival. The common U.S. rituals of Christmas, many adapted from other cultures, feature decorating a tree, sending cards, and giving gifts.

The mixture of the secular and the religious in Christmas is shown in the figure of Santa Claus as developed in his modern form in the United States. The term *Santa Claus* derives from "Saint Nicholas," the name of a Catholic bishop in fourth-century Asia Minor. The saint was renowned for his generosity to the poor. Saint Nicholas helped a man's three daughters raise their dowries by tossing bags of gold down his chimney. Hence, Santa today is said to come down a chimney with gifts. In the United States Santa took on his current form, complete with a stomach that shakes like a bowl full of jelly.

The custom of Christmas trees in England and the United States stems from 1841, when Prince Albert of England brought the custom to England from his native Germany when he married Queen Victoria. From the royal castle of Windsor the custom spread quickly throughout the realm. The custom was spread to the United States the next year by Dr. Charles Frederick Minnegerode, professor of Greek at the College of William and Mary.

Ritual Celebrations

Church attendance is customary for Christians on Christmas. People generally hold a feast after church. The day is one of family celebration and remembrance. People decorate a tree with religious, family, and secular decorations. Greenery such as holly shrubs and wreaths generally is used in decorations. The blood-red holly berries are a sign of Christ's bleeding, death, and suffering while wearing the crown of thorns. Christmas carols are sung in many places. Children are taught that Santa Claus brings presents to good children. He signifies the spirit of gift giving, a means of promoting solidarity. In the United States Santa comes on Christmas Eve, whereas in much of Europe he comes on his feast day of 6 December. In the spirit of the holiday, many children are taught by their parents to leave milk and cookies for Santa as he completes his rounds.

In Belgium, for example, people hold a big feast on Christmas Eve. The feast begins with a drink and then seafood and stuffed turkey. People already have given the big gifts on the feast day of St. Nicholas on 6 December. On Christmas Day, after a meal featuring sweet bread in the shape of the baby Jesus, members of a family distribute small presents either under a tree or near a fireplace hung with stockings. Another feast may follow.

In Brazil, Papai Noelle (Father Christmas) brings presents on Christmas Day. The wealthy share a feast of ham or turkey or similar treats. The poor share chicken and rice. In general, Brazil shares many Christmas customs with the United States.

Finnish people also share many customs with people of the United States. However, there are differences. Father Christmas lives in the northern part of Finland, north of the Arctic Circle. People send letters to him at that address. The Finns have a theme park near the home of Father Christmas. There are three holy days of Christmas in Finland: Christmas Eve, Christmas, Day, and Boxing Day. On Christmas Eve people eat rice porridge and plum fruit juice for breakfast. People clean their houses. Then a spruce tree is decorated. *The Peace of Christmas*, a Finnish story about Christmas, is broadcast on radio and television. At night the traditional Christmas dinner is eaten. It includes casseroles: macaroni, rutabagas, carrots, potatoes, and ham or turkey. Christmas Eve is also a day to visit cemeteries. People decorate gravesites, and the cemeteries seem to take part in the celebration. A family member dressed as Father Christmas distributes presents on Christmas Eve.

Although Easter is the most solemn and important of Christian holidays, Christmas has become the most popular, commemorating the incarnation of God in human form. Only by Christ being a man who was also God could his suffering and death make sense to Christians as an act of redemption.

The image of a baby born in a manger to a virgin has proven immensely appealing. The tableau has been reenacted by countless Christians over the centuries and has inspired masterpieces. The images of the holiday are familiar to non-Christians as well. The magi, the angels, Joseph in the background, the young mother and the babe, complete with manger animals, are part of many cultures.

The secular aspects of Christmas seem a natural adjunct to the holiday. From its beginnings the holiday has assimilated traditions from many peoples: Romans, Persians, Germans, Asians, and Africans. The assimilation continues to the present day, attesting to the popularity of the holiday, a time dedicated to peace and goodwill.

Frank A. Salamone

Further Reading

Cheal, D. J. (1987). The private and the public: The linkage role of religion revisited. *Review of religious research, 28*(3), 209–223.

Coffin, T. P. (1974). *The illustrated book of Christmas folklore*. New York: Seabury Press.

Dickens, C. (1914). *A Christmas carol*. London: J. M. Dent & Sons.

Gillis, J. R. (1996). *A world of their own making: Myth, ritual, and the quest for family values*. New York: Basic Books.

Glazier, S. D. (Ed.). (1999). *Anthropology of religion: A handbook*. Westport, CT: Praeger.

Hutton, R. (1994). *The rise and fall of merry England: The ritual year, 1400–1700*. Oxford, UK: Oxford University Press.

Irving, W. (1900). *Old Christmas*. Philadelphia: Dodd, Mead and Company.

Lippy, C. H. (1994). *Being religious, American style: A history of popular religiosity in the United States*. Westport, CT: Praeger.

Maus, C. P. (1938). *Christ and the fine arts: An anthology of pictures, poetry, music, and stories centering in the life of Christ*. New York: Harper & Brothers.

Newall, V. (1989). A Moslem Christmas celebration in London. *Journal of American Folklore, 102*(404), 186–194.

Plotnicov, L. (Ed.). (1990). *American culture: Essays on the familiar and unfamiliar*. Pittsburgh, PA: University of Pittsburgh Press.

Spicer, D. G. (1958). *Festivals of western Europe*. New York: H. W. Wilson.

Van Dyke, H. (1906). *The first Christmas tree*. New York: Charles Scribner's Sons.

Clothing and Rituals

Humans have always engaged in rituals. There is little doubt that some form of specialized dress or adornment was worn for these rites, as clothing and ritual are closely allied. Rituals are often accompanied by carefully defined clothing worn only by those directly involved as participants and observers. To participants, ritual clothing communicates eight significant ideas:

1. It makes the invisible, visible by facilitating an understanding of the supernatural.
2. It permits and enhances communication and communion with the supernatural.
3. It is a means of transformation from the real into the ideal.
4. It organizes social groups by conferring authority, legitimizes rites of passage, and reveals group inclusion or exclusion.
5. It signifies shared beliefs.
6. It subsumes individual identity within a larger, shared consciousness.
7. It confers an agreed-upon identity with its own role and expectations of behavior.
8. It symbolizes a quest for power over oneself, a group, nature, or the supernatural.

How and where humans first began to cover, or adorn their naked bodies is unknown. Modern scholars have many theories regarding how this first happened, but no single theory accounts for the range of dress and adornment that has developed. Most experts suggest that clothing arose from our need for ritual, sexual attractiveness, authority, and identification. For example, clothing can identify gender, group membership, social rank, and economic status. They argue that modesty and protection are artificial concepts that arose *after* the creation of clothing for the previous reasons, but are not themselves the reasons for their creation. Julian Robinson differs, suggesting that enhancement, alteration, and beautification of the body is an inborn trait. Given the visual record of humans using artificial additions to the body for tens of thousands of years, it is reasonable to believe that sexual attraction, identification, authority, ritual and an inherent trait are all interconnected and responsible for clothing.

Making the Invisible, Visible

According to Lawrence Langer, "the discovery of scrapers, awls and needles in the graves of Neanderthals dating from more than 75,000 years ago" provides the earliest evidence of a link between clothing and ritual (Langer 1959, 107). Langer suggests that the needles found in these graves demonstrate belief in an afterlife where needles would be needed for sewing. Early humans had developed formalized behavior requiring specialized clothing, and they believed they would need such ritual clothing in the afterlife. This suggests that early humans had conceptualized the existence of unseen, not fully understood forces, and had developed behaviors to propitiate them. This ritual clothing is likely to have been masks.

The cave paintings of Trois-Frères and Lascaux in southern France support Langer's theory. They contain images of apparently masked humans. Many believe the mask to be the oldest form of clothing. Langer says these masked figures might be the first documentation of the medicine man—men who held power because of their ability to control spirits or their special relationship to invisible and honored supernatural forces. Others suggest that masks represent an attempt to connect to the natural world that was the focus of early hunter-gatherer societies. Early human dependence on nature and lack of control over it may have led to rituals linking human dependence to these forces. Such rituals may have resembled those of the Aborigines of Australia who use facial painting—a form of masks—in their rites.

Andreas Lommel describes the Aborigines' belief in "increase" and each individual's spiritual connection to a living plant or an animal. Humans are expected to increase the numbers of their linked plant or animal, and ceremonies help ensure this. Andreas states, "while they do not wear representational masks, other aspects of masking are present" (Lommel 1981, 60).

Others speculate that these masked cave figures were an attempt to propitiate the spirit of the slain animal and to honor the hunter. Although the evidence is inconclusive, these figures are likely wearing specialized clothing. They are likely engaged in ritual behavior intended to make unseen forces or spirits visible and therefore comprehensible. Lommel suggests that these Paleolithic images provide evidence for development of the Shaman concept.

Communication and Communion

The development of Shamanism represents an evolutionary step in ritual clothing. Early cave paintings are relatively simple attempts to represent masked figures. The more complex concept behind Shamanism is reflected by the more complex ritual clothing associated with Shamans. In Shamanic cultures, the group is aware of powers or forces beyond human control with which humans must communicate and negotiate. Nunley and McCarty describe the costume of the Shaman as a "type of armor, designed to protect the Shaman while he is interacting with the Spirit World" (Nunley & McCarty 1999, 276).

Shamans have been integral to many religions in many cultures, and their ritual costumes are similar to the clothing of their societies. Their costumes are all typified by visual ornamentation, often in the form of appendages or fetishes. These power symbols are meant to impress observers and facilitate interaction with spirits. Fetishes may be pieces of bones, feathers, stones, fish scales, sacred totems, or symbols or objects valued by the community. The complete Shaman costume collected by Carl Heinrich Merck on Billing's 1787–1794 CE expedition across Russia includes an extraordinary collection of fetishes. Nunley and McCarty describe this garment (likely from the Siberian territory of the Evenki) as a stunning display of power, with nearly 30 kilograms of "brass appendages representing the sun and moon, life-size copper masks, bronze and iron bells, small iron objects and leather-covered, copper, doll-like spirit helpers" (Nunley & McCarty 1999, 277). These symbolic images and objects likely hold power for the Shaman and facilitate communication with powerful spirits. Many cultures use small doll-like objects as spirit helpers to assist the priest or protect his spirit when he leaves the natural world and interacts with the supernatural. These objects are essential in this transition. It is a short step from wearing appendages that assist communication to wearing objects, like masks, to transform the wearer into something more than human.

The Power to Transform

Masks are a vehicle of celebration and an instrument of revelation. They may comprise simple face painting or be elaborate and abstract three-dimensional objects that dwarf the human body. The image or face may be representational and easily identified or totally abstract, relying on culturally shared signs and symbols to convey its identity. All masks, however, are a means of transformation into the state of "other" or "Not I."

Early humans used masks in many ceremonies, marking activities such as initiations, war, harvest, and hunting. In wearing a mask it is thought that a spirit, power, or something "other" inhabits both the mask and the wearer.

W. T. Benda describes the power of this transformation as the "obliteration of the personality of the wearer. That we can only perceive the creature the mask represents and not the person who wears it is what gives masks their sense of mystery and magic" (Benda 1944, 1). This transformation—"I am not myself"—is fundamental to all cultures that wear masks. When the masked person becomes the "other," he or she presents a false face to convey a truth. It does not matter whether the masked figure is engaged in a religious or theatrical ritual; observers overlook the wearer and accept the "other" as the true entity. Their revelations will be considered as carefully as if they were pronouncements from actual beings. Benda suggests this powerful response is because people read faces as a "true and infallible index to human's souls" (Benda 1944, 2). Artificial, larger-than-life faces thus carry more weight in triggering responses.

Nunley and McCarty regard the power of masks as their ability to terrify, intimidate, mystify, and transform behavior. The mask provides a barrier behind which to project strength and hide weakness, a mirror on which the imagination creates the face of unseen powers. The mask also creates a layered identity: the wearer simultaneously exists on multiple levels, and the ritual transports participants from ordinary life to the extraordinary.

Confirmation of Authority within Social Groups

Ritual clothing also exists outside of religious connotations, for example, specialized clothing associated with confirmation of authority in a group. The ritual clothing of secular authority reflects the unique relationship between social and religious authorities: both use symbolic garments and adornments as a visual manifestation of earthly and spiritual power. It is worth noting that the Robes of State used for the coronation of Queen Elizabeth II of England, for instance, are based on the liturgical garments of the Roman Catholic Church during the Byzantine era. Ruth Rubinstein defined authority as that which can create what is permanent, stable, and of lasting value to the group. Having authority entails concern that group goals are being met. It assumes the existence of hierarchy and inequality in the group. The need to distinguish those with authority led to the creation of symbols of authority, conferred when the group recognizes the individual's elevation in status. The crown of a king, a tiger's pelt, or a general's golden stars are all symbols of rank and its inherent authority.

Rites of Passage within the Social Group

Rites of passage are a means of moving from one physical state to the next. These rituals accompany major transitions in life, the seasonal cycle, and cycles in social groups. The ritual provides stability in the midst of change and the ritual clothing serves as a link to the participants of previously successful transitions. Frequently these specialized garments, in style or color or both, represent a change from the norm. As a society redefines the individual, the participant's new status is recognized through these garments or adornments.

John Mack finds that masks are employed in rites of both health and change, such as ceremonies of birth, death, and developing maturity, to convey changed status.

Temporary adoption of special clothing can mark rites of passage. Best-known in Western culture is the white bridal gown and veil marking the transition from single to married womanhood. In the female religious orders of the Roman Catholic Church, the dress of the novice and postulant signify their current, temporary status as they progress to taking final vows. Wearing black for specified periods indicated the formal observance of mourning in past centuries; today this custom has been so reduced that mourning dress may only be worn during the funeral rite itself.

While rites of passage may be marked by temporary changes in clothing, other rituals employ *permanent* changes in dress. In Western culture, wearing a special ring on a specified finger can mark a rite of passage: the wedding, engagement, graduation, and sovereign's ring are all essentially permanent additions to one's physical self. In Victorian England, a young lady awaited the day she could wear her hair up, as her brother longed for long trousers; both symbolized maturity and acceptance into adulthood. Such clothing changes were not casual; rather, they reflected social consensus that the appropriate time had come.

Seasonal cycles have resulted in ritual-based clothing, such as the costumes worn on the night of All Hallow's Eve, masks associated with Mardi Gras and Lent, mummers at Christmastime, and the white gowns and candle lit-wreaths of Saint Lucia's Day.

Whether temporary or permanent, the garments associated with rites of passage reflect their society, revealing group standards of beauty and symbols of the ideal. This attempt to surpass the norm unites participants, linking them to their pasts. This leads to pronouncements that love is eternal, all brides are beautiful, and every young man may become a leader among men.

Inclusion and Exclusion within the Social Group

Ritual body decoration takes many forms, but the most universal may be tattooing. Tattoos or scarification (for those with dark skin) have long indicated inclusion and exclusion. Rufus Camphausen notes that since major monotheistic religions believe humans were created in God's image, these religions tend to avoid body alteration or make it taboo. Nature-based or pantheistic religions tend to have few, if any, prohibitions against altering the body. Tattooing is also used for tribal identity, beauty, and personal expression. Whether for religious or social reasons, the time, place, manner, and design of these "marks of civilization" are carefully controlled by the society. In many ways these marks convey the same layers of meaning as a uniform does. A sailor acquires the image of an anchor, a teen adds his gang affiliation to his body, a girl has her ears pierced as a sign of maturation, or a Maori leader has his personal sign emblazoned on his face. Each expresses inclusion by overtly acknowledging membership in a group.

Among cultures that use scarification and branding, Julian Robinson attributes the practice to an attempt to meet group standards of beauty. Many cultures believe that reinforcing personal beauty is an attempt to achieve the divine, and prescribe how these marks are to be acquired. An individual's acquisition of the marks is directly connected to the person's desirability as a sexual or matrimonial partner.

At the other end of the spectrum are marks meant to exclude. Camphausen calls these the marks of Cain and, like marks of civilization or inclusion, their possessors have no choice as to the time, place, method, or design of the symbol. These are marks used to brand slaves, replace personal identity with a number (as with concentration-camp prisoners), and identify murderers and other criminals. The recent popularity of multiple piercings, neo-tribal tattooing, and scarification represents a ritual of exclusion for disaffected youth. While these youth have chosen to exclude themselves, society has tacitly agreed to do so as well.

Whether as marks of inclusion or exclusion, the practice is accompanied by pain. Having the procedure done for purposes of adornment or group inclusion is an ideological choice. However, when the procedure is done for purposes of punishment or exclusion, it is considered shameful. Self-determination and individual and group consent are necessary for a positive connotation. Understanding the nuances of group and individual participation is required in order to fully understand the visual result and to correctly interpret the meaning of the marks. This is necessary in order to understand these marks as ritually based and not as just another teenage or outsider fad.

Shared Beliefs

One purpose of ritual clothing is to communicate shared beliefs and status in a designated group. Many groups wear sacred or symbolic clothing. The yarmulke is reserved for male members of the Jewish faith; the caped gown and organdy cap define female members of the Plain People. Less obvious signs of shared beliefs are the wearing of a cross, a crucifix, or a Star of David. Symbols and garments closely connected to specific faiths are not casually selected and worn, as they indicate membership in specific groups with clear-cut membership rules. A secular example is the academic hood and robe conferred upon those meeting the requirements a specific degree: the color and cut announce rank and field of expertise to those who know the code.

Stephen Scott best explains why clothing is chosen to express shared beliefs and history in his comments on the dress of the Plain People: "Their intent is to create a system for living, including dress, that is faithful to their beliefs and serves as an effective hedge against assimilation into the world" (Scott 1986, 22). Whether it is the dress of Mennonites, a nun's habit, or the special undergarments worn by Mormon husbands and wives, ritual clothing identifies particular groups of believers.

Dehumanization of the Individual

Prescribed or uniform clothing can dehumanize the individual. In place of personal identity, the uniform substitutes group identity or the personification of supernatural forces; those who accept the uniform agree to assume the visual identity of the group. Observers and participants consequently assume that those wearing specific ritual clothing have particular expertise or a set of unique group skills. This explains why a monarch clothed in Robes of State ceases to be an individual and becomes the personification of the country: She is no longer Elizabeth Alexandra Mary Windsor, but has become "H. M. Elizabeth II, by the Grace of God, of the United Kingdom of Great Britain and Northern Ireland, Queen, Defender of the Faith, Head of the Commonwealth." Another woman loses her own identity and is seen only as a nun—a faceless woman in an outmoded habit of black. Whether secular or religious, ritual uniform signifies a public persona understood by both participants and observers.

Agreed-upon Identity and Expectations of Behavior

Ritual attire also creates or reinforces an agreed-upon identity and expectations of behavior. Those who wear religiously based clothing preserve their archaic forms of dress because they understand and accept that their clothing separates them from secular standards. For example, vestments clearly communicate priests' close relationship with God or the spirits, and people expect these individuals' actions to reveal spiritual values. Many religious of various faiths have now adopted secular dress for daily activities so they can blend in and work more effectively in the secular world. Roman Catholic nuns have spoken of the freedoms they gained in exchanging the centuries-old habit for contemporary dress. They can shop, or work outside schools or hospitals without having to meet the ideal expectations created by their ritual clothing. However, sacred rituals still require the use of symbolic clothing. The liturgical vestments of Roman Catholic priests were codified in the Byzantine era as appropriate for celebrating the Sacraments. Though the chasuble, cassock, alb, cincture, and maniple all originated in the dress of the Imperial Roman middle class, it is now inconceivable that the chasuble, once outerwear for ordinary people, should be worn for anything other than celebrating a Sacrament.

Quest for Power

Dress and adornment can also signify a quest for power over oneself, a particular group, nature, or the supernatural. Nancy Etcoff and Jennifer Craik have examined what drives humans to adorn their bodies. Craik speaks of the tendency to regard the body as a barrier separating the inner self from the outer world; she believes this relationship is expressed through what and how clothing is worn. Etcoff believes there is a universal passion for adornment because of a spiritual longing to have "an outer representation that matches our dreams, and visions, and moral aspirations" (Etcoff 1999, 14). Both scholars have come to see fashion as an attempt to create a form to represent the ideal that a culture reveres in its spiritual form. If ritual clothing reflects acceptance of the symbol of the ideal, the infinite variety of ritual clothing and adornment reflects the vast diversity of those images.

Craik quotes Roland Barthes, who regards clothing as a substitute for the body, partaking "of man's basic dreams, heavenly and craven, sublime and sordid; by its weight a garment becomes wing or shroud, enchantment or authority" (Craik 1994, 16).

Nearly every form of dress and adornment has served as a form of ritual clothing. These have represented the power to interact with the supernatural because people believed in the power of that symbol to gain the protection of benevolent forces, ward off malevolent spirits, attain personal salvation, or lead the group. Individuals and cultures identify those who seek these goals by defined dress and adornments: the nun's habit, the penitent's sack cloth and ashes, and the politician's campaign button.

The Power of Ritual Clothing

Scholars agree that body coverings communicate powerful messages, and that ritual clothing is the most powerful. Specialized, ritual clothing reflects complex belief systems concerning forces neither fully known nor grasped. It enhances communication and negotiation with supernatural entities. Ritual garments and masks can add to one's identity, transforming it into the "other." Social organization, hierarchies, authority, rites of passage, and inclusion or exclusion are all marked by the adoption of ritual clothing. Uniform dress reveals shared beliefs, status, and history. A ritual uniform depersonalizes the individual and confers an agreed-upon, corporate identity that raises expectations of behavior on the part of both participant and observer. Ritual clothing can also denote a personal, social, and cultural quest for power.

What is clear is the deliberate nature of ritual clothing. As sign and symbol it reflects the ability and need to communicate complex ideas, identification, and membership to both participants and outsiders. It maintains traditions, defines the community, and serves as a bridge for future generations.

Kathleen Gossman

See also Asceticism; Body and Rituals; Food and Rituals; Humor and Rituals; Performance, Ritual of

Further Reading

Barnard, M. (1996). *Fashion as communication.* London: Routledge Press.

Bell, Q. (1976). *On human finery.* New York: Schocken Books.

Benda, W. T. (1944). *Masks.* New York: Watson-Guptill Publications.

Camphausen, R. C. (1997). *Return of the tribal: A celebration of body adornment.* Rochester, VT: Park Street Press.

Craik, J. (1994). *The Face of fashion: Cultural studies in fashion.* New York: Routledge.

Etcoff, N. (1996). *Survival of the prettiest.* New York: Anchor Books.

Gurel, L. M. & Beeson, M. S. (1975). *Dimensions of dress and adornment: A book of readings.* Dubuque, IA: Kendall/Hunt Publishing Company.

Hollander, A. L. (1978). *Seeing through clothes.* New York: Viking Press.

Huxley, F. (1974). *The way of the sacred.* Garden City, NY: Doubleday and Company, Inc.

Langer, L. (1959). *The importance of wearing clothes.* London: Constable and Company, Ltd.

Lommel, A. (1981). *Masks: Their meanings and functions.* London: Ferndale Editions.

Lurie, A. (1981). *The language of clothes.* New York: Random House.

MacGowan, K., & Rosse, H. (1923). *Masks and demons.* New York: Harcourt Brace and Company.

Mack, J. (1994). *Masks and the art of expression.* New York: Harry N. Abrams.

Mayer-Thurman, C. C. (1975). *Raiment for the Lord's service: A thousand years of Western vestments.* Chicago: The Art Institute of Chicago.

Nunley, J. W. &, McCarty, C. (1999). *Masks: Faces of culture.* New York: Harry N. Abrams.

Ribeiro, A. (1986). *Dress and morality.* London: B.T. Batsford Ltd.

Roach, M. E., & Musa, K. E. (1980). *New perspectives on the history of Western dress.* New York: NutriGuides, Inc.

Robinson, J. (1998). *The quest for human beauty.* New York: W.W. Norton & Company, Inc.

Rubinstein, R. P. (1995). *Dress codes.* Boulder, CO: West View Press.

Scott, S. (1986). *Why do they dress that way?* Intercourse, PA: Good Books.

Vlahos, O. (1979). Body: *The ultimate symbol.* New York: J.B. Lippincott Company.

Commemorative Rituals

Commemorative rituals are ceremonies that honor the memory of a person, place, or event. Primarily, they function to presence something from the past in the minds of participants, often thorough vocal or bodily participation. Commemorative rituals can be distinguished from others in terms of the central role of memory; the symbolic, temporal, or physical distance from that which is commemorated; the importance of speech or related symbolic gestures; and the patterned, often formalistic, constraints of commemorative performance.

Mediation and the Types of Commemoration

Commemorative rituals are among the most widespread and universal genres of religious ritual worldwide, and can be said to include everything from the common worship practices of the world's major religions, to the ritual dances honoring the ancestors of Australian Aborigines, to the supernatural displays of mediumship at a séance. Central to each kind of commemorative ritual is a mediation of the past and the present. For example, in a séance ritual a medium attempts to help a spirit or soul of an individual who has died communicate with participants who are presently living. Similar mediations occur in yearly rituals like Judaism's Yom Kippur, in which

A woman lighting a candle on 18 September 2001 at a spontaneous public memorial in Union Square for the victims of the 9/11 terrorist attack on the World Trade Center. COURTESY OF STEPHEN G. DONALDSON PHOTOGRAPHY.

A roadside shrine in southern Greece in 2003 marks the location of a motor vehicle accident. COURTESY OF DAVID LEVINSON.

participants ritually fast in remembrance of the reconciliation with God, or the Mexican Day of the Dead, in which participants honor the memory of loved ones with parades and pilgrimages to the graves of deceased friends and relatives. Other rituals like the Catholic Mass or Protestant Sunday worship service, as well as daily rituals like Islamic prayer, are also commemorative because of their mediating functions.

Because death is an ultimate recalcitrant fact of human life, perhaps the most recognizable and universal of commemorative rituals is that of a funeral in honor of an individual who has died. Funerals, shivahs, and wakes attempt to remind participants of someone who has passed, frequently through the evocation of the individual's character and personality, social roles, and past actions and deeds. Related to the funeral is the memorial service, which, unlike a funeral or wake, can honor the memory of an important event or hallowed place. For example, the destruction of the World Trade Center in the United States on 11 September 2001 has been commemorated in numerous memorial services since that time. In these commemorative rituals participants were invited to remember not only the deceased, but the past event and former place of the event as well. These kinds of rituals are significant because they indicate commemoration can also function to lament, blame, and criticize.

Symbolic Gesture and Communal Bonds

A symbolic act or gesture must be used in order for a commemorative ritual to effectively evoke the memory of a past person, place, or event. This act or gesture may be a symbolic representation of the commemorative object or certain patterned movements of the body (e.g., dance). In the West, speeches, speaking, or other forms of utterance, such as litanies and incantations, are the most common kinds of stimuli for memory in a commemorative ritual.

Some of the oldest extant views on speaking and commemorative rituals are found in the work of ancient Greek orators and rhetoricians, who described the central role of ceremonial oratory (variously, "epideictic" or "panegyric") as that of praising or blaming some past person or event. For example, in his treatise on the art of oratory, *On Rhetoric*, Aristotle suggested that in ceremonial speaking one should either speak of virtue and honor or vice and shame; to fail to do so violates the

Veterans march in the Memorial Day Parade in Great Barrington, Massachusetts in 1999. COURTESY OF KAREN CHRISTENSEN.

expectations of an audience or participants. Insofar as participants have expectations about commemorative rituals, it is also frequently said in ancient rhetorical texts that commemorative speaking is usually a celebration of communal bonds in relationship to the commemorative object. Although commemorative rituals may praise a person or condemn a common enemy, as a general rule they tend to highlight that which the participants share in common. Thus the goal of most commemorative rituals is to bring the past into the present for the celebration of communal bonds.

The Constraints of Commemoration

The ceremonial character of commemorative rituals implies that there are formal restraints informed by social custom and etiquette that are not typically violated. For example, at a memorial service or funeral, in general it would be inappropriate for speaker or ritual leader to focus on him- or herself instead of on who or that which is to be remembered. In the West, it is common at a funeral for participants to speak of the deceased, to reference his or her essence as passing on into a celestial or otherwise supernormal reality, and to stress the continuance of life (spiritual or otherwise) in the wake of death.

The *epitaphios* or funeral oration prized by the ancient Greeks provides a good example of the constraints of commemorative ritual. Thucydides' account of Pericles' funeral oration at the end of the first year of Peloponnesian War (431 BCE) describes Pericles addressing a mixed audience of Athenians. Although the primary purpose of the ritual was to honor those who died in the war, Pericles quickly articulates the honor of the fallen soldiers to Athenian ancestry, and later to the superiority of Athenian government. As in most eulogies, Pericles asks participants to remember the deceased as well as those loved ones who are still living, ultimately for the glory of Athens as a whole. This manner of linking the passing of a person or group of persons to a much larger purpose or cause is a formal necessity of any eulogy. Knowledge, tacit or otherwise, of the form is required of participants and, if the form is violated, would wrongly focus attention on the violation instead of the commemorative object and/or larger cause or purpose.

The specificity of commemorative rituals—their mediating and memorial functions, the importance of speech or symbolic gesture, and their formal constraints—however, seems broad enough to include a number of practices that may not seem prima facie commemorative in character. For example, one might describe a popular music concert as a commemorative ritual insofar as participants behave in certain formal ways (musicians and their audiences rehearse the form of call and response, for example) that attempt connect the present with aspects of the past (for example, a hit song). This classificatory problem is not new. The ancient Greeks had some difficulty deciding whether commemoration should be isolated to a particular kind of *place* (such as a sacred location) or could be expanded to include a variety of ceremonial occasions regardless of location. Similar to the problem of defining "religion," one's answer to the question of whether something counts as a commemorative ritual ultimately depends on its meeting the three criteria described here and, of course, the context of discussion.

Joshua Gunn

See also Academic Rituals; Death Rituals

Further Reading

Aristotle. (1991). *On rhetoric: A theory of civic discourse* (G. A. Kennedy, Trans.). New York: Oxford University Press.

Carmichael, E., & Sayer, C. (1992). *The skeleton at the feast: The Day of the Dead in Mexico.* Austin, TX: University of Texas Press.

Lanham, R. A. (1991). *A handlist of rhetorical terms* (2nd ed.). Berkeley: University of California Press.

Metcalf, P., & Huntington, R. (1992). *Celebrations of death: The anthropology of mortuary ritual.* New York: Cambridge University Press.

One nation: America remembers September 11, 2001. (2001). New York: Little Brown & Company.

Thucydides. (1954). *The history of the Peloponnesian war* (R. Warner, Trans.). New York: Penguin.

Turner, V. W. (1995). *The ritual process: Structure and anti-structure.* New York: Aldine de Gruyter.

Communitas

"*Communitas*" is a Latin term popularized by Victor Turner in his important and highly influential work, *The Ritual Process: Structure and Anti-Structure*. As he explains, he chose this term rather than "community" since the common denotation of that term implies a location or, perhaps, a gathering of individuals at a particular location. It should also be noted that "community" also implies "structure," in the sense that what is being referred to is a "standard" or "ordinary" grouping of "citizens" engaged in the various "everyday" activities that generally comprise what is known as a "community." *Communitas*, however, refers to a particular mode of social relations that obtains between individuals who share a common bond, that bond being their shared ritual movement from one well-defined social category to another, passing through, as it were, a distinctly "non-structural" or "antisocial" stage found at the interstices of these two categories. This particular mode of social relations is characterized by notions and behavior that serve to differentiate these individuals from their fellow citizens, allowing them to engage in behaviors that are generally taboo, socially unacceptable, or exceptional to some degree. Thus, "*communitas*" is manifestly "anti-structural."

Turner notes that *communitas* is conceptually located within culture between categories in liminality, on the margins or edges of culture in marginality, and on the "cultural underbelly" in inferiority. Liminality refers to that transitional period common to most rituals that is considered to be neither here nor there, i.e., "betwixt and between" two social categories; the initiate, for example, is temporarily caught between two well-defined social statuses or positions. Marginality is evident in situations where, for example, women or "structural outsiders" (individuals, for example, who are part of the group by virtue of marriage rather than consanguineal ties) in traditional societies are allowed to assert themselves with impunity. Finally, inferiority here is spoken of in the sense of an autochthonous people who have been politically subjugated yet are considered by the dominant group to be spiritually powerful.

A feeling of "community" that crosses religious boundaries is created by the placement of this memorial bouquet at a monument at the entrance to the Jewish cemetery in Frankfurt, Germany. COURTESY OF ELIAS LEVINSON.

Communitas and Liminality

Of the three, it is liminality that is particularly germane to a discussion of rituals, religious or otherwise. (Of course, all rituals are "sacred" in a general sense.) Arnold van Gennep first used the term "liminality" to designate the transitional period of *rites de passage* that falls between the initial stage of separation and the final or third stage of reaggregation, when initiates, for example, are returned and reincorporated or assimilated once again into society proper, only this time they now exercise all the rights and privileges of their new social status or position.

By definition, of course, liminality falls literally in the interstices of structure. That fact is crucial to understanding the general anti-structural (or antisocial in a broad sense) nature of the liminal period. Thus, for example, all individuals undergoing a particular rite commonly all dress the same or may not wear anything at all; they will generally all be treated the same; and they will often be addressed not by their personal names but a group-oriented appellation. Clearly, the liminal period, falling as it does between the cracks of "proper" and recognized social states or statuses (unmarried/married, alive/dead, child/woman, outsider/adherent), involves a general "leveling" of rights, rank, and privileges that is entirely antithetical to the "normal" or structural state of affairs. Turner (1997, 106), for example, notes the following "binary opposites" where the first represents *communitas* and the second structure: equality/inequality, absence of status/status, humility/just pride of position, silence/speech, and total obedience/obedience only to superior rank, just to mention a few. It should not be assumed here, however, that the "liminite" is powerless in a general sense. After all, if one is "outside" structure, he or she is not controlled by it. Consider, for example, the "hippies" and "flower children" of the sixties, quintessential liminites who staked out a social position that was distinctly antistructural or, in their terms, "antisocial." Falling outside the purview of proper culture, so to speak, they engaged in activities that were socially unacceptable in a general sense, for example, the consumption of psychoactive substances and rather unrestricted sexual practices.

The power, so to speak, of *communitas* is also evident in the interplay between structure and *communitas*. Turner notes that both processes are essential for the "well-being" of each other. In fact, one might view society diachronically as a manifestation of the dialectic process involving this continual interplay between structure and *communitas*.

One important example of this process might be referred to as "the normalization of *communitas*." Consider, for example, the "mourning" ritual practiced in the Orisha religion of Trinidad. According to James Houk, the individual "pilgrim" involved in the ritual gains certain knowledge regarding spirits, rituals, etc., during a series of spiritual travels. The information and knowledge gained during mourning, however novel or traditional, or, put another way, however heretical or heterodox, eventually becomes part of the complex of beliefs and practices that comprise the Orisha religion. It is in this sense that *communitas* is normalized. The subversion of standard social roles that occurs during mourning allows even neophyte and rank and file adherents to influence the religion along idiosyncratic lines, since everyone's experiences are equally valid and, thus, equally important. Looked at in this way, the *communitas* of mourning periodically revitalizes the structure of the belief system. In a similar way, Turner speaks of the purging and purification effect *communitas* has on structure.

In a broad and general way, it is during such religious rites that mythology is legitimized, the strong become weak, the weak strong, and traditional status categories are reinforced by contrasting them with the potential anarchy and statuslessness of liminality. In an important sense, without structure there is no *communitas* and without *communitas* there is no structure.

James Houk

See also Communitas, Rites of; Liminoid; Passage, Rites of

Further Reading

Alexander, B. (1991). *Victor Turner revisited: Ritual as social change*. Atlanta, GA: Scholars Press.

Bell, C. (1992). *Ritual theory, ritual practice*. New York: Oxford University Press.

Geertz, C. (1973). *The interpretation of cultures*. New York: Basic Books.

Houk, J. (1995). *Spirits, blood, and drums: The Orisha religion in Trinidad*. Philadelphia: Temple University Press.

Turner, V. (1977). *The ritual process: Structure and anti-structure*. Ithaca, NY: Cornell University Press.

van Gennep, A. (1909). *The rites of passage* (M. Vizedom & G. Caffee, Trans.). London: Routledge and Kegan Paul.

Communitas, Rites of

In the 1960s Victor Turner adapted the word "communitas" from Paul Goodman's usage, which connoted town planning on community lines. Turner uses "communitas" extensively in anthropology to mean a relational quality of full, unmediated communication, even communion, between people of definite and determinate identity, which arises spontaneously in all kinds of groups, situations, and circumstances. The *Random House Webster Unexpurgated Dictionary* (1998) defines "communitas" as: "*Anthropol.* The sense of sharing and intimacy that develops among persons who experience liminality as a group." Turner first noted this phenomenon—then not recognized in the social sciences—in the healing ritual of Chihamba among the Ndembu of Zambia in 1953. He observed and experienced it among the Chihamba patients who were in passage between illness and health, and also found it among novices changing from childhood to adulthood, and in other changes in social status. Furthermore he recognized it in many different societies among those in betwixt-and-between circumstances, those going through some threshold or limen in life together, that is, in a time of liminality.

Description

The bonds of communitas that are felt at liminal times are undifferentiated, egalitarian, direct, extant, nonrational, existential, and "I–Thou" (in Martin Buber's sense). The original sense of communitas is spontaneous and concrete, not abstract. The experience of communitas matters much to the participants. It does not merge identities; the gifts of each person are alive to the full, along with those of every other person. Communitas liberates individuals from conformity to general norms. It is the fount and origin of the gift of togetherness, and thus of the gifts of organization, and therefore of all structures of social behavior, and at the same time it is the critique of structure that is overly law-bound. Communitas should be distinguished from Durkheim's "mechanical solidarity," which is a bond between individuals who are collectively in opposition to another solidary group. In "mechanical solidarity," unity depends on "in-group versus out-group" opposition. But in the genesis and central tendency of communitas, communitas is universalistic. Structures, like living species, become specialized; communitas, as in the case of the biology of the human species and its direct evolutionary forebears, remains open and unspecialized, a spring of pure possibility as well as giving release from day-to-day structural role-playing, and it seeks oneness. This does not involve a withdrawal from multiplicity but eliminates divisiveness and realizes nonduality. Communitas strains toward universalism and openness; it is richly charged with feeling, mainly pleasurable. It has something magical about it. Those who experience communitas feel the presence of spiritual power.

Victor Turner emphasizes, first, "spontaneous communitas": a feeling that comes unexpectedly like the wind and warms everyone to each other. It defies deliberate cognitive and volitional construction and is at the opposite pole to social structures, that is, the role sets, status sets, and status sequences consciously recognized and regulated in society and closely bound up with legal and political norms and sanctions. Communitas or the feeling of communion or oneness is therefore often expressed in rituals of reversal in which the lowly and high-ups reverse social roles.

After the inception of spontaneous communitas a structuring process often develops and a cycle of communitas/structure/communitas ensues. For example, religious vision becomes sect, then church, then a prop for a dominant political system, until communitas resurges once more, emerging from the spaces of freedom often found in betwixt-and-between situations. Revivals are of this nature.

Much of religious observance consists of "normative communitas," the attempt to capture and preserve spontaneous communitas in systems of ethical precepts and legal rules. These are often gathered in documents of "ideological communitas," in which are formulated the remembered attributes of the communitas experience in the form of a utopian blueprint for the reform of society. Yet in the stories usually recorded within them reside the seeds of the realization of spontaneous communitas once again, whether these consist of poems, sacred history, sincere accounts of visions, or even music and art. In the works of prophets and artists we may catch glimpses of the unused evolutionary potential of communitas, a potential not yet externalized and fixed in structure.

Sources of Communitas

The spaces of freedom in society from which communitas emerges are various. Communitas breaks into society (1) through the interstices of structure in *liminality*, times of change of status; (2) at the edges of structure, in *marginality;* and (3) from beneath structure, in *inferiority*. Liminality, marginality, and inferiority frequently generate sacred accounts, symbols, rituals, philosophical systems, and works of art.

Liminality

Liminality is the process of midtransition in a rite of passage. During the liminal period, the characteristics of those passing through are ambiguous, for where they find themselves has few or none of the attributes of either the past or the coming state. They are betwixt and between. In nonindustrial societies their secular powerlessness may be compensated for by a sacred power—the power of the weak, derived on the one hand from the resurgence of nature when structural power is removed, and on the other from the experience of the sacred. Much of what has been bound by social structure is liberated in liminality, notably the sense of comradeship and communitas. The kind of people in our society who are liminal are teenagers, students, trainees, travelers, those with new jobs, and people in times of major disaster. In Western society there is a paucity of ritual for these occasions; nevertheless, new or spontaneous rituals sometimes arise. The birthday party is a common example of a regular rite-of-passage ritual.

Marginality

Marginality is a category whose individuals often look to their group of origin, the so-called inferior group (see below), for communitas, and to the more prestigious group in which they mainly live for their structural position. Marginals may become critics of the structure from the perspective of communitas; many writers, artists, philosophers, and postmoderns are marginals, as well as New Agers, environmentalists, gays, and those in monastic orders.

Inferiority

Inferiority is a value-bearing category that refers to the powers of the weak, countervailing against structural power, fostering continuity, creating the sentiment of the wholeness of the total community, and positing the model of an undifferentiated whole whose units are total human beings. The powers of the weak are often assigned in hierarchic and stratified societies to women, the poor, original inhabitants, and outcasts, as well as members of minorities, holy mendicants, children, and human rights advocates such as Mahatma Gandhi and Nelson Mandela. To quote Liz Locke (1999, 3): "The non-athletes, the readers, the musicians, the skate rats, the gamers, the geeks, the metal-heads, the ravers, the stoners, the net-heads, the writers, the outcasts, the refugees—we find a way to create communities."

Communitas and Pilgrimage

The journey to sacred shrines, usually undertaken by large groups of religious people seeking help at a faraway saint's tomb or birthplace, is an activity in which communitas flowers. Friends are made and a sense of sacredness grows as the days of travel go by. The religion and the forward urging of the people, often in collective prayer, together produce an elated sense of sisterhood among all, something that draws pilgrims to come again year after year. While the pilgrimage situation does not eliminate structural divisions, it attenuates them and removes their sting. Moreover, pilgrimage liberates the individual from the obligatory everyday constraints of status and role, defines her as an integral human being with a capacity for free choice, and within the limits of her religious orthodoxy presents for her a living model of human sisterhood and brotherhood. It should be noted that the study of this element in pilgrimage has been critiqued by Michael Sallnow and John Eade (1991), who turn back to the structured stage of communitas development and claim that conflict is endemic in pilgrimage and that religious power hierarchies decide the major outcome of pilgrimage, so that pilgrimage has the effect of enhancing the existing power structures of society.

The Presence of Communitas

Negative capability, that is, an open readiness without preconceived ideas, provides the circumstances. There exists a democracy and humility about communitas: no one can claim it as their own. This is seen in Victor Turner's vision of it as residing in the poor and inferior, a gift coming up from below. As for the concrete circumstances, they can be found when people engage in a collective task with full attention. They may find themselves in flow, that is, they experience a merging of action and awareness—a crucial component of enjoyment. Flow is the holistic sensation present when we act with total involvement, with no apparent need for conscious intervention on our part. There is a loss of ego; the self becomes irrelevant. In the group, what is sought and what happens is unity, seamless unity, so that even joshing is cause for delight and there is often much laughter.

The benefits of communitas are joy, healing, the gift of "seeing," mutual help, religious experience, the gift of knowledge, long-term ties with others, a humanistic conscience, and the human rights ideal.

Communitas takes place in the rituals of Africa and other preindustrial cultures, and also in churches, temples, mosques, and shrines all over the world, achieved by collective prayer. Pentecostal and charismatic churches seek and find moments of universal love, praying for the sick. Sufi brotherhoods in India, Pakistan, and Afghanistan, in intense, collective, submissive chants to Allah, find that sense of unity. Communitas, not always achieved, is sought in the world Olympic games, where the finely tuned human body is the common factor, an achievement possible for all humans. The presence of communitas in music and the change of consciousness in groups are two themes in need of further study.

Other Definitions

The term "communitas" has been further elaborated by later anthropologists, particularly Roy Willis and Stephen Friedson citing African ritual. They refer to a time of "intersubjective objectivity," "a space of communitas" (Willis 1999, 120), when people are tuned in to one another and live together through the same flow of experience. In a Lungu healing rite Willis himself experienced this liberated communitas. He was aware of being lifted out of normal consciousness into a state where ordinary perceptions of time and space were drastically altered. The participants, including himself, were all in relation, different versions of each other, but there were no fixed boundaries to selfhood, there existed a permeability and flexibility between self and other, an infinite reflexivity, with a sense of everything flowing within the all-encompassing rhythm of the drum (Willis et al. 1999, 103). Stephen Friedson (1996), similarly participating in Malawi ritual, tells how the spirits caused his "self" to expand, creating a space within him, an opening, a clearing, where he became aware of a rich lived experience of the equiprimordiality of human being and world. This was spiritual communitas, both experiences showing how this can develop between anthropologists and practitioners of religion.

A prime example of communitas has been described by Matt Bierce (personal communication, April 2001), who cites jam sessions in Victor Turner's terms: liminality and communitas. He says of his jamming group

> We have been writing songs together for six years now and our cooperative powers have grown immensely. We are intimately aware of each other and our abilities, tendencies, favoritisms, styles, moods, and emotions. This intimacy allows us a form of jamming or improvisation that I think is a rare and cultivated closeness bordering on telepathic intuition. Above all else, we are friends. In the context of a jam, we communicate in a way that superceded speech and cognitive logic, in a language of suggestions, weavings, liminal stances, pattern formations and dissolutions, patience, intensity and calm, and private exploration. You have to give yourself totally, without reservations. It's not enough that you believe this or that is going to happen. By beholding behind the closed eyes of your co-musicians and in sensing the nerve impulses and the movements of the muscles in their bodies, you will attain a security in relation to what is going to happen. We are also working together to keep the song whole or coherent. This often happens as one new pattern is woven into the mix, that others pick up on its inherent beauty, and find ways to integrate what they are doing into this new structure. Strummings and pluckings are added on by other instruments until a new structure is implicitly agreed to. Once this new structure is found and woven in, the improvisation really can commence. The conscious mind is put on the back burner and the unconscious is given more control. One has to become like a child.

And he adds, "It almost becomes like a trance, a religious experience."

Understanding communitas entails a recognition of a certain kind of medium in which we all live that is permeable from person to person and which nourishes what is "spiritual." The nature of this consciousness, in healing or music for instance, is felt when connecting with others. A kind of power exists that is implicit in this connective "spirit" between people. We can tap into shadowy abysses where there is a "reservoir," a rising and flooding medium that can waken the existing spirit connections into activity, a kind of power store that can join people. Then the soul is in tune with others. Souls in communitas may even connect with the dead; may experience the power of switching back and forth in time; may receive and send unmistakable messages where vitally needed; and are conscious of purposes throughout the spiritual web—a huge visionary purpose sometimes.

The implications follow that if one responds to communitas one can no longer treat another human being as an object, because each person is too much part of the other. We find ourselves, as in the Copernican revolution, smaller than we thought, even on a par with the animals and not above them. We exist in a vast interchange of spirit personality—often glimpsed, sometimes seen clearly in the acts of spirit sociality. The social itself becomes a matter of intuitions passed between people and a joyous sense of bonding, sometimes providing the power of collective healing and of acting in visionary harmony.

Edith Turner

See also Communitas; Liminoid

Further Reading

Buber, M. (1958). *I and thou.* (R. G. Smith Trans.). Edinburgh: Clark.

Durkheim, E. (1895). *The rules of sociological method.* Glencoe, IL: Free Press.

Eade, J., & Sallnow, M. J. (Eds.). (1991). *Contesting the sacred: The anthropology of Christian pilgrimage.* London: Routledge.

Friedson, S. M. (1996). *Dancing prophets.* Chicago: University of Chicago Press.

Locke, L. (1999, May–July). Don't dream it, be it. *New Directions in Folklore, 3,* 1–3.

Stinmetz, S. (Ed.). (1998). *Random House unabridged dictionary.* New York: Random House.

Turner, V. W. (1969). *The ritual process: Structure and anti-structure.* Chicago: Aldine.

Turner, V. W. (1974a). *Dramas, Fields, and Metaphors.* Ithaca, New York: Cornell University Press.Turner, V. W. (1974b). Pilgrimage and communitas. *Studia Missionalia, 23,* 305–327.

Turner, V. W. (1982). Liminal to liminoid in play, flow, and ritual. In *From ritual to theatre: The human seriousness of play* (pp. 20–60). New York: Performing Arts Journal Publications.

Turner, V. W. (1992). Variations on a theme of liminality. In *Blazing the Trail* (pp. 49–65). Tucson: University of Arizona Press.

Turner, V. W., & Turner, E. L. B. (1978). Appendix A: Notes on processual symbolic Analysis. In *Image and pilgrimage in Christian culture: Anthropological perspectives* (pp. 243–255). New York: Columbia University Press.

Willis, R., Chisanga, K. B. S., Sikazwe, H. M. K., Sikazwe, K. B., & Nanyangwe, S. (1999). *Some spirits heal, others only dance: A journey into human selfhood in an African village.* Oxford, UK: Berg.

Crisis Rituals

Crisis rituals are called rites of intensification. These are employed when an unfavorable change has affected the group, or the group faces a danger or calamity of some kind. Such situations spread anxiety, uncertainty, and fear that can be alleviated through the performance of mass rituals that provide security and hope by reinforcing social ties and pointing to the transcendent dimension beyond everyday experience.

Individual Crisis Is Community Crisis

In traditional village communities, a problem experienced by an individual or family becomes a community problem. An illness in a Jordanian village studied by anthropologist Hilma Granqvist brought the members together in collective support that helped restore the sick person's vitality. Bringing flowers to someone in a hospital or food to the home of a sick person are Western equivalents. The death of someone disrupts a community even more, and collective rituals help reinforce social bonds, relieve tensions, and commemorate the dead person. For example, women in the Trobriand Islands distribute large quantities of banana-fiber skirts and banana leaves upon the death of a relative, and in America, a fund for some social purpose is often established at the passing of a notable person, to keep his memory alive.

Among a Melanesian group, the anthropologist Bronislaw Malinowski observed a commemoration in which people were required to eat some of the dead person's flesh. This ritual cannibalism was performed with "extreme repugnance and dread" and was usually followed by violent vomiting, but it was "felt to be a supreme act of reverence, love, and devotion." Outlawed by the government but still done in secret at the time of Malinowski's study, the act was considered a sacred duty that expressed "the longing for all that remains of the dead person and the disgust and fear of the dreadful transformation wrought by death" (Malinowski 1954, 49–50). Death rituals make the loss of a person less disruptive socially while helping the community readjust.

Some cultures' response to crime is highly ritualized. An eyewitness account of a Turkish execution in Jerusalem in the late nineteenth century depicts the mother of the slain person drinking some of the blood of the murderer after his execution, exclaiming, "My son is avenged!" (Granqvist 1965, 126–27). Capital punishment in the United States carries some of this public outrage, but among Southwest Native American tribes, a man who has killed an enemy, even in self-defense, "must purify himself for sixteen days, to cure his spirit of the madness of shedding blood" (Erdoes 1976, 35).

Social Change as Crisis

New situations or practices, caused by some larger social change, may also threaten people's security and thus meet with resistance. In the early 1980s many organizations in America began to implement new management practices. Sociologist Rosabeth Moss Kanter studied these and recommended rituals to ease the pain of change. According to her, people should have a chance to say good-bye and mourn the loss of the old ways with rituals like file-burning ceremonies or celebrating the company's history. Facing the unknown can create anxiety; that is one reason for ritualistic celebrations of the New Year that help people reaffirm their faith in the future.

Also in the 1980s, many American communities experienced economic decline. When Flint, Michigan, was declared by *Money* magazine to be the worst place in the United States to live, prominent citizens gathered in the public square and ritually burned the offending magazines in an effort to reaffirm their vitality as a community.

Collective Calamities

Epidemics or natural disasters, such as floods, fires, or earthquakes, also call forth a collective response. Although these may involve more practical help than ritualistic behavior, religious rituals, such as special prayers offered in houses of worship, are usual. Many Native American tribes engage in rain dances that involve songs and petitions with the intent of manipulating nature through the symbolic power of rituals. Among the Pueblo Indians, for example, "all prayers, ceremonies, and dances… are essentially prayers for rain" (Erdoes 1976, 11).

War is met with special ceremonies in most societies, generally to show the society's might to the enemy. Special attire, beating of drums, and chanting are usual in tribal warfare. But even Western societies parade their military in a show of strength. It is also a time when leaders must address the public to reassure them of their security and to denounce the enemy. Nowhere has this been as evident as in the aftermath of the 11 September 2001 terrorist attacks on the United States. The president's speeches acquired extra importance, and countless people posted flags on their cars and by their houses to show their loyalty to the country. In some other countries, U.S. flags have been ritually burned to show the people's contempt toward the United States and its policies. Such an act is tantamount to burning the enemy in effigy, a practice that goes back to the shattering of the enemy in clay figurines in the ancient Near East.

Political domination by a foreign power and internal domination of one group by another are further examples of serious crisis situations for a society. The Tamang communities of Nepal have experienced both. In a threefold ritual of both secular activities (dance-skits) and religious rituals (exorcisms and the production of power *wang,* or retreat), they sought to reaffirm their society and to express resistance to the dominating forces. These activities generated symbolic power that "is an elementary form of power produced in the activity of ritual itself" (Holmberg 2000, 927).

Rituals Generate Hope

Whether the community is rallying together to collectively mourn a loss, to face social change in the company of others, or to respond to a natural disaster or human-made crises such as war, terrorism, or domination, the rituals employed constitute a form of collective action that can create a more optimistic outlook that something can be done about the situation. These rituals embody the horizontal dimension of social affirmation and the vertical dimension of spiritual renewal. Both of these sources provide strength and a new vision that helps alleviate fear and confusion and enables the community to look ahead with hope.

Sara Kärkkäinen Terian

See also Death Rituals; Ritual as Communication; Television and Ritual; Witchcraft

Further Reading

Erdoes, R. (1976). *The rain dance people: The Pueblo Indians, their past and present*. New York: Alfred A. Knopf.

Granqvist, H. (1965). Muslim death and burial: Arab customs and traditions studied in a village in Jordan. Helsinki, Finland: Centraltryckeriet.

Holmberg, D. (2000). Derision, exorcism, and the ritual production of power. *American Ethnologist 27*(4), 927–949.

Kanter, R. M. (1983). *The change masters*. New York: Simon and Schuster.

Kanter, R. M. (1985). Managing the human side of change. *Management Review 74*, 52–56.

Leavitt, S. C. (2003). Cargo beliefs and religious experience. In J. Bradley, & D. W. McCurdy (Eds.). *Conformity and conflict: Readings in cultural anthropology*, (11th ed.). Boston: Allyn and Bacon.

Malinowski, B. (1954). *Magic, science, and religion*. Garden City, NY: Doubleday.

Murray, C., & Sanders, P. (2000). Medicine murder in Basutoland: Colonial rule and moral crisis. *Africa 70*(1), 49–78.

Weiner, A. B. (1988). *The Trobrianders of Papua New Guinea*. New York: Holt, Rinehart, and Winston.

D

Day of the Dead

In Latin America the Day of the Dead (celebrated on the first two days of November) is a day of communal joy when communities use art, dance, music, food, and prayers to honor the dead. The day provides an opportunity for younger generations to learn their history and folkways as well as the respect of their ancestors.

Since pre-Columbian times folk festivals have been primary vehicles through which the people of Latin America have expressed their dreams and fears, amused their gods, and honored their ancestors. Through the years the indigenous cultures of Latin America, such as those of Mexico and Guatemala, have assimilated and adapted elements of the European conquerors to form the picturesque and complex folk traditions of today. Men and women, young and old, indigenous and nonindigenous maintain these links to the past.

The Day of the Dead *(El Día de los Muertos)*, also known as "All Souls' Day," is most prominently celebrated in Mexico but also to a lesser extent in regions of Guatemala, Bolivia, El Salvador, and Peru. In an area one town hosts the day, which involves the surrounding towns and their products, foods, and crafts, thus enriching all the towns. Traditions are preserved as people honor the dead and pass on their folk knowledge to the younger generation. The younger generation will be the caretakers of their cultures, their language, and their religion.

In Mexico the Day of the Dead is a week-long celebration; the first two days are used to honor the spirits of deceased children. During these two days children take part in the celebration, which features candies, such as the famous sugar skulls, and papier-mâché skeletons, which often reflect political satire. The first day of November is also a day to honor all Christian saints and martyrs. Pope Boniface IV introduced the day in the seventeenth century. It was originally celebrated in May but was moved to November by Pope Gregory III in the eighteenth century. This day is also known as "All Saints Day" *(Día de Todos los Santos)*, when many Latin American people go to mass to celebrate the Catholic feast. The second day of this festival is the official celebration of the dead, "the time of family reunion not only for the living but also the dead" (Carmichael and Sayer 1991, 14). Paradoxically, this is a joyful day when all the spirits return and spend a day with the living. "People in Mexico believe that the deceased deserve a vacation as much as the living do, so once a year they return to earth for family fun" (Milne 1965, 163). The living welcome the souls of the dead for a few brief hours of colorful activities that the dead once enjoyed in life. The present, past, and future are reconciled.

Cemeteries Decorated

Throughout the celebration cemeteries vibrate with colorful marigolds, candles, and food baskets. The celebration features symbolic themes such as food made with corn; copal (fossil tree resin) incense is burned throughout the cemeteries; and the living perform religious rituals. Musicians play traditional music; masked dancers perform in front of the Catholic churches. In Tancoco, Mexico, professional

DAY OF THE DEAD ON THE YUCATAN PENINSULA

While Day of the Dead rituals across Mesoamerica contain many common elements, there is also variety from community to community. The followjng example is of the Tzeltal of the Yucatan Openinsula.

... This altar is usually located in the house corridor. The altar is cleaned regularly and adorned with flowers by the women, and a candle or two is lighted on propitious days of the week, or to ask the house Saints for protection against witchcraft.

On the first of November, "day of all the dead" according to the Catholic calendar, a ceremonial offering of food to the spirits of the deceased is placed on this altar. It is in memory of the spirits who lived in the house in the immediate past, and who are supposed to come to enjoy the food and the fact that they are being remembered by the household. The ritual is performed only for the immediate generations. It is not the worshipping of one's ancestors, for it is for people who are not necessarily related by kinship, but for those who resided in the house. (Second wives, for example, are expected to offer food to the deceased first wife of their husbands if they lived in the same dwelling.)

Afterwards, the food is distributed among the living relatives, *compadres* and neighbors, and all members of the household go to the cemetery.

At the cemetery, the tombs are cleaned, repaired, adorned with marigolds, fruit and other food, and the family pays for the performance of a *responso*, funeral oration, read by a part-time specialist in such matters.

If these rituals are not performed, the dead come back to their life stage, the house, and wander aimlessly among the living, scaring people, giving them bad dreams, or taking the lives of children.

Source: Hunt, Muriel E. V. (1962).
The Dynamics of the Domestic Group in Tzeltal Villages: A Contrastive Comparison.
Chicago: Chicago University Library, Department of Photoduplication, Microfilm Thesis No. 9048, p. 113.

chanting *rezanderos* (prayer makers) and women wailing at gravesides are commonly seen.

In Guatemala traditional dances such as the Deer Dance *(La Danza del Venado)* are performed; this dance is performed with colorful costumes and deer masks. In a small region of Santiago Sacatepequez, the boys have spent months building huge kites *(barriletes)*, which they fly in a cemetery on the morning of 2 November.

In Bolivia and Peru people bring food to the cemeteries on 2 November and perform traditional dances all day. "In the village of Huarocondo, Peru the indigenous people take offerings of roasted pig, tamales, potatoes, corn, and eggs to the church to be blessed by the priest and left for the dead" (Milne 1965, 163).

Marigolds

Yellow symbolized death among the pre-Hispanic people; therefore, marigolds are profuse at the celebration. In some regions of Mexico the facades of houses are decorated with *papel picado* (intricately cut-out paper) and orange-yellow marigold flowers, and petals line the pathway between the cemetery and houses so that the dead can find their way home, where they will find tables set up as altars decorated with flowers, candles, offerings of saintly pictures, photos of the deceased, and Day of the Dead bread. The bread comes in many forms; one form is round, which symbolizes the shape of the human soul; another form is a flat, soft, cookie-like bread covered with red sugar; red symbolizes eternal life. Sugar skulls, sweets, and alcohol are sometimes added, depending on the economic status of the family.

Ofrendas is a pre-Hispanic practice of giving gifts to the dead. Pre-Hispanic Maya farmers buried their loved ones with an array of objects such as plain and painted pottery, jewelry, and copal incense. Bloodletting was conducted where their loved ones

Afro-mestizo households altar for the Day of the Dead in the community of El Cerro, Costa Chica, and Querrero. The flowers and candles are set mostly on the floor. Special foods including breads, fruits, and sweets are set out on plates for the shrines.
COURTESY OF BEATRIZ MORALES COZIER.

were buried to evoke a good harvest season. Today these offerings take the form of an elaborate feast for the souls. The cemeteries are decorated and immersed in a blanket of copal smoke. For some cultures copal incense brings back the spirits to the living world; for other cultures it symbolizes the departure of the spirits. The living make an array of offerings to the dead to nurture and renew their friendship and urge them to return the next year.

In summary the rituals of the Day of the Dead throughout the Americas remind everyone that death is not the end of life but rather the renewal of life. "It is a ritual that promotes rebirth" (Paz 1985, 51).

Mara Cosillo-Starr

See also Death Rituals

Further Reading

Carmack, R. M., Gasco, J., & Gossen, G. H. (1995). *The legacy of Mesoamerica history and culture of a Native American civilization.* Upper Saddle River, NJ: Prentice Hall.

Carmichael, E., & Sayer, C. (1991). *The skeleton at the feast the Day of the Dead in Mexico.* Austin: University of Texas Press.

Carrasco, D. (1990). *Religions of Mesoamerica cosmovison and ceremonial centers.* Prospect Heights, IL: Waveland Press.

Drew, D. (1999) *The lost chronicles of the Maya kings.* Berkeley and Los Angeles: University of California Press.

Garciagodoy, J. (1998). *Digging the days of the dead: A reading of Mexico's Día de Muertos.* Niwot: University of Colorado Press.

Horn, R. (1997). *Posquest coyoacan: Nahua-Spanish relations in central Mexico, 1519–1650.* Stanford, CA: Stanford University Press.

Kelsey, V. (1952). *Four keys to Guatemala.* New York: Funk & Wagnalls.

Milne, J. (1965). *Fiesta time in Latin America.* Los Angeles: Ward Ritchie Press.

Nutini, H. G. (1968). *San Bernardino contla: Marriage and family structure in a Tlaxcalan municipio.* Pittsburgh, PA: University of Pittsburgh Press.

Paz, O. (1985). *The labyrinth of solitude: Life and thought in Mexico* (L. Kemp, Trans.). New York: Viking Penguin. (Original work published 1961).

Schele, L., & Freidel, D. (1992). *A forest of kings: The untold story of the ancient Maya.* New York: Quill William Morrow.

Death Rituals

Death rituals or mortuary rites provide people with a means to deal with the loss and disruption caused by the death of a person. In many parts of the world the rituals form a sequence that may take place over a considerable period of time, as the body of the deceased is transformed from life and goes through a potentially dangerous or polluting state until it reaches a more inert condition. The rituals may also be intimately connected with culturally specific notions concerning rebirth, fertility, ancestral spirits, or the immortality of the soul. An immaterial essence or a soul is often conceived of as having to undergo a

ROBERT HERTZ ON DEATH RITUALS

Below is an excerpt from *Death and the Right Hand* by Robert Hertz, who conducted ethnographic religious and folklore studies in Indonesia and Polynesia during the early twentieth century.

> **But where a human being is concerned the physiological phenomena are not the whole of death. To the organic event is added a complex mass of beliefs, emotions and activities which give it its distinctive character. We see life vanish but we express this fact by the use of a special language: it is the soul, we say, which departs for another world where it will join its forefathers. The body of the deceased is not regarded like the carcass of some animal: specific care must be given to it and a correct burial; not merely for reasons of hygiene but out of moral obligation. Finally, with the occurrence of death a dismal period begins for the living during which special duties are imposed upon them. Whatever their personal feelings may be, they have to show sorrow for a certain period, change the colour of their clothes and modify the pattern of their usual life**

Hertz, Robert. (1960). A Contribution to the Study of the Collective Representation of Death. In *Death and the Right Hand.* Translated by R. and C. Needham. Aberdeen, UK: Cohen and West, p. 27. Originally published 1907.

journey after death, and rituals are performed to help it reach its destination.

The earliest systematic anthropological treatment of death rituals was by J. J. Bachofen in 1859. His study of symbols connected with fertility and femininity in ancient Greek and Roman funerary rites was later taken up by Sir James Frazer in *The Golden Bough* (1890), which includes a discussion on the regeneration of fertility through the killing of divine kings. Robert Hertz used ethnographic material from Indonesia and Polynesia to adopt a different approach. He looked at attitudes toward bones and flesh, the preparations that take place between a provisional burial following death and the final obsequies (known as "double obsequies" in the anthropological literature), the journeying of the soul, and the rituals observed by the mourners. Hertz argued that the socially constructed death rituals orchestrate the collective representation of death. The sequence of temporary and secondary burials permits the social group to readjust while the soul of the deceased is incorporated into the society of the dead. Hertz saw this incorporation as an initiation.

The physical occurrence of death is in itself a process or transition. Hertz discussed cases in which the proclamation of the successor to a ruler is not announced until the final obsequies have taken place. In Liberia a deceased ruler was finally buried on the death of the successor. This meant that the reign of the successor was coterminous with the temporary burial of the predecessor. In effect, the "ex-king, 'who is not considered to be really dead', watches over the successor and helps him in his function" (Hertz 1960, 129). This attitude toward the death of divine rulers was carried to an extreme in the Andes during the fifteenth and sixteenth centuries. Each Inca ruler ensured that his or her property was retained by the estate of his or her descent group and the body of the deceased ruler was prepared in a bundle of textiles. The ruler's retainers continued to maintain the agricultural production of the estate in order to observe a cycle of sacrifices to "feed" the mummy bundle, which was ritually offered food and drink. Hence it was recorded that Inca mummies presided over the marriage of their children or even contracted a "ghost" marriage, when Rawa Ocllo married the mummy of Wayna Capac to legitimate the claim of her children.

Archaeological Evidence of Death Rituals

Archaeologists have long been interested in burial practices because they form an important part of death rituals. Since the early twentieth century, a

The corpse of a Hindu is cremated in Varanasi, India in 1996.
COURTESY OF STEPHEN G. DONALDSON PHOTOGRAPHY.

particular form of treating human bodies known as Chinchorro, named after a beach at Arica, northern Chile, has evinced a great deal of interest. The prevailing arid conditions have permitted the good preservation of human remains, which were either allowed to dessicate naturally or were artifically mummified. Chinchorro mortuary treatment was long-lived, lasting from 7,000 to 1,500 BCE. The body of the deceased person was prepared in an extended position. In the most complex examples, the body was skinned, dismembered, and reconstituted, reinforced with sticks. Externally, skin was replaced on the body and was coated with black manganese paint (the so-called "black mummies") or with red ochre ("red mummies"). As an alternative to the red type, the skin was wrapped around the limbs and, in the case of children, around the torso as well ("bandage mummies"). The mummies are found in collective groups in an area extending along the coast of the far south of Peru and the far north of Chile.

Archaeologists distinguish between inhumation, in which case the corpse may be interred in a flexed or extended position, and cremation, which involves burning the body. Hertz considered cremation and the later disposal of the burned bones to correspond with the practice of provisional and final burials. He saw mummification as fitting into the same scheme. Instead of allowing the flesh to decay and then burying the bones, the embalmers prepared a mummified body that would not decay further and consigned it to the final burial. The Chinchorro mummies would thus seem to provide another example of Hertz's thesis. However, he also argued that the death of children does not give rise to the strong emotions or complex rituals that are accorded to adults. In his view children are not yet fully incorporated into the social order, so "there is no reason to exclude them from it slowly and painfully" (Hertz 1960, 84). Among the Chinchorro mummies, children were accorded special treatment after death. An emphasis on elaborate child burials lasted until about 500 BCE in the south-central Andes.

A common form of burial in the pre-Hispanic Andes was to place the body in a flexed position. Between about 450 BCE and 175 BCE, people living on the Paracas peninsula in the south of Peru buried the flexed corpse in a funerary basket, wrapped with heavily embroidered garments and plain cotton cloths. The production of funerary textiles would have involved many people in the community. One of the most long-lasting iconographic elements that they developed in the embroidery included the trophy head, and its symbolic counterpart, the bean. Germinating beans must have evoked ideas concerning death and rebirth.

The Role of Cloth in Death Rituals

The attention lavished on the Chinchorro and Paracas mummies exemplifies an aspect of death rituals mentioned by Raymond Firth: the rituals are performed by and for the benefit of the living, not the deceased. Firth discussed the case of a young man who was lost at sea after sailing from Tikopia, an island east of the Solomon Islands in the Pacific Ocean. Remarking that the funeral took place in the absence of a corpse, he reiterated a comment by Hertz that the rituals do not merely function as a hygienic means of disposing of the dead. When a person is lost at sea, Tikopia custom is to wait at least a year. If no news concerning the person arrives, the death rituals are performed with mats and bark-cloth but without the body of the deceased. Tikopia people explained to Firth that they spread the grave-clothes "to make the lost one dry" (Firth 1971: 62). They are providing dry garments for the spirit of the deceased, whose wet clothing is clinging round it after drowning at sea.

As indicated by these examples from Chinchorro, Paracas, and Tikopia, cloth or garments for wrapping the deceased play a prominent role in death rituals in many parts of the world, and have done so throughout time. Several contributors to the book *Cloth and Human Experience* (edited by Annette B. Weiner and Jane Schneider) point out this connection. Mourners, too, often wear special clothes.

Gillian Feeley-Harnik observes that among the Merina and Betsileo in the Malagasy highlands of Madagascar, relatives of the deceased honor important ancestors through an elaborate process of exhumation, rewrapping in new shrouds, and reburial. In western Madagascar, the Sakalava people wash a deceased person and place kapok drenched in cologne in the orifices of the corpse. They wrap the body with untailored garments known as *lamba,* then place it in a plain wooden coffin. After a few days they place a piece of white cloth over the coffin and carry it to a cemetery adjoining the local community for burial. The act of burial is accompanied by prohibitions that include not using the name of the dead person. Other prohibitions are observed by the spouse of the deceased, who remains inside the house and stays silent, only speaking in a whisper to close kin of the same sex. If the spouse leaves the house, he or she wraps completely in clothing and only leaves a single opening for one eye. This prohibition is observed for four to five weeks by a widower, longer in the case of a widow. According to Feeley-Harnik (1989, 84), Sakalava mourning rituals "support the inference that wrapping up, social formality, linguistic restraint, and depersonalization are ultimately associated with death, while speaking asserts the renewal of life and naming establishes familiar relations."

Late-Twentieth-Century Theoretical Developments

Maurice Bloch and Jonathan Parry encouraged the contributors to the volume *Death and the Regeneration of Life* to reconsider the two theoretical approaches represented by Bachofen and Hertz. These traditions converge on the concepts of rebirth that often feature in death rituals. Bloch and Parry consider it important to combine sociological and symbolic analysis. They take issue with Hertz's understanding of the character of the collective response as a group reasserts the social order after the disruption caused by the death of one of its members. In their view, and in contrast with Hertz, the "social order is a *product* of rituals of the kind we consider rather than its cause" (Bloch and Parry 1982, 6).

In many societies the putrescence or pollution of death is associated with women. Such an association is not universal. Olivia Harris indicates that it does not apply among the Aymara-speaking Laymi of highland Bolivia. She argues that Laymi death rituals tend to obscure the role of the dead in the agricultural cycle. In a further development of the theme, Peter Gose discusses Andean rituals as part of a cultural construction of economic processes that incorporate specific metaphysical assumptions. He explores one of the assumptions made by the people of Huaquirca, Peru, which has to do with "sowing as burial." On the day of a burial a group of male affines of the deceased wash the dead person's clothes by trampling them with their feet in a river. This work is an inversion of the normal practice, which is usually done by women using their hands. Moreover, the work follows a pattern. It is divided into three periods, separated by two bouts of drinking, which is how agricultural labor is performed. Gose argues that "clothes washing" in the Quechua language can be made to sound like a double entendre for "earth washing" or irrigation. The homology set up between irrigation and clothes washing, he explains, is matched by a perceived relationship between sowing ritual and the deceased as seed.

Ethnographic Fieldwork and Death Rituals

Ninteenth- and early-twentieth-century publications on death rituals were mostly written by authors who did not conduct sustained ethnographic fieldwork. The importance accorded to fieldwork after the 1920s has resulted in what Jack Goody (1962, 13) called "a degree of ethnographic myopia." However, the section on late-twentieth-century theoretical developments has demonstrated that anthropologists now attempt to understand death rituals in a manner that incorporates carefully contextualized fieldwork within a sensitively conceived theoretical framework.

Maureen MacKenzie's study of secret, sacred string bags known as *men amem* and their role in death rituals among the Telefol of central New Guinea reveals much about Telefol concepts of gender. The body of a deceased person is laid on a bed of leaves on a mortuary platform constructed in one of the gardens belonging to that person. These leaves consist of red-colored *iluh*, which women wrap round the umbilical cord of their babies, and *driim*, which have male associations, deriving from an avenue of hoop pines leading to the men's house, marking a male path only the initiated can use. If the deceased is male, softened taro leaves are placed in the mouth, and if female, red ochre clay is similarly placed. The Telefol consider red ochre clay to stand for the procreative menstrual blood of their creator ancestress, Afek. A ritual specialist informs the spirit of the deceased that the villagers wish it to stay amongst them as an ancestor spirit, and not to go to the Land of the Dead as a ghost spirit. He plants a red cordyline bush in order to establish the garden as taboo for the next four or five months. Its crops are left to whither and decay. As the red flesh of the deceased on the mortuary platform decomposes, the white bones are revealed. In due course, the specialist uses a pair of wooden tongs to place the potent bones in an open-looped string bag lined with *iluh* and *driim* leaves. He selects the skull, jaw, radius and ulna, finger, ankle and wrist bones, and also the pelvis if the deceased was a woman. The used string bag, the product of women's labor, becomes a *men amem*, in which the ancestor spirit is reborn inside its protective, womb-like abode. According to MacKenzie, the ritual specialist carries the *men amem* in a fashion that parallels the manner in which women carry their babies. He does this as part of a ritual procession to hang the *men amem* in a man's house, or from the back wall of a woman's house in Telefolip village. This is followed by a night of feasting and dancing, during which the people test the efficacy of the ancestor spirit. If they think the spirit has deserted them for the Land of the Dead, they discard the bones. Only the *men amem* of benevolent ancestors are retained.

The esoteric procedures used for producing *men amem* are taboo to women, who might understand the death rituals as a means men use "to tap ancestral power for the collective well-being of the whole community" (MacKenzie 1991, 187). However, MacKenzie observes that women's subversive role in community rituals is expressed in the *men amem*. They make the string bag, which serves as a symbol of both productivity and reproductivity and of nurturance and procreativity. Women's beliefs concerning conception focus on the notion that they transform red womb blood into white fetal bone. Hence MacKenzie concludes that women possess power that is primary and biological, while men ritually manipulate women's power in elaborating the secret *men amem*, which are taboo to women, but which express the complementary gender roles of Telefol rituals.

MacKenzie's ethnography shows us that anthropological interpretations of death rituals do not, perhaps, help us to understand the demarcation between life and death, which some people deliberately attempted to blur, as did the people of Liberia and the Incas in the case of their monarchs. However, a study of death rituals does illuminate how human beings define their humanity in a culturally specific manner.

Penelope Dransart

See also Commemorative Rituals; Day of the Dead

Further Reading

Aufderheide, A. C., Muñoz, I., & Arriaza, B. (1993). Seven Chinchorro mummies and the prehistory of northern Chile. *American Journal of Physical Anthropology 91*, 189–201.

Bachofen, J. J. (1967). *Myth, religion, and mother right: Selected writings of J. J. Bachofen* (R. Manheim, Trans.). London: Routledge.

Barley, N. (1995). *Dancing on the grave: Encounters with death*. London: John Murray.

Bloch, M., & Parry, J. (Eds.). (1982). *Death and the regeneration of life*. Cambridge, UK: Cambridge University Press.

Dillehay, T. D. (Ed.). (1995). *Tombs for the living: Andean mortuary practices*. Washington, DC: Dumbarton Oaks Research Library and Collections.

Dransart, P. (1997). Afinidad, descendencia, y la política de las representaciones de género: ¿Quién fue la *Quya* de Ataw Wallpa? [Affinity, descent and the politics of representations of gender: who was the *Quya* of Atawallpa?]. In D. Y. Arnold (Ed.), *Más allá del silencio: Las fronteras de género en los Andes* (pp. 475–490). La Paz, Bolivia: Instituto de Lengua y Cultura Aymara and Centre for Indigenous American Studies and Exchange.

Dwyer, J. P. (1979). The chronology and iconography of Paracas-style textiles. In A. P. Rowe, E. P. Benson, & A.-L. Schaffer (Eds.), *The Junius B. Bird Pre-Columbian textile conference* (pp. 105–128). Washington, DC: The Textile Museum and Dumbarton Oaks.

Feeley-Harnik, G. (1989). Cloth and the creation of ancestors in Madagascar. In A. B. Weiner& J. Schneider (Eds.), *Cloth and human experience* (pp. 73–116). Washington, DC, & London: Smithsonian Institution Press.

Firth, R. (1971). *Elements of social organization*. London: Tavistock Publications. (Original work published 1951).

Frazer, J. G. (1890). *The golden bough: A study in comparative religion*. London: Macmillan.

Goody, J. (1962). *Death, property, and the ancestors: A study of the mortuary customs of the LoDagaa of West Africa*. London: Tavistock Publications.

Gose, P. (1994). *Deathly waters and hungry mountains: Agrarian ritual and class formation in an Andean town*. Toronto, Ontario, Canada; Buffalo, New York; & London: University of Toronto Press.

Harris, O. (1982). The dead and the devils among the Bolivian Laymi. In M. Bloch & J. Parry (Eds.), *Death and the regeneration of life* (pp. 45–73). Cambridge, UK: Cambridge University Press.

Hertz, R. (1960). A contribution to the study of the collective representation of death. In *Death and the right hand* (R. Needham & C. Needham, Trans.). Aberdeen, Scotland: Cohen and West. (Original work published 1907).

MacKenzie, M. (1991). *Androgynous objects: String bags and gender in central New Guinea*. Amsterdam: Harwood Academic Press.

Niles, S. A. (1999). *The shape of Inca history: Narrative and architecture in an Andean empire*. Iowa City: University of Iowa Press.

Standen, V. G. Temprana complejidad funeraria de la cultura Chinchorro (norte de Chile) [Early funerary complexity in the Chinchorro culture (north of Chile)]. *Latin American Antiquity 8*(2), 134–156.

Weiner, A. B., & Schneider, J. (Eds.). (1989). *Cloth and human experience*. Washington, DC, & London: Smithsonian Institution Press.

Wise, K. (1995). La ocupación Chinchorro en Villa del Mar, Ilo, Perú [The Chinchorro occupation at Villa del Mar, Ilo, Peru]. *Gaceta Arqueológica Andina 24*, 135–149. An English translation is available at http://www.nhm.org/research/anthropology/Pages/chinchorro.

Divali

Divali is the festival of lights celebrated by Hindus and Jains (adherents of a religion founded in India based on the ideals of nonviolence, discipline, purity, and enlightenment) during October or November, according to the lunar calendar. Divali is also known as "Dipavali," which means "row of lights" and refers to little clay oil lamps that are lit at twilight during Divali and that are understood to welcome Lakshmi, the goddess of good fortune, into homes and businesses, which, it is hoped, she will grace during the coming year.

Associated Myths

Various myths are associated with the celebration of Divali. One of the most common myths relates the return of the hero prince Rama to his home in Ayodhya after rescuing his wife Sita from her abductor, the ten-headed demon king Ravana. Rama is a human incarnation of the god Vishnu and Sita, an incarnation of Vishnu's wife Lakshmi, whose epithet "Shri" refers to a kind of beauty associated with prosperity and well-being. When Rama and Sita were forced to leave Ayodhya by political intrigue, the royal capital withered. With the return of Sita, its greenness and fertility also returned. Welcoming Rama and Sita home, the citizens of Ayodhya lit lamps to light their way and to represent their joy at knowing that their hero and heroine, veritable embodiments of goodness and righteousness, had returned to assume governance and bring prosperity. The lesson related in this myth, the triumph of good over evil, is often taught to children at home and in schools on the days before Divali, when goodness is often explicitly associated with the light of wisdom triumphing over the darkness of ignorance, the source of evil.

Another myth frequently told at Divali is that of the churning of the milk ocean. The gods and demons were fighting, as they perpetually do, and when the demons appeared to be getting the upper hand, the god Vishnu suggested to the gods that they churn the ocean to acquire the nectar of immortality. Vishnu took the form of Kurma, the tortoise, whose back supported Mount Mandara, the churning stick. From the churned ocean came the nectar but also the auspicious Lakshmi, whom Vishnu chose her as his consort.

A third myth relates the story of Vamana, the incarnation of Vishnu as a dwarf, who secured from the demon Bali a promise that he could have as much territory as he could cover in three strides. Vishnu then grew into a giant, claimed the world, and cast the demon Bali into the underworld, from which he is allowed to return only during Divali to bestow more gifts on human beings.

Divali Ritual

People typically understand Divali as beginning a new year. They precede it with days, even weeks, of intense preparation, which typically includes a thorough housecleaning. Homes usually receive a new coat of whitewash or paint. Lakshmi is attracted only to homes and businesses that glisten with cleanliness and reflective light.

In some places worshipers wait until the auspicious hour appointed by Brahman (a Hindu of the highest caste) priests to light the lamps welcoming Lakshmi on Divali, but recently many enthusiastic Divali celebrants have begun lighting lamps for days before Divali. Firecrackers can be heard for weeks in most Indian cities—so much so that local newspapers post health advisories for asthma sufferers due to the toxins released by firecrackers. In Trinidad children typically "burst bamboo" by igniting chemicals in freshly cut stalks. These festivities have been pushed weeks back to Vijayadashmi, the festival that in southern India celebrates Rama's victory over his demon foe but that in northern India also celebrates the date when the goddess Durga subdues her demon adversaries.

During the days leading up to Divali, and especially on the day of the festival, shops typically reduce their prices with hopes of ending the year with a strong balance. The first customer of any day of the year is often considered a manifestation of Lakshmi, with whom bargaining should not be pressed to the point of losing the sale. The first-customer rule is especially important on Divali, when sales in stores operating on this holiday are often construed as indications of Lakshmi's favor.

On Divali, temples for Lakshmi and for Rama or Vishnu are typically filled with devotees paying special homage to Lakshmi and seeking her blessing. In addition, many devotees worship Lakshmi in their homes. In Trinidad special Sunday services are devoted to goddess worship (which often associates Lakshmi with Durga), and worshipers typically conduct special prayer sessions for Lakshmi in their homes. Throughout the world Lakshmi devotees typically make or buy and distribute sweets to friends and neighbors as an expression of generosity and the importance of shared prosperity. In India stores that typically sell other goods are frequently transformed into sweet shops to accommodate public demand.

In the United States and other diaspora (a scattering of a people) regions, Divali has become an occasion in which temple associations and students in universities put together cultural performances that represent Indian presence and culture in the diaspora setting. These performances often include recitals of classical dance, including Bharat Natyam, and folk dances, especially Bhangra, a folk dance that has been mixed with elements of reggae, hip-hop, rock, and disco by youth residing in regions inside and outside India.

Associated Rituals

Although practice varies among diverse populations, some important celebrations are held before and after Divali. Just before Divali is Dhan Teres (Wealth-Thirteenth), on which the purchase of precious metals is considered particularly auspicious. The day after Divali night is celebrated in some parts of India and elsewhere with the worship of Krishna, who is another incarnation of Vishnu. On this day Krishna is said to have lifted up Mount Govardhana to use as an umbrella. In this way he protected the cowherders of Vraj from the torrential rains sent by the king of the gods, Indra, who had previously captured all their cows and was envious of the people's infatuation with Krishna, the cows' rescuer. The next day is Bhai Duj (Brother-Second), on which sisters express affection for the brothers who protect them throughout their lives.

On Divali worshipers of Lakshmi affirm the passage of time through a celebration of the auspicious new year while recognizing the pursuit of *artha* (good fortune), a value recognized by Hindus and Jains as one of the legitimate pursuits of human life. On this holiday *artha* is symbolically associated with the light of wisdom, expressed through righteous behavior and given full expression in the myths of the divine Rama and of Vishnu, whose incarnations restore righteousness when it is threatened by demonic forces.

Lindsey Harlan

See also Hinduism

Further Reading

Babb, A. (1996). *Absent lord: Ascetic and kings in a Jain ritual culture.* Berkeley and Los Angeles: University of California Press.

Cort, J. (2001). *Jains in the world: Religious values and ideology in India.* New York: Oxford University Press.

Eck, D. (1982). *Banaras: City of light*. Princeton, NJ: Princeton University Press.

Dimmitt, C., & van Buitenen, J. (1978). *Classical Hindu mythology: A reader in the Sanskrit Puranas*. Philadelphia: Temple University Press.

Harlan, L. (in press). Reversing the gaze in America: Parody in Divali performance at Connecticut College. In K. Jacobsen & P. Kumar (Eds.), South Asians in the diaspora: Histories and religious traditions. Leiden, Netherlands: Brill.

Divination

Divination is a ritual process of attempting to obtain information from hidden—"occult"—sources. Although specific techniques vary greatly, divination systems are universal. In any society there is the general belief that everything that exists, has existed, or will exist is known by God or some other spiritual beings, or that such knowledge is inherent in the cosmos as a whole, or both, and that people can obtain details of such knowledge. Divination systems can be classified according to their underlying cosmological (cultural beliefs about the nature of the universe) premises—magical or spiritual, and their methods—mechanical or sensory but these categories overlap. Priests and shamans routinely perform divination, and some societies have professional diviners; but certain forms of divination can be performed by anyone; hence "diviner" is a role, not necessarily a status, in society. Divination always involves communication with a supernatural agency, and in texts on religion it may be discussed under "religious communication."

Magical or Spiritual Methods

All cultures have beliefs in five basic principles of magic, and any of these can be seen as underlying divination systems: (1) a concept of dynamic supernatural power that exists in varying degrees in all things, material or ethereal; (2) beliefs in natural forces, "engines" of nature separate from spiritual beings, energized by their own power and mechanically doing what they were programmed to do at their creation. The forces are conceptualized as supernatural agencies that operate independently of others but can be affected by them or by people using magic; (3) a coherent universe in which all things and events, past, present, and future, are stored and interconnected as if by invisible threads or pathways; (4) symbols—things or actions that stand in for and take on the qualities, especially the specific powers of other things or actions; and (5) principles of similarity and contact described by nineteenth century folklorist Sir James George Frazer in his classic discussions of sympathetic magic in the 1911 edition of *The Golden Bough:* things or actions that resemble or have been in direct contact or association with other things or actions have a special causal relationship with each other. Magic is believed to work by the activation of natural forces through the symbolic projection of power along links in the cosmic network.

Basic to all methods of divination is a formulation of the practitioner's intent, expressed in words—spoken, written, or thought. Words are powerful symbols that embody their own meaning; when spoken, they are activated and projected by the intent, the voice, and the breath of the speaker. Thoughts are similarly projected, although their power may be weaker than their spoken forms. Thus, the practitioner's intent may be projected through the ether to its target; or the intent may be directed at and embodied in some medium that becomes a vehicle to carry it to its supernatural destination. The meaning in words or thoughts is presumed to be "understood" by the agency or cosmic system being addressed. How the answers are received by the diviner varies greatly; the diviner may "hear" the answer or otherwise receive it sensorially; more commonly, the diviner will deduce the answer through culturally determined interpreta-

Predicting the future by "reading" signs in objects such as cards, bones, and tea leaves is a common form of divination across cultures. In this photo taken in London in 2003, a tarot reader provides his service. COURTESY OF KAREN CHRISTENSEN.

DIVINATION IN CENTRAL THAILAND

As is suggested by the etymological linkage between "fate" and "planet," much of the cognitive basis of the Divinatory System lies in astrology (*hooraasaad*). A villager's unique hour, day, date, month, and year of birth, and the [supposed] position of the planets and stars at that moment in time, are used by a divinatory doctor (*mau duu*) to determine the villager's horoscopic status. Various doctors use various formulae in calculating a horoscopic status, and the entire consultation process between doctor and client is often suffused with an air of mystic complexity [which serves to provide a potential excuse for the doctor—conscious or otherwise—in case his prediction fails to materialize]. Horoscopy does not, however, by any means exhaust the culture's repertory of divinatory techniques. Palmistry and numerology, for example, are also used, and a wide variety of omens (*laang*) are considered relevant to this or that type of consequence.

A villager's ritual behavior subsumable under the Divinatory System is often of a voluntary and ad hoc character, in the sense that if and when he feels anxiety he will seek the services of an appropriate divinatory doctor. In addition, there are various life-cycle events and ceremonies in connection with which he is culturally expected to seek such services whether he feels pronounced anxiety or not. Events such as top-knot cuttings, weddings, and a monk's leaving the yellow robes are precisely timed so as to be auspicious in terms of the individual's horoscopic status. This temporal aspect of divination is often associated with a spatial aspect. For example, when I decided to leave the monkhood, my horoscopically-derived instruction (roeg) not only prescribed that the resignation ceremony must occur on a certain day and at a certain hour, but also required that I depart from Wat Bang Chan in a certain auspicious direction.

In a very real sense, then, the Divinatory System locates the individual in time and space, and indicates to him likely paths to fulfillment within the complexities of these dimensions. Indeed, it is not unusual to hear divinatory doctors and other better-informed villagers using predestinational terms, such as "path of life" or "line of destiny" (*phrommalikhid*).

Source: Textor, Robert B. (1973).
Roster of the Gods; An Ethnography of Supernatural in a Thai Village. New Haven, CT: Human Relations Area Files, pp. 33–35.

tions—"readings"—of specific natural processes occurring either spontaneously or after human manipulation. An omen is a sign of supernatural portent revealed to the diviner through some unusual or unexpected event in nature. An oracle is any method of divination or vehicle of revealed information, including a specially gifted person.

Magical methods address the cosmic forces directly and may be distinguished from methods that invoke and address spirits. Unlike the forces of nature, spirits are generally conceptualized as willful and sentient beings, able to make decisions—including whether to obey human command. Anyone can learn and safely perform magic; but dealing with spirits involves risks and hence is the prerogative of priests and shamans, trained religious specialists who have learned methods of protecting themselves. Spirits are universally presumed to have knowledge that is hidden from people, and they can be persuaded to part with it. Requests for knowledge may be addressed to the Supreme Being or to the lesser specialized divinities, the gods; but in some areas, particularly Africa and Asia, people preferentially address their ancestors, the souls of departed lineal relatives who are regarded as members of the family. The supplication may be conveyed to ancestors through words spoken heavenward or to an earthly repository of the spirit or to a sacrificial animal or object whose soul or essence will carry the meaning to the spirit. The answer may come directly in words heard by the diviner or the client in a normal waking state or in sleep or in a ritually and perhaps drug-induced altered state of consciousness (ASC); or the spirit's answer may be revealed through some omen in nature or through a cultural device such as the biblical Urim and Thummim (sacred lots used in early times by the Hebrews, 1 Samuel 14:41–42).

Another premise underlying divination, particularly rituals to determine why something has happened, is that everything in the cosmos has a reason for happening; concepts of chance, randomness, or coincidence may be absent from people's thinking.

Scapulimancy and Ifa Divination

A classic example of magical divination is scapulimancy among the caribou-hunting Montagnais-Naskapi people of northern Labrador, as described by the anthropologist Frank G. Speck in the 1930s. Scapulimancy (reading patterns of cracks and marks in an animal shoulder blade) was used in many areas of the world and was a highly developed art in medieval Europe. Among the Montagnais-Naskapi it had various uses, among the most important of which was to guide hunters. Success in the hunt was critical to survival, especially in winter; but the territory was large, and the game might be anywhere. The diviner described a map of the territory on a caribou scapula, then asked the bone where its brothers were, and the patterns of cracks that appeared as it dried over a fire indicated where the hunters should go. This method illustrates classic principles of magic: the scapula was part of the actual animal hunted, thus magically connected to it.

A complicated system of divination directed at spirits is the Ifa system of the Yoruba people of Nigeria in Africa. Ifa is the Yoruba god of wisdom, commander of 256 lesser spirits called *"odù,"* among which all knowledge is divided in the form of long epic poems. Each *odù* is represented by a named combination of eight double or single marks, in two vertical rows of four each. The diviner, the *babalawo* (father of secrets), through a long apprenticeship, has memorized the entire literature and the corresponding marks. The first sixteen *odù* are senior and are represented by sixteen palm nuts, which the diviner passes quickly from one hand to the other, trying to transfer all the nuts. According to the success of his passes, he makes short marks with his fingertips in wood dust spread on a flat board in front of him—if two nuts remain after a pass, he makes one mark; if one nut remains, two marks; if none or more than two, no marks—until he has the signature of the particular *odú* in whose body of knowledge the answer to the problem resides. The Yoruba have a quicker—and less costly—method of Ifa divination in which a string of eight flat ovals is cast, and the signature of an *odù* appears immediately; but this is considered far less reliable because it is too quick and spirits, like people, can make mistakes. Similar systems operate elsewhere in West Africa and the Caribbean.

Other Types of Divination

Forms of divination rituals vary tremendously around the world and are known by a variety of labels. Some types can be defined. Strictly mechanical types, for which the supplicant needs no special innate ability, include varieties of "lots": blindly drawing straws or marked bits of paper or other objects from piles of many; casting or throwing flat-sided or oblong objects and reading the way they fall; reading the patterns of tea leaves at the bottom of a cup; dealing cards, and so forth. In west Africa casting the four valves of a kola nut is a method commonly used, addressed either to the cosmic forces or to spirits. There are five possible combinations, each named and meaningful. Other mechanical types include observing the behavior of objects floating in water or other liquids, of oil dropped onto water, or of objects suspended by strings, often over or in some source of power such as sacred places or scripts; and noting the direction spinning objects indicate when they stop.

Some mechanical forms of divination require a period of study to learn meanings of variations on observed behaviors. Many Western diviners claim knowledge of great divination powers in Tarot cards. Haruspication entails observation of natural things, from *haruspices*, ancient Etruscan specialists who examined the entrails of sacrificial animals to determine the gods' disposition and also interpreted natural phenomena, especially thunder and lightning, and prescribed remedies for the problems they detected. Just as doctors diagnose disease through interpretation of superficial symptoms in the patient, many people believe that features of certain parts of one's body may mystically reveal broader information about one's current and future health and general fortune to a trained specialist, such as in palmistry and iridology (diagnosis by patterns in the iris of one's eye).

Numerology (the study of the occult significance of numbers) and hermetic methods require esoteric knowledge of numbers and formulas—the name is derived from Hermes Trismegistus, regarded in medieval Europe as the Greek variant of the Egyptian Thoth, god of wisdom and writing. The ancient Chinese I Ching, a complicated system of lots and geometric figures whose configurations reveal the most intimate interconnections of the cosmos, requires lengthy study, as does astrology, an ancient method of divination depending on the belief that planetary and celestial objects and their apparent movements directly affect events on Earth. Persons skilled at such esoteric methods can exercise great power, especially in semiliterate society, because their wisdom is impossible to challenge by the unlettered. This kind of wisdom is hence awesome and potentially dangerous. A meaning of the word *wise,* as in the Latin word *magus,* was "having occult knowledge"; this is the meaning in the Bible: the Lord "frustrates the omens of liars and makes fools of diviners; … turns back the wise, and makes their knowledge foolish" (Isaiah 44:25, NRSV). In the Judaic scriptures such enterprises were viewed as vain and dangerous deviations from the absolutism of God's word; divination and prophecy, especially by omens or dreams, were capital offenses, as declared in Deuteronomy 13:1–5; compare such acts to divinely sanctioned divination by lots, the Urim and Thummim. Clearly, also, such easily corruptible power as could come to the diviner was detrimental to the functioning of egalitarian society.

Various forms of divination are used to identify persons guilty of some offense, especially a supernatural offense such as taboo violation or witchcraft. Trials by some sort of ordeal, from a test of physical strength, pain, or endurance, to the ingestion of poison, may be conducted under the presumption that evil, which is contrary to nature, will thus be revealed or that the innocent will have supernatural help or protection. In some instances both the accuser and the accused undergo the trial. A case well known in the social sciences is that of the Azande of central Africa, who have different categories of divination, distinguished by complexity (and cost), objectivity, and reliability. The rubbing-board oracle is a smooth piece of wood over which another piece of wood, lubricated with special fluids, is rubbed back and forth while names or questions with yes/no answers are spoken. The answers are indicated as the top piece of wood sticks or slides easily. To consult the termite oracle, considered more reliable because it is completely natural, in the evening a person inserts into a termite mound two sticks cut from different trees; the answer is revealed in the morning by how the termites have eaten either stick. Most reliable, and most expensive, is the poison oracle. A strychnine-based poison is prepared from plant extract, a question is presented to it, and it is forced down the throat of a chick, whose survival or death determines the answer.

Another natural method is employed by the Dogon people of Mali in Africa: A series of symbolic designs is drawn in sand between a fox's hole and some bait; in the morning the pattern of the fox's tracks is examined. Some methods involve beliefs in powers that flow in all things and the Earth itself, such as the Chinese concept of *qi* (chi) or the British "leylines"; detecting the directions and intensity of such powers can aid in diagnosis of some problem, as in the Chinese and New Age geomantic system of *feng shui* (the ancient science of balancing the elements within the environment).

Names for some forms of divination end in "-mancy," deriving from the Greek and Latin word *mantia* (divination) from the Latin verb *manere* (to handle), for example, *chiromancy* (palm reading), *geomancy* (divining by lines or figures or geographic features), *necromancy* (consulting spirits of the dead), *oneiromancy* (interpreting dreams), *onomancy* (divining by the letters of a name), and *scapulimancy*.

Some people distinguish between divination and prophecy, divination being narrow and specific in scope and prophecy being much broader, indeed, cosmic in scope. However, prophets really are supernaturally gifted diviners, their insight believed to come directly from some divine source, often revealed in a dream or vision. Some forms of divination are believed dependent upon some special "gift," an innate sensory ability that may be inborn or acquired. Shamans have the capacity of ecstasy, a specific altered state of consciousness achieved by projecting their souls out of their bodies into the spirit world. There the shaman's soul negotiates with the appropriate spirit for the desired information. Such negotiation may require physical struggle. A form of ASC that is probably universal is possession, in which a spirit enters a person's body and reveals secret knowledge through him or her. A spirit medium is a person whose body is a vehicle for such a spirit, a "channel" in New Age parlance, such as the famous Oracle at Delphi in Greece, or the woman of Endor, who raised the spirit of Samuel for the disguised King Saul (1 Samuel 28). Clairvoyant or clairaudient persons claim to be "sensitive" to messages from the spirit world. The stereotypical Western "fortune teller" receives visions by gazing intently at a crystal ball; crystals, believed to house concentrated cosmic power, have long been used in magic. Other methods, such as dowsing for ore or water and consulting the Ouija board, involve both mechanical and sensory skills.

Explanations

Most social and psychological explanations of divination are based in functions that the process is seen to serve to particular people in particular situations. Scholars agree that people regard the world as vast and indifferent and potentially chaotic and that divination serves the important social function of giving individuals a sense of control and certitude. Anthropologist Omar K. Moore, in his classic interpretation of Naskapi scapulimancy, proposed also that divination serves to randomize social decision making; and the sociologist George K. Park added that divination can vary according to specific social context but that in general divination removes the burden of a critical decision from the human level, much like flipping a coin. Divination as personal communication with gods, spirits, or the forces of the cosmos can be seen to serve the same comforting functions that have been suggested for other religious phenomena.

Phillips Stevens Jr.

See also Azande; Magic; Shamanism; Sorcery; Yoruba

Further Reading

Bascom, W. R. (1969). *Ifa divination: Communication between gods and men in west Africa*. Bloomington: Indiana University Press.

Bascom, W. R. (1980). *Sixteen cowries: Yoruba divination from Africa to the New World*. Bloomington: Indiana University Press.

Burnett, C. (1996). *Magic and divination in the Middle Ages: Texts and techniques in the Islamic and Christian worlds*. Aldershot, UK: Variorum.

Evans-Pritchard, E. E. (1937). *Witchcraft, oracles and magic among the Azande*. London: Oxford University Press.

Frazer, J. G. (1911–1915). *The golden bough: Vol. 1. The magic art and the evolution of kings* (3rd ed.) London: Macmillan.

Moore, O. K. (1957). Divination: A new perspective. *American Anthropologist*, 59(1), 69–74.

Park, G. K. (1963). Divination and its social contexts. *Journal of the Royal Anthropological Institute*, 93(2), 195–209.

Peck, P. (Ed.). (1991). *African divination systems: Ways of knowing*. Bloomington: Indiana University Press.

E

Easter

Although Christmas, celebrating the birth of Jesus Christ, is the more popular holiday, Easter, celebrating the resurrection of Jesus Christ, is the more central holiday of Christianity. Without the belief in the resurrection, as Saint Paul noted, there would be no Christianity. In Latin and Greek Easter is called Pascha; it is the oldest Christian observance, aside from the Sabbath. In fact, the Christian Sabbath very early on came to be regarded as a weekly commemoration of the resurrection.

The English term Easter for Pascha probably came from the name for the Anglo-Saxon goddess of spring, according to the Venerable Bede, an Anglo-Saxon eighth-century priest. It is another example of the manner in which Christianity borrowed and built on traditional feasts for the celebration of its own feasts. Certainly the secular side of Easter has the aura of fertility rites, with the Easter bunny providing a blatant example.

Controversies

One of the major historical controversies involving Easter among the faithful has been the date of the feast. There is no record of the actual date on which the crucifixion of Jesus took place. Therefore, there is no acceptable date for the resurrection. There are theological arguments regarding the actual date of the first Easter, the date on which they say Jesus rose from the dead. Most theologians argue that if Jesus were indeed crucified on a Friday, then Passover would have fallen on a Thursday as the Synoptic Gospels have it. Both 30 and 33 CE had Passover on a Thursday.

There are many theologians who accept a date of Friday, 7 April, in the year 30 CE as the correct date of the crucifixion. But there are some problems with the acceptance of this date. It contradicts the Gospel of John, which give a three-year period to the public ministry of Jesus. Those who support this early date for the crucifixion argue that the Synoptic Gospels of Matthew, Mark, and Luke state a one-year period of ministry.

Those theologians who oppose the early date prefer 3 April, in the year 33 CE. But this date also causes problems. Saul, later Saint Paul, does not seem to have enough time to persecute Christians. It leaves little time for his persecution, conversion, and three-year absence from Palestine. There is also the question of when Paul would have had time for his work in Jerusalem.

In the West, Christians celebrate Easter on the first Sunday after the first full moon of spring. This was the compromise settled upon by the eighth century. The Eastern Church, however, uses a slightly different calculation. Thus, the dates of Easter in the East and West rarely coincide. There has been some talk of fixing the date of Easter as the second Sunday in April but so far the various branches of Christianity have reached no agreement.

The Centrality of Easter

The feast of Easter is so important that there is preparation before and after to emphasize its importance. There is Lent, with its forty days of fasting, and the

EASTER IN A SERBIAN VILLAGE

As early as two or three o'clock in the morning, villagers arise on Easter Sunday, pack a breakfast in their carrying sacks or wicker baskets, and set out over the dark lanes for the church. Upon entering church, each person kisses the icon and places an offering of hyacinths and other spring flowers on the side. Soon the little church is filled to overflowing with a capacity congregation that will not occur again until the following year. Individual candles are lighted from a great taper on the altar, and the villagers, bearing their flickering lights, form a procession following the priest outside the church and moving three times around it. Communion is given when they return inside, and at sunrise the service is over. People step out into the early morning sunshine joyously calling, "Hristos vaskrese!" (Christ is risen!) and receiving the reply, Vaistinu vaskrese!" (Indeed He is risen!). The fast is broken by a picnic in the yard, and men press one another to sample their best rakija and wine. Children and adults alike enjoy the game of tapping Easter eggs, colored with homemade onionskin and berry dyes, and collecting those they have won by cracking them in the contest.

***Source*: Halpern, Joel M. *A Serbian Village.* (1958). New York: Columbia University Press, p. 241.**

fifty-day Easter season ending with Pentecost, the celebration of the coming of the Holy Spirit. For Christians, Easter replaced Passover and signifies their redemption and the forgiveness of sins.

The original Sunday vigil service, the first celebration of Easter by Christians, was comprised of psalms and Scripture reading, and provided a pattern for the Easter vigil service. The vigil is kept in both Eastern and Western Churches. The vigil in the Roman Church has the blessing of the new fire, lighting of the Paschal candle, lesson, blessing of the baptismal font, baptisms, and finally the Easter Mass. The vigil is traceable to the third century.

In the early church baptism was performed only once a year, at Easter. The Lenten period was one of preparation of catechumens. They were instructed in the tenets of the Christian faith. At the Easter vigil, the priests baptized the catechumens. Easter was thus a period in which people died to their sins and were resurrected with Jesus Christ. The symbolism is still found in the Easter services of various Christian churches.

Eastern Orthodox and Russian Orthodox churches begin their vigil services with a procession, which symbolizes a search for the body of Christ. Eventually, there is the cry, "Christ is risen!" The priests display the Easter Eucharist. Candles and lamps now provide light where there was no light when the procession started. This light symbolizes Christ as the light of the world.

Lent

Lent as a forty-day period of fasting has a long history in the church, as does the exclusion of Sunday in the Western Church and Saturdays and Sundays in the Eastern Churches. Beginning in the late 400s, Lent begins on Ash Wednesday, the Wednesday before the first Sunday in Lent. In the early days of the church, great sinners wore sackcloth and sprinkled themselves with ashes as a sign of repentance and in hope of being restored to the church at Easter. At Rome, from the late fifth century, the fast began on Wednesday before the first Sunday in Lent. By the ninth century public penance was dying out and the tradition of placing ashes on the foreheads of all the faithful began. It is a reminder of the brevity of life and the need for penance.

Holy Week is the last week of Lent. Fittingly, the church of Jerusalem would organize strikingly dramatic ceremonies at various sites connected with the passion of Jesus. Many of these ceremonies spread rapidly to other places. The Palm Sunday procession and the Good Friday veneration of the cross are two examples of these ceremonies.

Holy Thursday marks the institution of the Eucharist at the Last Supper, Christ's final meal with his apostles before his death. The washing of the feet is now a common part of the ceremony, depicting the humility of Jesus and his mission of service. Good Friday commemorates the crucifixion of Jesus and his redemption of sinners. The entire week serves to emphasize the significance of Easter Sunday itself.

Pre-Christian Origins of Easter

Most Mediterranean cultures celebrated the spring equinox. Common to all of these celebrations was the idea of fertility. Cybele, the Phrygian fertility goddess, for example, had a consort named Attis who was believed to have been born via a virgin birth. Attis died each year and was resurrected between 22 and 25 March. Attis, who is also Orpheus, was a center of the influential Cybelene mystery cult focused on Vatican Hill in Rome. Interestingly, Christians and devotees of Attis celebrated their holidays on the same day and argued bitterly over which was the imitation and which the prototype. Another pre-Christian influence on Easter was the record of the life of Krishna. Krishna is the second person in the Hindu trinity. Christians countered that the devil had created false trinities to confuse people.

Popular Celebrations

Like Christmas, Easter has managed to attract a number of popular customs to itself. The Easter bunny that distributes Easter eggs to young children is well known. It was German immigrants who brought the Easter bunny to America. There are also Easter chocolate animals, Easter eggs colored by the family, the Easter ham or lamb, family events, and the Easter bonnet worn to the Easter service. Many Christians who have not been to a religious service since Christmas will troop to their churches for Easter services.

The Easter egg predates the Christian celebration of Easter. The eggs are a symbol of rebirth. For Christians it was an easy step to take the Egyptian, Greek, Roman, and almost universal symbol of eggs as a sign of life and adapt it as a sign of the risen Christ. Before people began painting eggs, they wrapped them in gold foil, put the wrapped eggs in leaves and boiled them. The eggs then took on a gold color. The same effect was reached using flowers, and the color of these flower petals would be transferred to the eggs. It is a short step to the modern Easter basket with colored eggs and chocolate animals.

Even the hot cross bun has a pre-Christian origin. The word "bun" comes from the Saxon word "boun" meaning sacred ox. An ox was sacrificed to the Mother Goddess Eastre. Its horns were represented on the ritual bread for Eastre's feast. Later devotees decorated the bread with a symmetrical cross representing the moon. The buns were taken by Christians who used them to remind people during the Lenten season of the crucifixion of Jesus.

Sunrise services for Easter have their origin in the sun worship of pre-Christians. Worshippers of Baal would gaze at the rising sun to gain his favor. The practice came into Judaism of early morning services and the prophet Ezekiel remarks on it.

In England and Germany children roll eggs down a hill on Easter mornings. The tradition is traced to imitating the rolling away of the stone that protected the cave in which Jesus was placed. The custom came to the United States and Dolly Madison, James Madison's wife, organized the first White House egg roll. According to Dolly Madison, Egyptian children used to roll eggs against the pyramids. Therefore, she invited children to come to the Capitol and roll eggs down its hilly lawn. The Civil War interrupted this practice but it was resumed after the war. The egg rolling moved to the White House in 1880 to preserve the Capitol lawn. Only war has interrupted the custom. Easter Monday, the day of the egg roll, is the only time tourists are still allowed to wander over the White House lawn.

The Easter parade derives from the American custom of buying new clothes and walking around their towns after church attendance. There are a number of these parades, the most famous of which is that of New York's Fifth Avenue.

These and other traditions are reminders of the fertility symbols associated with the old pre-Christian feasts. The bright colors of the Easter eggs represent the sunlight of spring, whose return after a long winter is most welcome. These eggs are frequently used in egg rolling contests or given as gifts to friends.

In addition, to "pagan" rituals there is a fair share of Jewish rituals associated with Passover. The very word Pascha derives from the Hebrew term for Passover, an important feast in the Jewish calendar. Passover is a reminder of the flight of the Israelites from Egyptian slavery. Many early Christians regarded Easter as a new aspect of Passover, indeed as a perfection or completion of it. The Messiah, in their view, was Jesus. The prophecies foretelling his coming were completed in his arrival. For many years, Christians celebrated Easter around the time of the Passover, just as the first Easter had occurred.

Frank A. Salamone

Further Reading

Borg, M. J. (Ed.). (1997). *Jesus at 2000*. Boulder, CO: Westview Press.

Butler, J., & Stout, H. S. (1998). *Religion in American history: A reader.* New York: Oxford University Press.

Cheal, D. J. (1987). The private and the public: The linkage role of religion revisited. *Review of Religious Research, 28*(3), 209–223.

Colgrave, B., & Mynors, R. A. B. (Eds.). (1969). *Bede's ecclesiastical history of the English people*. Oxford, UK: Clarendon Press.

Davis, C. F. (1999). *The evidential force of religious experience*. Oxford, UK: Oxford University Press.

Davis, S. T., Kendall, D., & O'Collins, G. (1998). *The resurrection: An interdisciplinary symposium on the resurrection of Jesus*. Oxford, UK: Oxford University Press.

Glazier, S. D. (Ed.). (1999). *Anthropology of religion: A handbook*. Westport, CT: Praeger.

Heinze, R. (Ed.). (2000). *The nature and function of rituals: Fire from heaven*. Westport, CT: Bergin & Garvey.

Hutton, R. (1994). *The rise and fall of merry England: The ritual year, 1400–1700*. Oxford, UK: Oxford University Press.

Hutton, R. B. (1996). *Stations of the sun: A history of the ritual year in Britain*. Oxford, UK: Oxford University Press.

James, E. O. (1963). *Seasonal feasts and festivals*. New York: Barnes & Noble.

Lippy, C. H. (1994). *Being religious, American style: A history of popular religiosity in the United States*. Westport, CT: Praeger.

Maus, C. P. (1938). *Christ and the fine arts: An anthology of pictures, poetry, music, and stories centering in the life of Christ*. New York & London: Harper & Brothers.

Pannenberg, W. (1977). *Jesus, God, and man* (L. L. Wilkins & D. A. Priebe, Trans.). Philadelphia: Westminster Press.

Rahner, H. S. J. (1971). *Greek myths and Christian mystery*. New York: Biblo and Tannen.

Rust, E.G., (1996). *The music and dance of the world's religions: A comprehensive, annotated bibliography of materials in the English language*. Westport, OH: Greenwood Press.

The Venerable Bede. Sherley-Price, L. (Trans.) (1955). *A history of the English church and people*. Harmondsworth, UK: Penguin Books.

Spicer, D. G. (1958). *Festivals of western Europe*. New York: H. W. Wilson Co.

Ecstatic Worship

Ecstasy derives from the Greek term *ekstasts*, meaning "to be outside of oneself." The term describes a state of mind characterized by loss of bodily awareness and contact with reality, insensibility to fire and sharp objects, intense excitement, and loss of self-control. Ecstasy curbs bodily functions. It is often associated with a feeling of being under the control of an outside force or of being possessed by a supernatural being or divine power. In complete ecstasy a person is guided only by emotion. The term may also refer to lesser emotional experiences stemming from serious events or extreme stress. Various kinds of ecstasy are described in the literature:

Motoric ecstasy is induced by bodily movement and dancing, and may occur suddenly and disappear after a short period. After a period of extreme activity the ecstatic experience may end in fainting.

Mystical ecstasy is not induced intentionally, but may occur suddenly in the context of the adoration of a supernatural being or after prolonged meditation and purification. This ecstasy is a personal experience, sometimes taking place in a lonely and quiet place. It is frequently associated with visions, and may result in prophesies or the utterance of messages supposed to derive from supernatural sources. Ecstatic experiences of mystics and saints are of this type.

Toxic ecstasy is provoked by psychedelic drugs. Another type of ecstasy is based on psychic automatisms or trance-like states, objectifying the contents of the mind, and includes phenomena such as automatic writing and revelations (messages form the supernatural world). Hypnosis may trigger such experiences. Divination practices are often associated with these phenomena.

Religion and Trance-like Ecstasy

As demonstrated by Bourguignon (1973, 1976) and Goodman (1988), ecstatic behavior is important in religious rituals in cultures around the world—among gatherers, hunters, agrarians, pastoralists, and more advanced societies. Bourguignon found religious trance in about 90 percent of the ethnic groups studied from all continents.

Religious trance, including daydreaming, lucid dreaming, and meditative states, is an altered state of consciousness that may be induced by hypnosis. According to Rouget (1985), ecstasy and trance constitute the opposite poles of a continuum, linked by an uninterrupted series of possible intermediary stages. Ecstasy, according to this author, is characterized by immobility, silence, solitude, sensory deprivation, and hallucinations, while trance is described in terms of movement, crisis, sensory over-stimulation, amnesia, and lack of hallucinations.

Various degrees of trance are described in the ethnographic literature. For a long time trance behavior was considered abnormal or insane, but culturally informed study of institutionalized rituals leading to religious trance from around the world has debunked this view. Trance can be induced voluntarily in religious communities, and the faithful learn how to react to certain stimuli in specific ways.

Trance comprises institutionalized, culturally patterned altered states of consciousness. Methods used to induce this include singing, drumming, hand clapping, rattling, reciting of special formulas, gazing at candles, spinning on one's axis, smelling incense, or hyperventilation. Rouget (1985) studied the importance of music to inducing trance in many cultures, finding that certain rhythms or songs may create a conducive emotional climate for the adept. Many societies use psychedelic drugs for this purpose, and such drugs were already in use in Paleolithic times. According to Goodman (1988), these stimuli by themselves do not produce the shift from one state of consciousness to another; rather the expectation that this will happen leads to the ecstasy. Imaginatively, the entranced identifies with the spirit that will possess him or her. After a prolonged period of trance, the person—responding to other stimuli—wakes up, often claiming complete amnesia. The ability to experience altered states of consciousness is a psycho-biological capacity of the human species, but though anybody may become entranced, the socio-cultural context is important.

Psychological and Biological Explanations

The medical anthropologist Lex (1979) describes the bodily changes that occur during ritualistic altered states of consciousness. Entranced people perspire, tremble, and may fall to the ground, and their blood pressure decreases while their heart rate increases. One can observe a drop in stressors, such as adrenaline and cortisol, and EEG tracings reveal brain activity different from that of normal, waking adults. Those in religious trances manifest changes in emotional expression, hyper-suggestibility, modification of central-nervous-system function, intense excitation, altered body images, perceptual distortions, feelings of rejuvenation, and a disturbed time sense. Each of these characteristics may be of greater or lesser significance, depending on the cultural context in which they appear. Those experienced at entering trance can prolong the altered state of mind for a long time.

The context of ecstatic behavior depends on what is expected in a given religious community. Communal trance events take place when an entire group escapes from reality, via rituals that often culminate in dances and emotional expression. Upon waking up, the entranced report positive feelings of joy and happiness; they feel purified and in better health. Others may feel extremely tired or even faint. In some cultures, before waking up completely, the entranced remains in a semi-trance characterized by childish behavior. In West Africa and among African Americans this state is called WERE o ERE.

The first experience of ecstasy may be frightening, so initiation should be gradual initiated for the trance experience to be positive. In case of possession trances, the role of the spirit has to be learned. Ritual trance is culturally patterned according to religious and social traditions and is an institutionalized form of sacred altered consciousness.

Trance, Possession Trance, and Non-trance Possession

Bourguignon (1977) distinguishes between *trance* and *possession trance*. The later refers to the impersonation of spirits and the discontinuity of personal identity, while trance proper is considered to be an individual unpatterned state of consciousness. Historical and ecological factors and the degree of societal complexity are important in shaping ecstatic behavior. The entranced may play an otherwise unavailable role: suddenly they become the center of attention in their congregations. Lewis (1966) describes spirit-possession cults in relation to deprivation and marginalization. In rituals of spirit possession, women and other powerless groups can exert mystical pressure on superiors, when no other sanctions are available. Douglas (1970) believes that trance is a form of dissociation welcomed when society is weakly structured. The inarticulateness of social organization in itself gains symbolic expression in bodily dissociation.

Some religious communities interpret trance behavior as possession by evil spirits that have to be exorcized, as these spirits constitute a threat to the

ECSTATIC WORSHIP IN ETHIOPIA

The following text describes in much detail the ecstatic worship that is a core feature of the Zar healing cult of the Amhara of Ethiopia.

In the corners, more types of incense were burning than before. In addition to "etan" (frankincense), the domestic Ethiopian "bukbuka" was sending up clouds of perfumed smoke. Leaves of "wogart," believed pleasing to the zar that causes headaches and neuralgic pains, were occasionally placed on the clay incense burners. From time to time, some imported pebbles of yellow sulfur ("kabre" or "din") sent up acrid smoke. But the sweet odor of most types of incense predominated most of the time.

About 8:30, the drummer brought his heavy drum down from beneath the solioly built roof, and began to drum slowly, rythmically, still subdued. The curtain was lowered, but the shadow of Lady Salamtew behind it could still be vaguely seen. Suddenly raucous grunts began to be heard from behind the curtain, emanating from Woyzaro Salamtew. This meant that her first major zar had arrived, and was beginning to descend into her, performing the magical coitus. Her joyshouts became louder, higher pitched, turning to shrieks, quicker and quicker. She was beginning to perform the "gurri" victory dance of the zar who had conquered her.

Immediately the women devotees began to handclap rythmically, gradually quickening their tempo, in time to the twisting and turning of Lady Salamtew's body. The twisting began like an embrace, with her head thrown back, rotating movements of the chest, followed by a rythmic forward bump of belly and hips. Her ecstatic shrieks varied from pain to exultation (like the "ellel" of women in the Coptic church service). Encouraging shouts came from individual women in the audience, and some raised their holiday-reddened palms in prayerful joy. As the climax approached, the jerky twisting of Lady Salamtew's body gradually changed to smoother movements of the limbs. She was now well in tune with her zar, and he was comfortable within her. The excitement in the audience changed to warm and glowing emotion at the same time. Then Lady Salamtew emitted a loud scream, and dropped in a heap. The drum stopped abruptly. There was a sudden hush in the audience. The strong sweet odor of generously burned incense pervaded the consciousness and its smoke leisurely curled upward.

It was only a matter of minutes before Lady Salamtew recovered. Her brother pulled the curtain to one side. Her eyes were bright with curiosity as she glanced about the house as if she had just arrived. She had lost her absent-minded appearance, for now the zar acted and spoke through her. Suddenly she appeared to notice the foreigner for the first time, smiled and waved a friendly greeting. Her voice was still husky, but warm, as she called out "how are you" in understandable Amharic, rather than her esoteric "zar language"; this was a courtesy, though she used the female familiar gender (the zar often uses the inverted genders in address). She further inquired whether the foreigner was sitting in comfort, and how his health was today (hinting at the "ailments" he had used as a pretext). Then she ordered the handmaidens to offer the foreigner talla (barley beer), and coffee, on one of the zar coffee trays.

She then proceeded to greet the individual zar doctors and devotees as if she had been absent a long time. Each rose and bowed deeply to her. Barley beer was now passed around freely, while coffee beans were being roasted and crushed, in preparation for the next intermission.

Refreshed and heartened, the male zar doctor serving as poet now began to chant the hymns he had composed in honor of "aweliya" the chief male zar of Lady Salamtew. The rythm was as formal as the hymns chanted by the dabtara in the Coptic Abyssinian church, but contained Arabic loanwords borrowed from the traders vernacular. The audience quickly leaned the response and accompanied the responsive chant with rythmic handclapping....

Source: Messing, Simon D. *The Highland-Plateau Amhara of Ethiopia.* (1957) Doctoral dissertation, University of Pennsylvania. pp. 635–637.

individual and the community. In other cases, the possessing entities are believed to be good spirits to be treated with special consideration, so as to induce them to help the faithful. It is supposed that the spirits completely possess the body of the entranced whose own soul is temporarily absent: the medium is "mounted" by the spirit. The spiritual entity speaks through his or her mouth, giving advice or solving the problems of the faithful. Sacrifices are offered to the spirit, especially when healing or consolation is required.

Non-trance possession is considered to be provoked by evil forces that take possession of an innocent human being. Such possession can be permanent, so the evil forces must be exorcized (even the Catholic Church has rituals for this). However, many cases of so-called possession have pathological causes and should be treated by psychiatrists.

Examples

In the history of religion, many founders of religious groups claimed to have received divine guidance in order to legitimize their teachings. In pre-Christian times, the Pythia of Delphi, who claimed to receive messages from Apollo, was the most famous oracle of the Mediterranean world. Oracle practices are still common in Africa and Asia, where they persist in the hands of diviners who use a great variety of techniques.

Ecstasy plays an important role in Sufism, an Islamic spiritual movement that originated in the ninth century. A dervish—one kind of Sufi devotee—experiences unification with Allah when whirling for extended periods under the guidance of a master.

Ecstatic behavior is common in the religious practices of African societies south of the Sahara. Mediums are initiated into the cult of a particular divinity, who, on certain ceremonial occasions, takes possession of the faithful and speaks from their mouths. In other ethnic groups, the spirits of dead ancestors possess mediums to offer advice and cure the sick. Trance states are facilitated with singing, drumming, hand-clapping, bodily movement, dancing, and incantations. As it is believed that the soul of the entranced leaves the body while the spirit is present, they are not held responsible for their acts and do not remember what happened during trances.

In African-American cults, religious ecstasy and spirit possession are very common and follow the pattern of African practices. In the Cuban Santeria and Brazilian Candomblé a large group of initiated members often fall into trance at the same time. In Haiti, often a number of ecstatic dancers simultaneously perform the Voodoo rituals. In African-American religions, the initiation ceremonies or initial possession experiences are often of the nature of a cure for mental afflictions. In these cults, ecstatic religion is offered as therapy for the initiated. Under the guidance of a leader, what could be regarded as an involuntary possession illness develops into a controlled religious exercise (Lewis 1971).

Among hunters and gatherers, religious trance is clearly observable, especially during healing ceremonies. The medicine man or shaman goes into trance to contact the spirits of nature or of the dead, who help him to solve his clients' or patients' problems. North American Indian shamans enter religious trances to go on a spirit journey to the sky where their spirit helpers reside. South American shamans induce trance by smoking tobacco or drinking or sniffing hallucinogenic substances, such as *ebena*. Mexican shamans use hallucinogenic mushrooms (peyote) for the same purpose. Chilenian Mapuche shamans (Machi) are women who inherit their protective spirits matrilineally. When possessed by a familiar spirit, her own soul wanders and may be captured by witches who use it in their evil deeds. It is important to note that while African and African-American mediums are possessed by spirits who manifest themselves in their bodies, Amerindian shamans go on spiritual voyages to consult familiar spirits who live in the sky or secluded places.

Possession cults are also reported from China, Japan, and India in the context of Buddhism, Shintoism, and Hinduism, respectively. In these cultures it is often ancestor spirits that manifest themselves in the mediums.

In Pentecostal churches, "baptism by the Holy Spirit" can be interpreted as a ritual trance that proves that the believer is converted to the new faith. According to Goodman (1972), this unique personal experience of the divine power in one's body changes one's attitudes towards fellow men and the universe. It is legitimized by belief in the divine origin of the glossolalia, or speaking in tongues (the involuntary utterance of apparently meaningless phrases and syllables), that accompanies this baptism. This altered state of consciousness is provoked by suggestion, autosuggestion, rhythmic music, and body movement. The believer temporarily represses personal problems and henceforth considers him or herself to be a true member of the congregation. While baptism by the Holy Spirit is usually only experienced once in a lifetime, glossolalia is frequently practiced by pastors and the faithful during ordinary religious services. Many, seeking new ways to express their feelings in a religious context, have been attracted to Pentecostalism and it emotion-laden rituals.

The charismatic movements of other Christian churches are home to similar concepts and practices. In this context Christian enthusiasm is closely related to spirituality and is a product of an inherent human tendency.

In New Age groups, adherents search for illumination, using mind-altering techniques, drugs, and meditation to reach a state of ecstasy, interpreted sometimes as unification with the universe. Various New Age groups differ in their rituals and belief systems, but ecstatic experiences are sought by most of them. The New Age movement is becoming very commercialized, and ecstatic cults of this kind in modern Europe and the United States offer pseudo-religious rites in workshops, organized by so-called shamans, magicians, or parapsychologists. Followers of these cults aim to abandon reality by achieving a consciousness in which the reaction of the mind to external stimuli is inhibited or altered. The self-styled cult leaders teach their disciples techniques for this purpose and the roles they are expected to play in the congregation.

Final Considerations

The metaphysical meaning of trance states and ecstasy has been described by many authors of diverse backgrounds. According to Lewis (1971) possession trance is a psychodrama, an escape from harsh reality. Shamanism may contribute to mental health by stabilizing the incidence of nervous disorders. Possession trance indicates that the spirits are mastered by humans, or that God is not only with people, but in people. Weber (1963) claims that ecstasy is characteristic of the formative stages of religion, before behavior becomes routine. This explains why in modern Christianity, with the exception of charismatic groups, trance and ecstasy are rarely observed, while these phenomena are common in African, Amerindian, and Asian religions. Bourguignon (1978) regards possession-trance cults as expressions of anxiety. The great success of Pentecostalism today could be explained by the fact that in a time of crisis people search for religious experience that provides a profound emotional catharsis and a commitment reaching deep into the unconscious.

Angelina Pollak-Eltz

See also Possession and Trance

Further Reading

Bourguignon, E. (Ed.). (1973). *Religion, altered states of consciousness and social change*. Columbus: Ohio State University Press.

Bourguignon, E. (Ed.). (1978). *Possession*. San Francisco: Chandler and Sharp.

Douglas, M. (1962). *Purity and danger*. New York: Praeger.

Eliade, M. (1964). *Shamanism*. Princeton, NJ: Princeton University Press.

Fuest, P. (Ed.). (1972). *Flesh of the Gods*. New York: Praeger.

Goodman, F. (1972). *Speaking in tongues*. Chicago: Chicago University Press.

Goodman, F. (1988). *Ecstasy, ritual and alternate reality*. Bloomington: Indiana University Press.

Lewis, I. M. (1971). *Ecstatic religion*. Baltimore: Penguin.

Lex, B. (1979). The neurology of ritual trance. In E.D. d'Anggili, C.D. Laughlin, Jr.; J. McManus, & T. Burns (Eds.), *The spectrum of rituals: A biogenetic structural analysis*. New York: Columbia University Press.

Pollak-Eltz, A. (1994). *Religiones afroamericanas—hoy*. Planeta. Caracas, Venezuela: Universidad Santa Rosa de Lima.

Pollak-Eltz, A. (2002). *Estudio antropologico del Pentecostalismo en Venezuela*. Caracas, Venezuela: Universidad Santa Rosa de Lima.

Rouget, G. (1985). *Music and Trance*. Chicago: University of Chicago Press.

Weber, M. (1963). *The sociology of religion*. Boston: Beacon Press.

Epiphany

The Epiphany is one of the oldest and most important feasts in the Christian calendar. Its name derives from the Greek *epiphaneia*, which means "manifestation," and it celebrates the manifestation of Christ's divinity. The celebration of divine manifestation is neither original nor exclusive to Christianity; the Greeks, for instance, referred to Zeus alternately as Epiphanes and held celebrations called epiphanies in honor of his apparent divine nature. The Christian notion of divine manifestation centers on a number of distinct events in the life of Christ; specifically, the nativity, the visit of the magi, his baptism, and the miracle at the wedding of Cana. While each of these events was the focus of the Epiphany celebration early in its history, the feast came to be associated in the East fundamentally with Christ's baptism and in the West with the visit of the magi.

Epiphany is celebrated on 6 January. The date is significant for a number of important reasons. Initially in the East, the feast commemorated both the nativity and Christ's baptism. It was thought to correspond to the winter solstice and so drew on non-Christian, i.e., Egyptian, rituals of celebrating the lengthening of days. The origin of the Christian celebration dates roughly to the third century in Egypt. The Orthodox Church refers to the day as Theophany, a commemoration of Christ's baptism as the most thorough manifestation of God incarnate. In the West, the nativity celebration developed first. Early Western Christians began to celebrate the nativity on 25 December, a day that marked the occasion for the Roman festival of the sun. As Christ's birth was seen as the delivery of the "light of the world," it was made to correspond with the Roman feast. It was not until the fourth century that most Eastern sects adopted the Roman liturgical calendar and distinguished between the nativity and the Epiphany, marking separate feasts for Christ's birth and the manifestation of his divinity. It is also evident that, during the fourth century, the Western Church recognized the Epiphany as a separate feast. Cyril Martindale notes that "about the time of the diffusion of the December celebration in the East, the West took up the Oriental January feast, retaining all of its chief characteristics, though attaching overwhelming importance to the apparition of the Magi" (Martindale 2003, 4). Certain Coptic sects continued through the fifth century to celebrate the two feasts simultaneously; at present, only the Armenian Church continues to celebrate both events on 6 January.

The Feast of the Epiphany is also known by other names. Because of its early association with the nativity, it is sometimes called "Little Christmas." In England and Sweden, it is celebrated as "Twelfth Day," as it is believed that twelve days after his birth, Christ made his divinity manifest to Gentiles with the visit of the magi. With specific reference to the visit of the Eastern kings, it is known also as "Three Kings Day." The Ethiopian Orthodox Church celebrates Timqat (Epiphany) on 19 January as one of the highest holy days, and in Italy the festival of Befana is a remembrance of events associated with the visit of the magi. Various cultural festivities connected with the Epiphany are described in the section on cultural celebrations below.

While the Twelfth Day traditionally marks the end of the Christmas season, the Epiphany begins a new season, the Epiphany season, in the Ordinary Time of the Christian calendar (that is, the calendar ascribing ordinal numbers to Sundays in liturgical seasons other than Advent/Christmas and Lent/Easter). The Epiphany season begins with the celebration of the Epiphany and ends on the Feast of the Transfiguration, the last Sunday before the beginning of the Lenten season on Ash Wednesday. The transfiguration is the moment when Christ reveals himself to his disciples as the Son of God, and as such it is often considered to be an archetypical epiphanic or theophanic episode, the ultimate vision of Christ in heavenly glory. The Epiphany season is thus framed by distinct celebrations of divine manifestation. In addition to this liturgical significance, the Epiphany or Twelfth Night traditionally marks the beginning of the pre-Lenten Carnival, ending with the Bacchanalian festivities of Mardi Gras.

Epiphany in Orthodox and Western Christianity

In the Orthodox tradition, as already noted, Epiphany or Theophany came to be regarded as the feast commemorating Christ's baptism. The day both commemorates the physical event of Christ's baptism by John in the River Jordan and anticipates final reconciliation with God through baptism of the Spirit. In his *Discourse on the Day of the Baptism of Christ*, St. John Chrysostom, archbishop of Constantinople, describes the meaning of Theophany for the Orthodox believer. He writes, "it is necessary to say that there is not one Theophany, but two: the one actual, which has already occurred, and the second in the future, which will happen with glory at the end of the world" (2003). The actual Theophany is Christ's own baptism with water, on which occasion he is made known to the world; the other is the manifestation of his divinity through the Holy Spirit as the one by whom all Christians are ultimately baptized. Chrysostom explains further that John's baptism with water is a form of cleansing or repentance, while Christ's spiritual baptism is a baptism of redemption.

As water is the physical sign of spiritual cleansing and purification, the Feast of the Epiphany is characterized by a ritual blessing of the water in the Orthodox Church, as well as in the Byzantine Catholic rites. The ritual itself dates to the fourth century. Saint John Chrysostom specifies that on the feast commemorating Christ's sanctification of the nature of water, those who obtain the blessed water should "carry it home and keep it all year." The liturgical rite of sanctifying water invokes the manifestation of the Trinity at Christ's baptism. At the end of the service, the priest immerses a cross in the blessed water, raises it for the community to see, and recites a dismissal hymn, remembering that at Christ's baptism the voice of the Father bore witness to the Son and that the Spirit descended, in the form of a dove, to signify the enduring presence of God through baptism. As in the ancient custom, members of the community take the sanctified water home to drink and bless their houses.

The distinction between Christmas and the Epiphany had already been codified in the West by the time of Saint Augustine (354–430). Augustine's sermons on the Epiphany provide clear evidence of this and of the fact that the feast had come to commemorate the adoration of the magi. Each year Augustine would deliver a sermon on the Feast of the Epiphany, in which he would distinguish the angelic heralding of Christ's birth to the shepherds and the adoration of the magi, who were guided to Christ by a brilliant star and who, in his view, represent the entire Gentile world. In one sermon, for instance, he writes: "Only a few days ago we celebrated the Lord's birthday. Today we are celebrating with equal solemnity, as is proper, His Manifestation, in which he began to manifest Himself to the Gentiles. On one day the Jewish shepherds saw him…. on this day the Magi coming from the East adored Him" (Augustine 1952, 164).

Moreover, throughout his sermons, Augustine clearly emphasizes the central notion of divine manifestation by focusing on how the infant Christ's divinity was shown—through angels, a star, and not a human pronouncement but by "the power of the Word made flesh." What is significant is that the magi, to whom Augustine repeatedly refers as the "first fruits of the Gentiles," recognized an infant as divine. The magi, it is said, returned home following a route different from the one by which they had arrived; for Augustine, this "change of way meant a change of life." While the day itself commemorates the visit of the magi, its significance is far more general; namely, it represents the universality of the Christian message and the change or conversion that occurs in those who personally experience the manifestation of Christ's divinity. In this respect, Giovanni Battisti Cardinal Montini suggests in one of his Epiphany homilies that the feast is a "difficult one," for it "relates more to a concept, the concept of revelation, than to a single, specific fact" (Montini 1964, 99).

Cultural Celebrations Associated with the Epiphany

There are numerous cultural festivities and rituals associated with the Epiphany. While all of them bear some relationship to the specifically religious rituals and services held on the Feast of the Epiphany, others have developed a more secular character. In Greece, for instance, there is a clear connection between the Orthodox sanctification of water and the festival held on 6 January. During the festival, young men dive for a cross that, after having been blessed by a priest, is thrown into the water. The diver who retrieves the cross is presumably blessed with good fortune for the year. Timqat, the Ethiopian festival commemorating Christ's baptism and celebrated on 19 January, is also an occasion to revere the ark of the covenant. Each church has a *tabot*, a symbol of the true ark, which Orthodox Ethiopians believe is in Aksum at the Church of St. Mary of Zion. On the eve of Timqat, called Ketera, the *tabot*s from the various churches are shrouded in ornamental coverings and brought to a nearby body of water; in Lalibela, for instance, the festival takes place on the banks of the River Jordan. During the night, Mass is said followed by a festival of food and drink, and before dawn the priest blesses the water and sprinkles it on the crowd. With much fanfare, the *tabot*s are then returned to their respective churches.

Celebrations of Three Kings Day or Twelfth Day are especially common in Spanish- and German-speaking cultures and countries. On the eve of the Epiphany in Puerto Rico, for example, children, believing that the magi will visit their homes, leave food and water for the Three Kings and their camels in hope of receiving gifts in return. In German-speaking countries, doorways are blessed with holy water and decorated with the initials of the Three Kings, CMB (Caspar, Melchior, and Balthasar); the initials also stand for the Latin expression *Christus mansionem benedicat* ("Christ bless this home").

The Italian legend of La Befana (a name that phonetically resembles Epiphania) has endured for many centuries. The story has it that on their way to visit the

Christ child, the magi stopped at the home an old woman (Befana, as she is called) to ask directions. They invited her on their journey, but the old woman dismissed them quickly and returned to her housework. Realizing that she should have accompanied them, she unsuccessfully searched for the kings. Along the way she gave each child she encountered a small gift hoping that one would be the Christ child. On the Feast of the Epiphany, as the legend goes, the woman sets out to find the Christ child again, this time stopping at children's homes to leave gifts for them.

Literary/Aesthetic Appropriation of the Concept of Epiphany

James Joyce famously appropriated the concept of epiphany for distinctly literary and aesthetic purposes. In his early work *Stephen Hero,* he offers the following definition of epiphany: "a sudden spiritual manifestation, whether in the vulgarity of speech or of gesture or in a memorable phase of the mind itself…. it was for the man of letters to record these epiphanies with extreme care, seeing that they themselves are the most delicate and evanescent of moments" (1944, 188). While abandoning the specifically theological idea of divine manifestation, Joyce retains the defining character of an epiphanic episode—a thing's manifesting itself as what it essentially is, but only as revealed to an apprehending mind, for the mind itself must be active in the process of discerning a thing's nature. Utilizing scholastic distinctions borrowed from Aquinas's aesthetic theory—that integrity, symmetry, and radiance are requisite elements of beauty—Joyce suggests that the writer/artist can intellectually abstract an object from its surroundings and first view it as one integral thing (integrity), then recognize it as being a thing with an organized structure (symmetry), and finally recognize, most clearly, that it is that thing which it is. "*Claritas* is *quidditas,*" he says. Clarity is the very "whatness" of a thing. This is the moment of epiphany.

Alexander R. Eodice

See also Orthodoxy

Further Reading

Attridge, D. (1990). *The Cambridge companion to James Joyce.* Cambridge, UK: Cambridge University Press.

Augustine. (1952). *Sermons for Christmas and epiphany* (T. C. Lawler, Trans.). Westminster, MD: Newman Press.

Chrysostom, J. (2003). *Discourse on the day of the baptism of Christ.* Retrieved July 21, 2003, from http://orthodox.net/theophany/theophany-chrysostom.

Denis-Boulet, N. M. (1960). *The Christian calendar.* New York: Hawthorn Books.

Joyce, J. (1944). *Stephen hero.* New York: New Directions Publishing.

Montini, G. B. C. (1964). *Homilies on Christmas and Epiphany.* Baltimore: Helicon Press.

Company. Online edition copyright 2003 by Kevin Knight. (Original work published 1909)

Mastrantonis, G. (1996). *The feast of the epiphany: The feast of lights.* Retrieved month day, year, from http://www.goarch.org/en/ourfaith/articles/article8383. Copyright Greek Orthodox Archdiocese of America.

Reumann, J. (1972). *Understanding the sacred text.* Valley Forge, PA: Judson Press.

Eucharistic Rituals

The Eucharist is the church's commemoration of the life, death, and resurrection of Jesus and celebration of his sacramental presence to the community under the appearances of bread and wine. From the earliest days of the church Christians have gathered on Sunday, "the Lord's Day," to celebrate the Eucharist. The word "Eucharist" means "thanksgiving" (Gk. *eucharistein*); the ritual is also called the Mass (by Roman Catholics), the Sacred Liturgy (Orthodox), the Lord's Supper (Protestants), or sometimes referred to simply as "Holy Communion."

Eucharist as Ritual

Essentially the Eucharist is a sacred meal that through narrative and ritual recalls a past salvific event so that the community might enter into it and experience its power. The ritual of the Eucharist has often been summarized by the New Testament liturgical formula: "he took bread, said the blessing, broke it, and gave it to them" (Mark 14:22, all citations from New American Bible: The Catholic Study Bible Edition). Four ritual moments are evident here: the presentation of the gifts (taking), the eucharistic prayer (blessing/giving thanks), the breaking of the bread or "fraction rite"

Communion is one of the seven sacraments of the Catholic Church. The ritual is the receiving of bread and wine (symbolizing the Body and Blood of Christ at the Last Supper). Here, two girls celebrate their First Communion. COURTESY OF FRANK SALAMONE.

(breaking), and sharing the bread and wine (giving). At its heart is the eucharistic prayer, a thanksgiving narrative for the great works of God in creation and particularly for the life, death, and resurrection of Jesus introduced by the Preface and concluded by the Great Amen (see the early 3rd century Apostolic Tradition of *Hippolytus*). It includes an invocation of the Spirit (epiclesis), institution narrative ("he took bread…"), memorial of Christ's sacrifice (anamnesis), and the Great Amen of the faithful.

Origin of the Eucharist

The antecedents of the Eucharist include the Jewish Passover supper, the practice of praying a blessing before and a thanksgiving after meals, the table-fellowship tradition so important in the ministry of Jesus, and the Last Supper. The Passover was a ritual commemoration of the exodus from Egypt (Exodus 13:3–16), still celebrated by Jews. In the time of Jesus, there was a ritual element to most Jewish meals; the head of the household would open a meal with a blessing pronounced over the bread *(berakah)*, such as "Blessed are you O Lord, our God, king of the universe, who has given us bread from the earth." Similarly, at the end of the meal he would pray a grace that often included another blessing, a thanksgiving, and a supplication *(birkat ha-mazon)*.

Sharing a meal in the culture of the Near East has long been a symbol of communion, as it is for many people today. The meals Jesus shared with his disciples, with others, and with the multitude in the accounts of the miracle of the loaves were a sign of their inclusion in the "kingdom of God" that was so central to his preaching. He excluded no one. He was frequently criticized by the religious leaders of the day because he shared meals with the "tax collectors and sinners" (Mark 2:16; Matthew 10:19), to offer them a share in the blessings of salvation. On the night before he died Jesus shared a final meal with his disciples. Scholars debate whether this was a Passover meal. At this Last Supper, he gave a new meaning to his table-fellowship tradition, identifying the bread and wine of the table with his body and blood to be broken and shed in his approaching death, and promising them a renewed fellowship beyond his death (Mark 14:22–25 and parallels).

After his death his disciples continued to share meals in his memory and came to recognize him as present with them in a new way in the breaking of the bread (Luke 24:35; compare Acts 2:42). The church's eucharistic ritual combines the Jewish synagogue service for the "Liturgy of the Word" (Luke 4:16–21) with the Lord's Supper for the "Liturgy of the Eucharist."

The Meaning of the Eucharist

The Eucharist has been celebrated with a diversity of styles by different Christian traditions and since the Reformation has been differently understood by the various churches. The Orthodox eucharistic liturgy is celebrated with great solemnity. The altar or table is placed behind an iconostasis or icon screen that partly conceals it from the assembly. After the Second Vatican Council, the Roman Catholic eucharistic ritual was renewed; it is now celebrated in the language of the people, the priest or presider faces the assembly, and the faithful take a more active role and receive both the bread and the cup. Protestant traditions have also been affected by the liturgical movement and some are moving toward more frequent celebration.

Most significant for understanding the meaning of the *Eucharist is the World Council of Churches'* text,

Baptism, Eucharist and Ministry (referred to as BEM or the Lima text). Formulated by the WCC's Faith and Order Commission, which included Catholic, Orthodox, and Protestant theologians, it was approved at Lima, Peru in 1982. In describing the Eucharist under five aspects, BEM seeks to present a theological vision of Eucharist acceptable to most Christian traditions.

First, as a *thanksgiving* to the Father, the Eucharist gives thanks in the great eucharistic prayer to God for the work of creation and redemption.

Second, the Eucharist is the *memorial* (anamnesis) of Christ's sacrifice and the sacrament of his body and blood. Though they understand it differently, most Christians recognize Christ's real presence, given in the bread broken and the cup shared, according to his words "This is my body.... This is my blood."

Third, the Eucharist is an *invocation* of the Holy Spirit *(epiclesis)* on the gifts of bread and wine that they might become the sacramental signs of his body and blood, and on the community of the church that it might be empowered to fulfill its mission.

Fourth, the Eucharist is the *communion (koinōnia)* of the faithful, who by sharing the one bread and the common cup are brought into communion with Christ and with one another in his body, the church. The Eucharist is a sacrament of the unity of the community in Christ; therefore any division, whether based on economic status, race, sex, or confession, is contrary to the reconciliation of the God's people in Christ (compare 1 Corinthians 11:20–22; Galatians 3:28). The liturgy of the Eucharist ritualizes this communion in the Body of Christ by the mutual forgiveness of sin, the sign of peace, intercession for all people, sharing in the eucharistic bread and wine, and by taking communion to those who are sick or in prison.

Finally, as a meal of the kingdom, the Eucharist both symbolizes and anticipates the coming of the kingdom in its fullness. As Christians have been reconciled to one another by God's grace, so they are signs of Christ's love for all and especially for the outcast when they work for justice, love, and peace. When Christians cannot celebrate at the same table, the witness of their Eucharist is diminished.

Thomas P. Rausch

Further Reading

Baptism, Eucharist, and ministry. (1982). Geneva, Switzerland: World Council of Churches.

Emminghaus, J. H. (1978). *The Eucharist: Essence, Form, Celebration.* Collegeville, MN: Liturgical Press.

Kilmartin, E. (1965). *The Eucharist in the Primitive Church.* Englewood Cliffs, NJ: Prentice-Hall.

Kilmartin, E. (1998). *The Eucharist in the West: History and Theology.* Collegeville, MN: Liturgical Press.

Raymond, J., Rordorf, W., Blond, G., Jourjon, M., Hamman, A., Mehat, A., Saxer, V., Jacquemont, P., & Metzger, M., (1978). *The Eucharist of the early Christians.* New York: Pueblo.

Talley, T. J. (1976). From *berakah* to *eucharistia*: A reopening question. *Worship 50,* 115–137.

Evil Eye

The evil eye is the belief that people can cause harm to others by simply looking at them. This belief is common in several regions of the world and is accompanied by the use of a variety of ritual objects as well as ritual behavior to both ward off the effects of the evil eye and to reverse the harm it causes. The harm is most typically illness, accidents, death, or the destruction of valuable property. The evil eye is believed to have originated in the ancient Near East. The oldest written reference to it is a Sumerian cuneiform tablet dating to about 3000 BCE. From there the evil eye spread west to societies bordering the Mediterranean and east to the Indian subcontinent. From the Mediterranean it spread up the Atlantic coast of Europe as far north as Scotland. The belief was and remains most powerful along the Aegean coast of Greece and in southern Italy. Belief in the evil eye did not develop in sub-Saharan Africa, East Asia, or the Americas, although it was brought to the Americas by settlers from Spain and Italy. The evil eye is mentioned in the Old Testament (Proverbs 23, 28) and New Testament (Mark 7) and is a custom in many Islamic societies. However, even in societies where the evil eye belief is strong, not all people believe in it, and therefore not all people are potential victims. As in witchcraft and sorcery, one must believe in the evil eye to also believe that one has been the object of it.

At the heart of the evil eye belief is envy. Virtually everywhere it exists, people believe that people cast the evil eye when they feel envious about some characteristic or possession of the victim. The belief is most common in societies where there are marked differences in wealth and therefore groups who have reason to envy others. Those who cast the evil eye are

Strings of beads of various shapes and designs, all meant to ward off the evil eye, hang in a shop in Athens, Greece in 2003. Note their proximity to Greek Orthodox religious paintings.
COURTESY OF KAREN CHRISTENSEN.

most commonly envious of a person's wealth, stylish home, nice furnishings, smart or attractive child, or productive domesticated animals. In most places people believe that the evil eye is not cast on purpose but rather that it is simply a predictable component of feeling envious. For example, among the Santal people of India, people say that "Nothing happens to so and so; they are earning exceedingly; they will surely have no trouble. This speech of theirs takes effect. Then these people become ill; their cattle die, and they get much suffering" (Mukherjee 1962, 288). In a few places, particularly southern Greece and Italy, the evil eye accusation is more specific, and certain people (often the elderly and outsiders such as tourists) are believed to have the power to cast the evil eye and to do so deliberately.

Given the long history of the belief and its wide distribution around the world, it is not surprising that people employ a long list of ritual actions to ward off the effects of the evil eye and to reverse the harm it has caused. Warding-off measures include saying, singing, and chanting incantations; wearing amulets in the form of necklaces, religious symbols, pins, ribbons, and bracelets; avoiding people who may cast the evil eye; avoiding situations that may provoke the evil eye; repeating ritualized sayings; making specific hand gestures; burning herbs; and hanging protective objects on one's house. Amulets made specifically to ward off the evil eye usually are of a particular color, such as blue or red, and shape, such as a cat's eye or horseshoe.

The harmful effects of the evil eye are also varied, although the effects often involve the object of the envy (often a child or prized animal) becoming ill, plants withering, a valued object being damaged or destroyed, men becoming impotent, the milk of nursing mothers drying up, and a family suddenly experiencing general misfortune. In evil eye societies all of these events can trigger a belief that someone has cast the evil eye and that ritual action should be taken to reverse the effect. The ritual action is typically some form of a ceremony performed in the home, sometimes with the assistance of a religious healer. Across cultures many of the curative rituals involve the use of water, such as divining in a bowl of olive oil to identify the caster, feeding or bathing a victim in holy water, or spitting at the caster. This widespread use of water to cure is in accord with the anthropologist Alan Dundes's theory that the evil eye belief is about "drying up" and the loss of life.

In the contemporary world the evil eye belief is less common and less intense than in the past, perhaps because in many of the societies where it was once common there is more opportunity for upward social mobility and less reason to be envious of others.

David Levinson

Further Reading

Dundes, A. (Ed.). (1981). *The evil eye: A folklore casebook.* New York: Garland.

Maloney, C. (Ed.). (1976). *The evil eye.* New York: Columbia University Press.

Mukherjee, C. (1962). *The Santals.* Calcutta, India: A. Mukherjee and Co.

Exorcism

The word *exorcism* comes from the Greek word *exorkizein,* meaning "to drive out by solemn command or oath." As a religious ritual exorcism generally is the expulsion of a demonic spirit or some other evil

A KOREAN EXORCISM MANUAL

In every Korean book-stall will be found a little volume called "The Six Marks of Divination," or sometimes "The Five Rules for Obtaining the Ten-thousand Blessings." It represents some of the grossest superstitions of the Korean people. It is the common people who make great use of this book, but the woman of the upper class is almost sure to have a volume hidden about the house, from which to cast the horoscope of her infant sons and daughters. It is a curious mixture of Buddhism, spiritism and fetichism. One can see at a glance how Buddhism has joined forces with the original elements in Korean religion to form a conglomerate that will suit all tastes.

[...]

It will be seen that this book which we are describing is like a domestic medicine book in our own land. Those that cannot afford to hire a *mudang* to cure them will have recourse to its pages, and this accounts for the enormous sale which the volume enjoys. It affirms that the human body is subject to two kinds of diseases,—those which can be cured by medicine and those that require exorcism. Some people have foolishly tried to cure both kinds by drugs. The hermit Chang laid down the rules for exorcising the demons of disease, and he wisely said that if in any case exorcism does not succeed, it is certain that the disease is one that must be cured with medicine. Note the implication that exorcism should be tried first, which is a pretty piece of special pleading in behalf of the profession. The book tells on what days of the month special diseases are likely to break out, and the name of the spirit that causes them. Whichever one it is, the work must be begun by writing the name of the imp on a piece of white or yellow paper (according to the day on which it is done) together with the narne of the point of the compass from which the spirit comes, wrap a five-cash piece in this paper and throw it out of the door at the imp. These imps are supposed to be the spirits of people that have died, and they are specified as spirits of men who have died by accident away from home, aged female relatives, yellow-headed men, perjurers, men who have died by drowning and so on to the end of the list. In each case the exorcist is told to go a certain number of paces in some particular direction and throw the cash. The hermit wisely confined himself to diseases that will pass away in a few days by themselves, but it is a pity he did not exorcise the whole troop of devils with a good dose of castor oil.

***Source*: Hulbert, Homer B. (1906).**
***The passing of Korea*. New York, Doubleday, Page and Co., pp. 425, 428–429.**

influence by the use of classic principles of magic and/or the assistance of a more powerful spirit. Rituals of exorcism are probably universal to the world's religions. They have been especially prominent in Christianity since the time of Jesus; less so in Judaism and Islam. Exorcism was central to Catholic liturgy until the Second Vatican Council of the mid-1960s, after which it was considerably marginalized; but since the 1980s rituals of exorcism have increased and have been instituted in conservative Protestant denominations. The reality of the evil influence remains in the realm of cultural belief; but exorcism actually benefits believers through the same principles as psychotherapy.

Religious Altered States of Consciousness

All religions regard the direct experience of the sacred as important and recognize certain altered states of consciousness as manifestations of such experience. Recent advances in neuroscience describe the nature and physiological bases for various altered states of consciousness, generically called "ASCs" or "trance states," which are not only drug-induced states but also states induced without drugs; social scientists have recorded their cultural explanations. In world ethnology (comparative cultural study) three fundamental trance states are recognized as central to religious experience: ordinary trance, ecstatic trance, and

Two women seemingly possessed by demons undergo a ritual of exorcism in Tamil Nadu, India, 1988. COURTESY OF RICHARD J. CASTILLO.

possession trance. In all such states people behave abnormally but in culturally sanctioned ways. All cultures believe that supernatural entities contain dangerous communicable power, fatal in full strength; as God warned Moses, "you cannot see my face, for no one shall see me and live" (Exodus 33:20, NRSV). Even so, "the skin of his face shone" when Moses returned to his people, who were terrified (34:29), and he veiled himself for subsequent consultations with God. Lesser degrees of supernatural power can cause trance states, which occur occasionally in religious rituals. The ordinary trance state can result from being in close proximity to a divinity or with something that contains such power, such as holy water. In such a state a person's soul and personality are suppressed. The person loses control of many faculties, and he or she exhibits a variety of abnormal physical and behavioral traits. The person may twitch and babble; the eyes may roll back; the person may drool or froth at the mouth.

"Ecstatic," "enthusiastic," "charismatic," and other terms may be applied to any experience of a religious ASC; but "ecstasy" or "ecstatic trance" is the term given to the self-induced ASC experienced by shamans, who are religious specialists traditionally in Asian, Arctic, and New World indigenous societies. The physiological state may be similar to that of ordinary trance, although it is frequently drug assisted; but people believe that the shaman's body is empty of its soul, which has left on a specific mission into the spirit world.

Universally people believe that spiritual agencies can enter into and "possess" people. Possession by deities may be voluntary, actively sought by participants in ritual, as described by anthropologists in many examples from the traditional world; such possession is central to Pentecostal forms of Christianity. In all such cases the possession state is entered and exited voluntarily, the person's transition assisted by previous practice and by his or her belief and zeal, group support, rhythmic and percussive music, exuberant dance, and perhaps flashing lights, odors, or other sensory stimuli. Generally, behavior during possession is similar to that described for ordinary trance, but different spirits have their own characteristics, and there may be specific cultural differences. People invariably report positive experiences. Participation in so-called possession cults is therapeutic, especially for people in situations of social and economic hardship.

Demonic Possession

Sometimes spirit possession may be involuntary. It may be contagious and may spread from those who have sought it to others nearby. It may spread throughout a society or between societies in collective hysterias, especially in times of rapid social change. Most dangerous is "spirit attack." In cultures throughout the world spirits may attack people for many reasons, including anger, protection of self and territory, or the compulsion to deliver a message to the living, as in the case of the girl of the Yakima Indian tribe of Washington State described in a classic article by American psychiatrist Mansell Pattison. She wanted to be a normal high school girl and to participate in her parents' Presbyterian church, but she was harassed by the ghost of her grandfather who, the diviner determined, wanted her to be a shaman as he had been. Also, in probably all cosmologies (systems of cultural beliefs about the nature of the universe), evil spirits stand outside human social mores and attack and possess people out of pure meanness. Results are always unpleasant, ranging from mild discomfort to violent seizures or lasting mental or physical illnesses.

Thus, people take care to avoid spirits and to take specific defenses against them. The habitats and normal behaviors of most spirits are known. Spirits around the world are preferentially nocturnal, and so people take special precautions when they are abroad at night. Spirits generally avoid fire and bright lights, so people going out at night invite others to accompany them, carry lights, and make some noise—converse in low voices, whistle, or occasionally kick the undergrowth to announce their presence in advance to any unwary spirit (and to the neighbors, who will be unnerved by suspicious sounds outside). Spirits may be repelled by certain odors, herbs, amulets, signs of protection granted by other spirits, and so forth.

However, in spite of such precautions, spirits may attack and possess people. Sometimes possession manifests itself in ways easily explainable to Western medicine: epileptic-like seizures, schizophrenic-like sensory hallucinations. Often possession is fairly subtle, manifested in mood changes, loss of appetite and energy, some wasting physical condition; possession is diagnosed, perhaps through divination, only after other explanations and treatments have failed. As in voluntary possession, specific behaviors during possession by demons vary across cultures. Notable are differences in language: in Western cultures demons speak in low, gravelly voices, with frequent obscenities, especially sexual and scatological.

ASCs are real; whether or not spirits are real, voluntary collective ritual states of possession are explainable and have positive effects on people. However, the cultural concept of involuntary possession presents some problems to the analyst. It is difficult to understand how possession by a mean spirit might have positive socio-psychological features—until its remedy, exorcism, is considered.

Demon Exorcism

Exorcism—the "driving out" or "casting out" of an unwanted supernatural presence or influence—is also explainable in both neurobiological and cultural terms. The process covers many sorts of "driving out." The exorcist, who is a religious specialist—a priest or shaman—expels the spirit or other intruding element, and the process is successful when the victim is convinced that this has happened. As in group possession, the process is strengthened by social support. Exorcism is rarely a solitary ritual; the principal practitioner is invariably accompanied by several others, and all, including relatives and friends who might not be immediately present for fear of contagion, know that the ritual can work. Exorcism—"witch doctoring"—has been identified as a form of psychotherapy. Failure is explainable in many ways, but the efficacy of the ritual is not questioned.

In preparation for the ritual, the exorcist goes through whatever purification or sanctification ritual is standard before any instance of direct confrontation of the supernatural, and afterward he must go through a standard desanctification process. Exorcists may use spiritual and/or magical methods. The exorcist may invoke some powerful spirit for assistance—as Christians invoke Jesus, to exorcise "in its name"; or he may call the spirit into himself so that the summoned spirit is the agent of exorcism, working through the possessed exorcist. If the exorcist is a shaman he may use ecstasy in the ritual. He may lie down near the patient and go into his ecstatic ASC so that his soul can directly confront the possessing spirit. Accounts by shamans of such spiritual confrontations reveal that the shaman's soul uses some of the same techniques as a priest-exorcist.

Among the exorcist's techniques are some forms of magic. Universally, people believe in the power of spoken words, especially names. Names are intimately associated with and come to embody something of the essence of the thing named. By learning and using names of things in nature, people can control them. Most spirits are known by generic or attributive labels; gods are known by titles. However, spiritual beings capable of intervening directly in people's affairs may have their own "personal," hidden names. By naming the spirit the exorcist establishes his first measure of control over it. Through his specialized knowledge of mythology and cosmology the exorcist may also have knowledge of some weakness in that spirit, some failing in the spirit's past, or some quirk in its behavior. By verbalizing this knowledge the exorcist further strengthens his control. Also, by invoking the names of more powerful spirits or gods, perhaps ones who have bested the offending spirit in some contest in the past, the exorcist confirms his dominant position. He is thus able to command the spirit.

The exorcist's constant activity, commands, and revelations of his knowledge of the spirit may be designed to distract the spirit's attention from certain stratagems that the exorcist or his assistants now carry out. These stratagems are designed to trick the spirit or to make its habitation unbearable. Food, objects, colors, and aromas known to be enticing to spirits may be placed in strategic locations in "spirit traps." Acrid smoke from burning incense or herbs may attract, or repel, the spirit.

Possession is frequently conceptualized as a "hot" state, especially in areas of the world where medical ideas are based in concepts of systemic balance or harmony. A first step may therefore be to "cool" the victim, either by actually lowering body temperature, as in a cooling bath, or symbolically by a "cool" substance such as ashes, powder, the liquid from a land snail (in west Africa), and so forth. This step may not be designed to make the victim more comfortable but rather the spirit less so.

Toward this end the victim may be physically abused—alternately dunked in hot and cold water, exposed to inclement weather, denied food and drink, even physically beaten—while the enticements are laid out within the spirit's reach. An elaborate and widespread method of tricking the spirit is to persuade it that it is possessing the wrong body. A dummy may be constructed to resemble the victim, set in the victim's house, and surrounded with his or her favorite or intimate things and relatives, who have been coached in the ruse; all act as if the dummy is the possessed person. The spouse may even pretend to have sex with the dummy. Meanwhile the victim has been stripped of any recognizable attire, disguised, and hidden.

Immediately when the spirit leaves the victim and enters the dummy or whatever trap has been set for it, the trap is sealed, covered with something that inhibits spiritual activity, and quickly taken outside the village. It is burned, left at a crossroads, or thrown into the bush. In some cultures in Africa and Asia, when the spirit has let go, priests or shamans who have developed the ability to "see" into the spirit world attack the spirit with special weapons. Or the exorcist may draw the spirit into himself, typically by arousing its anger so that it attacks. The exorcist, who is adept at handling possession, will be quickly helped by his assistants while the patient is carried away from the scene. The exorcist does personal battle with the spirit and, victorious, banishes it. An important point to note is that the victim, his family, and many of his immediate social network participate actively in all stages of the ritual.

Exorcism of a demon from a person can be an elaborate, long, and expensive ritual; and herein is one social/psychological explanation: the patient is the focus of attention throughout the process. Thus, demonic possession and exorcism might be good for a person who feels socially neglected. For Pattison's Yakima girl and her parents, ritual banishment of the spirit of her grandfather clearly helped resolve her intercultural ambivalence.

Exorcisms of Other Forms of Evil

Exorcism may be performed to drive out other forms of evil. Witchcraft in the ethnological (cross-cultural) sense is an evil power that develops in some people and works evil through supernatural means. Western witches were believed able to send demons into people, and exorcisms of the victims were required. In many cultures the witchcraft power can work independently of its host, who may not know that he or she is a witch until the fact is revealed through divination. Because witches are evil, antisocial, and feared, people do not want to be witches; and a person revealed to be one may seek to be exorcised. Exorcisms of witches employ means similar to those of spirits; but they might also try to change the witch's own personality and disposition. Witchcraft is believed to be activated by negative emotions; positive, cheerful, and compassionate attitudes are not conducive to its success. So the witch may make loud spoken resolutions of reformed behavior and may spit or force himself or herself to vomit, helping to expel the power while undergoing whatever torment the exorcist may be inflicting on his or her body.

Sometimes people's houses or lands are polluted by some evil and need to be exorcised and cleansed after a possession, a haunting, an attack by a sorcerer, or violation of a taboo. Sometimes the whole community or the entire cosmos might be conceived of as overtaken by evil, as in some cosmologies that are governed by a concept of a balanced universe, such as the Asian *yin/yang* (*yin* is the feminine, passive principle in nature that in Chinese cosmology is exhibited in darkness, cold, or wetness and that combines with *yang* to produce all that comes to be; *yang* is the masculine, active principle that is exhibited in light, heat, or dryness and that combines with *yin* to produce all that comes to be). If the eternally conflicting tensions are drastically out of balance, a massive ritual of exorcism might be required, such as the great Eka Dasa Rudra, the Ceremony of the Eleven Powers, in Bali.

Exorcism in the Christian Tradition

Of the relatively few religious concepts of negative afterworlds, the Christian hell is by far the most severe, with its horrible punishments and ranks of demons commanded by Satan, who is the sworn enemy of God and Christ and dedicated to the subversion of humankind. Fears of societal infiltration by Satan have dominated Christian history. The Christian underworld and possession by demons developed directly out of the Zoroastrianism (a Persian religion founded in the sixth century BCE by the prophet Zoroaster) of the Persian king Cyrus the Great, who was conceived as exemplary hero and messiah (Isaiah 45:1; 2 Chronicles 36:11–23), the liberator of the Jews from Babylon in 539 BCE, and the rebuilder of the Temple. However, mainstream Judaism, true to its traditional scriptures, absorbed no such tradition of demonology. By the sixteenth century Jewish theology, especially through Kabbalah (or Cabala), the mystical system of obtaining occult knowledge, had resurrected a marginal tradition of demonic beliefs in the forms of the *dybbuk* (a wandering soul believed in Jewish folklore to enter and control a living body) and was interested in variations on the *golem* (an artificial human being in Hebrew folklore endowed with life), correlating directly with Christian demonology and persecution in the late Middle Ages. Some Islamic traditions allow for possession by and exorcism of spirits *(jinn)*, and *zar* and *bori* possession cults (named for particular types of possessing spirits) have flourished in some areas, allowing valuable psychological release from economic and social hardship for both men and women. However, of the three main Western religions, exorcism is most central and elaborate in Christianity.

Prior to Catholicism's Second Vatican Council of 1962–1965 Exorcist was one of four minor orders to which every new priest was ordained. Catholics distinguished between possession, the active presence of a demon within a person, and obsession, the harassment of a person and the pollution of a person's surroundings by a demon; persons thus tormented by demons were labeled "demoniacs," "energumens," "ecstatics," or "bewitched" (*maleficiati*, recipients of *maleficium*, diabolical evil influence), depending on the specific nature of their afflictions. The sacrament of baptism was both an exorcism of the taint of original sin and a defense against future evil influence; and both the priestly rite of blessing and the layperson's ritual of crossing oneself are forms of exorcism. After Vatican II exorcism was to be used sparingly, only as a last resort after medical diagnosis and treatment had failed. The old Roman Ritual of Exorcism remained—now in the vernacular, no longer in Latin—although the exorcist was allowed great latitude, depending on the nature of the case. Words were to be the primary means of exorcism, as Jesus had exorcised demons by command; of course, the priest was to undergo sanctification and investment of sacred garments, and he was to hold a Bible and crucifix, used like the magical power objects in exorcisms everywhere, and he had constant access to holy water.

Popular fascination with demons and exorcism in modern times received a huge stimulus by the 1971 publication of William Peter Blatty's book, *The Exorcist*, and the movie in 1973; this stimulus increased public receptivity to Malachi Martin's sensational 1976 book, *Hostage to the Devil*. In the 1970s fears of coercive cults and child abductions were followed by fears of murderous Satanic cults, which spread to all Christian areas of the world from 1980 to the mid-1990s. In his 1986 Summer Sermons Pope John Paul II assured Catholics that Satan is real, and in March 1990 New York's Cardinal John O'Connor acknowledged that some exorcisms had been conducted and condemned heavy metal music and other elements of popular culture as Satan inspired. In April 1990 ABC-TV's *20/20* broadcast an actual exorcism conducted by Roman Catholic priests. Renewed fervor over millennial prophecies in the Bible's Book of *Revelation* contributed to new cases of demon possession and new rituals of "deliverance" among branches of mainline Protestant churches that had historically scoffed at the Catholic preoccupation with demonology. Such rituals—including "deliverance by proxy," in which a stand-in for the reluctant actual victim receives the treatment—have become new forms of group therapy among some congregations. Historically demon possession and exorcism, like witchcraft, dangerous cults, and other expressive forms of religious beliefs, rise and fall as barometers of the collective social mood.

Phillips Stevens Jr.

See also Altered States of Consciousness; Catholicism; Divination; Healing; Magic; Ritual Specialists; Satanic Rituals; Shamanism; Sorcery

Further Reading

Cuneo, M. W. (2001). *American exorcism: Expelling demons in the land of plenty*. New York: Doubleday.

Goodman, F. D. (1981). *The exorcism of Anneliese Michel*. New York: Doubleday.

Goodman, F. D. (1988). *How about demons? Possession and exorcism in the modern world*. Bloomington: Indiana University Press.

Levack, B. P. (Ed.). (1992). *Articles on witchcraft, magic and demonology: Vol. 9. Possession and exorcism*. New York: Garland.

Lewis, I. M. (2003). *Ecstatic religion: A study of shamanism and spirit possession* (3nd ed.). London: Routledge.

Martin, M. (1976). *Hostage to the devil: The possession and exorcism of five living Americans*. New York: Reader's Digest Press.

Nauman, St. E., Jr. (Ed.). (1974). *Exorcism through the ages*. Secaucus, NJ: Citadel Press.

Pattison, E. M. (1977). Psychosocial interpretations of exorcism. *Journal of Operational Psychiatry*, 8(2), 5–19.

Prince, R. (Ed.). (1968). *Trance and possession states*. Montreal, Canada: R. M. Bucke Memorial Society.

Ward, C. (1989). Possession and exorcism: Psychopathology and psychotherapy in a magico-religious context. In C. Ward (Ed.), *Altered states of consciousness and mental health: A cross-cultural perspective* (pp. 125–144). Newbury Park, CA: Sage.

F

Fasting *See* Asceticism

Food and Rituals

When the nineteenth century paragon of materialism, Ludwig Feuerbach, said, "Der Mensch ist, was er ißt" ("A man is what he eats."), he wanted to uncover the material basis of human existence. The dictum has since gained a surplus of meaning, as humans do not merely consume food, but also chew on it with their minds and spirits. They attach meaning to eating, and hand it down through the generations by means of rituals.

Food Preparation and Rituals

To understand rituals surrounding food, one must visit the kitchen, or venture even farther to a slaughterhouse. In Roman Europe, the kitchen was inhabited by lares (household gods), and the oven was endowed with magical powers in ancient myths. In China, the kitchen god is respected, as the deity guards family well being year round. In Jewish traditions, meat is obtained through proper slaughtering (*shechitah*), which requires a humane manner of killing. The laws of *shechitah* mandate that slaughter be carried out by a qualified person and only after appropriate benedictions.

Food and Rituals in Daily Meals

Rituals are commonly associated with worship, sacrifice, and festal occasions; however, the daily meal is rich in rituals, as well. In ancient Rome, a portion of the meal was customarily thrown into the fire as an offering to the gods. In America, coffee, which gained popularity in the spirit of resistance to British colonial tea marketing, has become a ritual of waking up.

Various cultures have their own rituals surrounding meals. Each culture values its proper way of setting the table, and a slight infraction could cause much offence. The table setting and seating can reflect the polity of the society, whether hierarchical or egalitarian, or whether different genders should site closely together. The table setting may also communicate respect toward or avoidance of the dead. In the Korean traditional table setting, the bowl of soup is not placed left of the bowl of rice, since that is the placement on the table for the dead. It is commonly known that in the Chinese cultural tradition, any combination of four is to be avoided, as the word "four" is a homonym with "death" in Chinese.

Rituals at Festive Meals

The ritual aspect of food becomes prominent on festal occasions. From palace to peasants' village, feasts display the choice food the celebrants can afford. The extravagance fit for the festive mood is combined with dishes filled with traditional significance. Festivities are made manifest in rituals, some governed by the calendar and others by the rhythms in life.

Feasts controlled by the calendar mark important points in the cycle of time, or commemorate historic events. Virtually all cultures celebrate New Year's Day (though the actual day of the beginning of the year varies from one culture to another) with a meal that

THE CHINESE STOVE GOD

The Stove God, Tsao Chun, is not a god of the culinary arts, nor is his location above the stove a matter of convenience or coincidence. In northern Taiwan the large brick cooking stove on which most meals are prepared stands as a substantial symbol of the family as a corporate body. Possession of a stove identifies a family as an independent entity. The new independent segments of a recently divided household often share many of the facilities of a single house, including, occasionally, the kitchen, but independent families never share a stove, not even when the heads are brothers. When brothers divide their father's household the eldest inherits the old stove, while his younger brothers transfer hot coals from the old stove to their new ones, thereby inviting the Stove God to join them. For this reason, family division is commonly spoken of as *pun-cau*, "dividing the stove." In the view of most of my informants, the soul of a family, its corporate fate, is somehow localized in their stove. When a shaman informed one family that there were "ants and other things" in their stove, they demolished the structure and threw the bricks into the river. A neighbor explained, "There was nothing else they could do. A family will never have peace if they don't have a good stove."

Source: Wolf, Arthur P. "Gods, Ghosts, and Ancestors." (1974). In Arthur P. Wolf, editor. _Religion and Ritual in Chinese Society_. Stanford, CA: Stanford University Press, pp. 133–134.

features a variety of traditional delicacies, ranging from ham, poultry, and pickled herring, to black-eyed peas, carrots, and rice, all of which are associated with a wish for good luck for the new year (Gay 1996, 176).

In Christian traditions, the birth of Jesus is celebrated as a fixed feast of Christmas on 25 December, and homemade cookies and candies are shared among friends and relatives with the greeting of a merry Christmas. Easter is the movable feast of the resurrection of Jesus, and brings forth dyed eggs and colorful confections which symbolize new life. Traditionally, the pre-Easter season is observed with fasting, and Easter morning breaks the fast.

Jewish festal celebrations feature food items imbued with symbolic meaning. Honey symbolizes hopes for a "sweet" new year on Rosh Hashanah. Poultry dishes break the fast on Yom Kippur. Cheese on Shavuot marks the spring harvest, as well as the days of Exodus when the people of Israel did not have time to prepare meat. *Hamantaschen* (Haman's pockets) recall the story of Haman, who attempted a pogrom on the Jewish people. Oil and latkes for Chanukah recall the story of how a small portion of oil kept the temple lamp burning for eight days.

Throughout the world, harvest feasts are celebrated with sumptuous meals. In America, turkey is prepared in various ways according to the customs of various ethnic immigrant communities.

In less well-known examples of ritual meals, a "day of cold meal" is observed in China and Korea with a cold meal to mark the beginning of a new agricultural cycle. On the "fifth day of the fifth month" by the lunar calendar, rituals hoping for a bountiful harvest are performed.

In addition to annual celebrations, the feasts of full moons are monthly festal occasions in regions where the lunar calendar is in use. For weekly ritual meals, one may cite North American Sunday brunch and dinner, as well as the Jewish Shabbat meal.

Another group of feasts is celebrated in conjunction with rites of passages. In Korea, the birth of a new baby is celebrated with the soup of kelp (mistakenly called seaweed), as the plant symbolizes good luck. Among Catholics and Protestants (except Baptists), infant baptism (commonly called christening) is followed by a party. Other important transitions in life, such as graduation, ventures, and promotions, involve generous sharing of food, by which the host seeks to quell the jealousy of others, divine and human, and invite their blessings.

The beginning of a person's life is celebrated by an annual birthday. In the West the birthday cake is topped with lighted candles, which are blown out along with a wish. In Korea, where age is not counted by the number of birthdays, but by the number of New Year's Days one has celebrated, eating a meal on the first day of the year becomes an important ritual activity that marks growth or aging.

Many cultures mark the passage of a child into adulthood with meals. Children become adults when they are allowed to have food and drink forbidden to children. *Bar/Bat mitzvah* in the synagogue and confirmation in the church are readily observable examples of initiation rituals that are associated with celebratory meals.

The wedding feast is an important part of the ceremony, and food is served as wishes of happiness and fertility are made. While the types of food vary among many cultures, modern day weddings cannot omit the ritual wedding cake.

Funerals are often followed by meals. Food is shared as a sign of the solidarity of humanity for the survivors, for whom life has to go on. In China and Chinese related cultures, as part of the commemoration of the dead, food and water are placed outside for their journey after life.

Food and Gods

Since antiquity, food has been integral to religious services, and the ritual aspect of food becomes dominant in the context of worship. In worship, one seeks to communicate with the divine world through food. The New Year celebration in China includes placing sweet food on the mouth of the kitchen god, so that the deity may utter sweet words on behalf of the family. In the ancient Near East, the worshipper was expected to feed gods their daily meals. In the Epic of Gilgamesh, the gods are starved during the cosmic flood, and as soon as the first worship is offered, the gods converge on the sacrificial food like flies. In the Hebrew Bible, the phrase of "food of God" survives; however, God's need for victual is polemically downplayed, as God appears as the provider, not the provided for.

In religion, gods are not only guests, but assume the role of eternal breadwinners, as they are responsible for the supply of food. Worshippers recognize that their deity provides food for them, and the constancy of provision is regarded as indicative of the relationship between the deity and the worshippers.

The role of the providing deity is prominent in fertility cults. The myths of the dying and rising deity recall the cycle of seasons, and fertility cults often seek to impel the nature gods to yield abundant produce. The mythic cycle of Baal in ancient Canaan is a good example, as Baal dies with the dry summer and rises with the rain. The use of dairy products as offerings in diverse cultures ranging from the Hittites to the Romans indicates the concern with fertility in rituals.

In Chinese culture, a ritual meal is an essential part of "ancestor worship" (a term coined by Herbert Spencer in 1885). Respect for ancestors is expressed through rituals and victuals arranged in accordance with the prescribed order of ancestor worship, drawing upon spiritual influences from Confucianism, Buddhism, Taoism, and shamanism.

Food and the Words of Rituals

Rituals often include spoken words, which explain and even determine the nature of the act of ritual eating. Accompanying stories may narrate memorable events, such as deliverance from the bondage of Egypt at Passover, or the reversal of fortune in the face of pogrom recorded in the Book of Esther.

In the Judeo-Christian tradition, meals start or end with a prayer commonly known as "grace." The early-Christian Qumran community had the practice of concluding meal with thanksgiving, and one of the earliest Christian documents, the Didache, prescribes a grace after meal, as well.

In the Christian Eucharist, the words recited over the elements are central to the meaning of the food. In most Reformed traditions, the bread and wine *symbolize* the sacrifice of Jesus. In the Roman Catholic tradition, the doctrine of transubstantiation maintains that the words of consecration by the priest change the *substance* of the elements; while their form remains the same, the bread actually becomes the flesh of Jesus, and the wine the blood of Christ.

Food, Rituals, and Social Boundary

The place of food in various rituals makes it clear that food is not only a source of nutrients, but part of a social language that articulates social relations in a stylized fashion. Ritual foods expose who is included and who is excluded, and who is related to whom as well as how.

In covenantal relationships, the two parties of a covenant often engaged in a covenant meal. Ancient Near Eastern treaty documents indicate that pacts were concluded with ritual meals. Pledging allegiance through a ritual meal is the background of the Jewish apocalyptic Book of Daniel, which tells how the young men of Judah refuse to eat the royal portion (*patbag* is the Persian loanword). Instead, they insist on a diet of vegetables and water. Since the kosher laws do not require vegetarianism, one suspects that something else was involved in the refusal; by refusing to accept the royal portion, the men are refusing to pledge allegiance to the foreign king.

In a comparable story in the *Shi-ji* by the ancient Chinese historian Si-ma-qian, two men starve themselves to death, refusing to eat anything from the land of the king to whom they could not pledge their allegiance. In the Bible, the book of 2 Kings ends with a puzzling note on the release of King Jehoiachin, who is last seen at the royal table of the Babylonian king Evil-merodach (Awil-Marduk). The ritual of eating at the table of the king of Babylonian communicates the status of the vassal of the exiled Judean king.

Ancient dietary laws not only state what one cannot eat, but also with whom one cannot eat. New relationships are established through meals, and severed by refusal to eat together. For a long time, Christians banned outsiders from the Eucharist table. The Didache (9:5) cites Matthew 7:6 ("Do not give what is sacred to the dogs") as the basis for refusing the elements except to those baptized. Jewish dietary law functions as a sign of observant Jews, and in the first century, the Pharisees were found to display contempt for a group called the people of the land (*'am ha-aretz*), too poor to abide by the legal tradition required for the meal fellowship of *havurah*. Harris (1985, 86) speculates that the boundary of expansion of a religion coincides with the area where the required dietary law is realistic.

The seminal work of Douglas (1966) redefines the notion of the profane as the violation of boundaries established by cultural norms. In ancient Israel, which considered the cloven-hoofed ruminant as one category, the pig (cloven-hoofed, but not ruminant) crosses the boundary, and pork is unclean. Fish that live in the water but have no fins are likewise unclean.

Crossing the clear boundaries established by food can also highlight the gaining of acceptance, as those deemed excluded are welcomed into the fellowship of the table. The expansion of Christianity was characterized by the transgression of social boundaries established in terms of food, first set forth in the vision of Peter in the book of Acts. In a vision, Peter is commanded to eat the unclean, and as Peter refuses, God says to Peter, "What God has made clean, you must not call profane" (Acts 10:15). The first ecumenical council at Jerusalem set forth the Jewish–Christian relationship mainly in terms of food: "For it has seemed good to the Holy Spirit and to us to impose on you no further burden than these essentials: that you abstain from what has been sacrificed to idols and from blood and from what is strangled and from fornication. If you keep yourselves from these, you will do well. Farewell" (15:28–29).

Food for Further Thought

In the Hebrew Bible, the relationship between God and humanity is articulated in terms of food: "You may freely eat of every tree of the garden; but of the tree of the knowledge of good and evil you shall not eat, for in the day that you eat of it you shall die" (Genesis 2:16–17).

In cross-cultural interactions, cultural codes of behavior concerning food can be a hurdle, and potentially cause offense. Yet, by gaining an understanding of another culture's rituals concerning food, one may find the most effective way to appreciate and be appreciated by members of that culture.

Humans do not just consume food. They relish it, and attach special meaning to the food served. Rituals bring out this meaning in a stylized manner, as they are repeated to render their traditional service of adding to the flavor of life.

Jin Hee Han

See also Agricultural Rituals; Asceticism; Blood Rituals; Body and Rituals; Haircutting Rituals; Identity Rituals; Marriage Rituals; Passage, Rites of; Puberty Rites; Purity and Pollution; Scatological Rituals; Witchcraft

Further Reading

Badia, L. F. (1979). *The Dead Sea people's sacred meal and Jesus' last supper*. Washington, DC: University Press of America.

Baumgarten, A. I., Assmann, J., & Stroumsa, G. G. (Eds.). (1998). *Self, soul, and body in religious experience.* Studies in the history of religions (*Numen* Book Series), 78. Leiden, Netherlands: Brill.

Bynum, C. W. (1987). *Holy feast and holy fast: The religious significance of food to medieval women.* Berkeley, CA: University of California Press.

Camporesi, P. (1989). *The magic harvest: Food, folklore and society*. (J. Krakover Hall, Trans.). Cambridge, UK: Polity Press.

Counihan, C., & van Esterik, P. (1997). *Food and culture: A reader*. New York and London: Routledge.

Curran, P. (1989). *Grace before meals: Food ritual and body discipline in convent culture*. Urbana and Chicago: University of Illinois Press.

Davis, R. H. (Ed). (1998). Images, miracles, and authority in Asian religious Traditions. Boulder, CO: Westview Press.

Douglas, M. (1966). *Purity and danger: An analysis of the concepts of pollution and taboo*. London and New York: Ark Paperbacks.

Fieldhouse, P. (1986). *Food & nutrition: Customs & culture*. London: Croom Helm.

Harris, M. (1985). *The sacred cow and the abominable pig: Riddles of food and culture*. New York: Simon & Schuster.

Khare, R. S. (Ed.). (1992). *The eternal food: Gastronomic ideas and experiences of Hindus and Buddhists*. Albany, NY: State University of New York Press.

McGowan, A. (1999). *Ascetic eucharists: Food and drink in early Christian ritual meals*. Oxford Early Christian Studies. Oxford: Clarendon Press.

Maguire, E. D, Maguire, H. P., & Duncan-Flowers, M. J. (1989). *Art and powers in the early Christian house*. Illinois Byzantine Studies, 2. Urbana and Chicago: University of Illinois Press.

Mennell, S. (1985). *All manners of food: Eating and taste in England and France from the Middle Ages to the present*. New York: Basil Blackwell.

Reynolds, P. L. (1999). *Food and the body: Some particular questions in high medieval theology*. Studien und Texte zur geistesgeschichte des Mittelalters (Studies and texts on the intellectual history of the Middle Ages), 69. Leiden, Netherlands: Brill.

Ringgren, H. (1973). *Religions of the ancient Near East*. (J. Sturdy, Trans.). Philadelphia: The Westminster Press.

Schmitt, E. (1991). *Das Essen in der Bibel: Literaturethnologische Aspekte des Alltäglichen* (Eating in the Bible: Literary and theological aspects of the commonplace). Studien zur Kulturanthropologie (Studies in cultural anthropology), 2. Hamburg, Germany: LIT.

Shuman, A. (2000). Food gifts: Ritual exchange and the production of excess meaning. *Journal of American folklore, 113*, 495–508.

Toussaint-Samat, M. (1992). *A history of food*. (A. Bell, Trans.). Cambridge, MA: Blackwell.

Visser, M. (1991). *The rituals of dinner: The origins, evolution, eccentricities, and meaning of table manners*. New York: Grove Weidenfeld.

G

Gender Rituals

In some sense all ritual is gender ritual. As long as people live gendered lives, their experience of the world, and thus of ritual, will be gender dependent, whether or not the rituals they perform explicitly relate to gender. Religious rituals often make gender distinctions in their actions, and many rituals can only be performed by men or by women. However, this article defines gender rituals as those rituals whose major purpose is to establish, reaffirm, or problematize gender.

Defining and Theorizing Gender

Before examining gender rituals it is important to understand what is meant by "gender." Until recently it was agreed that gender could be defined vis-à-vis sex, sex being biologically determined, while gender was culturally acquired. Similarly, many cultures viewed "male" as closer to culture and "female" as closer to nature, with the result that nature was considered inferior to culture, and women inferior to men.

This gender-versus-sex dichotomy was eventually critiqued by feminists as too simplistic and beside the point. Most famously, perhaps, Judith Butler has argued:

> Gender ought not to be conceived merely as the cultural inscription of meaning upon a pregiven sex (a juridicial conception); gender must also designate the very apparatus of production whereby the sexes themselves are established. As a result, gender is not to culture as sex is to nature; gender is also the discursive/cultural means by which "sexed nature" or "a natural sex" is produced and established as "prediscursive," prior to culture, a politically neutral surface on which culture acts. (Butler 1990, 7).

Thus Butler would contend that the widespread belief that sex differences are *natural* indicates the very success of such a system. In understanding Butler it is important to realize that for her nothing exists before culture. There can be no natural sex because sex could not have been conceived or spoken of before the existence of cultural constructs.

So how does one study gender if it is always a result of culture? According to Daniel Boyarin, when studying gender one is "investigating the praxis and process by which people are interpellated into a two- (or for some cultures more) sex system that is made to seem as if it were nature, that is, something that has always existed" (Boyarin 1998, 117). Studying ritual is an intriguing way to understand how this cultural conscription of gender occurs, as many rituals play an important role in establishing, reaffirming, and problematizing gender and provide an outlet for participants to discuss and internalize the meaning of gender differences in society.

Establishing Gender through Ritual

Religious rituals that establish gender usually occur early in life. While many religious traditions treat young children as somewhat androgynous beings, there are traditions in which gendered existence begins at birth. An example of this is seen in Judaism. The first event after the birth of a baby boy is a *bris*, or

GENDER RITUALS AND GENDER ROLE AND STATUS

How gender rituals are carried out—and whether they occur at all—reflect often-complicated gender relations in the society. The following example concerning the role of Hopi mothers in their son's lives and initiation ritual and other life event rituals suggests the complexity of gender relations in Hopi society where women exercise considerable power and influence.

Whereas the division of labor tends to force a son very close to his father it serves to pull him somewhat apart from his mother. This does not mean that there is a weakening of affection, but it does imply that a mother's influence over her son is greatest in the early years of his life.

Hopi mothers are notoriously over-indulgent towards their children. I have often seen them deny themselves even a taste of some particular dainty at meals in order that a child may have more for himself; and I have seen little boys, old enough to know better, strike their mothers viciously while their parents assumed an air of indifference in order that those present might not note how badly they were hurt physically and mentally. Mothers often scold and threaten punishment, but only rarely do they make good their threats.

As a boy outgrows his childish fits of temper he begins more and more to appreciate his mother's position in the household and to rely on her advice. At this stage she generally encourages him not to be lazy, to go with his father and uncles into the fields, and to comport himself in a manner befitting a good Hopi.

When the time comes for a son's initiation into the Katcina cult, the mother helps choose his ceremonial father, and after the ceremony she brings food to the home of her child's sponsor. When a boy is old enough to go into his Tribal Initiation, the mother makes special cakes for his ceremonial father.

A mother's word counts heavily but is not necessarily final in a man's choice of a bride. During the actual wedding ritual a mother plays a very active part, and when a son goes into housekeeping she gives him various useful gifts and helps carry water to his new residence.

Even after marriage, when a man has left his mother's household and has gone from a subordinate position in his family of orientation to a more dominant one in his family of procreation, he does not feel that he has severed his ties with his natal home. He is always welcome to drop into his mother's house for meals, to bring friends there for entertainment, and to leave harness, tools, or other equipment in the mother's house if it happens to be more conveniently located than his wife's. Furthermore, if a mother becomes a widow her sons are expected to raise crops for her even if they happen to be married and primarily occupied in working their wives' farms. It is regarded as highly disgraceful for married sons to neglect a widowed mother.

The birth of children to a married son again brings his mother into prominence, for it is she who first washes and cares for the tiny infant, and it is she who conducts the ceremonies that lead up to the naming rites on the twentieth day. On that occasion she takes charge of the proceedings and is the first of many eligible women to bestow a name referring to her clan on the baby.

Source: Titiev, Mischa. (1971).
Old Oraibi; a study of the Hopi Indians of Third Mesa.
New York, Kraus Reprint Co., p. 19. (Originally published 1944).

ritual circumcision, which traditionally occurs eight days after birth. The purpose of the *bris* is to remember and re-enact the covenant made between God and Abraham (Genesis 17:1–14). It is through circumcision that boys are welcomed into the covenant and inherit the promises of abundance and land. Traditionally, this covenant was made between God and the male descendants of Abraham, and because the action of

Indian sadhus perform a ritual to ensure health and prosperity for clients by worshipping the Divine Female Principle in the form of young virgins. Himalayas, India, 1988. COURTESY OF RICHARD J. CASTILLO.

the ritual involves marking the male body, there was historically no parallel ceremony for girls. Although the overt purpose of the *bris* may be to commemorate Abraham's promise to God, it also serves to segregate boys and girls at an early age by indicating that being male is a prerequisite for full participation in Jewish rituals.

In many cultures, puberty, or coming-of-age, ceremonies have almost always been explicitly rituals of gender. These rituals, which Arnold van Gennep would label "rites of passage," welcome the initiates into the world of adults. While some cultures have celebrated parallel puberty ceremonies for boys and girls, most have emphasized either the male or the female in coming-of-age ceremonies. However, it is not just this division that marks these ceremonies as gender rituals. The very point of these rituals is to celebrate differences. Children become adults and begin living as distinctly gendered when their differentiated sex organs develop into their mature form at puberty. This explains why many of these rituals occur around puberty, although social and biological adulthood are not always considered synonymous.

Although some would assume that in a traditionally patriarchal world, coming-of-age ceremonies would be more common for boys than for girls, there are a surprising number of such ceremonies for girls. Among the best-known girls' puberty ceremonies is the Kinaaldá ceremony that the Navajo traditionally perform for girls at each of their first two periods. According to Bruce Lincoln, the Navajo celebrate a girl's menarche "because it indicates that she is ready to bring forth new life" (Lincoln 1981, 17). It is a girl's becoming a woman and thus her ability to bear children that is celebrated in such rituals. Thus, these rituals help establish her as a gendered being and emphasize those traits considered properly feminine in her culture—in this case fertility.

In the Kinaaldá ritual the girl becomes the Changing Woman (a fertility goddess) through songs, dress, and action. Her transformative power can especially be seen in the action of the initiated girl as she places her hands on younger girls, lifting them up to help them grow. Just as the Changing Woman is concerned with growth and the life cycle, so the initiand (new initiate) develops these concerns in part through this ceremony. Once the girl has undergone the Kinaaldá ceremony she is expected to be ready to marry and have children: at this point she is a woman, as the ceremony has affirmed the physical status she has already reached.

Reaffirming Gender through Ritual

Many religious rituals serve to reaffirm adults' gendered existence. Whether or not these rituals indicate equality or oppression, they do affirm differences between men and women. These differences do not necessarily relate to physical characteristics, as some puberty ceremonies do, but often re-establish the characteristics that the religious tradition considers properly masculine or feminine. To be socially accepted a man must often behave in masculine ways and a woman in feminine ways, and this is learned through ritual.

One common reaffirming ritual is the wedding ceremony. In many religious traditions men and women (both the wedding couple and their guests) play slightly different roles during the ceremony, roles that specifically relate to the ways in which men and women should behave in marriage. In a traditional Iraqi Muslim wedding, the actual ceremony takes place between the bride's father and the bridegroom. The father gives his daughter to the groom and asks whether the groom accepts the daughter according to the law of God and the prophet Muhammad. Once the groom has accepted her, the father gives his blessing, and those assembled recite the first chapter of the Qur'an. On the wedding night, usually after a day of festivities, the bride is delivered by her family to the groom, who greets her by washing her feet and praying. The wedding ceremony is a microcosm of the traditional marital relationship where the major public decisions are made by the men. Women are respected and loved by their husbands, but that affection is shown only in private. Finally, as the recitation of the Qur'an and the prayer indicate, the relationship between husband and wife will be guided by devotion to God and the example of the Qur'an. Thus, the very ritual of the wedding reinforces the cultural notions of masculinity and femininity and the relationship between men and women.

Some theorists suggest that our daily lives include cultural rituals not commonly regarded as religious that reaffirm gender. For instance, James McBride has argued that football games can serve as religious rituals that reaffirm gender for men who play or watch them, by tapping into anxieties associated with masculine gender in American society. According to McBride, "Football is a masculine ritual that symbolically plays out men's unresolved separation anxiety—the desire for and hostility toward the mother in every woman and the woman in every mother.... The basic structure of the game, pitting opposite teams against each other, mimes the binary opposition of father/mother, phallus/not-phallus" (McBride 2001, 135). In this theory, it is the relationship between the mother and son, and the very definition of masculinity that is being replayed on the football field. While few people would consider football a traditional religious ritual, McBride contends that its collective nature defines it as religious ritual.

Problematizing Gender Through Ritual

Religious ritual can also work to problematize traditional beliefs about gender or the relationship between sex and gender. One of the most basic ways in which ritual problematizes gender is through inversion: When men perform typically feminine actions or women exhibit masculine traits gender roles are questioned.

An example of gender-inversion ritual is "male menstruation," or sympathetic menstruation. Although men do not literally menstruate, in some cultures men ritually cause themselves to bleed or vomit so as to replicate the natural processes of women. In some cultures this only happens during initiation or puberty rituals, but some men perform such bleeding throughout their lives. Male menstruation can be accompanied by transvestism and doing traditionally female work, as in the case of the Northern Mejbrats in Western New Guinea. Ashley Montagu's description of the Australian Aborigines indicates that in some cultures it is even common for ritual surgery involving subincision of the penis to be performed upon boys so that they can imitate the female genitalia.

Why do these men ritually imitate women, and what does this gender-bending mean? First, according to Matthea Cremers, ritual inversion can serve "as an affirmation of masculinity and a way for men to rid themselves of contamination by females" (Cremers 1989, 85). By showing that they can imitate what is naturally unique to women, men negate any of women's potential superiority. Second, imitation of women may also indicate men's envy of the power they believe women naturally possess through their sexual organs.

Roman Catholic ordination rites accomplish such gender-bending, although not through strict ritual inversion. Although only men are permitted to become Catholic priests, the gendered language associated with the priesthood emphasizes the traditionally feminine characteristics that priests should exemplify, including submission and compassion. Even more explicitly, priests are considered to be "brides" of Christ. Clearly physical womanhood is not necessary in order to portray the ideal of femininity; however, physical manhood does seem necessary in order to portray the Priest's relation to Christ. One major Roman Catholic argument against ordaining women is that the priest must be an icon of Christ when performing the sacraments Christ instituted, and as an icon the priest must resemble Christ physically, maleness being an important component of this resemblance. As it is never argued that priests should be Hebrew or circumcised so as physically to resemble Christ, it is clear that gender is an important issue in the priesthood. It may be that the traditional feminine ideal of being submissive brides of Christ is balanced by physical masculinity, indicating that Roman Catholic priests are regarded as somewhat gender neutral, a notion reinforced by their vow of celibacy. In this example ritual thus problematizes gender so that the ritual participant may transcend it.

The Future of Gender Rituals

Particularly as a result of the women's movement of the 1960s and 1970s, there have been several changes in the acceptance of gender rituals throughout the world. In the West, reform movements within major religious traditions, especially Judaism and Christianity, have sought to de-emphasize the importance of gender in religious ceremony. This shift is especially clear in the case of Judaism, where ceremonies for girls have often been created to parallel the *bris* and bar mitzvah rituals for boys. Several Christian denominations have begun to ordain women, thus largely negating (or possibly complicating) the gendered distinctions formerly present in ordination rituals.

Another consequence of the women's movement has been the Western feminist critique of gender rituals throughout the world. Many American and European women have decried the practice of genital mutilation performed during some female initiation ceremonies. In addition, Western feminists have argued that unequal marriage and divorce ceremonies, female infanticide, *suti* (widow burning), and other religious or cultural practices oppress women and should be stopped. While many such rituals have been banned, at least in some areas, some women defend these practices theologically and do not find them oppressive.

Many feminist efforts have gone toward establishing strict equality for women in religious matters, but some religious feminists have worked to create rituals that celebrate gender differences, instead of sameness. Women in the women's spirituality movement have especially concentrated on empowering women through religious ritual. This empowerment may begin early, as many spiritual feminists have created menarche rituals for their daughters. These rituals emphasize the girls' feminine characteristics and introduction into womanhood. Spiritual feminists do not limit their celebration of womanhood to adolescence. In the feminist spirituality worldview all rites of passage are gender rituals, as womanhood is celebrated in all of them, including birth ceremonies, weddings, and menopause rituals. Women are empowered in these rituals through symbolism, chanting, gifts, and ritual activities such as dancing, which emphasize a connection to the Goddess and the creative abilities of women.

Not just the women's movement has complicated gender rituals. Same-sex wedding rituals have toppled many preconceived notions of gender relations within marriage, and transgender individuals have forced a rethinking of the very definition of gender and its relation to religious ritual. There are also men's spirituality groups that have focused on empowering men through religious rituals. While gender rituals will continue to shift in meaning and shape, clearly they will always be an important aspect of religious ritual.

Kelly Therese Pollock

See also Birth Rituals; Body and Rituals; Haircutting Rituals; Identity Rituals; Marriage Rituals; Passage, Rites of; Puberty Rites; Purity and Pollution; Ritual as Communication; Scatological Rituals; Witchcraft

Further Reading

Bourdieu, P. (2001). *Masculine domination* (R. Nice, Trans.). Stanford, CT: Stanford University Press.

Boyarin, D. (1998). Gender. In M. C. Taylor (Ed.), *Critical terms in religious studies* (pp. 117–135). Chicago: The University of Chicago Press.

Brooks, G. (1995). *Nine parts of desire: The hidden world of Islamic women.* New York: Anchor Books.

Butler, J. (1990). *Gender trouble: Feminism and the subversion of identity.* London: Routledge.

Chaves, M. (1997). *Ordaining women.* Cambridge, MA: Harvard University Press.

Cremers, M. (1989). Two rivers of blood: Female and male menstruation. *Anthropology UCLA, 16*(2), 72–94.

Elmberg, J. (1959). Further Notes of the Northern Mejbrats (Vogelkop, Western New Guinea). *Ethnos, 35*(1–2), 70–80.

Fuss, D. (1989). *Essentially speaking: Feminism, nature, and difference.* New York: Routledge.

Lincoln, B. (1981). *Emerging from the chrysalis: Studies in rituals of women's initiation.* Cambridge, MA: Harvard University Press.

McBride, J. (2001). Symptomatic expression of male neuroses: Collective effervescence, male gender performance, and the ritual of football. In E. M. Mazur, & K. McCarthy (Eds.), *God in the details: American religion in popular culture.* New York: Routledge.

Montagu, A. (1970). *The natural superiority of women.* New York: Collier Books.

Ortner, S. (1974). Is female to male as nature is to culture? In M. Rosaldo, & L. Lamphere (Eds.), *Woman, culture, and society* (pp. 67–87). Stanford, CT: Stanford University Press.

Plaskow, J. (1990). *Standing again at Sinai: Judaism from a feminist perspective.* San Francisco: HarperSanFrancisco.

Sutcliffe, S., & Bowman, M. (Eds.). (2000). *Beyond New Age: Exploring alternative spirituality.* Edinburgh, UK: Edinburgh University Press.

van Gennep, A. (1960). *The rites of passage* (M. B. Vizedom & G. L. Caffee, Trans.). Chicago: University of Chicago Press.

Glossolalia

The term "glossolalia," (from the Greek *glossa*, "tongue," and *lalia*, "to talk") literally means "speaking in tongues." In the Christian Pentecostal tradition, the phenomenon of speaking in tongues refers to an ecstatic religious experience, inspired by the Holy Spirit, which is characterized by the excited utterances of an alien, incomprehensible language. In the religious sense, glossolalia is a gift from God; it is indicative of a unique relationship between the speaker and God. Behavioral scientists generally view glossolalia as fundamentally a psychological phenomenon that lacks the salient features of genuine human language—syntactic structure, semantic meaningfulness, and representational quality. In this regard, speaking in tongues is not properly a linguistic act, but more akin to babbling.

Glossolalia as the Gift of Tongues

The New Testament provides a textual justification for the belief in the power to speak in tongues. With tongues of fire on their heads, the apostles were said to be "filled with the Holy Ghost, and began to speak in other tongues, as the Spirit gave them utterance" (Acts 2:3–4, RSV). The event of the first Pentecost as recorded in Acts thus marks the origin of the Christian idea of glossolalia. As described in Acts, the apostles spoke languages that were understood by hearers as their own native tongues. The implication here is that the languages spoken by the apostles were clearly recognizable human tongues; the spiritual mystery is that they spoke in languages they had never learned. While this may strictly be defined as *xenoglossy* (speaking in a language with which one has no prior familiarity), the operative theological idea is that this ability is a gift of the Holy Spirit.

In 1 Corinthians 12–14, the matter is explained differently. In the Pauline sense, speaking in tongues, while clearly a spiritual "gift," is to make incomprehensible utterances while in a state of religious ecstasy. The string of utterances, which may resemble an intelligible human language, always requires an interpretation by one endowed with the correlative gift of understanding; for glossolalia is not, under this view, simply a human language but perhaps the "language of angels." Because of the nonhuman, spiritual nature of the language, it is, by definition, not humanly understandable. It is, however, a sign of an individual's unique relationship with God, a kind of prayer, incomprehensible to the speaker but understood by God.

This latter idea serves a dual purpose in Paul's narrative on speaking in tongues. Despite his recognition that speaking in tongues is a gift, Paul warns that it is not to be overestimated and that it can, in fact, have destructive consequences. While the individual communicates directly with God ("he that speaketh in an unknown tongue speaketh not unto men, but unto God" [1 Cor.14:2, KJV]), to the external community speakers of tongues may appear to be mad (1 Cor. 14:23).

Paul does value the gift of tongues, but primarily as a form of prayer inspired in an individual by the Spirit alone; that is, understanding on the part of the speaker and others is absent ("if I pray in an unknown tongue, my spirit prayeth, but my understanding is unfruitful" [1 Cor. 14:14, KJV]). For this reason, the gift of tongues is inferior to other spiritual gifts.

Paul provides a hierarchy of spiritual gifts, in which the gift of tongues is the lowest. The gift of prophecy is far superior to that of tongues because it combines the spiritual with human understanding and, most important, because it speaks to others. Prophecy edifies, exhorts, and comforts (1 Cor. 14:3, KJV) and, in this way, serves to strengthen the community of believers. The highest of all gifts is love, for, whether one speaks in tongues or prophesies, without love, language is reduced to "sounding brass or a tinkling cymbal" (1 Cor. 13:1). One's individual faith and capacity to understand must, in Paul's sense, be informed by charity or else one is nothing (1 Cor. 13:2).

Despite the strenuous limitations the Pauline narrative places on the value of speaking in tongues, Pentecostal Christians view it as an extraordinary sign of one's spiritual baptism. For some strong Pentecostals, speaking in tongues is a necessary element in the conversion experience and Christian rebirth. Others, like Pentecostal or charismatic Catholics, share the view that speaking in tongues is a gift and sign of one's baptism, but do not see it as a requirement for full initiation into the Christian faith.

Glossolalia as Psycholinguistic Pathology

From a nonreligious and behavioral scientific perspective, glossolalia is a kind of psycholinguistic pathology. It is marked by the repetition of semantically and syntactically unintelligible, meaningless utterances. Even though the speaker may believe the utterances to be meaningful, from this standpoint, glossolalia lacks linguistic structure and cognitive content. While it may resemble a language, in large measure because the utterances resemble phonetically familiar sounds, there is no criterion of meaningfulness that can be employed in deciphering its cognitive value. Some hearers suggest possible meanings, but there is no independent mode of verifying such claims, as there is no discernible representational relation between the glossal utterances and the perceived world. Glossolalics themselves simply report that even if no one understands their utterances, God does.

Despite phonetic similarity and the occasional recognizable word in its string of utterances, glossolalia fails to meet other significant criteria for discerning linguistic structure. Glossolalia lacks a unique vocabulary and so it is not lexically ordered; it lacks systematic semantic representation of common human experience, which accounts for why it is not understandable by ordinary language users; and it is characteristically nonreflexive, that is, one cannot explain the nature of glossolalia by speaking in tongues.

What exactly constitutes the cause of glossolalia is a matter of considerable theoretical debate. Psychologists have variously proposed to explain the phenomenon in terms of certain disorders; e.g., schizophrenia, neurosis, psychosis, hysteria, or even epilepsy. Most agree that, irrespective of its cause, glossolalia itself is a linguistic aberration.

Ongoing Controversies

There is a seeming incommensurability between the theological and psycholinguistic conceptions of glossolalia. Whether glossolalia is a spiritual gift and sign of one's baptism or a kind of pathology is a fundamental disagreement. There are also disagreements internal to each of these perspectives. Theologians continue to debate the value and necessity of the gift of tongues, and behavioral scientists, while agreeing on the aberrant nature of glossolalia, continue to offer widely diverse theories as to its cause.

Alexander R. Eodice

See also African-American Churches; Altered States of Consciousness; Ecstatic Worship; Pentecostalism

Further Reading

Brown, L. B. (Ed.). (1973). *Psychology and religion.* Baltimore: Penguin Books.

Ford, J. M. (1971). *Baptism of the spirit: Three essays on the Pentecostal experience.* Techny, IL: Divine Word Publications.

Goodman, F. D. (1972). *Speaking in tongues: A cross-cultural study of glossolalia.* Chicago: University of Chicago Press.

Kildahl, J. P. (1972). *The psychology of speaking in tongues.* New York: HarperCollins.

Lovekin, A. A., & Malony, H. N. (1985). *Glossolalia: Behavioral science perspectives on speaking in tongues.* New York: Oxford University Press.

Martin, I. J. (1960). *Glossolalia in the apostolic church: A survey study of tongue-speech.* Berea, KY: Berea College Press.

Mills, W. E. (1985). *Glossolalia: A bibliography* (Studies in the Bible and early Christianity 6). Lewiston, NY: Edwin Mellen Press.

Samarin, W. J. (1972). *Tongues of men and angels: The religious language of Pentecostalism.* New York: Macmillan.

Greco-Roman

The term *Greco-Roman* refers to the thought and character of the ancient civilizations of Greece and Rome. These two civilizations and the sensibility that emerged from their combination influenced the history of Western civilization in virtually every significant respect. Throughout the period from the time of the Greek poet Homer, about 850 BCE, to the mature development of Christian thinking, represented largely by the early Christian philosopher Augustine's writings in the fourth and fifth centuries, the fundamental elements of Greek and Roman thought set the foundation for the educational, political, social, artistic, literary, scientific, and religious ideas and institutions that have come to constitute the core of the Western canon. One of the hallmarks of the Greco-Roman world is the increasing emphasis that came to be placed on the quality and character of human rationality. Human rationality was the great achievement of classical Greco-Roman thought, whether manifested as the ability to create social organization, design columns and arches, perfect the human form in sculpture, generate theories about the nature and structure of reality, develop philosophies of human will and action, or have insight into the nature of the divine.

Both Greek culture and Roman culture were unquestionably rooted in a spiritual tradition centered

The Theseion, or Temple of Theseus, overlooks the agora, the ancient marketplace of Athens. A Doric temple dating from fifth century BCE, it was originally the temple of Hephaistos, the god of smiths and metalworkers. Like many Greek and Roman sacred sites, it later was used by other religions: as a Byzantine church, a graveyard, and in the nineteenth century as a pilgrimage site for worshippers at Easter. COURTESY OF KAREN CHRISTENSEN.

on the relationship between the human and the divine (gods). The gods, however, were less supernatural and more hypernatural in that they had qualities essentially associated with human physical, psychological, and moral characteristics. Although there was no single theory of human personhood that defined the Greco-Roman period, there was a universal sense of having to understand nature and humans' place in it. Broadly construed, then, the Greco-Roman world was characterized by the most sanguine attitude about the human being's ability to understand what it means to live in world in which the forces of nature, the demands of fate, the possibility of contingency, and the rigors of civic and communal life pose complex intellectual challenges. The modalities with which the ancient thinkers faced such challenges were wide and varied; they included epic and lyric poetry, tragedy and comedy, scientific theorizing and metaphysical speculation, and moral and historical reasoning.

Fundamental Elements of Intellectual Life

Early Greek civilization emerged after the so-called Dark Ages (c. 1100–900 BCE) and after the collapse of the Mycenaean civilization (c. 1900–1100 BCE). The earliest literary works of this period are the great epic poems of Homer: the *Iliad* and the *Odyssey*. These works not only provide insight into the ancient Mycenae traditions and chronicle events in the lives of its most legendary heroes, but also lay the foundation for Greek religious and ethical thought. Rooted in an oral and bardic (relating to a poet) tradition, Homer's verses rhapsodically relate the events associated with the Trojan Wars. The *Iliad* tells of the Battle of Ilium (at Troy in modern Turkey) and the heroic efforts of Achilles; the *Odyssey* tells of the travels of Odysseus after the siege and collapse of Troy and his thoughts of returning to Ithaca and his wife Penelope. Homer's poetry also introduces into literature the pantheon of the Olympian gods, whose relationships to each other and to humans characterize the world and human action as mixtures of chaos and stability, reason and passion, wisdom and warfare. These two fundamental aspects of the Homeric epic poem—putting forward heroic actors as exemplars for human action and casting natural events as the consequences of the actions of the gods—set the stage for later Greco-Roman thought. That is, they demonstrate that, even in its earliest stages, the classical mind-set was geared to explaining the events of nature and the character behind human action.

Moreover, the Homeric epic, structured as it is in poetic meter and textured by figures of speech such as metaphor and simile, lent itself to memorization and became the prime educational source for the education of youth in early Greek culture. In this respect the Homeric epic set the stage for two important strands in the ancient Greek conception of education—the technical and the ethical. Education was for the dual purpose of training in various technical crafts, that is, warfare, sports, and oratory, and providing the means whereby one could learn to live virtuously and attain to the sort of courageous action as was exemplified by the Homeric heroes. The distinction in meaning between the Greek terms *techne* (technique) and *arête* (excellence or virtue) reflects these emphases. Over time the concept of *arête* became the primary goal of education.

The development of intellectual life in ancient Greece in the sixth century BCE led to important shifts in both outlook and language. Although religion had become a civic responsibility, as it was later for the Romans, certain thinkers began to focus not on the gods but rather on nature itself in an effort to discover the underlying structure of the universe and explain natural events. The problem was set: How can people account for the events in nature in a purely natural way; what is the source of stability in an apparently ever-changing world? The earliest thinkers to ponder such questions were from the Ionian coast and thought primarily in materialistic terms, that is, that there is an underlying physical substance, which can be rationally known as the essence of the material world. First among such thinkers was

Thales (c. 585 BCE), who thought everything is made of water; others proposed different subtheories. Democritus (c. 460 BCE), for instance, argued that the universe is composed of irreducible particles called "atoms," the concatenation (linking) of which accounts for all things physical, perceptual, and psychological. More important than the actual content of what was thought is the fact that such thought marked a radical departure from the poetical imagination and signaled the advent of scientific investigation. With this emphasis these early pre-Socratic (prior to the Greek philosopher Socrates) philosophers established the foundations for modern scientific theorizing.

Other Philosophies

Not all philosophers of that period were materialists. Pythagoras (c. 580–485 BCE), for example, viewed the universe in formal mathematical terms. All things, he suggested, are explainable, not through the discovery of some material substratum but rather through the rational discovery of numerical relationships. He had observed, for instance, that musical tones are functions of mathematical ratios and generalized that this is true of the whole cosmos. In contrast to both pre-Socratic materialism and Pythagorean idealism or formalism was the thought of Heraclitus (c. 545–485 BCE). Heraclitus argued that all things are in a constant state of change or flux and that this is the fundamental nature of the universe and, further, that through the use of reason people can reconcile the opposition that naturally occurs in the changing world. Attendant to this shift in focus was a shift in the nature of language itself. The poetic character of Homeric language seemed insufficient to provide such explanations; language became more discursive. This engendered increased speculation and was the condition for the possibility of understanding language itself as capable of representing reality to the knowing mind.

In the fifth century BCE a group called the "Sophists" completely rejected the idea of theoretical speculation and focused instead on teaching practical skills that would lead to material success. They were itinerant teachers who, for a fee, would instruct the youth in the art of oratory. Not only did they reject the idea of theoretical speculation, but also they rejected the idea that language is essentially representational; instead they viewed language as fundamentally performative and persuasive in nature. Although skeptical about the possibility of knowing reality as it is, the Sophists were most optimistic about human potential. Protagoras (c. 481–411 BCE) suggested that "man is the measure of all things." The Sophists were remarkable figures in that they rejected both the idea that human affairs are controlled by the gods and the idea that reason can know reality as it is; reality is simply what human beings take it to be.

Socrates (c. 470–399 BCE) steadfastly rejected the Sophists' view. He argued that underlying their standpoint was a warped conception of education because it relied too heavily on the idea of *techne* and ignored the possibility of *arête.* From the Socratic point of view it is possible not only to use language to persuade others to do something, but also through language to understand the very nature of goodness and virtue, the understanding of which begins with the recognition of one's own ignorance. Language is not just conventional, as it was for the Sophists, but rather it is the vehicle whereby terms may be objectively defined and truth rationally discovered. What marks this Socratic move as original is the idea that the pursuit of knowledge, through the use of reason, is itself a prime virtue.

After Socrates, Plato (c. 427–347 BCE) recast philosophical thought in a systematic way, utilizing many of the ideas that had preceded him. He speculated that the observable world is not fully real, that it is changeable and contingent. Underlying this world is an unchanging world of "forms" or "ideas," to which the mind bears necessary resemblance and relation. Through rational knowledge the mind can represent objects, and language can secure truth. In order to know, Plato proposed, one must believe something, it must be true, and the mind must be able to provide an intellectual justification for why it is true. Such justification is provided only by reference to the "forms," which are not just mathematical abstractions but rather idealized concepts of justice, beauty, and goodness. Reliance solely on observation of the physical, as was the case for the pre-Socratic materialists, or solely on the rhetorical aspect of language, as was the case for the Sophists, would prevent the discovery of truth and inhibit humans from acting according to principles. In his *Republic,* a work about both education and political organization, Plato proposes that social hierarchy itself is determined by rational ability.

Aristotle

The philosopher Aristotle (384–322 BCE), in rejecting the duality of worlds in Plato's philosophy, argued that the natural world is one in which form and matter are inseparable, all objects have an essential form or function that defines how they exist materially in the natural world. All things in nature must, he further suggested, have a natural material cause. Aristotle added to this the principle of final causality, that is, the notion that there is, for each kind of object, a natural end toward which it tends. Aristotle used this fundamental principle to explain not only physical objects but also ethics. All things have a purpose, defined by their function, and the purpose of being human is, according to Aristotle, to attain happiness. The unique function of being human is the ability to reason, through whose proper exercise happiness may be achieved. Moreover, Aristotle saw this as the means for understanding how to live with others in friendship and civic community.

During the Hellenistic period, stretching roughly from the death of the Macedonian king Alexander the Great in 323 BCE to the conquest of Macedonia by the Romans in 146 BCE, intellectual attitudes took a more critical and skeptical turn. People known as "Skeptics," for instance, rejected the idea that people are capable of knowing anything with certitude and that, in order to attain to a life of quietude, people must give up on the useless quest for certainty. Epicureanism and Stoicism were the most influential theories emerging from this period. The Epicureans argued that, in order to attain happiness, people must desire simple things, keeping pleasures moderate, and focus on building enduring human relationships. Stoicism argued that nature itself is rational and that through a proper understanding of it people can discover the principles that order human conduct. Nature, as it is a reflection of God's reason, is lawfully ordered. People, through the use of their own reason, can discover this rational order of nature and freely choose to act accordingly.

The Roman intellectual tradition borrowed much from the Greeks. This is perhaps most evident in considering the poet Virgil's *Aeneid* in relation to Homer's *Iliad* and *Odyssey*. Virgil (70–19 BCE) tells the story of Aeneas, who flees Troy upon its destruction and travels to Italy, where he must quell resistance and ensure the permanency of Rome. Like Odysseus and Achilles in Homer's epics, Aeneas is a traveler and a warrior. He is destined by the gods to perform his tasks, and the conflict of his desires and his destiny accounts for much of the *Aeneid*'s content.

Whereas the Greeks were inclined to high levels of speculation, the Romans had a much more measured and practical sense about the value of philosophical ideas. In this regard, it is not surprising then that the two philosophies that exercised the greatest influence on Roman thought were Epicureanism and Stoicism. The Romans, given their heightened sense of civic responsibility and the value they placed on practical life, were inclined toward seeing supreme value in simple and elegant theory. Lucretius (98–58 BCE) elaborated the fundamental principles of Epicureanism in his poem *De rerum natura* (On Nature). In that poem he argues for materialism and endeavors to show that the gods do not control human affairs. Only nature has control over human life, and much of it happens by chance. The goal then is simply to seek pleasure in ordinary life. More important to the Romans than Epicureanism was Stoicism. In opposition to Lucretius stood the statesman and philosopher Cicero (106–43 BCE), who steadfastly held to the Stoic idea of an orderly universe directed by rational intelligence. Cicero, popularly known as Rome's greatest orator, believed that the capacity to reason is the human manifestation of the natural principle of order. Further, he believed that, when properly directed, reason leads to a strong sense of duty and self-discipline, which are necessary for a well-balanced social order among citizens. The emperor Marcus Aurelius, who ruled Rome from 161 to 80 BCE, was one of the most ardent representatives of the Stoic standpoint, arguing that there is a single natural law to which human reason must conform.

The concept of natural law is one of the greatest legacies of Greco-Roman thought. Natural law, with its rejection of the idea that the actions of multiple gods control human affairs and its sense of a single law giving force and rational intelligence, provided medieval Christian philosophers with a foundation for the development of a natural theology and a justification for monotheism. Further, it continues to provide a normative structure for the determination of right moral action and just social conduct.

Alexander R. Eodice

Further Reading

Cary, M., & Haarhoff, T. J. (1963). *Life and thought in the Greek and Roman world.* London: Methuen.

Cochrane, C. N. (1944). *Christianity and classical culture: A study of thought and action from Augustus to Augustine.* New York: Oxford University Press.

Copleston, F. (1962). *A history of philosophy: Vol. I. Greece and Rome.* Garden City, NY: Image Books.

Cornford, F. M. (1932). *Before and after Socrates.* London: Cambridge University Press.

Grant, R. M. (1952). *Miracle and natural law in Greco-Roman and early Christian thought.* Amsterdam, Netherlands: North-Holland Publishing.

Guthrie, W. K. C. (1960). *The Greek philosophers from Thales to Aristotle.* New York: Harper Torchbooks.

Havelock, E. A. (1967). *Preface to Plato.* New York: Grosset and Dunlap.

Jaeger, W. (1973). *Paideia: The ideals of Greek culture: Vols. I & II* (G. Highet, Trans.). Oxford, UK: Oxford University Press. (Original work published 1933)

Nietzsche, F. (1962). *Philosophy in the tragic age of the Greeks* (M. Cowan, Trans.). Chicago: Gateway Editions.

Rommen, H. (1955). *The natural law* (T. R. Hanley, Trans.). London: B. Herder Book Co.

White, H. (1973). *The Greco-Roman tradition.* New York: Harper & Row.

H

Haircutting Rituals

The importance of haircutting ritual derives from the inherent quality attributed to hair, which is seen as a repository of vital powers. Therefore, this type of ritual is present in most belief systems, primarily in two major forms: as a part of initiation ceremonies or rites of passage, or as an act by which the person subjected to it is deprived of his or her social status. This deprivation can either be voluntary and self-imposed, in fulfillment of a vow or as a sign of grief or renunciation of the world, or it can be forced upon the person by the society or an interested adversary and as a means of degradation or restraint.

Initiation Ceremonies

Numerous world religions include haircutting among the rituals that mark the passage from one stage to another within the life cycle of an individual. It is particularly characteristic of initiation to manhood, though in some cultures it was also applied to girls. Thus, in Homeric times the male adolescent was termed *kouros*, and the female one *koure*, words that with all probability derived from the verb *keiro*, "to shear." In Athens of the classical period, three days in September or October were dedicated to the festivities of Apaturia, during which the members of *phratria* ("brotherhood" of citizens) introduced new members: their wives or children. The crucial day was the third one, called *koureion*, on which young boys and girls were shorn and their hair sacrificed to Zeus and Athena as a sign of entering upon a new stage of life, in which they would take full social responsibility. A parallel rite for the wife, called *gamelion*, was likewise accompanied by hair offering and served to make the marriage public.

Passage into maturity was marked by similar ceremonies in other cultures. Thus, in early medieval Japan the ritual of *genpuku*, putting on the garments of an adult, included the act of shaving the front hair, which was performed by a godfather who gave the new name to the young noble at the occasion. In Jewish culture, the initiation traditionally takes place on the child's third birthday: even though the Torah does not explicitly mention it, rabbis usually interpret the passage about not picking fruit from a tree for the first three years as giving a clue to the proper date for the ritual. In Islam, the child is sometimes dedicated to a saint, at whose sanctuary the hair-clippings are then offered.

Vows

In certain respects, taking a vow can be understood as a form of initiation. By this ritual act a person may enter another modus of being or another stage in spiritual development, though it might be voluntary and not necessarily required by the society as a part of the life cycle. The Nazirites in the Old Testament made a vow not to cut their hair until the end of the determined period, when it was ceremonially shaved at the tabernacle (Numbers 6:1–18). The Qur'an defines as one of the rules for pilgrimage *(hajj)* that hair should not be cut until the destination has been reached. Vows involving hair were sworn by women of Greek antiquity for safety in perilous situations: thus, Hygeia, goddess of health, was given offerings of women's hair before or after childbirth and Ptolemy's wife Berenice cut off her tresses and laid them on Aphrodite's altar in fulfillment of the vow made for the victory of her husband in war against the Assyrians in 247 BCE.

In Christianity, haircutting ritual accompanies taking of lifelong vows, those of ascetic life; likewise, in Buddhist faith it symbolizes the passage from the worldly to the holy life. Ancient cults had similar rituals: Plutarch mentions the "shaven head-crowns" as a mark of the votaries of Isis. However, clerical and monastic tonsure in Christianity (after having experienced several variants) was given its specific form as symbolizing the crown of thorns worn by Christ.

Even though female ascetics could cut or shave their heads as well, it was required that they should thereupon immediately enter strict enclosure and cover their heads: *Codex Theodosianus* (fourth century CE) reports the case of a group of women who cut their hair "contrary to divine and human laws" (since they continued their life of free-roaming asceticism) and were punished with the interdiction of access to the church. The shorn head was associated with adultery or prostitution and indicated sexual licentiousness, even though the idea behind the haircutting of female ascetics was precisely to annihilate one of the principal feminine adornments and a cause of temptation.

Grief and Mourning

Sacrificial offering of hair in ancient cultures was akin to its cutting as a sign of mourning. Widows of pharaonic Egypt buried hair-locks with their deceased husbands in order to protect them in the afterworld. In Greek antiquity, the head was shaved in grief and contrition: the Argonauts sheared their hair when they realized that they had killed King Cyzicus by mistake and Herodotus reports that the *neoteroi* of Miletus shaved their heads as a sign of mourning upon hearing the news of the destruction of the befriended city of Sybaris, whereby they acted as representatives of their polis.

Forceful Haircutting as Degradation

Apart from the fact that forceful haircutting constitutes an act of physical violence by itself, the humiliation it implies was intensified in those cultures, which attributed special powers or honor to hair. Medieval Germanic cultures appear outstanding in this respect. Shorn hair was a sign of slavery (as in a number of other cultures) and incompatible with high social status, in particular with royalty: cutting of a man's hair disqualified him from being eligible for the throne and represented humiliation that could be regarded as worse than death. A special sacral significance might have been attached to hair in the dynasty of the Merovingians, the "long-haired kings." Gregory of Tours (539–594) related in his *Historia francorum* the story of two brothers being murdered after their grandmother preferred their death to the option of having their hair cut. In fact, the dynasty was also extinguished by the tonsuring of Childeric III (743–751).

It is interesting that *Leges Burgundionum* (sixth century CE) imposed penalties and compensation for cutting off woman's hair. Burgundians were unique among the German peoples in allowing women to act as *Eideshelfer* (guarantors of other persons' oaths), which meant that they possessed a legal standing. Therefore, the cutting of hair obviously had the consequence that the *decapillata* or *detracta* (woman deprived of her hair by shearing or even scalping) suffered detriment or loss of her legal personality.

Charms and Magic

A number of cultures nurtured beliefs that binding and loosening as well as combing of hair could activate occult forces. Therefore, women suspected of witchcraft were rendered harmless by cutting their hair, which is reflected in the custom of the Inquisition to shear the accused before the torture. Hair clippings were also used for seductive, destructive, or healing sorcery, together with other detachable or extractable parts of the body, such as nail-clippings, saliva, blood, or semen. The act of haircutting often implied liminality that placed all participants in the ritual in imminent danger. Sir James George Frazer described feasts with human sacrifices held by Namosi tribe of Fiji on the occasions of chieftain's hair being cut. Among the Maoris, chieftains were forbidden to cut their hair, and with other members of the tribe various protective spells were uttered and taboos imposed.

From Samson to Sumo

The well-known story of Samson and Delilah (Judges 16:19), which received an interpretation according to Freudian theory as an act of ceremonial castration, rests upon the idea that is common even to various world cultures: namely, that cutting of hair deprived its owner of his vital energies, virility, honor, or even individuality. In a sense, these implications are present today in a number of rituals, from the shearing of military novices to the ceremonial cutting of the topknot suffered by defeated sumo wrestlers. Hair regained much of its significance with the hippie movement, when it became an outright symbol of opposition to the establishment. The ritual connotations discussed in this article may thus help to explain the emotional sway of the most famous haircutting scene in the modern era: the one in the movie *Hair,* in which Berger undergoes a brief reconciliation with society before he is ultimately sacrificed to it.

Marina Miladinov

Further Reading

Bächtold Stäubli, H. (1931). Haar [Hair]. In E. Hoffmann-Krayer et al. (Eds.), *Handwörterbuch des deutschen Aberglaubens* [Hand dictionary of the German faith] (Vol. 3, pp. 1239–1288). Berlin and Leipzig, Germany: Walter de Gruyter.

Frazer, J. G. (1922). *The golden bough: A study in magic and religion.* New York: Macmillan.

Hallpike, C. R. (1986). Hair. In M. Eliade & C. J. Aam (Eds.), *The encyclopedia of religion 5–6,* (pp. 154–157). New York & London: Collier Macmillan.

Herold, R. (1985). Jugend, Sexualität und Heiratsverhalten im Japan der Tokugawa- und Meiji-Zeit [Youth, sexuality, and marriage behavior in Japan in the Togukawa and Meiji eras]. In Müller, E. W., & Drechsel, P., (Ed.), *Geschlechtsreife und Legitimation zur Zeugung* [Sexual maturity and legitimation to conceive], (pp. 683–715). Munich, Germany: Verlag Karl Alber.

Hoyoux, J. (1948). Reges criniti, chevelures, tonsures et scalps chez les Mérovingiens [long-haired kings, hair, tonsures, and scalps of the Merovingian dynasty]. *Revue belge de philologie et d'histoire 26,* 479–508.

Kaufmann, E. (1955). Über das Scheren abgesetzter Merowingerkönige [Haircutting of deposed Merovingian kings]. *Zeitschrift der Savigny-Stiftung für Rechtsgeschichte-Germanistische Abteilung 72,* 177–85.

Kennel, S. A. H. (1991). Women's hair and the law: Two cases from late antiquity. *Klio 73*(2), 526–36.

Leach, E. R. (1958). Magical hair. *Journal of the Royal Anthropological Institute 88,* 147–64.

Morgenstern, J. (1966). *Rites of birth, marriage, death, and kindred occasions among the Semites.* Chicago: Quadrangle Books.

Trichet, L. (1990). *La Tonsure: Vie et mort d'une pratique ecclésiastique* [The tonsure: Life and death of a church practice]. Paris: Éditions du Cerf.

Wallace-Hadrill, J. M. (1982). *The long-haired kings.* Toronto, Ontario, Canada: University of Toronto Press. (Original work published 1962)

Zoepffel, R. (1985). Geschlechtsreife und Legitimation zur Zeugung im Alten Griechenland [Sexual maturity and legitimation to conceive in ancient Greece]. In E. W. Müller (Ed.), *Geschlechtsreife und Legitimation zur Zeugung* (pp. 319–401). Munich, Germany: Verlag Karl Alber.

Hajj

The hajj is the fifth pillar of Islam and its most elaborate ritual. It is essentially a highly structured pilgrimage to Mecca, where Muslims believe that Abraham and Ishmael built the Ka'ba, the first temple dedicated to God. Surrounded with pomp and pageantry, the hajj is a compelling symbol of the solidarity of the worldwide Muslim community—the *Ummah.* All Muslims should complete the hajj at least once in a lifetime if they are physically and financially able. It is enjoined in the Qur'an: "And pilgrimage to the House is a duty unto Allah for mankind, for him who can find a way there" (3:97). The hajj consists of a series of symbolic rituals performed together by all pilgrims; the Prophet Muhammad determined these rituals shortly before his death.

The pilgrimage to Mecca has been traditionally divided into two. The *'umra* (visitation), sometimes called the "lesser pilgrimage," takes place in and near the sacred mosque in Mecca and can be done at any time of the year. The other is the hajj (pilgrimage), done in the month of Dhū-al-Hijjah (the twelfth month of the Islamic calendar). The hajj entails a series of symbolic rituals designed to bring the faithful as close as possible to God. Muslims from all over the world come together to perform these sacred rituals, and no distinction is made between rich and poor. For several weeks before the commencement of the hajj, millions of Muslims come to Mecca. Before moving into the sacred landscape around Mecca, pilgrims enter a state of ritual purity (*ihrām*) by performing a ritual ablution (*ghusl*) and expressing their intention (*niyya*) to perform the hajj, and ultimately wear a white seamless garment also called an *ihrām.*

The devout disposition of someone who is to embark on the hajj is documented in a popular novel—*Midāq Valley*—by one of Egypt's foremost writers, Najīb Mahfūz. The main character in the novel, Ridwān Husseini, who is renowned for his piety, is about to go to Mecca and he describes his anticipation as a period of intense joy. He describes his longing for Mecca, how he anticipates drinking from the well of Zam Zam, and how he longs to visit the grave of the Prophet and pray in the holy garden. He passionately describes his vision of Mecca and the peace that comes with completing the hajj. Part of his ultimate desire is to walk through the lanes of Mecca and recite verses from the Qur'an, just as they were first received as if he were hearing a lesson given by Allah.

Performing the Hajj

Before the hajj officially starts, all male pilgrims put on special clothing called *ihrām*, consisting of two white pieces of cloth covering the upper and lower parts of the body (this clothing can also be used as the shroud in burial ceremonies). Female pilgrims have more freedom in what they wear as long as they wear something modest. The uniformity of the *ihrām* symbolizes the solidarity of all people before God: this is the way people will appear when they stand before Allah on the Day of Judgment. In the state of *ihrām* it is absolutely forbidden to have sexual relations, kill any living creature, or remove hair from the body. It is a state of complete purity and consecration. The state of *ihrām* is also analogous to what Arnold Van Gennep has described as the liminal phase (betwixt and between) in rites of passage, the phase between the old status and the new. It is a state of purity when certain things and behaviors are no longer permitted.

> On their way to Mecca, pilgrims recite the *talbīya*:
> I am here, O my God, I am here!
> I am here, Thou art without any associate, I am here!
> Praise and blessing belong to Thee, and Power.

When they get to Mecca, pilgrims recite these verses from the Qur'an:

> And say: "My Lord, lead me in with a just ingoing, and lead me out with a
> Just outgoing; grant me authority from Thee, to help me."
> And say: "The truth has come, and falsehood has vanished away: surely
> Falsehood is ever certain to vanish." (17:80–81).

The initial exercise of the hajj, the *tawāf*, is performed at least twice, upon first arriving in Mecca and just before leaving after completing all the other rituals. The *tawāf* is the sevenfold, counterclockwise circumambulation of the Ka'ba, the cube-shaped "House of God" (*Bayt Allah*). During this process, many pilgrims also try to touch the black stone (*al-Hajar al-Aswad*), a meteorite believed to be from heaven and placed by the prophets Ibrahim and Ishmael in one corner of the Ka'ba. Legends hold that Abraham and Ishmael used to circle the Ka'ba in this way. Muhammad used to touch the black stone whenever he went around the Ka'ba, and it is very common to see pilgrims kiss it and meditate near it. Given the huge crowd circling the Ka'ba, not all pilgrims can get near the stone, so they simply extend their arms toward it and devoutly recite, "I am here, O my God, I am here." The Ka'ba was a pilgrimage site even before the emergence of Islam; however, before his death, Muhammad claimed the site for Muslims and purged the Ka'ba of all pagan idols. The Ka'ba is sometimes described as the earthly example of God's throne in heaven, and the *tawāf* is often likened to the human imitation of the angels' circling his throne in worship.

The next ritual after the *tawāf* is the *sa'y*, when pilgrims run between the two hills of Safa and Marwa. This reenacts an episode in the life of Abraham and his family, when Abraham had abandoned Hagar and her son Ishmael in the desert. When Ishmael cried out for help, Hagar in frustration ran seven times back and forth between Safa and Marwa searching for water. Meanwhile, Ishmael kicked his feet into the ground and mysteriously produced a spring of water. The spring, later called the well of Zam Zam, is believed to have divine powers, and pilgrims drink from it during their stay in Mecca. Pilgrims customarily take some of the water of Zam Zam as a souvenir for friends and family members unable to perform the hajj themselves.

The next stage in the pilgrimage is for pilgrims to assemble on the plain of Arafat, southeast of Mecca, where Muhammad delivered his farewell sermon. From noon to sunset, pilgrims engage in prayer and continuous devotion (*wuquf*). Many believe that this is the best time to experience the presence of God in the world, as this is when God is closest to the world. The assembly at Arafat also allows Muslims from all over the world to engage in serious discussions about the condition of and challenges to Islam in the world.

After sunset, pilgrims move their tents to Muzdalifa, an open area on the way back to Mecca. Pilgrims pray intensely and also collect forty-nine stones to throw the following day at a symbol of the devil.

On the tenth day of Dhū al-Hijjah, pilgrims proceed to the adjacent valley of Mina. At Mina, pilgrims perform two rituals that commemorate the spiritual virtues of Abraham. First, pilgrims reenact Abraham's rejection of Satan's temptation by throwing stones at a tall stone pillar (*jammah*) symbolizing the devil. This stoning ceremony recalls an event that happened when Abraham and Ishmael were going to the place where Ishmael was to be sacrificed. The devil quietly spoke to Ishmael, telling him not to obey this divine command. Ishmael then picked up some stones and threw them at the apparition of the devil. The second ritual act involves an animal sacrifice (*qurbān*) commemorating how God allowed Abraham to sacrifice a sheep in place of his son. Likewise, Muslims around the world offer their own animal sacrifices in a celebratory ritual known as the feast of sacrifice (*'īd al-adhā*) or the Great Bairām. The feast lasts three days, and whoever sacrifices an animal must share a third of the meat with poor people, a third with a neighbor, and the rest with his or her household. After the sacrifice, pilgrims must have a ritual haircut, known as the *taqsīr*, that indicates the end of most of the restrictions of the state of *ihrām*. The white garment may be discarded, but sexual intercourse is still strictly forbidden.

For the next two or three days, until the twelfth or thirteenth day of Dhū al-Hijjah, pilgrims go back and forth between Mecca and Mina. They now have a more flexible schedule, and may perform one or more *tawāf* and *sa'y* in Mecca. At this time pilgrims, in a visit known as *ziyāra*, go to the Prophet's tomb in Medina. (The Hadith says: "Whoever visits my tomb, my intercession will be granted to him.") In these final days, male pilgrims can wear their regular national dress or local Arabian garb, testifying to their gradual return to the ordinary world.

Significance of the Hajj in the Modern World

The essence of the hajj is a pilgrimage undertaken with the humble intent of coming closer to God. The pilgrimage is rich in symbolic rituals that profoundly renew solidarity among the *Ummah*. These rituals have multiple meanings and implications that can only be interpreted by delving into the Qur'an, the Sunnah of the Prophet, and local legends.

The hajj is the most compelling reminder of Islam's message of unity. During the hajj, pilgrims passionately discuss the role of the *Ummah* and the challenges facing Muslims worldwide; they are supposed to return to their respective countries as renewed believers. The radical change in the political profile of Malcolm X after he went on the hajj pilgrimage is one compelling modern testimony to the transformative power of the hajj.

Akintunde E. Akinade

See also Islam; Liminoid; Pilgrimage

Further Reading

Denny, F. M. (1994). *An introduction to Islam.* Upper Saddle River, NJ: Prentice Hall.

Esposito, J. L. (1998). *Islam: The straight path.* New York: Oxford University Press.

Firestone, R. (1990). *Journeys in holy lands: The evolution of the Abraham-Ishmael legends in Islamic exegesis.* Albany: State University of New York Press.

Peters, F. E. (1994). *The Hajj.* Princeton, NJ: Princeton University Press.

Hanukkah

Hanukkah (also spelled Chanukah), meaning "dedication," is an eight-day celebration that begins on the night of the twenty-fifth day of the month of Kislev in the Hebrew calendar, which can fall between late November and late December. Hanukkah represents the victory of faith over tyranny and in particular commemorates the rededication of the Jewish Temple in 165 BCE, after its desecration by the Syrian oppressors. Hanukkah also represents a rededication of oneself to living according to God's commandments.

Hanukkah is among the most joyous Jewish holiday, and its eight days are days of rejoicing. Morning prayers each day include the recitation of Hallel (praise), while "grace"—*birket hamezon*—is recited after every meal. The home is decorated festively. Central to the celebration is the lighting of a menorah, a nine-branched candelabrum on which candles are arranged in a straight line, when the first evening stars become visible. One candle is lit on the first

THE HANUKKAH BLESSINGS

The first of the three blessings marks the beginning of Hanukkah:
Baruch ata Adonai elohenu melech ha olam, asher kiddishanu b'mitzvotav v'tzivanu l'hadlik ner shel Hanukkah.
Blessed are you our God, Ruler of the world, who makes us holy through your mitzvoth and commands us to kindle the Hanukkah lights.

The second blessing is:
Baruch ata Adonai elohenu melech ha olam, she asa nisim l'avoteinu, beyamim ha-hem, bazmah ha zeh.
Blessed are you our God, ruler of the world, who worked miracles for our ancestors in the days long ago at this season.

The third blessing is reserved for the first day:
Baruch ata Adonai elohenu melech ha olam, sheheheyanu, v'kiyimenu, v'higiyanu, lazman ha zeh.
Blessed are you our God, ruler of the world, who has given us life, sustained us, and has brought us to this season.

evening, two on the second, and so on through the eight nights of the festival. Blessings are recited before the candles of the menorah, three on the first and two on each night thereafter.

Lighting the menorah candles is followed by singing hymns and other joyous songs. Family and friends exchange gifts, children receiving gifts such as *Hanukkah gelt*—chocolate coins covered with gold foil. Children also play games, including a game of chance played with a traditional cubic spinning top called a dreidel. Hanukkah is also a time of special foods, especially foods fried in oil, such as potato pancakes (*latkes*), Hanukkah dough-balls, marshmallow dreidels, and jelly-filled doughnuts (*sufganiyot*).

Historical Status of Hanukkah

Hanukkah is not required by the Torah; rather, its origins are recorded in the books of Maccabees. These recount how the Syrian king, Antiochus VII, imposed pagan religious practices, including sacrificing pigs in the sanctuary of the Temple in Jerusalem and erecting an altar to Olympian Zeus on the great altar of the Temple. In response, Jews, led by the Maccabee family, rebelled against Antiochus. When the Jews prevailed and the time came to relight *N'er Tamid* (the Eternal Flame) to light the Temple, only enough undefiled oil could be found to last one evening. The menorah was lit and miraculously burned for eight days until more sanctified oil could be found.

Current Status of Hanukkah

Two factors have recently enhanced the prominence of Hanukkah in Judaism, starting in the second half of the twentieth century. The first is the rebirth of Israel, where the secular origin of the holiday and its emphasis on themes of rebellion against oppression and of martyrdom made it a holiday readily adopted by both religious and secular Jews. The second has been the influence (especially in the United States) of the celebration of Christmas on the Jewish celebration of Hanukkah during the same season.

Sociocultural Context of Hanukkah

Each of the traditional foods, games, and rituals of Hanukkah are filled with special meanings derived from Jewish history and culture.

Gelt is the Yiddish word for gold. *Hanukkah gelt* is the tradition of gift giving during Hanukkah that arose in the Middle Ages when local Jewish teachers received gifts of money. The most common contemporary form of *Hanukkah gelt* for children is chocolate coins wrapped in gold foil. These recall how, twenty-two years after the Temple had been recaptured, the Syrian king, Antiochus VII, recognized the right of Simon the Maccabee to mint coins for his country.

The tradition of special Hanukkah foods began in the Middle Ages with the eating of cheese delicacies that recalled the story of Judith, who fed cheese to the leader of the Jews' enemies. Sephardic Jews in particular continue to eat dairy foods as an important Hanukkah observance. Although the story of Judith belongs to a later era than that of the Maccabeean revolt against Antiochus, it has a similar theme of Jewish survival in the face of oppression and was popularly linked to Hanukkah. Eventually, foods fried in oil became central Hanukkah foods, the oil symbolizing the oil that burned in the Menorah of the Temple during the miracle of Hanukkah.

As a religious symbol, the modern menorah is rooted in the menorah of biblical times. The first Jewish menorah, used in the Tabernacle when the people of Israel were wandering in the desert, had seven branches. When the Temple replaced the Tabernacle, a menorah illuminated the sanctuary of the Temple. After the destruction of the Temple in 70 CE, a nine-branched menorah began to be used in celebrating Hanukkah. Eight of its nine branches represent the eight days of Hanukkah, while the ninth serves as the *shamash* (servant branch). Among Ashkenazic Jews, the *shamash* candle holds the flame from which the other branches are lit; Sephardic Jews light the candles with a separate match or candle, and the *shamash* is lit last. Also, in the Sephardic tradition the head of the household lights the candles while other members of the household watch, while in the Ashkenazic tradition children often light their own candles. Oil was originally burned in Hanukkah menorahs, but gradually candles have replaced oil in most Jewish families.

A dreidel is a cubic spinning top that children use in a game of chance. The four sides of the dreidel are decorated with the Hebrew letters *nun*, *gimel*, *hei*, and *shin*. In the game, these letters represent four words that in German begin with the equivalent letters: *nichts* (which means, take nothing), *ganz* (take everything), *halb* (take half), and *shtell* (put in). The game is begun by each child placing some *Hanukkah gelt* in a common pot and then spinning the dreidel in turn either to win nothing, win part or all of the pot, or place more *gelt* into the pot. Religiously, the four letters of the dreidel are understood as an anagram for the Hebrew sentence, "*Nes Gadol Hayah Sham*" (A great miracle happened there), referring to the miracle of Hanukkah when the menorah of the Temple burned for eight days with only enough sanctified oil for one day.

Richley H. Crapo

See also Judaism

Further Reading

Lutske, H. (1986). *The book of Jewish customs*. Northvale, NJ: J. Aronson.

Schauss, H. (1938). *The Jewish festivals: From their beginning to our own day* (S. Jaffe, Trans.). Cincinnati, OH: Union of American Hebrew Congregations.

Stern, C. (Ed.) (1994). *On the doorposts of your house: Prayers and ceremonies for the Jewish home*. New York: Central Conference of American Rabbis.

Unterman, A. (1981). *Jews: Their religious beliefs and practices*. Boston: Routledge & Kegan Paul.

Hawai`i

The Hawai`i of today is quite different from the Hawai`i before contact with the Western world. British navigator James Cook's visit to the islands in 1778 was the beginning of a radical change in Hawaiian culture and religion. However, some of the ancient religious rituals continue today. To understand rituals in Hawai`i today, rituals of precontact Hawai`i must be examined.

Prior to Western contact, the indigenous belief system in Hawai`i focused on the idea that sacred powers reside in nature. The polytheistic religious system in pre-contact Hawai`i was similar to the Hawaiian social class system in that there was a complex social ranking of both people and deities who were considered to be ancestors to the Hawaiian people. There were main gods (Lono, Kane, Kanaloa) local or regional gods, demi-gods (men with magical powers), volcano gods and goddesses (Pele and her

THE GODDESS-MISTRESS OF THE HULA

In Hawaii the place of Areoi as entertainers in great part was taken by the *hula* dancers. The *hula* was also semi-religious in its nature, and appealed very widely and powerfully to the Hawaiian emotions and imagination. It was combined song or recitative and dance, the songs and recitations relating to mythology, with which was naturally interwoven the history of the people and their everyday life, as naturally as gods and goddesses mingled with mortals.

The *hulau* was the special hall for the performance of the *hula*, a large building, containing a *kuahu* (shrine) for the deity whose presence was invoked at the performances. The goddess-mistress of the *hula* was Laka:

In the forest, on the ridges
Of the mountains, stands Laka;
Dwelling in the source of the mists.
Laka, mistress of the *hula*,
Has climbed the wooded haunts of the gods,
Altars hallowed by the sacrificial swine,
The head of the boar, the black boar of Kane.
A partner he with Laka;
Woman, she by strife gained rank in heaven,
That the root may from the steam,
That the young shoot may put forth and leaf,
Pushing up the fresh enfolded bud,
The scion-thrust bud and fruit toward the East,
Like the tree that bewitches the winter fish,
***Maka-lei*, tree famed from the age of night.**
Truth is the counsel of night –
May it fruit and ripen above.
A messenger I bring you, O Laka,
To the girding of the *pau*.
An opening festa this for thee and me;
To show the might of the goad,
The power of the goddess,
Of Laka, the sister,
To Lono a wife in the heavenly courts.
O Lono, join heaven and earth!
Thine alone are the pillars of Kahiki.
Warm greeting, beloved one,
We hail thee!

***Source*: Andersen, Johannes C. (1928).**
***Myths and Legends of the Polynesians*, New York: Dover Publications, Inc., pp. 445–446.**

brother Kanehekili), specific deities for specialized professions, and, finally, each Hawaiian family had an aumakua, a family god of either animal or human form, who was considered to be an ancestor. Even though Christianity has become the predominant religion of Hawaiians, there are still many people in Hawai`i who worship *Pele,* and give homage to *Ku* and *Lono*. Most notably, many people in Hawai`i today celebrate the *makahiki*, a season devoted to *Lono,* the god of peacemaking, humility and caring for the land. Some of the ancient religious rituals continue today. The earth cycle began with birth, and ended with death, the commencement of the existence of the spirit in the Unseen.

Rituals Surrounding Birth

The `Aha`aina Mawaewae feast was celebrated within a day after the birth of a family's firstborn *(hiapo)* to safeguard the boy or girl and provide for his or her optimal upbringing. The word *Mawaewae* can be translated as "clearing the way." This feast dedicated the child to the ancestral guardians; if it was not performed, people believed that the firstborn would grow up unruly and headstrong. The feast set the child's feet *(waewae)* on the way *(ma)* of the spiritual flow of the responsible elders. Not only did this feast bless the firstborn, but also it blessed his or her unborn siblings. The feast focused on the consumption of specific foods by the mother. These foods included mullet and taro, both of which were related to the god Lono. The mother also ate shrimp, kala seaweed, and crab; in Hawaiian the words for these foods relate to loosening a hold or grip. These foods from the sea were thought to free the child from bad influences.

Afterward there was a feast for the friends and family members who came to honor the *hiapo* with gifts. The *`aha`aina palala* was a ritual celebration that involved the composing of chants *(mele)*, hula performances, and the presentation of gifts. In precontact days people came from great distances to pay homage to the *hiapo,* especially if he or she was the firstborn child of a chief. Gifts were given in abundance, from food to woven *lauhala* mats and *kapa,* a cloth made from shredded bark and used for clothing and other uses prior to Western contact. The amount of gifts was so excessive that storehouses needed to be built to house them. The *palala,* both the celebration and the feasting, often lasted for several days.

The Feast of the Fullness of the Year *(`Aha`aina Pihi Makahiki)* was any kind of celebration of an anniversary, but the most important anniversary was the first birthday of a firstborn child. The most important feature of this feast was the chanting of *mele* composed in honor of the child and other chants regarding his ancestors and family *(`ohana)*. Relatives gathered with gifts to celebrate the birthday.

The Baby Luau

The Feast of the Fullness of the Year is an ancient celebration that continues in Hawai`i today as the baby luau (feast), which is held when the baby reaches one year of age. The baby luau is a feast of Hawaiian food, music, dancing, and flowers during which family and friends gather to celebrate the new child's entry into the family. The baby luau follows tradition in that Hawaiian chants and dances often are performed. A baby luau always includes gifts. Choosing a pig and baking it in the *imu* (ground oven) is the most important part of the celebration today.

For ancient Hawaiians the life cycle extended from the birth of a firstborn child in one generation to the birth of a firstborn child in the next generation. In precontact Hawaii, families *(`ohana)* did not consider normative transitions such as growing up, getting married, and getting divorced as genuine phases of the life cycle. Consequently, in precontact Hawai`i the rituals associated with the life cycle centered around life and death.

Rituals Surrounding Sickness and Death

Hawaiian beliefs arose out of sensory, emotional, and mental experiences of people in precontact Hawaii. Sickness and death were perceived to be a result of psychic factors at play in a person's life. Sickness could result from natural factors, disgruntlement of a relative, spoken curses, the displeasure of an *`aumakua* (guardian spirit), or sorcery. The kahuna (priest) was most concerned by problems with a *`aumakua* because they needed to be appeased by prayers and offerings that were dependent on the particular *`aumakua* that was involved. Prior to performing rituals to appease the *`aumakua,* however, the kahuna would perform *ho`oponopono,* a ceremony that focused on a spiritual cleansing and restoration of harmony in the family. After there was peace within the family, it was possible for the kahuna to deal with appeasing the *`aumakua.* Often the kahuna paid close attention to dreams because the *`aumakua* frequently provided instructions to the kahuna as to how to treat the patient and restore psychic harmony. (*Ho`oponopono* is still used in Hawai`i today, both in the family and in the workplace, to facilitate interpersonal interactions.)

While working to remove the disturbing influences that made a person sick, the kahuna would require the *ho`omalu* (period of quiet), during which the family would concentrate on only one thing: the recovery of the patient. During this time peace had to be maintained both within the family and within the community, or else quarreling would break the *ho`omalu* and the kahuna would have to start again.

The *wai huikala* (water of purification) was needed for a *kala* ceremony, which were performed to dedicate hula altars, homes *(hale)*, or canoes or to purify a house after someone had died. Sea water, with a touch of turmeric, was used for this ceremony. People who had been in contact with a dead person or had been to a funeral needed to be sprinkled with *wai huikala* before entering the house. This ceremony is still occasionally practiced.

After death the *`uhane* (spirit) leaves the body; however, ancient Hawaiians believed the spirit leaves from the corners of the eyes, where tears originate. The *`aumakua* was believed to lead the *`uhane* to the *leina* (the leaping place), which was a point overlooking the sea. Generally it was believed that the spirit is safe with the *`aumakua* in the Unseen.

After death bodies were either buried or bundled and hidden. Bodies that were to be buried were put into a shed built away from the house until they were disposed of. A body was placed into a fetal position with the face down to the knees. However, because the *`uhane* was most closely associated with bones, burial was not the usual practice. A relative was assigned to tend to the corpse, removing the decaying flesh until the bones were left. Then the bones could be cleaned, made into a bundle tied with sennit cords, and taken to the final hiding place, which was generally identified with the family's *`aumakua.*

As a form of ritual worship, some *`uhane* were made into controlled spirits who had *mana* (spiritual power). The *`unihipili* were spirits of dead who were kept because of love and affection. They were tied to the real world through a connection to a keeper or place. Physical fragments of the deceased, including bones, fingernails, hair, and other relics, were kept in a calabash or bundle and hidden away. The spirits were called on by worshiping *(ho`omana).*

For Hawaiians who had been connected to Pele during life, their bones were wrapped with red and black *kapa* and taken to the priests of Pele. Deceased relatives of Kanehekili were wrapped in black *kapa,* and the priest, also dressed in black *kapa,* called on Kanehekili until a bolt of lightning struck the body, and it vanished. People who were related to reptiles *(mo`o)* orwater spirits took their dead, wrapped in yellow *kapa,* to a stream where they prayed until the *mo`o* appeared; then they lowered the body into the stream, where it became *mo`o.* For a family connected to sharks, the body was presented to the sharks wrapped in a *kapa* designed with markings related to the sharks; this allowed the family members to recognize their relative, a shark *`unihipili.* It was through this process that spirit guardians were made through the rituals associated with death.

The death feast *(aha`aina makena)* was convened to publicly grieve over the death of a loved one and to mourn the passing of the spirit. Mourners brought an abundance of food to prepare. Wails and lamentations for the departed were frequent. On the one-year anniversary of the death, Hawaiians held a memorial feast called the "*`aha`ina waimaka,*" which refers to the gathering at the time of death when members of the family came together out of respect and love for the deceased. The *`aha`ina waimaka* was one of the most important occasions because it marked the end of mourning and celebration of the living.

Death in Contemporary Hawaii

When Westerners arrived in Hawaii, they brought diseases that devastated the population. By the time plantation labor was needed in the nineteenth century, labor had to be imported from many countries, primarily from Asia. In Hawai`i today two-thirds of the population have Asian roots. As a consequence, funerals in Hawai`i reflect a mix of religious and ethnic backgrounds. People commonly believe that after a long and full life, the decedent passes into another level of existence, and his or her passage may be celebrated by a funeral, followed by cremation or burial.

Whereas people wear black to funerals throughout most of the Western world, in Hawaii, where East meets West, funeral traditions vary. For the population with Catholic roots, especially the Filipino population, black clothing is requested. However, the most common form of dress for mourners is aloha attire, which is colorful, often light-colored Hawaiian prints on dresses and shirts. The connection between dark clothing and death is not as ingrained in Hawaii, where Asian religions coexist with Christianity, and the color white is associated with death in some Asian cultures. The attitude toward death in modern Hawai`i is similar to that in old Hawai`i in that people believe that the dead person is truly passing on to another stage of existence. As with the precontact custom, the memorial gathering of the family members one year after a person's death is common, as is the weekly tending of gravesites, much like the tending of the deceased's bones in preparation for the transition to the spirit world.

In the twenty-first century Hawaiian residents live in the contemporary world, but they continue to utilize rituals from what they refer to as "the Old Ways." Rituals from precontact Hawai`i are still present, although in different forms. Incorporating all of the ethnic, cultural, and religious diversities that exist in Hawai`i is a major goal of the culture today, and to reach that goal, *ho`oponopono,* a practice begun as a ritual for healing, has come to be a useful practice for the modern world.

Linda Arthur

See also Micronesia; Yoruba

Further Reading

Arago, J. (1823). *Narrative of a voyage around the world 1817–1820.* London: Treuttel and Wurtz.

Beaglehole, J. C. (1955). *The journals of Captain James Cook on the voyages of discovery.* Cambridge, UK: Cambridge University Press.

Bray, D. K., & Low, D. (1990). The *kahuna religion of Hawaii.* Garberville, CA: Borderland Sciences Research Foundation.

Daws, G. (1974). *A history of the Hawaiian Islands.* Honolulu: University of Hawai`i Press.

Handy, E. S., & Pukui, M. K. (1958). *The Polynesian family system in Ka`u, Hawai`i.* Wellington, New Zealand: The Polynesian Society.

Healing and Rituals

Healing illness is among the oldest and most widespread uses of religious ritual. Religious healing possibly is the oldest profession, with ritual the primary tool of religious healers. In the contemporary world the use of religious belief and ritual to heal is often labeled "spiritual healing" or "faith healing." Often ritual as engaged in by the patient, family and friends, or both is meant to complement rather than replace scientifically based medical treatment. Modern medicine recognizes that physical well-being, emotional well-being, and spiritual well-being are interrelated and that the use of ritual to enhance spiritual health may therefore also benefit emotional and physical health. Although there is much diversity across religions, all religions include a belief in the healing power of religion and ritual practices designed to heal or enhance other forms of treatment. Christian Science, for example, places great faith in religious healing, primarily through prayer. Other approaches to healing found across religions include touching, reading religious texts, employing ritual objects such as beads or a cross, administering liquids, and observing dietary restrictions.

Supernatural Theories of Illness

One reason why religion and ritual play a major role in the treatment of disease is the widespread belief that at least some diseases are caused by supernatural forces. One survey of a world sample of societies indicates that in almost every society (137 out of 139 studied) some illnesses are believed to be caused by supernatural agents. Attribution of disease to supernatural forces is found among people in all regions of the world and is especially deep in East Asia and the Mediterranean region. In modern, Westernized societies most illness is attributed to natural causes, although supernatural forces are still commonly believed to have some potential influence, as indicated by prayers routinely offered for the ill and by the placement of chapels in hospitals. In non-Western societies attribution of illness to supernatural forces is much stronger, with 53 percent of these societies linking all or most illness to supernatural forces, including witchcraft and sorcery. Supernatural explanations of disease across cultures fall into three categories: mystical, animistic, and magical.

Mystical explanations include beliefs about fate, ominous sensations (dreams, sights, and sounds that cause illness), contagion, and mystical retribution as causes of illness. The common element in all of these is the belief that disease is caused by some supernatural force (but not a specific supernatural being) that operates in response to and punishes the victim, who has violated religious rules. Belief in fate and ominous sensations as causes of illness is not especially common around the world, but mystical retribution and contagion are frequently mentioned in a large minority of cultures.

Mystical retribution occurs when a person behaves in an immoral way, and especially when a person violates a major taboo. For example, in Sri Lanka in the Indian Ocean people believe that serious illness might come to a man who violates sexual mores by having relations with a woman who is a

An elderly woman and a young girl in the healing chamber of the Santeria de Chimayo in New Mexico. The small, rural church draws thousands of pilgrims each year, many of whom take with them the healing earth which continually refills the hole in the floor of the chamber. COURTESY OF JOANNE CALEGARI AND DAVID LEVINSON.

relative. Contagion occurs when an illness results from a person coming into contact with a ritually polluting object or person. In all cultures beliefs and rules dichotomize (divide into two) animate and inanimate objects and behaviors as either ritually pure or ritually unclean. If an object is classified as ritually unclean, it is also usually thought to be potentially ritually polluting, and a person who comes into contact with the object may become ritually polluted and then become ill through the process of contagion. Because contact can cause illness and death, there are always rules that restrict contact with the polluting object.

Animistic explanations are those by which disease is believed to be caused by the action of a supernatural being such as a spirit, wandering soul, or ghost of an ancestor and to take the form of soul loss or spirit aggression. Soul loss as an explanation for illness arises from the widespread belief that the soul in certain circumstances leaves the body and then returns while the person is alive. Soul loss is also tied to the widespread belief that the soul leaves the body when a person dies. Thus, it is important that the soul return because the person will die if it doesn't. Sometimes soul loss is good because the soul will look over the physical body and protect it from harm. However, in about 20 percent of societies people believe that losing one's soul temporarily causes illness. In another 10 percent of societies people believe that sorcerers can cause a person to become ill or to die by causing the soul to leave the body. Restoring the soul usually requires the expertise of a healer who through rituals can diagnose soul loss as the cause of the illness and then bring the soul back.

Spirit aggression is the most common supernatural explanation for illness and death around the world. In over 60 percent of societies people attribute at least some illness to the maliciousness of spirits, and in 42 percent of societies spirit aggression is the primary explanation for illness. These societies tend to be those where spirits and other supernatural agents are believed to be active in human affairs in general and where much ritual activity is devoted to dealing with the spirit world. Typically, major spirits and gods are not seen as concerning themselves with matters such as disease; minor spirits, ghosts, and the souls of ancestors who are unhappy with the behavior of the living cause disease. For example, the Dani people of Papua New Guinea believe that the ghosts of deceased ancestors lurk about the villages looking to cause disease, and thus Dani sorcerers devote considerable ritual activity to driving the ghosts into the forest, where they can do little harm to humans.

Magical explanations for disease attribute illness and often death to the deliberate actions of humans who use ritual magic to cause others to fall ill or die. The three most common forms of ritual magic are the evil eye, sorcery, and witchcraft, all three of which are common around the world. For example, the Zande people of west Africa say that "his condition is bad," meaning that witchcraft is present.

Witchcraft attribution is not found everywhere around the world. It is most common in the Mediterranean region, sub-Saharan Africa, and among Native Americans. Where disease is believed to be caused by witches, ritual mechanisms always are available to protect oneself and to reverse the harm caused by witches. People commonly wear protective objects such as charms on clothing, repeat prayers, and hold public rituals to remove disease from the community. In addition to trying to ward off witchcraft, people will be vigilant for clues that help them detect the presence of a witch, such as the distinctive sound of a witch's footfalls and unusual activity by animals. Curing illnesses caused by witches is a serious matter that requires the skill and knowledge of a religious healer. Sometimes the healer is a generalist who deals with all supernatural matters; at other times he or she might specialize in using ritual to reverse the harm caused by the witch.

Sorcery is another fairly common explanation of illness around the world and tends to occur in societies that do not attribute illness to witchcraft. Sorcery is most common in Native American cultures in North and South America. Sorcery relies on the use of spells, formulae, and incantations by a trained sorcerer who intentionally seeks to make someone ill, usually in service to a client. However, sorcerers also cure illness, and in most societies curing is the bulk of their work.

The evil eye is the belief that a person can cause harm to another person or the person's property by simply looking at that person or the property. This harm may come in the form of sickness, an accident, or destruction of property such as a valuable pot, a dwelling, livestock, or crops. Wherever people believe in the evil eye, it is almost always linked with envy. People who are wealthy or attractive are often the targets of the evil eye, and the destruction of valuable possessions is a widespread result of "casting the evil eye." Across cultures and throughout history people have believed in the evil eye mainly in cultures that produce social and physical goods that can be envied.

Given the widespread belief that the evil eye can strike anytime an individual envies something about a person, it is not surprising that thousands of preventive measures are taken to ward off its effects. Incantations are sung, chanted, recited, and spoken to ward off the evil eye. Amulets in the form of charms, necklaces, crosses, pins, and ribbon in thousands of varieties are worn on the body or attached to clothing. The intervention of a professional curer such as a sorcerer, exorcist, or priest may also be required.

Healers and Ritual Healing

Across cultures people who heal disease include professional healers, informal healers, and magico-religious healers. Professional healers, who are formally trained and paid for their work, rarely employ ritual healing. Informal healers, who are often family members, may employ rituals but on a limited basis. Magico-religious healers, who are sometimes labeled "folk healers," are healers whose role and status are based on their innate or learned ability to control the supernatural forces that cause illness. They are usually paid for their services, and those who are successful can attain much status in their communities. They often use ritual to communicate with the supernatural world as a method of treating illness.

There are several types of magico-religious healers. Some, such as shamans, shaman/healers, and magical healers, focus their efforts on treating illness. Others, such as priests, mediums, and sorcerers, might treat illness, although they also devote time to other religious activities. In many societies people have access to more than one type of magico-religious healer, with each type specializing in certain types of illness. For example, the Aymara people of Peru consult six types of magico-religious healers, all of whom use ritual magic to cure illness: magician, sorcerer, doctor, diviner, chiropractor, and midwife.

Shamanism is a system of religious beliefs and practices that rest on the belief that many events on Earth are caused by supernatural forces and that therefore human contact with and control of the supernatural are necessary to control life on Earth. The shaman specializes in contacting and controlling the supernatural, and curing illness is one reason why he or she does so. Shamans may be male or female, old or young, and good or evil. Shamans can contact and control spirits and through the spirits use the shamans' power to cure illness. A shaman cures through a ritual known generically as a "séance." A séance is a ritual conducted by the shaman during which the shaman is possessed by a spirit or travels to the spirit world and serves as a medium of communication between humans and the spirit world. The séance is a magical performance in which the shaman uses a combination of power over the spirits, knowledge, physical strength and stamina, performing talents, and an altered state of consciousness to convince the audience of his or her powers and to achieve the goal of the séance, which is often to cure a sick person.

As part of his or her communication between the spirit world and human world, the shaman arranges a sacrifice that will appease the spirit and thereby cure the disease.

Similar to shamans are shaman/healers, who are typically full-time, trained, professional healers in large, settled communities. Unlike shamans, who are ritual generalists, shaman/healers specialize in the treatment of disease or even the treatment of only certain diseases. An example is the *zar* doctor, found in north African cultures such as the Amhara of Ethiopia. A *zar* doctor is the leader of a *zar* cult and treats mental illness, primarily in women, although men may also use the *zar* doctor's services. A *zar* doctor diagnoses and treats the illness and then involves the patient with the doctor's *zar* cult, a form of therapy group that provides protection for life. A *zar* is a spirit that may be either harmful or benevolent. Harmful spirits possess humans through magical coitus and cause illness, including mental illnesses such as fatigue, depression, seizures, and mood disorders. *Zar* doctors treat while in a trance and while possessed by their *zar* spirit. They diagnose illness by interpreting the words of the possessed victim, by causing the victim to become possessed again, or by observing the possession as it occurs. After a *zar* doctor knows what has caused the spirit to be displeased, he or she negotiates an offering with the spirit, which is paid by the patient. The patient then becomes a member of the *zar* doctor's cult, which provides lifelong protection from the spirit. Cult members attend treatment sessions for other patients, which involve the burning of incense, drumming, poetry recitations, and possession.

Mediums are another type of magico-religious healer. Mediums derive their power from possession by a supernatural force such as a god or spirit. Mediums typically spend most of their time predicting the future or explaining the past, although some also conduct rituals to cure illness.

In addition to these healers, religious specialists with more general roles in the community, such as priests, ministers, imam (prayer leaders of mosques), and rabbis, may be involved in healing. For example, they often provide comfort to the sick and their families, lead prayer for the sick, and sometimes even conduct exorcism rituals.

David Levinson

See also Evil Eye; Exorcism; Magic; Shamanism; Sorcery; Witchcraft

Further Reading

Atkinson, J. M. (1992). Shamanisms today. *Annual Review of Anthropology, 21,* 307–330.

Balzer, M. M. (Ed.). (1990). *Shamanism: Soviet studies of traditional religion in Siberia and central Asia.* Armonk, NY: M. E. Sharpe.

Dundes, A. (Ed.). (1981). *The evil eye: A folklore casebook.* New York: Garland.

Eliade, M. (1972). *Shamanism: Archaic techniques of ecstasy.* Princeton, NJ: Princeton University Press.

Evans-Pritchard, E. E. (1937). *Witchcraft, oracles and magic among the Azande.* Oxford, UK: Clarendon Press.

Fuller, R. C. (1989). *Alternative medicine and American religious life.* New York: Oxford University Press.

Koenig, H. G., McCullough, M. E., & Larson, D. B. (2000). *Handbook of religion and health.* New York: Oxford University Press.

Levinson, D., & Malone, M. J. (1980). *Toward explaining human culture.* New Haven, CT: HRAF Press.

Mair, L. (1969). *Witchcraft.* New York: McGraw-Hill.

Maloney, C. (Ed.). (1976). *The evil eye.* New York: Columbia University Press.

Marwick, M. (Ed.). (1970). *Witchcraft and sorcery.* Harmondsworth, UK: Penguin.

Mascie-Taylor, C. G. N. (1995). *The anthropology of disease.* New York: Oxford University Press.

McClain, C. S. (Ed.). (1989). *Women as healers: Cross-cultural perspectives.* Piscataway, NJ: Rutgers University Press.

Murdock, G. P. (1981). *Theories of illness.* Pittsburgh, PA: University of Pittsburgh Press.

Winkelman, M. (1986). Magico-religious practitioner types and socioeconomic conditions. *Behavior Science Research, 20,* 17–46.

Winkelman, M. (1990). Shaman and other 'magico-religious' healers: A cross-cultural study of their origins, nature, and social transformations. *Ethos, 18,* 308–352.

Hinduism

Hindu rituals pertain not only to life but also to the afterlife and have become a culturally constructed system of sequences of acts. These rituals endow a legitimacy that is recognized and accepted by society. These rituals are also organized events having a beginning and an end, command attention, promise continuity and stability, and are accepted by believers.

GLOSSARY OF HINDU TERMS ASSOCIATED WITH RITUAL

Aachaman	a symbolic purification of body
Abhisheka	anointing or consecrating by sprinkling water
Arati	a step in worshipping by waving the lamp before a deity
Arya-samaj	a reformed Hindu group, does not believe in worshipping idols
Aasana	offering a seat of honour
Aavahan	invocation of a deity
Deepa	a lamp or light
Dhupa	aromatic smoke offered to a deity
Diwali	festival of lights
Gandha	perfume, fragrant substances offered to deities
Ganesha	elephant-headed god
Homa	rite of oblations into consecrated fire
Japa	repeating prayers/mantra in an undertone
Kalash	consecrated water in a pitcher
Kumbha Mela	religious gathering held every 12 years in fours places
Naivedya	an offering of food presented to a deity
Navaratri	nine-day festival in honour of the Goddess Durga
Parikrma	reverential salutation and circumambulation from left to right around a deity
Pitra-Tarpan	honouring ones deceased parents, grandparents and ancestors
Puja	worship-service, ceremony of worship
Purohit	family priest
Sanatan-dharma	traditional Hindus believing and worshipping many deities
Snana	ablutions
Tirtha	place of pilgrimage or shrine dedicated to a deity on or near a river
Upachara	worship procedure
Upanayana	sacred-thread ceremony, initiation into studentship
Visarjana	departure of the invoked deity, de-consecration of *Puja*
Vrata	vowed observation of austerity done together with keeping a fast
Yaga	related to *homa*, putting oblations into consecrated fire
Yajamana	a host (who invites a priest to conduct worship-service)

During the centuries rituals helped Hindus to carry forward traditions, values, and beliefs that have shaped current religious practices.

Many Deities, Many Days

Traditional Hindus believe in *sanatan-dharma* (worshiping many deities). Hindus have an elaborate system of rituals for everything related to a religious function, be it performing a simple *puja* (worship), conducting a complex sacrament ceremony, fasting, celebrating festivals and fairs, bathing in sacred rivers or lakes, going on a pilgrimage, or conducting a complex ceremony marriage. In addition, Hindus have the largest number of *vrata* (fasts) and festivals; according to P. V. Kane, there are about one thousand religious activities durng the Hindu calendar year. Every date in the Hindu calendar and every day of the week are marked for some kind of worship. For example, the weekdays are named after seven of nine

Richard Castillo and an Indian sadhu perform a ritual of initiation at a location of spiritual power on the bank of the Ganges River, Himalayas in northern India, 1988. COURTESY OF RICHARD J. CASTILLO.

planets to be worshiped. These nine planets, called "Navagrahas," are the Sun, Moon, Mars, Mercury, Jupiter, Venus, Saturn, Rahu, and Ketu. The seven days of the week have derived their names from the first seven planets; Rahu and Ketu are the ascending and descending nodes of the moon. Among these nine planets, Saturn, Rahu, and Ketu are considered inauspicious and maleficent; thus, they need to be propitiated. Hindus regard these planets as having the greatest astrological significance, influencing a person's life cycle in many ways. Thus, in all rituals these planets are invoked and worshiped. In addition, each day of the week is named after a planet; for example, Sunday is for the Sun God, Monday is for Lord Shiva and the Moon, Tuesday for Hanuman and Mars, Wednesday for Mercury, Thursday for Jupiter and Gurus, Friday for Venus and various goddesses, and Saturday is named for Saturn planet and Shani God, the son of Sun God. Moreover, in every month several auspicious occasions call for a special worship and fasting; for example, the eleventh day of the Hindu calendar is called "Ekadashi" and is a day when fast is kept and *puja* is done in the late afternoon or early evening. There does not appear to be any object on Earth or in heaven that a Hindu is not prepared to worship; these objects include the planets, rocks, mountains, trees, shrubs, rivers, seas, reptiles, birds, wild animals, domesticated animals (especially cows and bulls), good or evil demons, bad spirits, ghosts, spirits of ancestors, any number of divine entities and deities, and departed souls. Although there is regional variation and worships and rituals specific to areas or villages, Hindus perform their rituals with great thoroughness. For example, the traditional marriage ceremony starts at midnight and continues for hours.

There are four forms of rituals: (1) *Japa* is repeating the name of a deity or a mantra to invoke a deity. Generally it is done privately in a home, a temple, or in some sacred place where a devotee repeats the name of a specific deity or a mantra. *Japa* is of three kinds. In the first, the devotee speaks the name of the deity or the mantra; in the second, the devotee speaks the name or the mantra, but no one hears; and in the third, nothing is spoken, but the name or the mantra is repeated in the mind. Generally, a devotee uses a *mala* (rosary) for this purpose. (2) *Homa* is offering oblations (offerings) into a sacred fire by invoking deities; this ritual can be a part of a specific worship in a home, a part of group worship, or a part of some sacrament ceremonies. (3) *Puja* is a worship service conducted with sixteen steps. The role of a priest is important in suggesting the appropriate and most auspicious day and time (the priest also acts as astrologer) for conducting a specific worship. (4) *Pitra-tarpan* (ancestor worship, also called *"shraaddha"*) obligates Hindus to honor their ancestors at least once a year when a fortnight is reserved for this purpose around the months of September and October. The service is conducted generally at the bank of a river or lake by offering at the minimum libations of water to one's deceased parents and other ancestors; the service is similar to the one performed at the time of cremation, although less rigorous. In addition, one should visit Gaya (Bihar Province) after the death of one's parents to perform this service.

Puja

The most important of all Hindu rituals is called *"shodasha-upachara-puja"* (worship-service which can be performed in several steps). However, before performing these steps, one should perform five preliminary steps after the priest has announced to all present the purpose of the ceremony: (1) symbolic purification *(aachaman)* of one's body and the place of worship by the priest and the host or couple for whom the service is being performed. The priest then consecrates the ritual utensils, flowers, bell, and other items needed for the service. (2) Seeking the blessing of the Mother Earth to begin the service. (3) Worship of Lord Ganesh (the deity to remove obstacles), which is always done at the beginning of a *puja*. (4) *Kalash-puja* (consecration of water in a jug). (5) Invocation of the nine planets to come and take their seats at the service. In some instances, Matrikapujan (worship of seven mother-goddesses) is done just before the start of the main sixteen-step worship service.

After the five preliminary steps the sixteen steps of *shodasha-upachara-puja* are performed: (1) performing *aavahan* (invoking the deity); (2) performing *aasana* (offering deity a place of honour at the ceremony); (3) offering Arghya water to drink; (4) offering water to wash the hands and feet of the deity *(padya)*; (5) performing *snana* (bathing of the deity, either with Ganges River water or with five items called *"panchamrita"*: milk, yogurt, *ghee* (clarified butter), honey, and sugar); (6) anointing the deity with fragrance; (7) performing *abhisheka* (anointing with water); (8) performing *vastra* (offering of new garment); (9) performing *pushpa* (offering of flowers); (10) performing *dhupa* (offering of incense); (11) performing *deepa* (offering of light by a lamp); (12) performing *naivedya* (offering of food); (13) offering *tambula* (betel leaf with nuts, clove, and spices); (14) performing *parikrama* (offering a reverential salutation by circling the divine image clockwise or, if the worshiper cannot circle the divine image, by standing still); (15) performing *aarati* (salutation to the deity by waving a lamp); and (16) offering flowers to the deity and praying for its return.

After this service the priest applies a vermilion paste to the foreheads of the host and his family members, and wraps a sacred thread around the hands of the host and his family. The sixteen steps are the mirror image of the welcome accorded to a guest by a Hindu family in ancient times. The guest was called "Atithi-Deva" (a godly person whose arrival was unknown). Of course, there are regional and linguistic variations in these steps. If a person is not able to perform such an elaborate worship service, a *puja* can be done in five or ten steps. The five-step *puja (panch-upachara)* consists of offering water, flowers, incense, light, and food; the ten-step *puja* consists of washing the feet of the deity, bathing and anointing the deity with fragrance, and offering garment, flowers, incense, light, food, and prayer. Each step has its own mantra, which is recited by the priest. In case of an emergency or the unavailability of material for worship, there is a provision for *labdha-upachara,* which is worshipping with whatever is available (such as water or flowers). These steps are performed not only to offer proper respect to the deity but also to carry out a vow that the host *(yajman)* took to get his wish fulfilled.

Rites (Sacraments)

Sixteen to forty rites *(sansakars)* are prescribed for Hindus. The following sixteen are considered important: (1) *garbhadhana* (conception of the child), (2) *punsavana* (consecration of the child in the womb), (3) *simantonnayana* (parting the hair of the pregnant woman), (4) *jatakarma* (birth of the child), (5) *namakarana* (naming the child), (6) *nishkramana* (taking the child out of the home for the first time), (7) *annaprashana* (feeding the child solid food for the first time), (8) *chudakarna* (giving the child's first haircut), (9) *karnabedha* (piercing the child's ears), (10) *vidyarambha* (the child going to school), (11) *upanayana* (sacred-thread ceremony), (12) *vedarambha* (study of Vedic literature), (13) *keshanta* (shaving of the boy's beard), (14) *samavartana/snana* (end of the child's education), (15) *vivaha* (marriage), and (16) *antyesthi* (cremation rite). For each of these sacraments scriptures have prescribed elaborate rituals. However, in the course of time these rituals have declined because individuals have been unable to perform some lengthy procedures and have incurred heavy expenses. Of these sixteen four are to be performed before the birth of the child, but nowadays practically no one performs them. Of the remaining twelve the following six are considered crucial and are observed by many Hindus: (1) name giving, (2) offering of solid food to the child, (3) the child's first haircut, (4) the sacred-thread ceremony, (5) marriage, and (6) cremation. Of these six the sacred-thread ceremony, marriage, and cremation require extensive rituals. For example, the marriage ceremony has about thirty-four steps, starting with the invocation and invitation of all deities so that the ceremony is concluded without any problem (the presence of deities indicates a divine witness). Then come the welcome of the bride and groom and his family and guests, confirmation of the wedding by the exchange of garlands between the bride and groom, *gauri-pujan* (worship of goddess Gauri and Parvati, consort of Lord Shiva by the bride, gifts to the bride from the groom's family), *panigrahana* (giving away the daughter), *agni-pradakshina* (going around the fire by the couple), *saptapadi* (taking seven steps to promise each other [to be friends for life, to take care of each other in sickness and health, etc.]), and placing of *mangalsutra* (a necklace on the wife [a symbol for married women]). Before the marriage party departs for the groom's house, several other ceremonies are performed. However, due to constraints of time, many of these steps have been shortened; nevertheless, an abbreviated marriage ceremony still takes about two hours. While the marriage ceremony is being performed, songs and dances are performed, and an atmosphere of gaiety and fun with food and drinks continues.

Vratas (Fasts)

Hindus undertake numerous *vratas* (fasts); some of these fasts are to fulfill a vow or to observe a special *puja*. For each *vrata* there is specific worship service. For example, married women keep the following four *vratas:* (1) *vat-savitri,* which is worshipping the banyan tree to ensure a long life for their husbands by fastening a sacred thread around the tree; (2) *gangaur,* a fast that is kept mostly by women in Rajasthan Province when they worship the goddess Gauri, consort of Lord Shiva; (3) *karva-chauth,* which is kept for the welfare of their children and husbands by worshipping the family of Lord Shiva and the moon without drinking a drop of water until night, when the fast is broken after seeing the moon and greeting their husbands; and (4) the Haritalika Teej fast, which is dedicated to the goddess Parvati (also called "Gauri") without drinking water or eating food for twenty-four hours. On the other hand, a fast is recommended for both men and women on at least four major occasions. (1) Shivaratri is when worshipers gather at Shiva temples and after worship keep a vigil during the night by chanting and group singing. (2) Navaratri are the nine days of fasting, done twice a year, although for Bengalis, the autumn Durga *puja* is most important. (3) Krishna-Janmastami (the eighth god-reincarnation) is the celebration of the birth of Lord Krishna. (4) Rama-Navami celebrates the birth of Lord Rama. (5) Makar-Sankranti, the only Hindu festival based on the solar calendar, celebrated each year on the fourteenth of January when the Sun enters into the zodiac sign of Capricorn commencing its northern course. In addition, some people fast on the eleventh day of the Hindu calendar month called "Ekadashi" and on other days identified for worshipping a deity in different regions of India.

Festivals

Like fasts, Hindu festivals differ among regions and linguistic groups. Four festivals are most famous: (1) Maha-shivaratri is the worship of Lord Shiva; devotees fast and visit a Shiva temple. (2) Holi is when people throw colored water on each other and sing songs. It is a harvest-related festival with overall fun-filled activities. (3) Dashahra is celebrated on the tenth day of autumn Navaratri as a victory of Rama over Ravana. (4) Diwali or Dipavali is the festival of nights, when the Goddess Lakshmi is worshipped; on that dark night millions of lights shine on housetops, doors, windows, temples, and other buildings. Fireworks are displayed, and earthen lamps are lit all over. Gifts are exchanged, and sweets are distributed.

A regional festival is Rath-yatra, which includes a procession of the three deities Balarama, Krishna, and Subhadra taken out in a massive chariot in Puri, where millions take part (the word *juggernaut* originates from this procession). Puri is a place where the rigor and conservatism of the Hindu religion are set aside as Hindus of all castes and creeds dine together without any distinction of high and low. The Ganesh Chaturthi festival worships Lord Ganesh, the remover of all obstacles in life, and is celebrated mostly in Maharashtra and western India. In addition, there are three major crop-related festivals. (1) Baisakhi is celebrated mostly in Punjab in April or May when the winter crop is in and farmers are happy to celebrate the fruits of their labor. (2) Onam is a festival of Kerala province in India, celbrated in August and September to celebrate the arrival of the monsoon crop with boat races. (3) Pongal, in January, is a four-day festival of the harvest season that features cooking new rice in milk and worshipping the Sun, the Earth, and cattle.

Kumbha-Mela

Of various bathing rituals, Kumbha-mela [It means that on that auspicious day and time, gods are pleased to send nectar inside a pitcher (Kumbha) which descends symbolically on to the Earth, and those who take the bath on that time, their sins are cleansed] is a ritual when millions take a holy dip in the waters at Allahabad (where the Ganges and Yamuna Rivers merge), at Haridwar (where the Ganges River descends from the mountains and starts its journey to the southeast), at Ujjain at the Shipra River, and at Nasik at the origin of the Godavari River. These Kumbha-melas take place every twelve years in these four cities. During the 2001 Kumbha-mela in Allahabad, 35 million people bathed. There are processions of *sadhus* (ascetics), hermits, and other religious people; some of them ride elephants, horses, or other kinds of mounts.

Sacred Baths

All religious functions require Hindus first to take a bath. But when a temple is on the banks of a river, one ought to take a holy dip in the river and then visit the temple. Rivers are revered; there are many temples on their banks. The most sacred river of all is the Ganges, which, according to Hindu mythology, originated in heaven but now flows from a glacier source in the Himalaya Mountains. Ganges water is used in all religious rituals to convey gratitude and respect to gods and goddesses. To take a bath in the holy waters of the Ganges, especially on auspicious days, is to have one's sins washed away. Six other rivers are considered sacred: Yamuna, Godavari, Narmada, Sindhu (now in Pakistan), Kaveri, and Saraswati (which vanished some time ago). One finds temples dotted on the banks of these rivers as well as others. When people visit these rivers, they perform religious rites, including the worship of their ancestors. *Panda*s (professional and mostly hereditary priests) assist pilgrims with the rites.

Pilgrimage

Hindus claim to have the largest number of sacred places. From Mount Kailash in the Himalayas in Tibet to the southernmost tip in Kanya Kumari and from Dwarka in the west to places in Tripura in the east, there are thousands of places that are considered sacred by all Hindus without distinction of caste or language. For Hindus pilgrimage to sacred places constitutes an important aspect of spiritual upliftment and religious duty. Some places of pilgrimage are of local importance; some are of regional importance. The rest are of national importance; all Hindus are enjoined to visit these at least once in their lifetime. They are (1) the four Dhams (special or holy place and a seat of religious authority) (Badrinath, Puri, Dwarka, and Rameshwaram), (2) the seven sacred cities (Varanasi, Haridwar, Ayodhya, Mathura, Kanchi, Ujjain, and Dwarka), (3) the seven sacred rivers for a holy dip, and (4) Gaya in Bihar for *pitra-tarpan* (worship of ancestors, particularly after the death of one's parents). Many sacred places are located at the confluence of rivers; others are difficult to reach, such as Vaishnava Devi in Jammu, Amarnath in Kashmir, Kailash in Tibet, and Kedarnath and Gangotri in the Himalayas. Some mountaintops are also considered sacred; the Himalayas are supposed to be the holiest place for religious penance and austerities.

The most important aspect of such pilgrimages is not only to awaken the feeling of national unity despite many languages, but also to strengthen the catholicity of the Hindu religion. Pilgrimages, especially when transportation was not extensive, afforded Hindus an opportunity to know each other and to appreciate different customs and traditions within the same religion. In the past, when people began or ended a pilgrimage, they were given a big sendoff or welcome home because much of their journey was on foot, and the odds of their return were not good. In places of pilgrimage such as in Haridwar, Badrinath, Kedarnath, Varanasi, Pushkar, Kurukshetra, Rameshwaram, Puri, and Dwarka, the local *panda*s keep a register of visits by pilgrims; and when the descendants of pilgrims visit these places, they can see the names and signatures of their ancestors.

Hindu rituals are the expression of traditional beliefs, sentiments, aspirations, hopes, and fears, including the acknowledgment by community elders that an event has taken place. In ancient times, in the absence of written documentation, these rituals sanctified an event and accorded to it a legal standing. However, over time, these rituals have declined in prestige and acceptance. Mantras recited during rituals are in Sanskrit, which most people don't understand. Because of the use of Sanskrit and the obscure nature of religious rituals, people taking part in them are indifferent. What have survived are some elaborate rituals that give religious sanctity to a ceremony, which is conducted by a priest whose profession is not well respected by the masses.

Onkar P. Dwivedi

See also Divali; Purity and Pollution

Further Reading

Haridas Bhattacharya, H. (Ed.). (1956). *The cultural history of India: Vol. 5. The religions*. Calcutta, India: Ramkrishna Mission, Institute of Culture.

Hindu Sanskriti Anka of Kalyan (Special Vol. 24). (1950). Gorakhpur, India: Gita Press.

Kane, P. V. (1973). *Dharmashastra Ka Itihas* [History of Hindu Scriptures]: *Vol. 4*. Lucknow, India: Uttar Pradesh Hindi Sansthan.

Mishra, R., & Mishra, L. (1994). *Nityakarma-Puja Prakash*. Gorakhpur, India: Gita Press.

Pandey, R. B. (1949). *Hindu samskaras: A study of Hindu sacraments*. Banaras, India: Vikrama Publications.

Singh, C., & Nath, P. (1999). *Hindu festivals, fairs and fasts.* New Delhi, India: Crest Publishing House.

Singh, C., & Nath, P. (1999). *Hindu manners, customs and ceremonies.* New Delhi, India: Crest Publishing House.

Tachikara, M., Hino, H., & Deodhar, L. (2001). *Puja and samskara.* Delhi, India: Motilal Banarsidass.

Humor and Rituals

One can examine the rituals found in humor and the humor found in rituals. The line between the sacred and the profane is not as clearly delineated as the French sociologist Emile Durkheim suggested because divinity is often found in the secular, and the profane is often found in the sacred. The contraries (sacred clowns) found in a number of Plains Native American cultures are an example of the mixture of the sacred and the profane filled with humor. These contraries reverse the normal order of the universe, saying "Goodbye" for "Hello" and "I'm glad I did it!" for "I'm sorry." Contraries (a category of men among Plains Indians) paint themselves in motley colors, clean themselves with sand, and then stride off through the river.

These contraries pretend to be cold on the hottest summer day and warm in the depth of winter. They expose themselves naked in winter while bundling up in buffalo robes in summer. Arapaho clowns moan and groan when picking up lightweight things and refuse to notice the weight of heavy objects. There are many examples of the ways in which contraries reverse the usual order of things. They may talk backward, as Koshari (Hopi Kachinas) contraries do, or feign fear of the safe events of life, as Mayan clowns did.

The point of a ritual is to call attention to the everyday and to force people to think about it. Contraries demonstrate the fact that violations of norms cause humiliation. However, the fact that contraries violate these norms is what makes them sacred. In addition to living lives of ritual contrariness, these clowns often participate in more formal religious rituals. Tohono O'odham (Papago) clowns, for instance, squeak and sing while begging food from participants during rituals. During rituals fellow dancers pretend to castrate their contraries and play at beating them.

These sacred clowns through their play call attention to the sacredness of performance by relieving the solemnity that often accompanies worship. They are free to do whatever they will, including mocking the occasion and defiling religious rituals and sexual mores. They may dress in rags, as Pueblo Native American clowns do when they mock the kachina (deified ancestral spirit) dancers. These clowns will burlesque the ceremony, stumble, fake eating excrement, and even put up false gods for worship. The shamans will sometimes join in the fun, provoking laughter from the worshippers.

Music, Humor, and the Sacred

Music is often humorous by intent. Salsa, for example, is a "feel good" music that conveys its humor in ritualistic ways that rely on incongruity. It is a hybrid of the metallic sound of the U.S. jazz trumpet and the five-beat rhythm of the Cuban bongo. Salsa is basically identified with Puerto Ricans—its major performers and innovators—in the United States. It is so popular because it addresses the events of everyday life. It uses English and Spanish in a manner familiar to the way Puerto Ricans do. Moreover, it is filled with good humor. It seeks to strengthen ties, through humor, between Puerto Ricans and other Americans. In common with all good humor, it defies definition.

Ritualistic humor is also used in the blues and calypso. That humor serves the purpose of cultural criticism. It is not merely clever wordplay. Certainly, clever wordplay is part of the performance and humor. However, the humor is part of a critique of the dominant classes who repress otherwise-powerless people. It is also an attack on corrupt social structures and their leaders by the powerless people. The blues and calypso were created on plantations. The blues was formed on cotton plantations of the U.S. South after emancipation, and calypso was formed on the urban margins of the sugar plantations in Trinidad after liberation. The blues and calypso can be seen as extensions of the jokes of the harlequin (buffoon) and similar performers who form marginalized classes in Germany.

Calypso is, in fact, a powerful force in Trinidadian life. What's more, it helped change the interpretations of the attempted coup in 1990 by Abu Bakr and his followers. The attempted coup was reinterpreted through the humor of his calypso performance as an occasion when youth banded together and used their humor, love of freedom, and calypso to triumph over a threat to the freedom so generally prized in Trinidad. Calypso was put forward as a means to bring about peace in Trinidad and the world itself through mocking war and political pretensions.

Trinidadians are a people of many races and ethnic groups. Occasionally disputes break out, but the cultural ideal is one of unity through diversity. Moreover, they are a people committed to freedom. Their long history of resistance to oppression has made them wary of threats to that freedom. Louis Regis said, "The national ideology that arises from all of these factors is that Trinidadians see themselves as an amalgamation of diverse, expressive, free, creative, peaceful peoples who have learned to live with one another despite their differences" (Birth 1994, 165–178).

Calypso performers in the 1991 carnival used the opportunity to involve their audiences in a reaffirmation of Trinidadian commitment to freedom and diversity. They employed humor in their performances, including pointing invisible guns at the sky and imitating the followers of Abu Bakr by shooting at the sky. Their bullets, however, were the bullets of *soca* (soul calypso) and would bring peace, rather than violence, to the world.

Humor in music is a common phenomenon. It is, however, not a surprising one. Both humor and music are played and involve recombination of common elements. The Yanomami people of South America use music at their feasts to express joy and promote solidarity. People dance two by two to music in a singsong manner, much in the style of children.

The combination of humor and music does indeed make the medicine go down just a little easier. Certainly the connection between humor and religion has been noted elsewhere. After all, among other things, religion seeks to assert the essential unity between opposites while being most concerned with those areas of apparent disjunction that disturb everyday life. Mythlike stories containing humor provide a safe distance from which people can examine the subversive elements of life. As the main character in the movie *Punchline* asserts, humor is too serious to joke about. It allows people to treat dangerous topics in a fashion that distances people from contact. However, as moralists from the ancient Greek philosopher Plato to the present warn, performance does not provide that safe distance. Something about music, dance, and drama reaches to the unconscious of people and speaks to them nonrationally about the essentials of life. At that level, apparent contradictions merge: subversion and affirmation, humor and seriousness, laughter and tears—each of these pairs is perceived as merely a transformation of the same underlying sacred reality. Both halves of an opposing pair are needed to understand life within a particular culture. Such transcendence frightens many people. It is because of the inherent awesomeness of the sacred that many of its practitioners appear as fools. By appearing as fools—in the mode of U.S. jazz musician Dizzy Gillespie or his alter ego, Jon Faddis—they encourage people who might otherwise be afraid to do so to approach them. In this manner, performance often takes on characteristics that reveal its intimate relationship with the sacred. Consequently, being at a performance holds the potential for subverting and disturbing a person's view of reality. Additionally, because that disturbance routinely occurs at an unconscious level and uses a culture's core symbols, it is difficult to defend against and is "subversive" in a totally literal sense simply because it undermines people's defenses and turns people upside down.

Jazz has struggled throughout its history to remain in that authentic carnival mode, one of Dionysian (relating to the Greek god of wine) joy baring its soul in public places. Therefore, it has been most frequently found as ambiguous, locked in sacred conflict with its own inner pull toward reason and its innate obligation to question reason itself through public performance, a performance that inevitably attacks all that is inherently wrong in society while revealing its contradictions, often concealing its hostility through humor.

Part of the joy of jazz performance is its constant inside comments to the hip and the square and the humor that such comments generate. Jazz singers Marion Cowings and his wife, Kim Kalesti, for example, noted the absurdity of the failure of most of the participants in a New York State African studies meeting to attend a free jazz concert. Cowings and Kalesti found it poignantly humorous because while the participants professed their adamant allegiance to multiculturalism they could not walk a few yards to attend a free concert that demonstrated the multiculturalism they had so passionately professed only a few moments before. Such ravishing music results from the very competition for its control that forms its sociocultural setting. It is music of contraries, and the creative tension that the attempt to reconcile those contraries produces ensures its originality and ingenuity. This use of humor as a ritualistic part of a music that its performers consider sacred touches on the need for humor in presenting the sacred.

Humorous Art and Religion

Humor and art have been coupled for about as long as art has existed. The ritual masks used for religious ceremonies provide ample evidence of the humor involved in art and religion. The exaggeration found in many of these masks is certainly meant to be humorous. Certainly, in ancient Roman religion, the mosaic of the god Priapus weighing his extended penis on a balancing scale is meant to be humorous.

In ancient Egyptian art going back to 2400 BCE, there were humorous depictions of sacred clowns and other entertainers—acrobats, jugglers, and animal acts. The clown has been part of theater for many centuries. The ancient Greeks had clowns with shaved heads who wore padded costumes. These clowns oversaw serious dramas and mimes. Throughout a play they commented on the action, entertaining distracted audiences. Hard as it is to imagine today, clowns interrupted the serious works of the ancient Greek dramatist Sophocles and other serious artists by throwing nuts at the crowd. Clowns who wore ragged patchwork robes and pointy hats similarly distracted ancient Roman audiences. These clowns mocked the serious actors. These actors in turn made the clowns the butt of their jokes.

The tradition was maintained in English medieval mystery plays. These plays made clear the connection between the sacred and the profane. They represented mysteries in the life of Christ but often contained buffoons or pranksters. These buffoons and pranksters had to be able to fool the devil. They pleased the rustic farmers who comprised most of the audience because they outwitted those who were supposedly their superiors. They also wore distinctive clothing, separating them from their audience.

The connection between humor and the sacred is carried on in stories told in virtually every culture of the world. The Kina and the eighteen Kuna of Panama, for example, delight in the interplay of verbal art and humor. Verbally artistic language for the Kuna, in ritual and in everyday speech, involves an actualization of various potentials of speech play with regard to both text and performance. There are speech plays in which nicknames describe relationships to animals, for example, and then these nicknames are used metaphorically in rituals.

Humor helps bring people closer to the sacred. Thus, levity and even seeming disrespect by designated tricksters, such as clowns, can relieve the tension that rituals produce. Lightening the heavy burden of getting the ritual correct can make approaching the ritual easier. The most powerful religious practitioner in a Nigerian village, the Bori doctor, was also the most humorous. He constantly disrupted sacred events, even his own, by introducing slapstick and verbal play into his routines.

The juxtaposition of contradictory elements marked humor for the Austrian neurologist Sigmund Freud. He knew that only the sacred and the temptation of the sacred can be truly funny. Humor shows the closeness of the sacred and the profane and the sacred in the profane. Undermining reality puts people on the brink of questioning what is socially and culturally real and threatens their smugness. Sacred clowns perform a vital social function.

Frank A. Salamone

See also Inversion, Rites of; Misrecognition and Rituals; Music; Performance, Ritual of; Scatological Rituals; *Star Trek* Conventions

Further Reading

Bell, C. (1997). *Ritual: Perspectives and dimensions.* New York: Oxford University Press.

Benson, J. (1994). *The rise of consumer society in Britain, 1880–1980.* London: Pearson Publishing UK.

Best, G. D. (1993). *The nickel and dime decade: American popular culture during the 1930s.* Westport, CT: Praeger Publishers.

Birth, K. (1994). Bakrnal: Coup, carnival, and calypso in Trinidad. *Ethnology 33*(2): 165–178.

Driver, T. F. (1998). *Liberating rites: Understanding the transformative power of ritual.* Boulder, CO: Westview Press.

Gossen, G. H. (Ed.). (1993). *South and Meso-American native spirituality: From the cult of the feathered serpent to the theology of liberation.* New York: Crossroad.

Grotjahn, M. (1966). *Beyond laughter: Humor and the subconscious.* New York: McGraw-Hill.

Hancock, M. E. (1999). *Womanhood in the making: Domestic ritual and public culture in urban south India.* Boulder, CO: Westview Press.

Hunt, N. R. (1999). *A colonial lexicon of birth ritual, medicalization, and mobility in the Congo.* Durham, NC: Duke University Press.

Kendall, L. (1987). *Shamans, housewives, and other restless spirits: Women in Korean ritual life.* Honolulu: University of Hawaii Press.

McDaniel, L. (1998). *The big drum ritual of Carriacou: Praise songs in rememory of flight*. Gainesville: University Press of Florida.
Mio, J. S., & Katz, A. N. (Eds.). (1996). *Metaphor: Implications and applications*. Mahwah, NJ: Lawrence Erlbaum Associates.
Pelling, H. (1960). *Modern Britain, 1885–1955*. Edinburgh, UK: T. Nelson.
Pitts, W. F. (1996). *Old ship of Zion: The Afro-Baptist ritual in the African diaspora*. New York: Oxford University Press.
Salamone, F. A. (1976). Religion as play: Bori, a friendly witchdoctor. In D. F. Lancy & B. A. Tindall (Eds.), *The anthropological study of play* (pp. 147–156). Cornwall, NY: Leisure Press.
Salamone, F. A. (1976). Religious play in a small emirate. In A. Bharati (Ed.), *Human: Actors and audiences* (pp. 6–13). Berlin, Germany: Mouton.
Schechter, W. (1970). *The history of Negro humor in America*. New York: Fleet Press.
Sherzer, J. (1990). On play, joking, humor, and tricking among the Kuna: The Agouti story. *Journal of Folklore Research, 27*(1–2), 85–114.
Snowman, D. (1977). *Britain and America: An interpretation of their culture, 1945–1975*. New York: New York University Press.
Webster, H. (1948). *Magic, a sociological study*. Stanford, CA: Stanford University Press.
Ziv, A., & Zajdman, A. (Eds.). (1993). *Semites and stereotypes: Characteristics of Jewish humor*. Westport, CT: Greenwood Press.

Hunting Rituals

By using such elements as stylized ceremonies, taboos, prescriptions for proper behaviors, and myth, hunting rituals map the relations between the human and animal worlds. While economic concerns often motivate hunting rituals, how these rituals are understood and symbolized varies dramatically between cultures. In general, one performs hunting rituals and obeys prescriptions to insure ongoing hunting prosperity, or, in other words, to maintain a relationship between prey and community that convinces the prey (or their divine caretakers) to continue offering themselves to satisfy communal alimentary needs. Ritual authenticity is the responsibility of the entire community, not just the hunters: a community member's breach of taboo, for example, can affect hunting success as much as the failure of a hunter to kill his prey in the proper manner.

Ritual Elements

Stylized ceremonies may include wearing specific clothing and body paint in preparation for the hunt, ritual reenactment of a killing (either symbolic or literal, as in the case of the Siberian bear feast, mentioned later), and prescribed customs for greeting returning hunters, consuming the meat, and disposing of leftover portions from the kill. In the view of sub-arctic American Indian hunters, throwing animal remains to the dogs instead of following traditional ceremony could lead to animals fleeing hunting areas, weapons becoming ineffectual, or disease spreading in the human population.

Taboos are prohibitions, restrictions, or the designation and setting apart of certain objects (physical or abstract) as sacred and thus illicit in profane application. Ritual hunting behavior often involves taboos on language, sexual interactions, and gender-specific behaviors. Language taboos reveal much about indigenous perceptions of animals. For instance, teasing or insulting the beaver has been taboo among many North American groups. Historically, they believed that beaver could hear and understand human conversation and, if offended, would cease to offer themselves to be killed. Proscriptions on sexual relations vary according to stage of the hunt and across populations. Intercourse was taboo for men and women of the Saami people of Northern Swedish Lapland in the seventeenth century for three days following a successful bear hunt. On the other hand, representatives of the Mandan of the North-American plains had multiple sexual partners in preparation for the buffalo hunt. With only a buffalo robe and genital-covering turtle shell to cover her nakedness, a woman representing Buffalo Woman would dance with experienced hunters who represented the buffalo bulls. When the dance was finished, young women would approach these older men (chosen by the women's husbands) and invite them to "walk with the buffalo." When the older man accepted, he had intercourse with the young wife, thereby transferring his buffalo power to her. She then would transfer that buffalo power to her husband, again through sexual intercourse.

Hunting rituals often prescribe norms for the proper hunting, killing, consuming, and disposing of animals, both in grand ceremony and daily life. In many communities, cultural stipulations require

THE POWER AND DANGER OF THE BEAR HUNT

The following extract of text describes the taboos associated with the bear hunt of the Lapps (Saami) of northern Scandinavia.

The dangerous tabu attaching to the dead bear and the prophylactic character of most customs practised at the bear-feast are confirmed by several other rites. When the men at last return home with the slain bear, they are awaited by the women who, to receive them in a seemly way, have dressed themselves in their best clothes. The men do not enter into the "kota" through the ordinary, bigger door, but through the smaller door on the opposite side. The women have their heads covered because the men are still charged with the dangerous power proceeding from the body of the bear. Moreover, they look at the men only with one eye and through a brass ring, and they spirt their whole face with the blood-like alder juice so that it is turned quite red. For safety's sake they have previously spirted alder juice on their own face and made cross marks on it. It is easy to see that all these measures are prophylactic in character. The wonderful power ascribed to the alder and the blood-like alder juice has been pointed out before, and the ceremonial spirting with this magical liquid seems to have occurred especially as a rite of the bear-feast.

To what extent the men who took part in the bear hunting were afterwards "tabued," especially in their relation to the women, appears moreover from the fact that for three days they were prohibited from sleeping with their wives. The man who "ringed in" the bear and thus was considered to be tabued in a special degree must wait five days before he can approach his wife. These precautions also are due to the desire of the men to protect their wives against harmful influences.

A peculiar ceremony which must be touched upon with a few words is performed with the skin of the bear after it has been stripped off. Rheen says that "they place the skin of the bear upon a stump and allow their wives, who are blindfolded on this occasion to shoot at a mark on the skin, with bows and arrows. The woman who is the first to hit the mark, i.e., the skin of the bear, will win the prize before all others. It is also regarded as an omen that her husband will be the first to get a bear."

***Source*: Karsten, Rafel.**
***The Religion of the Samek: Ancient Beliefs and Cults of the Scandinavian and Finnish Lapps.* (1955).**
Leiden, Netherlands: E. J. Brill, p. 120.

hunters to deny responsibility for their participation in killing. After killing a bear, the seventeenth-century Saami sang the bear song, in which they pretended to be from countries other than their own in case the dead bear's spirit was ill-disposed toward them. Other Northern groups claimed not to have fashioned the weapons used to kill the bear, and some informed the dead bear that they had not speared it themselves, but that it had slipped and fallen on their knives. Regarding the consumption and killing of animals, some sub-arctic tribes prohibited menstruating women from eating flesh. As recently as 1979, Kirk Endicott reported that the Batek Negritos of Peninsular Malaysia, although relatively unreligious, had to cook all animals killed by blowpipe with no seasoning except salt and without any other food, or else the hunter's dart poison would become ineffective.

Mythic stories are intimately related to hunting rituals: they are incorporated into and retold within them, in addition to justifying them. Myth explains the primal relationships between humans and animals that form the foundation of ritual practices. There are many variations among Northern tribes of a myth in which a native woman marries a bear man and is transformed into a bear. One Orochon (of East Siberia) version has a woman captured by a bear man; thereafter, she appeared to people as a bear. Despite her visiting women in the forest who were picking berries and asking them to tell her brothers not to mistake her for a regular bear, one day she is shot. Before dying, she instructs the hunter how to perform the bear-play ceremony (Kwon 1999, 382). In a similar vein, the Aleuts decorated their bodies and kayaks to appeal to sea otters' human qualities. Success in the hunt depended on the moral probity of the hunter and his family. The myth that gave rise to these perceptions involved an incestuous brother and sister who committed suicide. To assuage their parents' grief, a divine being created sea otters to became judges of human morality (Krech 1981, 126).

Reservations about Fidelity to Ritual

Traditional bear-hunt rituals among Northern peoples are typically of four main types: preparation for the hunt, often concerned with the purification of the hunter; leaving the camp, with a focus on gaining supernatural permission to enter hunting grounds; the kill, generally encompassing the idea that the animal freely offers itself; and return to camp, with more acts of purification, women ceremonially welcoming hunters back into the domestic world, and the proper disposal of animal remains. Yet while leading anthropologists agree that bear-hunting societies *claimed* to follow these tenets, actual levels of adherence to ritual law varied. The noted scholar of religion Jonathan Z. Smith questions the likelihood that these (or any ritual hunting practices) were faithfully observed.

Smith questions whether a hunter who accidentally kills his prey in a ritually unacceptable manner would actually leave the meat to rot. He also examines the logistical feasibility of some requirements: does a hunter really have time for incantations between first sighting the prey and thrusting his weapon? Further, is it believable that promises made in some traditions, such as to withhold meat from women and dogs, would be followed in practice? Is it plausible that a hunter who has spent years developing his skill would not boast of his prowess, instead giving credit to the animal itself or members of a neighboring people? Smith suggests that the Siberian Bear Festival is an attempt to bridge this gap between idealized and actual hunting behavior.

The Siberian Bear Festival

One of the best-documented and most complex hunting rituals is the Siberian Bear Festival, also known as bear feasts, playing the bear, and bear play. The ritual begins when a hibernating bear is awakened and killed and the cub (or cubs) is taken back to the village. Initially, the whole community helps feed the new bear. Eventually, a host family adopts the cub and raises it as a family member (it is even reported that native women breast feed the cub), though once its claws develop it is kept in a cage. The cub is kept for three to four years, until it reaches sexual maturity. (An Orochon elder from Sakhalin Island reported that the community determines sexual maturation as the moment when the bear begins to play with its genitals.)

About a mile from their dwellings, male members of the tribe prepare a ritual site for the killing; this area is considered taboo for women. The bear is let out of its cage and taken to visit each family in its foster village. At the home of the ritual host, the bear is given food and water and cleansed through prodding with a stick. Women now participate, coming out of their homes dressed in ceremonial clothing and beating a drum made of a tree trunk.

Next the bear is led to the ritual site and tied between two tree trunks. The bowman shoots arrows first over the treetops, then into the bear's heart. Once the bear is dead, its head is set beside a fire, skinned, and the eyeballs thrown far away. Afterwards, the body is carried back to the encampment, where the flesh is boiled and consumed by all. The feast lasts fifteen to twenty days, while sexual tensions build and are often indulged (sexual purity is required before the killing). Once the flesh is consumed, the men of the host group move to a new location, where they cook and consume the bear's head. The eldest man gets the honor of eating the tongue. The ceremony ends with a final smoking of the skull (Kwon 1999, 375–380).

American Indian Rituals

Before the devastation of the American Indians of the Northern Plains, their hunting rituals focused either on promoting the capture of animals for food or acquiring animals' power for specific purposes, such as war. Ceremony and tepee decorations were replete with mythical references to a time when boundaries between humans and animals were less clear or even non-existent. Often people dressed as and imitated animals to reinforce this impression. In some cases, current understandings of the separate roles of humans and animals were reversed in myth. For example, buffalo were believed to have been the primary species, feeding upon the flesh of humans who lived under ground, until one day a human escaped the hunt and slept with a buffalo maiden who resembled a beautiful woman. She instructed the young man how to prepare weapons that would allow his people to defend themselves. When humans next emerged aboveground, armed and able to fight the buffalo, the power structure was reversed.

Given the difficulty of distinguishing humanity from the rest of creation, hunting rituals may have lessened the cognitive dissonance of killing living creatures by providing a structure, often reported as dictated by the animals themselves, which made the killing acceptable to the prey. As long as communities followed hunting prescriptions, they received a salve to their consciences that their behavior was not overly hurtful and assurance that the animals would continue to make themselves available for communal nourishment.

Controversy and Misconceptions

Scholarly debates over the comparative importance of mythic and economic motivations for hunting practices have been particularly controversial in regard to the excessive hunting practices of the subarctic American Indians French colonial trappers were hunting animals for fur at rates that would soon lead to extinction. Native groups eventually joined in this hunting spree, and scholars disagree as to why. Calvin Martin (1978) posits that epidemics beginning in the sixteenth century were regarded by American Indians as a breach of contract with the animals. While natives had maintained the sanctity of various taboos and adhered to religious rites, animals had broken faith by causing disease. The resulting disillusionment left natives vulnerable to the economic temptations presented by French trappers. If animals failed to maintain their part of the bargain, natives were under no obligation to keep theirs and were ideologically free to benefit from the lucrative fur trade. Those who disagree with Martin argue that animals were never blamed for disease. Rather, ritual breach resulted in a scarcity of game. Shamans, sorcerers, deities, and the French might all be blamed for disease, but not animals. Martin, however, cites evidence that natives felt animals may have been culpable in this regard. Others argue that real epidemics were not experienced by natives until the 1630s—after the commencement of over-hunting. Many of Martin's opponents insist the motives for excessive participation in the fur trade were economic. Natives saw that the French were hunting at a rate that made sustainable hunting an impossibility: the Penobscot, for instance, reportedly felt that white hunters' over-exploitation of the beaver was inevitable, and that their only recourse was to take advantage of the resource before all hunting opportunity disappeared.

Contemporary Trends

Although the last bear rituals were performed on Sakhalin Island in the 1950s, the native anthropologist Chuner Mikhailovich Taksami attempted to revive the ceremony in the early 1990s. There is currently a renewed emphasis on the religious aspects of hunting among American Indians as environmentalists rally to restrict their ability to hunt. Framing the issue in terms of religious tradition rather than livelihood lends the American Indian position more political clout. Many hunting rituals have fallen out of practice in the modern world. However, even where rituals are no longer performed, and their mythical counterparts are known only to elders and anthropologists, still there survives in the minds of many peoples the faint memory of an earlier understanding.

Kate Holbrook

See also Agricultural Rituals; Sacrifice and Offerings

Further Reading

Endicott, K. (1979). *Batek negrito religion: The world-view and rituals of a hunting and gathering people of peninsular Malaysia*. Oxford, UK: Clarendon Press.

Flores, D. (1991). Bison ecology and bison diplomacy: The Southern Plains from 1800–1850. *Journal of American history*, 78, 465–485.

Harrod, H. I. (2000). *The animals came dancing: Native American sacred ecology and animal kinship*. Tucson: The University of Arizona Press.

Kent, S. (Ed.). (1996). *Cultural diversity among twentieth-century foragers: An African perspective*. Cambridge, UK: Cambridge University Press.

Krech, S. (1999). *The ecological Indian: Myth and history*. New York: W. W. Norton & Co.

Krech, S. (Ed.). (1981). *Indians, animals, and the fur trade: A critique of keepers of the game*. Athens: University of Georgia Press.

Kwon, H. (1999). *Play the bear: Myth and ritual in East Siberia. History of religions*, 38, 373–387.

Martin, C. (1978). *Keepers of the game: Indian-animal relationships and the fur trade*. Berkeley: University of California Press.

Middleton, J. (Ed.). (1967). *Myth and cosmos: Readings in mythology and symbolism*. Austin: University of Texas Press.

Nelson, R.K. (1983). *Make prayers to the raven: A Koyukon view of the northern forest*. Chicago: University of Chicago Press.

Schweitzer, P. P., Biesele, M., & Hitchcock, R. K. (Eds.). (2000). *Hunters and gatherers in the modern world: Conflict, resistance, and self-determination*. New York: Berghahn Books.

Smith, J. Z. (1980). The bare facts of ritual. *History of religions*, 20(1–2), 112–127.

Iban

The word *Iban* is commonly used to identify (1) the Bornean people who identify themselves as "Iban" and (2) their language and other commonly shared cultural products. Ibans are found in all political territories of Borneo—Sarawak, Sabah, Kalimantan, and Brunei—and other countries in southeastern Asia. The island of Borneo, the third-largest island in the world, is home to between 150 and 200 self-naming or autonymic societies, of whom the Iban are the largest, numbering about 600,000. Ibans have two traditional ritual specialists: shamans and bardic (relating to a tribal poet-singer) priests. The former have responsibilities for healing, the latter, for almost all other rituals.

Iban Rituals

Ibans observe numerous religious rituals, including more than one hundred major festivals and scores of lesser rituals. The rituals include cyclical (annual) rituals and life-crisis rituals.

The cyclical rituals of greatest significance are those related to the annual agricultural cycle, in which a sophisticated technology is reinforced with elaborate rites, leaving little to chance. From the selection of rice seeds to the storage of the harvest, no act of this complex system of farming is performed without appropriate rituals. Seeds are blessed with offerings and prayers, and in areas where wet rice is cultivated and seedlings are transplanted, the young plants are treated as and called "rice children." In a ritual blessing, bardic-priests precede young women carrying the seedlings in finely woven blankets around the longhouse veranda (Iban social and ritual communities). The intention of the blessing is to convey fertility to plant and bearer. Rituals are performed to alert the god of agriculture and earth that humans intend to enter his domain. After planting, fields are ritually tabooed for three days lest anyone offend the earth or plants. Approximately two dozen rituals accompany each named phase in the growth and development of rice plants. When the rice is mature, a preliminary ritual is performed to alert the rice that its time of sacrifice is at hand. Seven stalks with panicles (flower clusters) are tied around with a red thread and are cut with a finger knife. Harvesters then wait three days before the actual harvest begins. The senior woman must set the pace for harvesting, and it is believed that she conveys fertility to the rice. On the last day of the harvest, clothing worn by members of each family is brought to the field and placed over the harvest baskets so that the rice will recognize the body odor of the member of the household. In some areas rice can be stored only by the senior woman and only during the waxing of the moon to ensure that the stored rice will magically increase. Likewise, in some areas the farming year concludes with a Festival of the Peak of the Year, which marks the end of the agricultural cycle and is an occasion for asking blessings upon residents of the host community. Even among Ibans who have converted to the Christian faith, many of the traditional agricultural rituals are retained.

Festivities and Memorials

The months after the storage of rice are spent in festivities and the performance of memorial rites. A highly mobile people who practice ambilineal (tracing through either male or female line) descent and ambilocal residence (meaning a couple can choose to live with either the husband's or the wife's family, or on their own), Ibans have kin scattered in up to a dozen communities. Festivals provide an opportunity to renew acquaintances and strengthen relations. Memorial rites vary regionally. Among Iban of southwestern Sarawak, the Festival of the Ancestors (Gawai Antu or Festival of Spirits or Festival of Heads) is an important rite that combines features of both cyclical rituals and life-crisis rituals. Unlike many societies in southeastern Asia, Ibans do not exhume and rebury their dead. The festival is an opportunity to honor all family members who have died since the last festival and is regarded as crucial because these persons are believed to directly affect the productivity of rice plants. Among Ibans of north central Sarawak the festival is of secondary importance. The Festival of the Ancestors may take up to five years to plan and to accumulate the resources needed for hosting such an event. One month prior to the festival women weave baskets in which gifts will be presented to the ancestors. On the first day of the festival members of the host community and relatives who have come to assist them in preparing for the hundreds of guests who will arrive shortly engage in cockfighting. The cockfighting is symbolic of a contest between the living and the dead and an occasion of much enjoyment for participants. Guests from as many as a dozen communities arrive and, after bathing and donning their best clothes, are led into the longhouse. Women enter the family apartments of kin or friends, and men walk the length of the house, being plied with rice wine by each host family. From the far end of the veranda men are led back to seats of honor along the outer wall. More drinks are served, and hosts wave cockerels over the heads of the guests, intoning prayers that, should the travelers have seen any omen bird or other inauspicious sign, they will be covered by the sacrifice of the bird. About 10 P.M. warriors, preferably men who have taken a human head, dramatically clear a path between the otherworld and the longhouse. Ancestors are invited, and not long after teams of six bardic priests begin their chanting of the praise of rice in its various forms, as a symbol of life and as a gift of the ancestors. For an hour or so they chant in every fourth or fifth family room before moving onto the common veranda, where they walk up and down, traversing the length of the veranda, until about 3 A.M. About 8 A.M. warriors and other respected older men drink the most sacred rice wine in an act of sharing with the ancestors. The festival concludes on the third day as wooden frames, like small A-frame structures, are taken to the nearby cemetery and gifts presented to the ancestors.

Life-Crisis Rituals

However one may regard the Festival of the Ancestors, life-crisis rituals begin with the prebirth and postbirth taboos observed by pregnant women and their spouses and continue with rituals observed for the newborn infant. Husband and wife may not perform any act that would jeopardize the life of the fetus or newborn.

Other than rituals of the initiate's journey and adolescent girls' taking up weaving, few rituals mark physical and social changes related to puberty. Until about the middle of the twentieth century Iban men were expected to undertake an initiate's journey in which they demonstrated their cunning and skills by living off the land for from three months to three years. When headhunting was common among Bornean tribes, the initiate's journey was the occasion when a man might acquire his first head trophy. Such experiences were attended by numerous rituals, including an elaborate system of augury (divination from omens) and offerings. As hundreds of other societies did, Ibans sought guidance from the calls and flight of particular birds. A particular call might force initiates to call off their journey, as might the sighting of a bird on the left side of a path. Offerings were made for every activity of major or minor importance. In the words of one Iban man, "We do nothing without first providing offerings to the spirits." (Nuing anak Kundi, conversation, 15 August 1960) For Ibans of north central Borneo the rituals related to warfare remain of supreme importance.

For young women weaving was an analog to headhunting and was acknowledged as such by Ibans. Weaving also functioned as a highly ritualized technique to distinguish more able and affluent Iban families from poorer ones. By tradition a young woman could take up weaving only after she had a "culture-pattern dream" (Lincoln 1935). After such a dream she would seek confirmation and support from her family, and her mother either would take on the daughter as an apprentice or would make arrangements for the daughter to study with a master weaver. In any case, one of the early important rituals to be performed on behalf of the novice weaver was the invocation of the spirits of ancestral weavers, the presentation of offerings to the spirits of weaving, and the "laying on of hands" to convey the beneficence of such spirits to the new weaver.

The next rituals of importance are engagement and marriage. Engagements are arranged by the parents of a couple and involve negotiations about postmarital residence. Parents of a single child usually will insist that the newlyweds live with or near them, especially if the parents of the child whom their daughter or son will marry have several siblings. In marriage relatives and friends from several longhouses are invited, and there is much merriment. Marriage is called "splitting the betel nut" by Ibans. This phrase refers to the ritual of exchanging brass boxes that are tied up with gold threads and contain betel nuts. The threads are tied with numerous knots and may require up to an hour to untie. When the betel nuts have been removed, they are split and then rolled as dice might be, with a "reading" being done of the nuts. If the nuts land flesh side up, the newlyweds will have a son; if the nuts land skin side up, the newlyweds will have a daughter.

Rituals for Health and Success

Ibans have created two major officiants: bardic priests and shamans. Bardic priests are employed for all of the major agricultural rituals, as well as rites celebrating bravery and memorializing the dead. Bardic priests are persons of remarkable memory.

All Ibans have been exposed to shamanic rituals from early childhood onward. Further, it is unlikely that any Iban growing up in rural areas at some distance from modern medical facilities was not treated by a shaman. Shamans are psychotherapists who practice a form of transactional analysis (a system of psychotherapy involving analysis of individual episodes of social interaction for insight that will aid communication). Imploring their spirit-familiars or spirit guides who instruct and assist the shaman in dealing with patients' souls, they treat the souls of their patients by employing a hierarchy of rituals that generally is effective.

Ibans are part of "the luminous web" (Taylor 2000). Nothing happens without cause, and, as often as not, the cause is spiritual in nature. Rituals are performed for every imaginable activity in the hope of appeasing spirit beings and ensuring success.

Vinson Sutlive

See also Agricultural Rituals; Calendrical Rituals; Taboo

Further Reading

Lincoln, J. S. (1935). *The dream in primitive cultures*. Baltimore: Williams and Wilkins.

Sather, C. (2001). *Seeds of play, words of power: An ethnographic analysis of Iban shamanism*. Kuching, Malaysia: Tun Jugah Foundation.

Sutlive, V., & Sutlive, J. (2001). *The encyclopaedia of Iban studies*. Kuching, Malaysia: Tun Jugah Foundation.

Taylor, B. (2000). *The luminous web*. Cambridge, MA: Cowley.

Identity Rituals

Identity rituals locate an individual within a particular tradition in contrast to other traditions. Identity rituals are specific to a cultural system. Such rituals function on what the Greek philosopher Aristotle called an "optative-exclusive" principle: As a person opts for *this*, a person excludes *that*; as a person chooses one identity, a person inevitably excludes others. Thus, a person is that person and not someone else. Similarly, by being a Roman Catholic, one is not a Hindu or a Mormon. This is precisely the function of identity rituals: to avoid confusion and to create and maintain a sense of order. (The English writer Samuel Johnson observed that the person who attempts to be everything to everyone ends up being nothing to anybody.)

This said, it is crucial to acknowledge that the six billion people on Earth have created just over six thousand ways of defining what it means to be "human." Not surprisingly, most autonyms—the ethnic terms that people call themselves, such as *Hopi* or *Navajo* or *Iban*—mean "human." In recognizing the plurality of ways in which people believe and behave, it is just as important to accept the fact that these wider ritualized ways are not right or wrong, only different. All people create identities, but the values that each person associates with an identity will be different from those of any other. Identity rituals help alleviate anxiety about belonging and counting. Rituals exist among all people to affirm that each member does belong to this group or that and that in one way or another each person counts. Prestate (tribal) societies generally have been more tolerant of all people than have state-organized societies. Prestate societies have treated members as more or less equal, with possibly some status distinctions. States are based upon myths of accommodation and rituals of

PERSONAL IDENTITY THROUGH THE VISION QUEST

Among some Native American groups, a person begins to establish as identity as a shaman through a vision quest, as described below for the Thompson Indians of the Northwest.

As an example of the more common form, I will present that of the Thompson. The Thompson complex is more nearly that of the Klamath but is even simpler. The vision quest, which takes place at puberty, is essentially the prerogative of boys, although girls may obtain some slight powers. Hence shamans are men and but few women. The vision is sought in the mountains where the boy remains praying, dancing, running about, and fasting. His training does not end with the vision, but continues after power has been acquired, the whole being directed toward magical training for adult life. In fact the powers bestowed by the spirits are specifically for particular professions and arts. The spirits are legion: natural phenomena, animals, birds, and a random collection of objects. The seeker sometimes receives power from the same spirit as his father and shamans sometimes directly inherit their powers. It does not appear that the shaman novice establishes himself by a performance of fixed kind, nor do the shamanistic seances, though they include feats like those of the Klamath, occur only in midwinter.

***Source*: Spier, Leslie. *Klamath Ethnography.* (1930). Berkeley: University of California Press, 242.**

differentiation. For example, in ancient Sumer there was a myth that the health and well-being of the ancient Mesopotamian city of Akkad depended upon the amicable relations among people of different backgrounds—shepherds, farmers, traders, and the like—while the rulers set themselves apart. Such behavior makes one feel that one is special and belongs to a privileged class.

Fundamentalism of any religion—Hinduism, Judaism, Christianity, Islam—provides an identity to the "true believer" and a powerful sense of belonging. Members believe alike and behave alike. Uniformity supercedes unity but at an enormous price. With an emphasis on a limited selection of "fundamentals" such religious conservatism requires individuals to suspend critical judgment and individual thinking and to accept the teaching of the leader.

Identity rituals establish features and create boundaries that, although invisible and permeable, are nevertheless real. As inclusive as one's community may attempt to be, certain beliefs and behaviors set it apart from others. Some major religions are open and inclusive, whereas others do not permit nonbelievers to participate in their rituals. Muslims do not permit non-Muslims in their mosques. Some Christian denominations practice "closed communion" (an oxymoron!), that is, they do not permit members of other denominations to share the Eucharist (the Lord's Supper). In both cases the intention of Muslims and Christians is to maintain the identity and integrity of their community.

In the story of the Exodus, Yahweh (the Hebrew god) chose slaves who had no identity and, by revealing for the first time the divine name, also gave identity to the people of Israel. This identity was confirmed by the covenant at Sinai—an identity ritual—and marked by the practice of circumcision. Jews still reaffirm this covenant annually when they observe Passover. The unity of Jews and a primary source of religious identity are phrased in the question asked at Passover: "Why is this night different from all other nights?" to which the answer is given, "We were slaves in Egypt"—a ritual identification with ancestors who lived more than three millennia earlier.

Basic Cultural Orientations

Each culture provides its members with basic orientations to self, other people, the material world, time and space, values, and norms. Identity is a process by which people learn who they are by interacting with

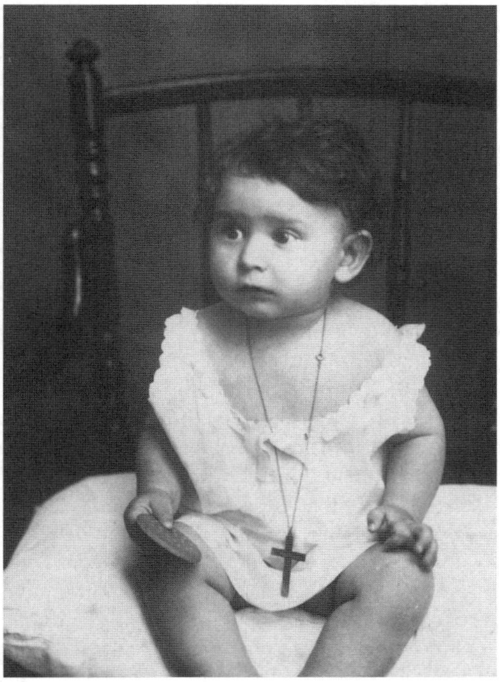

In this old family photo a young Greek Orthodox child is wearing a large cross. Public display of the cross identifies Christians around the world. COURTESY OF BERKSHIRE PUBLISHING GROUP.

other people, and their learning is affected by all of the other orientations—the material world, time and space, values, and norms.

The Nature of the World

For a majority of the world's societies religion is not some extramural institution, limited to rituals performed on holy days. Rather, for most of the world's societies religion is part of a total way of life, of what philosophers refer to as an ontological (relating to existence) scheme, an all-embracing system, in which no action is not part of the all-inclusive framework. Members of such religious systems are condescendingly referred to as "pagans," or only slightly better than believers in a traditional religion. Naturists (persons who traced all religious symbols to natural phenomena) of the nineteenth century, such as the English Orientalist Max Müller and the Scottish scholar William Robertson Smith, were understandably dismissed for their efforts to explain all religious systems in terms of natural phenomena. However, postmodern thinkers would do well to recognize the insights that such naturists provide: that all people are part of natural systems and are subject to forces beyond human comprehension.

A Search for the Self

Contrary to the writings of some social scientists, all people have a sense of self-awareness. This sense is one of the characteristics that makes people human. Americans, as beneficiaries of the Enlightenment (the period during the 1700s in Europe and the United States when humanity was emerging from centuries of ignorance into an age of reason, science, and respect for humanity) and of the emphasis on independence, are perhaps more individualistic than are other peoples. An overemphasis on independence can be destructive, as the French writer Alexis de Tocqueville observed in the nineteenth century. People find out who they are through interaction with other people, not through privacy or privatization, as popular as both are. As people try to "find themselves," to discover who they are, the insight provided by U.S. philosopher Alan Watts is correct when he writes that "trying to define yourself is like trying to bite your own teeth." People do not define themselves or discover themselves alone—they do it through interpersonal interaction. As people are aware of themselves and of others, they form identities but always within the contexts and moments in which they live.

Identity formation is a lifelong process of "negotiations" among the biological inheritance that people receive from their parents, the groups to which people belong, and the world within which people live. Just as identity formation is never finished, so, too, it is potentially dynamic or fluid. As people change group settings, their identity also may change. This is true also for ethnic identity. Tisza is a group, established in Washington, D.C., to perform Hungarian dance. Most of its members are not descendants of Hungarian ancestors. In fact, the leaders of Tisza are not Hungarian. The identities of both groups of people—Hungarian and non-Hungarian— are changed as they perform the dances.

Within the context of religious systems individuals and groups develop and elaborate rituals by which they create and convey identity to each other. Identity rituals locate individuals in relation to other people, the material world, and time and space and reflect the values of a group that become normative.

Identity rituals help people resolve their ambivalence about their mortality. On the one hand, people are quick to dismiss earlier generations while treasuring their own. Some identity rituals and the social theologies they represent give a sense of self-transcendence to believers, the assurance that in the world mediated to them by their culture, life has meaning and purpose. Nihilism (annihilation) has been protested by people from Neanderthals to twenty-first-century urbanites. Neanderthals were the first people to bury their dead, on whose cheeks they rubbed iron-rich dirt to give a life like appearance and to whom they provided toolkits for the afterlife. With such rituals people still try to establish their identities and ensure immortality in the memory of others.

The author of children's books, Richard Eyre writes:

> Our parents cast long shadows over our lives. When we grow up, we imagine that we can walk in the sun, free of them. We don't realize, until it's too late, that we have no choice in the matter; they're always ahead of us.
>
> We carry them within us all our lives—in the shape of our face, the way we walk, the sound of our voice, our skin, our hair, our hands, our heart. We try all our lives to separate ourselves from them, and only when they are gone do we find we are indivisible.

So are people tied by common bonds of inheritance that make them uncommonly human while also commonly natural. Yet, people have considerable anxiety about who they are and why they are. People live in a world that is divided along numerous fault lines—female and male, young and old, black and white, brown and yellow. Some such fault lines are physically based, cultural creations. That is, they are not "natural" or "inevitable." Rather, they occur because of human decisions or indecisions.

Identity and Other People

In prestate societies, with relatively few categories available for the location of individuals, identity often has been tied to relationships and, in particular, to success in reproduction. Teknonymy is a ritualized practice by which those men and women who have contributed to the continuity of the group receive the honorific teknonyms "Father of So-and-So" or "Mother of So-and-So." In those societies practicing teknonymy ancestors are accorded particular prestige and are regarded as unseen presences who, although invisible, are much aware of everything their descendants do.

Among some societies, prior to the availability of information about reproduction, conception was believed to be a spiritual process. For example, among the Australian aborigines, impregnation was thought to have been done by clan spirits. By a mysterious process the clan spirit, which resided in the clan water hole, created a blood clot within a woman, and the clot developed into the fetus. Identity was established through conception because the infant was recognized as having been fathered by an ancestral spirit.

Among the BaGanda people of Uganda in Africa, a widow took up a vigil at the graveside of her deceased husband and remained there for up to two years or until, it was believed, the husband had been reborn in an infant. Similarly, the Ibans of Sarawak, Malaysia, believe that life recycles through a series of stages, from person to spirit, from spirit to dew, from dew to rice, from rice to person. With this confidence, girls are named for their maternal great-grandmother; boys are named for their paternal great-grandfather. In order to be certain of the name to be used, balls of rice are placed on the floor with the name of a great-grandmother or great-grandfather assigned to each, depending on the gender of the infant. The first ball that a chicken pecks is taken to be the name to be given the child.

In several societies in southeastern Asia, when infant mortality rates were as high as 50 percent, infants often were given repulsive names—"Buffalo Dung," "Worm," "Maggot"—in the hope that predatory spirits would be repulsed by the names and leave the children alone. Then, when a child was three or four years old, the child would be given a more ordinary name. In the same region ritual name changing was common. If a person suffered from ill health or had a run of bad luck, he or she might ask to have his or her name changed. The folk belief was that a person's fate changed as the name was changed. When individuals or groups have converted to Islam or Christianity, it has been common for them to take either an Arabic name, such as "Abdul Rahman," or a Western name, such as "Jeffrey" or "Stanley," to indicate their new status. Saul of Tarsus, upon his conversion to Christianity, took the name of "Paul," and much earlier, Jacob, "the Cheat," had his name changed by God to "Israel" (Prince with God).

Identity has most commonly been based on physical appearance or culture. Racism, however, is a relatively recent phenomenon. The concept of "race" as a scientific category appeared in 1775 in the doctoral thesis of the German anthropologist Johann Blumenbach. This is not to say that people had been unaware of differences based on physical appearances or language or culture. However, not until the eighteenth century was the fiction of race made the basis for identifying and sorting people. Anthropologists have rejected race as a meaningful category of study but recognize the persistent nature of race as a basis for identification and discrimination. People no longer force other people to sit in the back of the bus or drink from separate water fountains, but rituals for separating people endure. They are not unique to Caucasians.

Space and Time

Identity has often been tied to one's place of birth or one's place of residence. The god of Israel originally was associated with Mount Sinai, so much so that five centuries after the Exodus, the prophet Elijah fled to Mount Sinai to find Yahweh. A couple of centuries earlier, King David lamented events that overtook him, forcing him to leave Jerusalem and God. The psalms written in Babylonia expressed the sense of alienation that the Jewish exiles felt and how they longed for their homeland. The anthropologist George Peter Murdock regarded residence as the most important variable in the analysis of social and personal identity.

Identity rituals locate individuals in space and time. As much as people want to believe that they transcend the influences of time and aging, the reality is that people are a product of the time during which they grew up and reached their social maturity. This fact was presented in a film by Morris Massey entitled *What You Are Is Where You Were When,* with the thesis that one's personality is fairly well set by the time one reaches age twenty-one. (Happily, Massey produced a sequel, *What You Are Is Not What You Are Going to Be,* acknowledging changes in personality.) One's social philosophy is bound to be different depending on whether one lived through the Great Depression, World War II, the McCarthy era, the 1960s, or Watergate. The religious idioms and images, the rituals and languages of different traditions (such as Roman Catholic, United Methodist, Unitarian, Muslim, and Buddhist) inevitably reflect circumstances in the world around the particular tradition.

The predominant forces of the twenty-first century are the state and the corporation. Each force has taken on a larger-than-life quality, and each assumes powers that seem impossible to challenge. To be associated with either, especially in an official way, conveys distinction and identity that mark the individual as well as a person of power. The rituals associated with entrance into and progress within the state or the corporation resonate with echoes of humans' tribal past. A former CEO of the Continental Group, formerly a major insurance company as well as the owners of Hallmark Greeting cards and Manufacturers Trust Bank, shared with the author the parallels between the rites of the boardroom and the potlatch (ceremonial feast) of the Kwakiutl people. Although one is located on Wall Street and the other in British Columbia, the processes and ends are the same.

For people in some parts of the United States, football and other sports take on what may be described as a religious nature. If by *religion* is meant "activities and attitudes related to ultimate issues," sports have become just short of all consuming for many Americans. Students and alumni identify with the successes and failures of their favorite teams, and at many colleges coaches' salaries exceed those of presidents. Salaries paid to professional athletes are disproportionate to their social contributions but an example of Jesus's observation that "where your treasure is, your heart will be also" (Matthew 6:21). In contemporary society the philosopher Reuel Howe has written that people identify people in terms of what they do and evaluate them by what they have.

Another identity ritual is associated with patriotism. National identity has various manifestations, and Americans possibly are more zealous in the expression of their love of country than are citizens of any other country. The floods of emotion after the terrorist attacks on the World Trade Center and the Pentagon are characteristically American. The song "God Bless the U.S.A." was played and sung repeatedly in gatherings great and small.

Caught up in the groundswell of ritual responses, it may be difficult for Americans to recognize that nationalism is a source of identity for citizens of other countries as well. As people sing "God Bless America" and "America, the Beautiful," they must remember in the words of the hymn composed by the late theologian Georgia Harkness, "... but other lands have sunlight, too, and clover, and skies are everywhere as blue as mine" (Harkness 1934).

Every person lives with a sense of self-awareness that is enriched or diminished in response to orientations provided by her or his culture. People learn who they are in community, and in association with others people participate in the identity rituals of infancy, childhood, adolescence, and adult life to discover who they are and who they may become.

Vinson Sutlive

See also Naming Rituals; Personal Rituals

Further Reading

Daner, F. J. (1976). *The American children of Krsna: A study of the Hare Krsna movement*. New York: Holt, Rinehart and Winston.

Eyre, R. (1993). *Utopia and other places*. London: Bloomsbury Press.

Hallowell, A. I. (1955). The self and the behavioral environment. In *Culture, personality, and experience* (pp. 75–100). Philadelphia: University of Pennsylvania Press..

Harkness, G. (1934). This is my song. In *The United Methodist Hymnal* (pp. 437). Nashville, TN: United Methodist Publishing House.

Howe, R. (1963). *Herein is love*. Chicago: Judson Press.

La Barre, W. (1968). Personality from a psychoanalytic viewpoint. In E. Norbeck, D. Price-Williams, & W. McCord (Eds.), *The study of personality: An interdisciplinary appraisal* (pp. 65–87). New York: Holt, Rinehart and Winston.

Initiation Rites

See Gender Rituals; Passage, Rites of; Puberty Rites

Inversion, Rites of

Rites of inversion are ceremonial or formal acts or events at which participants symbolically turn the world, as they know it, upside down. That is, participants, whether by choice or obligation or both, deliberately engage in ordered disorderly conduct. Inherent in the logic of inversion is the recognition that the conditions and events that make up such rites are unusual and temporary. These rites are ritual events intended to reverse persons' social positions, public roles, and patterns of everyday life for a prescribed amount of time. Such forms of institutionalized disorder can be found in most cultures spanning from "primitive," "tribal," agrarian-based societies to "complex," industrial or postindustrial societies, from Africa to Brazil to Trinidad to the United States. The specific aspects of these rites vary across both time and space in regard to which roles are highlighted for inversion (e.g., men becoming women, humans becoming deities, kings becoming peasants). There are, however, certain functional and structural similarities for the development and use of rites that negate a culture's "normal" order, regardless of whether or not these rites are meant to invert the order of everyday life or the "sacred" cosmological (relating to a branch of metaphysics that deals with the nature of the universe) order.

The very notion or act of inversion, reversal, or symbolic transformation is dependent on the existence of a collectively understood, although not necessarily collectively endorsed, social order. A culture's social order is predicated upon its taken-for-granted status ascribed to it by its "community of believers." The basic elements of social order are understood as "the way things are." The central categories that establish this order—and the classification systems that legitimize it—symbolically imply its negation. That is, each category within a classification system implies its opposite. Anthropologist Claude Levi-Strauss and his fellow structuralists recognized binary opposites as natural and inherent elements that form the structure of myths and rituals. Whether or not the recognition of binary opposites is a universal, innate faculty of the human mind, as structuralist interpretations contend, or merely a residual effect of language itself, inversion relies on the acknowledgment of the relationship between opposites. The manipulation of a culture's classification system allows those both observing and participating in rites of inversion to express the taken-for-granted order's negation, its reversal.

The social order of a culture is made up of events, actions, and material objects that are defined, in part, by their location within a classification system. A classification system functions as a code for cultural knowledge. These events, actions, and material objects within the code, however, help determine only one side of the system. A culture's social order is also determined by those events, actions, and material objects that signify and exhibit deviance, defiance, disorderliness, and dirt. The anthropologist Mary Douglas describes these "dangerous" aspects as "polluting" mechanisms. Because both order and disorder are embedded in any culture's social order, community members learn "both the conventional means of articulating orders and rules *and* the counteractive patterns by which those very conventions may be profitably and recognizably transformed" (Babcock 1978, 27). As such, the construction of celebrations of ritualized disorder, which valorize and sanction danger, pollution, and taboo, develops naturally out of the legitimized, normative social order. Again, rites of inversion can be understood as being the antithesis of a people's idealized normative social order, yet existing as part of a culture's overall way of life. Rites of inversion highlight and signify the symbolic relationship between order and disorder.

The Function of Inversion

There is no all-encompassing functional definition or explanation of rites of inversion. Their functions are context dependent, constitutive of a culture's power structures, gender relations, mythic narratives, cosmological belief systems, geographical and environmental localities, and historical origins. Although specific functions of these rites may serve different purposes, the primary intent of rites of inversion—systematic role reversal and transformation—is similar between cultures. The functions of these rites have been a subject of debate for anthropologists and "natives" alike. Rites of inversion can be used for a number of purposes, such as collective tension management or catharsis, conservative social control, adult forms of play, or catalysts for rebellion or revolution. Often the function is dependent upon *who* is participating and *what* they are inverting.

Rites of inversion can be used like a steam valve to release built-up tension. Although the actions associated with reversals or inversions might look like protests against the established, normative social order, the South African anthropologist Max Gluckman claims that "they are intended to preserve and strengthen the established order" (Gluckman 1965, 109). From his classic study of rituals of rebellion in southeastern Africa, he suggests that these rites have a cathartic aspect to them in that they help purge the social system of tensions and potential disruptions that develop due to inequalities necessary to the sustainability of the system as a whole. In these moments of catharsis, behaviors invert, contradict, or rescind the commonly held cultural codes, values, and norms. While presenting an alternative to the normative social order, these types of inversion provide at atmosphere for releasing either one's idlike (relating to the division of the psyche that is the source of psychic energy derived from instinctual needs and drives) instincts or the strain of one's social position, high or low.

Cathartic rebellion can function as a means for maintaining social control. If the tensions of the underclasses, the nonruling classes, are released and consequently eliminated or diminished by participating in "state"-sanctioned rites of inversion, so, too, might the underclasses' impetus for social reform and revolution be squandered. In fact, this was a concern of Marxist thinkers such as the Russian Leon Trotsky in regard to European seasonal folk rebellions and of members of the Frankfurt School, who saw inversion-like factors linked to the conspicuous consumption of mass cultural artifacts. The Frankfurt School, a Hegelian and Marxist oriented group of philosophers and social scientists, believed that the culture industries of the ruling class devised particular marketing techniques that help foster regular patterns of consumption. As such, a sale on a certain luxury item might lure those that cannot typically afford such an item to it. This "price inversion" is designed to appeal to the "wants" rather than the "needs" of the non-elite classes.

Because rites of inversion are defined by and represent temporary reversals of everyday norms, values, and social positions, normative social rules are put aside. As such, rites of inversion imply a certain degree of flux and uncertainty. Such ideas of uncertainty, and their depiction through representative rites, can be related to times prior to the creation of a religion's cosmology or, for that matter, to the creation of the cosmos itself. Associated with acts of creation and the dynamic process of creation is the idea of play. Uncertainty is inherent in the logic of play. This does not mean that play is lawless or without structure. All games have rules, although some rules can be "played" with, bent, stretched, or broken more easily than others. Similarly, rites of inversion are structured and controlled but are often enacted as forms of adult play.

A certain amount of playfulness is involved when inverting one's social position or gender identity. This does not mean that these inversions are taken less than seriously. Transvestitism (men dressing as women or vice versa) is common in many types of symbolic inversion around the world. Often, sexual rites of inversion add elements of play in the form of homosexual relations and other forms of traditionally taboo or inverted libidinous acts. The play forms of rites of inversion are aided and abetted by the generally nonrestrictive and inclusive environments where the threat of social humiliation, degradation, or punishment is blunted. In such a relatively free environment, new roles and new ideas can be acquired, albeit temporarily, and played with; this inversion, however, has consequences after the rite or event has concluded.

Although inversion tends to reinforce the normative order and is implicated into the structure of that order as its negation and is thereby limited in regard to its revolutionary potential, rites of inversion do question the validity of the existing order. These rites often up-end normative hierarchical positions by leveling out social and sacred inequalities. Mocking, mimicking, satirizing, and ridiculing the culture's taken-for-granted categories and conceptions are techniques for inverting social roles. As these acts help define symbolic boundaries necessary for the functioning and maintenance of a community's worldview, they also question the efficacy and absoluteness of the normative order. "Clown or trickster or transvestite never demands that we reject totally the orders of our sociocultural worlds… rather, they remind us of the arbitrary condition of imposing an order on our environment and experience, even while they enable us to see certain features of that order more clearly simply because they have been turned inside out" (Babcock 1978, 29). Because inversions show the plasticity and flexibility of seemingly concrete social positions, there is room for the development of revolutionary reform-oriented impulses within the borders of these rites.

Examples of Inversion

It might be an overstatement to say that rites of inversion exist in all cultures and all religious institutions. However, such a statement would not be too far off track. Examples of these rites are seen in Carnival festivals (marking the last days before Christian Lent) in the European medieval period and its variations in the West Indies, the La Havre Islands of Nova Scotia, and Indonesia, among others. Enmeshed in the public drunkenness and topless exhibitionism, New Orleans's Mardi Gras celebrations have become a secularized, although arguably still religious, version of Carnival, successfully maintaining its integral symbolic inversions.

Ritualized "clowning" is a common characteristic of inversion rites. Often these activities involve wearing masks and costumes. Men and women wear costumes or uniforms associated with roles other than one's own, whether it's as a "stranger" to the community or deity of the community. More than simply play-acting, wearing costumes helps participants become someone or something else. In many religious institutions masked "strangers" go from house to house, asking villagers for alms. Clowning can be a means for ritualized philanthropy. Examples of masked "strangers" can be found in the Christmas celebrations in Newfoundland and visits by the Japanese *namahage* (strangers), Hopi "ogres," Inuit *naluyuks* (clowns), and Eastern Cherokee *boogers* (beasts).

Research Directions

Because rites of inversion exist in many religions and cultures across both time and space, studying these rites may prove to be a valuable means of cross-cultural research. By recognizing the similarities in function and structure, as well as the differences, people can gain a better understanding of the human experience on a universal level. As for particular regional or cultural studies, these rites, which present the negation of the normative social order through mockery, masking, and symbolic metamorphosis, can help outsiders and insiders alike recognize the specific elements that make that culture or religion work.

Michael Ian Borer

See also Humor and Rituals; Rituals of Rebellion; Scatological Rituals

Further Reading

Babcock, B. (Ed.). (1978). *The reversible world: Symbolic inversion in art and society*. Ithaca, NY: Cornell University Press.

Bakhtin, M. (1968). *Rabelais and his world*. Cambridge, MA: MIT Press.

Bateson, G. (1958). *Naven*. Stanford, CA: Stanford University Press.

Billington, S. (1991). *Mock kings in medieval society and Renaissance drama*. Oxford, UK: Clarendon Press.

Cohen, A. (1993). *Masquerade politics: Explorations in the structure of urban cultural movements*. Berkeley and Los Angeles: University of California Press.

Dirks, R. (1987). *The black Saturnalia: Conflict and its ritual expression on British West Indian slave plantations*. Gainesville: University of Florida Press.

Douglas, M. (1966). *Purity and danger: An analysis of concepts of pollution and taboo*. London: Penguin.

Eco, U., Ivanov, V. V., & Rector, M. (1984). *Carnival!* The Hague, Netherlands: Mouton.

Falassi, A. (Ed.). (1987). *Time out of time: Essays on the festival*. Albuquerque: University of New Mexico Press.

Gluckman, M. (1963). *Order and rebellion in tribal Africa*. New York: Free Press.

Gluckman, M. (1965). *Custom and conflict in Africa*. Glencoe, IL: Free Press.

Handelman, D. (1990). *Models and metaphors: Towards an anthropology of public events*. New York: Cambridge University Press.

Huizinga, J. (1970). *Homo ludens: A study of the play element of culture*. London: Paladin.

Kinser, S. (1990). *Carnival, American style*. Chicago: University of Chicago Press.

Le Roy Ladurie, E. (1979). *Carnival in Romans, 1579–1580*. London: Scholar Press.

Mintz, J. (1997). *Carnival song and society: Gossip, sexuality and creativity in Andalusia*. New York: Oxford University Press.

Norberk, E., & Ferrer, C. R. (1979). *Forms of play of native North Americans*. St. Paul, MN: West Publishing.

Ostor, A. (1980). *The play of the gods: Locality, ideology, structure, and time in the festivals of a Bengali town*. Chicago: University of Chicago Press.

Turner, V. (1969). *The ritual process: Structure and anti-structure*. Ithaca, NY: Cornell University Press.

Twitchell, J. (1992) *Carnival culture: The trashing of taste in America*. New York: Columbia University Press.

Islam

The nature of Islamic rituals is different from that of other religions. The rituals in Islam fall under the category of *'ibada* (submissive obedience to God) and form a necessary part of religious worship and practice, as opposed to the *mu'amalat* (mutual relations amongst humans). Therefore, unlike other religions, the main object of religious rituals in Islam is not only to bring the believer spiritually closer to God, but also to carry out religious practices as laid down in theory by the Muslim jurists (*fuqaha'*). Thus, the rituals must be observed as prescribed by the Islamic Law (*shari'a*), which is the totality of God's commands that regulate all aspects of life of a pious Muslim. Because the *shari'a* is based upon the Qur'an (the Holy book of Muslims), the Hadith (a narrative record of the sayings or customs of the Prophet Muhammad and his companions), and *Ijma'* (general consensus and practice of the early Muslim community), a Muslim is obliged to observe these rituals as regulated by the shari'a laws, otherwise juristically the act of worship is considered invalid.

The mosque is the focal point of communal worship for Muslims around the world. This mosque is located in Capetown, South Africa. COURTESY OF FRANK SALAMONE.

The rituals in Islam constitute the essential aspect of worship and religious practices. Among the wide range of rituals, the five pillars (arkan) are the most important. Rites (*manasik*), namely, the acts of worship regarding birth, marriage, and burial that play an important part in the life of Muslims are also ratified as rituals, and they are likewise to be observed as the religious practices. In general, all these rituals and rites are the same with very minor and insignificant differences in the Sunnite and Shi'ite sects and their various schools of thought.

The five pillars of Islam are the foundation of Muslim life. Their observances form the backbone of faith. The first pillar is the profession of faith (*shahada*). As a Muslim, one must profess his faith in the religion of Islam by reciting the formula "There is but one

ISLAM AS A WAY OF BEING

The following extract of ethnographic text describing women's lives in a Kurd village in Iraq indicates that significance of Islam to its adherents.

> **For those fortunate to be able to make it, the pilgrimage is a form of foreign travel that has no counterpart elsewhere. Once more it means entering a great religious association, enduring with others the rigours of the journey and with them assuming a state of sanctity or initiation. The stay in Mecca constitutes a series of ecstatic experiences which women and men who have taken part in them never cease to talk about. These experiences set their mark on the soul and are later outwardly manifested by the clothing rules referred to. In the five daily prayer periods, in the thirty days of the fast, and on the days of pilgrimage, women enter the great congregation of the orthodox on an equal footing with men. These events are such a break in the daily life that they must be considered a spiritual luxury, quite incompatible with the wretched life pattern of our industrialised community. The demands made by Islam on the time of the individual cannot be reconciled with our Western rhythm of life. In return, these demands give to daily life a spiritual content extremely difficult [to] replace anything else whatever. When even a hard-working housewife like the young woman I saw in Bokha whose daily work covered husband, child, house, mulberry plantation and the milking of goats twice daily in the mountains, felt that she had the right to take the time to say her daily prayers before preparing dough for bread making or before loading the heavy goatskin of water on her back, it must give her a feeling of human worth in the middle of her inhuman labours. She possessed the right and the duty to collect herself five times daily, to be silent and to consider spiritual matters, and nothing in the world could deprive her of this. It is not surprising that the Islamic Kurdish women conducted themselves with calm and dignity. So long as certain inviolable areas of time and thought exist for them, the daily drugery will never be able to engulf them entirely.**

***Source*: Hansen, Henny H. *The Kurdish Woman's Life: Field Research in a Muslim Society, Iraq.* (1961). Copenhagen Ethnographic Museum Record, No. 7. Kobenhavn, Denmark: Nationalmuseet, p. 152.**

God (Allah) and Muhammad is His messenger." Strictly speaking, without the profession of faith, one cannot be considered a Muslim.

The second pillar is prayers (*salat*). According to the actual practice of Muhammad (*sunna*), one must pray five times a day. These prayers are held (1) before sunrise (*fajr*) (2) at noon (*zuhr*) (3) shortly before sunset (*'asar*) (4) immediately after sunset (*maghrib*) and (5) before going to bed (*'isha'*). While praying one must face towards Mecca. It is recommended that male members of the Muslim community join the congregational prayers that are regularly held in the mosques. Females can pray at home. One must join Friday noon prayer, which is congregational. Before the prayer, one must perform the ritual of ablution (*wudu'*) consisting of washing the mouth, face, hands, feet and so forth.

Almsgiving

The third pillar of Islam is almsgiving (*zakat*). All Muslims are obliged to help poor and needy people by giving them 2.5 percent of their net savings at the end of the Muslim calendar year.

Fasting (*sawm* or *siyam*) is the fourth pillar: observing fast from dawn to dusk during Ramadan, which is the ninth month of the Muslim calendar. During the fast, one is not allowed to eat, drink or smoke and must not commit any sin.

Pilgrimage (*hajj*) is the fifth pillar of Islam. It involves numerous rituals and also quite a few rites. Every adult Muslim who is physically fit and financially able to afford to undertake a journey to Mecca must perform the ritual of pilgrimage once in his lifetime. It is performed in the twelfth month (*dhu al-hijja*)

Muslim celebrants at a festival marking the birth of Muhammad in Rawalpindi, Pakistan in August 1996. COURTESY CF STEPHEN G. DONALDSON PHOTOGRAPHY.

of the Muslim calendar year and lasts for ten days from the first to the tenth day of the month. The important rituals in performing the pilgrimage are that one wears two seamless woolen or linen sheets (*ihram*), cutting of hair and walking clockwise seven times around Kaaba (a stone building in the court of the Great Mosque at Mecca) (*tawaf*). After performing these rituals and running seven times between Safa and Marwa (*sa'y*), male members of the Muslim community may cut their hair and can come out of ihram. At the end of the ritual of pilgrimage, Muslims offer animal sacrifice at Mina, located between Arfat and Mecca. Obviously this is in remembrance of Abraham (Ibrahim in Arabic) who was willing to sacrifice his son Ishmael (Isma'il in Arabic) in obedience of the command of God. In the Qur'an, in contrast to the Hebrew Bible, God asked Abraham to give sacrifice of his son Isma'il and not his son Isaac.

Minor Rites

The following are minor but important rites (*manasik*) concerning circumcision, birth, marriage and burial. After the birth of a child, the words of *adhan* (call to the prayer) are recited in the right ear of the child and his head is shaven. Every male child is circumcised any time between eight days and ten years after he is born. This is again in remembrance of Abraham (Ibrahim) with whom the rite of circumcision is associated as it being an outward expression of the covenant between God and human beings. This is because Muhammad is considered to be the descendent of Abraham through the lineage of Ishmael (Isma'il) and also that Muhammad claims to bring the same message in a renewed form that was given to Abraham. Although marriage (*nikah*), in practice, is arranged by the parents of the bride and groom, it is, as the Qur'an prescribes, a legal contract between husband and wife and must be witnessed by two people. The groom is supposed to a give the bride dowry (*mahr*) that will become her property. After a person dies, the body of the deceased is washed, then the corpse is wrapped in the white unsowed cloth and is carried in a wooden bier to the grave and placed in it. Thereafter, the prayers are said for the salvation of the deceased in the hereafter.

Husain Kassim

See also Buddhism; Catholicism; Hinduism; Jainism; Judaism; Ramadan

Further Reading

Johansen, B. (1999). *Contingency in a sacred law*: Legal and ethical norms in the Muslim *Fiqh*. Boston: Brill.

Lane, E. W. (1966). *Manners and customs of the modern Egyptians*. New York: Dutton.

Schacht, J., & Bosworth, C. E. (1974). *The legacy of Islam*. Oxford, UK: Clarendon Press.

Wilkinson, P. (1999). *Illustrated dictionary of religions*. London: DK Publishing.

J

Jainism

Jainism is a religion that was founded in India around the seventh century BCE. It is based on the ideal of nonviolence toward all living creatures (*ahimsa*) and urges a path of discipline, purity, and enlightenment. It is one of the three ancient Indian religions; the others are Hinduism and Buddhism. With these other two religions, Jainism had great influence on Indian philosophy, logic, art, architecture, and sciences such as mathematics and astronomy.

Although Jainism shares some ideas with Hinduism and Buddhism, it is an independent religion, not an offshoot. Its name comes from the Sanskrit word *ji*, meaning "to conquer." Jains must conquer bodily passions and even bodily ways of knowing in order to reach enlightenment. Those few people who have conquered these distractions are Jina (Conquerors). The followers are Jaina (followers of the Conquerors).

History

Jainism originated in the Ganges River basin of eastern India, an area of robust religious debate and study at the time. As Jainism began, Buddhism also began in conjunction with other religions that opposed Brahmanic (relating to a Hindu of the highest caste traditionally assigned to the priesthood) teachings. These religions shared a desire to renounce the world. Their adherents opposed what they saw as a shallow ritualism. All of these new religions promoted asceticism (strict self-denial as a measure of spiritual discipline), which urged abandoning ritual and taking social and domestic action. Moreover, they sought illumination as a means of ending the rounds of rebirth they viewed as part of life.

Parshva, a seventh-century BCE teacher, was the earliest historical Jain figure. He founded a religious community based on Jainism's principles of worldly abandonment and nonviolence. He was, according to Jains, the twenty-third ford-maker—one who leads people across the streams of rebirths to illumination. The last ford-maker of the early age was Vardhamana, or Mahavira, the Great Hero. He was the last teacher of "right" knowledge, faith, and practice. He was a contemporary of the Buddha, who lived in the fourth century BCE.

Mahavira was a member of the warrior class, the son of a chieftain. Like Buddha, he gave up his high status to become an ascetic. From the age of thirty to his early forties he lived alone, deep in prayer and ascetic works. He then converted eleven followers, each of whom was a Brahman. Indrabhuti Gautama and Sudharman, his disciples, are considered by Jains to be the founders of the Jain monastic community. Jambu, another disciple, is the last person of the current age to gain enlightenment, according to Jains.

Jainism grew rapidly. By Mahavira's death there were fourteen thousand monks and thirty-six thousand nuns. Although Jainism had numerous schisms, only one had any lasting significance. This schism involved the White Robe and Sky Clad sects. The White Robes argued that the appropriate apparel for monks and nuns is white robes, whereas the Sky Clad sect argued that monks—but not nuns—should be naked. This schism led to one regarding whether a person can attain illumination from a female body. That schism continues to the present.

Doctrines and Rituals of Jainism

In Jainism complete liberation comes only when a person has achieved liberation from the body, and the soul has become purified and perfect. The accumulation of bits of material (*karmans*) impedes perfection. *Karmans* come as a result of numerous reincarnations and a person's actions. Jain rituals seek to move their adherents closer to perfection. These rituals involve disciplined and virtuous practices of nonviolence.

White Robe monks can have some personal possessions—their robes, begging bowls, a cloth over their mouths to prevent swallowing tiny insects, and a whiskbroom. In one ritual a monk who has been in service for a long time presents these possessions to a new monk. Monks take a number of vows. Basically they vow to avoid injuring any life form. They also vow to refrain from lying, stealing, having sexual intercourse, and owning anything other than the items they receive upon becoming monks. Regulations aid monks in keeping their vows.

Monks have six "obligatory actions" that are vital parts of monastic ritual. These actions are equanimity (balance), praise, obeisance, confession, resolution to avoid sinful activities, and abandonment of the body. Each of these actions is overseen by a preceptor, or teacher. The culmination of a monk's life is ritual starvation in which the monk lets go of his bodily life, aiding his soul. This ritual starvation is not common in modern times.

The *samayika* is the most important of the six obligatory actions. It is a meditative and renunciatory ritual of limited duration that strengthens laymen's—and Jainism emphasizes the role of men—adherence and ability to follow Jainism's virtues. Until recent times, Jainism followed life-cycle rituals of the local area rather than its own birth, marriage, and death rituals.

Laymen must observe eight basic rules of behavior. These rules have varied in place and time but generally include (1) avoiding eating at night and (2) eating a diet that excludes meat, wine, honey, and fruits and roots that shelter life forms. Laymen also observe twelve vows. These vows enjoin followers to refrain from being violent, lying, stealing, and committing adultery and to be content with limited possessions. Additionally, Jains are counseled to avoid traveling unnecessarily, engaging in harmful activities, and pursuing pleasure. They are to fast, offer aid and gifts to monks, help the poor and other Jains, and to die if they cannot observe the major vows.

Jains also have rituals for worshiping, or paying homage to, liberated souls, monks, and the Scriptures. Tirthankara, located in a central shrine room of temples, is the center of most image rituals. Tirthankara, a liberated soul, is the "builder," one who has conquered all earthly desires. Prayers cannot influence liberated souls, but their presence reminds people of people's obligations to seek perfection. In addition, daily rituals include singing hymns, saying prayers, repeating sacred formulas, saying the names of liberated souls, and praying before statues. Flowers, fruit, and rice are offerings to the bathed images.

The Jain religious calendar has significant days called "*parvan*." These are days with periods of fasting and festivals. Each liberated soul has five major events in life, and Jains commemorate these events: descent into the mother's womb, birth, renunciation, attainment of omniscience, and final emancipation.

The most important period in the ritual year is the period when monks and nuns leave the monastery or convent and settle in the community for four months, usually from late July to early November.

However, Mastakabhisheke (Head Anointment) is the most famous Jain festival. It occurs on a twelve-year cycle at the Digambara sacred complex at Shravana Belgola in India. As many as one million people attend the festival. A seventeen meter-tall (55.77 feet) statue of Bahubali—who was noted for his strength, both physical and in performing the Jain austerities—is anointed with such things as water, milk, and flowers.

Pilgrimage

Jains have a number of pilgrimage sites in India. Sites with shrines significant for their association with liberated souls are Parasnath Hill and Rajgir in Bihar State, Shatrunjaya and Girnar Hills on the Kathiawar Peninsula, Shravana Belgola in Karnataka State, Mounts Abu and Kesariaji in Rajasthan State, and Antariksha Parshvanatha in the Akola District of Maharashtra state. Local temples have depictions of these shrines, and regional shrines also substitute for pilgrimage sites.

Location

Until recently Jainism was almost totally limited to India. However, recent waves of immigrants have carried it to the United States and United Kingdom.

About 4 million Jains live in India. Even with Jainism's recent spread overseas, only about 100,000 live outside of India.

Jains used their long-established trading links in eastern Africa to settle in that region. However, anti-Indian feeling and the persecution of former dictator Idi Amin Dada led them to flee to other countries. Jain settlers in the United Kingdom built the first Jain temple outside of India in Leicester. Jains needed this temple to preserve their identity. Jains also established organizations in Europe and the United States to promote and explain Jainism. Publications, such as *Jain Digest* and *Jain Spirit*, promote Jain ideals of nonviolence, vegetarianism, and environmentalism.

Frank A. Salamone

See also Divali

Further Reading

Banks, M. (1992). *Organizing Jainism in India and England.* Oxford, UK: Oxford University Press.

Dawson, C. (1948). *Religion and culture.* London: Sheed & Ward.

Hemacandra. (1998). *The lives of the Jain elders* (R. C. C. Fynes, Trans.). Oxford, UK: Oxford University Press.

Humphrey, C., & Laidlaw, J. (1994). *The archetypal actions of ritual: A theory of ritual illustrated by the Jain rite of worship.* Oxford, UK: Oxford University Press.

Humphrey, C., & Laidlaw, J. (2000). Intellectual *ahimsa* revisited: Jain tolerance and intolerance of others. *Philosophy East & West, 50*(3), 324–347.

Laidlaw, J. (1995). *Riches and renunciation: Religion, economy, and society among the Jains.* Oxford, UK: Clarendon Press.

Littlefield, D. F., & Parins, J. W. (1984). *American Indian and Alaska Native newspapers and periodicals.* Westport, CT: Greenwood Press.

Moore, G. F. (1913). *History of religions.* New York: C. Scribner's Sons.

Prentiss, K. P. (1999). *The embodiment of Bhakti.* New York: Oxford University Press.

Javanese

With more than 110 million inhabitants, Java is the most populous island in Indonesia, the world's largest Muslim-majority nation. Java has a diverse religious landscape, comprised of innumerable villages, ancient royal centers, port towns, and ethnically mixed industrial cities. Most ethnic Javanese live in rural villages, but there are significant parallels between religious practice in the towns and in the countryside. The rural-urban axis has always been an important dimension of Javanese civilization.

Most Javanese identify themselves as Muslims but the importance they give to the Islamic aspect of their cultural identity varies enormously. This variation is a source of perennial controversy for scholars and for Javanese themselves. The problem is not just one of definition—of deciding what counts as Islamic or native Javanese—but of making sense of cultural variation and, beyond that, of living together harmoniously in spite of differing beliefs and practices. Unsurprisingly, Javanese rituals have figured prominently in comparative discussions of plural culture, Islam, syncretism (the combination of different forms), and ritual meaning.

Historical Background

A first step in understanding religious variation is understanding history. Until the sixteenth century most of Java was divided into kingdoms that, culturally, were a blend of Hindu, Buddhist, and indigenous Javanese elements. With the coming of Islam—a gradual and sporadic process beginning in the 14th century—a distinction arose between the inland agrarian Hindu-Buddhist realms and the Islamizing coastal merchant states. The contrast between a more orthodox north coast and a syncretist heartland persisted even after Islam had become the dominant faith throughout Java. (An enclave of Hindu-Javanese culture survives in the Tengger highlands of East Java.) Reflecting that history, many Javanese today distinguish between (1) practitioners of a syncretist tradition of "Javanism" composed of folk beliefs, Islam and Indic mythology and (2) pious Muslims who stress the Islamic part of their cultural heritage.

Since Indonesia's independence from the Netherlands in 1949, the pattern of religious variation has been colored by party politics and the intervention of authoritarian government. Following the anti-communist massacres of 1965–6 and a turn toward officially recognized religions, many syncretists opted for a purer form of Islam, whereas up to 2 million chose to redefine their ancestral rituals as Hindu or to make a clean break and become Christians. In recent decades, modernization, urbanization, and a sustained revival of Islam have weakened the appeal of Javanism, whether in its rural or courtly (originating from the royal courts) varieties.

Ritual Constituencies

Ritual life in the village centers on the home and the mosque or the prayer-house. A separate focus is the shrine dedicated to the village guardian spirit or founding pioneer. Such shrines are the scene of thanksgiving meals and divinations presided over by the caretaker or a spirit medium. At the annual Village Cleansing, puppet shows and other entertainments are held in honor of the guardian spirit. Depending on the local religious politics, such activities may be obstructed, tolerated, or patronized by pious Muslims.

The balance—or tension—between Islamic piety and non-Islamic or syncretist practices characterizes any given community. In the most integrated villages, such as in parts of rural East Java, pious Muslims and Javanists (plus middling types) live cheek by jowl in relative harmony, even participating in each others' domestic rituals. Such integration has been achieved partly by means of a rich symbolism that permits a variety of interpretation. This is best seen in the most frequently celebrated ritual, the prayer-meal (*slametan*).

The Slametan

The format varies in different parts of Java, but in most *slametan*s a group of neighboring men sit around a mat laden with symbolically significant foods and offerings while the host's delegate burns incense and makes a speech of dedication to the ancestors, local spirits, the Prophet Muhammad, and, of course, the host's family. This dedication is composed of formulas that mean different things at different levels. For example, a dish of red and white porridge may signify Adam and Eve, one's parents and ancestors, male and female, or Everyman and Everywoman. Which of these meanings is most important—the Islamic, mystical, or familial—will depend on a participant's cultural orientation; but the ritual form is shared. The event closes with an Arabic prayer spoken in unison. The Islamic ritual frame is said to "contain" the Javanese essence or meaning. Similarly, in the state cults of the central Javanese courts, esoteric Indic and Sufi notions of the union of the soul with God are enveloped in an exoteric (overt, public) "container" of Islamic liturgy (rites prescribed for public worship). In areas where pious—and especially reformed—Muslims predominate, specifically Javanese elements of *slametans* and other rituals may be eliminated. Mortuary feasts have a more narrowly Islamic character, involving collective prayers and chanting.

The Ritual Calendar

*Slametan*s may be held to inaugurate a house, to thank the ancestors for a harvest, to reconcile family members after a quarrel, to assure success in school exams, or to promote recovery from illness. They are also integrated with rites of passage (to mark seven months of pregnancy, birth, circumcisions, and weddings), with the cycle of rice production, and with the Islamic calendar of holy days. The most important of these include 12 Mulud (third month), the Prophet Muhammad's birthday and the occasion of a state ceremony at the royal palaces when large cones of rice are distributed among the people; 27 Rejeb (seventh month), a feast commemorating the Prophet's ascension to heaven; 1 Ruwah (eighth month), a prayer-meal in honor of the ancestors; 29 Ruwah, eve of the annual Fast, when family graves are strewn with flowers to commemorate the dead and ask their blessing; and Lebaran, the holiday following the annual Fast when migrants return home and villagers ask each other's forgiveness for the year's accumulated offenses. Lebaran is celebrated on a large scale in the courts of Yogyakarta and Surakarta. As always in Javanese public rituals, the goal of social harmony is key to the event.

Apart from these universal Javanese rituals, pious Muslims also perform the canonical rituals of Islam such as the five daily prayer sessions, Friday mosque worship, and periodic recitations of the Qur'an (the holy book accepted by Muslims as divinely revealed to the Prophet Muhammad).

An Exorcism

Finally, no account of Javanese rituals would be complete without mention of the *wayang* (shadow puppet play). Indeed, one of the most important of all rituals is the *ruwatan*, a shadow play performed to exorcise children born in inauspicious combinations (such as girl-boy-girl, five boys, only child). The play tells the story of the birth and banishment of Kala, a monster who preys on human beings and is the source of disaster in the world. The play's celebration is at once an explanation of misfortune, a ritual protection, a demonstration of social status (whether the sponsor be a peasant or an army general), and a moment in a vast cycle of mutual exchange—most rituals in Java record a detailed ledger of contributions and returns. Rich or poor, great or small, the Javanese rarely has to wait long for an invitation to a ritual.

Andrew Beatty

See also Africa, West; China: Popular Religion; Iban; Islam

Further Reading

Beatty, A. (1999). *Varieties of Javanese religion: An anthropological account.* Cambridge, UK: Cambridge University Press.

Geertz, C. (1960). *The Religion of Java.* Glencoe, IL: The Free Press.

Headley, S. C. (2000). *From cosmogony to exorcism in a Javanese genesis.* Oxford, UK: Oxford University Press.

Hefner, R. W. (1985). *Hindu Javanese: Tengger tradition and Islam.* Princeton, NJ: Princeton University Press.

Keeler, W. (1987). *Javanese shadow plays, Javanese selves.* Princeton, NJ: Princeton University Press.

Koentjaraningrat. (1985). *Javanese culture.* Singapore: Oxford University Press.

Woodward, M. R. (1989). Islam in Java: *Normative piety and mysticism in the sultanate of Yogyakarta.* Tucson: University of Arizona Press.

Judaism

Judaism is rich in tradition while abounding with great diversity of interpretation among its various denominations (Modern Orthodox, ultra-Orthodox, Reform, Conservative, and Reconstructionist). Observant Jews experience life as an intense covenantal relationship between God and God's chosen people. Thus, Judaism is frequently described as a way of life. The Jewish way of life is guided by the divine instruction found in the Torah. The Torah acknowledges God as the creator of the universe; therefore, all of life is sacred. The practical consequence of this belief is that the mundane details of existence (the passage of time, space, eating, and attire, to name but a few) become charged with the sacred. Throughout the course of an ordinary day, a Jewish life is full of potential for placing one's self in the presence of God. Prayer and ritual in Judaism are centered on the institutions of family and synagogue and guided by sacred texts and a liturgical calendar.

Sacred Texts and Major Prayers

The Torah is the foundational sacred text for Judaism. It contains the first five books of the Bible. When the Torah is combined with the books of the prophets, *Nevi'im,* and the wisdom literature, *Kethuvim,* the canon of the Jewish Bible is complete and is known by the acronym TaNaKh (Tanakh)

Jewish interpretation of the biblical texts proceeds through the lens of another sacred text, the Talmud. There are two versions: the Babylonian and the Palestinian (c. fifth and fourth century CE, respectively). The Talmud consists of the Mishnah, a second-century CE collection of oral law (halakah), and commentaries on Mishnah called Gemara. Together the Tanakh and the Talmud guide Jewish practice.

The Amidah and the Shema provide Jews with their most sacred of prayers that begin and end each day. The Amidah is a series of nineteen blessings and the Shema begins with a recitation of Deuteronomy 6:4. The Shema is a confession of faith in the oneness of God; it is also proclaimed on one's deathbed.

Sacred Covenant

Maintaining the covenant in Judaism involves correct relationship with God and one's fellow human being; the religious and ethical domains are not separate for the Jew. Perhaps the most familiar of the biblical covenants are those that God makes with Noah, Abraham, and Moses. In Genesis 9:8–17, God promises that never again will there be a flood to devastate the earth. The sign of the covenant is the rainbow. In Genesis 17:2–3, God commands Abraham, "Walk in My ways and be blameless. I will establish my covenant between me and you." The sign of this covenant is infant male circumcision, a necessary ritual of Jewish life known as the *brit milah.* Finally, God initiates a very specific covenant with Moses on Mount Sinai (Exodus 19), with God giving the Ten Commandments (the Decalogue). Each covenant becomes more detailed. Indeed, the Mosaic covenant is traditionally said to specify 613 *mitzvot* (Hebrew plural for a command of the Torah). While these *mitzvot* organize an observant Jewish life, many of them only applied in ancient Judaism while the temple was still standing.

Temple

While all space is sacred because it is created by God, there is some space that is particularly sacred. In the ancient biblical period, the temple in Jerusalem was perceived as the holy center of the universe, for it was understood as God's own house. The temple, the holy city Jerusalem, and the land of Israel comprised the most sacred of spaces.

The building of the temple commanded by God (see 2 Samuel 7:13; 1 Kings 5:19) provides a reference point for conveniently dividing the history of ancient Israel into three periods: (1) around 1800–1000 BCE; (2) 1000–586 BCE; and (3) 515 BCE – 70 CE. The first period constitutes the formative period from the patriarchs through the settlement in the land of Israel. The second period is known as the First Temple period, for it marks the era of King Solomon's (tenth century BCE) building of the temple. The Babylonian destruction of the temple and the forced exile of the Jews conclude this period. The Second Temple period, 515 BCE–70 CE, marks the reconstruction of the temple and the restoration of the Jews to the land. The Roman destruction of the temple completes the Second Temple period.

The fall of the Second Temple in 70 CE initiates the Diaspora (Greek for "scattering"). The Jews are left without a homeland until the emergence of the independent State of Israel in 1948. Throughout the Diaspora, however, the site of the temple, Jerusalem, and Israel remain important sacred spaces for Jews. In the contemporary world, they remain a religious focal point for most Jews though only the remnant of the temple, the Western Wall, remains, while control of Jerusalem and the boundaries of Israel continues to be a source of social, political, and military strife.

Synagogue

With the fall of the temple, rabbinic Judaism began to emerge. Cycles of prayer replaced the temple sacrifices that were no longer possible. The development of the synagogue accelerated and it became the center for Jewish community life, worship, and study. Today, the various denominations subscribe to different views regarding the expectation of a Third Temple in a messianic age but there is no doubt that their synagogues are vital centers of Jewish life.

The ritual space for synagogue prayer is focused on the *amudah* (the reading table for the proclamation of the Torah), the *bima* (pulpit), the *aron hakodesh* (the ark or, literally, holy chest that contains the scrolls), and the *sifrei Torah* (the Torah scrolls). Certain prayers at synagogue require a minyan, a group of ten adult males over the age of thirteen. Women are now counted toward a minyan in some Reform and Conservative congregations.

Sacred Dress

The tallith (prayer shawl) and the tefillin (phylacteries) are some of the more familiar ritual garments of synagogue prayer. Both accessories are the result of biblical precepts, both are worn during morning prayer, and their use was formerly restricted to men. The requirement to wear tallith comes from Numbers 15:38–39. The text commands that fringes with a cord of blue be added to one's garments so that when one looks at the fringes one is reminded of God's commands and the covenant. Tefillin are also of ancient origin and vary in appearance. They are small boxes with straps that wrap around the head and the left arm and they contain scriptural passages.

The skullcap (*kippah* or yarmulke) is not a biblically prescribed mode of dress. Wearing the *kippah* is not restricted to synagogue. The Talmud explains that the head covering is necessary because it would be improper for men to have bare heads in God's presence. Head coverings vary by region and tradition and can be much more elaborate than the skullcap. Currently, some denominations and congregations are allowing women the option of wearing the *kippah* at synagogue.

Home: Sacred Space, Food, and Rites of Passage

Perhaps the most distinctive feature marking the sacred space of a Jewish home is the mezuzah. The mezuzah is a small container filled with the words from Deuteronomy 6:4–9 and 11:13–21 that command its use. It is placed on the right side of the door to the dwelling.

The concept of food as sacred also helps to demarcate a Jewish home. The laws of *kashrut* are detailed and complex; however, the basic division of food is into the categories of kosher ("proper") and *trefah* (indicating an animal killed improperly, even if they are not on the Hebrew Scripture lists of approved foods). Further, dairy and meat are regularly separated, while during Passover all products containing a leaven are removed from the household and an entirely new set of cooking implements is used.

Believing that all of life is sacred, observant Jews have rituals to accompany major life events. One such ritual, the aforementioned *brit milah*, welcomes a baby boy into the covenant of circumcision while baby girls may be welcomed by a *brit habat* (covenant of the daughter), an innovation of the past thirty years in response to feminism. The so-called coming-of-age rituals, bar mitzvah and bat mitzvah (son and daughter of the commandment), are actually not necessary to achieve the status of a young man or woman obligated to follow Jewish law. A boy achieves the status by turning thirteen and a girl by turning twelve. The ceremonies, however, have become an important rite of passage.

Marriage has two aspects. The ceremony is known as the *kiddushin* (literally, "sanctification"), thus reflecting the belief that marriage is holy. The marriage canopy (*khupah*) and the ritual smashing of a glass to recall the destruction of the temple are central features of the wedding ceremony. The *ketubah* indicates the contractual nature of marriage; historically the marriage contract provided economic protections to the woman in the event of a divorce.

End-of-life rituals are as specific and important as those at any other stage of life. The following are but a few of the fundamental elements of the rituals surrounding death: (1) *keri'ah*, the ritual rending of garments; (2) the designation of a *shomer* ("watcher"), one who remains with the body from death to interment; (3) a funeral that includes the Mourner's Kaddish, psalms (frequently 23 and 91), and the *el mal'e rachamim*, a memorial prayer; (4) burial within twenty-four hours if possible; (5) shivah, the seven-day period of mourning, *sheloshim*, the thirty-day period of mourning, and *yarzeit*, the one-year memorial of death.

Sacred Time

A clear articulation of sacred time provides a method for drawing close to the divine. Sacred calendars delineate daily, weekly, monthly, and annual religious obligations. Jewish sacred time assures its adherents that their timely observance of prayer binds them together in a community dedicated to God and the fulfillment of the covenant.

Sabbath

The weekly observance of Sabbath (Shabbat) is considered a most holy obligation prescribed in Exodus in the Decalogue. Keeping Sabbath involves rich home-based rituals and synagogue services. From sundown Friday to sundown Saturday all work ceases (the Talmud specifies activities constituting work). The festive Friday evening meal involves special prayers for lighting the candles, blessing the wine, and blessing the two loaves of challah bread. A similar sequence of prayers occurs during specified Saturday meals.

In the synagogue, Sabbath services generally follow the structure of the daily morning, afternoon, and evening services. An additional service, though, is sometimes added directly after the morning service. An annual cycle of Torah readings is followed. Sabbath is personified as a queen and a bride. She is welcomed as a festive period of peace, study, and companionship. The traditional greeting is "Shabbat Shalom!"

Lunar Year

The civil year is currently 2003 CE. In Jewish sacred time, however, the year is 5763 of the era of creation. A lunar rather than a solar calendar organizes Jewish time. A lunar month consists of either 29 or 30 days, thereby creating a year of 354 days. In order to account for the difference between the lunar and the solar year, an extra month is added to the year seven times in a nineteen-year cycle. The extra month, Adar II, is inserted into the calendar in the spring. This insertion is known as a leap month and sometimes the year itself is called a leap year. Lunar dating and the names of the months of the Jewish year are derived from ancient Babylon.

Annual Pilgrimage Festivals

The Torah mandates three annual pilgrimage festivals: Pesach (Passover) beginning on the fifteenth day of Nisan, *Shavuot* (Pentecost) beginning on the sixth day of Sivan, and Sukkoth (Booths or Tabernacles) beginning on the fifteenth day of Tishvi (see Leviticus 23). The temple at Jerusalem was the focal point for these festivals. By the late Second Temple period, Jews far from Jerusalem would attempt to make a pilgrimage at least once. The three festivals were originally tied to the harvest cycles of ancient Israel.

After 70 CE, the importance of Pesach, *Shavuot*, and Sukkoth does not wane though the temple sacrifices are no longer possible. The fundamental religious meanings of the holidays are emphasized. Pesach, or

Passover, celebrates the exodus from Egypt, the passage from slavery to freedom. It is a feast of national liberation. For Jews living outside of Israel, a common prayer is "Next year in Jerusalem!" which signifies the ongoing centrality of the sacred city. *Shavuot* commemorates the giving of the law to Moses on Mount Sinai. Occurring fifty days after Passover, *Shavuot* is also known as Pentecost. Sukkoth memorializes the forty years of Jewish wandering in the desert and living in temporary booths. Consequently, this holiday requires the erection of a sukkah, a temporary dwelling for the week-long celebration. Sukkoth is a festive time celebrating both the possibility of redemption and the autumn harvest. Children participate in the building and decoration of the sukkah, to which ordinary daily patterns of meals and prayers are transferred.

Autumn High Holy Days

Sukkoth, Rosh Hashana, Yom Kippur, Shemini Atzereth, and Simchas Torah take place in the autumn. Rosh Hashana marks the new year though it occurs on the first two days of the seventh month of Tisri and not during the first month of the year (Nisan). It inaugurates the "days of awe," the ten-day period between Rosh Hashana and Yom Kippur. The sounding of the shofar (ram's horn) is a distinctive highlight of the Rosh Hashana services. It inaugurates a celebration of God's creation of the world as well as a period of self-examination, repentance, and recognition of the need for God's mercy. To symbolize the purity of new creation and forgiveness of sin, bright white liturgical robes are worn by the cantor and rabbi while observant Jews will also wear a white robe called a *kittel*. Meals are characterized by dipping bread and apples in honey to signify the prayer for a "good and sweet year." The liturgy is lengthened by the addition of three blessings *(berakhot): malkhuyot, zikhronot, shofarot*. The three blessings highlight, respectively, God's creative sovereignty, God's care for human beings, and God's self-revelation at Sinai.

The days of awe preceding Yom Kippur are a time of repentance and turning toward God (*teshuvah*), prayer and study (*tefillah*), and acts of charity (*tzedekah*). Yom Kippur requires a day-long fast. The wearing of leather shoes, sexual contact, and bathing are also prohibited. A special candle burns in remembrance of deceased parents and children are blessed before the evening service begins. There are five services throughout Yom Kippur. The famous opening evening service is called Kol Nidre ("all vows") and it is a legal recitation that voids all religious promises made during the previous year. This service recognizes that human beings often fail to fulfill their intentions; in essence, God grants one a fresh start for the New Year. Yom Kippur is a day of judgment and a day of atonement intended to bring the believer back into correct covenantal relationship with God.

Shemini Atzereth and Simchas Torah are related holidays that follow the conclusion of Sukkoth. In some locales the two holidays are celebrated simultaneously on the day after Sukkoth while other traditions observe the holidays on successive days. Shemini Atzerett has biblical roots (see Numbers 29:35) and is associated with prayers for rain. Simchas Torah has developed into the dominant festival. It is a celebration of the conclusion and the recommencement of the reading of the annual Torah cycle. The celebration includes seven festive processions of the Torah.

Winter Holidays

Hanukkah, Tu Bi-Shevat, and Purim fall roughly during the winter months. Hanukkah is an eight-day festival commemorating the Maccabean victory over Antiochus IV during the period 165–163 BCE. Antiochus profaned the temple with idols in addition to prohibiting circumcision, Sabbath observance, and Torah study. The Hasmonean family under the leadership of Judah "the Hammer" Maccabee (Judas Maccabaeus, d. 160 BCE) led the successful revolt against Antiochus. When the temple was back under Jewish control, the victors found one undesecrated jar of oil left by the High Priest Onias. The holy oil was expected to last only one day but it burned for a week. Thus, Hanukkah celebrates the rededication of the temple to God and the "miracle" of the oil. The familiar symbol of the menorah is the key to this festival of lights.

Tu Bi-Shevat was historically a new year's celebration marking the first blooming of the trees. With the exile from the land of Israel (*eretz yisrael*), this annual event also became a way to signify a connection to Israel. People in the Diaspora mark the occasion by eating fruits and grains common to Israel while school children in Israel plant trees.

Purim creates a riotous carnivallike atmosphere replete with role-reversals, masquerades, drinking, and noise-making. The megillah (scroll) of Esther is read with the entire congregation taking parts. Purim commemorates Queen Esther and Mordecai's successful rescue of the Jews from Haman's plan to exterminate the Jews within the realm of King Ahasuerus.

Spring/Summer Commemorations of Persecution and Independence

Yom Ha-Shoah, Yom Ha-Atzma'ut, Yom Yerushalayim (occurring between Passover and Pentecost), and Tisha B'Av collectively memorialize the darkest and perhaps the brightest moments in Jewish history. Yom Ha-Atzma'ut and Yom Yerushalayim are Israeli Independence Day and Jerusalem Independence Day, dating from 1948 and 1967, respectively. Yom Ha-Shoah was established in 1951 to be a solemn day of mourning for the six million Jews murdered under Hitler's "final solution." Tisha B'Av involves the only other fast on the Jewish calendar that is as long as the Yom Kippur fast. It is the holy day that recalls the destruction of the First and Second Temples.

Elena G. Procario-Foley

See also Hanukkah; Passover; Yom Kippur

Further Reading

De Vaux, R. (1961). *Ancient Israel* (Vols. 1–2). New York: McGraw-Hill Book Company.

Heschel, A. J. (1996). *The Sabbath: Its meaning for modern man*. New York: Noon Day Press.

Lamm, M. (2000). *The Jewish way in death and mourning*. New York: Jonathan David Publishers.

Robinson, G. (2000). *Essential Judaism: A complete guide to beliefs, customs, and rituals*. New York: Pocket Books.

Seltzer, R. M. (1980). *Jewish people, Jewish thought: The Jewish experience in history*. New York: Macmillan Publishing Company, Inc.

Solomon, N. (1996). *Judaism: A very short introduction*. Oxford, UK: Oxford University Press.

Strassfeld, M. (1985). *The Jewish holidays: A guide and commentary*. New York: Harper and Row Publishers.

Wylen, S. M. (1989). *Settings of silver: An introduction to Judaism*. New York: Paulist Press.

Wylen, S. M. (1996). *The Jews in the time of Jesus*. New York: Paulist Press.

K

Kwanzaa

Kwanzaa (first fruits) is a pan-African holiday celebrating culture, history, community, and family. "Kwanzaa" is a Swahili word, and this language is used for all the rituals, principles, symbols, and greetings associated with this holiday. In the United States, it is celebrated for seven days from 26 December to 1 January. It has its origins in the first-harvest celebrations often held in late December in ancient and modern African societies, including Egypt, Ashantiland, and the Zulu empire.

Kwanzaa's African-American form, blending African and American customs, was created by Maulana Karenga in 1966 to help re-root and reconstruct African culture, and to promote unity, empowerment, and self-determination among African Americans. The introduction of Kwanzaa was timely, as it meshed with the growing interest among African Americans in connecting with their African heritage. Today, Kwanzaa has a place in mainstream American culture, and is recognized by schools, business, and government, complete with published greeting cards and a U.S. postage stamp.

Though Kwanzaa and its U.S. practice have been likened to a religion, in that they are rooted in an ideology having its own symbols and rituals and linked to the importance of the Creator, it is an African American *cultural* holiday. While Riley (1995) describes it as a spiritual holiday, it is not incongruent with belief in Christianity, Islam, or Judaism. Indeed, many African Americans who embrace Christianity celebrate both Christmas and Kwanzaa.

Creativity combines with history, politics, economics, mythology, and cultural values to shape the principles of Kwanzaa. Kwanzaa builds on the five traditions of the African first-fruits celebration: reaffirmation of family and community bonds; giving thanks for the beauty and bounty of creation; commemoration of the past and of ancestors; recommitment to cultural ideals; and celebration of good—good life, family, community, and culture.

The Nguzo Saba

Each day of the seven-day holiday focuses on one of the seven guiding principles or Nguzo Saba: the first day focuses on *umoja* (unity), the second, *kujichagulia* (self-determination), the third, *ujima* (collective work and responsibility), the fourth, *ujamaa* (cooperative economics), the fifth, *nia* (purpose), the sixth, *kuumba* (creativity), and the seventh day on *imani* (faith). Each day can be celebrated with poetry, personal histories and stories, African folktales, quotations, and proverbs.

The Seven Symbols

The number seven is sacred in many African cultures that celebrate Kwanzaa. As with many of the original celebrations, in the U.S. festivities last seven days, are based on seven principles, and use seven symbols. The seven symbols are the *kinara* (candle holder) which symbolizes ancestors, *mishumaa* (candles), *mkeka* (placemat), *mazao* (fruit and vegetables) representing the crops, *muhindi* (ear of corn, typically one for each child in the gathering), *zawadi* (gifts), and the *kikombe cha umoja* (communal cup of unity).

The Rituals of Kwanzaa

While the basic values of Kwanzaa stay the same, the specifics of the rituals and the rituals themselves are open to interpretation, creation, creativity, and shaping into individual family traditions. Several rituals are typically part of Kwanzaa, including a special greeting, statement of the daily principles, lighting the seven candles, offering libation to ancestors, eating, entertainment, and giving gifts.

Ritual Activities

A special daily greeting in Swahili is used during Kwanzaa to reinforce awareness of the principle for the day. One is greeted with, "*Habari gani*?" meaning, "What news?" or "What's happening?" The response is the principle of the day, for example, "*umoja*" on the first day or "*kujichagulia*" on the second.

The family gathers, often at mealtime, to discuss the day's principle. The candle for that principle is lit by the person who will lead the discussion, or by another family member. Additional activities may be included in the celebration of the principle.

Lighting candles (*mishumaa*) is a daily part of the week-long celebration. There is one candle for each day, one for each principle. The first candle is lit on day one; that candle and a second one are lit on day two, and so forth. A black candle in the center of the ceremonial candelabrum—kinara—represents the people in unity; the three red candles on the left represent struggle, and the three green candles on the right represent the fruits of the future. The black candle is lit on the first day; the remaining ones are lit alternating left and right, suggesting movement from struggle to the fruits of the future.

The pouring of libation (*tambiko*) is important in celebrating Kwanzaa. The purpose is to remember and honor ancestors, acknowledge those who came before and paved the way, recognize links to the past and the legacy for the future, and instill in children the value of honoring elders. The cup (*kikombe*) is filled with water, juice, etc., and a libation statement, usually including a roll-call of deceased family members, or champions of the African and African-American legacy, is recited. The statement is made by an elder, in deference to his or her presumed wisdom and life experience. Images of love, achievement, strength, and struggle are evoked, reaffirming commitment to achievement. The libation is poured into a bowl of leafy green vegetables. The elder drinks from the cup, and then engages the group in a call to unity or *harambee*. In small family gatherings the cup is then passed down to the youngest member in age-descending order.

The feast—*karamu*—is celebrated on the eve of the last day of Kwanzaa. A variety of foods are shared within the family or a larger group, and the venue is decorated using African motifs and the red, black, and green colors of Kwanzaa. Entertainment is part of the celebration.

The last day of Kwanzaa is the day of meditation, Siku ya Taamuli, when the focus is on assessment, reflection, and recommitment. Gifts (*zawadi*) are usually given on this day to children, and sometimes to other family members. Gifts usually include books or artifacts of African or African American culture.

Families typically adapt the Kwanzaa celebrations, and this is consistent with two of its principles—*kuumba* (creativity) and *kujichagulia* (self-determination). Maintaining the original spirit of Kwanzaa is what is most important.

Susan D. Toliver

See also African-American Churches; Yoruba

Further Reading

Anderson, D. A. (1992). *Kwanzaa: An everyday resource and instructional guide*. New York: Gumbs and Thomas.

Danquah, J. B. (1928). *Gold Coast: Akan laws and customs and the Abuakwa Constitution*. London: George Rutledge and Sons.

Gamble-Gumbs, I. (1998). *How to plan a Kwanzaa celebration: Ideas for family, community, and public events*. New York: Cultural Expressions.

Gluckman, M. (1938, January 11). Social Aspects of First-Fruits Celebrations and the South Eastern Bantu. *Africa*, p. 1.

Harris, J. B. (1995). *A Kwanzaa keepsake: Celebrating the holiday with new traditions and feasts*. New York: Simon and Schuster.

Karenga, M. (1998). *Kwanzaa: A celebration of family, community and culture*. Los Angeles: University of Sankore Press.

Karenga, M. (1988). *The African American holiday of Kwanzaa: A celebration of family, community and culture*. Los Angeles: University of Sankore Press.

Karenga, M. (1977). *Kwanzaa: Origin, concepts, practice*. Los Angeles: Kawaida Publications.

Lynfield, B. (1997, December 31). Kwanzaa lights up as African-American holiday. *Christian Science Monitor, 90*, p. 12.

Madhubuti, H. R. (1972). *Kwanzaa: an African-American holiday that is progressive and uplifting*. Chicago: Third World Press.

McClester, C. (1997). *Kwanzaa: Everything you always wanted to know but didn't know where to ask.* New York: Gumbs and Thomas. (Original work published 1985)

McNair, M. O. (1998) *Kwanzaa crafts: Gifts and decorations for a meaningful and festive celebration.* New York: Sterling Publishing.

Riley, D. W. (1995). *The complete Kwanzaa: Celebrating our cultural harvest*. New York: Harper Collins.

L

Language, Literacy, and Ritual

All religious practice is ritual, from a Roman Catholic mass in the Vatican to Balinese preparations for a sacred rite of renewal. Ritual is shaped by the way practitioners manage the tools of their trade, including prayer, sacred texts, and offerings, creating forms of worship that are both familiar and dynamic. How has literacy changed religious ritual? In what ways is language manipulated to provide insight and guidance in the face of change or conflict? This article examines how information and education become part of sacred practice, with special focus on the evolving form of the Iglesia Autóctona in Chiapas, Mexico.

Divining the Word

In May 2002, the women of Cerro Verde, a small community in the southern jungle of Chiapas, Mexico, gathered in their tiny Catholic *capilla* to consider the words of St. John.

David, a catechist, led the service. The little town sees a priest twice a year, if that. So the only person in the community prepared to interpret the reading from St. John was David—catechist, activist, father, farmer, and ex-political prisoner.

"Unless you believe in *Jesu Cristo*," intoned David. "You will not enter into the kingdom of heaven." Clear enough.

"Unless you believe in *Jesu Cristo*, you will not enter God's kingdom here on earth."

"Unless you believe in *Jesu Cristo*, we'll all wind up victims of Plan Puebla Panamá, and a huge dam will be built, and all our land will be under water."

The shift happened so fast, it was easy to miss the transition from the realm of the soul to that of earthly struggle. This was liberation theology at its most basic. At times, liberation theology uses elaborate commentary to link scripture to the plight of the poor. Here in Cerro Verde, however, there was no time to be elaborate: the rains had come, the church was dark and cold, and the Mexican government was involved in a development plan that could irrevocably change rural life.

Across the state in the Highlands, the members of a Maya women's weaving cooperative met to install a new president. A Roman Catholic priest, dressed in blue jeans and a plaid shirt, stood behind a makeshift altar, intoning the opening prayers of the mass in Spanish and Tzotzil Maya. Before the altar, over 1000 thin, white tapers burned, tended by a Maya shaman (*h'lol*), who recited ancient forms of prayer concurrently with the priest. About halfway through this hybrid service, the priest departed from the order of service, and asked the attendees to break into small groups, to reflect on what characteristics the new president would need in order to be a good leader of her cooperative, in this time of change.

Both these services reflected acceptable practice in the Iglesia Autóctona—the "native" or indigenous Roman Catholic Church in Chiapas. This is a religious tradition where the seeds of Roman Catholicism flower differently in each niche of belief, linguistic tradition, spiritual leadership, and social-political need. Thus, the "autochthonous" church may be distinctly Maya in one setting, and distinctly secular in others. It derives its ritual form from Roman Catholicism, its discourse from Liberation Theology, and often,

RITUAL AS A POLITICAL FORCE

In Latin America, ritual is sometimes a combination of religion and political action. Meeting together to reflect on the implications of Plan Puebla Panamá—a massive infrastructure project spanning from Mexico to Panama—and to ask for guidance and understanding, a San Cristóbal congregation prayed:

We call to you Lord
in the long hours
when almost nothing happens as we would hope
and much happens as we would not want...

We feel confused
but not lost.
We don't ask you for relief:
we ask to know how to share with you the Vigil in the Orchard.
we ask to know how to counter the threats of those who plot projects
to benefit dark interests.

***Source*: "Taller Plan Puebla Panamá." (2002, July 3). Workshop materials, Diocese of San Cristóbal de las Casas, Chiapas, México.**

its—ceremonial content from Maya customs. It reflects the right and capacity of the poor to think and reflect for themselves.

The Iglesia Autóctona and the Chiapas Conflict

The Iglesia Autóctona is derived from the tenets of liberation theology, a form of Catholicism that has permeated Latin America and accompanied Latin American sociopolitical struggle since the early 1960s. In spite of these shared roots, the form of worship in Chiapas is unique, differing from that of other Central American movements born during the last decades of the twentieth century.

Chiapas, an agrarian and primary resource state on the southern border, has experienced escalating political tension and violent strife for decades, culminating in the Zapatista uprising on 1 January 1994. Coinciding with the signing of the North American Free Trade Agreement (NAFTA), the rebellion responded to long-standing patterns of exploitation and discrimination in this region of rich land and poor people.

The Zapatista uprising began with ten days of fighting in 1994, followed by a cease-fire that led to stillborn peace accords in 1996. Since that time, low intensity warfare has continued, peaking with the massacre of 45 women, children and men in the village of Acteal in December 1997.

In July 2000, Vicente Fox defeated the candidate of the Partido Revolucionario Institucional (PRI) becoming the first opposition president of Mexico in 71 years. One month later, the PRI was also defeated in Chiapas as a coalition candidate was elected governor. Though Fox vowed to end the war in Chiapas "in fifteen minutes," and the Zapatistas traveled to Mexico City in March 2001 to address the Mexican Congress, little has changed. The full peace agreement has not been honored and new indigenous rights law does not recognize indigenous autonomy. In spite of the continuing conflict, non-Zapatista and Zapatista communities-in-resistance try to live peacefully and autonomously in several areas of the state.

Shaping Ritual and Practice

The Roman Catholic Church has played a major role in the expression of social conscience and in the struggle to find a lasting peace in Chiapas. The Church took shape under the tutelage of Bishop Samuel Ruíz García who arrived in the diocese of San Cristóbal de las Casas in 1960 (Meyer 2000). Like other Latin American Roman Catholic leaders, he admits that he was born into the full flowering of faith in the company of the poor and marginalized. This reflects a basic insight of liberation spirituality, that the poor hold a privileged place in God's greater plan. According to Samuel Ruiz, their gift to us is that they allow us to accompany them in their struggle.

Underlying currents of Maya thought and world-view have shaped the Chiapas church. These include the notion of complementary dualism, the use of divination in the form of prayer-guided questions that seek to shed light on life's problems, and the concept of *madre tierra* as a guide to appropriate environmental relationships. Of these, it is the acceptance of complementarity that separates the San Cristóbal church from other forms of liberation Catholicism.

The concept of complementary opposition and dualism refers to opposed elements that together comprise a whole, and is a key to the Maya world view. The elusive primary deity of Mesoamerica is a Dual God, the primary unity being made up of two opposed and interdependent entities. Indeed, as Gary Gossen notes, ancestors, deities, and ritual personages are given a "bisexual honorific title" translated as "fathers-mothers" (Gossen 1996, 316). Duncan Earle points out that, "A balancing of dual and opposed elements is woven throughout the religion, the world view and the social order, and appears in poetry and mythic sagas like the Popol Vuh" (2001, 2).

In her ethnography of San Pedro Chenalhó, Christine Eber describes the place of complementary dualism in Maya daily life: "Pedranos say that men and women are indispensable to one another. Without *jnup/jchi'il* (my complementation, companion, or spouse), one cannot be a true man or woman (Eber 1999, 67).

The church's accommodation to the particular circumstances of Maya daily life and belief has evolved in the settings where it once sought to impose its own language and conception of faith. As explained by Samuel Ruíz García during an interview in 1999:

> "You know," he said. "We believe in the Catholic Church that there is holy succession reaching back to the apostles. When priests and deacons are ordained, they are ordained in a line reaching back to Jesus Christ, an apostolic succession. Now all of the apostles were men…." Don Samuel gave a little shrug. "But Mary, she was the mother of Jesus, she was almost an apostle….
>
> "When we ordain deacons these days," he continued. "We commission the couple, husband and wife." He paused on the word commission, a canon-safe word. "They serve together in the communities, and then the husband dies. At first, we tried to appoint a new deacon to replace him, but the people said, 'Padre, we already have a good deacon.' So we said to ourselves, 'yes, this works,' and so ministry is given to both men and women." (Simonelli 2001, 2)

Among the Maya, the ministry of being a healer, or *h'ɔl*, has always been given to both men and women, complementarily and simultaneously. For the emerging indigenous church to work within the Maya world view, it had to reflect in its tangible and real expression, the way in the opposite is resolved in the whole.

Using Literacy and Language in Ritual: Countering Globalization

The form of worship, ritual, and prayer found in the autochthonous church is not simply another version of syncretism or "folk" Catholicism. Though anthropological analyses have described the resulting form as an "imperfect mix" (Mauer Avalos 1993, 228) or sloppy Catholicism, this is not the case. It is a product of "the process of destruction, dialogue, negotiation, accommodation, and creativity that occurred when the Christian spiritual traditions of Iberia encountered the vast and varied wonder that was America" (Gossen 1993:19). It is, as Duncan Earle notes, an act of "appropriating the enemy," a conscious construction of resistance for the Maya. Arising initially as a "politically correct" formulation, it allowed them to continue their own practices under the guise of acceptable ritual, especially during periods of extreme oppression. Yet if we examine the homilies and writings of official Roman Catholic practitioners in the diocese, it appears that contemporary Maya religious practice in Chiapas has co-opted the conquering religion.

As in other parts of Latin America, a key to actual worship has been the use of catechists as leaders of worship. In the absence of priests and deacons, in remote areas ritual and practice have been shaped by necessity. Ritual has had space to develop on its own, in regions rife with political struggle and armed conflict. Drawing on scripture as a basis for reflection, prayer is guided by both the form of discourse familiar in Christian prayer and by the use of literary couplets that hearken back to ancient Maya writing.

In a gathering that included a presentation by a government spokesman, a reading from scripture (Mathew 7: 15–17, 19–20) was used to guide reflection on the issue of mega development:

> Beware of false prophets: they come unto you with the skin of lambs, but within are fierce wolves.
> You will recognize them by their fruits: Do you harvest grapes from thorns of figs from thistles?
> The same happens with a healthy tree: it gives good fruit, while a bad tree produces bad fruit.
> Cut the whole tree that does not give good fruit, and throw it into the fire. Therefore, by their works will you know them.

Though reflection can begin with prayer, catechist leaders and their congregations are not dependent on scripture and prayer alone in analyzing on-going events. As in the case of Plan Puebla Panamá, up-to-the-minute government documents and internationally generated critiques are downloaded from the internet in the cities and find their way into the mountains and jungles, carried by pastoral representatives who demand briefings from the diocese. Arriving at rural outposts of belief and worship, these documents are summarized and presented to the congregation, somewhere after the gospel and before the place where the communion occurs in formal Roman Catholic worship.

Literacy and Information as Order and Preservation

The Chiapas experience is unique in form, though it parallels the use of language and literacy in Hindu worship in Bali. There is a tradition of using poetry and theater to teach sacred writings and morality to the masses, including the incorporation of *wayang* or shadow puppetry. As early as the 1970s, Hindu priests realized the value of using the media to bring religious messages to the masses. As depicted in Ira R. Abrahms's film, *Three Worlds of Bali*, this was especially important in the preparations for *Eka Dasa Rudra*, an island-wide ceremony that occurs once a century to control the forces of good and evil. In 1963, an abortive attempt to hold the ceremony out of cycle and during serious political conflict took place. When the ceremony was finally held in 1979, manipulation of language and information helped it to occur peacefully, while at the same time, making the transformation of demons into beneficent spirits possible.

Not all religious practitioners view literacy and information as an asset. Though radio broadcasts were used to warn reservation dwellers of the religious-based dangers of going outdoors during an eclipse, a Navajo *hatali* or medicine man in Canyon de Chelly, Arizona expressed distrust of documentation of religious practices. Even though many intricate ceremonies could become lost, he refused to permit his descriptions and sacred stories to be recorded.

In Bali, as in Chiapas, however, literacy has provided a secular content to religious practice, one in which all can share in the analysis of social-political threats and struggle. At the same time, discourse and ritual have converted the secular to the sacred, whether it is the construction of protest against global mega-development or guidance for the new president of a cooperative. To separate church from state, ritual from daily practice, is to view the spiritual as an institution, rather than a permeating philosophy of life. In the autochthonous church, God is present in a tiny chapel, in a cooperative's headquarters, in a diocesan meeting with a government representative. In Bali, priests used literacy and information technology to protect against heretical co-option of religious practice by secular political figures. Ritual takes form as believers use a varied set of tools to make sense of a changing world. Literacy becomes the nourishment that keeps belief alive in everyday life.

Jeanne Simonelli

Further Reading

Avalos, E. M. (1993). The Tzeltal Maya-Christian Synthesis. In G. H. Gossen (Ed.), *South and Meso-American native spirituality: From the cult of the feathered serpent to the theology of liberation* (pp. 228–230). New York: The Crossroad Publishing Co.

Bricker, V. R. (1981). *The Indian Christ, the Indian king: The historical substrate of Maya myth and ritual.* Austin: University of Texas Press.

Earle, D. (1990). Appropriating the enemy: Maya religious organization and community survival. In L. Stephen & J. Dow (Eds.), *The politics of popular religion in Mexico and Central America* (pp. 115–142). Washington, DC: American Anthropology Association.

Earle, D. (2001). Mesoamerica through a maya gaze: Three thousand years of culture, resistance and accommodation. Unpublished field course and reading guide for fieldwork in cultural anthropology, Wake Forest University, Winston-Salem.

Eber, C. (2000). *Women & alcohol in a highland Maya town.* Austin: University of Texas Press.

Eber, C. (2001). Buscando una nueva vida: Liberation through autonomy in San Pedro Chenalhó. *Latin American Perspectives, 28*(2), 45–72.

Gossen, G. H. (1993). Introduction: On the human condition and the moral order: A testimony from the Chamula Tzotzil Maya of Chiapas, Mexico. In G. H. Gossen (Ed.), *South and Meso-American native spirituality: From the cult of the feathered serpent to the theology of liberation* (pp. 414–435). New York: Crossroad Publishing.

Gossen, G. H. (1993). *South and Meso-American native spirituality: From the cult of the feathered serpent to the theology of liberation.* New York: Crossroad Publishing.

Gossen, G. H. (1996). The religions of Mesoamerica. In R. M. Carmack, J. Gasco, & G. H. Gossen (Eds.), *The legacy of Mesoamerica: History and culture of a Native American civilization* (pp. 290–319). Upper Saddle River, NJ: Prentice Hall.

Gutierrez, G. (1984). *We drink from our own wells.* Maryknoll, NY: Orbis Books.

Gutierrez, G. (1988). *A theology of liberation* (Rev. ed.). Maryknoll, NY: Orbis Books.

Hernández-Castillo, R. A. (2001). Building a utopia: The hopes and challenges of the women of Chiapas. In R. A. Hernández-Castillo (Ed.) & L. Beneria Surkin & J. Beneria Surkin (English Eds.), *The other word: Women and violence in Chiapas before and after Acteal* (pp. 113–134). Copenhagen, Denmark: International Work Group for Indigenous Affairs.

Lansing, J. S. (1994). *The Balinese.* New York: Harcourt Brace.

Meyer, J. (2000). *Samuel Ruiz en San Cristóbal.* Mexico, DF: Tusquets Editores.

Morkovsky, M. C. (1993). *Guerilleros*, political saints, and the theology of liberation. In G. H. Gossen (Ed.), *South and Meso-American native spirituality: From the cult of the feathered serpent to the theology of liberation* (pp. 526–547). New York: Crossroad Publishing.

Nash, J. C. (2001). *Mayan visions: The quest for autonomy in an age of globalization.* New York: Routledge.

Ross, J. (2000) *The war against oblivion: The Zapatista chronicles 1994–2000.* Monroe, ME: Common Courage.

Schieffelin, B. B, Wollard, K. A., & Kroskrity, P. V. (1998). *Language ideologies: Practice and theory.* New York: Oxford University Press.

Simonelli, J. (1997). *Crossing between worlds: The Navajo of Canyon de Chelly.* Santa Fe, NM: SAR Press.

Simonelli, J. (2001, November). *Complementaridad: Realities of gender in contemporary Mesoamerica.* Paper presented at the Annual meeting of the American Anthropological Association, Washington, DC.

Simonelli, J. (2002). The scent of change in Chiapas. In L. S. Wallbridge & K. Sievert (Eds.), *Personal Encounters: A Reader in Cultural Anthropology* (pp. 46–52). New York: McGraw-Hill.

Sobrino, J. (1988). *Spirituality of liberation: Toward political holiness.* Maryknoll, NY: Orbis Books.

Liminoid

The concept of liminoid or liminoid state was introduced to the discussion of rituals by anthropologist Victor Turner in the 1970s and has remained an important part of discussion ever since. This concept stems from the liminal phase of rites of passage that describes a sacred, ambiguous, and dangerous marginal state. The sharp demarcation between labor and leisure in industrial and post-industrial societies has effected the transfer of this individual-oriented tribal ritual foreground of rites of passage to the context of group-oriented performance and social drama. The secularization of this state of being allows the liminoid creator to be flexible and innovative with social heritage to provide a reinterpretation or reconstruction of society. Thus, performance can be used, like ritual, to advance society as a whole through educating the audience about the resolution of social problems presented on stage.

Ritual and Rites of Passage

While ritualistic rites of passage were studied and described by many from the first generations of anthropologists, it was Victor Turner (1920–1983) who emphasized them as culturally generative while also being the social "glue" described by Radcliffe-Brown. Turner's fieldwork in the 1950s on rituals of the Ndembu in Africa was heavily influenced by Arnold Van Gennep's writings on ritual and "rites of passage" from which the concept of the liminal and liminoid emerges.

Rites of passage are cultural tools used to demarcate changes in place, state, social position, and age; in Van Gennep's view, the rites of passage accompanying these changes in state are demarcated by three phases: separation, margin, and aggregation. The phase of separation symbolically detaches the ritual subject from a previous state in social structure and/or cultural conditions. Often, rites of passage mark a transition to adulthood with a traumatic separation event, such as circumcision.

The key to any ritual drama is found in the point of conflict that marks the climax of separation. From this traumatic point of departure, the individual enters a transitional or marginal ritual state. This phase is like a threshold because the ritual subject is in neither one space nor another. Hence, this phase is also called liminal, after *limen*, the Latin word for threshold. The liminal phase is marked by ambiguity, both symbolic and literal, because the present state of the ritual subject is unlike either the past or future states. For instance, a child undergoing the rites of passage associated with puberty is not a child anymore, yet he or she is also not an adult. During this liminal phase, the societal ideals of the group are exposed and the liminal aspect of ritual then becomes a gateway to understanding the social organization and values of the group.

The liminal is intriguing because of its amorphous nature. This indefinite time of transition between states is one of great power. Liminal entities are "betwixt and between" the ascribed and hierarchical positions of the laws of society and ceremonies of culture. There is a strong component of cultural and ritual symbolism attached to liminal phases and entities that are frequently associated with cycles of birth and death—a sort of death with rebirth, from tomb to womb. The liminal phase serves to erode and then reform the ritual subject, now imbued with power and knowledge to assume a new state. In Turner's examination of what was commonly dismissed as an interstructural or interstitial period, he discovered an entire new world of symbols and meaning. The aggregation, or reaggregation, phase is the conclusion of the passage across the threshold into a new state. This implies that ritual is functional and processual in the development and creation of society at the level of the individual who experiences the reinforcement of norms and cultural traditions through liminal education.

Leisure Genres and Transformation to the Liminoid

Brian Sutton-Smith inspired Turner to study play and then drama as a form of ritual in increasingly socially complex and industrialized societies where ritual and rites of passage were much less defined, let alone practiced. Sutton-Smith describes play, or leisure, as periods of separation from society that are timeless and from which new symbols, models, and paradigms emerge. These newly emergent forms loop back to society, thus making this concept of leisure the dialectic partner of ritual. Applying Sutton-Smith's ideas to ritual and liminality, Turner takes the liminal out of the individually-focused rite of passage and places it into the context of social drama and industrialized society. He thereby defines leisure and play as liminoid, with the feedback becoming culturally generative through the experience of the audience and participants.

Social and aesthetic dramas are liminal because they contain ritual action, or a core that restores behavior. Turner's interest in performance as liminal leads him to the deduction that performance is a paradigm of process. From his work with Richard Schechner, a performance theorist, Turner isolated a thread of thought that continued beyond his theory of ritual in the theater: the notion that "if" is the gateway to imagination through which society leaves reality behind.

Performance in industrialized societies is the gateway for reform, while the liminal function makes that performance a ritual of becoming. Thus, the liminal aspect of ritual is supplanted by the *liminoid*, in which performers are free to create symbolic power through that feedback loop to society that ultimately either reinforces or reinvents important values and traditions. The key difference here is that the liminal—an obligatory state of being for the ritual participant in a rite of passage—is sacred and holy, while the liminoid is completely secularized and devoid of the concept of obligation or rite of passage. The liminoid is a dynamic event involving creator, performer, and audience who cooperate voluntarily, but together generate culture either through the reinforcement of cultural norms and traditions or through redressing social ills.

Communitas and the Generation of Culture

Part and parcel of the liminoid is communitas, which describes a social relationship of corporate liminality, or egalitarian comradeship. Communitas leads one from the subjective experience into vital and total relations with humans, generating myths, symbols, metaphors, rituals, philosophy, art, and religion. This is a state of evolutionary potential, internalized and unfixed in structure that exists in a dangerous dialectic with structure. As much as communitas is necessary as generative of cultural innovation, it cannot sustain humanity because of a seemingly inescapable human need for materialism and organization. And so, the danger of this dialectic is a maximization of one leading to a minimization of the other which can lead to extremes, such as despotism and revolution.

The underlying essence of a continuous human bond is inherent in the notion that one must gain experience through ritual transition. There can be no human society unless each level of the social structure is aware of the experience of the lower levels of the same structure, having experienced them prior to being elevated by the imbued knowledge from liminality, or in the case of industrialized nations, the liminoid. Persons born to high social ranks are not legitimized without the transient humility of a rite of passage from one state to another. The theoretical implication is that social life, and thereby social drama, is a dialectical process involving experiences of opposites.

Performance and Social Drama

The role of theatre, or performance, in industrial nations is more than simply an Aristotelian emotional catharsis because it reinterprets or reconstructs society. The study of social dramas is the building block to analyzing theatre, or performance, as the function of ritual in these societies. Social drama is defined as the place where conflict is enacted through the assertion of paradigms representing various groups or individuals. Social dramas are an inherent part of all societies. From gender roles and class boundaries to ethnic groups, cults, and sects, society is rife with the potential for a breach in social relations. Once a breach occurs, it causes a crisis that is eventually resolved through redressive processes. Redressive processes consist of political processes (ranging from deliberation to war), legal-judicial processes (arbitration to court), and ritual processes (divinations to sacrifice). The result is reconciliation or an agreement to disagree.

With the increased complexity of human culture, the point of resolution in social drama can be explored through theatre. Liminality is generative in that it provides alternative programs that serve to free behavior and social action from a performative modality. Theatre is a secular judge with a sacred character. It can cross-culturally relive lived experience and explore experiences not yet lived. Theatre assigns meaning to macroprocesses by making decisions and enacting their outcomes. Ultimately, performance and drama deal with crises, schism, conflict, and ultimate resolution. This pattern of drama is transformative but in a special way. Events in theatre are not real. Events in theatre enact imagined potentialities, or these alternative programs.

Performance offers the power to take social convention to extremes within a contained, or controlled environment, the consequences of which do not impinge directly on ordinary life. This power is likened to hypothesis testing in the scientific method, whereby ritual offers a test pattern for events that may or may not work to redress complaints, such as social inequity or political domination. In either case, the hypothesis is being tested and the audience as a group is led toward an inevitable conclusion based on the data presented by the creator. The liminoid phase is voluntary and experienced in communitas, but ultimately forces the group to enter an ambiguous state filled with possibility and danger. There must be sincerity in the performance and there must also be relevance to the audience for culture to be effectively regenerated. The key to understanding the liminoid in leisure forms as ritual for industrialized societies lies in the intersection with the liminal. Here, the individual or particular experience is transcended out of ritual and rites of passage and universalized in this sacred space of performance. At this liminoid phase, one's own crises are seen in abstraction to the level of the universal and, as such, removed or distanced from emotion and bias. At this level then, the resolution of the universal concept of the crises becomes one's own existential reality and the process is complete with the reintegration into society, or crossing over the threshold.

Cultural Relevance

The concept of the liminal emerges from the ritual of non-industrial societies. The appearance of a sharp demarcation between work and leisure time in industrial and post-industrial societies transforms the liminal to the liminoid. Removed from ritual and generated in leisure, liminoid genres do not lose their ritual power because the notion of communitas is retained and is culturally generative. Furthermore, additional power is garnered from the presence of a voluntarily participating audience. Keeping in mind the power of communitas, the audience must find a performance to be culturally relevant and, together with the performers, engage in a mutual suspension of disbelief. Finally, by analyzing the structure of the ritual, or liminoid genre, one can understand the collective experience of the audience and the transformation they undergo. This concept of pleasure time and mutual experience lends credibility to theatre and film as artistic genres that involve the participants in a processual dynamic that creates meaning. By transcending particular causes of social drama, a universal experience is explored which allows liminal entities, those betwixt and between, to understand perspectives unavailable during non-ritual time.

The thesis that underlying these postulations as to the functions of ritual and their component symbols is that each society's social life is based on that society's unique model of life, which thereby, is enacted in ritual. In other words, rituals reflect the ideals and strivings of a particular society, ideals such as calling leaders to account, secularizing values and beliefs, or revealing typical conflicts and suggesting remedies. Performances such as theater or film foster the deeper aspects of growth and development that, in industrialized societies, ritual has ceased to provide. They do this by probing a society's weaknesses through exposure of the status quo in the context of the larger world.

Kara C. Hoover

Further Reading

Ashley, K. (Ed.). (1990). *Victor Turner and the construction of cultural criticism: Between literature and anthropology*. Bloomington: Indiana University Press.

Ashley, K. M. (Ed.). (1990). Victor *Turner and the construction of cultural criticism*. Bloomington: Indiana University Press.

Babcock, B. (1987). The arts and all things common: Victor Turner's literary anthropology. *Comparative criticism*, 9, 39–46.

Clifford, J. (1988). *The predicament of culture: Twentieth century ethnography, literature and art*. Cambridge, UK: Harvard University Press.

Schechner, R. (1985). *Between theatre and anthropology*. Philadelphia, PA: University of Pennsylvania Press.

Schechner, R., & Appel, W. (Eds.). (1990). *By means of performance: Intercultural studies of theatre and ritual*. Cambridge, UK: Cambridge University Press.

Schechner, R., & Schuman, M. (Eds.). (1976). *Ritual, play, and performance: Readings in the social sciences/theatre*. New York: Seabury Press.

Turner, V. (1962). *Chihamba the white spirit: A ritual drama of the Ndembu*. Vol. 33. Manchester, UK: Manchester University Press.

Turner, V. (1967). *The forest of symbols: Aspects of Ndembu ritual*. London: Cornell University Press.

Turner, V. (1968). *The drums of affliction: A study of religious progresses among the Ndembu of Zambia*. Bath, UK: Oxford University Press.

Turner, V. (1969). *The ritual process: Structure and anti-structure*. Chicago, IL: Aldine Publishing Company.

Turner, V. (1974). *Dramas, fields, and metaphors: Symbolic action in human society*. Ithaca, NY: Cornell University Press.

Turner, V. (1982). *From ritual to theatre: The human seriousness of play*. New York: Performing Arts Journal Publications.

Turner, V. (1985). *On the edge of the bush: Anthropology as experience*. Tucson, AZ: University of Arizona Press.

Turner, V. (1986). *The anthropology of performance*. New York: PAJ Publications.

Turner, V. (1992). Blazing *the trail: Way marks in the exploration of symbols*. Tucson, AZ: University of Arizona Press.

Turner, V. W., & Bruner, E. M. (Eds.). (1986). *The anthropology of experience*. Urbana: University of Illinois Press.

M

Madagascar

The Malagasy people (numbered at 16.4 million in 2002) of Madagascar believe in an afterlife, and this is the most basic of all traditional beliefs and the foundation of the traditional Malagasy social structure. All Malagasy groups believe in a unique and supreme God who is called by different names: the Zanahary (Creator) or Andriamanitra (Sweet, or the Lord Who Smells Good). This fact contradicts the commonly observed traditional ceremonies in Madagascar, in which the Malagasy people call the spirits of their ancestors for blessing, leading outsiders to misinterpret the religions in Madagascar as polytheistic. This misinterpretation ignores the social structure of the Malagasy. The traditional religion is neither animistic (giving souls to nonliving matter) nor polytheistic. It is monotheistic, worshiping only one god. The spirits and of the dead serve only as intermediaries between the living and God.

The traditional social structure in Madagascar is strongly hierarchical according to the age and the gender of each individual. At the top of this hierarchy is the oldest man, the patriarch who rules the whole community. He has no administrative function, and his social position is not an elected one. His morality and integrity are the only criteria on which he is chosen. He is believed to represent the group lineage of the community and therefore is the closest to the ancestors' world in the afterlife. On the other hand, the ancestors are believed to intermediate between the supreme God and the living and are conceived as having the power to affect the fortunes of the living for good or evil. Surprisingly, there is no struggle for power between the living and the dead in that the ancestors are considered to have more authority over the members of a family. In some regions of Madagascar—for example, in the northwest among the Sakalava—the deceased monarchs still rule the community and are described as "gods on Earth."

The concept of *tanindrazana* (the land of the ancestors) reveals the respect of the living Malagasy people for their ancestors. The island was even described as the "ghost island" by travelers in the sixteenth and seventeenth centuries. The Malagasy people believe that life on Earth is only a part of the cyclical form of life as a whole. They believe that the invisible world is the mother's realm and that the living world is the father's realm. A newborn therefore comes from the mother's womb and lives in the father's world and at death returns to the mother's world. Rites of passage confer to the newborn social identity, which is defined most of the time according to the father's lineage. However, one point should be emphasized: The Malagasy people do not believe in reincarnation. They believe that the newborn comes to this visible world because of the ancestors' blessing.

Rites of Passage

Rites of passage include circumcision of young males, the bridewealth ceremony during the traditional marriage for girls, the funeral, and the second burial. All of these rites are characterized by the separation of the individual from the mother's lineage (at the circumcision for a boy and at the marriage for a girl) and the integration into the father's lineage. The girl will join her father-in-law's lineage. At a funeral the inverse of this process occurs: separation from the father's lineage and integration into the mother's lineage. However, it is important to note that not every dead person becomes an ancestor. The second burial (*famadihana*) among the highland ethnic groups is performed to give the dead the identity as ancestors. The word *famadihana* can be translated as "returning the corpse," which is the second burial ceremony. During this ceremony, which can last two days or more, the corpse is wrapped with new shrouds. Famadihana is the final step of the funeral rituals in the highlands because the dead will enter the realm of the ancestors afterward. In coastal areas the royal relics bath represents the second burial. Anthropologist Gillian Feeley-Harnick (1991) described the royal relics bath among the Sakalava in western Madagascar, where it is performed every four or seven years. It is also an opportunity to entertain relationships with the dead relative. Construction of sumptuous family tombs, especially in southern Madagascar and in the highlands, shows this link between the living and the dead. It reflects, as well, the higher position of the dead in the community because the tombs are usually built of stone, whereas the houses of the living are built of only brick and wood. Among the Sakalava the tombs are decorated with carvings showing explicit sexual activity. These carvings are meant to illustrate the life-giving force, or fertility, of the ancestors. The emphasis in the minds of the people, however, is not on the afterlife but rather on the relationship of the dead with the living and the role of the former as bearers of power and authority.

All ethnographies (cultural studies) of the Malagasy find ceremonies of spirit possession occurring in all ethnic groups. Besides funeral ceremonies, spirit possession is the only way to communicate "directly" with the ancestors. Feeley-Harnick (1991) insists on the importance of *tromba* (spirit possession) among the Sakalava. Throughout the history of this group, the spirits of deceased monarchs have governed the daily life of the living Sakalava. She even describes the awkward situation when the French invaded that part of the island in the late nineteenth century and found a teenage boy ruling the community. The French were obviously ignorant of the actual authority of the deceased monarchs over the living. Such anecdotes occurred all over the island during the precolonial, colonial, and postcolonial periods. An official seeking popular support during election campaigns has always sought ancestral support first. Richard Huntington (1978) and Maurice Bloch (1986) have mentioned the Malagasy concept of the soul of a recently deceased person, the *lolo,* which is said to be the *angatra* (ghost of the unknown dead).

The most striking manifestations of the traditional religion in Madagascar are spirit possession ceremonies, funeral ceremonies, the *famadihana,* and circumcision. However, those ceremonies are only the overall manifestations of the traditional beliefs in Madagascar and hide a more crucial point about the survival of Malagasy society per se.

Double Identity

According to statistics, 41 percent of the Malagasy people declare themselves to be Christian and 7 percent Muslim. These statistics suggest that 52 percent of the Malagasy people follow the traditional religion. In addition, surveys in the city and in the countryside show that those percentages are biased in that most of the Malagasy people are reluctant to admit that they follow the traditional religion, and even when they admit it, they assume that they are also Christians, a typical syncretism (combining different forms) of religions. This reluctance is a result of attitudes formed during the French colonization period, when the indigenous beliefs were considered primitive and archaic and Christianity the religion of progressive people. During the reign of King Radama II (1861–1863), who allowed missionaries to teach in Madagascar, a revival of the traditional belief, *ramanenjana,* occurred in the capital city Antananarivo. It seemed that many people were obsessed by the spirit of the deceased Queen Ranavalona I, who persecuted the Christians. After the baptism of Queen Ranavalona II (1868–1873), the missionaries were convinced of their success, but they did not realize that the Malagasy were following the religion of their queen, not the Christian religion. After the independence of Madagascar from France in 1960, the Malagasy cultural identity was reclaimed in accordance with traditional beliefs.

Serge Ratsirahonana and Patricia Wright

See also Crisis Rituals; Possession and Trance; Rites of Passage

Further Reading

Bloch, M. (1968). Tombs and conservation among the Merina of Madagascar. *Man, 3,* 94–104.

Bloch, M. (1971). *Placing the dead: Tombs, ancestral villages, and kinship organization in Madagascar*. London: Berkeley Square House.

Bloch, M. (1986). *From blessing to violence, history and ideology in the circumcision ritual of the Merina of Madagascar*. Cambridge, UK: Cambridge University Press.

Dina, J. (2001). The Hazomanga among the Masikoro of southwest Madagascar: Identity and history. *Ethnohistory: Vol. 48.*

Feeley-Harnik, G. (1986). Ritual and work in Madagascar. In C.P. Kottak (Ed.), *Madagascar, society and history*. Durham, NC: Carolina Academic Press.

Feeley-Harnik, G. (1991). *A green estate, restoring independence in Madagascar*. Washington: Smithsonian Institution Press.

Lambeck, M. (1998). The Sakalava Poiesis of history: The past through spirit possession in Madagascar. *American Ethnologist, 25*(2), 106–127.

Middleton, K. (1999). Circumcision, death, and strangers. In K. Middleton (Ed.), *Ancestors, power, and history in Madagascar: Vol. 20. Studies of religion in Africa*. Leiden, Netherlands: Brill.

Raison-Jourde, F. (1999). Social competition and the control of sacred places in rural Imerina: The case of Ankadivoribe. In K. Middleton (Ed.), *Ancestors, power and history: Vol. 20. Studies of religion in Africa*. Leiden, Netherlands: Brill.

Sharp, L. (1990). *The possessed and the dispossessed: Spirits, identity, and power in a Madagascar migrant town*. Berkeley and Los Angeles: University of California Press.

Southal, A. (1986). Common themes in Malagasy culture. In C.P. Kottak (Ed.), *Madagascar, society and history.*. Durham, NC: Carolina Academic Press.

Wrong, M. (1995, December). A loving dance of death. *World Press Review, 42*, 41–42.

Magic

Scholars agree that the concept of magic is universal and of central importance to understanding religious belief and ritual. There is, however, considerable disagreement as to just what magic is and what it signifies. For the public, too, the term has many meanings. In its broadest sense, the term denotes any belief, behavior, or phenomenon that seems to exceed people's presumptions about the workings of the physical world. The term can refer to the trickery employed by stage magicians; it can mean an inherent ability to change form or visibility or location; or it can denote a romantic, awe-inspiring, or wondrous quality.

Complicated systems of numerical or algebraic notation that since Classical times have purported to reveal solutions to "occult" mysteries, such as those used in astrology, alchemy, Kabbala, and Rosicrucianism, have been called "high magic," to distinguish them from the "low" or simple magic of unlettered people. Such forms have also been called "Hermetic" magic, the term deriving from the name Hermes Trismegistus, Greek variant of the Egyptian Thoth, god or principle of writing and written wisdom (from a time when writing itself was regarded as a magical skill). These so-called "occult sciences" were revived in the late nineteenth century by European and British occult groups, notably the Ordo Templi Orientalis and Aleister Crowley's Hermetic Order of the Golden Dawn. The term was often spelled "magick" by the Crowleyites, and by later adherents to various forms of modern paganism, notably Wicca, in whose rites sympathetic magic is central. Especially since the latter half of the twentieth century, the term "magic" has come to refer to anything considered "psychic," "paranormal," "occult," or "New Age." It may refer to any concept of supernatural power, or to anything that seems miraculous. Frequently its connotation is negative, referring to ideas of sorcery, witchcraft, demonic invocation, or any other activities expressly forbidden by religious tradition, such as the "abominable practices" condemned in the Bible, e.g., Deuteronomy 18:9–12.

Magic in World Ethnology

Nineteenth- and early twentieth-century scholarly discussions of magic assumed its distinction from religion and debated its place in the evolutionary development of human thinking. Anthropologist E. B. Tylor in his *Primitive Culture* (1871) regarded it as a "pernicious delusion," the efforts of people in "the lowest known stages of civilization" to make sense of their world. He did, however, acknowledge its symbolic logic and place within a cultural/religious system. Folklorist Sir James George Frazer in the third edition of *The Golden Bough* (1911–1915) also emphasized the erroneous assumptions in magic, regarding it as the earliest stage in the progression of human thinking through religion to science, but his discussion of the underlying principles of magic are still valuable today. Sociologists Marcel Mauss and Henri

AN OJIBWA MAGICIAN AT WORK

The following ethnographic account describes a seance or magical ceremony conducted by an Ojibwa magician in the Great lakes region in the 1930s. Such ceremonies were routinely conducted to make contact with and communicate with the spirit world.

With the exception of a few brief agitations of the tent from time to time by the masters of the winds, the other spirits were so tardy in making their appearance on this occasion that I thought the seance was going to be a failure. The conjurer engaged in brief bits of conversation with members of the audience during this period. "Nothing is coming (kanesa)," he kept mumbling over and over again. But different members of the audience kept encouraging him. "Don't give up," "Wait a little longer," they kept saying. And the conjurer would reply saying that he was doing his best. Among other things he was heard to say, "I'd be glad to hear you for a while." This was addressed to the pawaganak. Finally there was a more continuous agitation of the structure and a spirit came in who sang a song. This was kamandinizawit, the master of scapulimancy, although I did not know this at the time....

Soon several members of the audience began calling for mikinak, the Great Turtle. "Mikinak! Mikinak! Where's mikinak?" the Indians shouted and, as soon as he arrived, a gentle ripple of laughter swept over the audience. Mikinak talks in a throaty nasal voice not unlike that of Donald Duck. It is extremely characteristic and very easily distinguishable from other voices that emanate from the tent. His popularity with the audience was manifested throughout the evening by the almost constant stream of repartee which took place between members of the audience and this pawagan when he was present.... Often the Indians will pass a plug of tobacco into the tent just for mikinak to enjoy a smoke. When smoking he has the peculiar habit of emitting a long uninterrupted whistle.

The special function of mikinak in the conjuring tent, however, is to act as a sort of intermediary between the other spirits and the conjurer and to serve as a messenger. He it is who is sent on long journeys to distant parts of the country to find out the information requested by members of the audience. When anyone wishes to ask such a question, it is customary to call the skabewis to one's side and state the inquiry to him, at the same time giving him a small quantity of tobacco. The skabewis then goes to the conjuring lodge, repeats the question to the conjurer, and hands him the tobacco. This tobacco is a fee, not a sacrifice. On this occasion I said I wanted to know how my father was, as he had been very ill and I had received no mail. After the conjurer had been told my inquiry he repeated it aloud and someone in the audience called out, "send mikinak!" And in a moment or two mikinak started on his journey to Philadelphia.

***Source*: Hallowell, Irving A. (1942). *The Role of Conjuring in Saulteaux Society.* Publications of the Philadelphia Anthropological Society, Vol. II. Philadelphia: University of Pennsylvania Press, pp. 44–46.**

Hubert in *A General Theory of Magic* (1902–1903) stressed the social and practical dimensions of magic, as distinct from the spiritual nature of religion. Noting that it involves a belief in a mystical communicable power, they took the Melanesian-Polynesian concept of *mana* as representative of a universal way of thinking, manifested in the modern world in the concepts of "luck and quintessence." Emile Durkheim in his *The Elementary Forms of the Religious Life* (1912) agreed with Mauss that magic is opposite to religion, but saw magic as individual and religion as social. He argued for a reverse of his predecessors' evolutionary progression: magic, said Durkheim, must come later than religion, arising from the individual's seizing the methods of religion for his own use, and addressing both natural forces and spiritual beings.

These various early interpretations were "armchair" theories, based on reports of others and interpreted through European systems of thinking. With the development of modern anthropological fieldwork and the refinement of ethnographic description, beginning with Bronislaw Malinowski's influential work in the Trobriand Islands of Melanesia in 1915, anthropology became more aware of the nature of culture and the specifics of cultural meaning. Malinowski's fieldwork yielded the first detailed ethnographic study of a traditional magical system, his two-volume *Coral Gardens and Their Magic* (1935). A survey of academic perspectives on magic is provided by Daniel O'Keefe in his *Stolen Lightning* (1982).

Most studies of magical acts and beliefs describe them with little discussion of how people think they work. Understanding what is going on in a magical worldview is important, because it reveals basic human ways of thinking. Anthropologists have identified five concepts that, because they are found universally and at all stages of human history, most usefully describe beliefs and practices termed "magic"; any act or belief is magical if it combines some of these concepts.

1) Foremost is the concept of a communicable supernatural *power*, universally believed to exist in all natural and supernatural things. The animate have more of this power than do the inanimate, the living have more than the dead, people have more than animals, spirits have more than people, and the Supreme Being has so much that simply being in its presence can be dangerous. The Biblical concept of God's "glory" is illustrative. For example, Moses' demand that God reveal His glory to him is denied: "you cannot see my face, for no one shall see me and live" (Exodus 33:20, NRSV). Nevertheless, Moses terrified his people when he returned to them because "the skin of his face shone, because he had been talking with God" (34:29), and he veiled himself for subsequent meetings. The shepherds receiving the news of Christ's birth were similarly "terrified" when "the glory of the lord shone around them" (Luke 2:9). Power that emits light is evident also in the halos over the heads of saints in medieval religious art, and the alleged "aura" that, according to New Age beliefs, emanates from people. Similar ideas of power are central to all supernatural belief systems. The Melanesian and Polynesian concept of *mana*, borrowed by modern New Age beliefs, is well-known, as is Chinese *qi* ("chi"). Power in people and in anthropomorphic deities is concentrated in certain body parts that can have particular importance in magical concepts. The eyes, mouth, hands (especially certain fingers), and genitals are probably universally important; others, such as the breasts, anus, and soles of the feet, might be regarded as having positive or negative power depending on the culture.

2) *"Forces"* in nature, often regarded as supernatural agencies in their own right, as distinct from spiritual entities: Not to be confused with measurable forces such as gravity, electromagnetism, or the strong and weak nuclear forces, these "forces" are conceptual only, but represent a likely universal concept. Forces have power, and can be conceptualized as the engines of nature; they are in all things, programmed since Creation to act in specific ways, either individually or in concert with others. They respond to spiritual direction; indeed, when people pray to supernatural beings for some tangible return, they are asking the beings to motivate the appropriate forces of nature. And these forces respond to direct manipulation through magic.

In many belief systems "forces" and power may seem to merge, as in *mana* and *chi*, in the Iroquois *orenda*, Malay *kramat*, Indian *brahma*, Greek *dynamis*, *ashé* among the Yoruba of West Africa and its Caribbean derivatives (*aché*, *axé*), *karma* and *chakras* in Hindu and Buddhist systems, the alleged "energies" in Therapeutic Touch and Reiki, and ideas of flowing streams of power in the earth, like "leylines" in Britain and earth energies addressed in the Chinese geomantic system of *feng shui*.

3) *A coherent, interconnected universe* in which everything is actually or potentially interconnected both spatially and temporally: Everything that has happened, is happening, or will happen has been preprogrammed into the system, and evidence of it is discoverable.

4) *Symbols* are critical in magic: Words, thoughts, things, or actions that both represent other things or actions and take on the qualities of the things they represent. The American flag is a good example; if the flag is intentionally damaged, more than its material is harmed. If the symbol's referent has power, the symbol becomes powerful. Though some powerful symbols seem to be universal—eggs, horns, the color red, and representations of powerful body parts—most are understandable only within their specific cultural context. Words are powerful symbols, critically important in magic. Speech is powerful: the word is activated by the life force and the intent of the speaker. It is borne on his or her breath, and carries the power of its meaning directly to its target. Unspoken thoughts can have similar, though

probably weaker, effect; this belief explains telepathy, telekinesis, and the projection of "psi energy." Names are especially powerful in magic; names are intimately associated with their referents, and to have the name of a thing or a person is to have some control over it.

5) *Frazer's principles*: In the third edition of his twelve-volume work on kingship and religion, *The Golden Bough* (1911–1915), J. G. Frazer set down his classic discussion of "sympathetic magic" which provides the best explanation of how the magical symbol is believed to work. Influenced by the philosophy of Positivism, Frazer and other nineteenth-century thinkers postulated natural processes as invariable "laws" (today they are more generally referred to as principles). Thus sympathetic magic operates according to the "law of sympathy" which has two subtypes: the "law of similarity"—things or actions that are similar to others have a causal relationship; and the stronger "law of contact"—things or actions that have been in contact with others, spatially or temporally, retain a connection after they are separated. He called the first type homeopathic magic, and the second, contagious magic. The concept of homeopathy had for long been in use to describe processes that seem to operate according to principles of similarity or imitation (it governed Samuel Hahnemann's development of homeopathic medicine a century earlier). The "similarity" between the magical act and its referent may be obvious—the color red symbolizes blood, and hence life and vitality; eggs and phallic or vulval symbols embody reproductive power—or it may be understood only within its specific cultural/linguistic context. Frazer's principle of "contact" is applicable in cases where things might not be physically touching, but exist in some sort of association with each other. Examples are: an athlete who ate certain foods for breakfast and did well in his event, eats that same meal for breakfast on subsequent competition days; a baseball hit out of the park by a champion to win a World Series takes on extraordinary value.

So, magic involves the use of symbols to project power along the network of natural interconnections to affect particular forces of nature. This anthropological definition of magic does not involve spirits. Spirits are generally conceived as sentient and willful beings, and the human invocation of them is risky business: they might not obey, and their power is especially dangerous to people. Frazer recognized this problem, but allowed the involvement of spirits in the magical act, especially when magic and religion are intertwined. He asserted that spirits respond dumbly to the act of magic, as do the forces of nature. However, it seems cross-culturally more accurate to recognize spirit invocation and command as a distinct activity operating under a different set of premises.

Magic in Other Supernatural Contexts

Any of the above principles of magic are operative in six common supernatural concepts and practices.

The magic act: involving open, public, "good" magic performed for individual or collective benefit but harming or depriving no one. It is generally believed that the natural order of things is good, and magic helps the natural forces along paths they would likely go anyway, as in farming, hunting, gambling, and love magic.

Sorcery: In the anthropological sense, sorcery is evil or "black" magic, conducted for harmful or selfish ends. A classic example is the misnamed "voodoo doll," an image representing a person that is somehow damaged, with the intention of inflicting similar harm upon the victim. Sorcery operates contrary to the natural order, and is hence supernaturally dangerous; it is antisocial, and hence is often prohibited by law. For both reasons, sorcery is clandestine, not easily demonstrable, and is often more feared than real.

Blessing and curse: Both are forms of verbal magic. The spoken word is universally powerful and respected. Blessing is the direct expression of a positive hope that good fortune may befall a person, and it is universally welcomed. Curse is a form of sorcery, a direct verbal expression of a negative intention, and is always dreaded. Both are forms of direct speech, and should not be confused with spirit invocation, such invoking God to bless or damn a person.

Taboo and pollution: "Taboo" derives from the Melanesian/Polynesian *tabu*, meaning containing so much *mana* as to be dangerous, and hence avoided. In the magical sense, taboo means avoiding an unwanted magical connection, in fear of causing an unfortunate outcome (for example, in some cultures a pregnant woman should not carry a water pot); or the consequences of mixing two different kinds of power. The result of violating taboo is pollution, including defilement or "uncleanness" in the Biblical sense (see the ritual avoidances prescribed in *Leviticus*). Concepts of taboo accord with the ways peoples everywhere classify their worlds according to certain dichotomous opposites (such as male/female, sickness/health, living/dead, east/west, culture/nature, sacred/profane), ensuring that things of one class are kept separate from things of another.

Divination: Another universal practice, divination is a process of seeking hidden ("occult") answers to questions. Questions may be addressed to spiritual beings, and answers received in a variety of ways. Strictly magical methods are commonly used, depending on the fundamental magical principles of symbols, power, and a coherent interconnected cosmos. Words, containing their own meaning, activate the interconnections in nature and pry loose the answers, also revealed in nature through interpreting some omen or sign.

Magical protection, often apparently similar to the first item, active magic: It is universally believed that power may be harnessed from one source and used in another way. Clear examples of this are using religious symbols, such as the Cross or Star of David, actively to promote good fortune, or as protective or apotropaic devices. Amulets, charms, fetishes, and talismans are different terms for magical devices that contain power to effect good results or to deflect evil influences. Real animal horns or representations of horns are widely used to protect against a variety of evils: human supernatural evil from sorcery, witchcraft, or the Evil Eye; spiritual evil, such as demons or vampires; or general misfortune; or as "good luck" charms, such as horseshoes suspended over the doorway of a house. Words are powerful as counter-magic, and written words are especially effective charms because of their permanence.

Magic is intertwined with religion, both as the individual expression of the collective religious rite, or as complementary to it. A priest addressing a deity may wear colors in sympathy with the seasons: in Africa, a priest's dark robes may help rain clouds to gather; pale blue robes promote clear skies.

Magical Thinking Today

Contrary to the expectations of many modern scholars, as the methods and principles of science and technology spread, magic is unlikely to disappear from human thinking and behavior. Magic serves vital human psychological functions of explanation and control, functions that may increase in importance in an increasingly complex world. Many superstitions people still observe are explainable by the foregoing discussion of the principles of magic and its various operations. The taboo concerning the number thirteen, especially Friday the thirteenth, derives from the Christian story of the Last Supper of Jesus and the classic principles of taboo: there were thirteen people at that table, the Crucifixion occurred on a Friday, and people consciously avoid the possibility of re-establishing any of the cosmic connections associated with those terrible events. Breaking a mirror is image magic. Opening an umbrella in the house brings the wild elements of nature into the tranquility and order of domesticity, as does putting a hat on a bed. Stepping on a crack may transmit damage to oneself. A sneezing person is temporarily vulnerable, and another's verbal blessing, even invoking the blessing of God, brings protection in a magical way.

Many of today's New Age beliefs, and the increasingly popular "alternative" and "complementary" medical practices, are based in magical thinking. A clear example is homeopathy, based on the principle of "similars," whose founder Samuel Hahnemann explicitly declared the activity of "dynamic" forces left behind after successive dilutions had removed all particles of the original substance. Similarly, many very popular therapies based on various ideas of "energy," such as Reiki, Therapeutic Touch, Distant Healing, Tai Chi, and acupuncture, demonstrate basic principles of magic. Old and new systems of magical divination, such as astrology and Feng Shui, abound. Pill and candle manufacturers, and purveyors of crystals, know that people associate certain colors with physical conditions: red is active, stimulant, cardiovascular; pale blue or green are sedative; beige or orange represent skin; white is all-purpose. Magic "works" through people's cultural expectations—the famous placebo effect.

A Neurobiological Basis?

Today there is another explanation for the persistence of magical thinking. The five principles of magic described above are absolutely universal: they are found in all cultures in all historical periods, and there is evidence for them in prehistory as well. Anthropologists have long known that when a custom is found to be universal, they are justified in looking beneath the cultural level for an explanation, into the evolutionary biology of the species. As Frazer showed, imitation is central to magic. Students of learning processes have long known the basic role of imitation in primate and human communication, and recent studies have suggested that other intelligent animals, such as dolphins, are adept imitators. Now Marco Iacoboni and his colleagues at the Brain Mapping Center at the University of California at Los Angeles have described specific brain mechanisms associated with imitation. Magical thinking may be fundamentally and biologically human.

Phillip Stevens, Jr.

See also Prayer; Sorcery; Wicca; Witchcraft

Further Reading

Douglas, M. (1966). *Purity and danger. An analysis of the concepts of pollution and taboo*. London: Routledge and Kegan Paul.

Durkheim, E. (1915). *The elementary forms of the religious life* (J. W. Swain, Trans.). New York: George Allen & Unwin. (Original work published in French in 1912)

Frazer, J. G. (1911–1915). *The golden bough: Vol. I, Part I. The magic art and the evolution of kings* (3rd edition). London: Macmillan.

Hand, W. D. (1980). *Magical medicine*. Berkeley: University of California Press.

Iacobani, M., Koski, L. M., Bras, M., Bekkering, H., Woods, R. P., Dubeau, M. C., Mazziotta, J. C., & Rizzolatti, G. (2001). Reafferent copies of imitated actions in the right superior temporal cortex. *Proceedings of the National Academy of Sciences*, 98(24), 13995–13999.

Iacoboni, M., Woods, R. P., Brass, M., Bekkering, H., Mazziotta, J. C., & Rizzolatti, G. (1999). Cortical mechanisms of human imitation. *Science*, 286, 2526–2528.

Malinowski, B. (1935). *Coral gardens and their magic* (Vols. 1–2). London: George Allen & Unwin.

Mauss, M. (1972). *A general theory of magic* (R. Brain, Trans.). London: Routledge & Kegan Paul. (Original work published in French with Henri Hubert, 1902–1903).

O'Keefe, D. L. (1982). *Stolen lightning: The social theory of magic*. New York: Vintage Books.

Stevens, P., Jr. (2001). Magical thinking in complementary and alternative medicine. *The Skeptical Inquirer*, 25(6), 32–37.

Mardi Gras

Mardi Gras, whose name is taken from the French words for "Fat Tuesday," is also known as "Carnival" and is the final day of the season of Carnival. Rendered from a variety of Latin forms (*carnelevarium, caro vale,* or *carnem levare*), the word *carnival* essentially means "to get rid of flesh meat." At least one source departs from this common understanding of *carnival* and traces it to the words *carrus navalis* (cart of the sea) (*Ecologist* 2002, 61), thereby drawing references to the festive floats of Carnival as well as to the pre-Christian roots of Carnival celebrations. Mardi Gras is also known as "Shrove Tuesday" from the past tense of *shrive,* an Anglo-Saxon word meaning "to confess, to ask forgiveness of sins." Finally, the German words *fasching* and *fastnachtsdienstag* correspond to carnival and Shrove Tuesday respectively. The notions of indulging, not eating meat, and confessing point to the season after Mardi Gras: the annual Christian observance of Lent, which is a period of fasting, prayer, and penitence lasting forty days.

Dates

Mardi Gras is always the day before Ash Wednesday. The date is determined by the date of Easter. For Western Christianity, Easter is the first Sunday after the first full moon occurring on or after the vernal equinox. In many places of the world, however, Mardi Gras implies not only the Tuesday before Ash Wednesday but also an entire season of Carnival that can begin as early as 6 January after the Feast of Epiphany.

Contexts

Mardi Gras celebrations have antecedents in pre-Christian pagan customs tied to the changing seasons, the coming of spring, and New Year's festivals. A sixth-century Athenian tribute to Dionysus (the Greek god of wine) involved the first float, and carnivals developed with Roman festivals such as the Bacchanalia. Such ancient festivities celebrated fertility and the expectation of plenty with the new spring.

Christianity transformed these popular rites of spring into pre-Lenten events because they were inappropriate for the spiritual and physical asceticism (strict self-denial as a measure of spiritual discipline) of Lent. Further, on a practical level, ritualizing the consumption of forbidden foods prior to Ash Wednesday—early on meat, fish, eggs, cheese, butter, milk, and alcohol were forbidden during Lent—prevented food from going to waste in an age before refrigeration. The festive atmosphere of "clearing the shelves" with family and friends helped to give rise to

Mardi Gras celebrations. The elements of excess common to Mardi Gras celebrations echo their ancient pagan antecedents but also provide a counterpoint to the deprivations of Lent. Christians, however, understand that the true celebration of excess comes only after the preparation of prayer and Lent that culminates in Easter Sunday's celebration of God's saving love.

Meanings

Two theses are frequently used to generalize the meaning of Mardi Gras, whether medieval or modern, in New Orleans or Venice: the subversion thesis and the containment or safety-valve thesis. The subversion thesis contends that Carnival has the ability to bend, challenge, or even temporarily nullify the sociopolitical structures of a city or religious community. Cross-dressing and role inversion are traditional manifestations of such behavior. The medieval Feast of Fools associated with the Church's observance of the Circumcision or the Epiphany offers a prime example of such behavior. Gladman's Riding represents an example of an extreme form of the subversion thesis. In 1443 in Norwich, England, local merchant John Gladman dressed as the king and rode into the city with a group of armed men dressed as his courtiers. Gladman powerfully conveyed a message to the local authorities through role inversion. The containment thesis focuses on the temporary and seasonal nature of Carnival and argues that ritualized subversive behavior is a safe and legal way to sublimate dissatisfaction with one's sociopolitical status and powerlessness; it is a safety valve that does not pose a threat to power structures.

Scholarship at the end of the twentieth century is beginning to challenge these two theses as a somewhat facile approach that misses the deeper meanings and individual contexts of distinct local Mardi Gras customs. Further, at least one ethnological (cultural) study seriously challenges the subversion explanation of Mardi Gras and repudiates the idea that the U.S. Carnival showcases excessively inappropriate and lewd public behavior.

A variation of the choice between subversion and containment theses describes Mardi Gras celebrations as demonstrating differences within wholeness. In other words, Carnival can be used both to highlight and diffuse opposite and competing segments of society and to bring those segments into a whole, albeit one of creative tension. Finally, some Christian scholars argue that the laughter of Mardi Gras is theologically necessary as part of a measured balance with work and prayer and as a symbol of the social inversion represented in Jesus's life and parables.

Around the World

Celebrations of Mardi Gras are held around the world: in Venice, Italy; Nice, France; Rio de Janeiro, Brazil; and New Orleans. Each city has websites detailing its Mardi Gras balls, parades, and other events. Although these cities arguably sponsor the most famous Carnival seasons, theirs are by no means the only major celebrations. Sydney, Australia, for example, is gaining notoriety for its Gay and Lesbian Mardi Gras. In fact, a casual search of the World Wide Web using the key words "Mardi Gras" produced almost a half-million hits. This number points to the popularity and diversity of Mardi Gras celebrations around the world. Many Mardi Gras celebrations have become important tourist attractions and therefore have less to do with religious preparation and Lent than with the strength of the local economy. The enthusiasm for Carnival generated by the development of Mardi Gras has, in fact, spawned Carnival celebrations that are not at all connected by the calendar to Ash Wednesday.

Customs

The variations among Mardi Gras celebrations are vast and have to do with climatic, regional, ethnic, and national differences. Some traditions originated with the practical concerns of Lent in mind. Thus, the need to consume butter, eggs, and milk resulted in the creation of pancakes, a treat in medieval England. Medieval English festivities included pancake races, football games, morris dancing (a form of folk-dance involving complicated steps, bells, and scarves which originated with the Moors of Spain but was widely developed in England), mumming (a type of festive folk-theater that featured the death and resurrection of one of the characters and masked actors; it has antecedents in the medieval sword dance and the themes of mumming are connected to the rebirth of the earth after winter), and racing in large groups to the churches.

The basic elements of food and drink, dance and drama, costume and disguise, games and performer-spectator interaction remain the staples of Mardi Gras throughout an overwhelming array of national and regional differences. New Orleans is an example of how intense differences can be within even a single region. The vast parades of New Orleans are a specifically urban Mardi Gras. The rural areas of southwestern Louisiana provide a very different Mardi Gras experience.

Elena G. Procario-Foley

See also Catholicism; Easter; Humor and Rituals; Inversion, Rites of; Music; Performance, Ritual of

Further Reading

Gulevich, T. (2001). *Encyclopedia of Easter, Carnival, and Lent*. Detroit, MI: Omnigraphics.

Huber, L. V. (1989). *Mardi Gras: A pictorial history of Carnival in New Orleans*. New York: Pelican.

Humphrey, C. (2001). *The politics of Carnival: Festive misrule in medieval England*. New York: Manchester University Press.

Kinser, S. (1990). *Carnival, American style: Mardi Gras at New Orleans and Mobile*. Chicago: University of Chicago Press.

Lindahl, C. (Ed.). (2001, Spring). *Journal of American Folklore, 114*(452).

Ludwig, J. B. (1976). *The great American spectacles: The Kentucky Derby, Mardi Gras and other days of celebration*. New York: Doubleday.

Martin, C. (1999). Carnival: A theology of laughter and a ritual for social change. *Worship, 73*(1), 43–55.

Santino, J. (1994). *All around the year: Holidays and celebrations in American life*. Urbana: University of Illinois Press.

Yancey, P. (1993, April). From Carnival to Mardi Gras. *Christianity Today, 37*(26), 64.

Marriage Rituals

Marriage perhaps involves rituals more elaborate than those of any other life event in most cultures. The bewildering variety of such rituals makes generalizations difficult, but placing the rituals in their larger cultural context shows some similar features in their functions and symbolisms. Because in preindustrial cultures religion covers all spheres of life, most marriage rituals there place the sexual and economic aspects of marriage also in a religious context, celebrated and perpetuated by ritual practices.

Marriage is a universal institution, but defining it adequately presents a challenge. One authoritative definition focuses on perhaps the most common characteristic—children: "Marriage is a union between a man and a woman such that children born to the woman are recognized legitimate offspring of both parents" (Royal Anthropological Institute 1951, 110). Other definitions generally emphasize that the marital union is socially and legally recognized and establishes a family as a social unit that regulates sexual activity, produces and raises children, implies some reciprocal rights between the spouses and between them and their offspring, and constitutes a basic economic unit. In short, marriage could be seen as a set of rights that gives access to the spouse's sexuality, labor, and property, although not all of these aspects are necessarily present in all marriages.

Anthropological literature on rituals places marriage in the category of life crises because it marks a transition from one phase of life to another. Indeed, in many cultures it is the most important rite of passage into adulthood. In most cases it is a happy occasion, celebrated universally by music, dance, food, and drink. In India a flute starts playing early in the morning a day or two before the wedding day, and continues for two or three days, changing tunes at appropriate times, and people sing specially composed songs. In a Zapotec (ancient Mesoamerican civilization) wedding ritual in Mexico a band of musicians plays from early morning on the wedding day throughout the ceremonies, which last until early next morning. Special messengers invite key people to the wedding, people hold processions between the bride's and the groom's house, the village president's house, the godfather's house, and the church; people eat four special meals, and two men stage "the dance of the turkey," each holding a turkey by its wings (with its feet on the floor) and dancing from the patio to a village-road intersection, joined by two women carrying baskets. There are fireworks, candles, gifts, and candies and cookies.

Elaborate rituals are typical in traditional, preindustrial societies that practice arranged marriage and that establish large kinship groups as major economic and political units. Modernization tends to increase secularization and correspondingly to decrease the ritualistic dimensions of the marriage event. Symbolically, however, even in Western societies vestiges of rituals connected with ancient customs remain, such as asking for the prospective bride's hand and giving away the bride.

LOVE MAGIC

The use of magical means to win the affection of a man or woman is common across cultures. The following is an extreme example of a magical technique used by desperate men in Central Thailand.

The use of dangerously polluted material in love magic occurs when a man resorts to the strongest magical means known to ensure the love of a woman. It entails putting but a single drop of *namman phraaj*, the fluid which magical practitioners extract from certain corpses, in the food of the woman. Upon swallowing the food, she will become totally enslaved to the man. This occurs only rarely, because *namman phraaj* is rare. Only a specialist with great magical powers will try to obtain the liquid from the corpse of a person who died inauspiciously, preferably from the most dangerous kind of corpse: that of a woman who died whilst pregnant or during childbirth. Reputedly, in the deep of the night the lay magical specialist approaches the place where such a corpse lies. He should grasp the dead body firmly in his arms, and extract some liquid from the skull by holding a lighted candle under the chin of the cadaver. A terrible struggle may ensue before the corpse releases some of this *namman phraaj*. The liquid is extremely dangerous, and in present times there are only a few men who are reputed to possess it. Only a desperate man will try to use it as love magic, for whilst it certainly causes a woman to be enslaved to a man, it may make her very ill at the same time. It is said that she may become mentally deranged for the rest of her life by consuming some of the liquid.

***Source*: Terweil, Barend J. (1975).**
Monks and Magic; An Analysis of Religious Ceremonies in Central Thailand.
Scandinavian Institute of Asian Studies, Monograph Series, 24. Lund, Studentlitteratur; London: Curzon Press, p. 144.

Rituals Leading to Marriage

Rituals of marriage begin long before the actual wedding ceremonies. Whether the bride and groom fall in love or someone makes the match, meeting involves ritual. Dress, makeup, hairstyles, ornaments, and other efforts to enhance personal appearance are often ritualistic efforts to attract the opposite sex, as are flirtations of various kinds. Young men in the Trobriand Islands of the southwest Pacific Ocean may decorate themselves with Johnson's Baby Powder, and girls like to put flowers in their hair or a garland around their neck. Nuer youth around Sudan in Africa attend dances and afterward sit in the tall grass around the dancing ground and exchange endearments, the young men flattering their girlfriends, who are "decked with flowers and ornaments and anointed with oil for dancing" (Evans-Pritchard 1951, 52). In another context a Nuer young man leaps behind his oxen to show his masculinity and chants poems to the girl, especially if he is interested in marrying her. Courtship may not lead to marriage—most young people have several such relationships—but it is recognized as a prelude to marriage. Parents have a final say to approve the marriage, and usually no objection is voiced if the man owns cattle.

Arranged marriage is sometimes characterized as parents choosing a set of in-laws. The attention is not as much on the feelings of the prospective marital partners as on the kin network that is established or that has to be maintained by the impending marriage.

The matchmaker is most often the father of the bride or of the groom (often at the prompting of the mother), a maternal uncle, or some other trusted person—often a Brahman (a Hindu of the highest caste traditionally assigned to the priesthood) or a barber in traditional Indian cultures. The transaction begins with negotiations between the parents. The young people may or may not know one another or meet at this stage. In one tradition in Upper Egypt, a potential mother-in-law comes to the house of the bride-to-be to assess her suitability. Love marriage is considered irrational and therefore suspect, although young

A Jewish bride and groom dance the hora—a traditional Israeli folk dance—with friends and family at their wedding reception. COURTESY OF MARCY ROSS.

people increasingly meet at universities or work places, fall in love, and demand and get their way.

In the warrior culture of the Sambia of Papua New Guinea an ideal warrior—one who ideally has killed another human—captures a woman, steals a wife from the enemy tribe. For the !Kung of the Kalahari Desert of South Africa, however, killing two large animals suffices to define a man as an adult who is ready to marry. The man asks his parents to arrange a marriage. He may be ten years older than his prospective bride, most likely a teenager. The girl's parents also stress the demonstrated hunting ability of their prospective son-in-law because the hunter whose poisoned arrow hits the animal first receives the hide, which is used to make pubic coverings for both men and women.

In the !Kung society and in many others, furthermore, parents may arrange a son's marriage during infancy—sometimes before the prospective bride is born. The marriage is then consummated and celebrated when the spouses come of age. This custom usually occurs in societies in which cousin marriage is considered ideal; it ensures that the wealth stays in the extended family.

Premarriage Rituals

Courtship customs (or their absence, e.g., seclusion of the sexes practiced in some Islamic societies) have a ritualistic character, but a series of more specific rituals usually starts when the relatives have agreed to the marriage. The first stage is the formal betrothal. In a Yoruba community in Nigeria, representatives

An American bride and groom in traditional wedding attire perform a Celtic hand-wrapping ceremony as part of their marriage ritual in 2001. COURTESY OF BECCI SEARLE-SCHRADER.

of the man's lineage gather at the compound of the woman's lineage. They offer kola (a beverage made from the seed of the kola tree) and other refreshments, perhaps even some money. The woman's representatives share these to show their acceptance of the betrothal. In Christian betrothals there, the man presents his fiancée with a Bible and a gold wedding band. This custom is not much different from a U.S. engagement in which the man presents a ring to his prospective fiancée as he proposes to her. In Africa, however, the man does not kneel in front of the woman, as is the idealized custom in the United States.

A bridal shower is a special prenuptial tradition in the United States. A close friend or relative invites a group of friends together as a surprise to the bride. The friends gather in an informal atmosphere in someone's home and "shower" the bride with small personal or household items that she will need as a married woman. This custom has both functional and symbolic meanings as the woman is about to enter a new phase in life. Games played during the evening often symbolize the bride's fertility and future reproductive role. The groom's friends organize a sometimes rowdy bachelor party that symbolizes the end of the groom's freedom, independence, and responsibility solely for himself. Lately, both the prospective bride and groom may attend the wedding shower, and some women organize bachelorette parties for the bride.

The Yoruba betrothal marks the transfer of rights to the woman and the beginning of a series of obligations between the two lineages. The man now calls the woman his wife and has sexual relations with her. He also presents gifts of agricultural produce or money to her father or helps in some labor each year until the woman moves to her husband's home. This phase takes place when the bridewealth (wealth transferred from the groom's family and kin to the bride's family) is completely paid off. The ceremony marking this point in the process is also celebrated with gifts and refreshments.

Tying the Knot

Marriage is a contract in most cultures, defined by either tribal laws or the laws of modern nation-states and recognized by the public. A ritualistic signing of the contract in the presence of witnesses and/or religious or civil authorities is part of most wedding ceremonies. In a temple wedding in India the officiating Brahman fills out the temple marriage register that has been signed by the groom and witnessed by at least one other important person, such as a village president.

Common expressions such as "tying the knot" illustrate the solidity and permanence of this contract, and the exchange of rings in Western cultures becomes a physical symbol of the bond. Historical records show that even in clandestine marriages in medieval England that were performed without clergy, some ritual was involved, including witnesses, gifts, and sometimes a wedding ring. Church weddings involved vows, blessing of the rings, and a public ban (legal or formal prohibition) read several weeks ahead of time to preclude any objections to the marriage.

Wedding ceremonies generally include a public declaration that confers a new status to the spouses as mature adults. The officiating clergy declares the couple as husband and wife by "the authority vested in me" by the state, witnesses must sign the contract, wedding bells ring, and pictures may be printed in the newspaper to mark the event. Thus, even in religious ceremonies there is a secular authorization by the state, and the public is given a chance to voice its objections if necessary. "To *be* marriage, the institution requires public affirmation" (Cott 2000, 1).

The degree of formality in marriage contracts and associated ceremonies, however, ranges from none at all among the Inuit of northern Alaska and Western cohabiting couples to several days of transactions and celebrations among people in many parts of the world, such as Mexico, the Middle East, Asia, and Africa. The Nuer carry out an official, public marriage ritual in three basic stages that are spread over several months—the betrothal, the wedding, and the consummation—and some additional ceremonies complete the marriage contract years later. In many preindustrial societies marriage involves a long process.

Symbolic rituals are used to express the new unity of the couple. In many U.S. weddings the bride and groom together light a unity candle. *Tali*-tying is a common ritual in India, and in some ceremonies the bride's father ties the couple's right hands together with a scarf. In a Tamil Brahman wedding seven steps taken by the couple around a sacrificial fire make the marriage binding, although other ceremonies take place as well. This symbolism apparently is more prevalent in cultures that emphasize marital unity—or where the law dictates what a marriage is; many other cultures focus more on alliances among and between kin groups than on the special relationship between the spouses.

Symbolic or Unusual Marriages

Symbolic marriages extend the meaning of marriage beyond the usual union between a living man and a living woman. The Nuer practice a "ghost marriage" in which a male kinsman marries a woman in the name of a man who died before having any heirs, and the bride is thus legally the ghost's bride. In northern Japan a memorial practice of a "bride-doll marriage" emerged during World War II in which the soul of someone who has died before being married—represented by the dead person's picture in a glass box—is married to a spirit spouse embodied in a consecrated figurine in the same box, a doll "which is believed to have been animated with the miraculous power of Jizo, a prominent Buddhist Bodhisattva [deity]." The "couple" is enshrined in the temple from five to thirty years, during which "Jizo is believed to guide the dead person, stranded between worlds, toward successful rebirth and eventual salvation" (Schattschneider 2001, 854).

Another example of a symbolic marriage is a token prepuberty marriage in central India in which a physically immature girl is "married" to an object such as an arrow from a tribal group or a wooden rice-pounder. One of her male relatives acts on behalf of the object, and the event is celebrated for two days with ceremonies that involve all other rituals except gifts. The girl will later have a regular marriage, but not going through the ceremony before puberty makes the girl permanently unclean.

The Nuer also practice a form of marriage in which one woman marries another. The marriage rituals are the same as in a regular marriage, but the woman-husband gets a male kinsman or friend to beget children on her behalf and to assist in some chores. The woman who chooses to marry this way is usually barren and counts as a man; she may even marry several wives if she is rich, and her children address her as "father." This is not the same as a homophilic marriage, a same-sex marriage, legalized so far only in Denmark, Greenland, Sweden, and Norway.

Rituals Relating to Sexuality and Fertility

Sexuality is present in most marriages throughout the world, and the marriage bed is sometimes decorated for the wedding night, although in some cultures the couple are not supposed to engage in sexual relations the first night, or even for a while. Indian marriages employ a ritual bath for purification of both bride and groom, and they change into new clothing for the rest of the ceremony.

Although the bride's femininity is usually emphasized in the marriage context, curiously in some cultures the bride must become masculine at least for part of the ceremony. In an old Tamil Brahman tradition on the fourth day of the wedding the bride was dressed up as a boy and made to speak to the bridegroom somewhat rudely. Sambia grooms first see their brides in a group ritual. The brides are dressed in bark capes and lie flat, their faces on the ground, while the grooms, in full warrior garb, stand stiff and cast their stony faced gazes to the sky. Looking at the women's faces would contaminate them and show their inner panic. They have been isolated in young men's clubhouses, engaged in prescribed homosexual activities, so marriage with its heterosexual contact is a new and scary experience; it takes some time before the marriage is consummated. To make the transition easier, the bride's dress is similar to that of the boy initiates in the clubhouse. When the groom finally has sex with his wife—after her menarche (the onset of menstruation) ceremony—he must perform a nose-bleeding after each menses of his wife to purify himself of the pollution created by having sex with a woman.

Sexuality is also part of the requirement in Islamic and Christian cultures that the bride be a virgin. Among the Kanuri people in northeastern Nigeria, virginity of the bride is the ideal; a virgin bride is considered prestigious and commands a high price, thus girls often have to marry older men who can afford them. In most societies a double-standard allows a man to have premarital or extramarital sex, but the woman must be a virgin at marriage and faithful to her husband afterward. Sambia men normally continue their homosexual relations for some time, but the birth of the first child confers a full status to men as fathers and requires them to settle down. Thus, marriage and the onset of fatherhood constitute final rites of passage into manhood.

Symbols of fertility are part of marriage rituals everywhere. A bridal couple in the United States is often showered with rice—or lately bird seeds—as a symbol of fertility.

In India bamboo is considered such a symbol, so the wedding canopy is supported by bamboo poles, and a mango twist is tied together with the bamboo pole because mango, too, is associated with marriage and fertility. In many societies marriage is simply a continuation of the sexuality and fertility rituals that begin with puberty rites. These rites are society's attempt to control sexual relations. It is in the society's interest to channel sexuality toward reproduction.

Economic Rituals

Marriage is everywhere also an economic transaction, and this aspect is observed ritually in many societies, especially those in which the kinship group is a major economic and political unit. Arranged marriage is the norm in such societies, and marriage negotiations between the two sets of kin focus on the financial aspects of the deal, often with mutual suspicion until understanding has been reached. Bargaining may continue even into the wedding festivities.

The best-known economic customs relating to marriage are dowry and bridewealth. Dowry is given to the woman from her parents as an advance on her inheritance, and it is hers, although often administered by her husband. In case of divorce, she will take it with her. It establishes a conjugal fund. Dowry is most common in Asia and some European countries and generally in agricultural or pastoral societies. It reflects the status of the woman at marriage, and a good dowry can gain a desirable husband.

Bridewealth, on the other hand, is paid to the bride's family, in part to compensate it for the loss of a worker. Among the Nuer ideal bridewealth is forty cows, to be paid in installments, but few can afford such a high price. Bridewealth is often referred to as "brideprice," but that term may be misleading because most societies resent the idea that the woman is purchased. It is rather a form of circulating the wealth; the bride's brother can then pay his bridewealth at his marriage.

Bridewealth is more common in Africa, where most societies practice it. Dowry and bridewealth, however, need not be mutually exclusive; a combination is often used. The ritualistic part of these arrangements involves visits and negotiations between the two sets of kin and sometimes special displays of the items.

Other economic aspects of marriage include marrying within one's own social class—a concern for the rich even in Western societies to keep the wealth in the family. Cousin marriages in many societies, such as the Fulani in Africa, not only strengthen family ties but also solve the problem if the family has difficulty coming up with bridewealth. Research has shown that marriage between relatives is more frequent when there is scarcity of cattle; bridewealth demands appear to be reduced with close-kin marriage. It is also worth noting that in societies where polygyny is legal (one man with two or more wives), it is not practiced very widely because few men can afford several wives. As to wedding ceremonies, they are most elaborate with the first marriage; subsequent marriages may take place fairly quietly.

Marriage Rituals in Times of Change

Marriage represents the launching of the most universal institution—the family. The rituals by which marriage is celebrated are as diverse as the cultures of which they are a part, but in various ways they all celebrate and strengthen the couple's unity and kin network. By their religious dimension they help reinforce the meaning of the event.

Old rituals are in danger of being gradually eliminated as more and more people around the globe emulate Western ways. At the same time, however, there is a new appreciation of tradition, and many people—especially in the diasporas (scatterings of people)—seek to employ their native rituals in the celebration of life events, whereas others create new rituals and traditions. Wedding ceremonies are a rich part of cultural heritage and help establish the new family entity on a firm cultural footing. With increasing geographical mobility, change, and globalization, rituals give a sense of permanence and continuity that can provide a feeling of security and stability in times of social change.

Sara Kärkkäinen Terian

See also Gender Rituals; Passage, Rites of

Further Reading

Boodhoo, S. (1993). *Kanya dan: The why's of Hindu marriage rituals.* Singapore: Mauritius Bhojpuri Institute.

Burch, E. S. (1970). Marriage and divorce among the north Alaska Eskimos. In P. Bohannan (Ed.), *Divorce and after*. Garden City, NY: Doubleday.

Cohen, R. (1970). Brittle marriage as a stable system: The Kanuri case. In P. Bohannan (Ed.), *Divorce and after*. Garden City, NY: Doubleday.

Cott, N. (2000). *Public vows: A history of marriage and the nation.* Cambridge, MA: Harvard University Press.

Douglass, L. (1992). *The power of sentiment: Love, hierarchy, and the Jamaican family elite.* Boulder, CO: Westview Press.

El Guindi, F., & Hernandez Jimenez, A. (1986). *The myth of ritual: A native ethnography of Zapotec life-crisis rituals.* Tucson: University of Arizona Press.

Evans-Prichard, E. E. (1951). *Kinship and marriage among the Nuer.* New York: Oxford University Press.

Fried, M., & Fried, M. H. (1980). *Transitions: Four rituals in eight cultures.* New York: W. W. Norton.

Good, A. (1991). *The female bridegroom: A comparative study of life-crisis rituals in south India and Sri Lanka.* New York: Oxford University Press.

Goody, J. (1973). Bridewealth and dowry in Africa and Eurasia. In J. Goody & S. J. Tambiah, *Bridewealth and dowry.* Cambridge, UK: Cambridge University Press.

Goody, J., & Tambiah, S. J. (1973). *Bridewealth and dowry* (Cambridge Papers in Social Anthropology No. 7). London: Cambridge University Press.

Gough, K. (1959). The Nayars and the definition of marriage. *Journal of the Royal Anthropological Institute, 89,* 23–34.

Hampshire, K. R., & Smith, M. T. (2001). Consanguineous marriage among the Fulani. *Human Biology, 73*(4), 597–603.

Hanawalt, B. A. (1986). *The ties that bound: Peasant families in medieval England.* New York: Oxford University Press.

Herdt, G. (1987). *The Sambia: Ritual and gender in New Guinea.* Fort Worth, TX: Holt, Rinehart and Winston.

Kensinger, K. M. (Ed.). (1984). *Marriage practices in lowland South America.* Chicago: University of Illinois Press.

Malinowski, B. (1929). *The sexual life of savages in north-western Melanesia.* New York: Halcyon House.

Mann, K. (1985). *Marrying well: Marriage, status and social change among the educated elite in colonial Lagos.* New York: Cambridge University Press.

Pasternak, B. (1983). *Guests in the dragon: Social demography of a Chinese district 1895–1946.* New York: Columbia University Press.

Roy, B. (1984). *Marriage rituals and songs of Bengal.* Calcutta, India: Firma KLM Private.

Royal Anthropological Institute of Great Britain and Ireland. (1951). *Notes and queries on anthropology* (6th rev. ed.). London: Routledge and Kegan Paul.

Rugh, A. B. (1984). *Family in contemporary Egypt.* Syracuse, NY: Syracuse University Press.

Schattschneider, E. (2001). "Buy me a bride": Death and exchange in northern Japanese bride-doll marriage. *American Ethnologist, 28*(4), 854–880.

Singh, K. (1993). Foreword. In S. Boodhoo, *Kanya dan: The why's of Hindu marriage rituals.* Singapore: Mauritius Bhojpuri Institute.

Stone, L. (1979). *The family, sex and marriage: In England 1500–1800* (Abr. ed.). New York: Harper and Row.

Tambiah, S. J. (1973). Dowry and bridewealth and the property rights of women in South Asia. In J. Goody & S. J. Tambiah (Eds.), *Bridewealth and dowry.* London: Cambridge University Press.

Martial Arts

Martial arts include a wide range of practices from many Asian countries and religious traditions. They range from Chinese *wushu* (sometimes inaccurately called "kung fu") to Korean tae kwon do and a variety of Japanese arts: karate, aikido, kendo, *iaido, naginata,* and judo. Almost all martial arts are connected with some religious or spiritual belief system, although their origins also lie in the practical need that people had to defend themselves without weapons.

The popularity of martial arts in the West seems to wax and wane depending on the current crop of action films and television shows. Some have become more like Western sports, with competitions, rankings, and scoring systems, whereas the appeal of others is the way they combine physical training with a more traditional focus on social, philosophical, and spiritual development. Some, such as *iaido,* a Japanese martial art using swords, are practiced by a relatively few skilled people. Others, such as karate and tae kwon do, are popular with schoolchildren and with women for self-defense.

The ancient origins of martial arts are thought to lie in religious combat rituals, imitating the gods who were able, according to myth, to triumph without weapons. Early styles in Japan were associated with the Japanese religion Shintoism and with Mikkyo, an esoteric form of Buddhism, and some forms of Chinese *wushu* are categorized as Daoist/Buddhist. Many martial arts developed within the confines of temples, which were places of refuge during the troubled periods when martial arts tended to develop most quickly. The temple of Shaolin, in China, for example, became a sort of university where martial arts experts lived together, shared their knowledge, and trained their students.

One aspect of the development of modern "sport" forms of traditional martial arts is the desire to eliminate the spiritual or mystical elements. This transformation—sometimes referred to as "sportification"—is intended to make martial arts more like Western sports, in which competing and winning are the only goals. For example, the idea of *chi* or *ki* (universal energy or breath concentrated in a person's center) is basic to martial arts practice. This idea can be translated into physiological terms as the center of gravity, but in traditional practice *ki* is far more than a physical spot or force, and the *ai* in *aikido* can be translated as "harmony" or "love."

Self-mastery and self-knowledge are important goals in martial arts practice, and the student is guided in a variety of ways in personal development as well as physical training. The practice of *zazen,* the basic seated meditation of Zen Buddhism, has been incorporated into a number of modern martial arts because it can easily be used out of context, without any demand on the student for a particular religious affiliation.

The practice of martial arts contains a variety of ritual elements. In aikido, the *dojo* (practice room) includes an altar with a photograph of the founder, Ueshiba Morihei (1883–1969), a scroll with calligraphy, and fresh flowers. Students bow to their instructor, to the photograph, and to one another, and in many clubs clap two or four times at the beginning and end of the session. This clapping is a traditional way of warding off evil spirits.

Some gestures in *naginata* have no practical martial arts purpose but are instead intended to ward off evil spirits and direct their force to the attacker or to offer prayers to the dead.

In tae kwon do, a Korean martial art that is also an Olympic sport, sessions typically begin and end with a few minutes of meditation, a lecture on good conduct (rather like a sermon), and the recitation of an oath. Here is an example:

> Tae Kwon Do Oath
> I shall observe the tenets of tae kwon do.
> I shall respect the instructors and seniors.
> I shall never misuse tae kwon do.
> I shall be a champion of freedom and justice.
> I shall build a more peaceful world. (*Christensen & Levinson 1996, 1006*)

Even the clothing worn in martial arts connects them to their traditional religious roots. Unlike clothing in modern Western sports, which changes over time to provide greater protection or improved performance, most martial arts clothing is traditional, often beautiful, and may appear heavy and impractical. In a number of martial arts, for example, training is done in a cotton jacket and pants with a heavy divided skirt, the *hakama,* on top. The traditional clothing offers protection but might be said to be, at root, more like the traditional dress of the Amish than like that worn by competitive runners or rugby players.

Physical activities have often had strong religious significance—among the ancient Greeks, for example. The religious significance of traditional martial arts and their focus on mind-body interaction appeals to many participants and gives these forms of physical activity a depth and a complexity that provide both physical and mental benefits.

Karen Christensen

See also Sport and Ritual

Further Reading

Donohue, J. (1994). *Warrior dreams: The martial arts and the American imagination*. Westport, CT: Bergin and Garvey.

Muromoto, W. (1999). Mudra in the martial arts. Retrieved June 23, 2003, from http://www.furyu.com/onlinearticles/mudra.html

Melanesia

Melanesia has no traditional religion and no series of common rituals regulated by a liturgical (relating to rites prescribed for public worship) calendar. This region of the southwestern Pacific Ocean is culturally and linguistically one of the most diverse on Earth—according to some authorities it is home to one-half of the world's cultures. This variety is reflected in the region's wide range of cosmologies (branches of metaphysics that deal with the nature of the universe), belief systems, and associated ritual practices. Even people who speak the same language may vary in the rites they follow; indeed, these rites may vary in the same community from one occasion to another. Melanesians show a fascination for new ritual forms, and rapid fashion changes have characterized their practices with the arrival of new cults and the demise of old ones, evidenced most dramatically during the past century or so by their rapid embrace of Christianity.

Spirits of the Dead and Forest Spirit Rites

Melanesia's teeming cultural diversity notwithstanding, there are ritual themes common to large parts of the region. A common class of rites relates to beliefs that the spirits of deceased relatives, both the recently dead and the long dead, may intervene, for good or bad, in the lives of human beings. People attempt to manipulate or control these spirits through rites and observances. The spirits can strike from the invisible plane on which they exist, causing people to fall ill and sometimes die. The spirits all too regularly assault the living without any cause, as the frequent occurrence of sickness and occasional death in any community demonstrate. Such sickness frequently triggers the performance of rites to appease these spirits. Although these rites vary widely in their form, they commonly feature an offering—often of food—to the spirits, and occasionally an animal, maybe a valuable pig, is slaughtered. People often believe that such spirits frequent certain places. So people may erect shrines at those places for the spirits to occupy and then perform rites for the spirits. Sometimes these shrines contain relics, such as the skulls of deceased kin or supernatural stone objects, which people manipulate during rituals, such as smearing them with blood. The mortuary rites that attend the disposal of a corpse, which often comprise a long, drawn-out series, also aim to placate the spirits of the recently dead, which many people believe to be

A community mission church in the West Sepik Province of Papua New Guinea. At one time the rituals of the church differed across regions but now have become increasingly blended as the churches have come under Melanesian control. COURTESY OF PAUL SILLITOE.

particularly virulent and dangerous. A funeral is a hazardous time for all and may feature rites to drive the new spirit away with exhortations not to harm its living relatives. These rites may appear perfunctory compared to those of some other religious traditions. Other spirits may also attack the living and cause sickness and death. A common class is forest spirits: malicious ghouls thought to inhabit remote locales. The rituals performed to exorcize these spirits are often similar to those performed to cure persons attacked by the spirits of the dead.

Success Rites

On other occasions Melanesians may call on the spirits of the dead or other supernatural forces to promote success in some venture. People commonly perform small rites in gardens at key stages during their cultivation, such as when planting crops, to encourage a good harvest. Similarly, when hunting or fishing, particularly if going after elusive or dangerous quarry such as shark or dugong (an aquatic mammal), men may perform small rites over traps on the beach. When making things, especially those that feature complex technological processes or those associated with hazardous activities, people may engage in rites to ensure success. Coastal communities, for example, commonly perform rituals when building and launching oceangoing outrigger canoes to ensure the safety of those who sail in them. In the Balim Valley of central New Guinea men perform a ritual when they erect a 10-meter (33.33 feet) high defensive watchtower overlooking enemy territory, placing a miniature bow and arrows at the base and calling on the spirits of the dead to ensure its effectiveness. The exchange of wealth is another context when people are frequently eager to exert some degree of control. On important social occasions throughout Melanesia people exchange valuables such as seashells, pigs, and cash, including bridewealth at marriages and mortuary payments at funerals. They are eager to exercise some direction over these sociopolitical events, success in which commonly determines social status. They may make a small offering at a shrine to the spirits of the dead.

Sorcery and Witchcraft Rituals

Another class of rituals concerns the activities of people who resort to supernatural means to inflict illness and death on others. These activities involve rites both to cause others grief and to make better those people who are attacked. Sorcery involves the attempt to bring about sickness and death by the conscious manipulation of effects, often personal effects associated with the victim such as things that he or she has touched or owned—food leftovers, hair clippings, and so forth. Again the rites vary widely in their content from place to place. Someone can learn the necessary procedures and then set out to attack victims through the manipulation of the prescribed rites and spells. In some places people use toxic substances to poison their enemies; in other places they rely on the symbolic manipulation of appropriate objects, sometimes ritually mimicking the victim's ensuing agonies. Alternatively there is witchcraft, which is the result of an inborn malignant power over which those so empowered commonly have no conscious control. They may even be unaware that they possess the power. People often believe that this malignant power leaves witches when they are asleep to perpetrate its evil deeds and may take terrifying forms, such as the flying witches of the Trobriand Islanders, who breathe fire and destruction from their pubic hair. No one can learn rituals and become a witch; a person either is or is not one. However, one can learn divination rites to detect both witchcraft and sorcery attacks and perhaps even to defend people from such misfortune. One can also learn rites believed to cure the unfortunate victims of such attacks.

Large Well-Being Cults

Other rituals concern community distress and well-being, as opposed to individual distress and well-being. These rituals may seek to promote fertility and ward off disasters. These rituals are larger in scale and more dramatic, sometimes featuring the construction of large cult houses. They may seek to appease spirit forces that hold sway over large regions, such as the spirit of a red- or pale-skinned woman associated with sky-beings, which is a widespread belief in parts of the New Guinea highlands. People may perform such rituals in response to a region-wide threat or catastrophe, such as an imminent famine (e.g., triggered by an adverse El Niño climatic anomaly) or a natural disaster (e.g., a devastating tectonic event such as volcanic eruption or tidal wave). These rituals appear to be subject to rapid changes, with new cults sweeping through regions every generation, perhaps reflecting people's perception of the ineffectiveness of previous rituals to protect them against such overwhelming forces and people's search for something more effective. These rituals relate to widespread concerns throughout Melanesia about Armageddon-like threats, concerns that people have subsequently transferred to missionary-taught Christian doctrine about the day of final judgment. These large cults vary widely both between regions and, subject to fashion cycles, within regions. Dances at which people decorate themselves colorfully with paint and plumes are common, as is the slaughter of animals, largely pigs, while knowledgeable persons engage in prescribed ritual procedures, maybe hidden from view in some sanctum.

Initiation Rituals

Another class of community-wide rituals found in some regions concerns initiation, largely to mark the passage of males to adulthood. Again these rituals vary widely. Some rituals to mark this change of social status are dramatic. Adults may thoroughly frighten initiates, subjecting them to terrifying ordeals as they introduce them to sacred knowledge. Adults may beat initiates with sticks or stinging nettles, pierce their nasal septa or ear lobes to accommodate ornaments (e.g., seashells), thrust abrasive leaves into their nostrils to induce bleeding or flexible canes down their throats to cause bloody vomiting, and slash or circumcise their penises. On the Sepik River initiates are subjected to a painful operation on upturned canoes during which numerous small cuts are made on their torsos to heal as small ridges mimicking the corrugated backs of crocodiles associated with the spirit world. These rituals are associated with majestic cult houses that contain many carved objects, some sacred, such as bamboo flutes, which are introduced to the young men during the rituals. People direct the violence at others in some places, such as the extensive swamplands that extend across central southern New Guinea, where in the past, people embarked on head-hunting raids against neighbors to secure human heads, likened to seed coconuts, necessary in initiation rituals to "germinate and grow" strong young men. One reason put forward for these dramatic rituals is that they "produce" strong warriors, inculcating into young men a tolerance of physical pain and encouraging ferocious personalities, necessary in the context of their violent tribal polities. In other regions, such as that of the Ok speakers of the central mountains of New Guinea, the emphasis is on the transmission of sacred knowledge over many years, men passing through a series of stages during their lives as they acquire more knowledge; here rituals focus on smaller cult houses.

Christianity

Many Melanesians today are Christians. The region has been subjected to the evangelical attentions of missionaries since the latter part of the nineteenth century. Many communities have a small church *(lotu)* and observe Christian rituals as taught by the missionary denomination that preaches in their locale, these denominations having divided up Melanesia into areas of influence, with people worshiping according to the liturgy of Catholics, Methodists, Seventh-day Adventists, Lutherans, and so forth. The churches have increasingly come under local Melanesian control. As this happens syncretism (combining different forms) becomes progressively more evident between Christian and traditional Melanesian beliefs, such as mixing of Christian and Melanesian doctrines about the end of the world. This is particularly evident in cargo cults that coincide at several points with the Christian religion as proselytized across Melanesia, particularly in Christianity's foundation with a Son of God prophet figure, beliefs in an afterlife, paradise, and so on. There was an effervescence of millenarian (relating to a millennium) talk and activity throughout Melanesia with the approach of the third millennium CE, fueled by missionaries whose churches subscribed to similar beliefs, with people saying that in the year 2000 the world would come to a cataclysmic end with unlimited prosperity for believers.

Millenarian Cults

Cargo cults anticipate an apocalyptic millennium in the near future. They have been described as typical Melanesian religious occurrences. They predict that those who follow the specified ritual manipulations and observances will receive rewards, notably an abundance of manufactured goods, and enjoy a better material life after a supernatural intervention in the near future. The term *cargo cult* originates from the frequent use of the pidgin word *kago* by participants to describe the returns they believe their activities will bring them. *Kago* derives from the English word *cargo,* though it has a wider and uniquely Melanesian nuance. The cults are small-scale and short-lived affairs. However, similar movements may recur repeatedly in the same region, each new one rising from the remains of previous failed ones whose millennial promises came to nothing. During their brief existences cargo cults give rise to intense and furious ritual activity, which may disrupt orderly social life. They usually feature messianic leaders. These leaders play a significant role in creating cults, rising up to direct their activities, recasting what people have absorbed of European ideas (in which mission-taught Christianity usually features prominently) in the light of traditional belief and moral expectations, reinterpreting myths, and manipulating associated symbols to promulgate a highly appealing syncretic message. The ritual activities inspired and directed by these "prophets" may divert people from subsistence tasks, even forbid such tasks, and encourage the pursuit of preparations for the coming millennium. This response is understandable because they are predicting the end of the world, perhaps in a cataclysm, which makes continuing with such everyday tasks appear pointless. Out of the upheaval a new order will emerge, perhaps ushered in by the return of the participants' ancestors, with sufficient goods for all and eternal prosperity. The rituals vary widely in form. On the southern islands in the Vanuatu chain people have cleared airstrips and created an imitation control tower and bamboo landing lights like a regular aerodrome at which cargo-laden spirit aircraft could land. They have conducted military-like parades calling on the spirit of a volcano to help them and erected a series of red crosses at which people can make necessary offerings. Sometimes people revive defunct customs and stage large dances as part of their cargo cult rites.

The future probably holds further locally inspired interpretations of Christianity, rooted in southwestern Pacific Ocean culture and experience, as the people of Melanesia continue to adjust to the teachings of colonial missionaries, finding themselves living today in independent nation-states and better able to adapt what they have learned to their cultural expectations.

Paul Sillitoe

See also Taboo

Further Reading

Bateson, G. (1958). *Naven.* Stanford, CA: Stanford University Press.

Lawrence, P., & Meggitt, M. (Eds.). (1965). *Gods, ghosts and men in Melanesia. Melbourne, Australia:* Oxford University Press.

Lindstrom, L. (1993). *Cargo cult.* Honolulu: University of Hawaii Press.

Sillitoe, P. (1998). *An introduction to the anthropology of Melanesia: Culture and tradition.* Cambridge, UK: Cambridge University Press.

Sillitoe, P. (2000). *Social change in Melanesia: Development and history.* Cambridge, UK: Cambridge University Press.

Stephen, M. (Ed.). (1987). *Sorcerer and witch in Melanesia.* New Brunswick, NJ: Rutgers University Press.

Swain, T., & Trompf, G. (1995). *The religions of Oceania.* London: Routledge.

Trompf, G. W. (1991). *Melanesian religion.*Cambridge, UK: Cambridge University Press.

Tuzin, D. F. (1980). *The voice of the tambaran.* Berkeley and Los Angeles: University of California Press.

Worsley, P. (1957). *The trumpet shall sound.* London: Macgibbon & Kee.

Micronesia

Micronesia, in the Pacific Ocean east of the Philippines, has never been a unified reality linguistically or politically. In the past these islands and atolls (coral islands consisting of a reef surrounding a lagoon) were divided into geographic portions by the colonial powers. Today all—except Guam, which remains a U.S. territory—are independent nations: Commonwealth of the Marianas, Kiribati (Gilberts), Republic of the Marshall Islands, Republic of Palau, Republic of Nauru, and the Federated States of Micronesia, which includes the states of Kosrae, Pohnpei, Chuuk, and Yap and the neighboring atolls. The distance from Tobi (south of Palau) up to Guam and then southeast to Tarawa (Kiribati) is roughly 6,400 kilometers. The hundreds of populated islands are either sand or coral atolls only a few feet above sea level or "high" volcanic islands. The populations can vary from twenty-five to twenty-five thousand. The high islands with large populations have the demographic potential for elaborate ritual.

Definition and Assumptions

Ritual is acted-out belief, often with reference to the supernatural. The term *acted-out belief* needs some qualification. Belief has no priority over ritual. It may well be that a verbal explanation of religion does not exist or has been lost over time. Perhaps ritual itself articulates in action what cannot be said in words. This often seems to be the case in ritual possession and trance.

"Reference to the supernatural" is also difficult to define. It is something, somewhere, or somebody whose existence is beyond the ordinary, beyond what a Eurocentric definition might call "the empirically verifiable." Sometimes in Micronesia the natural and the supernatural get bound together in a pretty tight relationship. For example, the resetting of broken bones and associated massaging certainly have an empirical dimension, that is, did the bones heal correctly? But where is the source of the healer's power: learned through dreams given by the ancestors.

In Micronesia it is difficult to distinguish between magic and religion, among magicians, sorcerers, and priests. In the past, Micronesians recognized this blending of what early anthropologists saw as different categories. Frequently in their languages, islanders use a generic term to cover what Eurocentric thinking might term "sorcerers," "magicians," "mediums," "oracles," and "priests."

The Chuuk-speaking islands of Guam, for example, have a convenient all-embracing term for those ritually blessed by supernatural agencies: They are all *sowu* (experts, specialists, or masters). Western anthropologists struggle to distinguish the *sowu* who are priests, sorcerers, or magicians. The Yapese also had a similar all-embracing term: *tamaron*. There could be *tamaron* who performed rituals for good fishing or *tamaron* who went to the hut of pregnant women to bless and ensure their successful delivery. In short, the distinction between magician and priest—and all the in-betweens of sorcerer, doctor, healer—is largely a Western problem, not a Micronesian one.

Most of the rituals described here died out by World War I but lingered on in the remote atolls, and new data was described shortly after World War II.

Main Features

Several rituals are noteworthy: the death and mortuary ritual; healing and curing; divining using possession and trance; ritual or sacred dancing; religion in the service of the governing polity and in war; and ritual for good crops. Only Yap appears to have had a ritual calendar, determined by the priests at the shrines, but the workings of the calendar were not well remembered in 1910 when Wilhelm Mueller from the Hamburg expedition did research on Yap. On Pohnpei the priests at the old ritual centers were in some way involved in determining the calendar, but little is known of the Pohnpeian and Yap calendars

The death and mortuary ritual had a deeply religious dimension, unlike rituals pertaining to puberty

RELIGIOUS RITUALS AND ECONOMIC ACTIVITY ON TRUK (CHUUK) IN MICRONESIA

All economic activities in Truk are—or at least were until recently—surrounded by religious customs or ritual activities such as the use of magic and observation of tabu regulations. For example, men should have no sexual intercourse for two weeks prior to the planting and harvesting of *Runa*, *oni* or *ke*; they should not eat fish, turtle, or kon of any kind before going to the field to plant these three crops. The crops would be watery if these rules were not observed. A person who wishes to cut a breadfruit must call the *son mai*, i.e., a practitioner who specializes in breadfruit magic. The *son mai* prepares a magic medicine for those participating in the work. Should this be omitted the Truk believe other breadfruit trees in the community will lose their fertility. The magic which prevents such a calamity is called *safein apatapat en uan mai.*

***Source*: Hall, Edward-T., & Pelzer, Karl J. (1946). *The Economy of the Truk Islands: An Anthropological and Economic Survey.* Honolulu, HI: U.S. Commercial Company, Economic Survey, p. 62.**

and marriage. The period between death and burial (often three to four days) was described as a time when the deceased was transformed into a potentially good or helpful or harmful spirit. On Chuuk and Yap this potential for good or evil was expressed in a belief of two souls. Especially on the Chuuk-speaking islands relatives of the deceased waited for a good spirit to possess one of the assembled kin and become the oracle or medium for the group. The sign of the good spirit staying or returning was seen when a kinsperson of the deceased fell into an altered state of consciousness (trance), possessed by the spirit of the dead person.

Almost every region in Micronesia had some kind of shrine to honor the ancestors. The Kiribati (like the Chamorros of the Marianas) kept the skulls of their kin, often talking to them as though they were still alive. The Chuuk-speaking islands had miniature shrines hanging from the house rafters, many in the shape of a double-hulled canoe, although the double-hulled canoe was never seen in Micronesia, only described in some myths. From the shrine the spirit-ancestor would descend and sit on the shoulder of its chosen medium. This medium often worked his or her way into a trance state and took on the voice and gestures of the ancestor for whom the medium was "the canoe." The possessed medium could spontaneously berate the living, answer questions from the living, predict future events, or just retire into a lethargy with unrecognized mumblings.

During the funeral ritual of the Palauans, a group of senior women would gather, and one would hold a bundle of *sis* branches; when the woman holding the *sis* branches began to shake (or the *sis* without human help shook), the leading female kin would query the spirit of the deceased about the cause of death. The Palauan funeral ritual also had a patently secular purpose. If the deceased were a title holder, the title would be passed on to the next eligible kin during the period of mourning. If the senior women were not satisfied with the candidate, they withheld transfer of the title until a suitable candidate was found.

Of the many rituals performed to meet crises, warfare stands out, especially for Kiribati, Palau, and Chuuk. Chuuk warfare ritual was in the hands of the *itang*, sometimes called the "warrior-priests" (Goodenough 2002). Their main job was to plan battle strategy, invoke the power of the gods, and stimulate their followers to bravery and audacity in battle. An *itang* was no rear-echelon chaplain. An *itang* stood ahead of the first line of warriors or, if the battle were at sea, stood in the leading canoe. On land he would erect an effigy, often the corpse of a deceased enemy pierced with spears pointed at the opposing force. Standing next to the effigy, he began a chant calling on the gods to bring bravery, audacity, and victory to his troops. The ritual must have been noisy because he would chant, and at the end of each verse, all the troops would cry out the last syllable or word of the verse. Of course, the *itang* of the opponents was doing the same. In a curious paradox the *itang* could be skinned alive if captured or could stop the battle by standing between the opposing forces and saying, "stop." When the colonial German government banned warfare and demanded the surrender of rifles and ammunition, warfare ceased, and the *itang* lost their main job (why they did not revert to traditional weapons such as the spear or throwing club is curious). The *itang* are still identified in the Chuuk lagoon, but their main function now is as a repository of traditional lore and lineage histories; they are the warrior-priests turned oral historians.

However, by far the most common Micronesian rituals performed to handle life crises were healing and curing. These rituals both diagnosed the sickness and offered healing, which generally involved a combination of natural or human-made ingredients and specific chants or prayers. For the Chuukese the expert was *sowusáfey* (medicine expert). These *sowusáfey* included both local *sáfey*, still referred to in English as "local medicine," and hospital *sáfey*. To the outsider the role of *sowusáfey* might appear to be an achieved status, that is, learned. However, for the Chuukese and other Micronesians being a healer is an ascribed status because the gods or spirits have chosen this person and given him or her the physical formula of ingredients, the means of application, and the chants or prayers to accompany the ritual. In the Chuuk tradition, a spirit is behind every sickness, so a medium must first ascertain the causing spirit. A common method was divination through knots in coconut palm frond or the pattern of scattered small stones; in more serious cases, the *wáátawa* (possessed spirit-medium) was sought out and questioned. If the symptoms were well known, the *sowusáfey* might go directly to administering the medicine. Ultimately the *sowusáfey*'s knowledge and skills came from the ancestor's spirit, either in dreams to him or her directly, or were learned from kin who had received the formula in a dream or perhaps even purchased it from somebody in contact with the ancestor-spirits. The religious element of Micronesian healing is focused on where the sickness and the medicine came from: from the spirit world where one can get the skill to heal or to harm.

In reality every *sowusáfey* was also a sorcerer. The *sowusáfey* had to protect himself and his clients; hence the *sowusáfey* had a bag of dirty tricks to keep the enemy at bay (sorcery). The work of the *sowusáfey* was not a private affair between the master of medicine and the sick person. Often, after the *sáfey* had been prepared, the *sowusáfey* administered it in the presence of the family, the lineage, or, in the case of small atolls, the entire population. On Pohnpei the medicine and healing were once administered by the lower-ranking priests, who called upon the spirits while in a trancelike state and were possessed by one or more spirits. They would touch the body of the sick person to ascertain what spirit was inside causing the illness. Healing ritual was Micronesian-wide and in all probability still is. Christianity may have driven the chants underground or into a mumble of sorts, but this writer has recorded the chants that contemporary *sowusáfey* have received in a dream or through a spirit-possessed relative.

Predicting and Calculating the Chances

Much of Micronesian ritual involved predicting the future and assessing the odds of doing something. Divination is a strong theme in much ritual. The best two examples of divination by official mediums come from Chuuk and Palau. In Chuuk the *wáátawa* was the chosen kinsperson on whom the ancestor-spirit descended from the *faar* (hanging altar) and who was at the service of his or her kin. On Palau the *korong* were likewise official mediums to the chiefs. Polish ethnologist Johann Stanislaus Kubary told of how the high chief of Melekeok asked the attendant *korong* what the gods said about Kubary's safety on a planned trip through the territory of an enemy chief. Kubary even offered to the gods, via the *korong*, gifts or sacrifices of his own clothes. These, too, the *korong* said, augured well for Kubary's planned trip. The Palauan *korong* carried out their roles in a variety of circumstances. They could be at the beck and call of the chiefs, as in the Kubary case. They could set up a private practice in their own residence or a nearby hut. There the rapid chewing and spitting of the slightly narcotic betel leaf may have stimulated a trance state during which the *korong* answered the petitioner's questions directly or through the interpretations given by his wife. Moreover, some of the villages of old Palau were ruled directly by the gods—and indirectly through the leading *korong* of the village. At times the *korong* competed with the chiefs for political power; sometimes the *korong* were the power behind the secular ruler.

However, for most Micronesians divination was open to anyone as a kind of do-it-yourself ritual. It was performed to decide on the favorable time, place, and action for almost every aspect of life on the basis of palm-frond knotting. The number of knots in a sequence of palm fronds formed a code that could predict the outcome of events.

Breadfruit Ritual

Equaling the medicine expert *(sowusáfey)* in importance was the *sowuyótoomey,* the breadfruit and fish "caller." Breadfruit is an important staple throughout Micronesia, although in the west (Yap and Palau) the taro plant is more important. Curiously, little or no grand ritual is connected with taro production. However, on many islands—especially the Chuuk-speaking islands—a good breadfruit harvest meant the difference between prosperity and starvation, hence the importance of the breadfruit ritual and its ritual leader, the *sowuyótoomey* (breadfruit caller). So important was the successful *sowuyótoomey* that his body or larynx might be mummified lest he take back the breadfruit spirits to the heavenly cornucopia of the south.

Each morning and evening the *sowusáfey* went about inspecting the breadfruit trees, blowing on his conch horn, watching for natural omens of a good or bad harvest, and making medicines for those who may have offended the breadfruit spirits.

On Pulowat the breadfruit goddess was believed to take the form of the conger eel *(Hewanu),* the same symbol used for the Kosraean breadfruit goddess and the Pohnpeian goddess, Ilake. Usually these eels were sea rather than coastal or reef eels, but sometimes they come close to shore. If one were found the priest was immediately called because he could perceive the mission of the eel, that is, to tell that someone of the *sowuyótoomey*'s group would die or to tell of a good harvest. The priest could "read" the eel's intentions, so the following ceremony could be one of mourning or of rejoicing. The eel was taken to the community house and put on a platform. Aromatic wreaths were hung on the platform by women, and men stacked offerings of coconuts. Later the *sowuyótoomey* took thirty men and the sacred eel to his own dwelling, where they stayed, sequestered from women. *Hewanu* told the priest if he were satisfied with work in the field. If *Hewanu* was satisfied, the priest would wrap the eel in mats and take him to a taboo spot on Elanelap Island, where presents were piled for the departing goddess.

Dancing as Ritual

Some early missionaries took exception to the frequent dancing at festivals, noting that some of the dances were lewd and even called "coitus dances." However, some early ethnographers (culture researchers) and early missionaries realized that some dances were sacred, inspired by the ancestors, communicated through the ancestors' medium, the *wáátawa.* The short-lived nativist (relating to a policy of favoring native inhabitants as opposed to immigrants) outbreaks in the Chuuk area were marked by outbreaks of dancing. These were a highly symbolic return to the old ways, the old religions. Sometimes the dance rods of the *wáátawa* hung from the canoe house rafters, bedecked with flower wreaths; sometimes the dance rods were lined up below the *faar,*the hanging, double-hulled miniature boat (or alter) where the spirits of the ancestors dwelt when they came back to Earth.

Rituals That Legitimized the Governing Secular Structure

In early Micronesia the relationship between the secular and the sacred was close; in fact, the priest and the chief might be the same person, as in the old Pohnpeian cultic centers of Wene and Salapwuk. On Palau the *korong* sometimes became so powerful in his own right that he outranked the leading chief's priests. Some villages on Palau were said to be ruled by the gods, and in these villages the *korong* became the de facto ruler. The nativist movement on Palau, Modekgnei, was a return to the ecstatic, almost-shamanic prophecies and healing of the old *korong.*

The most visible and imposing religious structures in service of the political regime are at Pohnpei's Nan Madol and Kosrae's Lelu, which are series of platforms and walls and tombs built of prismatic basaltic beams. These are among largest megalithic ruins in the Pacific.

The ritual at Nan Madol was as impressive as its architecture. Each year the priests of Nan Madol would bring a turtle *(wehi)* to the sacred enclosure next to the royal residence (the kings there were called the "Sau-Deleurs," masters of Deleur). The priests would kill the turtle and offer the guts to the sacred eel. Portions of the guts were given to the SauDeleur (or paramount chief, also known as the Nahnmwarki) and the priests. On one occasion in the 1830s one priest was miffed because he didn't get his fair share, so he slaughtered the sacred eels. The paramount chief thereupon declared the ritual ended permanently. One might say that it was a ritual support of the ruling regime. However, the SauDeleur dynasty had vanished more than a century before the last turtle-eel ritual.

Remains of the Old Rituals

Medicine and healing appear to be the strongest remnant. The second remnant is prominent in the Chuuk regions. The ancestors are still believed to come to the living, especially young girls, take possession of them, put them into an altered state of consciousness (trance), and offer unsolicited or solicited answers to family problems. Thus, the ritual behavior of the old *wáátawa* continues but not as an openly recognized religious status.

The dance tradition continues on Yap—and not just for tourists. The men of a village, for example, may perform a dance only for their village. They dance for themselves. They may even dance portions of the Roman Catholic ritual. Other islands may be reviving the dance tradition as a tourist attraction. Yap does not need to revive anything.

Experts do not agree on the extent to which the ceremonies of the Pohnpeian Nahnmwarkis, especially in the *sakau* (or *kava,* a shrubby pepper) ritual offering, reflect a sacred tradition going back to the ancient priestly centers at Nan Madol, Salapwuk, and Wene. Moreover, that ritual has already been debased by the commercial sale of *sakau* and the introduction of *sakau* houses.

The islands and atolls of Micronesia are trying to maintain as much of the old rituals as they can.

Jay Dobbin

Further Reading

Burrows, E.G. (1963). *Flower in my ear: Arts and ethos of Ifaluk atoll* (University of Washington Publications in Anthropology No. 14). Seattle: University of Washington Press.

Burrows, E. G., & Spiro, M. E. (1957). *An atoll culture: Ethnography of Ifaluk in the central Carolines.* Westport, CT: Greenwood Press.

Craig, R. D. (Ed.). (1982). *The Palau Islands in the Pacific Ocean* (M. L. Berg, Trans.). Mangilao, Guam: Micronesian Area Research Center.

Goodenough, W. S. (1986). Sky world and this world: The place of Kachaw in Micronesian cosmology. *American Anthropology, 88*(3), 551–568.

Goodenough, W. S. (2002). Under heaven's brow: Pre-Christian religious tradition in Chuuk. *Memoirs of the American Philosophical Society, 246,* 421.

Hanlon, D. L. (1988). *Upon a stone altar: A history of the island of Pohnpei to 1890* (Pacific Islands Monograph Series No. 5). Honolulu: University of Hawaii Press.

Hezel, F. X. (1983). *The first taint of civilization: A history of the Caroline and Marshall Islands in pre-colonial days 1521–1885* (Pacific Islands Monograph Series No. 1). Honolulu: University of Hawaii Press.

Lessa, W. A. (1966). *Ulithi: A Micronesian design for living.* New York: Holt, Rinehart and Winston.

Mauricio, R. (1993). *Ideological bases for power and leadership on Pohnpei, Micronesia: Perspectives from archaeology and oral history.* Unpublished doctoral dissertation, University of Oregon, Eugene.

Nason, J. D. (1978). Civilizing the heathen: Missionaries and social change in the Mortlock Islands. In J. A. Boutiler (Ed.), *Mission, churches and perspective* (ASAO Monograph No. 6, pp. 109–137). Lanham, MD: University Press of America.

Parmentier, R. J. (1987). *The sacred remains: Myth, history and polity in Belau.* Chicago: University of Chicago.

Peterson, G. (1990). *Lost in the weeds: Theme and variation in Pohnpei political mythology* (Occasional Paper No. 35). Honolulu: Center for Pacific Islands Studies, School of Hawaiian, Asian, and Pacific Studies, University of Hawaii.

Riesenberg, S. H. (1948). Magic and medicine on Ponape. *Southwestern Journal of Anthropology,* 4(4), 406–429.

Semper, K. (1873). *Die Palau-Inseln Im Stillen ocean* [The Palau islands in the satisfying ocean]. Leipzig, Germany: Brockhaus.

Spiro, M. E. (1958). Ghosts, Ifaluk, and teleological determinism. In W. A. Lesssa & E. Z. Vogt (Eds.), *Reader in comparative religion: An anthropological approach* (pp. 432–436). Evanston, IL.: Row Peterson.

Walleser, S. (1913). Religiose Anshauungen Und Gebrauche Der Bewohner Von Jap (Deutsche Südsee) (Religious beliefs and practices of the inhabitants of Yap [German South Seas]). *Anthropos, 8,* 607–629, 1044–1068.

Millennialism

On 22 October 1844, followers of William Miller, a Baptist farmer from upstate New York, gathered in churches and on hillsides from New England to Ohio to await the Second Coming of Christ. Several

THE GHOST DANCE

The Ghost Dance was a major millennial movement that was followed by many Native American groups in the Plains and Midwest in the late nineteenth century. Some of the key elements are described below in an account written several decades after the dances were repressed.

The dance with its creed, prescribing honesty, good will and peace, spread very rapidly and pilgrimages were now made from great distances to meet the Messiah, as had been done in the case of the Shawano prophet. In this way the ghost dance in the form then given to the people by Wovoka spread rapidly over a large area of the plains and the western plateau regions, but it seems not to have gone to any extent into the regions east of the lower course of the Missouri river, and hence did not come to the Minnesota and Wisconsin peoples. It is an interesting fact, however, that the dream dance appears to have come at about this same time from the Minnesota tribes to the Chippewa and Menominee of Wisconsin, and that while these two ceremonies are by no means the same there appear to be certain features common to the two which point to a possible connection between them.

The essential features of the ghost dance religion as they appeared in their most recent form, that taught by Wovoka, when compared with those underlying the dream dance show certain interesting similarities and differences as follows:

1. Both faiths have their origin in revelations, which come to individuals who are supposed to be especially endowed with occult powers, and who are given in these visions the creed of the faith and the ritualistic procedure of the ceremony with instructions to transmit them to their people.
2. The creed in each religion embodies certain ethical principles which call for a reign of peace, good will and justice, and for the equality of races and individuals.
3. The object sought by the worship in each case is the future, and secondarily the present, betterment of the individual participants and the race at large. This in the case of the ghost dance takes the form of an idea that a regeneration of the earth will shortly be in order at which time the Indians are to be given back their former life and are, together with their resurrected relatives and friends, to live upon the earth in a state of perpetual youth and under ideal conditions. This state of affairs is to come with the appearance of a Messiah upon the earth and will be heralded by signs. Various definite dates have been prophesied for its arrival and it is the failure of these prophesies which has caused the apparent abandonment from time to time of the faith, though the naturally religious feelings of the people quickly respond to new prophesies and new revelations of a similar kind. With the dream dance, on the other hand, it appears that, while a similar idea is the underlying principle, it has taken no such tangible form. The devotees are content to pin their faith to a promised new order of things, which shall be ushered in at an indefinite future date. The most important part of this faith is the hope of the devotees for reward in the ordinary spirit world in return for good deeds and upright living in the present world.
4. The desire of the devotees of each of these religions are expressed by means of invocations to the Great Spirit and by means of definite and fixed ritualistic ceremonies.

Source: Samuel A. Barrett.
The Dream Dance of the Chippewa and Menonimee Indians of Northern Wisconsin. (1911).
Milwaukee, WI: Milwaukee: Public Museum, pp. 297–298.

decades earlier Miller had come to the conclusion, based upon his reading of biblical prophecies, that Christ would physically return to Earth around 1843 to establish his millennial (thousand-year) kingdom. In 1832 Miller had begun lecturing on the subject in New York and New England, doing so mainly from church pulpits that were opened to him on account of his Baptist standing. Couched in the terms of the reigning revivalism of his day, Miller's "midnight cry" soon found a hearing. By 1843 believers were preparing for their meeting with Christ in earnest. Many sold or gave away all of their possessions and then gathered to await Christ's triumphant return. The failure of Christ to return on the first date that had been set led to a recalculation of the time line and the establishment of a new date with even greater assurance. As one of the last issues of the believers' newspaper, *Midnight Cry,* announced before that appointed October 1844 day, "Behold, the Bridegroom cometh! Go ye out to meet him!"

The vision of a millennial kingdom that Miller and his followers awaited was derived from the Revelation of Saint John, the last book of the Christian New Testament. Chapter 20 describes a coming millennium when Christ will rule with his followers over all the Earth, and evil will be restrained. The Christian conception of a millennial age under the reign of Christ at the end of history drew heavily upon the messianic traditions of Judaism that shaped early Christian belief and practice. In the book of Revelation the expected messianic age was seen to be universal in its historical and cosmic proportions, a concept that echoed one particular strand of earlier Jewish tradition. From this Christian concept the more general religious phenomenon of belief in a coming age of peace and righteousness to be established, usually by supernatural means, takes its name. Although millennial expectations can be found among many of the world's religions (especially Islam), they are most commonly identified with Christianity or are derived in part from contact with Christian sources. Hence their rituals usually bear Christian or quasi-Christian overtones.

Preparation for the imminent end of one age (Miller's followers called it their "robing") and proleptic (anticipatory) participation in the beginning of another constitute the ritual heart of millennialism. As with other rites of passage, the rituals of millennialism often entail cleansing of all impurities from the body and soul (repentance) as part of the preparation. Where many rites of passage are concerned with purity for the transition of an individual on a local plane, however, the rituals of millennialism tend to be collective and universal or cosmic in nature. (In the case of recent environmental millennialism, as in the radical group Earth First!, the cosmic dimensions have become especially pronounced.) The apocalyptic cleansing that millennialists foresee often takes the form of organized social (or environmental) violence, lending many millennial movements an ominous character. The belief in a coming cosmic battle between forces of good and evil, when cast in millennial terms, is easily historicized. In some cases adherents conclude that they are called to take up arms or to be prepared to engage in direct military action in the coming battle. More often millennialists believe that they are to suffer violence passively on a collective, historical scale as the world passes from one age to another. Ritual repentance and historic persecution are fused in meaning as a "cleansing" in preparation for the end.

Breaking of Taboos

Closely related to the themes of repentance and cleansing are what Peter Worsley has called the "ritual breaking of taboos" (1968, 250) practiced by millennial groups. Such activities are rooted in the millennialists' rejection of beliefs and values of the present and immediate past (many millennial movements extol the beliefs and values of a more distant past, which they foresee being restored in the coming millennial age). Old moral norms are ritually broken in expectation of the new moral norms that are soon to come. This is especially true of rituals surrounding practices of sexuality. Celibacy among the Shakers based in New England and "complex marriage" (or sexual communism) among the utopian Oneida community of upstate New York in the nineteenth century are examples of the norms of monogamous marriage being challenged on the basis of a millennial vision of an age to come.

Rituals of proleptic participation often entail forms of action that are meant not only to indicate, but also to actually hasten and even precipitate the coming of the new age. One example of this is the belief among U.S. Fundamentalist or Evangelical Protestants that Jesus Christ will return only after every living person on Earth has heard the Christian message of salvation. The nineteenth-century slogan "the evangelization of the world in this generation!" has been understood by many within the Fundamentalist and Evangelical communities as an imperative that will hasten the Second Coming of Christ. Although most Evangelicals would shy away from calling their evangelism or "witnessing" a form of ritual action, the ritualized character of these activities stands out when they are seen through the lens of millennial expectation that often accompanies them. Another example of precipitative behavior is found in the Native American Ghost

Dance of the last decades of the nineteenth century in North America. The prophetic founder of this revitalization movement, Jack Wovoka, taught that if Native Americans acted righteously toward one another and danced the traditional Native American round dance without ceasing, the Great Spirit would cause the Earth to swallow up the white invaders, the buffalo to return, and the land to be replenished. Thousands of Native Americans joined the movement and participated in the ritual of the Ghost Dance until the Wounded Knee Massacre in 1890 and the subsequent banning by the U.S. government of such religious movements among Native Americans.

Rituals among millennialists often have an egalitarian tone, pointing toward the structural inversion that such movements proclaim. The ruling saints with Christ in the millennial kingdom of the Revelation of Saint John are none other than those who were persecuted in the previous age. Among the so-called cargo cults of the South Pacific, expectations of coming cargo in the form of refrigerators and other manufactured goods signified the global redistribution of consumer goods and the knowledge that led to their production. The egalitarian beliefs of the Tonghak movement in Korea and the Taiping in China in the nineteenth century carried over into revolutionary action. In both movements any line that might have been drawn between ritualized religious practices and the everyday social world disappeared as they engaged in their anticolonial quest for social power on a national level.

This last observation points toward one of the more interesting characteristics of millennial beliefs and ritual practices. Almost all millennial movements conceptualize life in the coming age as being totally infused with religious or transcendent meaning. They envision the everyday world that is to come to be one of religious and ritual totalization. In the Revelation of Saint John life in the millennium will be an unending experience of worship. Among the Heaven's Gate cult adherents in the 1990s in the United States, spirituality and technology were completely fused. The Internet was their most important ritual vehicle for communication with the beyond, the coming age (called "the Evolutionary Level above Human") was one that was revealed through advanced technological means.

Transcendent Meaning

The millennial erasure of any line between the secular and the sacred, or the religious and the profane, serves to infuse everyday events on this side of history with a transcendent meaning far beyond what the uninitiated or unbelieving person is capable of perceiving. Members of the Korntal community, a nineteenth-century German Pietist (relating to a seventeenth-century religious movement originating in Germany in reaction to formalism and intellectualism) group holding millennial beliefs, would leave their coats each morning along the eastern edge of the fields into which they went to work. That way, if Christ were to appear that day in his Second Coming, they could snatch their coats up as they were ascending to meet him. The founder of the Korntal community, G. W. Hoffmann, described their millennial vision succinctly: "We wait, pray and prepare as if the Lord will come tomorrow; but we plant, build and work the earth as if it is still a thousand years away" (http://ourworld.compuserve.com/homepages/bg_korntal/gesch.htm).

For most millennialists, historical events are bursting with meaning that remains undisclosed to those outside the movement. What appear to other people to be common events in the everyday world, to the adherents of a millennial movement are rituals of the end. Historical events reported in the daily newspapers are revealed to have operating behind them suprahistorical (transcending history) figures and meanings that only those who hold to the particular millennialist vision or faith are privy to seeing and interpreting. Millennial movements of all forms tend to perceive history itself to be nothing less than a grand ritual acted out upon a cosmic stage, with suprahistorical (or heavenly) figures at work within and upon it, descending and ascending to the earthly plane where the nations now engage. Businessmen and businesswomen go on buying and selling, political rulers wage war and negotiate peace, people travel to and fro for work or pleasure, all the time oblivious to the fact that they are involved in a cosmic drama whose true dimensions are about to be revealed.

Secular Movements

The tendency to see in historical events suprahistorical meaning is the case even for the so-called secular millennialist movements of the past century, most notably Marxist Communism and Nazism. Both understood themselves explicitly to be all-consuming (or totalizing) philosophies compelled by millennial visions of the end of history. Both, therefore, imbued the day-to-day world of life under their regimes with ultimate ritual meaning. Human labor assumed transcendent meaning in the German political philosopher Karl Marx's philosophy, whereas its collective practitioners (the "working class") became the privileged agents of the construction of the new millennial age (the "classless society"). The ritual dimension of the historical terror carried out by the Nazis in central Europe is reflected in the language that is used to speak of their mass murder of 6 million Jews: "Holocaust" originally meant the burnt offering in a ritual sacrifice.

What do millennial believers do when their prophecies and visions of the imminent end of history fail to come true? Some simply abandon the belief in an imminent end and embrace other nonmillennial religious views or reject any further religious aspirations altogether. Others recalculate the expected time of the end and push the date for imminent change a bit farther down the calendar. For them the rituals of dating the end and preparing for its coming easily continue. Still others reinterpret the expected end in spiritual terms and claim that it did, in fact, happen but at a level that is not yet visible on the historical plane. Ritual changes must be introduced to signify discontinuity at the level of spiritual existence in such situations. Even a partially realized millennialism can have enduring effects in this regard. Looking for the next world, millennial movements often end up helping to transform the current world.

Dale T. Irvin

Further Reading

Barkun, M. (Ed.). (1996). *Millennialism and violence.* Portland, OR: Frank Cass.

Burridge, K. (1980). *New heaven, new Earth: A study of millenarian activities.* Oxford, UK: Basil Blackwell.

Cohn, N. (1961). *The pursuit of the millennium.* New York: Oxford University Press.

Festinger, L., Riecken, H. W., & Schachter, S. (1956). *When prophecy fails.* Minneapolis: University of Minnesota Press.

Numbers, R. L., & Butler, J. M. (1993). *The disappointed: Millenarianism in the nineteenth century* (2nd ed.). Knoxville: University of Tennessee Press.

Worsley, P. (1968). *The trumpet shall sound: A study of "cargo" cults in Melanesia* (2nd ed.). New York: Schocken Books.

Misrecognition and Rituals

Misrecognition is the process by which human action is attributed with meanings that are at best partial and distorted, and at worst, wholly mystified. The question of misrecognition in religious rituals asks whether practitioners' own understandings and reports of their actions provide a sufficient account of a ritual's motivations and meanings. The question is premised on the idea that ritual actors' own explanations are at best partial and sometimes even false. For example, participants in a ritual often report that it must be performed just so because the gods or ancestors founded it that way and because it has taken that form since time immemorial. An outside observer, contrariwise, might contend that the ritual was invented at a particular moment in history or borrowed from a neighbouring society and that it has changed substantially over time. Next, whereas a practitioner may report that a ritual's performance fulfils a divine obligation and entails no self-interest, an outside observer may note that through claims of "divine obligation," social hierarchies are created or maintained such that certain individuals profit in status, wealth, and power at the expense of others.

Such a posture entails viewing ritual critically. This posture resists accepting the self-reports of ritualizers at face value. Here is an example: A coronation ritual for a king represents that person as inherently and uniquely the spokesman of God, or even *as* a god. From an etic (outsider's) perspective, however, this misrecognizes as "natural" and inevitable what is contingent and socially produced. The same celebrated person in another context or another moment in history would be a commoner. Consider another example: Rituals of gift exchange may appear to be spontaneous acts of generosity expressing affection between one person and another. Yet, viewed with sufficient critical distance, gift giving can also be interpreted as the circulation of goods to tighten some social alliances and loosen others. Although misrecognized as an act motivated by individual sentiments of beneficence, gift-giving rites may be less self-sacrificing than self-interested. They can be viewed as a means of preserving useful alliances and storing up social credit that may be called upon in the future.

Pioneering Thinkers

This critical approach has its roots in the ideas of the German political philosopher Karl Marx. A key term adapted by Marx from reports of "primitive" religions was *fetishism. Fetish* was the derogatory term used by colonial traders to describe carved religious icons used in rituals by peoples living on the West African coast. Just as a simple piece of wood could be misrecognized as having great power, Marx argued, so the material objects that circulate in industrialized societies are also misrecognized. Whereas their actual value derives from their use, and from the labor of the human hands that made them, as fetishes they are considered to hold inherent value in and of themselves. As if by magic, a Mercedes-Benz is misrecognized as objectively endowed with power. In fact, that power was orchestrated by careful marketing and is dependent on a society that views cars as symbols of prestige. However, the work and hands that actually made the car and the strangeness of such a society are forgotten by the fetishists. The question of misrecognition and ritual takes a cue from Marx, then, to ask a fundamental question: How do religious rituals come to appear to be external to their human makers, ageless and authoritative, despite the fact that they were instituted by specific persons at a specific time and for specific reasons?

A student of Marx's ideas, the Italian philosopher Antonio Gramsci, expanded Marx's focus on economic life to culture, including religion, folklore, and ritual. Gramsci focused his study on the "common sense," embedded in everyday speech and actions, and how that construction of common sense both creates and conceals reality. In so far as this "common sense" exerts force, leading us to perceive and experience the world in predictable, socially learned ways. Gramsci referred to it as "Hegemony," a word he intended to denote something between influence and command. Hegemony is comprised of the actions and assumptions that are taken for granted: In the industrialized West it includes beliefs such as "time is money" or that patriotism is important for a good society. These commonsense beliefs are maintained through ritual acts. By standing habitually to sing the national anthem before a sporting event, actors internalize into their very bodies a posture of deference before the flag, quite apart from their conscious choice to do so. Placing a hand on the Bible in a court of law as a guarantor of honest speech likewise renders a sequence of positions habitual and thereby unquestionably real. Through such internalized routines, the guardians of the flag or the Bible (government officials, priests) are attributed with prestige, honor, and material benefits. Ritual actors fail to perceive not only that rituals maintain tradition, but also that they do so in ways that protect and extend the interests of some groups at the expense of others and that make such interests and group hierarchies seem legitimate, permanent, and natural.

Classical anthropology, whether the structural functionalism (a social theory in which the meaning of a cultural institution is said to reside in the function it plays in society's overall coherence and health) of the British tradition or the semiotic (relating to a theory of signs and symbols) structuralism of the French tradition, has also viewed ritual as misrecognition. In the work of British anthropologist A. R. Radcliffe-Brown, for example, ritual is viewed as a favorable route to maintaining social unity and consensus and reducing conflict. In the work of the French anthropologist Claude Lévi-Strauss, ritual is a way of cognitively ordering and classifying the human experience of the world. From both perspectives, ritual is again misrecognized as the obligatory carrying out of traditional, sacred obligations. Actors fail to see what a more detached, comparative observer might, namely that the key issue is generating and maintaining the social and cognitive order that human societies require. Although ritual action is one path to the creation and maintenance of such order, especially effective because it marshals the authority of gods, tradition, and the past, any particular action is arbitrary. Other kinds of action could easily replace rituals and would fulfill the same ordering function. In some societies legal procedures and political ceremonies, not ritual, regulate social consensus, and the members of such societies seem none the worse for the substitution. The implication is that religious rituals themselves are sufficient but not necessary. Individual sentiments of meaning and shared sentiments of affinity between people may in some cases emerge out of political, artistic or athletic movements, expanding the possible referents of what we consider as "ritual".

Recent Problems and Advances in Perspectives

How is a particular feature of human culture externalized and made to seem not merely plausible, but obligatory; not provisional or contingent, but rather permanent, essential, and even universal? One problem with the idea of misrecognition is that theorists have in general not developed arguments about how, exactly, this transformation from contingency to putative obligation occurs. One argument is that of the late social anthropologist Victor Turner. Turner argued that through rituals' use of symbols, rituals draw on distinct "poles" of reference to create meanings that seem uniquely real. On one end of a continuum lies a symbol's sensory pole, the physical experiences with symbols such as touching, immersing, dancing, ingesting, lifting, bowing, feeding, painting, and so forth. On the other end lies a symbol's ideological pole, the norms and values it represents, such as social unity or political authority. In the context of ritual performance norms and values are actually inscribed onto the participants' bodies. Norms and values are transferred to initiates through the bodily engagement with symbols, which in turn generates powerful sentiments of affinity and belonging. A key analyst of ritual, Catherine Bell, argues that this experience of bodily mastery makes participants experience ritual as empowering. The goal of ritual, in her view, is to initiate "ritualized agents," people who have thoroughly internalized the postures and procedures of a ritual as bodily, instinctual knowledge and are thereby distinguished from those who ritualize differently.

The most influential work on misrecognition and ritual in recent decades is that of the French social theorist Pierre Bourdieu. Bourdieu argued that misrecognition of ritual happens in part because ritual's shifting malleability is officialized and—through the application of special clothing, ranks, and uniform procedures—given the appearance of objectivity and unshakeable truth. He also demonstrated that economic interests and calculations involved in ritual are suppressed in order to perpetuate a collective faith in the social group. However, he broke new ground by arguing that misrecognition is maintained even when everyone knows—"sees through"—a ritual event, a phenomenon he called "miscognition." For example, at a political ritual such as a presidential nomination convention, everyone knows that each word uttered is carefully scripted by professional writers and TelePrompTered to speakers. Nevertheless, all participants act as though the nominee's speech were spontaneous and heartfelt in order to preserve cherished beliefs about their society, its political system, and the "sacredness" of the leader.

Even more importantly, Bourdieu made clear that ritualizations in the industrialized West are as liable to misrecognition as those of any less technologically complex society. If one form of misrecognition in ritual is to suppress, ignore, or forget the extent to which individual or class interests exert force in rituals, another form of misrecognition is to attribute *all* agency to economic self-interest. This presumes that all humans think in economic terms of profits and losses, a quality that may be distinctively characteristic of industrialized capitalist societies and not a universal human condition.

The Future of Misrecognition

In recent decades scholars of postcolonial studies have attacked the premises of misrecognition. If all knowledge systems are contingent and historical, rather than universal, how can Western analysts claim to occupy a neutral, objective ground from which to determine the "real" motivations and meanings of ritual? Does this not recapitulate the mistaken colonial notion that Europe and its descendants represent the center of the world, the makers of history, and the brokers of objective, scientific knowledge from whom others must learn? The discussion of misrecognition ends, then, where it began: with a critical inversion, now of the Euro-centric premises of misrecognition itself.

Paul Christopher Johnson

See also Communitas

Further Reading

Bell, C. (1992). *Ritual theory, ritual practice*. New York: Oxford University Press.

Bloch, M. (1992). *Prey into hunter: The politics of religious experience*. Cambridge, UK: Cambridge University Press.

Bourdieu, P. (1977). *Outline of a theory of practice* (R. Nice, Trans.). Cambridge, UK: Cambridge University Press.

Bourdieu, P. (2000). *Pascalian meditations* (R. Nice, Trans.). Stanford, CA: Stanford University Press.

Clifford, J., & Marcus, G. E. (Eds.). (1986). *Writing culture: The poetics and politics of ethnography*. Berkeley and Los Angeles: University of California Press.

Geertz, C. (1973). *The interpretation of cultures*. New York: Basic Books.

Gramsci, A. (1971). *Prison notebooks* (Q. Hoare & G. Smith, Eds. and Trans.). New York: International.

Lévi-Strauss, C. (1966). *The savage mind* (G. Weidenfeld & Nicolson, Ltd., Trans.). Chicago: University of Chicago Press.

Lincoln, B. (1989). *Discourse and the construction of society*. New York: Oxford University Press.

Marx, K. (1967). *Capital: A critique of political economy.* New York: International Publishers.

Mauss, M. (1967). *The gift: Forms and functions of exchange in archaic societies* (I. Cunnison, Trans.). New York: Norton.

Radcliffe-Brown, A. R. (1952). *Structure and function in primitive society.* London: Cohen & West.

Sahlins, M. (1976). *Culture and practical reason.* Chicago: University of Chicago Press.

Tambiah, S. J. (1979). A performative approach to ritual. *Proceedings of the British Academy, 65,* 133–169.

Turner, V. (1967). *Forest of symbols: Aspects of Ndembu ritual.* Ithaca, NY: Cornell University Press.

Monastic Communities

Within the Christian tradition monasticism is an institution of ancient origin that seeks to regulate a life dedicated to discipleship, usually by a group of individuals living in community. Because monastic life is simply an intensification of the basic baptismal commitment common to Christianity, many of the rituals found in monasticism are also practiced by Christians in general. Christian monasticism is found almost exclusively within the Roman Catholic and Eastern Orthodox churches, so the normal rituals of those churches are practiced in their respective monasteries. The liturgy (rites prescribed for public worship) of the Eucharist (communion) as practiced by monks differs only in details from its practice in all Catholic and Orthodox churches, for example, perhaps with more attention given to aesthetic or contemplative concerns.

The Liturgy of the Hours, a series of biblical prayers and hymns spread throughout each day, is considered an essential part of monastic life, although it is also practiced by nonmonastic clergy and even laity. Certain rituals, such as profession of religious vows or culpa (confession of faults), are generally unique to monastic communities or other religious orders that developed from monasticism. Besides these common rituals, individual monasteries may have their own customs such as special blessings or religious devotions that attract pilgrims.

Liturgy of the Hours

Also known as the "Divine Office," the Liturgy of the Hours is the ritual most closely associated with monastic life. The influential sixth-century *Rule of St. Benedict* states that nothing should take precedence over this form of prayer, which it calls "the work of God." The complete liturgy consists of seven prayer sessions ("Hours") spread throughout the day. The most prominent Hours are Morning Prayer (Lauds) and Evening Prayer (Vespers), usually held near dawn and dusk, respectively. Three shorter prayer times, known as the "daytime Hours," are called "Terce," "Sext," and "None," from the Latin names for the third, sixth, and ninth hours of the day. The prayer time known as "Vigils" was historically held sometime during the night, requiring monks to interrupt their sleep. This difficulty has often caused monastic communities to move Vigils to shortly after Vespers or before Lauds. The Hour known as "Compline" functions as an evening examination of conscience, but includes the elements common to the other Hours.

The individual elements of each Hour and their sequence are similar in each session. Members of the monastic community are seated together, often divided into two halves as on two sides of a chapel. The session begins with a brief invocation asking for the Lord's assistance. This is followed by a sung hymn. Then a few Psalms are recited or sung, with each half of the assembly often alternating verses. A short antiphon (a psalm, anthem, or verse sung responsively) is usually recited before and after each psalm. After all the psalms a brief passage from the Old or New Testament is read, with a short pause for individual meditation. At Lauds the silence is followed by the Canticle of Zecharia (Luke 1:68–79, NAB), sung or recited. At Vespers the Canticle of Mary or Magnificat (Luke 1:46–55, NAB) follows the period of silence. The Hour is concluded with prayers of intercession, the Lord's Prayer, and a concluding oration, often taken from the sacramentary for the day's Eucharistic liturgy. The shorter daytime Hours proceed from the Scripture reading and proceed directly to the concluding prayer, omitting the canticle, intercessions, and Lord's Prayer. The Hour of Vigils often features two longer readings, including one from nonscriptural sources such as prominent Church writers of the first three centuries CE. Some variation on this general structure can be found at individual monasteries. Monasteries may also choose to omit or combine some of these Hours because of time constraints. In general, monasteries of the Cistercian order attempt to keep all seven of the Hours, whereas Benedictine monasteries often omit some of the smaller daytime Hours.

SELECTION FROM THE HOLY RULES OF ST. BENEDICT

CHAPTER XVII

How Many Psalms Are to Be Sung at These Hours

We have now arranged the order of the psalmody for the night and the morning office; let us next arrange for the succeeding Hours. At the first Hour let three psalms be said separately, and not under one *Gloria*. Let the hymn for the same Hour be said after the verse *Deus, in adjutorium* (Ps 69[70]:2), before the psalms are begun. Then, after the completion of three psalms, let one lesson be said, a verse, the *Kyrie eleison*, and the collects.

At the third, the sixth, and the ninth Hours, the prayer will be said in the same order; namely, the verse, the hymn proper to each Hour, the three psalms, the lesson, the verse, the *Kyrie eleison*, and the collects. If the brotherhood is large, let these Hours be sung with antiphons; but if small, let them be said without a break.

Let the office of Vespers be ended with four psalms and antiphons; after these psalms a lesson is to be recited, next a responsory, the Ambrosian hymn, a verse, the canticle from the Gospel, the litany, the Lord's Prayer, and the collects.

Let Complin end with the saying of three psalms, which are to be said straight on without an antiphon, and after these the hymn for the same Hour, one lesson, the verse, *Kyrie eleison*, the blessing, and the collects.

***Source*: The Holy Rule of St. Benedict. (1949).**
Translated by Rev. Boniface Verheyen, OSB of St. Benedict's Abbey, Atchison, Kansas.
Retrieved 19 December 2002, from http://www.osb.orb/rb

Liturgical Seasons

Monks generally repeat the Prayer of the Hours each day, usually with special schedules for Sundays and church solemnities (days commemorating the lives of saints and days of liturgical importance). The 150 biblical Psalms may be distributed over a period of several weeks or less. The liturgy on Sunday is commonly more elaborate than on weekdays, often with embellishments such as incense or more elaborate melodies.

The overall arc of the liturgical year traces the life of Jesus Christ, from Advent's anticipation of his birth to remembrance of his death and resurrection at Easter. As the Prayer of the Hours progresses through the Church's year, it changes according to the season. The Church year begins with Advent, starting on the first Sunday of December. This season, which lasts until Christmas Day, is marked by a tone of anticipation. The Church recalls the people of Israel awaiting their messiah in Scripture readings and antiphons proper to Advent. The days immediately preceding Christmas are marked by the "O Antiphons"(messianic references from the Old Testament) at Vespers. In the relatively short Christmas season that follows, the proper prayers and antiphons of the Hours express the Church's joy at the newborn Son of God. From the close of the Christmas season in January until the beginning of Lent in late winter, the liturgical season is considered the "ordinary time" of the year. The season of Lent ushers in a spirit of repentance and preparation for Easter. The psalms, antiphons, and readings for Lent are selected around this theme. With the coming of Easter, the theme switches to joy at the resurrection of Christ. The Easter season lasts for seven weeks, after which the calendar returns to ordinary time for the balance of the liturgical year. Scattered throughout the year are solemnities. On these days particular psalms, readings, and prayers are selected to focus the Divine Office on the appropriate theme.

The quiet and serene courtyard of the Carmelite Cloister in downtown Frankfurt, Germany in 1990. COURTESY OF DAVID LEVINSON.

Historical Development

The Liturgy of the Hours is believed to have its origins partly in the Jewish roots of the earliest Christian communities. The Jewish custom of offering temple sacrifice in the morning and evening was probably carried over into the Christian Hours of Lauds and Vespers. Monasticism began to develop in the third century CE as a reaction to the increasingly popular acceptance of Christianity into mainstream society of the Roman Empire. The first monks were seeking a life of greater asceticism and dedication to prayer, following the command of Jesus to "pray always" (Luke 18:1, NAB). Beginning in the deserts of Egypt, early monastic communities did not yet possess the organized structure that would eventually develop, but life in these communities was already shaped around frequent times for prayer each day. Monasticism was influential on the Church from the fourth century CE onward, and in turn was influenced by the Church in the adaptation of the Roman hourly schedule to the Christian desire for frequent times of prayer. This combination led to the structure that the Prayer of the Hours has held to this day.

By the fifth century CE monasticism had, along with Christianity, spread to the western Roman Empire. The *Rule of St. Benedict* became the dominant guide for monastic life in the Roman Catholic Church and continues in this role today. The *Rule* describes the daily Divine Office in great detail, specifying at what times the Hours are to be held and when various Psalms are recited. Consistent with the flexibility that the *Rule* shows in most areas of monastic discipline, it allows the monastery's leader (the abbot) considerable latitude in adjusting the liturgy to the particular community's needs. This flexibility has allowed the *Rule of St. Benedict* to be used in monasteries of different cultures around the world but also accounts for the significant variation in how the Liturgy of the Hours is arranged in various monastic houses. Pope Gregory the Great (590–604 CE) played a major role in giving the Benedictine rule prominence in the western Church. He also transferred his name to the style of singing that has remained at the forefront of sacred Christian music for centuries: Gregorian chant. Also known as "plainsong" or "plainchant," this harmonically rich method of vocal prayer has been associated with monastic life since Pope Gregory's era. Recordings of monastic Gregorian chant enjoyed renewed popularity even in the late twentieth century.

The *Rule of St. Benedict* divides the daily schedule into distinct times for prayer and work. Through the second half of the first Christian millennium, as monasticism grew to a major role in European culture, finding an ideal balance between times for prayer and work proved challenging. The tenth-century monastic reform movement centered on the French abbey of Cluny was known for its lengthy and solemn Liturgy of the Hours. Partly in reaction to this, the twelfth-century Cistercian reform placed more stress on simplicity, manual labor, and poverty. Monasticism flourished during the high Middle Ages, followed by periods of decline punctuated by reform efforts continuing through the Renaissance. Many monasteries were destroyed in the sixteenth-century Protestant revolution, but the traditional practices of the Divine Office were maintained in the surviving monastic houses. The French Revolution and pre-Napoleonic suppressions also took their toll on European monasticism. After coming dangerously near to extinction, a nineteenth-century revival brought back the traditional forms of this monastic prayer, albeit in far smaller numbers than during its high medieval apex. The reforms of the Second Vatican Council (1962–1965) brought further changes to the language and styles of the Divine Office. Previously recited in Latin, it is now more likely to be in the local vernacular. The years after the council were marked by considerable liturgical experimentation in monastic communities, with varying degrees of success.

Monastic Profession

The process of formally entering into monastic life involves some unique ceremonies. A newcomer to a monastery, seeking to become a monk, starts his training with a one-year period known as a "novitiate." The start of this year is marked by a simple ceremony during which the monastic clothing, called a "habit," is given. This ceremony is generally attended only by the monastic community and takes place outside of Mass. At the end of the novitiate year, one who wishes to continue in monastic life takes vows of celibacy, obedience, and poverty for a limited period of time, typically three years. These vows, called "simple" or "temporary" vows, are marked by a profession ceremony. At the end of this period, the monk may be admitted to solemn vows. The period of temporary vows is a modern development because ancient monastic documents simply speak of vows following the period of apprenticeship. The *Rule of St. Benedict* does not describe the profession ceremony in any great detail, stating only that the newcomer writes out these promises in a document and signs his name in the presence of the monks and abbot. Modern-day profession ceremonies are usually celebrated during Mass and may include additional ceremonies added by the particular community. These additions may include covering with a shroud as a symbol of spiritual death and rebirth or giving of rings in women's communities as a sign of spiritual marriage.

Confession of Faults

The monastic ritual of confessing faults, known as "culpa," dates from the earliest documents. The *Rule of St. Benedict* mentions it as a disciplinary practice. Modern monastic communities may hold it as a formal meeting in chapel, including common prayer and a period for silent reflection. After each monk confesses individual faults, the abbot may conclude with an exhortatory blessing or suggest a common penance. This practice is not to be confused with the Roman Catholic Sacrament of Reconciliation (confession). The faults mentioned in culpa generally relate to community life and, unlike the matter of individual confession, are not considered serious sins. Culpa has also historically been practiced individually. In this case a monk would admit his faults privately to the abbot or another monk in authority. Private culpa as a formal practice is rare in contemporary monastic life.

Today and the Future

Individual monasteries often practice local customs that may include various rituals. Certain abbeys are centers of pilgrimage (e.g., Einsiedeln, Switzerland), with large public liturgies and devotions. Although present-day monasticism appears to be in a period of stagnation at best, recent decades have included an increased interest by lay Christians in the Liturgy of the Hours. Having lasted through centuries of growth and decline, the rituals found in monastic life seem likely to survive into the foreseeable future.

Matthew Kowalski OSB

See also Asceticism; Communitas; Communitas, Rites of

Further Reading

Chupungco, A. (1982). *Cultural adaptation of the liturgy*. New York: Paulist Press.

de Vogue, A. (1983). *The Rule of St. Benedict: A doctrinal and spiritual commentary*. Kalamazoo, MI: Cistercian Publications.

Field, A. (Ed.). (2000). *The monastic hours: Directory for the celebration of the work of God and directive norms for the celebration of the monastic Liturgy of the Hours*. Collegeville, MN: Liturgical Press.

Fry, T.; Baker, I.; Horner, T.; Raabe, A.; & Sheridan, M. (Eds.). (1981). *RB 1980: The Rule of St. Benedict in Latin and English with notes*. Collegeville, MN: Liturgical Press.

Hourlier, J. (1995). *Reflections on the spirituality of Gregorian chant*. Orleans, MA: Paraclete Press.

International Commission on English in the Liturgy. (1976). *Christian prayer: The Liturgy of the Hours*. New York: Catholic Book Publishing.

International Commission on English in the Liturgy. (1976). *The rites*. New York: Pueblo Publishing.

International Commission on English in the Liturgy. (1985). *The sacramentary*. New York: Catholic Book Publishing.

International Commission on English in the Liturgy. (1989). *Rite of religious profession*. Washington, DC: United States Catholic Conference.

Kardong, T. (1996). *Benedict's rule: A translation and commentary*. Collegeville, MN: Liturgical Press.

Mitchell, L. (1977). *The meaning of ritual*. New York: Paulist Press.

Nicholson, D. (1986). *Liturgical music in Benedictine monasticism: A post-Vatican II survey*. St. Benedict, OR: Mount Angel Abbey.

Ratzinger, C. J. (2000). *The spirit of the liturgy*. San Francisco: Ignatius Press.

Taft, R. (1986). *The Liturgy of the Hours in East and West.* Collegeville, MN: Liturgical Press.
Vagaggini, C. (1976). *Theological dimensions of the liturgy.* Collegeville, MN: Liturgical Press.

Mormons

The Church of Jesus Christ of Latter-day Saints was founded in 1830 in northwestern New York State by Joseph Smith and is headquartered in Salt Lake City, Utah. The movement crystallized around key differences with modern Christianity that members believe were received from Jesus Christ via a contemporary authoritative revelation starting with Smith and continuing through a present-day prophet. The main body of the movement—persecuted because of divergences of concept (principally continuing revelation, physicality of God and Jesus Christ, and the nature of their relationship to humans) and practice (principally economic and political communalism and polygamous marriage) with mainstream Christianity—was forced to move from major centers built successively in New York, Ohio, Missouri, and Illinois. By 1847 Church leaders established permanent headquarters in Utah in what was then a sparsely inhabited indigenous homeland and an abandoned northern frontier of Mexico. Between 1890 and 1910 Church leadership suppressed the earlier practice of polygamy.

Christians of other denominations early labeled the Church's members "Mormons," deriding their adoption of an additional book of scriptures, the Book of Mormon, which Church members then and now consider to be a record of God's ancient revelations to and interactions with religious groups somewhere in the New World between approximately 589 BCE and 421 CE. Initially a slur, the term "Mormons" stuck as an unofficial self-designator. The term is used by members for brevity and alternates with the acronym "LDS" (Latter-day Saints), a term reflecting the belief that the current church is a recent or "latter-day" "restoration" of the key aspects of organization, belief, and practice associated with the biblical, or former-day Christians, called "saints" by Paul and others.

Doctrinally and structurally, the Church focuses on the notions of authoritative interconnection through its priesthood and on "continuing revelation" from Jesus Christ, a combination that provides both structural coherence and a mechanism for continuing change, adaptation, and development among its membership of 11.4 million worldwide.

Categories of Ritual

Within the LDS Church ritual practices occur on daily, weekly, and annual cycles as well as on the longer cycles of a lifetime.

Daily Practices

Mormon sermons and classroom discussions encourage a member to build spiritual strength by kneeling privately in daily prayer and by studying the Scriptures thoughtfully and regularly, preferably at least once a day. Indeed, various scriptures admonish one to "pray always" inwardly, as one goes about one's activities, to help one make ethical decisions aimed at worthy goals. In addition to personal prayer, parents should gather their families daily for family prayer.

Weekly Practices

On Sundays (or, rarely, on other days if national law or regional culture so dictate), Mormons feel that they should attend church explicitly "to partake of the sacrament" and to "worship," "learn," and "strengthen" each other.

The set of "Sunday meetings" typically begins with the sacrament meeting. This meeting is framed with prelude and postlude instrumental music to transition members from secular to sacred time and space and with opening and closing songs that unite congregation members by singing together. An opening prayer and a closing prayer invoke God's presence and blessing on the congregation, its leaders, and the peoples of the world and commonly ask that God inspire the world's leaders to make wise choices. Within this frame members signal the ritual apex, "partaking of the sacrament," by maintaining absolute silence while a male age sixteen to eighteen (a "priest") recites the two prayers of the sacramental covenant through which members recommit weekly to "remember Jesus Christ" and "keep his commandments" so "that His spirit may be with them." Deacons, age twelve to fourteen, then "pass the sacrament" by distributing trays of "broken" bread and small cups of water to members in the congregation. After the administration of the sacrament one or two youths give brief sermons, and one or two adults give longer and more developed sermons.

Only the sacrament prayers must be recited exactly, the prayers being an "ordinance" for "renewal of covenants." All other "talks" (i.e., sermons) and prayers are given by either gender according to their own inspiration and construction, although what they choose to say usually conforms to widely shared expectations of appropriate spiritual content and phraseology. By delivering their individual insight in a clearly shared style, members both build the community and include themselves in it. During this hour—their most important weekly meeting—Mormons explicitly feel they should "sit together as a family," unless leadership obligations require them to "sit on the stand," the raised platform at the front of the chapel where leaders, clerks, and choir sit facing the congregation.

On the first Sunday of each month, called "Fast Sunday," the assigned talks (lay sermons) of the sacrament meeting are omitted, and the time is left open for members spontaneously to "bear their testimonies" in what is variously called "fast meeting," "testimony meeting," or "fast and testimony meeting." Members who feel inspired stand in the congregation or walk to the pulpit and express their faith, "knowledge," or personal assurance "that the Gospel is true" by relating some experience in which they perceive divine intervention, inspiration, or insight acquired in the process of living their life. Such affirmations manifest core LDS beliefs regarding agency (the belief that one must always be responsible for one's actions) and the necessity of continuously nurturing one's spirituality. Part of that nurturance involves fasting by abstaining from two meals prior to the meeting, an act that consciously symbolizes the domination of bodily needs by spiritual intents. Moreover, the monetary value of the meals omitted is to be donated to an LDS Church program that provides for the "needy" both locally and worldwide.

At the conclusion of the sacrament meeting members move to classrooms for Sunday School. For nearly an hour, under the guidance of a teacher using a manual that provides worldwide thematic consistency, class members read the Scriptures and discuss their implications. Mormons study the Old Testament one year and the New Testament the next, considering the Bible to be the record of God's revelatory interactions with Judaic tribes in the Old World. Mormons spend another year studying the Book of Mormon. This book uniquely defines Mormons because they consider it to be a record of God's revelatory interaction with and a partial history of a people (the Nephites) who built a civilization presumed to be somewhere in the New World. The Nephites, in Mormon belief, were subsequently wiped out by religious wars with tribal factions of different religious and cultural persuasion called "Lamanites." Mormons believe that some of the descendants of the Lamanite factions have survived and are represented among the indigenous populations of the New World. Finally, Mormons spend a year studying the Doctrine and Covenants, considered to be a record of God's revelations and interactions with "his children" in modern times. During Sunday School study hour, families split up as members go to class groups that are age related but gender mixed. Married couples generally sit together unless one spouse has a teaching obligation. In contrast to the sacrament meeting, where a talk is delivered with little overt interaction with or vocal response from the congregation, a good Sunday School teacher is highly interactive, and members discuss or even debate points of theology inferred from the Scriptures.

During the final hour participants reorder themselves in gender-specific study groups. Men gather in priesthood meeting and divide into age-graded components of the Priesthood. In Mormon social organization and practice, the Priesthood is divided into two major components, each with subdivisions: The first component, Aaronic Priesthood, includes subdivisions ("offices") of "deacons" (aged twelve and thirteen), "teachers" (ages fourteen and fifteen), and "priests" (ages sixteen and older but generally not older than nineteen). The second component, the Melchizedek Priesthood, is composed of Elders (age eighteen and older but generally not older than thirty-five or forty), and High Priests (age eighteen and older but generally not younger than thirty). During a priesthood meeting, each subdivision of the priesthood has a class taught by an adult. Topics of study have varied over the years, but at present men study a selection of the writings of one of the former leaders of the Church, a different one each year. Adult women pursue the same course of study under the auspices of the separate women's meeting, the Relief Society. Teen-age "Young Women" likewise study gospel topics in gender-separated age groups that match those of the Aaronic priesthood young men. Children from eighteen months to three years attend nursery for the two hours of Sunday School and Priesthood/Relief Society, during which they play, have activities, and learn basic social and religious concepts. Children ages four to eleven attend primary school in age-graded year groups composed of both genders. Children younger than eighteen months remain with their parents during Sunday School and priesthood/Relief Society meetings.

The ritual cycle continues through the week, although Mormons would be surprised to hear their weekday religious activities called "rituals." The Church encourages its families to regularly assemble on Mondays in their home to hold "family home evening," an event of family-centered entertainment, planning, learning, and devotion. The actual execution of the family assembly can be quite sporadic and its content highly dependent on the ages of the children in the family. However, the admonition to have regular family home evening on Mondays portrays the important religious emphasis on the family as the foundational unit of the Church and establishes the responsibility of parents to transmit the core value structure and the central practices of the faith to their children through familial ritual.

Once a week, designated adults organize an activities night for youth (ages twelve to eighteen) of the congregation. These activities may include sports competitions, domestic or occupational skills acquisition, hikes, cookouts, dances, or lessons regarding doctrine or personal ethics, with frequent emphasis on sexual morality defined as abstinence until marriage. Women may attend a weekly Relief Society Enrichment meeting which may be held at any time convenient to the cultural needs of a given region. Less formally, spouses are encouraged to nourish their marriage with time apart from other family routines, and some do so on a formal or informal "Friday night date."

Annual Cycle

Mormons also experience an annual religious cycle. Although they commemorate Easter and Christmas, for example, regular Sunday meetings tend not to be commemorative as much as instructional. The high points of instruction are the semiannual General Conferences. On the first weekends of April and of October, Church leaders from around the world speak to the membership during five two-hour sessions. These conferences are broadcast (with simultaneous translation into more than fifty languages) and sent via satellite to chapels around the world and to commercial television and radio stations that choose to sponsor them.

Life Cycle

Like all peoples and faiths, Mormons have a series of life-cycle rituals that marks progressive states of social maturation and links them with cosmological (relating to a branch of metaphysics that deals with the nature of the universe) ideas. The most important rituals are called "ordinances," meaning that they are considered binding covenants that must be authoritatively and correctly performed to be valid.

By custom (but not by covenantal requirement), the first life-cycle ritual is "blessing the child," or "giving the child a name." Shortly after birth at the parents' convenience, the parents bring the newborn to a Fast and Testimony Meeting. The father, a close kin, or a designated friend who "holds the Melchizedek Priesthood" (i.e., an ordained male lay leader) acts as "voice" for a prayer of inspiration that also blesses the child in various aspects of its future life. The person acting as voice and other "priesthood holders" (generally kin and friends of the family) stand in a circle, typically with right arms extended to the center under the child and left arms at rest or on the shoulder or back other participants. Thus, the child begins social life within the community at the center of a prayer circle that symbolically resonates with the prayer circle central in the performance of LDS temple ceremony.

Mormons baptize at age eight or older, the "age of accountability" in LDS belief wherein one can distinguish between right and wrong. The age limit emphasizes the core principle of agency in Mormon cosmology. Those members younger than age eight, or those who will not reach a mental equivalent of moral accountability, "have no need of baptism," being considered "innocent," "without sin," and therefore not in need of baptism (Book of Mormon/Moroni 8:8, 22). In Mormon concept baptism is a requirement for "admission to the kingdom of heaven." Through baptism, the child or repentant adult gains "remission of sins" and makes a covenant to abide by Christ's example and law and to "bear one another's burdens" (Book of Mormon/Mosiah 18:8–10).

After the baptismal service or at the next Sunday church service, the baptized person receives a second ordinance: the "laying on of hands for the gift of the Holy Ghost." In this ordinance the candidate is invited to "receive the Holy Ghost." That is, the baptized person is given the "gift of the Holy Ghost" but must actually make herself or himself receptive to receive its spiritual "promptings"—the heightened sense of inspiration and spiritual companionship—that in Mormon theology emanate from this "third member of the Godhead." Importantly, in this ordinance the person is confirmed a member of the Church of Jesus Christ of Latter-day Saints, whereas before he or she was not formally a member.

When a person is ready, minimally age twelve but usually sixteen or older, the person arranges the requisite worthiness interviews and makes an appointment to receive a "patriarchal blessing." In this ritual the "Stake Patriarch," a senior and spiritually distinguished and designated individual, gives the young man or woman a blessing. The blessing "declares a lineage" suggesting a spiritual adoption and affiliation with Old Testament promises to the patriarchs. Usually such a blessing also suggests the outlines of an individual's potential in different aspects of his or her future life, provided that "one lives worthily" and is "anxiously engaged" in making self and others better. The blessing typically touches on such matters as marriage and family, health, characteristics or attributes that need to be cultivated or improved, or strengths that should be taken advantage of or further developed in service to others. In Mormon thought the blessing comes from God, with the patriarch acting as "voice" and conduit for the inspiration. The blessing is recorded, transcribed, and given to the recipient in text form. Correlated with and paralleling patriarchal blessings, any member can request and receive a "priesthood blessing," in which a Melchizedek Priesthood holder acts as voice to deliver insight and blessing to a member facing difficulty, risk, uncertainty, or a perplexing decision. If possible, this blessing is given in the context of a family, by the requestor's father. It is then called a "father's blessing." In many families fathers give blessings regularly at the start of school or as children depart home, prepare for marriage, or engage in other new phases of their lives. Here the father is literally "the patriarch of the household," but service and guidance, rather than dominance, are the intended meaning of the word.

Missions and Marriage

A young man or woman may choose to go on a mission if he or she has maintained himself or herself worthy to go. The cultural life of the Mormon congregation, however, sends distinctly different messages to the two genders. Men are "expected" to go on missions. In Utah, for instance, about two-thirds serve for two years, Young women, by contrast, are advised that marriage is more important but that they "may" go on missions. About one-third of young women born in Utah serve missions for eighteen months. Among female Mormons, marriage becomes the more focal index of adulthood.

Ritually, upon accepting a mission call or immediately prior to a marriage, a person "enters the temple" to receive or "take out" his or her own endowment. The candidate is "washed and anointed" and dressed head to toe in white, the celestial color of purity and authority. The candidate joins a "company" of sacred fellow "journeyers," the same word used for the groups of Mormon pioneers as they crossed the United States wilderness seeking spiritual refuge to Utah. The company witnesses a dramatic presentation of God's use of law and social hierarchy to organize the Earth from the existing materials of the universe to populate it with plants, animals, and humans, and to endow those humans with the spiritual knowledge they need to deal with the continuous presence of both good and evil that they consciously chose in their pre-earth life to experience.

The endowment is an ordinance, and like all ordinances it presents a covenant in which God delivers accurate spiritual knowledge, spiritual empowerment, and a promise of future blessing via the ordinance. Simultaneously, the candidate promises Old Testament obedience to the Ten Commandments, with special emphasis on sexual and devotional fidelity within marriage, combined with New Testament dedication to making ethical decisions that improve the physical and spiritual welfare of the human community throughout the world. In contrast with the physical plainness of Mormon church buildings and Sunday church services, the temple is richly, densely, and visually symbolic and dramatic.

The endowed, and therefore spiritually adult, Mormon of either gender wears a garment of white (symbol of purity and authority) cloth in the form of a T-shirt and boxer shorts. Mormons see the garment as a spiritual reminder of the sacredness both of the body and of sexuality. Most believe that wearing the garment proffers a kind of spiritual protection in that it reminds them of their obligation to treat their body and their mind as a sacred temple vis-à-vis the world around about. Some believe that wearing the garment provides even physical protection. Some non-Mormons, interpreting this behavior through their own cosmology, judge the practice bizarre. Perhaps this is because, for most Americans, the human body is a physical object that produces sweat and odors; it contaminates. One must wash it frequently and perfume it to avoid offending others by bodily dirtiness. Therefore, one wears "underwear" to absorb the body's excretions, thereby preventing the contamination of one's clothes and of others. Underwear thus contaminated can hardly be thought of as sacred or as a reminder of good. Mormons, however, reverse the symbolism. The human body is inherently sacred and to be kept pure. The garment shields the body from the spiritual assaults of the world by reminding one of one's spiritual character and of one's covenant to try to be ethical with others. Such symbolism of one's religious devotion and orientation is, however, private. In Mormon thought one should not flaunt one's religious devotion before others by wearing externally visible signs of religious affiliation, such as crosses or amulets, because such can be construed as confrontational.

The culminating ritual in the ritual life cycle of the individual is "being married in the temple" "for time [earth-life] and eternity [after death]" to one's "eternal companion." Children born within an "eternal marriage" are "born in the covenant" and are eternally connected to those parents in a genealogically-connected family system that Mormons believe will reemerge in heaven after the deaths of successive generations. Mormons consider "temple marriage" the logical completion of the endowment sequence, in part because it connects their creative reproduction within marriage to the creative endeavor of God in the eternal cosmos. Couples of other religious backgrounds who investigate the Church and decide to become converts to the LDS faith are baptized, later endowed, and finally have their existing civil marriage "sealed" in a temple "for eternity" and their children likewise sealed to them. Family thus stands at the center of the cosmological symbol system in the temple, and the importance of family is replicated in the performance of daily "family prayer," weekly family home evening, and the nearly obligatory symbol of "sitting together as a family" in the most important church service of the week, the sacrament meeting..

In a little-discussed and rather murky area of Mormon theology, women become coholders of the priesthood through temple marriage, sharing it with their husbands. Only in the temple do women perform ordinances and serve as ordinance workers. Outside of the temple, which is to say "in the world" that is seen as both corrupt and spiritually incomplete, all ordinances are performed by men, although women pray, teach, and preach throughout the structure and exercise managerial leadership in the Church's auxiliaries: the Relief Society, Primary, and Young Women's organizations. In the temple, which is the Mormon's closest symbolic approximation of the nature of heaven, women are coequal with men. That coequality is further emphasized in a Mormon belief in the existence of a Mother-in-Heaven, a concept necessarily entailed also in the notion of sealing into family units that may "eternally progress" until acquiring coequal status with God.

Senior Members of the Church

Senior citizens have a highly respected place in Mormon culture and practice. "Active" senior males (as High Priests) are the primary lay ritual administrators in the congregation. After retirement from secular employment, couples or those of either gender by then single are often called to serve as temple workers who staff the activities of that central symbol of the Mormon community and life cycle. They may be called to serve "senior missions," where their life expertise and career expertise are used in local church leadership, humanitarian service, or proselytizing somewhere around the world. Such service activities enrich and broaden the scope of retirement. Some couples fulfill several such missions, interspersing them with periods at home visiting grandchildren, and continue to do so until incapacitated by ill health.

Death Rituals

Upon death the body of a Mormon is disposed of in accordance with each nation's legal requirements. Burial is preferred over cremation, but likely as a matter of U.S. cultural roots rather than theological preference. For a Mormon funeral in the United States, one may have a viewing, in which the deceased, if endowed, is dressed in the white clothing used in temple service. At the funeral service, close family members typically deliver memorial eulogies of the good life of the deceased. The funeral tone is usually happy, even humorous, reflecting Mormon belief that death is but an eye-blink transformation in the continued existence of an eternal spirit that is thereby reunited in eternal family with deceased parents and siblings or children who might have preceded them in death.

Mormons believe that their worthy dead will be received by Jesus Christ, or his deputized emissaries, and that they will be "actively engaged" in a kind of heavenly Works Projects Administration of missionary work to the spirits of the deceased of all times and places who did not have access to "the fullness of the gospel" during their earth-lives. Mormon heaven is thought to be as active, service oriented, kinship interconnected, and family centered as Mormon life on earth is.

Ritual and Cosmology

Mormon ritual encodes a distinct Christian cosmology that is quite different from the more widely known variants of Protestant and Catholic theology. In Mormon scriptural accounts of a divine apparition to Joseph Smith at the foundational "restoration" of the Church, God and Jesus Christ appear as—and in Mormon temple ritual are represented as—separate, embodied, resurrected beings. Mormons thus see humans as both substantially and conformationally similar to God, taking literally "in the image of God created he him; male and female, created he them" (Genesis 1:27, KJV). For Mormons the human connection to God is intimate indeed because, as one prophet said, "As man now is, God once was; as God now is, man may be" (Ludlow 1991: vol. 2:555).

Thus, in Mormon thought the creation of the Earth and of humans was not a special creation for God's pleasure, but rather part of a larger eternal process of great consequence in which the increasing refinement of humans is integral. Therefore, the daily and weekly practice of LDS church life places enormous emphasis on cultivation, maturation, and increasing spiritual refinement of both youths and adults. The notions are encoded in concepts of "eternal progression" and in ritual in at the temple wherein the individual joins a "company" (the same term applied to those who crossed the Plains as a group during the forced marches to refuge, 1830–1860) of persons who, in the older temples, moved physically "up" from room to room, each room symbolizing increasing refinement and increasing spiritual obligation as one moved from "worldly" toward "celestial" spheres. In modern temples the task is accomplished somewhat more passively, and virtually, by film and lighting as the company is taken on humankind's appointed course of progress from worldly to celestial obligation. In a word, temple ritual both dramatizes and synthesizes the purposes of life, and these are continuously reproduced in family and congregation through good teaching and example.

Mormon ritual encodes a further radical concept: that the underlying essence of humanness—called "intelligence"—is not created by God but rather exists as part of the eternal substance of the universe. This remarkable concept absolves God of the problem of having created the Hitlers, Pol Pots, and Charles Mansons of the Earth. In Mormon concept and ritual the "intelligence" or "will" or propensity to do either good or evil is uncreated because "intelligences" are eternal and are transformed later into "spirit children" of God and finally into embodied human beings involved in the natural processes of Earth life. Yet, one's intelligence is improvable, but only by the intelligence's own judicious contemplation of choice in the acquisition of knowledge and experience, primarily during Earth life.

Such notions give meaning to life and encourage efforts to be moral, to learn from one's mistakes, and to acquire education and wisdom in all its forms. In Mormon ritual cosmology the acquisition of ultimate knowledge and the development of spiritual power through proper connection to priesthood (by conferral or through marriage) and eventual godhood require ultimate responsibility and reliability. Hence the Mormon emphasis on covenant and on keeping commandments as a measure of character. Mormons do have a place in their theology for the concept of "grace," however, because no one is worthy or perfect in and of himself or herself, and therefore Christ's atonement is both necessary and freely available to all. In Mormon thought, nevertheless, grace is necessary and sufficient for salvation (admission to a good life in heaven) but grace is not sufficient for "exaltation," the term Mormons use for those who have proven themselves sufficiently trustworthy to be active participants in future divine creativity in an expanding universe.

Although Mormons see God and Jesus Christ as morally invariant, the human and cultural material they interact with is highly variant. Therefore, "the heavens have not closed." Thus, Mormon scriptures are added to, and other ritual practices are changed, "line upon line," as the people become more "ready" or receptive.

Ritual and the Social Reproduction of Community

Mormon ritual practices work together to instill the principles and procedures of the faith into members. Such is the explicit purpose of each congregation: to provide a nurturing support system in which the young will be able to grow up and become "strong in the faith." Yet, there is a decided tension between producing a community through effective socialization and having individuals authentically committed by individual choice. Hence the dual requirement of a nurturing community based on mutual service and willingness to "bear one another's burdens" *and* constant insistence that people must, through prayer and practice, "find out for themselves" whether what they are taught is actually true (James 1:5 KJV; Book of Mormon/Enos 1–11; Doctrine and Covenants 9:7–9). This internalization of commitment by personal epiphany—"having put it to the test" in order to "gain one's own testimony"—becomes the basis for continued authentic social reproduction of the LDS community. Such agentive commitment is the logical individual complement of continued social and ritual practice and the basis of Mormon success through missionary expansion.

Through this commitment men and women linked by eternal marriage anchor the institution of the spiritually reproductive family and staff the local ward and the broader LDS Church as a community support system. Their rituals encourage them to serve others, both inside and outside the church community, through community service and donations of labor and wealth to provide for the physical, spiritual, and educational needs of others, both Mormon and non-Mormon, around the world. Through ritual such efforts are dedicated not only to the living but also to the deceased of all times and places because, in LDS cosmology, all humans are spiritual brothers and sisters via an uncreated eternal connection to God, to Jesus Christ, and to each other as now-embodied morally accountable agents.

John P. Hawkins

Further Reading

Arrington, L. J., & Bitton, D. (1979). *The Mormon experience: A history of the Latter-day Saints*. New York: Alfred A. Knopf.

Bushman, C. (1997). *Mormon sisters: Women in early Utah* (2nd ed.). Logan: Utah State University Press.

Bushman, C. L., & Bushman, R. L. (2001). *Building the kingdom: A history of Mormons in America*. Oxford, UK: Oxford University Press.

Cooper, R. E. (1990). *Promises made to the fathers: Mormon covenant organization*. Salt Lake City: University of Utah Press.

Cornwall, M., Heaton, T. B., & Young, L. A. (Eds.). (1994). *Contemporary Mormonism: Social science perspectives*. Urbana: University of Illinois Press.

Eliason, E. A. (2001). *Mormons and Mormonism: An introduction to an American world religion*. Urbana: University of Illinois Press.

Givens, T. (2002). *By the hand of Mormon: The American scripture that launched a new world religion*. New York: Oxford University Press.

Hill, M. S. (1989). *Quest for refuge: The Mormon flight from American pluralism*. Salt Lake City, UT: Signature Books.

Leone, M. P. (1979). *The roots of modern Mormonism*. Cambridge, MA: Harvard University Press.

Mauss, A. L. (1994). *The angel and the beehive: The Mormon struggle with assimilation*. Urbana: University of Illinois Press.

McMurrin, S. M. (1965). *The theological foundations of the Mormon religion*. Salt Lake City: University of Utah Press.

O'Dea, T. F. (1965). *The Mormons*. Chicago: University of Chicago Press.

Ostling, R. N., & Ostling, J. K. (1999). *Mormon America: The power and the promise*. New York: HarperCollins.

Packer, B. K. (1980). *The holy temple*. Salt Lake City, UT: Bookcraft.

Roberts, B. H. (1965). *A comprehensive history of the Church of Jesus Christ of Latter-day Saints*. Provo, UT: Brigham Young University Press. (Original work published 1909–1915)

Shipps, J. (1985). *Mormonism: The story of a new religious tradition*. Urbana: University of Illinois Press.

Talmage, J. E. (1962). *The house of the Lord: A study of holy sanctuaries, ancient and modern*. Salt Lake City, Utah: Bookcraft.

Music

Music and rituals can be examined in two ways: first by looking at rituals within musical performance and second by looking at the role of music in the performance of sacred ritual. Both ways are simply different ways of looking at music as a spiritual medium. From perhaps its beginning, music has been found in conjunction with the sacred. Many philosophers and theologians have noted the power of music to move humans to a level above the ordinary. Some have welcomed its spiritual power, whereas others, such as the ancient Greek philosopher Plato, have warned against it.

MUSIC IN AFRICAN-AMERICAN LIFE

The three songs below exemplify folk and blues songs that have been so significant in African-American music.

Stones in My Passway

by Robert Johnson

I got stones in my passway and my road seems dark at night
I got stones in my passway and my road seems dark at night
I have pains in my heart, they have taken my appetite

I have a bird to whistle and i have a bird to sing
Have a bird to whistle and i have a bird to sing
I got a woman that i'm loving, oh, but she don't mean a thing

My enemies have betrayed me, have overtaken poor Bob at last
My enemies have betrayed me, have overtaken poor Bob at last
And there's one thing certain, they have stones all in my pass

Now you're trying to take my life and all my lovin' too
You have laid a passway for me, now what are you trying to do?
I'm crying, "Please, please, let us be friends"
Now when hear me howling in my passway, rider,
please open your door and let me in

I got three legs to truck on, whoa, please don't block my road
I got three legs to truck on, whoa, please don't block my road
I been feelin' strange 'bout my rider, babe, i'm booked and i got to go

St. James Infirmary

Folks, I'm goin' down to St. James Infirmary,
See my baby there;
She's stretched out on a long, white table,
She's so sweet, so cold, so fair.
Let her go, let her go, God bless her,
Wherever she may be,
She will search this wide world over,
But she'll never find another sweet man like me.
Now, when I die, bury me in my straight-leg britches,
Put on a box-back coat and a stetson hat,
Put a twenty-dollar gold piece on my watch chain,
So you can let all the boys know I died standing pat.
Folks, now that you have heard my story,
Say, boy, hand me another shot of that booze;

If anyone should ask you,
Tell 'em I've got those St. James Infirmary blues.

Swing Low Sweet Chariot

Swing low sweet chariot,
comin' for to carry me home,
swing low sweet chariot,
comin' for to carry me home,
comin' for to carry me home.

I looked over Jordan, and what did I see,
comin' for to carry me home,
a band of angels comin' after me,
comin' for to carry me home.

If you get there befo' I do,
comin' for to carry me home,
tell all my friends I'm comin' too,
comin' for to carry me home.

Whether welcomed or warned against, music has played a large role within sacred ritual and has also continued to contain spiritual messages within itself. These messages generally are presented in a ritualized manner by musicians, adding to their power in a number of ways. Ritual enhances security and encourages surprise by playing with the expected to evoke wonderment via displacement, or sublimation.

Ritual within Music

Many musicians assert that their music is spiritual. Whether they are associated with Santeria (a religion originating in Cuba), play Western classical music, or play jazz and the blues, they emphasize the spirituality of their music. For example, voodoo practitioners use the *Book of Dream and Mystery*. The book tells the meaning of dreams, finding hidden meanings behind dream symbols. Many of the symbols have a spiritual meaning behind them. A long line of spiritual scholars used the book to give credence to its techniques and lessons including the doctors and followers of voodoo to Albert the Great, the medieval teacher of the Italian philosopher Thomas Aquinas. The influence of voodoo in the blues is well documented, and many blues singers make reference to it. In fact, voodoo and other magic have drawn heavily from Christianity, inverting its forms, substituting obscene symbols for sacred ones. That is why spirituals were seen to be in opposition to the blues, and the blues was a secular version of the sacred. The two are intertwined, and each gains power from the other.

An old blues song such as Peter Clayton's *Root Doctor Blues,* for example, shows the relationship between the blues and voodoo quite clearly:

> I'm a first-class root doctor and I don't bar no other doctor in this land, (*twice*) My remedy is guaranteed to cure you, pills and pains ain't in my plan. (Oliver 1961)

The blues singer embraces the power of healing claimed by "root doctors" (voodoo doctors). The healing is a spiritual healing, one that also offers protection.

The opposite often takes place. The slick pastor who is more interested in picking the pockets of his parishioners is a commonplace in African-American folklore. The false spiritual leader who sells phony holy water in little vials and offers cures for ailments beyond his power has been satirized by U.S. musician

Men in a park in Beijing, China in 2002 perform traditional and highly ritualized Peking Opera. COURTESY OF KAREN CHRISTENSEN.

Louis Armstrong and other performers such as Flip Wilson. Many in the African-American community condemned Armstrong, for example, for revealing dirty linen in public, but blues and jazz singers believe in telling the truth in their music and in subverting accepted reality.

The ritual of blues music is easily stated. There are different kinds of blues, but the standard form has come to be twelve bars. The lyrics are generally in iambic pentameter. The problem is stated in four bars, repeated in four more, and then resolved. The anger felt by people is diverted into other channels that are filled with pathos and humor. The problems of people are resolved in the blues.

The blues provides a safety valve for dangerous emotions, allowing them to be expressed and dealt with, even in a disguised manner. The blues thus serves a survival function, diverting attention from dangerous enemies to those who can be more safely dealt with. Like other folk traditions, the blues serves a number of functions, from speaking with the divine to placating the divine. It aids in making sense of group rituals and in understanding the mysterious.

As in other folk music, in the blues elders teach youngsters the traditions, history, and the ways by which emotions can be expressed and the ways by which they cannot be expressed. Ideas about the life hereafter are common in the blues. There are also ritualistic ways of providing amusement, mocking pomposity, and easing one's pain. Archetypes of social life are found in blues songs, and people learn how to deal with them and make sense of their world.

The organ is an important instrument for rituals performed in many Christian churches. This highly stylized organ is in a cathedral in Madrid, Spain. COURTESY OF SARAH CONRICK.

In the United States, except for New Orleans and Savannah, mixing African religious music with European music was difficult because of the nature of Protestantism, although there was some mixture. From the earliest days, however, secular music had no difficulty in becoming syncretistic (combining different forms). Work songs, rooted deeply in African musical tradition, simply switched their references from work in West Africa to work in the United States.

Music as Part of Ritual

A Yoruba (a Niger-Congo language of Africa) proverb states, "The spirit will not descend without song." Music, then, is sacred and spiritual and a necessary part of anything else that is to be spiritual. The

African-American church is filled with the spirit, that is, with emotion. The dances and songs that are important parts of African religious rituals are part of the African-American experience. "Spirit possession," an integral part of these rituals, also became an integral part of Afro-Christianity. "Gettin' the spirit," "gettin' religion," and "gettin' happy" are different ways of proclaiming the same thing: being possessed by the spirit. Music is an indispensable part of that experience. Music helps one to get the spirit.

African-Americans made Christianity into a new thing, using its form but adapting it to their purpose. They did the same thing with religious music. They used its forms and instrumentation but bent them to their own styles and uses. The words, rhythms, and, yes, even the harmonies were African-American.

African-American spirituals were most likely the first truly indigenous African-American music. They were not simply African or European but rather an amalgam of both, produced by African-Americans in the United States. This music spread to others in the United States and became, often unconsciously, part of the general religious music of Americans. Many people agree that the Methodist Revival (movement that began in the eighteenth century and reached the south in the middle of that century), for example, began by trying to convert African-Americans and ended by converting Americans to African-American styles of worship. Much of this conversion came via African-American spirituals.

Attempts by African-American preachers to get rid of Africanisms in worship were doomed to failure. Dancing was too much a part of the ritual tradition to be eliminated by rules. Dancing was an integral part of African religious life and found its way back into the U.S. churches from which it was banned. The songs that accompany the dancing ritual may be sung by the dancers, but usually a band and singers center the others by singing and clapping. Then the spirit often moves people to express themselves in an energetic fashion.

A number of sources produced African-American Christian music. African ritual musics were adapted to Christian sources but maintained their close ties with Africa. Ring shouts, for example, were taken into Christian worship. The Ring Shout is a traditional African religious ritual practiced by slaves throughout the South. River cult ceremonies from Dahomey (today Benin) became part of the Christian baptism ritual. Many Christian spirituals were simply African melodies with Christian lyrics. *Swing Low Sweet Chariot* is one such spiritual with roots deep in Africa.

Folklorist Robert Farris Thompson has argued that the concept of "coolness" characterizes African-derived philosophy, art, ethics, and religion. Thompson points out that cool philosophy is a medium. From that medium come concepts about generosity, harmonization, balance, and completed work fit to be remembered by descendants. Coolness is a positive way of thinking, combining ideas of self-possession, stillness, vigor, therapeutic power, and social cleansing. In addition to the typical European connotations of coolness, there are African connotations. The Mandingo, of West Africa, for instance, call favorable divination results "cool." The Yako of West Africa have a ceremony called "cooling the village." This ritual is performed when there are violence and social disturbance in a village. The Yako use water and herbs in the ritual.

Jazz fans are used to the juxtaposition of the cool and the sacred. The "cool" element of musical ritual and of ritual behavior itself is manifested in every aspect of the black aesthetic. The quintessential cool jazz musician was Lester Young of the United States. But the jazz ethos does not apply simply to being cool. When the jazz community began to articulate black nationalistic ideas in the late 1950s and the 1960s, these efforts reached the apex of the cool aesthetic. The U.S. musician John Coltrane, for example, combined the elements of cool and sacred in his music. The combination of explicitly African elements with a sacred message in songs such as *Kulu se Mamma* and *A Love Supreme* is especially noteworthy. Fans considered this music to be a ritual of freedom and revolution, a kind of collective aesthetic spiritualism.

Music in the Ritual of Other Cultures

The concept of music as a sacred phenomenon that channels power to bring harmony to society is found in many cultures. Anthropologist Ellen Basso has studied the role of myth and ritual performance, including the role of music, among the Kalapalo people of Brazil. Basso has examined Kalapalo ideas about the relationship between sound and "orders of animacy." Orders of animacy constitute a hierarchical taxonomy (system of classification). The Kalapalo place musical entities, the most powerful of beings, at the top of this taxonomy. The acts of musical entities are found always and everywhere. They are not limited by place or time. They are unpredictable and have a multiplicity of feelings. They are dangerous entities; their danger is fed by their ability to produce music.

Music is the highest stage of animacy (possession) and hyperanimacy. The Kalapalo imitate the models that the musical entities present to them. Music gives performers a share of the power. Music also helps control dangerous power. It is in itself a power. It is, therefore, important in ritual performances. It helps people. Through ritual performances people can affect political life and, therefore, human relationships.

The Christian church has long understood this concept that music adds to the spiritual experience. Hence, there have been various arguments concerning the appropriate music to accompany rituals. Gregorian chant was the official music of the Church for many years because of a deep understanding of the power of music to provoke powerful emotions.

The term *Gregorian chant* in its strictest sense refers to the Roman form of early plainchant. It is thus distinguished from other types of plainchant, which it replaced. The chant style is termed *Gregorian* because tradition has it that Pope Gregory the Great (590–604) gave Roman chant its final arrangement. Although that tradition has been challenged recently, the term will remain. More important is why chant came to dominate ritual performance in the Roman church.

Gregorian chant is slow, imitating deliberate and reverent speech. It does not have a steady beat. Chant slows one's metabolism, relaxing the body, quieting the mind, and providing inner peace. Chant has neuropsychological benefits. It promotes strength and vitality and recharges the soul.

Music plays an essential role in rituals around the world. It accompanies ritual performance in all known societies. It is also often viewed as sacred in its own right, comprised of its own myths and rituals. The combination of music and ritual is a powerful force, reinforcing social solidarity, reaffirming the value of social harmony, supporting the norms and customs of the social group, and serving to maintain or reestablish social organization.

Frank A. Salamone

Further Reading

Bell, C. (1997). *Ritual: Perspectives and dimensions.* New York: Oxford University Press.

Crocker, R. G. (Ed.). (1990). *The early Middle Ages to 1300.* Oxford, UK: Oxford University Press.

Fellerer, K. G. (1961). *The history of Catholic church music* (F. A. Brunner, Trans.). Baltimore: Helicon Press.

Gabbard, K. (Ed.). (1995). *Jazz among the discourses.* Durham, NC: Duke University Press.

Glazier, S. D. (Ed.). (1999). *Anthropology of religion: A handbook.* Westport, CT: Praeger.

Harris, J. E. (Ed.). (1993). *Global dimensions of the African diaspora* (2nd ed.). Washington, DC: Howard University Press.

Hatcher, E. P. (1999). *Art as culture: An introduction to the anthropology of art* (2nd ed.). Westport, CT: Bergin & Garvey.

Heinze, R. (Ed.). (2000). *The nature and function of rituals: Fire from heaven.* Westport, CT: Bergin & Garvey.

Hughes, D. A. (Ed.). (1954). *Early medieval music, up to 1300.* London: Oxford University Press.

Jones, L. (Imamu Amiri Baraka). (1963). *Blues people: Negro music in white America.* New York: W. Morrow.

Oliver, P. (1961). *Blues fell this morning: The meaning of the blues.* New York: Horizon Press.

Steiner, R. (2000). The practice of conjuring in Georgia. In M. Fassler & R. A. Baltzer (Eds.), *The divine office in the Latin Middle Ages: Methodology and source studies, regional developments, hagiography.* New York: Oxford University Press.

N

Naming Rituals

Naming rituals in any religion provide opportunities for identification and celebration of the newborn. They are rich traditions passed on from generation to generation. Although naming rituals differ among religions, they usually act as a welcoming first step into particular religions. Some religions, namely those of Native Americans and Africans, utilize naming rituals throughout the lifespan. Recently, secular naming rituals have gained popularity, allowing people with no religious affiliations the opportunity to formally announce a child's name without religious rituals.

Christian Naming Rituals

Christians from around the world adhere to certain rituals in regards to naming. Although a universal ceremony related to the naming of a child does not exist, Christians partake in baptisms, also known as "christenings," when godparents bring the child to be welcomed as a member of the religious community. In this ritual the child's name is repeated in order to announce the child. The child often wears a gown that may have family significance, and his or her head may be anointed with oil and water. Baptisms are usually performed during the first year of life.

Christians observe several rituals when choosing a name. Traditionally, Christians should be named after saints or at the very least biblical figures. If this ritual is not enacted, then Christians are asked to provide a baptismal name (to be used at baptism) in addition to the nonsaint name. U.S. Catholics are required by Canon 761, decreed by Pope Benedict XV (1854–1922), to choose names from a list of satisfactory saints' names.

At confirmation ceremonies Catholics are asked to choose an additional name, again a saint's name (traditionally added after the middle name). Unlike at baptism, when the name is chosen by the parents, this name is chosen by the confirmed.

Jewish Naming Rituals

In the Jewish religion gender plays a role in the rituals of naming. For boys the *bris milah* has two steps: circumcision and naming. The ceremony is performed on the eighth day after birth and is required by the Torah (the body of wisdom and law contained in Jewish Scripture and other sacred literature and oral tradition). Often the parents are asked to explain the choice of name within the ceremony. The Hebrew name can be a translation of a nonreligious name or a different one altogether. Rituals of the ceremony include providing an empty chair representative of the prophet Elijah witnessing the ceremony, having the godparents present, and reciting blessings.

For a Jewish girl a ceremony known as *"simchat bat," "brit ha bat,"* or *"shalom bat"* is held in order to celebrate her identification. Although this ritual is not required by the Torah, it has been gaining popularity. Female Jewish children are usually named on the first Sabbath after the birth or at any Torah reading.

Details about how the child is named vary from region to region. For instance, European Jews name their children after a departed relative or friend. Living friends' and relatives' names are used by Sephardic (relating to the occidental branch of

THE NAMING CEREMONY OF THE KHASI OF INDIA

The naming ceremony of the child is performed the next morning after the birth. Certain females are invited to come and pound rice in a mortar into flour. The flour when ready is placed on a bamboo winnower (*u prah*). Fermented rice is mixed with water and is placed in a gourd. Some powdered turmeric is also provided, and is kept ready in a plantain leaf, also five pieces of *'kha piah*, or dried fish. The earthen pot containing the placenta is then placed in the *nongpei*, or centre room of the house. If the child is a male, they place near him a bow and three arrows (the implements of a Khasi warrior); if a daughter, a star or cane head-strap for carrying burdens. An elderly man, who knows how to perform the naming *puja*, which is called by the Khasis "*kaba jer khun*," places a plantain-leaf on the floor and sprinkles some water on it. He takes the gourd in his hand and calls a god to witness. The people assembled then mention a number of names for the child, and ask the man who is performing the *puja* to repeat them. This he does, and at the same time pours a little liquor from the gourd on to the ground. As he goes on pouring, the liquor by degrees becomes exhausted, and finally only a few drops remain. The name at the repeating of which the last drop of liquor remains adhering to the spout of the gourd is the name selected for the child. Then the *puja* performer invokes the god to grant good luck to the child. The father takes the pot containing the placenta, after having previously placed rice flour and fermented rice therein, and waves it three times over the child, and then walks out with it through the main entrance of the house and hangs up the pot to a tree outside the village. When he returns from this duty, before he re-enters the house, another throws water over the father's feet. The father, being thus cleansed, enters, and holds the rice flour to his mouth three times. Two people then, holding the dried fish by their two ends, break them in two. The powdered turmeric mixed with rice flour and water is applied to the right foot of the father, the mother and the child receiving the same treatment. The friends and relations are then anointed, the turmeric being applied, however, to their left feet. The bow, arrows, da, and u star are carefully placed inside the inner surface of the thatch on the roof, and the ceremony is over. Rice flour is then distributed to all who are present, and the male adults are given liquor to drink.

***Source*: Gurdon, Philip R.T. (1907). *The Khasis.* London: David Nutt, pp. 124–125.**

European Jews settling in Spain and Portugal) Jews. Both male and female naming ceremonies can be followed by a traditional Hebrew meal.

Hindu Naming Rituals

In the Hindu religion the naming ritual is called a *"namkaran"* and transpires on the twelfth day after the birth of the child. Some Hindu communities hold the naming ritual three months after the birth. Females in the Hindu culture tend to partake in the naming ritual more fully than males, especially in certain castes. The baby is placed in a cradle, and traditional songs are sung, making sure to rhyme with the baby's name. Often rice, sugar, and toys are brought to the ritual. Other rituals include giving new clothes, consecrating a gold object, and anointing.

The name of the child must include an even number of syllables for boys and an odd number of syllables for girls. Names as well as the rituals performed in the Hindu culture often reflect one's position in the caste system as well as the names of holy beings. Hindus believe that the more names a person has, the more he or she is protected from bad events. The caste system plays a significant role in how much or how little celebrating happens in regards to naming.

Islamic Naming Rituals

Islamic tradition holds that an Aqiqah ceremony (a sacrificial ritual) be held seven days after the birth of a child. The ritual can be private or can include family and friends. Several rituals surround this ritual,

Greek Orthodox parents and their daughter at her naming ceremony in Athens in the 1950s. COURTESY OF BERKSHIRE PUBLISHING GROUP.

including the naming of the baby. The baby's head is shaved as a sign of purification, and the hair is weighed so that a donation to the poor can be made on the part of the baby's family. The amount donated, if the family is able, is equal to the weight of the hair. Another ritual includes the slaughtering of sheep. Then the name of the child, as chosen by the parents or an elder member of the family, is formally announced. Names are often taken from the Qur'an (the book of sacred writings accepted by Muslims as revelations made to Muhammad by Allah) or from a list of highly regarded Muslims. Prayers and food are included in the naming ritual, which is viewed as a celebration. In some countries circumcision is also performed at this ritual, and for some Islamic cultures circumcisions are extended to girls.

Sikh Naming Rituals

The Sikh religion has aspects similar to those of Islamic and Hindu cultures. Sikhs hold a naming or christening ritual at which donations and prayers are offered. The ritual usually occurs within ten days of the birth. The first letter of the child's name is decided by randomly opening a book of hymns to reveal the first letter of the first word of the hymn. The name of the child, which is chosen by the family, is approved by the congregation with a shout. Additions to the ends of names for both boys and girls are utilized.

Native American Naming Rituals

Members of Native American cultures commonly have multiple names and thus a multitude of rituals associated with naming. Naming rituals differ from tribe to tribe. Male members of the Blackfoot tribe usually have three names: a birth name, a nickname, and a tribal name. For most Native American tribes the tribal name, sometimes called the "spirit name," is the most ritualistic. The boy in search of a spirit name is required to offer gifts such as tobacco and money (which are blessed) and to prepare the meal for the ritual. All leftover food must be burned. The spirits are called upon, and the name is repeated by both the leader of the tribe and the boy. The tribal name is then earned (not just given).

The Sauk tribe conducts a naming ritual at birth or several months after, depending on how long it takes for a name to be chosen. An elder is usually in charge of choosing the name. One ritual is placing a piece of the umbilical cord in a small pouch with other items. This pouch stays with the child for the rest of his or her life.

In the Hopi tribe a child is called a name by his or her paternal grandmother in addition to receiving other names from aunts on the father's side of the family. The name that "sticks" (Alford 1988, 37) is the one that is utilized by the parents of the child.

Native American names often reflect the animal world, and name changes throughout the lifespan are common. Often names are passed down from generation to generation, as in other religions.

Yoruba and Other African Naming Rituals

Often the traditional religions of Africa include hints of Islamic and Christian rituals. However, there are some differences. The Logbara people of Africa believe traditionally that a naming ritual should be held immediately after the detachment of the umbilical cord. However, often rituals are held four days after the birth of a male and three days after the birth of a girl. The females of the family discuss possibilities for names, but the mother makes the final decision, with her mother-in-law choosing a second name. Some traditions hold that the father should play a role in the naming or that children coming to the house of the baby should also suggest names. "At the naming ceremony the giving of the name makes the child an individual. As for Africans in general, so for Logbara, 'the name is the person'" (Dalfovo 1982, 121). Name changes and nicknames are common among the Logbara.

The Yoruba people of Africa believe that a baby must be named within nine days after birth in order to live longer than the parent of the same gender. In a naming ritual food and objects are presented to the baby, and the baby's name is announced. Often the ritual takes place outside. Ceremonially, the baby's foot is placed on the ground in order to represent the first step toward religion. Food is served afterward.

The Babukusu people of Kenya are given three names throughout a lifetime: an ancestral name, a childhood name, and an adolescent name. Chosen by the father or a maternal uncle, the ancestral name is the only name that is accompanied by ritualistic behavior. The Babukusu child is often named after relatives. After a prayer the uncle of the child places an iron or skin bracelet on the child's wrist: left for a girl and right for a boy. The bracelet is a sign of a connection to the ancestor the child is named after. Ancestral names provide a religious center and are often restricted from everyday usage and saved for special occasions. Therefore, the second and third names are used more commonly.

Pagan Naming Rituals

A common misconception categorizes the pagan religion as a secular tradition. However, the pagan religion is categorized by a belief in nature. The Wicca religion, based on ancient pagan beliefs, and shamanism, based on magical beliefs, also fall into the larger classification of pagan traditions. A naming ritual is important in the pagan religion. The ritual introduces the child not only to the community of pagans but also to a spirit world. The ritual should take place outside within nine days of the birth and might include a tree that was planted to celebrate the child's birth. Some pagans suggest that instead of nine days after, the ritual should take place when the parents feel physically ready or at the first new moon. An offering can be buried at the bottom of the tree to represent the linking of the child to the tree. Parents choose the name of the child, which is not required to be a pagan name. In the Wicca religion the baby obtains a mystical name. After the leader of the ritual has discovered if the parents have considered the matter of a name seriously and the parents have said yes, the baby's name is granted, and the baby is kissed, followed by the recitation of a pagan prayer. In some rituals the participants stand in a circle and chant the child's name.

Religious Naming Rituals in Context

Various religions have various naming rituals. Even within the same religion, rituals differ from culture to culture. The traditions of naming rituals continue to change while still reflecting the religious beliefs they were founded upon. Naming is an important and powerful force that grants newborns and older people alike the gift of an identity. Naming rituals provide humans with a reason to celebrate and to recognize the embedded beliefs of their religions. Like all religious rituals they are both sacred and necessary.

Diane M. Ferrero-Paluzzi

See also Crisis Rituals; Passage, Rites of

Further Reading

Alford, R. D. (1988). *Naming and identity: A cross-cultural study of personal naming practices*. New Haven, CT: Hraf Press.

Dalfovo, A. T. (1982). Logbara personal names and their relation to religion. *Anthropos*, 77(1–2), 113–133.

Diamant, A. (1994). *The new Jewish baby book names, ceremonies, and customs: A guide for today's family*. Woodstock, VT: Jewish Lights Publishing.

Gill, S. D. (1982). *Native American religions: An introduction*. Belmont, CA: Wadsworth Publishing.

Gill, S. D. (1983). *Native American traditions: Sources and interpretations*. Belmont, CA: Wadsworth Publishing.

Jordan, M. (2001). *Ceremonies for life: Birth and naming rituals, marriage and commitment celebrations, remembrance ceremonies*. New York: Collins & Brown.

Leslie, J. (1991). *Roles and rituals for Hindu women*. Rutherford, NJ: Fairleigh Dickinson University Press.

McLeod, W. H. (Ed.). (1984). *Sikhism*. Lanham, MD: Rowman & Littlefield.

Mibiti, J. S. (1969). *African religions and philosophy*. London: Heinemann.

Oduyoye, M. A., & Kanyoro, M. (Eds.). (1992). *The will to arise: Women, tradition, and the church in Africa*. Maryknoll, NY: Orbis Books.

Ongong'a, J. J. (1983, April). African names and Christian names. *AFER*, 25, 114–118.

Plaskow, J. (1990). *Standing again at Sinai*. San Francisco: Harper and Row.

Spirn, M. (1998). *Birth: World celebrations and ceremonies*. Woodbridge, CT: Blackbirch Marketing.

Walker, B. (1968). *The Hindu world: An encyclopedic survey of Hinduism* (Vol. 2). New York: Munshiram Manoharlal.

Native Americans: Arctic

Arctic Native Americans—the Inuit peoples—inhabit the northern North American coastline from Prince William Sound in southern Alaska westward and northward in Alaska and eastward across Canada to Quebec, Labrador, and Greenland. Most of this inhospitable 15,000-linear miles area north of latitude 60° N varies from sparse vegetation on plains to deeply cut fiords and glaciated mountains. The climatically harsh Arctic is free of ice for only three months in the summer, when the sun nearly always shines. The long Arctic winter is extremely cold, with light appearing only around midday. The Inuit traditionally endured a precarious existence, subsisting on sparsely available resources.

The word *Eskimo,* often used to refer to Arctic Native Americans, derives from the Abenaki word *Eskimantisc* and the Ojibway word *Asskimey.* The Abenaki and Ojbway are both Native North American tribes. However, it is considered a pejorative word that means "eater of raw meat." Arctic Native Americans refer to themselves by the terms "the People" or "the Real People"—*Inuit* in their vernacular. Three main Inuit groups subsist in the Arctic: the Yup'ik, the Inupiat Inuit, and the Greenlandic Inuit. The Arctic culture is based on maritime hunting, using many distinctive features such as toggle harpoons, kayaks, and tailored skin clothing. Social institutions were used to cement alliances. A division of labor, with men hunting and women sewing and raising children, was clearly evident. Religious beliefs were based on the spirituality of the natural world and strongly influenced the Inuit hunting and fishing lifestyle based on bearded seals, harp seals, and ring seals living along the ice edge. The Inuit did not have chiefs; they were a society of equals grouped into large families rather than tribes.

Their harsh, unpredictable environment led the Inuit to adopt an animistic/shamanistic (an ancient form of worship that includes magic, trance, mysticism, and respect for souls of animals) form of nature worship, interwoven with folklore, that pervades their entire culture. The shaman *(angakut)* is usually male but can be female in some Inuit tribes. Traditionally, the shaman functioned as doctor and priest, providing religious leadership by virtue of supernatural powers and a connection with guardian spirits, thus often as acting as intermediary with the animistic powers and the spirit world. The shaman had the most acute knowledge of taboos and observances and could interpret reasons for illness or lack of hunting success, divine the future, improve hunting conditions, control the weather, and ascertain who had broken a taboo that ultimately could gravely harm the community. Accompanied by drumming, Inuit shamans entered a trance, allowing the soul to leave the body and cover great distances to learn the causes of community problems. They wore masks to communicate with the spirits.

Despite regional variations among Inuit people, some other religious commonalities exist. All Inuit believed that inanimate objects such as rocks, mountains, and other landscape features have thinking, feeling, talking spirits *(anua).* The mercurial forces of nature were manipulated by these powerful spirits, who needed to be appeased. Inuit culture was shaped by the need to kill these spirits to obtain food and other life necessities; thus, a positive reciprocal relationship with these spirits was pivotal. Spirits were respected, and a positive relationship was paramount to the Inuit lifestyle, which was centered around religious rituals to preserve the equilibrium in nature. These rituals were preventive measures such as offerings, special signs, ceremonies, and taboos that were strictly observed to maintain a healthy society. Bad hunting, bad weather, illness, and death were deemed to be caused by evil spirits.

The Cosmos

The Inuit believe that the cosmos consists of four layers: the Sky world, the Earth, the Undersea world, and the Underworld. The weather spirits—Storm, Cloud, Wind, Snow, and Cold—can play tricks on people. The Inuit also believe that each person has at least three spirits. The first is the immortal spirit, which leaves a person's body at death and lives on in the spirit world. The second is the breath spirit of life, which ceases to exist upon death. The third is the spirit abiding in a person's name. Another spirit is the departed spirit, which has some influence and can affect the supply of game. The eventual destination of a spirit depends on the type of death endured by the deceased. Losing a spirit is considered offensive to other spirits and sometimes causes death. Because spirits exist in all people and animals, a complex system of taboos is observed to assure that animals will continue to make themselves available to hunters. Traditionally one taboo that is maintained today is that caribou-skin clothing could not be sewed in certain seasons. Another was that a slain seal had to be laid on fresh snow for butchering and given drink of fresh water. Seal meat could not be mixed with caribou meat. Many traditional rituals have been maintained and are performed before and after hunting expeditions to assure success. The majority of rituals focused on hunting and the land-sea dichotomy.

A huge force in Inuit culture is the *tunghat,* a mythical beast who lives on the moon and is seen only by shamans. Tunghat regulates fish and game animals because their spirits reside on the moon. Sedna (or Takanaluk) is the most important deity, except in northwestern Hudson Bay and western Alaska. Sedna is the generative underwater goddess spirit. She is deemed to be part fish and part human and is identified with natural forces and cycles relating to sea animals. Sedna's observations about improper behavior have governed the Inuit. This, too, is a reciprocal relationship. If taboos have been observed, Sedna releases sea animals to the Inuit hunters; if no sea animals are released, starvation ensues and threatens Inuit existence. The Inuit also confess their transgression of taboos. To appease Sedna and assure hunting success the Sedna Ceremony is held in the autumn by the Baffin Island Inuit. During a trance a shaman flies to Sedna's dwelling place and challenges her about releasing the sea animals. A determination of food availability also ensues between the people born in winter and those born in summer. The Sedna Ceremony also obliterates turbulent weather in order to secure better hunting.

The Mourning Observance of three to five days is a ritual (this is an old ceremony that has been around for thousands of years and continues today) that incorporated rigid taboos to counter the evil power of ghosts and to demonstrate esteem for departed souls. The Inuit maintain that the soul with its human desires and needs remains after death, therefore food, clothing, and implements are offered at the grave or at festivals. Securing and consuming food also has always been a feature following a death. Hunting did occur during mourning. Sharp knives could not be used for fear of injuring or cutting the ghost of the soul. The Feast of the Dead also expressed deference to and pacified a departed soul sometimes months or years after burial.

An important ritual was conducted whenever an animal was slain because every animal had its own taboo rituals. The Inuit believed that an animal's soul returns to the other world without a grudge if it is given water upon death. This kindness ensured a favorable report to Sedna, who would release more sea animals, ensuring a time of feast rather than famine. Another ritual was that of separating the land animals from the sea animals. Inuit could not use the same weapons to hunt land animals and sea animals.

Messenger Feast

The Inuit calendrical cycle had various festivals and feasts. The Messenger Feast lasted from four days to several weeks every January. A message was sent from a host village to another village, inviting it to the feast, which was like a potlatch (ceremonial feast marked by the host's lavish distribution of gifts). The feast was meant to celebrate life-cycle events, increase the animal population, and provide for dancing, competitive games, singing, feats of strength, and elaborate gift exchanges. Shamans wearing masks would dance. Sometimes children were initiated into their future adult roles during the Messenger Feast. Young people wore special masks and learned special dances. The Messenger Feast brought renewal, rebirth, and a reaffirmation of Inuit social values along with a much-needed social exchange.

The ritual of seal parties was held in the spring. This ritual occurred when the men came home with their first seals. The women distributed the seal meat and a variety of small household items.

Whaling was a highly ritualized activity. The whaling season ended with the captain acting as host of the four-day Whaling Ceremony, which took place in the Karigi (ceremonial structure). The Whaling Ceremony consisted of singing, distributing whale meat, skin, and blubber, dancing, competing in games, and making new clothes and kayak covers. The Inuit observed this ceremony because they believed that bowhead whales let themselves be taken and killed but must be placated. The ceremony was held to appease the spirits of the bowhead whales by returning their skulls to the sea, ensuring their immortality and allowing reincarnation. During the whaling season the captain's wife strictly observes the taboos; she pours water into the whale's mouth upon capture.

The five-day Bladder Feast was an annual purification feast held during the winter solstice. It was an atonement demonstrating respect for all the seals caught the previous year as well as an appeal to assure future hunting success. The Inuit premise was that the spirits of the seals move into their bladders when killed; thus, the bladders of the seals, as well as of walruses and white whales, were removed and harvested, painted, and hung in the men's houses. The bladders were offered food and water. Dances, drumming, song presentations, and purification rites were performed during the feast the men's houses and the inhabitants of the men's house took sweat lodges. At the culmination of the Bladder Feast the bladders were deflated, removed, and returned to the sea. A prayer was recited asking for the bladder spirits to be reborn to ensure new animals the following year. The bladder spirits were pressed to report their favorable experience to Sedna, who would likely release sea animals the next season. A potlatch would occur on the fifth evening. Village boys are led from house to house nightly and offered food by the women. Yet another ritual involves two older men feeding some boys a berry-fish mixture prepared and offered by the women. Women make new clothing for everyone, and the men make new dishes and new songs.

Caribou Festival

The Caribou Festival was held just before the spring hunting season and was ritually significant. Each group of Inuit had a shaman who called the caribou. The hunters observed taboos before and after the hunt. Rituals included women sewing new clothing for the men, people singing, people greeting the caribou, and people holding a variety of ceremonies and social festivities. The thanking of the caribou for their gift of nourishment to the group was an important facet of this festival.

Birth rituals were strictly observed. An infant had to be born in an abode separate from the family residence, otherwise the family residence had to be abandoned. After giving birth, the mother was isolated for one month if the child was a boy and two months if the child was a girl. The naming ceremony, conducted by a shaman, involved the reincarnation of departed souls through birth and naming because the Inuit believed that human souls live after physical death. The spirit of a recently departed family member would eventually reside in a newborn child who received the departed family member's name. The name would automatically transfer the family member's strength to the newborn. However, the newborn was not named (it has been done this way for thousands of years and they continue the practice) until the eighth day of life. If the newborn died before the naming ceremony, it was considered not to have lived.

As children grew, they learned Inuit values and beliefs through religious rituals and practices and then passed the rituals and practices on to their own children. Children listened to their elders and observed a strict code of conduct. No child could harm another child or an animal. They were taught to show respect for all living creatures. Children learned that life is dependent on accepting responsibilities.

Amulets were considered favorable magic because they warded off evil spirits. Amulets were a crucial aspect of Inuit culture and were considered as important as the tools for hunting expeditions. Whaling amulets consisted of images of the bowhead whale and were made from stone, ivory, or baleen (a horny substance found in two rows of plates along the upper jaws of baleen whales). As many as thirty amulets adorned the body or clothing of an Inuit. Amulets were also attached to hunting equipment or the conveyance used for hunting. The shaman usually instilled power in the amulets. Amulets were discarded if they did not prove beneficial, and other amulets would be worn.

Toward the end of the eighteenth century the Inuit began to have increasing contact with traders, explorers, and missionaries. The traditional Inuit were exposed to Christianity by Russians and Europeans. The majority of Inuit have converted to Christianity.

Annette Richardson

See also Shamanism; Vision Quest

Further Reading

Blodgett, J. B. (1979). *The coming and going of the shaman: Eskimo shamanism*. Winnipeg, Canada: Gallery.

Brody, H. (1987). *Living Arctic: Hunters of the Canadian North*. Vancouver, Canada: Douglas & McIntyre.

Bruemmer, F. (1971). *Seasons of the Eskimo: A vanishing way of life*. Toronto, Canada: McClelland and Stewart.

Coles, R. (1977). *The last and first Eskimos*. Boston: New York Graphic Society.

Damas, D. (1971). *The Eskimo*. Ottawa, Canada: National Museums of Canada.

Freuchen, P. (Ed.). (1961). *Book of the Eskimos*. Cleveland, OH: World Publishing.

Hirschfelder, A., & Molin, P. (2001). *Native American religions*. New York: Checkmark Books.

Hunt, N. B. (2002). *Shamanism in North America*. Toronto, Canada: Key Porter Books.

Lassieur, A. (2000). *The Inuit*. Mankato, MN: Bridgestone Books.

Mowat, F. (1980). *The desperate people* (Rev. ed.). Toronto, Canada: McClelland and Stewart-Bantam.

Spencer, R. F. (1959). *The north Alaskan Eskimo: A study in ecology and society*. Washington, DC: U. S. Government Printing Office.

Native Americans: Northeast

Although it is generally known that the U.S. holiday of Thanksgiving developed out of the religious rituals of some northeastern Native Americans, the religious practices of Native Americans of the Northeast are not generally well known. Between 1500 and 1750 several important religious concepts affected the nature of religious rituals and ceremonies among the speakers of both the Algonquian and Iroquoian languages. One of the most significant concepts was that the world was filled with mysterious, spirit-like entities, often called "manitou" among Algonquian-speaking tribes, who could be good or evil. Although manitou could be contacted by individuals through a process of fasting and suffering, sometimes manitou contacted individuals engaged in ordinary activities. Religious leaders (medicine men and medicine women) could elicit the aid of spirit helpers to cure and care for people, just as witches could to bring harm to people. People sought spiritual power by means of the fast, sacrifice, isolation, and dreams. Dreams were important in revealing spiritually powerful information. Among many groups sacred objects could be gathered into spiritually powerful medicine bundles.

Major Rituals and Festivals

Common rituals of the Northeast were world renewal festivals, curing ceremonies, and rituals to mark the cycle of planting and harvesting. Rites of passage were present among all groups. These rites marked an individual's passage through major life stages from birth to death.

Among cultivating groups such as the Shawnee and the six Iroquois tribes (Cayuga, Mohawk, Oneida, Onondaga, Seneca, and Tuscarora), the Green Corn Ceremony, also called the *"busk,"* was one of the most important rituals. Also practiced throughout the Southeast and prairies, the Green Corn Ceremony generally took place in August when it was first apparent that the annual crop of maize, the staple food of the Northeast, was going to provide adequate food for people. In addition to being a ceremony to give thanks, it celebrated the renewal of the world.

Many groups performed rituals to mark major acts associated with both the cultivating of crops and the gathering of wild plants. Among the Iroquois the ceremonial round included the Green Corn Ceremony and the Harvest, Midwinter, Maple, Corn Planting, and Strawberry Ceremonies. The Harvest Ceremony of Algonquian-speaking groups developed into the U.S. holiday of Thanksgiving. The Native Americans of the Northeast gave thanks to their creator, frequently identified as the sun but also as "Grandmother" among the Shawnee and as "Sky Woman" among many of the Iroquois.

Other Ceremonies

Among groups such as the Huron, the Feast of the Dead was held every few years to mourn all who had died since the last feast and in some cases to rebury the dead in a common grave. Especially important among the Iroquois was the Midwinter (or New Year's) Ceremony, usually held in early February. Either religious leaders or members of religious organizations performed curing ceremonies as needed. Among the Iroquois, the False Face Societies were important, and their members, wearing elaborately carved wooden masks, exorcised illness at the Midwinter Ceremony and other key times during the year. The seven-day-long Iroquois Midwinter Ceremony was presided over by two "keepers of the faith." A key element of the ceremony involved the sacrificing and burning of white dogs to demonstrate the people's thankfulness.

Ritual Changes over Time

With the steady destruction or depopulation of northeastern groups since the coming of Europeans, many demoralized northeastern tribes turned to Christianity or other new religions. One of the most significant religions was begun by a Shawnee, Tenskwatawa, brother of the great political leader Tecumseh. Together the brothers attempted to unify Native Americans in the early nineteenth century to stop the westward expansion of white Americans. Whereas Tenskwatawa's religion largely fell apart after the defeat of the Shawnee during the War of 1812, other religions succeeded. Most famous was the Longhouse

AN IROQUOIS GREEN CORN FEAST SPEECH

Thanksgiving speeches were an important component of the Green Corn Ceremony feast of the Iroquois. The following is the first speech given at the feast each year.

We return thanks to our mother, the earth, which sustains us. We return thanks to the rivers and streams, which supply us with water. We return thanks to all herbs, which furnish medicines for the cure of our diseases. We return thanks to the corn, and to her sisters, the beans and squashes, which give us life. We return thanks to the bushes and trees, which provide us with fruit. We return thanks to the wind, which, moving the air, has banished diseases. We return thanks to the moon and stars, which have given to us their light when the sun was gone. We return thanks to our grandfather He-no, that he has protected his grandchildren from witches and reptiles, and has given to us his rain. We return thanks to the sun, that he has looked upon the earth with a beneficent eye. Lastly, we return thanks to the Great Spirit, in whom is embodied all goodness, and who directs all things for the good of his children.

***Source*: Morgan, Lewis Henry. (1901).**
***League of the Ho-De-No-Sau-Nee or Iroquois*, Volume 1. Edited and annotated by Herbert M. Lloyd.**
New York: Dodd, Mead and Company, pp. 194–195.

religion of the Iroquois, which developed out of the chaos of Iroquois life after the American Revolution. Factionalized during the war and overrun by white settlers after the war, the Iroquois turned to alcohol and other destructive practices. At the end of the eighteenth century a Seneca man known as "Handsome Lake" began having visions. Out of his visions developed the Longhouse religion, which blended some elements of Christianity and U.S. values with traditional Iroquois religion and values. Although espousing many white U.S. practices, the Longhouse religion also reinforced traditional rituals such as the Midwinter Ceremony. The teachings of Handsome Lake have been recorded in symbols on the traditional wampum belts of the Iroquois and memorized and repeated by preachers of the Longhouse religion down to the present day. The religions of Tenskwatawa and Handsome Lake had common values regarding alcohol abstinence, greater self-sufficiency, and the need for Native American communities to rely less on help from white Americans.

Outlook in the Twenty-First Century

Both traditional religious societies such as the Iroquois False Face Societies and the Longhouse religion survive among northeastern groups. Many Christian denominations are also present, and since the 1970s many Christian churches have attempted to incorporate traditional, non-Christian elements into their rituals with predominately Native American congregations and to be more tolerant of Native Americans. Developed by John Hascall, who was a medicine man of the Ojibway people and a Catholic priest, the Sacred Circle drug and alcohol therapy programs incorporate elements of both Christianity and traditional Native American religion. Whether they are standing alone or incorporated into Christianity, many northeastern rituals will continue to exist.

Sharlotte Neely

See also Vision Quest

Further Reading

Morgan, L. H. (1962). *League of the Ho-De-No-Sau-Nee or Iroquois*. New York: Corinth Books.

Shimony, A. A. (1994). *Conservatism among the Iroquois at the Six Nations Reserve*. Syracuse, NY: Syracuse University Press.

Spindler, G., & Spindler, L. (1971). *Dreamers without power: The Menomini Indians*. New York: Holt, Rinehart and Winston.

Tanner, H. H. (Ed.). (1987). *Atlas of Great Lakes Indian history*. Norman: University of Oklahoma Press.

Tooker, E. (1970). *The Iroquois ceremonial of midwinter*. Syracuse, NY: Syracuse University Press.

Tooker, E. (1979). *Native North American spirituality of the eastern woodlands*. New York: Paulist Press.

Trigger, B. G. (Ed.). (1978). *Handbook of North American Indians: The Northeast*. Washington, DC: Smithsonian Institution Press.

Wallace, A. F. C. (1972). *Death and rebirth of the Seneca*. New York: Random House.

Weaver, S. M. (1972). *Medicine and politics among the Grand River Iroquois*. Ottawa, Canada: National Museum of Man Publications.

Native Americans: Northwest Coast

Native Americans of the Northwest Coast cultural area live in the coastal region of North America from southeastern Alaska to northern California. Within this area many Native American groups reside with much diversity of language and culture. However, certain rituals are common. These rituals fall into three primary categories: individual expressions through the guardian spirit complex, rites of passage, and communal ceremonies. All three categories of rituals are expressed though a broad range of ceremonies referred to as "potlatch" (a ceremonial feast marked by the host's lavish distribution of gifts). In the last 150 years many of these rituals have been blended with Christian beliefs.

Certain aspects of the natural environment are considered sacred in Northwest Coast religions. Sacred places include waterfalls and mountain lakes; sacred plants include red cedar, the boughs of which are a common component of ritual cleansing; sacred objects include masks, rattles, power boards or poles, which are activated by a spiritualist for divination, and drums.

Guardian Spirit Complex

Common to the belief systems of the Native Americans of the Northwest Coast is a complex of ideas centered around guardian spirits. Almost as much a part of the natural realm as of the supernatural realm, guardian spirits are manifested in both animate and inanimate forms. Often these spirits have been divided into "lay" spirits and "shamanistic" spirits, but these categories are not so clear-cut. Usually a "lay" spirit relationship is that between an individual and his or her guardian spirit that imparts some basic skill such as hunting, fighting, or fishing for men and basket making, berry picking, and weaving for women. The "shamanistic" spirit, on the other hand, gives certain individuals the ability to heal people (or harm them) either spiritually or physically. Spiritual healing involves a shaman traveling to the world of the dead to retrieve lost souls or removing foreign objects that have been placed in the ailing person's body by someone intending that person harm. This ritual takes various forms, such as the "spirit canoe" of the southern Puget Sound Salish people, in which the shaman and his spiritual helpers traveled to the land of the dead in a spiritual canoe, or the "soul catcher," a carved tubular object that is used to trap the patient's spirit. All major components of the belief systems of the Northwest Coast people are focused on an individual and his or her personal guardian spirit.

Guardian spirits of the Northwest Coast consist of both individual expression and hereditary rights. As do most Native Americans the people of the Northwest Coast acquire a guardian spirit during a period of self-sacrificing, fasting, and praying. Additionally, in the Northwest Coast an individual can encounter spirit helpers that "run in the family," that is, that are acquired by virtue of kinship. The guardian spirit complex is a relationship between a spirit power that gives some advantage in hunting, fishing, war, or some other specialized knowledge. Additionally, it is a personal relationship, one that is not readily divulged but that is expressed during the winter ceremonies in song and dance. Yet, despite the secrecy surrounding a guardian spirit's identity, people can often guess what spirit a person possesses based on that person's actions, skills, and abilities and on the words and movements of the songs and dances.

In past times an individual was sent at the age of puberty to a place of solitude to seek a guardianspirit. This spirit quest typically involved ritual fasting and bathing. Among most groups both boys and girls participated in this quest. If unsuccessful the young person would be sent out again. Some individuals sought more than one spirit, although it was said that only the strongest person could handle more than one. In addition to a person obtaining a spirit through

TLINGIT RITUAL PREPARATIONS FOR THE POTLATCH

"They always notify a year before so they can practice the dance, get ready for the potlatch". Formal messengers (nakani) are not sent at this time. "They send word there, that's all. 'You're invited.' They always notify a year before."

During this year the host chief prepared himself magically by bathing before dawn and by observing dietary rules. "They drink water so much a day, not much. They don't eat much." Presumably at the end a total fast was enjoined. The chief also had to be continent. His wife slept alone in their bedroom while he slept on the bench by the door of the house, although my informant did not know for how long. I did not learn whether other members of the host's group also observed similar taboos.

The host might also prepare the magical "medicine to be noticed ." Presumably this involved the root of some plant, as was customary in Tlingit "medicines," with which was placed a piece of something that had previously received favorable notice. This was to insure a successful potlatch.

The guests also took magical precautions, but these seem to have been most important for the song leaders and principal dancers, for I heard no specific mention of the guest chiefs in this connection. Swanton (1908, p. 438) specified of guests from Sitka on their way to a potlatch at Klukwan: "While they were going up the dance leaders had to fast for two days and for some time they had to keep away from women; otherwise they would not live long." I believe that this abstinence was because they were using a magical ingredient. One of my informants, who was a song leader in the group invited from Dry Bay to Yakutat in 1910, told how she and the two male song leaders were given the medicine 'no strength inside one,' and in consequence had to fast for a day. This was a tasteless piece of root which the song leaders held in their mouths while performing. This was to prevent them from making mistakes, and to attract favorable attention even if they sang and danced poorly.

Guests might also use "need medicine" or "looking at the sun medicine" so that they might be paid twice over at the potlatch. An informant was shown this plant by Sam George, a son of Dry Bay Chief George, the same chief who had prepared the medicine for the song leaders in 1910. "When they're having a potlatch, when they start paying off people from one end, then they come back again. If a person has that kayani ['medicine'], they give him another one [gift]. I think it's that'alatin nakw ['looking at medicine']. Sam George was surprised [that it worked]. His father or grandfather made it for him in a potlatch… [He was paid twice], even coming back."

***Source*: Laguna, Frederica-de. (1972).**
Under Mount Saint Elias; the History and Culture of the Yakutat Tlingit.
Smithsonian Contributions to Anthropology, Vol. 7.
Washington, D.C.: Smithsonian Institution Press, pp. 616–617.

this quest, guardian spirits could come unannounced when the person was ill or in mourning, in a dream, or as the result of a chance encounter. The guardian spirit concept remains a common aspect of Native American ritual and represents a complex expression that is highly individualistic. During times of ritual fasting and bathing the individual seeks a site of seclusion and sacredness. Sometimes these sites are sought anew, but often they are sites that family members know of. Ritual bathing also plays an important role in Northwest Coast ritual life. Because ritual bathing requires places with privacy and pure water, it is becoming an increasingly difficult pursuit in recent times due to environmental degradation and the encroachment of civilization. In recent times other means of acquiring a spirit have replaced the spirit quest. These means include shaman assistance and ritual induction.

Since the 1880s a religion known as the "Indian Shaker Church" has been present in the southern

Northwest Coast. This religion combines beliefs of the guardian spirit complex and Christianity. Shakers receive spiritual "gifts" from the holy spirit and use them to heal people. Shakers hold regular church services, during which members ring bells and sing as a form of prayer. Shakerism is considered a Christian religion by its practitioners.

Three general types of guardian spirit rituals exist in the Northwest Coast. All three involve sacred dances. In the north, among the Tlingit, Haida, and Tsimshian, ritual centers around dances demonstrating prerogatives inherited through the matrilineal (based on the maternal line) clan. Dances portray the symbols of the clans in the form of crests. These crests are also displayed on totem poles and house fronts.

In the central Northwest Coast, among the Wakashan speakers, winter dances center around the performances of secret societies. Membership in a society is by ritual induction, during which individuals are secluded while they learn the rules and obligations of the society. The most famous of the secret societies is the Hamatsa (Cannibal Dance). A ritual performance by members of the society is also called the "Hamatsa." The Hamatsa dancers are considered particularly powerful because during the ritual performances they interact with the dead, a practice that would be deadly to individuals who have not undergone the proper training and ritual preparation. Membership in these secret societies is considered highly prestigious. Much of their ritual is unknown to nonmembers, hence the term *secret societies.*

In the southern Northwest Coast, especially among the Coast Salish people, winter dances center on the individual demonstrations of guardian spirits. "Spirit dancers" perform song and dance, which are their personal property, not allowed to be used by others. The performances can be done to heal or to perform other tasks, but most importantly they are done to improve the individuals' well-being.

Rites of Passage

The principal rites of passage practiced in the Northwest Coast center around birth, child naming, marriage, and death. Typically these rites are conducted at a potlatch that varies in size according to the status of the individual and the individual's family. Rites of passage are conducted on behalf of individuals but require the participation of the larger kin group. Child naming, for example, requires the consent of family members to bestow an inherited name on an individual. A number of ceremonies mark rites of passage, including the performance of masked dancers, the use of ritual objects such as rattles, and the demonstration of inherited rites and privileges. Ritual preparation is an important component of rites of passage, usually involving cleansing through bathing, fasting, or scrubbing the body with the boughs of red cedar.

Communal Rituals

Some religious rites are conducted on behalf of the community as a whole. The most common and most famous was the First Salmon Ceremony, which welcomed the first catch of the season. The actual species varied from tribe to tribe, but generally the first-caught fish of the five species of salmon that were most important to the local village was the object of this ceremony. For example, the Coast Salish people of the mouth of the Fraser River in British Columbia depend on the sockeye salmon to a large extent and consider it most important to their livelihood; therefore, the sockeye is treated with reverence in this ceremony. The people believe that salmon live in the ocean in longhouses much like those inhabited by humans. Once a year the salmon don their fish clothing and swim up streams, where they would make themselves available to people. If salmon were treated with respect they would allow themselves to be caught and continue to return year after year. When the first salmon was taken each year the fish was brought into the village, where a ritual was conducted over it. It was sprinkled with eagle down and red ochre and ritually cooked. Members of the village all ate a small piece, and the bones were gathered and placed back into the water. The fish then resumed its living form and went to tell the rest of the species how it had been treated properly. From that point on members of the community are allowed to commence fishing for food to eat and store. No one is allowed to fish before this ceremony is conducted; therefore, the ceremony has conservation effects because it limits access. After a hiatus of several decades this communal ceremony is making a comeback in many communities throughout the Northwest Coast.

Other than the First Salmon Ceremony, communal rituals were few. Although rituals included the entire community and neighboring communities as participants, most rituals were conducted on behalf of an individual or a family.

Potlatch

The best-known Northwest Coast ceremony is the potlatch. The word *potlatch* means "to give" and has come to be applied by anthropologists and Native American people alike to ceremonies that involve the ceremonial redistribution of wealth goods. A potlatch is often held to mark certain life stages, such as child naming, a wedding, or a funeral; but other occasions could be marked by a potlatch. The northern Northwest Coast clans commemorate the building of a clan house or the raising of a totem pole with a potlatch, which validates certain rights to territory. Other people, such as the Kwakwaka'wakw (Kwakiutl), hold a potlatch to validate one's status or to mark one's entry into a secret society. For the Coast Salish a potlatch is held to make public one's spirit dance. Although the potlatch has entered into general anthropological parlance as a grandiose ceremony used to enhance an individual's status, potlatches take a variety of forms and served a variety of functions. The ceremonial redistribution of wealth goods takes place on numerous occasions; naming ceremonies, funerals, weddings, house raisings or totem pole raisings, and other functions are reasons for a potlatch. Although historical evidence overwhelmingly supports the contention that potlatching and the amount of wealth goods redistributed increased dramatically in the mid- to late 1800s, there is also evidence to support the contention that potlatching was an important part of the socioeconomic system prior to European contact. Certainly today the potlatch is the most important ceremony throughout the Northwest Coast and is a time when numerous rituals are conducted.

In the past a potlatch lasted several days and included guests from numerous surrounding villages. The host would recruit help from kin and fellow villagers because to host a potlatch single handedly would have been nearly impossible. Preparations often began a year in advance, with invitations being announced and the gathering of wealth goods begun. When the actual potlatch began the entire house was cleared out so that hundreds of people could be seated inside. Although a potlatch might last several days, the actual redistribution of wealth goods would be only a small part of the ceremony. Feasting, performances by masked dancers, speeches, and contests took place. In modern times, with many Native American people needing to working for a living, potlatches have been condensed into one day or a weekend, but the tradition has persisted. Today the potlatch remains the major setting of Northwest Coast ritual.

Daniel L. Boxberger

See also Native Americans: Northeast; Native Americans: Plains; South America: Highland; South America: Savanna and Tropical Forest

Further Reading

Amoss, P. T. (1978). *Coast Salish spirit dancing: The survival of an ancestral religion*. Seattle: University of Washington Press.

Amoss, P. T. (1987). The fish God gave us: The first salmon ceremony revived. *Arctic Anthropology*, 24, 56–66.

Barnett, H. G. (1957). *Indian Shakers: A messianic cult of the Pacific Northwest*. Carbondale: Southern Illinois University Press.

Barnett, H. G. (1968). *The nature and function of the potlatch*. Eugene: University of Oregon Press.

Boas, F. (1930). *Religion of the Kwakiutl Indians*. New York: Columbia University Press.

Drucker, P. (1965). *Cultures of the north Pacific Coast*. San Francisco: Chandler Publishing.

Goldman, I. (1975). *The mouth of heaven: An introduction to Kwakiutl religion thought*. New York: Wiley.

Jonaitis, A. (1999). *The Mowachaht whalers shrine*. Seattle: University of Washington Press.

Kan, S. (1988). *Symbolic immortality: The Tlingit potlatch of the nineteenth century*. Washington, DC: Smithsonian Institution Press.

Miller, J. (1999). *Lushootseed culture and the shamanic odyssey: An anchored radiance*. Lincoln: University of Nebraska Press.

Native Americans: Plains

Despite frequently being portrayed in films and other forms of popular media, the religious rituals of Plains Native Americans are not generally well known. By 1830, at the height of traditional Plains culture, the Plains Native Americans occupied the stretch from the Mississippi River in the east to the Rocky Mountains in the west and from southern Canada in the north to the Texas-Mexico border area in the south. By this time, several important religious

THE "MEDICINE" WOMAN OF THE BLACKFOOT

The most important functionary in the Blackfoot sun dance is a woman, known among the whites as the medicine woman, and upon a clear comprehension of her functions and antecedents depends our understanding of the ceremony itself. Accordingly, we shall proceed with as complete an exposition of her office as the information at hand allows. In the first place, a sun dance cannot occur unless some woman qualifies for the office. On the other hand, it was almost inconceivable that there should be a summer in which such a qualification would not be made. This attitude of our informants implies that public opinion had sufficient force to call out volunteers against their own wills. There was a feeling that an annual sun dance was, from a religious and ethical point of view, necessary to the general welfare, for which some individual ought to sacrifice personal comfort and property to the extent required by custom. As we shall see later, this was no small price to pay for a doubtful honor. This feeling was sure to express itself in the subtle ways peculiar to Indian society, if need be, to the direct suggestion of a candidate who in turn felt impelled to come forward as if prompted entirely from within.

As a rule, however, the woman qualifies by a vow. Oftimes, when a member of the family is dangerously ill, one of the women goes out of the tipi and raising her eyes to the sun calls upon it that health may be restored to the ailing one. In such an appeal she offers to make gifts to the sun, usually specifying that she will sacrifice a piece of cloth, a dress, a robe, an ax, etc., which are after a time, provided the sick one improves, hung in trees or deposited upon a hill. Such appeals are still made with great frequency. It is believed that unless the woman has been industrious, truthful, and above all, true to her marriage vows, her appeal will not be answered. Sometimes, when the woman addresses the sun she promises to be the medicine woman at the next sun dance. She herself may be ill and promise such a sacrifice in case she receives help. Again, she may, out of gratitude for the satisfactory way in which her prayers have been answered, announce her intention to take this step. In such a case, a fermal announcement is made to the sun. In company with a man, usually a medicineman experienced in the ceremonies, she steps out into the camp, where they face the sun whom the man addresses, explaining that as this woman asked for help in time of need and that in as much as it was granted, she in turn promises to be the medicine woman at the first opportunity. Some such formal announcement is made in every case where the prayers have been answered. By this formality, the vow receives public registry.

***Source*: Wissler, Clark. *The Sun Dance of the Blackfoot Indians.* (1918). New York: American Museum of Natural History, Anthropological Papers, Vol. 16, Part 3, pp. 231–232.**

concepts affected the nature of religious rituals and ceremonies. One of the most significant concepts was that everything, both animate and inanimate, has a spirit or consciousness. By seeking visions, Plains Native American men and women could contact and enlist the aid of guardian spirits, who typically manifested themselves as animals. The most sacred animal was the bison (buffalo), from which the Plains tribes got most of their food. Places were also sacred, some more than others because of their concentrations of spiritual power and importance in creation stories. These places were sometimes marked by medicine wheels made of stone. There are dozens of medicine wheels in the Plains, but the most famous is the medicine wheel in Wyoming's Bighorn Mountains. Medicine wheels are circles of stones dating from prehistoric times. Some are large, some are small, and many have features that line up with seasonal astronomical sightings. All have religious significance to the Plains tribes. Objects could also be sacred. Among many groups sacred objects could be gathered into spiritually powerful medicine bundles. The most sacred object was the calumet (pipe), often made from red catlinite stone. Religious leaders (medicine men and medicine women) were more skilled than most at connecting with spiritual power, although all men and women sought such power on their own as well.

Major Rituals and Festivals

The most important ceremony throughout the Plains was the sun dance, which probably originated with the Cheyenne and Arapaho and spread throughout the area to more than twenty groups. At its core the sun dance was a world renewal ceremony and therefore important to the entire tribe. Consequently, a sun dance typically was held when the entire tribe could gather in one place in the late summer when the bison were most concentrated and food was most plentiful. Despite being of concern to the entire tribe, a sun dance was usually sponsored by one man, often termed a "whistler" because of his use of an eagle bone whistle during the ceremony. The motivation for sponsoring a sun dance could range from wanting to ensure the well-being of the tribe to seeking spiritual power during a time of crisis to thanking the supernatural for some favor, such as the recovery of a critically ill child, to wanting extraordinary power to accomplish revenge against an enemy tribe. Because so many people gathered for a sun dance, preliminary activities could include the opening of medicine bundles or other activities of religious societies. Sun dances were also times for purely social activities.

One of the first acts of the sun dance was to select and erect a tall central pole surrounded by a large open-topped structure. One or more medicine men would supervise activities, prepare the key participant, and conduct the ceremony. With the moral support of his family and members of his warrior society, the key participant would often fast, pray, spend time in a sweat lodge, and seek visions in order to purify himself. The main activities of the key participant included self-torture. In the most famous sun dance self-torture typically the key participant's chest was pierced with bison bone skewers attached to leather cords fastened to the top of the sun dance pole. The goal was for the skewers to pull free while the key participant tugged at the skewers and danced around the pole, culminating in a vision. Sometimes the key participant's back or legs would also be skewered so that he could drag bison skulls as he danced. To show support, his friends from his warrior society might inflict lesser degrees of torture upon themselves, including the stripping away of skin as flesh offerings.

From the end of the nineteenth century into the 1930s, the U.S. government banned the sun dance. As a result the ceremony died out among some groups and became less elaborate among others. In general the number of sun dancers declined among most Plains groups until the late 1960s and the development of groups such as the American Indian Movement (AIM), who saw value in the traditional beliefs.

Other Rituals

Among other significant rituals of the Plains was the Calumet (or Pipe) Ceremony. The Calumet Ceremony was meant to instill peace in participants by the smoking of tobacco from a shared pipe. The Lakota Sioux Yuwipi Ceremony existed mostly to find lost objects or cure the sick. The Pawnee Morning Star Ceremony involved the sacrifice of a female captive, who, if cooperative, brought special blessings to the tribe. Rites of passage were performed among all groups. These rites marked an individual's passage through major life stages from birth to death.

Although the sun dance was important throughout the Plains, it was more important in the western Plains than in the eastern Plains (prairies). Living on the fringes of the Northeast and Southeast, prairie groups planted crops, mostly maize, and thus rituals associated with planting and harvesting were also important and held throughout the year. Some groups, such as the Pawnee, engaged in the harvest ritual known as the "green corn ceremony," more common in the Northeast and Southeast than in the Plains.

Astronomical observations were common throughout the Plains, and groups such as the Cheyenne referred to the Milky Way as the "Hanging Road," by which the souls of the dead proceeded to the afterlife. Astronomical observations told prairie groups when to plant or harvest their crops and when appropriate ceremonies should be held throughout the year.

Ghost Dance

With the near-elimination of the bison and severe human depopulation at the end of the nineteenth century, many demoralized Plains tribes turned to the new religion they called the "Ghost Dance." Ghost Dance participants danced for days and collapsed with visions of dead relatives who were to be resurrected. With the slaughter of Lakota Sioux Ghost

Dancers in 1890 at Wounded Knee, South Dakota, by the U.S. Army, the religion virtually ceased to exist. The promised resurrection of the dead and the return of the bison did not happen.

About the same time, however, yet another religion developed and still exists as the Native American Church. Combining some Christian ideas with Plains values such as vision questing, the Native American Church advocates the use of the hallucinogenic plant peyote during rituals. Although the Ghost Dance religion failed, the Native American Church has succeeded, not in promising the impossible, but in helping people cope with their problems.

Outlook in the Twenty-First Century

Both the sun dance and the Native American Church survive among the Plains groups. Many Christian denominations are also present among Plains groups, and since the 1970s many Christian churches have attempted to incorporate traditional, non-Christian elements into the rituals of churches with predominately Native American congregations. For example, it is common for people to smoke the calumet on the altar in churches and for churches to hold Christian sweat lodges. Sacred circles draw upon ceremonies of the past when participants sat in a circle around a fire. Sacred Circle drug and alcohol therapy programs incorporate elements of both Christianity and traditional Plains religion. Whether standing alone or incorporated into Christianity, many Plains rituals will continue to thrive.

Sharlotte Neely

See also Vision Quest

Further Reading

Crow Dog, L., & Erdoes, R. (1996). *Crow Dog: Four generations of Sioux medicine men*. New York: Harper.

DeMallie, R. J. (Ed.). (2001). *Handbook of North American Indians: Plains*. Washington, DC: Smithsonian Institution Press.

Frey, R. (1993). *The world of the Crow Indians*. Norman: University of Oklahoma Press.

Harrod, H. L. (1992). *Renewing the world: Plains Indian religion and morality*. Tucson: University of Arizona Press.

Hull, M. (2000). *Sun dancing: A spiritual journey on the red road*. Rochester, VT: Inner Traditions.

Kehoe, A. B. (1989). *The Ghost Dance: Ethnohistory and revitalization*. New York: Holt, Rinehart and Winston.

Lowie, R. H. (1982). *Indians of the Plains*. Lincoln: University of Nebraska Press.

Mooney, J. (1991). *The Ghost-Dance religion and the Sioux outbreak of 1890*. Lincoln: University of Nebraska Press.

Neihardt, J. G., & Black Elk. (2000). *Black Elk speaks: Being the life story of a holy man of the Oglala Sioux*. Lincoln: Bison Books of University of Nebraska Press.

Smith, H., & Snake, R. (1998). *One nation under God: The triumph of the Native American Church*. Santa Fe, NM: Clear Light Publishing.

St. Pierre, M., & Long Soldier, T. (1995). *Walking in the sacred manner: Healers, dreamers, and pipe carriers-medicine women of the Plains Indians*. Carmichael, CA: Touchstone Books.

Native Americans: Pueblo

The Pueblo Native Americans conceive of nature and the Creator as one. Pueblos revere the sky, Earth, and moon and recognize numerous supernatural spirits (Great Ones) living in the underworld, in the sky, or at the four cardinal points and animal spirits such as water serpents and spiders. Secret religious and fraternal societies are organized to venerate these spirits. Kachina (a deified ancestral spirit) and kiva (a semisubterranean chamber) societies' members dress up and impersonate the spirits having great power for good or ill. Pueblos conduct ritual dances in kivas or on village plazas to placate and venerate powerful spirits so they will bring rain, life, and good health. Ceremonies are divided into the summer and winter solstices, scheduled according to agricultural cycles. The Koshare, who entertain during ceremonies, ridicule evil spirits and embarrass those who have acted against tribal standards. The Pueblo people including Hopis, Zunis, Eastern Pueblos of the Rio Grande River, and Western Pueblos of the mesa and canyon area. Among these groups there is cultural unity, but four linguistic stocks, different forms of social organization, and variations in religious rituals.

Religion is the key to understanding Pueblo daily life in the arts, government, and society. Pueblos venerate a range of supernatural spirits, cosmic beings, animals, and ancestral spirits. Kachinas are represented by masked dancers who become the spirits

The kiva, or underground ceremonial chamber, has been, and continues to be, the place where the most sacred rituals are performed by the Pueblo peoples of the American Southwest. This photo is of the remains of a large and ancient kiva in Chaco Canyon, New Mexico. COURTESY OF DAVID LEVINSON.

represented by the masks. Because wearing a kachina mask is dangerous, a dancer must go through a ritual of separation from the mask after a dance. In the kiva there is a hole in the floor *(sipapu)* that represents the place of emergence of the people from the inner worlds. The prayers of the people return through the *sipapu* to the Great Ones of the underworld. Pueblos offer up prayers, make gift offerings, and hereditary clan and society priesthoods conduct rituals and ceremonies. Each priesthood worships some being and has a ritual, paraphernalia, and a calendar of ceremonies. The priesthoods ensure proper presentation of ceremonies.

Location

The Pueblo people live in villages of compact stone or adobe houses (pueblos) and are agriculturalists. They consist of four linguistic stocks: Tanoan, Keresan, Zunian, and Shoshonean. The Hopi (Peaceful Ones) speak a Shoshonean dialect and reside in northeastern Arizona in six villages. The Zuni, Acoma, and Laguna live to the east of the Hopis in what is now western New Mexico. Four other tribal groups of eastern Pueblo people—Tiwa, Tewa, Towa, and Keres—live along a 209-kilometer stretch of the Rio Grande. Residing in high desert villages in New Mexico and eastern Arizona, the Hopi and Zuni remained more isolated from European contact and so preserved more of their religious heritage.

Clans

Pueblo tribes are groups of clans who take their names from the natural environment. Religious motivations underlie most clan and society activities. Spiritual leaders of religious secret societies conduct ceremonies and perform rituals throughout the calendar year to seek rain, good crops, and tribal welfare. Among the Tewa, when the spirits are impersonated in ritual ceremonies, they reflect the social divisions of the winter and summer moieties (components). The winter moiety sponsors rituals concerning winter spirits who may be impersonated only by members of the winter moiety. The summer moiety sponsors rituals of the summer supernaturals and impersonates their spirits. Among eastern Pueblos along the Rio Grande the pueblo is divided into summer and winter people. Men's societies have responsibility for protecting the tribe and conducting fertility rituals. The roles of the priesthoods are those of healers. Members of ancient Hopi priesthoods function as clowns or fun-makers during sacred kachina dances.

Most Pueblos perform their religious rituals according to the solar cycle. Limited water supplies create among Pueblos a sense of uncertainty, which is reflected in their tribal mythologies and emergence on the earth. Insecurity is noticeable among Zuni and Hopi in the western areas because they live in an area vulnerable to water shortages. Pueblo people rely on irrigation to ensure crops. Life centers on religious rituals. A recurrent fear in the Zuni emergence account is of a barren land, and ceremonies focus on the coming and going of rain. The cycles of planting, maturing, and harvesting of corn dominate the symbolism of their intense ceremonial life.

Kachinas

Many Pueblo religious rituals and ceremonies supplicate the supernatural spirits for rain. The Hopi kachina Anak'china, a supernatural spirit shared by many eastern and western Pueblos, and the Zuni spirit Kokokihi are similar. They dance for gentle rain to nourish the corn crops. Hemis, recognized by his towering headdress, repeats a prayer for clouds and rain. Ahola, one of the major kachinas, represents Alosaka, the germ god, who has power over fertility and growth. At Zuni Pueblo in New Mexico, the Corn Maids come after Shalako, the annual ceremony held in December with prayers for health and fecundity of people, animals, and crops, and Pautiwa brings water so all the people may have good luck with summer rains. The snow kachina is another important source of water. Hopi believe that life is continuous after death because the deceased join the kachina spirits. Ancestors become rain-bringers, and this belief is woven into Hopi ceremonies.

Kivas

Among the Pueblo, guardian spirits and animals played important roles in their complex religious rituals. Kivas are thought of as the doorways to the underworld, the *sipapu* represents the place of emergence. Each pueblo had at least one kiva. Kivas began appearing in the Pueblo world about 750 CE, during the development of the first true pueblos from 700 to 900. Some people think the pueblo grew around the nucleus of the kiva, usually located in the plaza. By 1150 to 1300 a more dramatic, ceremonial life in the kivas developed. The kivas were constructed with walls of stone for men only and used as clubhouses or chapels for society members. At Taos Pueblo, New Mexico, the kiva societies have responsibility for conducting ceremonies, rituals, and dances.

Emergence

In Hopi lore the Earth always existed. Hopis were generated by the Earth, emerging through the *sipapu.* The *sipapu* has its origin in Hopi emergence accounts. Hopis came together in the subterranean Third World. They created an enormous reed plant, pierced the sky of the Third World, left the Third World, and escaped to the world above with all the animals. Two brothers, Spirit Masters, helped them. The Hopis and the animals finally emerged from the Grand Canyon. The land was dark and wet. The Hopis and animals tried to bring light to the world. Spider made the moon. Hopismade the sun from a bleached deerskin shield. Coyote opened a jar; sparks flew into the sky and became stars. Vulture flapped his wings, dried up the wetland, and formed land for the people. Spirit Masters formed grooves in the Earth, making valleys for the water to flow through. The Hopis formed into clans with animal names and settled in permanent homes. The place where the reed pierced the sky of the Third World is Sipaapuni, a side canyon in the Grand Canyon.

Pueblo people emphasize the importance of the Earth more than the heavens. The Pueblos originated with the emergence of people from the underworld. The Keresan people trace their origins to the underworld, from which they emerged through an opening and took up residence on the Rio de los Frijoles near its confluence with the Rio Grande. Among Taos Pueblos the most important ritual is the annual August pilgrimage to Blue Lake. The lake symbolizes the source of life, the place of emergence, and it is the origin of Taos's water supply. The Jemez Pueblo (Hemish) people also have accounts of their emergence from the underworld by way of Lake Hoa-sjela. The Tewa people speak of their emergence through a lake in the San Juan Mountains. The creation story of the Tiwa people credits Badger with digging a hole from one world to the next during emergence, allowing the people passage to the world above. In traditional dances men at Ysleta del Sur Pueblo, El Paso, Texas, wear badger skins and thus honor the one who helped the people make the journey.

Emergence accounts are useful in understanding Zuni religious beliefs and practices. The Sun took pity on people living underground in the dark Fourth World in the Southwest. The people could not see each other, could not breathe, and felt their way around. The Sun's two sons went to the Southwest, where the people wanted to know how to leave the darkness and agreed to follow the two sons in order to see father Sun. Branches from trees were used to make prayer sticks in preparation for the ascent. The bow priests led the way and emerged first, followed by those who carried medicine bundles. The two sons realized that the people had no mouths and could not eat or enjoy corn. At night the bow priests cut each face, making lips and a mouth for everyone. Everyone then ate corn and drank water. Witches followed the people, bringing them gifts of corn and death. The *koyemci,* a clowning society, emerged as the children of an incestuous couple: a priest's son and daughter. While crossing a river, children who were washed from their mothers' arms became kachinas. Water Spider stretched his legs and arms in the four directions. He was in the "middle place" and announced that this was where the people would live forever.

Hopi Rituals

The Hopi annual cycle of religious ceremonies and rituals is based on the agricultural calendar: planting and harvesting of crops. The Hopi ceremonial year is divided into two parts, based on the winter solstice and summer solstice. Hopis live in a harsh, dry region but have successfully cultivated corn, beans, squash, and melons. Their rituals center on the need for rain to bring life to the seeds. The great annual religious winter ceremonies of the Hopi are Pamurti in January, Powamu in February, and Palulukonti in March.

Powamu is a ceremony held for sixteen to twenty days of the second moon after the winter solstice. It is the bean-planting ceremony. Powamu celebrates the return of the kachinas to the pueblo because they have been away since July. A festival exorcises evil spirits; it is a purification and renovation of the Earth in preparation for the planting season; it is the advent of the spirits. A messenger goes from kiva to kiva announcing the onset of the festival. Prayer sticks are made and placed at shrines. Masks are painted. Beans and corn are planted in sand basins in all the kivas. The seeds germinate as they are warmed and watered. One morning Ahul, the sun kachina, arrives with the kachina chief. Ahul visits each kiva and gives blessings, prayers, and gifts of corn and bean sprouts to the kiva groups in retreat, and then everyone feasts.

In July Niman, the home ceremony, is conducted over the sixteen-day period after the summer solstice. At this ceremony the Hemis kachina enters the plaza carrying corn stalks from the first corn crop. These are symbols of the bounty that the kachinas have bestowed on the Hopi. The Homegoing Dance sends the kachinas to their homes in the San Francisco Peaks, west of the Hopi Indian Reservation, Arizona. After the Niman ceremony, the kachinas depart until the next December, when the cycle starts again.

Zuni Rituals

Among the Zuni are many secret societies whose functions pertain to warring, healing, hunting, agriculture, and religion. Cardinal directions play a key role in Zuni rituals. The Pihlakwe (bow priesthood) represents the west; the Shumekwe represents the east; Newekwe (Galaxy People) represent the upper region; Chitalekwe (Rattlesnake People) represent the lower region. Each society has its own set of rituals. Some are performed secretly; others are performed publicly as dances. A complex clan system is based on matrilineal (based on the maternal line) and matrilocal clans (geographical in nature, based on the home territory of the wife's kin group), encompassing all other social groups, including six kiva male societies. Priesthoods orders concerned with medicine, curing, and rain and the bow priesthood complete the social organization. The Shalako ceremony conducted in late November or early December is a component of the winter solstice ceremony. The Shalako ceremony begins when ten masked figures, the *koyemci* (sacred clowns), announce that in four days the *kokko*s (kachinas representing them) will arrive in the village. They also announce that in eight days the Shalako will commence. The Zuni Shalako kachinas are six giant messengers of the spirits. The large, birdlike kachinas dance in and around new homes, blessing them. They enter the ceremonial grounds south of Zuni, accompanied by members of a medicine society. All six Shalakos arrive at the ceremonial grounds, run back and forth over a racecourse, and plant prayer sticks to assure the health of the villagers and the fecundity of people and their animals and crops. The Shalako dance all night and return to their homes in Sacred Lake. The ceremony closes the Zuni year, and shortly afterward the New Year arrives at the time of the winter solstice, when a new cycle of religious ceremonies begins.

Pueblo Rituals

At Santo Domingo Pueblo, New Mexico, medicine men hold a spiritual retreat before a masked dance is held. Medicine men meet in the kiva, symbolically returning to Shipap, the place of people's emergence, to get the Mother to send the Cloud People. The medicine men return after four days, bringing the Shiwanna (Rain Makers) with them, and the masked dance is held. During the retreat the medicine men make kachina dolls for the girls and miniature bows and arrows for the boys. The medicine men redecorate and repaint the masks and prepare other paraphernalia for the masked dance. Eight medicine societies are integral to the spiritual life of Santo Domingo. The four major medicine societies—Flint, Cikame, Grant, and Boyaka—work cooperatively for the good of the people.

The Taos Pueblos developed their ceremonial year by dividing themselves into two groups: summer people and winter people. Summer people became responsible for ceremonies associated with the natural cycle of the summer season. Winter people became responsible for participation in winter rituals. Six kiva societies that are organized around Northside and Southside areas take responsibility for winter dances and summer dances. Kiva initiation ceremonies are completed in time for the August tribal pilgrimage to Blue Lake, Taos Pueblo, New Mexico. At Zia Pueblo, New Mexico, the Flint medicine society conducts rituals to heal and rituals to ensure sufficient water. At Picuris Pueblo, New

Mexico, the Northside people, associated with the cumulus cloud kiva, and the Southside people, associated with the sky kiva, take responsibility for rituals to ensure rain and successful hunting. At Tewa Pueblo, New Mexico, the people visit shrines located at the cardinal directions around the pueblo to pray to departed ancestors and to leave offerings of cornmeal or feathers for departed ancestors.

Spanish Conquest

Before the Spanish arrived in 1540 a council of leaders of religious societies governed each pueblo autonomously. The Spanish authorities and Franciscan fathers built missions and churches in each pueblo. They taught Roman Catholicism, Spanish and Latin languages, music, painting, and skills such as carpentry. The priests insisted that the Native Americans give up their religious practices, such as dances, songs, and masked celebrations, and their use of sacred cornmeal. The Pueblos connected Christian beliefs with their traditional spiritual practices and transformed Catholic saints James, Isodore, and Rafael into kachinas. The priests intensified their pressure on the Pueblos by the 1640s. They persecuted Pueblo priests, accused them of sorcery, flogged many, and hanged some. They raided the Native Americans' sacred chambers, defiled their altars, and burned their masks and feathers. In 1598 Juan de Onate and 129 settlers colonized the Zuni area. He suppressed the Pueblos' religious practices, enslaved some Pueblos, killed others, and exacted tribute from the survivors. These cruelties led to widespread Pueblo participation in the revolt of 1680. Pueblos burned the Catholic missions, killed the governor in Santa Fe, New Mexico, and murdered numerous Spanish settlers and Catholic priests. Pueblos under Pope, the San Juan Pueblo leader who planned and organized the revolt by making an alliance between most villages, drove the Spanish conquerors away until 1696. Persecution by Spanish priests and conquistadors encouraged Pueblos to keep secret their traditional beliefs. Because ceremonies with altars, fetishes, songs, and prayers would lose effectiveness if shared or adopted by others, secrecy was important in maintaining the power of traditional ceremonies. Persecution for their religious beliefs and a strong faith in the intrinsic value of their practices forced Pueblos to adopt others' beliefs.

Evidence of Roman Catholicism is visible throughout the pueblos of the Rio Grande region. To some extent this evidence shows the assimilation process as Pueblo people integrated Catholicism into their spiritual traditions. Catholic beliefs, the Mass, and holy days have been incorporated into Pueblo traditional practices. The calendar of festivals, rituals, and ceremonies shows this blending of Pueblo and Catholic religions. At Santo Domingo, New Year's Day is celebrated with a mass. The Pueblos also celebrate 6 January (the Feast of the Epiphany or "day of the kings"). In late January or early February they conduct a ceremony, Sandaro, that depicts the arrival of the Spaniards. In August they celebrate the traditional Corn Dance, an elaborate ceremony presented by the kiva societies in full strength. The Spaniards conquered the Pueblos, and the Pueblos absorbed the religion of the conquistadors but with much adaptation.

Rodger C. Henderson

See also Native Americans: Northeast; South America: Savanna and Tropical Forest

Further Reading

Adams, E. C. (1991). *The origin and development of the Pueblo katsina cult*. Tucson: University of Arizona Press.

Benedict, R. (1935). *Zuni mythology* New York: Columbia University Press.

Bunzel, R. L. (1973). *Zuni katcinas: An analytical study.* Glorietta, NM: Rio Grande Press.

Dozier, E. P. (1970). *The Pueblo Indians of North America.* New York: Holt, Rinehart and Winston.

Erdoes, R. (1976). *The Rain Dance people.* New York: Alfred A. Knopf.

Fewkes, J. W. (1985). *Hopi katcinas*. New York: Dover.

Goldfrank, E. S. (1927). *The social and ceremonial organization of Cochiti.* Menasha, WI: American Anthropological Association.

Gutierrez, R. A. (1991). *When Jesus came, the corn mothers went away: Marriage, sexuality, and power in New Mexico, 1500–1846.* Stanford, CA: Stanford University Press.

Hodge, G. M. (1993). *Kachina tales from the Indian pueblos.* Santa Fe, NM: Sunstone Press.

Mails, T. E. (1983). *Pueblo children of the Earth mother.* Garden City, NY: Doubleday.

Ortiz, A. (1969). *The Tewa world: Space, time, being, and becoming in a Pueblo society*. Chicago: University of Chicago Press.

Ortiz, A. (Ed.). (1979). *Handbook of North American Indians: Vol. 9. Southwest.* Washington, DC: Smithsonian Institution.

Parsons, E. C. (1939). *Pueblo Indian religion.* Chicago: University of Chicago Press.

Parsons, E. C. (1959). *Hopi and Zuni ceremonialism.* New York: Harper and Brothers.

Sando, J. S. (1976). *The Pueblo Indians.* San Francisco: Indian Historian Press.

Sando, J. S. (1992). *Pueblo nations: Eight centuries of Pueblo Indian history.* Santa Fe, NM: Clear Light Publishers.

Schaafsma, P. (2000). *Kachinas in the Pueblo world.* Salt Lake City: University of Utah Press.

Sedgwick, M. K. (1926). *The sky city: A study in Pueblo-Acoma Indian history and civilization.* Cambridge, MA: Harvard University Press.

Tyler, H. A. (1964). *Pueblo gods and myths.* Norman: University of Oklahoma Press.

Vecsey, C. (1996). *On the padres' trail.* Notre Dame, IN: University of Notre Dame Press.

White, L. A. (1973). *The Acoma Indians, people of the sky city.* Glorietta, NM: Rio Grande Press.

Nature Worship

Nature worship has been given a number of definitions, many of them erroneous. It is not, for example, "devil worship" or an excuse for sexual licentiousness. Nature worship is a religion based on forces and objects in nature. Although the forces and objects vary from culture to culture, they generally include the sun, moon, water, and fire. Above all, nature worship venerates the generative principle in nature.

Nature worship has been practiced for as long as there have been human societies. Some form of nature worship is found in every religion, although it is often somewhat hidden among so-called higher religions. The death and rebirth of a god, a blessing of plants, a great Earth goddess, the hidden meanings in church architecture, a horn of plenty at Thanksgiving celebrations—each reflects earlier beliefs in the generative principle in nature.

Examples of Traditional Nature Worship

The Ainu people of Japan believed that shapeless and invisible beings live in rocks, fish, trees, the sun and moon, and in fire. These objects and phenomena were sacred. The shaman maintained the link between humans and the supernatural powers of nature. Early anthropologists termed this type of belief "animism." One is tempted to dismiss any dying race as "primitive." At the end of a cultural evolution that lasted thousands of years, the Ainu world is on the verge of extinction, yet it once had great vitality. Its gods were as numerous as the phenomena of nature.

Many traditional peoples, such as the Tungus of Siberia, share these beliefs in the animating forces of nature. The Tungus, for example, believe that the bear has a special role in the destiny of humans. The bear resembles humans in many ways. It speaks and acts like humans and has compassion and suffers. The Tungus refer to the bear as the "exalted being that lives in the mountains."

Mana is another aspect of nature that has inspired awe. Mana is an impersonal power. Polynesians and Melanesians of the Pacific Ocean use the term *mana* to refer to those processes that influence nature and its working. Among societies—including Native American societies—that venerate the forces of nature mana is conceptually related to a number of other forces, such as the *orenda* of the Iroquois, the *wakan* of the Dakotas, and the manitou of the Algonquin. For Polynesians and Melanesians, however, mana means more than simply "impersonal power" or "supernatural power." Mana comes from people who use it, such as chiefs. Moreover, Polynesians, Melanesians, and Native Americans do not distinguish natural from supernatural realms of existence.

Many ceremonies among traditional peoples have addressed the generative principle in nature. Native Mexican populations venerated the vegetative spirit as the Great Mother of life. Japanese people had a cult of trees. European tribes worshiped stalks of grain or the generative power they symbolized.

Modern Nature Worship

Nature worship has recurred often in Western history. The Romantic movement of the nineteenth century, for example, followed the lead of the eighteenth-century philosopher Jean-Jacques Rousseau. This sophisticated pantheism was an attempt to recapture the imagined lost innocence of the noble savage.

Many sexual rituals that seemingly violate taboos, such as the coupling of uncles and nieces in New Guinea at specified times of the year, are fertility rituals seeking to have nature imitate the reproductive act.

The twentieth and twenty-first centuries have been marked by movements, such as Wicca, New Age religions, and even Greenpeace, that deify nature and seek to recapture, as the Romantics did, the lost link between humans and nature.

Adherents of the Wicca religion espouse pantheism and claim to see the divine in everyone. The word *wicca* comes from the Anglo-Saxon, meaning "to control nature to one's purpose." Most Wiccans celebrate eight sabbats (holidays) centered around the solar cycles, solstices, and equinoxes and *esbats* centered around the lunar cycles. On Halloween Wiccans honor the spirits of their ancestors. They also cast spells aimed at magically manipulating people or events to fulfill the desires of Wiccans. Some Wiccan witches meet in groups called "covens" or "circles," whereas others practice alone.

Young women have been attracted to Wicca because of its attention to the sacred feminine, nature worship, and its desire to empower young women. Wicca has rejected traditional male-dominated faiths that also have been environmentally unfriendly. Wiccans regard Wicca as a pagan mystery religion. It is also a nature religion. Wiccans adore a mother goddess and her horned consort. This mother goddess is the life force. She has been known as "Mother Nature," the Greek goddess Artemis, Gaia, and the Roman goddess Diana. Some Wiccans worship Jesus's mother Mary as the goddess.

The Green movement, which contends that the Western lifestyle is unsustainable, came into its own about thirty years ago. The Smithsonian Institution has corroborated the Green contention in arguing that the pre-Columbian Americas were in fact a sustainable environment, an Eden in which Native Americans lived in balance with the natural world. The Green movement desires to return to this imagined perfect balance through veneration of nature.

Anthropologists have basically given up the search for the origins of religion. However, whatever explanations early anthropologists had about the origins, the explanations had aspects of what people can still term "nature worship." Many of these aspects—totemic, animistic, or otherwise—have persisted in modern-day "higher religions" and social movements.

Frank A. Salamone

Further Reading

Allen, A. V. G. (1897). *Christian institutions*. New York: C. Scribner's Sons.

Bell, C. (1997). *Ritual: Perspectives and dimensions*. New York: Oxford University Press.

Chandler, R. C. (1999). Religion and politics in America: Faith, culture, and strategic choices. *Public Administration Review, 59*(2), 179.

Drake, D. (1916). *Problems of religion: An introductory survey*. Boston: Riverside Press.

Goldenweiser, A. A. (1922). *Early civilization: An introduction to anthropology*. New York: A. A. Knopf.

Hopkins, E. W. (1923). *Origin and evolution of religion*. New Haven, CT: Yale University Press.

Hutton, R. B. (1996). *Stations of the sun: A history of the ritual year in Britain*. Oxford, UK: Oxford University Press.

Kanoza, T. M. (1999). The Golden Carp and Moby Dick: Rudolfo Anaya's multi-culturalism. *MELUS, 24*(2), 159.

Lang, A. (1901). *Myth, ritual, and religion: Vol. 1*. London: Longmans, Green, and Co.

Lissner, I. (1957). *The living past* (J. M. Brownjohn, Trans.). New York: Putnam.

Meisenhelder, S. (1996). Conflict and resistance in Zora Neale Hurston's Mules and Men. *Journal of American Folklore, 109*(433), 267–288.

Noblitt, J. R., & Perskin, P. S. (2000). Cult and ritual abuse: Its history, anthropology, and recent discovery in contemporary America (Rev. ed.). Westport, CT: Praeger.

Schaefer, J. (2001). Appreciating the beauty of Earth. *Theological Studies, 62*(1), 23.

Steiner, J. F. (1943). *Behind the Japanese mask*. New York: Macmillan.

Stringer, M. D. (1999). Rethinking animism: Thoughts from the infancy of our discipline. *Journal of the Royal Anthropological Institute, 5*(4), 541.

Takayarna, K. P. (1998). Rationalization of state and society: A Weberian view of early Japan. *Sociology of Religion, 59*(1), 65–88.

Naven Ceremony

Naven is the central ceremony of the Iatmul, a Papuan tribe of the Sepik region of New Guinea in the western Pacific Ocean. *Naven* is a celebration of certain achievements of a sister's child (a *laua*) by the *laua*'s mother's brother (a *wau*). When the Iatmul were studied by anthropologist Gregory Bateson (1936), a *naven* could be initiated by a *laua*'s participation in life events ranging from major achievements, such as the *laua*'s first wearing of spirit masks or—in former times—first homicide, to minor achievements, such as the *laua*'s first catching of a fish. Today a *naven* is initiated by first-time events that have arisen due to contact with Western civilization, such as a *laua*'s first airplane trip or the purchase of an outboard motor for a dugout canoe. The basic characteristic of the ceremony was transvestite mocking of the other gender by the *wau:* A *wau* dressed as a decrepit old widow by wearing filthy rags. While so dressed, he was referred to as a "mother." A *wau* "mother" hobbles about, seeking "her child" (the *laua*) with the purported intent of rewarding the child for his or her accomplishment. The *laua* normally hides to avoid the spectacle of the *wau*'s self-degradation. When the *wau* finds his *laua,* he further demeans himself by rubbing the cleft of his buttocks down the length of the *laua*'s leg. In response, the *laua* is expected to quickly retrieve some valuables and present them to the *wau* to "make him all right." In major *naven* ceremonies the ritual behavior spreads beyond the relatives normally involved to others who are considered to be symbolically equivalent to them. During the *naven* ceremony the *laua*'s female relatives (excluding the mother) also engage in cross-dressing but invert the symbolism of the *wau*'s dressing in filthy rags by wearing fancy male attire. Wives of the *laua*'s elder brother are expected to beat the *laua.* The ceremony also includes other performances that emphasize cross-dressing and exaggerated sexuality. At the end of the ceremony the *laua* presents gifts to his maternal relatives and to other participants.

Social Tensions

Bateson saw the transvestite burlesquing of gender roles in the *naven* as an expression of social tensions between paternal and maternal kin. The Iatmul trace their ancestry patrilineally (through the paternal lineage). According to Bateson, Iatmul villages were characterized by weakness in their internal cohesion, and potential conflicts between members of their patrilineages and affinal (related by marriage) relatives threatened to limit the size that a village could reach without suffering from serious internal conflicts. Symbolically, the *naven* ceremony communicated the importance of the kinship link between the *wau* and the *laua.* In the absence of any institutional system of law to deal with internal conflicts, the *naven* ceremony's legitimating of the affinal relationships between *wau*s and their *laua*s minimized the likelihood of actual conflicts between patrilineally related kin and their affines. This permitted Iatmul villages to achieve larger populations than would otherwise have been possible. This contributed to village survival in a region of frequent intervillage warfare.

According to Bateson, processes in Iatmul society led to a strong system of cultural contrasts between males and females. The male ethos emphasized pride, self-assertion, harshness, and spectacular display. In contrast, the female ethos emphasized women's sense of "reality," cooperation, naturalness of emotional responses to experiences, an interest in routine behavior, and an informed attitude. This pattern of contrast in the normal roles of men and women involved male dominance being responded to with increased submissiveness by women. Bateson asserted that there was a tendency for this contrast in dominance and submission to grow progressively greater because the submissiveness of women was responded to by men with even greater dominance, a progressive change in Iatmul gender relations that Bateson referred to as "complementary schismogenesis." He defined *schismogenesis* as "a process of differentiation in the norms of individual behavior resulting from cumulative interaction between individuals" (Bateson 1958, 175–176). Bateson argued that the complementary schismogenesis of Iatmul male-female relationships resulted in hostility between the genders and that members of each gender held those of the other to be responsible for their own growing dominance or submissiveness. The process made it increasingly difficult for members of either gender to understand the emotional reaction of members of the other gender, and mutual jealousy between men and women was promoted.

According to Bateson, the *naven* ceremony provided a temporary, socially acceptable release from the strain of progressive schismogenesis. During the ceremony men and women were permitted to temporarily discard the ethos of their respective genders and behave according to the ethos of the other gender. It also made possible a public display of personal congratulations to the *laua.* Under normal circumstances a *laua*'s relatives could not express such public appreciation because forms of public display were lacking in the standard female ethos, and the expression of vicarious personal emotion was lacking in that of males. Thus, the ceremony provided women with the opportunity for public display of their emotions in an acceptable way and provided men with the opportunity for expression of vicarious personal emotion.

Metaphorical Dialogue

Anthropologist Eric Kline Silverman (2001) found that the *naven* ceremony was still being practiced in 1994 among the eastern Iatmul. The *naven* ceremony that Silverman observed in Tambunum village appeared to him to intensify the conflicts in Iatmul culture rather than bring closure to them, as Bateson had asserted. Participants seemed to Silverman to be genuinely mortified and shamed by the taboo violations to which they are subjected. In Silverman's view the *naven* ceremony is best understood as a metaphorical dialogue between two competing images of motherhood and the effect of these on Iatmul men's concepts of masculinity. The eastern Iatmul men with whom Silverman spoke expressed an idealized image of motherhood that is "nurturing, sheltering, cleansing, fertile, and chaste—in a word, moral. But men also fear an equally compelling image of motherhood that is defiling, dangerous, orificial, aggressive, and carnal—hence, grotesque. Masculinity in Tambunum is a rejoinder both subtle and strident, both muted and impassioned, to these contrary, embodied images of motherhood" (Silverman 2001, 2). Silverman portrays Iatmul men as experiencing intense nostalgia of infancy and a sense of personal identity that includes envy for women's capacity for motherhood. The symbolism of *naven* expresses the tragedy and pathos of the conflicted experience of Iatmul masculinity. In it Iatmul men mock the motherhood that they envy and long to be reunited with, and women mock the masculinity of men that denies them the nurturing abilities that they envy. In both ways, according to Silverman, it "exposes the fictions and fragility of manhood" (2001, 12) among the eastern Iatmul.

Richley H. Crapo

Further Reading

Bateson, G. (1932). Social structure of the Iatmul people of the Sepik River (Part III). *Oceania, 2*(4), 401–453.

Bateson, G. (1958). *Naven*. London: Wildwood House.

Helbig, M. (1991). *Kulturanthropologie und Psychologie sexueller Rituale—Naven (Papua-Neuguinea) und Tantra (Altes Indien, Nepal, Tibet)* [Cultural anthropology and psychology of sexual rituals] (Doctoral dissertation, Freie University, Berlin, Germany).

Silverman, E. K. (2001). *Masculinity, motherhood, and mockery: Psychoanalyzing culture and the Iatmul naven rite in New Guinea*. Ann Arbor: University of Michigan Press.

New Year's Celebrations

The New Year is one of the most universally celebrated events in society, both ancient and modern. Although dates and rituals vary according to culture, country, or religion, the New Year represents a turning point. This turning point is traditionally a time of celebration, renewal, and rebirth. The New Year is a transitional period between two worlds: that of the old year and that of the new year. The liminal (relating to a sensory threshold) period of the New Year in this sense is sacred time, a calendrical rite of passage. The New Year represents the beginning of new life, the beginnings of creation, and a renewal of power; it looks both backward with reflection to the past and forward with hope to the future. A common theme—out with the old and in with the new—is reflected in many of the rituals surrounding the New Year.

Timing of the New Year

The date of the New Year depends on which calendar or time-reckoning system is employed. The New Year can, therefore, occur in any month or season, but it occurs more frequently at certain times than others. In the ancient world time was reckoned by natural occurrences—the passage of day to night, season to season, harvest to sowing. The beginning of the year was not always a fixed date but rather was established by annual vegetation cycles or climatic occurrences.

Ritualistic Elements in the New Year

Although most cultures celebrate the turning of the year, customs and rituals vary. As with most religious rituals, New Year's celebrations include prayers or blessings such as acts of praise, thanksgiving, and supplication to a natural or supernatural force. The elimination of the old through fasting, purification, expulsion of sickness and evil powers, atonement, and forgiveness for past and future transgressions is a common element as well. These rituals restore harmony of nature and ensure that harmony in the upcoming year. Predicting the future is another common feature of New Year's celebrations.

In many cultures noisemaking is thought to ward off demons for the upcoming year. Often drums, noisemakers, or loud music is an integral component of celebrations. The stroke of midnight is accompanied by clapping, cheering, and sounding paper noisemakers. The practice of blowing the shofar

THE NEW YEAR IN KOREA

On New Year's morning salutations or calls are made on friends, acquaintances, and superiors. To this rule there must be no exception, on pain of rupture of friendly relations. The chief ceremony of the day is the sacrifice at the tablets of ancestors. Proceeding to the family tombs, if near the house, or to the special room or shelf in the dwelling itself, the entire family make prostrations. Costly ceremonies, with incense-sticks, etc., regulated according to the family purse, follow. This is the most important filial and religious act of the year. In cases where the tombs are distant, the visit must not be postponed later than during the first month. After the ancestral sacrifices, comes the distribution of presents, which are enclosed in New Year's boxes. These consist of new dresses, shoes, confectionery, jewelry for the boys and girls, and various gifts, chiefly cooked delicacies, for neighbors, friends, and acquaintances. For five days the festivities are kept up by visits, social parties, and entertainments of all sorts. The ordinary labors of life are resumed on the sixth day of the new year, but with many, fun, rest, and frolic are prolonged during the month.

***Source*: Griffis, William E. (1882). *Corea: The Hermit Nation*. New York: Charles Scribner's Sons, p. 297.**

(ram's horn) at Rosh Hashanah, the Jewish New Year, may also reflect this custom.

Ancient New Year's Celebrations

In the ancient Near East the New Year reflected the natural rhythms of the seasons and was celebrated twice yearly. One New Year was celebrated in the autumn when the first crops harvested were ritually blessed. An agricultural festival at harvest and at sowing was necessary to invoke the blessing of the gods for fertility and abundance, so rites of thanksgiving to the gods for providing a bountiful harvest accompanied celebrations of food and drink.

Another New Year was celebrated in the spring during the planting season. The spring rituals were a natural time for the New Year as the first new growth after a desolate winter appeared. Spring New Year's celebrations tended to represent a rebirth of nature and often commemorated the resurrection of a dying god. For example, among the ancient Canaanites the myth of the death and resurrection of the fertility god Baal—celebrating his triumph over the Canaanite god, Mot (Death) and the building of his palace—has been connected to the New Year's festivities in Canaan.

One of the most famous New Year's celebrations in antiquity was the *akitu* festival of Babylonia. This festival was celebrated continually for over two thousand years throughout ancient Babylonia and other cities in Mesopotamia. The *akitu* festival involved elaborate rituals, abundant prayers, sophisticated sacrifices, royal processions of the king and gods, recitation of sacred texts such as the *Enuma Elish* and the Babylonian creation myth, and lavish banquets. The earliest known *akitu* festival celebrated by the earliest inhabitants of southern Mesopotamia, the Sumerians, was an agricultural festival occurring twice a year: at the autumnal and spring equinoxes. Because the festival was celebrated at equinoxes, when days and nights were in balance, it was also symbolic of a "perfect balance" of the sowing and harvesting of crops.

Eventually the *akitu* festival became an annual national spring festival, combining its agricultural flavor with religious and political ideologies. By the first millennium BCE the festival was at its most developed stage, lasting for twelve days in Babylon, the capital of Babylonia. The participation of the king and the royal priesthood was mandatory. The temples of the gods underwent ritual purifications and exorcisms, were ornately decorated, and were filled with bountiful offerings. The statues of the gods were removed from their temples, and for this one time of the year, the citizens of Babylon were allowed access to the gods as they were paraded around the streets and into a special "New Year's House." Prophecies and oracles were issued for the upcoming year. Scholars have also speculated that the *akitu* festival included a reenactment of the primordial cultic battle between the chief god Marduk and the chaotic sea-monster goddess Tiamat, as detailed in the creation myth. Other indications point to a "sacred marriage" between the king and a priestess to promote fertility, especially in early New Year's celebrations. The *akitu* festival legitimized the Mesopotamian king. Mesopotamian mythology proclaimed that kingship was handed directly from the gods to the king. At the New Year the king, to reaffirm his divine sanction, underwent a ritual humiliation by being stripped of his symbols of power, forced to his knees, ritually slapped by the high priests, and required to swear an oath that he had not neglected his duties as king. After his kingship was renewed, he would "take the hand" of Marduk and lead the procession of the statues of the gods.

New Year in Ancient Israel

In ancient Israel two agricultural festivals likely acted as New Year's celebrations: a spring festival that commemorated the religious New Year and an autumnal festival that commemorated the civic New Year. The autumnal festival (1 Kings 8:2, 65) and the festival of the Lord (Judges 21:19), celebrated in the seventh month of Tishri, may have been indications of the New Year. Additionally, Ezekiel 40:1 records the beginning of the year as the tenth day of Tishri. After the Babylonian Exile (ca. 538 BCE) when the adjusted lunar calendar was adopted, the New Year was moved to the first day of the new moon in the month of Nisan. In Leviticus 25:9 the blowing of the shofar on the tenth day of the seventh month may designate the beginning of the New Year, as it does in modern Judaism.

The Mishnah (the collection of Jewish traditions that was made the basic part of the Talmud) records four New Years—the first of Nisan as the new year for kings and religious festivals; the first of Elul as the new year for tithing of cattle; the first of Tishri for the civil calendar, Sabbath, and Jubilee years; and the fifteenth of Shevet as the new year for trees (Tractate Rosh Hashanah. 1:1). The Tishri became the celebrated New Year because on this day all the world is judged (Tractate Rosh Hashanah. 1:2).

Other Ancient New Years

Solar and lunar observations also determined the New Year in the ancient world. In Egypt either the heliacal (relating to the sun) rising of the star Sirius, which occurred in July, or the flooding of the Nile in September marked the start of the New Year. The New Year's rituals at the temple of Edfu reveal that the statue of the god Horus was removed from his temple and exposed to the rays of the sun to reunite his body with his soul. At the New Year statues of Horus and his divine family were placed on boats in the Nile. Singing, dancing, and feasting lasted for a month until the statues returned to the temple.

The ancient Mediterranean world also had several New Years. The date varied in Greece, whereas in Rome it was celebrated at the spring equinox until 153 BCE, when 1 January became the civic New Year. Although this is the day of New Year in the secular modern world, not until the nineteenth century did most Western societies adopt this date, changing New Year's Day from 25 March to 1 January.

New Year's Celebrations around the World

In early northern European cultures the winter solstice was the common New Year's Day because it honored the rebirth of the sun god. The ancient Celts celebrated New Year on Samhain (summer's end). On this day the dead were honored because it is believed that on this liminal day the threshold between the world of the living and the world of the dead is open. Modern U.S. children celebrate this day as Halloween.

Modern Judaism celebrates the New Year during the autumn on the first and second days of Tishri. The first day, Rosh Hashanah (head of the year) also is the first day of the Days of Awe leading to Yom Kippur (Day of Atonement). On Rosh Hashanah God remembers and judges humans for their actions. The New Year is a time of introspection. Normally work is forbidden. Traditions include blowing the shofar in the synagogue and eating sweet foods such as honey and apples to ensure a good new year. On the first night of Rosh Hashanah a special greeting, "May you be inscribed and sealed for a good year," is said, referring to the Book of Life that God maintains.

The Islamic New Year, Al-Hijra, occurs on the first day of the Islamic month, Muharram. This date commemorates the Hijra, the date when the Prophet Muhammad emigrated from Mecca to Medina in Saudi Arabia in 622 CE, denoting the beginning of the Islamic age.

The Chinese New Year begins on the second new moon after the winter solstice. The festival lasts for approximately fifteen days. Several rituals are noteworthy. The first involves cleansing and purification of the home. Offerings are given to the ancestors, accounts are settled, debts are paid, and symbolic foods are eaten. Firecrackers and noisemakers chase away a mythical monster. Parades and lanterns provide colorful displays.

Although the celebration and timing of the New Year vary greatly, they represent a common theme of purging the past and looking forward to a time of peace and prosperity.

Julye Bidmead

See also Calendrical Rituals; China: Popular Religion; Divali

Further Reading

Bidmead, J. (2002). *The akitu festival: Religious continuity and royal legitimation in Mesopotamia*. Piscataway, NJ: Gorgias Press.

De Moor, J. C. (1972). *New year with Canaanites and Israelites* (Vols. 21–22). Kampen, Netherlands: Kok.

Eliade, M. (1959). *Cosmos and history: The myth of the eternal return* (W. R. Trask, Trans.). New York: Harper and Row.

Gaster, T. (1955). *New year: Its history, customs, and superstitions*. New York: Abelard-Schuman.

O

Oaths and Ordeals

Before the advent of common law and the jury system the guilt or innocence of an accused person was usually determined by oaths and ordeals under the auspices of the Church. Oaths were an invocation to God and were used in the context of a legal proceeding. An ordeal was a physical act that relied on divine assistance to determine guilt or innocence.

Oaths

The oath was a medieval concept that indicated that the person taking it swore before God, the just judge. Oaths were used as religious acts of virtue, appeals to divine judgment. An assertory oath called for God to witness a fact; a promissory oath called for God to witness a binding resolution; a contestatory oath invoked God's testimony (using God to swear to the oath) with the words "So help me God" or "Upon my soul." In the modern era, private oaths are used between individuals. Public oaths are divided into doctrinal decrees and canonical legislation that affirm an oath's legality. Oaths are also determined by political variances (different legal and geographical jurisdictions) that demand obedience to authority. Oaths are not taken as seriously as they were in previous centuries.

During the Middle Ages in Western civilization a variety of oaths was used. An oath of fealty (fidelity) swore a vassal's (subordinate's) loyalty to his lord. This oath was made on the Bible or a reliquary (a container or shrine in which sacred relics are kept) of a saint. An oath of homage (vow to be faithful and serve only the lord) and an oath of fealty were usually taken at the same time. Homage was granted by the lord to any vassal who received a fief (feudal estate) from his lord. A vassal granted fealty to a lord who had not granted the vassal land. The oath of fealty to the Crown was the paramount oath and superceded all others.

In jurisprudence, oaths are considered sacred because the accused declares his or her innocence before God. Centuries before the jury system was created, the accused charged by a litigant swore a solemn oath to be truthful in his declaration of innocence. People assumed that the person taking the oath of innocence was being truthful. Being truthful was known as "waging the law." The character of the accused had to be verified by a number of kin or friends who attested to his honesty and trustworthiness. These people were known as "compurgators." Local custom or the court, whichever had greater jurisdiction, decided on the number of oath helpers (a group of people who acted as witnesses to the character of the accused), but it was usually eleven, with the accused being a twelfth. Compurgators were usually kin who did not want the family reputation or worth to suffer for the crimes committed by a family member. The reputation of the accused and the compurgators was at stake if they lied. An oath was a serious undertaking in the medieval era because people feared God's wrath. Thus perjury was scarcely considered; guilty parties, people assumed, would not dare take an oath of innocence. Compurgation became the basis for law in many modern-day European countries because God would never declare an innocent person guilty.

A man participates in the Empalao ritual ordeal in Valverde de la Vera, Spain in the 1990s.
COURTESY OF BECCI SEARLE-SCHRADER.

Perjury and Ordeal

However, some people who took the oath of innocence perjured themselves and escaped punishment. Their perjury was a corrupt sin and the dishonesty became a personal struggle with God. If perjury could be proven, and if compurgation was denied by the presiding judge, then an ordeal was used as a means of justice to determine guilt. An ordeal was used to request God's clarification in ambivalent cases, to erase the evil from the community, and to declare reparation and punishment. An ordeal was also used if the case could not reach a just conclusion. An ordeal was always a last resort and used only if all other means had been exhausted. Ordeals resolved common offenses against the Church, the state, or the king.

The ordeal existed in classical antiquity. It was noted in the code of Babylonian king Hammurabi (d. 1750 BCE), which was used in Asia, Africa, and as far away as Polynesia. The ordeal was not used during the Roman era because Rome had a highly developed justice system. The ordeal emerged in Western civilization after the fall of the Roman Empire but had been used by German tribes. Salic (relating to a Frankish people of the fourth century CE) law documented the ordeal of the cauldron around 510. Gaul, Italy, Ireland, Frisia, and the Byzantine Empire also used the ordeal. Ordeals came into full custom in France under Emperor Charlemagne with the Capitulary of Aachen in 809, which stated that an ordeal was to be imposed if the truth could not be pronounced or was uncertain. Several types of ordeal emerged during Charlemagne's time.

An ordeal was based on the premise that omniscient God has witnessed a criminal act and that by his deciding guilt or innocence an innocent party will be protected because God will not let an innocent person lose an ordeal. Justice was an important societal element and had to fit in with God's ideal of a world free of sin. The accused was responsible to the injured party, and often restitution was included in the punishment.

The ordeal was a substitute for the oath of innocence. It was used only if guilt was not clearly proven and only in specific circumstances and against specific criminals. A bilateral ordeal involved the accused and the victim; a unilateral ordeal involved only the accused. The Church strictly administered an ordeal with a ritual. Before an ordeal took place, the accused would be sequestered for three days and would fast during that time. A religious service with prayer, Mass, or communion was performed. Priests blessed all the instruments that were used in an ordeal.

Regional variations determined the type of ordeal that the accused would endure. The type of ordeal also depended on the nature of the offense. Confessing to the offense was preferable, to all parties concerned, to undergoing an ordeal. Civil and Church authorities favored a confession because it meant repentance and salvation. If a person was found guilty after an ordeal the penalties were quite harsh.

Types of Ordeals

Mesopotamia and ancient Greece used the cold-water ordeal *(judicium aquae frigidae)*. Germanic tribes continued this type of ordeal, usually held in the autumn or winter. The accused was bound with hand and feet together, sometimes trussed to the knees. A rope was tied around the waist and attached to a pulley that flung the accused into a pool of blessed water, usually a river or lake. If the accused floated to the surface it meant he was rejected by the holy water and justly punished. If the accused sank it proved he had immunity to the holy water and would be pulled out before drowning and declared innocent. Emperor Louis the Pious of France prohibited this ordeal, but it continued unabated. Women were exempted from this ordeal because they had a higher fat body ratio; also fat men usually floated. The ordeal of coldwater flourished again in the sixteenth and seventeenth centuries during the witch phobia.

In the hot water ordeal *(judicium aquae caldaria)* the accused had to pick a stone from boiling water, usually in a cauldron. The scalded flesh was bound for three days. Upon examination if a blister appeared then the accused was considered guilty. If the scalded flesh had healed the accused was cleared of charges.

In the ordeal by hot metal *(judicium ferri)* the accused carried a red-hot iron or rod a set distance, usually nine to twelve paces. For a severe crime the iron would be two to three times heavier than for a less serious crime, especially if the offender had a bad reputation. The wounded hand was bound for three days with wax-covered rags, with an additional bandage of clean rags used to indicate that no one had tampered with the rags. After the third day the wounded hand was inspected. If the wound was clean the man was cleared of guilt because God had shown innocence. If the wound festered, discharged pus, or discolored then he was declared guilty and punished.

In a variance of the hot metal ordeal the accused had to walk over nine or more heated plowshares that were laid out on the ground at unequal distances. The accused was forced to walk blindfolded and barefoot. If unhurt the accused was declared innocent. Women were allowed to use the hot iron ordeal. In a variance of the metal ordeal an accused could take the ploughshare ordeal where he or she was forced to walk over the ploughshares blindfolded and barefoot. If unhurt the person, male or female, would be declared innocent. Ordeal by fire was also used by the Persians, Hindus, and Siamese. In West Africa the boiling oil ordeal first plunged the accused into cold water and then into boiling oil. If the accused was scalded, the accused was guilty. This ordeal was also used by the Japanese and the Ainus.

In the unilateral ordeal by cake *(judicium offoe)* or morsel of execration (the act of cursing or denouncing), the accused ate consecrated bread or wafer host (eucharistic bread) and sometimes cheese. The assumption was that the accused, if guilty, would die immediately after eating something holy. If he choked he was guilty.

The suspended loaf was another unilateral ordeal. A deacon baked a loaf of bread from meal and blessed water but included a stick of wood. The accused appeared with two witnesses. The bread was suspended between the witnesses. If the bread turned in a circle the accused was declared guilty.

Ordeal of the Cross

The ordeal of the cross *(judicium crucis)* was bilateral. The accused and the litigant stood with outstretched arms in front of a cross. The person who dropped his arms first was considered guilty. This ordeal was used extensively after the ninth-century capitularies (civil or ecclesiastical ordinances). It was most often undertaken by ecclesiastics. A unilateral variation was widely used. The accused was blindfolded and led to a large cross that had two canes on it. One of the canes held the symbol of the cross. If the accused chose the cane with the symbol of the cross he was deemed innocent; if he chose the other cane he was deemed guilty. In all ordeals the priest decided the guilt or innocence of the accused.

Yet another type of ordeal—trial by battle or combat—was brought to England after the Norman invasion in 1066. This ordeal was a battle between accused and accuser and was not restricted to the nobility or to knights. The accused and accuser fought to the death without rules. Sticks were the common weapons. The victor was declared the innocent party. In some cases the litigants were replaced by proxies who underwent the ordeal. Ordeal by battle eventually became the duel. The duel was established in 501 by Gundebald, king of the Burgundians. The loser was the guilty party, because the outcome of the duel was God's judgment. During the Viking era, as soon as a dueler's blood reached the ground he was defeated. The duel was seldom used, however, and fell out of favor.

The Church likely used ordeals to protect people and to provide mercy. Although ordeals were risky for the accused, recently examined records of ordeal indicate that most people were found not guilty. King William II of England (1056–1100 CE) was unhappy that men who had broken the forest laws had passed the hot iron ordeal despite their guilt. Thereafter he decided that God was too merciful, and William decided guilt or innocence of the accused.

The penalties for failing an ordeal were stiff. The accused always had the choice to confess and be spared an ordeal, however. The Church preferred confession because it led to repentance and salvation. A coroner was usually present at an ordeal.

The ordeal remained in favor as a legal tool until well into the thirteenth century in some countries. England's King Henry I allowed the ordeal as a method of trial. It became mandatory only under King Henry II in 1166, although English jurisprudence leaned more toward grand jury trials and by the thirteenth century had advanced significantly in common law. By 1215 ordeals by fire and water were forbidden by Pope Innocent III (1160/61–1216) in the fourth Lateran Council largely because theologians could not reconcile demanding a service from God and asking him to be the judge.

Pope Innocent III argued not only that compurgators had to be of good character but also that they had to swear their belief that the oath of innocence was true. This argument undermined the whole foundation of oath taking.

Annette Richardson

Further Reading

Arnold, M. S. (Ed.). (1981). *On the laws and customs of England: Essays in honor of Samuel E. Thorne.* Chapel Hill: University of North Carolina Press.

Bartlett, R. (1986). *Trial by fire and water: The medieval judicial ordeal.* Oxford, UK: Clarendon Press.

Goitein, H. (1923). *Primitive ordeal and modern law.* London: George Allen & Unwin.

Hogue, A. R. (1966). *Origins of the common law.* Bloomington: Indiana University Press.

Kerr, M., Kerr, H., Forsyth, R. D., & Pleyley, M. J. (1992). Cold water & hot iron: Trial by ordeal in England. *Journal of Interdisciplinary History, 22,* 573–595.

Lea, H. C. (1968). *Superstition and force: Essays on the wager of law—the wager of battle—the ordeal torture.* New York: Greenwood Press.

Lea, H. C. (1996). *Torture, ordeal, and trial by combat in medieval law.* New York: Barnes and Noble.

Pollock, F., & Maitland, F. W. (1968). *The history of English law before the time of Edward I* (2nd ed.). Cambridge, UK: Cambridge University Press.

Online Rites

A distinction must be made between religion online and online religion. In broad terms, religion online is the Internet as a medium for supplying information about, and services related to, religious groups and traditions that are already established and operating offline. Online religion, on the other hand, is the use of the Internet to create a dedicated electronic space in which visitors can participate in liturgy (rites prescribed for public worship), prayer, ritual, meditation, or other activities through computer-mediated communication. In this way online religion not only extends the ritual opportunities available to adherents, but also becomes a means of religious innovation.

Participating in "online rites," then, refers to participating in religious practices that have been either designed specifically for the World Wide Web (web) or modified for use on the web. Some virtual rites take place in real time through the use of Multi-User Domains (MUDs), computer-mediated environments used for online gaming, education, or socializing, usually text-based and often oriented around a particular theme (a castle, an enchanted forest, a university), where participants create characters called *avatars* to interact with each other and the environment. Another ways in which rites take place in real time is through the use of Multi-User Domain that is Object-Oriented (MOO), where object-orientation is a programming option that allows for an expanded range of interaction between participants and the computer-mediated environment, as well as chatrooms, or interactive websites; other virtual rites are designed to be downloaded to a home computer for use later by the participant(s). Whereas many websites that host virtual rites are designed to be used by a single participant, others establish specific times at which a variety of participants may gather in a shared, online ritual environment.

Online Worship Spaces

Hindus, for example, can visit sites such as www.pujaroom.com or www.onlinedarshan.com for online, interactive *pūjā*s (Hindu worship of a god or goddess that occurs online in some computer-mediated manner) dedicated to a variety of deities, including Ganesha, Rama, Krishna, and Durga. In these electronic worship spaces, computer-generated butter lamps (about the size of a tea light or small candle, these lamps traditionally use clarified butter (*ghee*) instead of wax) sit in front of an on-screen altar devoted to the particular goddess or god. Often, a wispy trail of incense or an iconostasis (altar frame) is visible in the background. Flowers in full virtual bloom are gathered before the altar, flanked by *arti* lamps (oil lamps which are used in the *puja* ceremony) and occasionally a bell. Devotees may click and drag these blooms to the feet of the god or the goddess; clicking and dragging also move the lamp for the *arti* ceremony; the altar bell is rung in similar fashion, as though calling the virtual family to worship. Online Darshan.com includes sound files of *arti* chants, along with Sanskrit transliterations and translations.

Roman Catholics who are attached to the Tridentine Mass (traditional Latin Mass of the Roman Catholic Church, enacted by the Council of Trent in the years 1545–1563), on the other hand, can visit websites such as www.latinmass-ctm.org and download the complete Latin Mass in either audio or video format. Then, in the privacy of their own home or office, they may participate in the rite of the Church as often as they wish. Although supporters of this practice regard an Internet mass as little different from masses that have been broadcast for decades over the radio or television—more sophisticated, perhaps, and with greater potential for interactivity, but essentially no different in kind—other Catholics maintain that the Church will never accept the validity of online liturgy and sacraments over those that take place in real life. Indeed, the Pontifical Council for Social Communications has declared that "although the virtual reality of cyberspace cannot substitute for real interpersonal community, the incarnational reality of the sacraments and the liturgy, or the immediate and direct proclamation of the gospel, it can complement them, attract people to a fuller experience of the life of faith, and enrich the religious lives of users" (Pontifical Council for Social Communications, 2002). Although the council acknowledges the potential benefits of online religion, the ritual mediation of grace is still held by the Roman Catholic Church to occur only in the face-to-face domain of the real world.

Neo-pagan (relating to non- and pre-Christian forms of worship) cyber-rites first appeared in the late 1980s on the computer network CompuServe. Now they vary from Wiccan (one branch of modern neo-paganism) versions of the online *pūjā* rooms to more elaborate rites that demand as much if not more imaginative energy from participants as do rites in real life. Indeed, many neo-pagans regard virtual reality as the next great platform on which the potential of magick (the neo-pagan spelling of magic, in order to distinguish their ritual processes from stage magic or illusion-craft) may be realized.

In a neo-pagan cyber-rite certain events occur online, whereas others occur in real life. Online, although participants may be separated by thousands of miles, each participant logs into a private chatroom that has been designated as the ritual site. Offline, each participant consecrates in some way his or her own physical working space for the rite: lighting candles or incense in the vicinity of the computer, placing ritual tools within easy reach, or perhaps casting a circle-within-a-circle—an individual expression of the larger ritual circle cast by the entire group. After the group has formed, participants may be invited to repeat the words of the rite as they appear on the screen: calling the corners (a sacred space is created by acknowledging the powers and spiritual guardians of the four cardinal points of the compass), invoking the goddess(es) and god(s), perhaps participating in a guided meditation on the particular Sabbat (eight holy days of the Neopagan ritual year, organized around the solstices, equinoxes, and the midpoints between them), Esbat (lunar cycle meetings of Neopagan groups which occur outside the ritual structure of Sabbats), or ritual purpose, and finally dismissing the powers and opening the circle (the ritual end to a Neopagan worship service).

A number of neo-pagans are also investigating the potential of "web-witching," that is, the use of the Internet not only as a site for online rites but also for magickal spellworking. JaguarMoon, for example (www.jaguarmoon.org), has been organized as an online teaching "cybercoven" (a Wiccan, or other Neopagan, working group that exists solely or primarily online) hived off from another online mother group, ShadowMoon (www.shadowmoon.org). Ritual classes and performance take place entirely on the web, and coven members communicate electronically. The organizers of both cybercovens hope the concept will become more acceptable to the neo-pagan community.

Issues

Among the many issues that inform any discussion of online rites, two are of particular importance. First is the issue of actual ritual performance in a virtual ritual space. An obvious problem with virtual rites, and part of the ongoing debate over their efficacy, is the lack both of physical proximity to other ritual participants and of a dedicated ritual space such as would be provided by a church sanctuary, a Buddhist meditation hall, or a consecrated circle. Few, if any, practitioners use their computers solely for online ritual purposes; in the increasing whirl of e-mail, online shopping, website construction, Internet research, gaming, and web surfing, virtual rites, then, become just one more thing for which computer, desk, and electronic work space is used. Critics of online rites also point out that an onscreen photograph of a forest, temple, or altar complete with cyberincense is not, in fact, a forest, temple, or altar. And the one can never—and should never—be substituted for the other.

Second is the issue of online efficacy. That is, do online rites mediate actual results? Clearly, the Vatican believes they do not, whereas many neo-pagan participants believe that they do. Although Zen Mountain Monastery (a Zen Buddhist Monastery and retreat center in the Catskill Mountains) has been working to launch an online program called "Cybermonastery," the abbot, John Daido Loori, wonders about its efficacy: "Is someone going to come to enlightenment on the Web? I doubt it, but you never can tell." (Zaleski, 1999)

Douglas E. Cowan

See also Hinduism; Paganism and Neo-Paganism; Performance, Ritual of; Television and Ritual

Further Reading

Brasher, B. E. (2001). *Give me that online religion.* San Francisco: Jossey-Bass.

Cobb, J. (1998). *CyberGrace: The search for God in the digital world.* New York: Crown.

Hadden, J. K., & Cowan, D. E. (Eds.). (2000). *Religion on the Internet: Research prospects and promises.* London: JAI/Elsevier Science.

NightMare, M. M. (2001). *Witchcraft and the web: Weaving pagan traditions online.* Toronto, Canada: ECW Press.

Pontifical Council for Social Communications. (2002). *The Church and Internet.* Retrieved June 4, 2003, from www.vatican.va/roman_curia/pontifical_councils/pccs

Rheingold, H. (2000). *The virtual community: Homesteading on the electronic frontier* (Rev. ed.). Cambridge, MA: MIT Press.

Turkle, S. (1995). *Life on the screen: Identity in the age of the Internet.* New York: Touchstone.

Zaleski, J. (1997). *The soul of cyberspace: How new technology is changing our spiritual lives.* San Francisco: HarperCollins.

Zaleski, J. (1999, Winter). Straight ahead: Jeff Zaleski interviews John Daido Loori. *Tricycle: The Buddhist Review 54* 48–54.

Orthodoxy

The word *orthodoxy* derives from the combination of two Greek words—*orthos* (right) and *doxa* (belief). *Orthodoxy* thus literally means "right belief." Although the word may be applied in other contexts—a person could, for instance, be described as an "orthodox conservative"—it is most frequently used to describe religious beliefs. In a generic sense of *orthodoxy,* in order for a belief to be right or correct, it must adhere to an external objective standard, which supplies a justification for the claim of the belief's correctness. From a religious standpoint, an ecclesial (relating to a church) authority must serve as the ultimate determinant of the rightness of religious belief. Those people who are, in this sense, orthodox religious believers measure their beliefs against such an external authority. The conformity of the belief to the external authority defines the belief as orthodox; beliefs that fail to conform sufficiently are at best heterodox (unorthodox) and at worst heretical.

Although people agree on the pattern of justification required to define a religious belief as orthodox, people disagree on what constitutes the legitimate ecclesial authority. Even the most cursory examination of different Christian denominations demonstrates that each views itself as orthodox. Roman Catholicism, the Eastern Orthodox Church, and Protestantism all stake claims to orthodoxy, but each has a different authoritative standard. Catholicism relies on Church dogma and tradition; the Eastern Orthodox Church professes to be purely apostolic, using the faith of the apostles as an ultimate source; and Protestantism claims that only the scriptural text itself *(sola scriptura)* can qualify as the authoritative basis of religious belief. Various senses of what counts as correct religious belief follow from adherence to different authoritative norms. Although the term *orthodoxy,* in its general sense, has one meaning, what qualifies as orthodox belief in a specific religious sense is highly contextualized.

The Schism between Eastern Orthodox and Roman Catholic Churches

The term *Orthodoxy* is often taken to refer to the Eastern Orthodox Church. The Eastern Orthodox Church (canonically the Orthodox Catholic Church) is actually a set of autocephalus (independent) churches, each with its own self-governing structure headed by a patriarch. The Eastern Orthodox Church, although unified around a set of doctrinal beliefs and norms for action seen as originating in the beliefs and acts of the apostles, developed as a set of distinct religious communities organized by nationality and geography. This development was not simply a function of cultural differences; more fundamentally, it was the result of a particular conception of church governance. Specifically, the early Eastern Orthodox Church fathers believed that all bishops were fundamentally equal and that each had authority over his own see (jurisdiction of a bishop), although there was recognition by Eastern patriarchs of the bishop of Rome and later of the patriarch of Constantinople as first among equals.

Although important doctrinal and theological differences had developed between the Roman Catholic and Eastern Orthodox Churches, spanning the fourth through the tenth centuries, the ultimate schism between the two in 1054 could be explained primarily in terms of irreconcilable differences regarding ecclesiastical authority. As the Roman Catholic Church gradually developed a structure of centralized authority that was ultimately codified in the power of the papacy, the Eastern Orthodox Church remained committed to the concept that all churches are equal and that doctrinal differences could not be settled by the dicta (formal pronouncements) of a single authority. Although not a rejection of the historical significance of Rome as the successor of the Apostle Peter's own church, this commitment was a rejection of the idea that Rome alone could have legal power over all of Christendom. The Eastern Church subscribed to the idea that such matters could be adjudicated only by agreement among the bishops.

A Greek Orthodox chapel on the Greek cruise ship Olympic Champion in the Adriatic Sea between the Balkans and Italy in 2003. COURTESY OF KAREN CHRISTENSEN.

Further, in rejecting the jurisdictional authority of Rome, the Eastern Church did not propose itself to be any less *catholic.* The catholicity of Eastern Orthodoxy was defined solely by the adherence to a common set of beliefs and practices rather than by allegiance to a singular, determinate church authority. Moreover, according to the Eastern Church such authority was rooted in tradition and thus lacked the biblical justification for a claim to orthodoxy. Despite its antipathy toward the central role of tradition in Roman Catholicism, the Eastern Orthodox Church itself, although claiming apostolic authority, derived many of its doctrinal concepts from the rich tradition rooted in the commentaries of the early Christian fathers and the teachings that emerged from the great ecumenical councils of the early Christian era. Nonetheless, the Eastern Orthodox Church firmly rejected the idea of a single earthly authority; thus, the separation between the Eastern Orthodox and Roman Catholic Churches was inevitably made permanent as a result of increasing legalism in Roman church matters, leading ultimately to the doctrine of papal infallibility, a notion loathsome to the Eastern ecclesiastical structure.

The *Filioque*

Both Roman and Eastern Orthodox Catholicism are grounded in the belief that Christ is one person with

Russian Orthodox women lighting candles in a church in Verhoturye, Siberia, Russia in November 2000. COURTESY OF STEPHEN G. DONALDSON PHOTOGRAPHY.

two distinct natures: divine and human. Although the Roman Catholic and Eastern Orthodox Churches were united against the sects of the Eastern Orthodox Church in Armenia, Syria, and Egypt—which denied that Christ was in any way human—other doctrinal and theological differences between them proved irreconcilable. Prime among these is the introduction of a small phrase called the *"Filioque"* into the Christian doctrines known as the Nicene Creed, a phrase indicating that the Spirit proceeds from both the Father and the Son. Although the theology of both the Roman Catholic and Eastern Orthodox Churches is essentially trinitarian (believing in the Holy Trinity of Father, Son, and Holy Spirit), the Eastern Orthodox Church accepted the idea that the Holy Spirit proceeds only from the Father, as originally stated in the creed; Rome had long accepted the idea that the Holy Spirit "proceeds from the Father and the Son." From the perspective of Eastern Orthodox theology, this is to confuse the nature of God the Father and God the Son; that is, the Son and Holy Spirit proceed only from the Father. Later in the eleventh century, after the inclusion of the *Filioque* was codified in the Roman rite and the papacy attempted to force, through the power of excommunication, a unified liturgy (rites prescribed for public worship) throughout all of Christendom, the Great Schism of 1054 marked a final separation between the Roman Catholic and Eastern Orthodox Churches. The inclusion of the *Filioque* thus cut to the heart of a deep theological controversy and, from the Eastern standpoint, demonstrated the aberrant nature of the Roman Catholic interpretation of the Holy Trinity.

The development of scholasticism—using deductive logic and Aristotelian principles to establish a natural theology that could, for example, prove the existence of God—in the West, with its rationalistic approach to reconciling faith and reason, during the medieval period further solidified the separation of the two Churches. Due in large measure to the Italian religious philosopher St. Thomas Aquinas's appropriation of Aristotelian (relating to the Greek philosopher Aristotle) principles in the thirteenth century, Western theology emphasized the use of human reason in determining the existence of God. Although Aquinas believed it is not strictly possible to know God's essence, he did assert that it is possible to prove the existence of God through purely rational argumentation. Such argumentation depends not on innate knowledge of God's existence, imbued in human nature by God's grace, but rather on the rational mind's ability to reason from observable features of the universe to the necessary existence of God. Orthodoxy holds that far from strengthening faith, such argumentation, because of its reliance on purely human abilities, actually serves to weaken Christian faith. It is especially pernicious, from the Eastern Orthodox perspective, to suppose that Christian faith can change in any way as a result of the rationalistic investigation of nature.

Orthodox Mystery and Iconography

Orthodox ritual and liturgy are rich in mystery and symbolism. Because of its strong antipathy to rationalism and naturalism, Orthodoxy self-consciously views itself in mystical or supernatural terms. Such a quality is manifest physically, for instance, in its liturgical services, where passages are chanted and not merely spoken, in the lavish vestments worn by priests, and, perhaps most significantly, in its iconographic (representing something by pictures or diagrams) art, which itself is seen as a kind of spiritual modality. In general, Orthodoxy sees its Church as a purely mystical body, the understanding of which cannot be attained through the development of a rational or natural theology. Thus, a highly symbolic liturgy and nonrepresentational art take on the significance of providing the faithful with some means of experiencing the supernatural.

Like Roman Catholicism, Eastern Orthodoxy is a sacramental religion (that is, based on the idea that the sacraments are signs of Christ's divinity that can help bring about salvation); however, its understanding and descriptions of some sacraments differ significantly from those offered in the Roman Catholic Church. Eastern Orthodoxy makes no effort to offer rationalistic explanations and holds that it is indeed impossible to supply such explanations for the meaning of sacramental mystery. Consider, for instance, differing explanations of the idea of the Eucharist (communion). In the Catholic Mass bread and wine are transformed by the performative act of consecration by a priest, Christ's surrogate, into the actual body and blood of Christ. With this transformation (transubstantiation) the elements of bread and wine cease to have any real significance because those elements literally, according to Catholic theology, become something else. In Eastern Orthodoxy, there is no conception of transubstantiation. The elements of bread and wine retain their physical status, that is, they undergo no substantial change but rather become through consecration signs of Christ's suffering. In retaining their purely physical quality, the bread and wine serve as a reminder of Christ's physical humanity, his having a worldly nature as well as a divine nature.

Unlike both Catholicism and Calvinism, Orthodoxy rejects the concept of original sin, the theoretical notion of which was most thoroughly developed by the early Christian church father Saint Augustine. The idea that there is collective human guilt is foreign to the sensibility of Orthodoxy. Christ's redemptive power, then, is construed not primarily as the forgiveness of original sin, but most fundamentally as overcoming death, which according to Orthodoxy is the real consequence of Adam's fall. Under the Augustinian view, evil is the privation of good, and human nature is inherently deprived of good through original sin; only through the will and grace of God could human goodness be realized at all. In rejecting this view, Orthodoxy places higher value on the idea of choosing good, which could be realized only through communion in the Church itself. The sacrament of baptism, a sign of Christ's manifestation as divine and a recalling of Christ's redemptive power over death, is then less a cleansing of guilt and more a mystical initiation into the Church, through which the real evil of death may be overcome. As in the case of the Eucharist, it is important to preserve the physical character of bodily cleansing with water because it is another reminder of the Incarnation.

Icons

The concept of God incarnate, the central Christian belief, is most symbolically represented in the Orthodox conception of icons. Icons are not mere depictions of religious events or venerable figures; they are artistic revelations of the Incarnation itself. Flat and ornately designed, icons do not resemble objects as they are in nature but rather as they might be after having undergone divine transformation. At once physical and transfigured, icons provide the faithful with a glimpse of the spiritual world. In the ninth century there was a movement by people within Orthodoxy itself to purge the Church of icons; these Iconoclasts were unsuccessful, and the veneration of icons became one of the enduring hallmarks of Orthodox religious practice. The annual feast of Orthodoxy itself celebrates this achievement.

The iconography of Orthodoxy also constitutes a repudiation of the value of naturalistic, three-dimensional images that adorn Roman Catholic churches. Such images resemble the human figure as it is in nature and in this respect are incapable of serving as mystical signs of the mystery of the Incarnation and signals of a transfigured state. Icons are venerated precisely because they are a means whereby the faithful come to regard themselves as made in the image of God.

Central to the practice of Orthodoxy is the notion of deification (theosis). The symbolic and mystical character of the Church's rituals serves as a reminder of the ultimate sanctification of human life. Through communion in the Church and participation in the liturgy, human life itself is transfigured, transformed, by the grace of God, into a divine nature. This deification is the ultimate promise of Christ's redemption because, according to Orthodox belief, it makes people like God and signals the victory over death.

Whose Orthodoxy?

The consequences of historical schism and reformation are apparent in the vast differences in liturgical practice, ecclesial structure, and theological interpretation among the Roman Catholic, Eastern Orthodox, and Reformed Protestant Churches. Despite this, there is an underlying unity of belief among those who, in a general sense, consider themselves Orthodox. For all such Christians it is an acceptance of those fundamental tenets set out in the Apostle's Creed, a prayer based on the fundamental tenets of Christian belief supposed to have been held by the twelve Apostles. Most generally, then, it is the very idea of an adherence to a common core set of beliefs that defines Orthodoxy. Acknowledgment of this essential creedal nature of Orthodoxy, although insufficient to resolve all religious differences, serves to unify various sectarian believers, especially as against those of modernistic temperament who would deny the value of a core set of beliefs, biblically and historically grounded.

Whether religious belief is possible without some commitment to a core set of fundamental beliefs is a question motivating contemporary research. Those who claim to be skeptics about Orthodoxy may be open to the argument that the skeptical position is self-defeating; that is, skeptics themselves may have replaced traditional Orthodoxy with a kind of Orthodox liberalism in religious matters. Under this conception the choice is not between Orthodoxy and non-Orthodoxy but rather between competing forms of Orthodoxy.

Alexander R. Eodice

See also Buddhism; Catholicism; Hinduism; Islam; Judaism; Protestantism

Further Reading

Bauer, W. (1971). *Orthodoxy and heresy in earliest Christianity.* Philadelphia: Fortress Press. (Original work published 1934)

Chadwick, H. (1967). *The early Church.* Baltimore: Penguin Books.

Chesterton, G. K. (1908). *Orthodoxy.* New York: Dodd and Mead.

Cohen, N. (Ed.). (1990). *The Fundamentalist phenomenon.* Grand Rapids, MI: William B. Erdman.

George, R. P. (2001). *The clash of orthodoxies.* Wilmington, DE: ISI Books.

Le Guillou, M. J. (1962). *The spirit of Eastern Orthodoxy.* New York: Hawthorn Books.

Meyendorf, J. (1966). *Orthodoxy and Catholicity.* New York: Sheed and Ward.

Pelikan, J. (1971–1989). *The Christian tradition: The development of doctrine: Vol. 1. The emergence of the Catholic tradition (100–600)* & *Vol. 2. The spirit of Eastern Christendom* (600–1700). Chicago: University of Chicago Press.

Pelikan, J. (1990). Fundamentalism and/or Orthodoxy? Toward an understanding of the fundamentalist phenomenon. In N. Cohen (Ed.), *The Fundamentalist phenomenon* (pp. 3–21). Grand Rapids, MI: Wm. B. Erdmans.

Schmemann, A. (1965). *Sacraments and Orthodoxy.* New York: Herder and Herder.

Ware, T. (1997). *The Orthodox Church.* New York: Penguin Books.

P

Paganism and Neo-Paganism

Paganism and Neo-Paganism are religions that practice, reclaim, or experiment with non- and pre-Christian forms of worship. The term *pagan,* from the Latin word *paganus* (country dweller), was used by early Christians to describe what they saw as the backward, unsophisticated practices of rural people who continued to worship Roman gods after Christianity had been declared the official religion of the Roman Empire in 415 CE. The term maintained a negative connotation until it was reclaimed by Romantic (relating to a literary, artistic, and philosophical movement originating in the eighteenth century) revivalists in nineteenth-century Europe. Inspired by the works of early anthropologists and folklorists, who attributed spiritual authenticity to pre-Christian Europeans and the indigenous people of the Third World, revivalists coined the term *neo-pagan* to characterize the religions they were creating. Today the terms *pagan* and *neo-pagan* are often used interchangeably by Neo-Pagans to emphasize the historical and cultural continuity they claim with their spiritual forebears.

Some Neo-Pagans distinguish between their own revival movement and what they call "paleo-paganism" and "meso-paganism." According to this distinction, paleo-paganism includes pre-Christian religions, whereas meso-paganism includes the religions of indigenous groups who were never fully Christianized and thus never lost contact with their polytheistic traditions. Thus, for example, the Roman state religion is paleo-pagan; indigenous Native American religions are meso-pagan; and the religion practiced by the Reformed Druids of North America is Neo-Pagan.

Contemporary Neo-Pagan traditions are diverse and include groups who reclaim ancient Sumerian, Egyptian, Greek, and Roman practices as well as those dedicated to reviving Druidism (the priesthood of the ancient Gauls) and the worship of Norse gods and goddesses. Traditions also include hermetic (relating to the works attributed to Hermes Trismegistus) groups such as the Ordo Templo Orientis (OTO), an occult society founded in Germany in the late 1800s to the revive magic and mysticism; cabalistic groups who study ancient Hebrew mysticism; and alchemists, who practice the spiritual refinement of the will. By far the largest subgroup within Neo-Paganism is made up of revival witchcraft traditions, including Wicca (revival witchcraft). Some Neo-Pagans may mix elements from these traditions with others borrowed from Native American and Afro-Caribbean spiritualities, yielding highly syncretic (combining different forms) traditions. It is therefore almost impossible to generalize accurately about Neo-Pagan ritual practice.

Ritual in Neo-Pagan Religions

Ritual is the most important form of religious expression common to Neo-Pagan religions. Neo-Pagans emphasize ritual because of the tremendous attention it received from early anthropologists, folklorists, and religious scholars, who saw it as a set of patterned behaviors intended to regulate humans' relationships with supernatural agents such as deities or ancestor spirits. Neo-Pagans have adopted this early

Stonehenge in southern England is probably the best-known symbol of pagan religion. Its location on a slight rise in the Salisbury Plain and mysteries about its origin and meaning add to its allure. COURTESY OF KAREN CHRISTENSEN.

anthropological concept; but because they generally see divinity as present in every living thing, ritual becomes a vehicle to achieve communion not only with deities, but also with nature, community, and the inner self. Neo-Pagan rituals are a form of communally created artistic expression that strives to give participants direct, transcendent experiences of the sacred.

Neo-Pagans use a variety of techniques to bring about these experiences. These techniques include meditation, music, dance, poetry, drumming, costumes, and handmade objects, as well as symbolic action and speech. The stimuli are designed to communicate with participants' unconscious minds, moving them toward both religious ecstasy and new cognitive understandings. The planning and coordination of a successful ritual become an art form in and of themselves, and participants may contribute by making objects for use in a ritual, playing instruments, singing, dancing, reciting poetry, or engaging in other art forms within the ritual context. Most Neo-Pagan rituals are participatory experiences; there is little separation between clergy and laity in these religions, and all who are present play a part in the ritual performance.

Structure of Neo-Pagan Rituals

Most Neo-Pagan rituals have a three-part structure: setting the stage for the primary action, performing the actual work of ritual, and reintegrating participants into the everyday world. This structure is grounded in the work of twentieth-century ritual scholars such as the French sociologist Arnold Van Gennep, who identified three principal stages of ritual, and Victor Turner, who described ritual as "liminal" (existing outside ordinary time and space). Most Neo-Pagan groups do not have regular meeting places such as churches or temples. Their rituals take place in private homes or in public parks and meeting places. Rituals usually begin by consecrating the space: a series of actions designed to put participants in a frame of mind that Neo-Pagans call "between the worlds," that is, between the sacred world and the everyday, mundane world. Neo-Pagan traditions differ in how they accomplish this, but they may use incense and saltwater to symbolically cleanse the space or mark the area in which the ritual will occur with a knife or sword blade drawn through the air or with a line of chalk on the ground. These actions symbolically separate the ritual world from the everyday world. Ritualists may then summon the spirits of the four cardinal directions (north, south, east, and west) and the elements associated with each one (earth, fire, air, and water). When the space and the participants are ready, other spiritual entities, such as deities, nature spirits, or ancestors, may be summoned into the sacred space to honor them, give thanks, or request their help for the ritual's principal goal.

The middle part of the ritual constitutes its core. It is here that the participants commune with the gods

A collection of ritual objects used in worship by a follower of Neo-Paganism in western Massachusetts in 2002. COURTESY OF KAREN CHRISTENSEN.

through dance, music, movement, and a technique called "guided meditation," in which a narrator tells a story that participants follow in their imagination. The story may feature a journey to an imaginary temple where participants encounter gods and goddesses and receive personal messages from them. During this part of the ritual participants may raise energy with their bodies by dancing and singing and direct it toward a prearranged goal, such as world peace.

The final part of the ritual is designed to thank and dismiss the entities with whom participants have communed and to prepare the participants to return to ordinary reality. Sometimes food and drink are shared by all present as a symbol of fellowship. In some traditions this act is said to help participants return to an ordinary state of consciousness after having experienced religious ecstasy. After the spirits have been honored and saluted, the sacred circle (the spiritually purified space wherein Neo-Pagan and Wiccan rituals are usually held) is opened, and participants return to ordinary time and space.

Types of Rituals

Neo-Pagans tend to value variety in their ritual experience, and no two rituals are ever quite the same, even within the same tradition or group. Nevertheless, rituals can be divided into several categories. These categories include calendrical rituals, initiations and other rites of passage, and rites of crisis.

Calendrical rites are those that mark changes in the seasonal cycle of the year, for example, the transition from winter to spring. These rites tend to recur around the same time each year. They are important in Neo-Pagan theology because pagans venerate the sacredness of nature, and the natural world is considered a metaphor for the human condition. Although many Neo-Pagan traditions follow the Wiccan yearly cycle of eight sabbats (holy days, usually corresponding to the solstices, equinoxes, and cross-quarter days between each solstice), there no single calendrical cycle is common to all forms of Neo-Paganism; rather, each tradition follows a yearly cycle linked to the religion or spirituality that it emulates. For example, members of the Fellowship of Isis in Los Angeles commemorate the Navigium Isidis, a historical ritual in which boats were launched in the Nile River delta to honor the goddess Isis during the month of March. At that time in old Egypt the Nile flooded its banks, bringing water and fertility to the land. In the absence of the Nile, U.S. practitioners gather at a beach along the Pacific Ocean, where they release into the waves small boats made of ice (which is nonpolluting) imbued with their wishes and dreams. Practitioners of Asatru, a form of Norse paganism, celebrate Walpurgisnacht, a feast sacred to the Teutonic goddess Walpurga, on the night between 30 April and 1 May. This feast, which marks the return of spring, is characterized by drinking, dancing, feasting, and jumping over a bonfire *(balefire)* for good luck.

Rites of passage mark changes in the life cycle and status of the individual. These rites include child-blessing rites, puberty rites, marriages and funerals. Neo-Pagan traditions have developed rites for all these occasions. For many Neo-Pagans the most significant rites of passage are initiations. Some traditions require members to undergo an initiation in order to become full participants; in other traditions, initiates gain status as they progress through a hierarchy of initiatory "degrees." During these rites, esoteric knowledge is communicated to the initiates by elders in the tradition, and often by the gods themselves through visions. Initiation rites are secret in that their structure and esoteric teachings are never communicated to outsiders; however, they have some common elements. Sometimes initiates are required to undergo physical, psychological, or spiritual testing, taking on tasks that are challenging to prove their commitment to a spiritual path. They may learn new religious material, spend a night camping under the stars, swim naked in the cold ocean, or be challenged to overcome a bad habit or face an irrational fear. Upon initiation initiates often assume a new ritual name that symbolizes their evolving religious identity. They emerge from these challenges strengthened in their faith, often with profound mystical experiences that affirm the rightness of their religious practice.

Rites of crisis are created in response to a perceived threat in the life of the community or the individual. During such threats Neo-Pagans believe that through ritual they can tap into divine energies and channel them toward a goal. They may rally to work for peace if it appears that a war is imminent or assemble to stop environmental degradation in a specific area; but they also gather around friends and family who face a serious illness, the loss of a job, or a personal transition. Their response on these occasions is to create rites to restore the balance between the human world, the natural world, and the divine. They perceive the crisis as evidence that this balance has been disrupted, and they see themselves as vehicles to bring about healing on many levels.

Sources of Neo-Pagan Rituals

Despite Neo-Pagans' attempts to recapture the authenticity of ancient religions in their rituals, most of their ritual materials are of fairly recent origin. Anthropological, folkloric, and literary texts provide many of the raw materials they weave into their new art forms. Individuals seeking to reconstruct a particular tradition may research libraries, journals, and ethnographies (cultural studies) for information about a past culture's rituals. In other cases living traditions provide elements to which Neo-Pagans give new meanings and interpretations consonant with their values and beliefs. Some groups, for example, color eggs for the spring equinox, arguing that the egg was a natural symbol of fertility and regeneration associated with the Teutonic goddess Eostar long before Christians adopted it for Easter. Neo-Pagans may also borrow elements from the mass media and popular culture for their rituals, although sometimes these elements are used tongue in cheek. One group enacted a series of rituals based on the television series *Star Trek* and its Klingon characters, complete with costumes and language. In this light-hearted spoof, the juxtaposition of tough warrior space aliens with the usually romantic language and structure of ritual made for a humorous performance. This kind of reflexivity (taking material out of its original cultural context) is typical of many Neo-Pagan rituals; practitioners maintain an awareness that they are reviving and recombining traditions and are always ready to comment on its inherent absurdity.

Neo-Pagans have been criticized by some Native Americans, who feel that Neo-Pagans are stealing and profiting from their cultural traditions. Although Neo-Pagans do borrow from many other cultures in creating their rituals, the majority do so without intent to profit from their actions or to defraud the public into believing that they are authentic practitioners of the ethnic traditions they borrow. Some apparent similarities between Neo-Pagan ritual and Native American spiritual practice stem from parallels between the European tradition of high magic, with its sacred circles and four cardinal directions, and certain Native American practices and beliefs. Other similarities are more clearly cases of appropriation, for example, the non-Native American "sweat lodges" that are popular at some Neo-Pagan festivals. In such cases, although Neo-Pagans may actually intend to honor Native American cultural traditions by imitating them, the decontextualization of Native American sacred practice can be irritating to its original practitioners, who perceive such decontextualization as disrespectful.

In general Neo-Pagan rituals are artistic, life-affirming performances that create a sense of community and connectedness for their largely white, sophisticated, middle-class practitioners.

Sabina Magliocco

See also Crisis Rituals; Passage, Rites of; Wicca

Further Reading

Adler, M. (1986). *Drawing down the moon: Witches, druids, goddess-worshippers and other pagans in America today*. Boston: Beacon Press.

Hanegraaf, W. J. (1998). *New age religion and Western culture*. Albany: State University of New York Press.

Harvey, G., & Hardman, C. (1995). *Paganism today*. New York: HarperCollins.

Hutton, R. (2000). *Triumph of the moon: A history of modern pagan witchcraft*. Oxford, UK: Oxford University Press.

Magliocco, S. (1996). Ritual is my chosen art form: The creation of ritual among contemporary pagans. In J. R. Lewis (Ed.), *Magical religion and modern witchcraft* (pp. 93–119). Albany: State University of New York Press.

Orion, L. (1995). *Never again the burning times: Paganism revived*. Prospect Heights, IL: Waveland Press.

Pike, S. (2001). *Earthly bodies, magical selves*. Berkeley and Los Angeles: University of California Press.

Vale, V., & Sulak, J. (2002). *Modern pagans*. Champaign, IL: Research Press.

Passage, Rites of

Rites of passage move participants from one social status to another. Rites of passage take a variety of forms: They may be explicitly recognized as formal rites (as in the case of a high school graduation), or the function of social transformation may be buried beneath other understandings of a process (as in the case of the gradual toughening of adolescents accomplished through middle school violence). They may be collective or individualized, they may be associated with religious symbolism and institutions or not, they may involve every person within a society, or they may be limited to members of a particular class, occupation, or subculture, and they may be mandatory or optional. Rites of passage share a recognizable structure and are important events for the reproduction of social values and institutions, including forms of power and inequality.

The Three-Stage Model of Arnold Van Gennep

The French anthropologist Arnold Van Gennep (1873–1957) developed a framework for understanding rites of passage in his classic book *The Rites of Passage.* Van Gennep described three stages to any rite: separation, transition, and reincorporation. In the separation stage the persons who are to be transformed are taken away from their normal lives, roles, and identities. For example, citizens who are to be reclassified as "marines" are removed to an island or swamp, then stripped of their most obvious physical marker of individual identity—their hair and clothes—at the onset of the rite of passage known as "boot camp." In some rites of passage, participants encounter a second level of separation—taken-for-granted norms of social interaction no longer apply in the new world in which they find themselves; these are replaced by new and unpredictable codes of behavior and a new language.

After participants are separated from society, they pass through a transition stage in which their old identity is stripped from them. They experience "liminality" (relating to a sensory threshold) or the condition of being "betwixt and between the positions assigned and arrayed by law, custom, convention, and ceremonial" (Turner 1977, 95). The symbolic anthropologist Victor Turner (b. 1920) wrote that, in liminality, society shows participants in rites of passage that they are blank slates, "clay or dust, mere matter, whose form is impressed upon them by society" (Turner 1977, 103). Thus, participants in rites of passage are not differentiated from each other—their previous statuses and individual positions in the social structure are concealed. This concealment may be expressed in nakedness or in the intensity of shared experience such as pain, as in circumcision rituals; shared humiliation, as in the hazing rituals of adolescent males in African warrior societies and U.S. military academies; or altered states of consciousness brought on by fasting, ecstatic dancing, sleep deprivation, or the ingestion of drugs. Often, participants are given the freedom to playfully overturn normal social conventions and taboos, demonstrating their position outside normal, everyday life. Monogamous sexual relationships are markers of individualized status, so participants in rites of passage often undergo forced sexual abstinence, or, as in the case of the *elima* ritual of the central African BamButi described by the American anthropologist—Colin Turnbull (1924–1994) or in the North American ritual of spring break, they may experience a temporary license for sexual promiscuity. In either case, sexuality is not allowed to separate individuals from the egalitarian community undergoing transition.

Some institutions and subcultures have tried to transform the ecstatic, "antistructure" (a temporary absence or inversion of everyday statuses, roles, and hierarchies) feeling of liminality into a permanent way of life. Turner describes monastic orders of the Middle Ages and the hippie subculture of the 1960s as efforts to create communities of ongoing liminality. Such communities are often considered dangerous by society as a whole because they threaten the order of established social categories. Eventually, Turner argues, such antistructural communities become institutionalized and lose their liminal qualities.

The final stage in a rite of passage is reincorporation. In this stage participants are welcomed back into normal, everyday society with a new status. This completion of the rite may be marked with a celebration, such as the hugs exchanged between parents and their children after a graduation ceremony or the parties that follow wedding ceremonies.

Rites of Passage and Identity

Rites of passage may involve symbols that convey a message about the shared cultural identity of the community that sponsors the rites. Modern Westerners often assume that their societies, unlike

FEMALE GENITAL MUTILATION IN AFRICA

Villeneuve in her study, "Les femmes cousues," divides the sequence of operations which Somali women undergo into three stages. (1) Excision of the clitoris and infibulation of the vulva before puberty; (2) the opening made by the husband for intercourse at marriage; and (3) subsequent openings for delivery of the child, after each of which the vulva is again partially closed. The initial operation takes place between the ages of six and eight at a small family ceremony within the hut to which the girl's mother invites female relatives and neighbours, men being rigorously excluded. The ceremony is in no sense a communal rite, and usually only one child is initiated, although sometimes two sisters may be operated on together. The whole operation—excision of the clitoris and infibulation of the vulva—takes about 20 minutes, and is performed at dawn by a Midgan woman. Infibulation, like circumcision, is a mark of adulthood and eligibility for marriage; even prostitutes are infibulated.

***Source*: Lewis, I. M. *Peoples of the Horn of Africa.* (1955). London: International African Institute, p. 135.**

the more "traditional" peoples formerly studied by anthropologists, lack cohesive rites of passage. In fact, the dispersal of rites of passage into numerous specialized rites and the solitary nature of many rites—such as the epic, transformative road trip of U.S. writer Jack Kerouac and thousands of imitators—symbolically reconfirm the cultural value of individualism in the West, especially in the United States.

In another example of a rite of passage of a Western subculture that symbolically expresses cultural values, Canadian anthropologist Daniel Wolf describes the ritual through which a Canadian outlaw biker gang transformed initiates into full-fledged members. The initiates were taken to a state park several hours away from home, then stripped naked, beaten, covered with a mixture of sludge and dirty oil from the motorcycles and urine and feces from the bikers, and finally reincorporated into the gang with hugs and a night-long party. This rite confirms the bikers' perceived distance from "normal" society and their sense of ultramasculinity based on toughness. Through the mixture of waste products from humans and motorcycles, the rite also symbolically transforms the men from normal humans into "bikers"—heroic hybrids of man and machine.

Rites of passage may also incorporate elements of the natural or social environment. For middle-class Americans, immersion in nature—through a liminal summer spent at camp or an epic canoeing trip down a wild river—often provides the context for a status-changing rite. Rites of passage often also involve altering the body through the infliction of marks such as tattoos or scarification or through the infliction of bodily pain. Julie Peteet, an anthropologist who studies gender in Palestinian society, describes a rite of passage that involves the ritual manipulation of the political environment as well as the infliction of bodily violence. Palestinian males in the occupied territories, whose traditional rites of passage involved risk-taking adventures, used their beatings at the hands of Israeli soldiers and prison guards during the uprising of the 1980s as identity-confirming rites of passage that became a necessary part of the cultural apparatus that transformed boys into men. Young men were separated from their families and brought to prison, where they experienced the liminality of shared hardship and violence with a community of fellow prisoners, then were reincorporated into their families through a celebratory feast. This rite reconfirms the Arab values of manhood and honor while simultaneously tying those values to the ongoing political and military resistance to occupation.

Rites of Passage, Gender, and Inequality

Many rites of passage are restricted to one gender—most typically males. Anthropologists have interpreted these rites in different ways. Psychological interpretations such as those proposed by U.S. psychologist Bruno Bettelheim (1903–1990) stress the way that these rites, such as male circumcision, function to resolve personal psychological problems such as "female envy." To fully become men, Bettelheim argued, boys must be separated from their mothers and must satisfy their unconscious envy of women by having their genitals cut.

Less psychologically inclined anthropologists focus less on purportedly universal unconscious drives and more on how specific cultures use these rites of passage to construct the meanings of the gender categories of male and female. U.S. anthropologist Gilbert Herdt's ethnographic (cultural) study of the Sambia people of Melanesia (islands of the southwest Pacific Ocean) shows how Sambia men believe that maleness and femaleness are fundamentally different qualities. Girls develop naturally into adult women, whereas boys need to acquire the essence of biological maleness from other males in cultural exchanges made in male secret societies.

The idea that boys must be made into men whereas women simply unfold is not universal, but neither is it unique to the Sambia. Boys are largely raised and nurtured by their mothers, yet they must at some point join the community of adult males. This movement from the asexual, female domestic sphere to the sexual, adult male sphere often calls for a jarring rite of passage that is not available for women. Societies may then define men as "more adult" or "more cultural" than women because women are not ritually transformed into culturally defined adults. Rites of passage thus play an important role in reproducing gender inequality. For example, feminist filmmaker and anthropologist Melissa Llewelyn-Davies argues that, among Masai herders of Kenya in Africa, men go through three formal life stages—childhood, warriorhood (an intense and glamorous liminal phase of men's lives), and adulthood—whereas women go through only childhood and adulthood. This additional male life stage provided by an institutionalized rite of passage provides the ideological basis for male control of livestock and production and women's subordinate status as "property." If rites of passage are key sites for the reproduction of gender inequality, then gender equality can be promoted by establishing rites of passage for women. In the United States the federal Title IX (1972), which guaranteed women equal access to one of the important rites of passage—high school and college athletics—is thus one of the most important vehicles for women's equality.

Historically, high school sports not only have reproduced gender inequality, but also they have naturalized inequality based on race and class. Educational anthropologist Douglas Foley shows, for example, how high school football in a Texas small town in the 1970s became a medium for the display of racial hierarchy and the power of the town's dominant families as white, economically privileged males were generally given the lead roles on football teams. Foley's analysis follows from the insights of other class-based analyses of socialization in industrialized nations—the rites of passage of upper-class boys (sports and the licensed "wildness" associated with organizations such as fraternities) prepare and qualify them for positions of power and privilege, whereas the equivalent, "rebellious" rites of passage of working-class youths are seen as "deviant" activities that alienate them from the power structure and prevent upward mobility.

Female Genital Operations

Rites of passage that involve cutting women's genitals have been the object of a great deal of controversy since the 1970s, when Western second-wave feminists such as Alice Walker began to attack these rites as violent expressions of male domination. Many African men and women responded angrily to these attacks, which they regarded as a form of neocolonial racism. Female genital operations are practiced across broad stretches of sub-Saharan and north Africa and take a variety of forms, ranging from minor, largely symbolic cuts to major operations such as clitoridectomy (removal of the clitoris) and infibulation (partial closure or sewing shut of the vagina). The meanings, histories, and cultural politics associated with these painful rites also vary from region to region. In an ethnographic account of a clitoridectomy rite practiced in western Kenya, Christine Walley, U.S. anthropologist, does not attempt to solve this controversial issue but argues instead that the debate needs to free itself from several problematic assumptions: the ethnocentric (relating to the attitude that one's own group is superior) assumption that female genital operations form a single monolithic tradition imposed on passive women by men and the idea that practices can only be judged in the context of their culture. Instead, Europeans and Africans must find a language to address these rites that appreciates the rites' diverse meanings and their connection to historical processes.

Implications

Van Gennep's three-stage model of rites of passage has proven to be a remarkably durable analytical tool. Increasingly, researchers do not think of the rite of passage as a distinct event whose features may be explained through a single, analytical vehicle such as Bettelheim's psychoanalytic model. Instead, the rite of passage serves as a lens that can be applied to almost any social situation—examples of separation, transition, and reincorporation can be found everywhere. The rite of passage model enables people to explore not only psychological issues, but also issues of gender, political power and resistance, emotion, group identity, and cultural symbolism. Although the term *rite* suggests a privileged connection to religious ritual, the multiplicity of rites of passage in the world shows how difficult it is to separate the exclusively religious sphere from the rest of social experience.

Ben Feinberg

See also Africa, West; Altered States of Consciousness; Birth Rituals; Crisis Rituals; Death Rituals; Gender Rituals; Liminoid; Marriage Rituals; Naming Rituals; Pilgrimage

Further Reading

Adams, A. E. (1993). Dyke to dyke: Ritual reproduction at a U.S. men's military college. *Anthropology Today, 9*(5), 3–6.

Arnett, J. J. (1996). *Metalheads: Heavy metal music and adolescent alienation.* Boulder, CO: Westview Press.

Bettelheim, B. (1954). *Symbolic wounds: Puberty rites and the envious male.* New York: Collier.

Bly, R. (1990). *Iron John: A book about men.* New York: Addison-Wesley.

Brain, J. L. (1977). Sex, incest, and death: Initiation rites reconsidered. *Current Anthropology, 18*(2), 191–207.

Foley, D. E. (1990). *Learning capitalist culture: Deep in the heart of Tejas.* Philadelphia: University of Pennsylvania Press.

Herdt, G. H. (1982). *Rituals of manhood: Male initiation in Papua New Guinea.* Berkeley and Los Angeles: University of California Press.

Llewelyn-Davies, M. (1981). Women, warriors, and patriarchs. In S. Ortner & H. Whitehead (Eds.), *Sexual meanings: The culture construction of gender and sexuality* (pp. 330–358). Cambridge, UK: Cambridge University Press.

Peteet, J. (1994). Male gender and rituals of resistance in the Palestinian *intifada:* A cultural poetics of violence. *American Ethnologist, 21*(1), 31–49.

Turnbull, C. (1961). *The forest people.* New York: Simon & Schuster.

Turner, V. W. (1977). *The ritual process: Structure and anti-structure.* Ithaca, NY: Cornell University Press.

Van Gennep, A. (1960). *The rites of passage.* Chicago: University of Chicago Press. (Original work published 1909)

Walker, A., & Parmer, P. (1993). *Warrior marks: Female genital mutilation and the sexual blinding of women.* New York: Harcourt, Brace and Company.

Walley, C. J. (1997). Searching for "voices": Feminism, anthropology, and the global debate over female genital operations. *Cultural Anthropology, 12*(3), 405–438.

Willis, P. E. (1981). *Learning to labor.* New York: Columbia University Press.

Wolf, D. R. (1992). *The rebels: A brotherhood of outlaw bikers.* Toronto, Canada: University of Toronto Press.

Passover

Each year all over the world Jewish families and congregations gather to celebrate an ancient religious ritual, the Passover (Pesach), commemorating the deliverance of the Jews from their bondage in Egypt (c. thirteenth century BCE). Passover was instituted to remember that Yahweh (the god of the Jewish people) is faithful to all his promises. This detailed ritual and weeklong feast take place on the same date every year, the fourteenth day of Nisan on the Jewish calendar (Exodus 12:6), usually in March or April.

Historical Background

In many ancient religious rituals people commonly sacrificed the eldest son to appease the local or national deity or deities for the sins of the nation or family. Many religious anthropologists see many similarities between the practices of other ancient Near East religions and the practices of the early Jewish worship of Yahweh.

Even the earliest pages of the Jewish Scripture have a record of this practice of sacrifice of the eldest son. Genesis 22:2 states: "Take now your son, your only son Isaac, whom you love, and go to the land of Moriah, and offer him there as a burnt offering on one of the mountains of which I shall tell you" (NRSV).

This theme can be found in the Passover narrative in the Book of Exodus. Yahweh hears the cries of his people who are in bondage in Egypt and remembers a covenant promise given to Abraham, patriarch of the nation (Genesis 12–17). This promise or covenant motivated Yahweh to free the nation of Israel from its bondage.

> He said further, "I am the God of your father, the God of Abraham, the God of Isaac, and the God of Jacob." And Moses hid his face, for he was afraid to look at God. Then the LORD said, "I have observed the misery of my people who are in Egypt; I have heard their cry on account of their taskmasters. Indeed, I know their sufferings, and I have come down to deliver them from the Egyptians. (Exodus 3:6–8a, NRSV)

This narrative describing the deliverance of the Hebrews from the land of Egypt starts a divine battle between the gods of Egypt and the monotheistic god of the Hebrew people, who states, "on all the gods of Egypt I will execute judgments: I am the LORD" (Exodus 12:12, NRSV). Yahweh in his deliverance of the Hebrew people sends ten plagues, which are an attack on each of the major gods of the people of Egypt.

The final attack is upon the supreme god of Egypt, Re, also known as "Amon-Re." The sacrifice of the eldest son to Re was one of the common practices in the worship of Re. As the Hebrew narrative develops, Yahweh attacks Re in the final plague when he sends darkness over Egypt and kills the entire firstborn male population of Egypt.

Moses (c. thirteenth century BCE), Yahweh's spokesman and prophet, tells the Hebrew people to follow a detailed ritual to protect themselves from the coming plague. This ritual includes dipping a hyssop branch into lamb's blood and sprinkling the door posts and lintel (i.e., door frame) of each Hebrew home. The Hebrew people were also to roast and eat the lamb from which they received the blood and to eat unleavened bread and bitter herbs. The Passover then was a ritual to allow the Hebrew nation's escape from the plague of the firstborn (Exodus 12).

This attack shows two interesting facets. The first is that the Hebrew Bible is attempting to show the superiority of Yahweh over the gods of Egypt. The second is that Yahweh does not want human sacrifice as part of Israel worship of him. Passover originated as the practice of sacrificing a lamb substituted for the practice of sacrificing the eldest son—echoing back to Yahweh's provision (Jehovah-Jireh) of a ram to Abraham in substitution for Isaac. Later in biblical writing the eldest son still belongs to Yahweh but is no longer sacrificed (Exodus 22:29).

Elements and Practice

Jewish practice is essentially the same as it has been for centuries. Each year on the fourteenth of Nisan Jews begin a weeklong celebration and feast beginning with a meal called the "seder" (from the Hebrew word for "order"). Prior to the meal a family cleans the house from all *chametz* or leaven. After this the seder can be performed.

The modern seder has many of the elements found in the biblical text and a few additions. The seder prayer book, called the "Haggadah," was revised by Rabbi Hillel (300 BCE) and comprises a service of thanks and the singing of psalms of praise. These psalms form the heart and structure of the meal. The meal includes roasted lamb, unleavened bread, and bitter herbs (Exodus 12, Numbers 9:11). The service also includes four cups of wine.

The elements of a modern Passover feast include singing psalms, saying a blessing, and reciting other material. The modern seder agrees substantially with what is laid down in the Mishnah, a commentary of the Jewish Bible. Three thick unleavened cakes, wrapped in napkins or placed in a cloth bag, are laid upon the seder dish; parsley and a bowl of salt water represent the hyssop and blood of the Passover of Egypt. Watercress or horseradish tops represent the *maror* (bitter herbs); *charoset* (a mixture of nuts and apples) duplicates the clay that the Israelites worked into bricks; *karpas* (vegetables) are also placed on the seder plate. Also placed on the table are *zeroa* (a roasted shankbone that is as a symbol of the paschal lamb, a Passover sacrifice in biblical times), *beitzah* (roasted or boiled egg) in memory of the free-will offering of the feast, and wine in a glass or silver cup for each member of the family and each guest. An extra cup of wine is filled for the prophet Elijah (ninth century BCE) as the Jewish people await their coming messiah.

The seder begins with the leader or master of the table washing his hands and dipping the bitter herbs into a dish of water; a prayer is said. Then the herbs are eaten by all in attendance. The middle piece of unleavened bread is broken to represent the affliction of the people of Israel while in bondage in Egypt. This bread is set aside to be eaten at the end of the seder. Then a series of responsive readings relating to

Israel's slavery in Egypt is read. Singing, drinking the cups of wine, eating from the seder elements, and saying prayers and blessings are part of the seder ritual.

Jews in other parts of the world have added elements. For example, Jews in Yemen recite together "who has chosen us above every people" and "He called us a community of saints, a precious vineyard, a pleasant plantation; compared to the host of heaven and set like stars in the firmament." German and Polish Jews read five portions of poetry at the end of the seder. In the Spanish language Sephardic (relating to the occidental branch of European Jews settling in Spain and Portugal) Jews living in Turkey recite extrabiblical legends about the Exodus that are not found in the Haggadah (ancient lore forming especially the nonlegal part of the Talmud). This meal of remembrance is ended with the drinking of the last cup of wine.

For Jews, the Passover is an identifying mark of their faith. To not celebrate the Passover seder is tantamount to not being a Jew (Numbers 9:13).

Christian Interpretation

Christianity, which began as a sect of Judaism, has one of its most important rituals—Holy Communion, also called the "Lord's Supper" or the "Eucharist"—rooted in Passover.

Jesus, born a Jew, and his Jewish disciples made their way to Jerusalem to participate in the annual Passover rituals. According to the New Testament, Jesus, anticipating his death, selected two of the seder elements to define his nearing end.

> While they were eating, Jesus took a loaf of bread, and after blessing it he broke it, gave it to the disciples, and said, "Take, eat; this is my body." Then he took a cup, and after giving thanks he gave it to them, saying, "Drink from it, all of you; for this is my blood of the covenant, which is poured out for many for the forgiveness of sins. I tell you, I will never again drink of this fruit of the vine until that day when I drink it new with you in my Father's kingdom." When they had sung the hymn, they went out to the Mount of Olives. (Matthew 26:26–30, NRSV)

The early Church as reflected in the New Testament canon saw Jesus as the promised messiah and deliverer of the Jewish people. Jesus was to deliver his people from their sins through his own death by crucifixion. This deliverance was not for the Jews only but rather for all nations of the world (John 3:16).

The death of Jesus is seen in terms of the shedding of his blood and the breaking of his body. Thus, the New Testament uses these terms as it speaks of Holy Communion. For Christians the bread of the seder was to signify the body of Jesus crucified, and the wine of the seder was to represent the blood of Jesus shed for the sins of those whom he would save and forgive.

Because of this adaptation of the seder Jesus is called by the New Testament writers "The Lamb of God who takes away the sin of the world!" (John 1:29, NKJV). This new ritual represents a new covenant for a new people, according to Christian believers. "Exodus 24:1–11 records the ratification of the old covenant between God and Israel on Mount Sinai, and it sheds some light on the words of Jesus used when he instituted the Lord's Supper… Jesus would refer to his own blood as the blood of the covenant and inaugurated a new phase of the history of redemption" (Mathison 2002, 192).

Passover is a central to the Jewish religion. It touches all the senses of the Jewish people. As each Jew gathers with family and other believers the Passover is celebrated to remember the history of their people, the faithfulness of their god to his promises to them. As the seder meal is eaten and the wine is poured and the psalms are sung, the taste and smell of the past help renew this feast of remembrance.

Patrick W. Malone

See also Blood Rituals; Crisis Rituals; Food and Rituals; Identity Rituals; Judaism

Further Reading

Bloom, H. (Ed.). (1987). *Exodus, modern critical interpretations*. New York: Chelsea House.

Clements, R. E. (1972). *Exodus, the Cambridge Bible commentary*. Cambridge, UK: Cambridge University Press.

Douglas, J. D. (Ed.). (1980). *The new Bible dictionary*. Wheaton, IL: Inter-Varsity Press.

Fredman, R. G. (1981). *The Passover Seder*. Philadelphia: University of Pennsylvania.

Freedman, D. N. (Ed.). (1992). *The anchor Bible dictionary*. New York: Bantam Doubleday Dell.

Goodman, P. (1961). *The Passover anthology*. Philadelphia, PA: Jewish Publication Society.

Kasher, M. M. (1962). *Israel Passover Haggadah*. New York: American Biblical Encyclopedia Society.

Kline, M. G. (2000). *Kingdom prologue*. Overland Park, KS: Two Age Press.
Mathison, K. (2002). *Given for you*. Phillipsburg, NJ: Presbyterian and Reformed.
Sarna, N. M. (1992). *Exploring Exodus*. New York: Schocken Books.
Segal, J. B. (1963). *The Hebrew Passover*. New York: Oxford University Press.
Stavans, I. (Ed.). (1998). *The Oxford book of Jewish stories*. New York: Oxford University Press.
Turretin, F. (1978). *The atonement of Christ*. Grand Rapids, MI: Baker Books.
Twerski, A. J. (1999). *From bondage to freedom*. New York: Shaar Press.
Wiesel, E. (1993). *A Passover Haggadah*. New York: Simon & Schuster.

Pentecostalism

Pentecostalism is a contemporary religious movement within the Christian tradition that emphasizes the work of the Holy Spirit within the life of the believer as manifested by the apostles shortly after the death, resurrection, and ascension of Christ. Pentecostals believe that the promised Holy Spirit, of which Jesus speaks in Acts 1:5 and whose initial coming is recorded in Acts 2:4, was not a one-time event and that the indwelling of the Spirit is a divine provision made for all Christians who seek the experience. Later in Acts chapter 2, Peter declares that the Holy Spirit, "is for you, for your children, and for all who are far away, everyone whom the Lord our God calls to him" (Acts 2:39, NRSV). The initial evidence of what is often referred to as "the baptism in the Holy Spirit" is generally (though not exclusively) regarded as speaking in tongues or glossolalia. This was the experience of the apostles on the day of Pentecost (hence the designation "Pentecostalism"), a traditional Jewish festival celebrated fifty days after Passover. The emergence of modern Pentecostalism constitutes what has been described as "the most dramatic development of Christianity" (Martin 2002, 1) in the last century.

Contemporary Origins

The late nineteenth and early twentieth century witnessed periods of intense evangelical and then later Pentecostal activity throughout both the United States and the British Isles. In Britain the Second Evangelical Awakening—a sustained revival that was particularly strong in Scotland—flourished between 1859 and 1860. Later, a significant concentration of religious fervor was demonstrated in the Welsh revival of 1904–1905, during which time it was reported that over 100,000 people were converted to Christianity. Similar religious revivals were taking place in North America.

Placing the religious fervor of this period into historical context, the increased intensity of an evangelical drive from within a number of established Protestant denominations could be seen as a reaction against the secularizing impulses of modernity. A growing concern amongst many evangelicals became the restoration of the church in what were perceived to be the "last days" before Christ's return. At such a time, Christ would "rapture" all true believers (transport Christians from the earth to heaven) and eventually cast judgment on the world. Part of the restoring of the church prior to this event was thought to be a return to the fervor and supernatural experiences of the New Testament church, in which miraculous events took place and many were added to the church daily.

A leading proponent of restoration theology was Iowa-born Charles Fox Parham, a former Methodist pastor. By 1901 Parham had established a Christian school in Topeka, Kansas, and it was there that one of his students, Agnes Ozman, received the baptism in the Holy Spirit and reportedly spoke in Chinese for the next three days. William Seymour, a poor and relatively uneducated African-American whose parents had been slaves, was greatly influenced by the teachings of Parham. His subsequent ministry in Los Angeles eventually led him to play a pivotal role in the Azusa Street Revival of 1906. The Azusa Street Revival is significant in the history of the Pentecostal movement because it is generally thought to have witnessed the first instance of a congregant speaking in tongues. Since these initial accounts, the Pentecostal movement, although diverse, has become a global phenomenon and has also permeated, to various degrees, many religious traditions, including Catholicism. It should be noted that Pentecostal sects had emerged in Britain prior to the Topeka and Los Angeles experiences. Conflicting with the Calvinism of the Church of Scotland, both McLeod Campbell and Edward Irving advocated the manifestations of the Holy Spirit as pertinent for the contemporary church. Campbell's ministry in Row, Scotland, and Irving's church in London both witnessed the outpouring of the Holy Spirit and speaking in tongues in the early 1830s.

Pentecostal Universals

The rise of Pentecostalism throughout the twentieth century is generally regarded as extraordinary, the most prodigious growth being concentrated in Latin America and Africa. Estimates suggest that nearly a half-billion people worldwide can be classed as part of the Pentecostal movement. Given its global status, Pentecostal practice and ritual expresses multifarious cultural forms. Even so, a number of universals can be identified as being integral to the Pentecostal believer's experience. They are (1) the baptism in the Holy Spirit with the subsequent exercising of the gifts of the Holy Spirit, (2) an eschatological emphasis, and (3) life in the Spirit.

The Baptism in the Holy Spirit

The account of the apostles' experience recorded in Acts 2 describes what is, for most Pentecostals, the initial baptism in the Holy Spirit. Generally, within the context of collective forms of worship, church attenders will pray for individuals to receive the baptism. Essentially, this experience is a manifestation of the Holy Spirit who, since their salvation, dwells within the believer. The subject is encouraged to simply praise God out loud and to be aware of any compulsion to utter unfamiliar sounds. When the baptism occurs, glossolalia will result. Taken from the Greek *glossais lalein*, the term means "to speak in tongues," and the language spoken is unknown to the subject. In Acts 2:4 we read, "All of them were filled with the Holy Spirit and began to speak in other languages, as the Spirit gave them ability." Although unknown to the speaker, the language may be understood by others; witnesses to the events in the "upper room" on the day of Pentecost were amazed at the fact that the apostles were declaring the greatness of God in their own native languages (verse 8).

Speaking in tongues is believed to fulfill two main functions. First, it is given as edification (a form of spiritual encouragement or building up) to others within a corporate setting. A further manifestation of the Holy Spirit occurs when the language(s) spoken is/are not understood by the hearers; in such a case God will bestow the gift of interpretation upon another believer, who then relays the message of the tongue dialogue in the common language of the group. The second function is a means for the individual to personally worship God; speaking in tongues is sometimes referred to as a "prayer language." One commentator describes it as a possible means to "vent the inexpressible" (Spittler 2002, 675).

Pentecostals believe that subsequent blessings or "gifts" (from the Greek word *charismata*) of the Holy Spirit can be bestowed on the believer. In 1 Corinthians 12:7–10, the apostle Paul instructs the church at Corinth that individuals may be blessed with various manifestations of the Spirit for the common good (verse 7). He then lists them: the gifts of wisdom, knowledge, faith, healing, miracles, prophecy, the discerning of spirits, tongues, and the interpretation of tongues. The gifts of the Holy Spirit are given to the church in order to strengthen and edify believers. The baptism in the Holy Spirit is regarded, generally, as a special anointing that empowers and enables Christians to live out their faith boldly and equips them in their mission to share the message of the gospel. In Luke 24:49 Jesus makes reference to the coming of the Holy Spirit as he instructs his disciples to, "stay here in the city until you have been clothed with power from on high."

Eschatological Emphasis

Eschatology is the study of the End Times; Pentecostalism can be regarded as a movement strongly related to a theology of the second advent, or Christ's return. Indeed, the Pentecostal experience itself confirms the imminence of Christ's return. In the book of Acts chapter 2, Peter stands to address the crowds who have just witnessed the first baptism in the Holy Spirit. Drawing from the prophet Joel, he states, "In the last days it will be, God declares, that I will pour out my Spirit upon all flesh, and your sons and daughters shall prophesy, and your young men shall see visions, and your old men shall dream dreams" (Acts 2:17; compare Joel 2:28).

Pentecostalism is integrally linked to the notion of the restoration of the early church in the End Times. Although interpretations pertaining to the exact sequence of events for the rapture of the church and Christ's Second Coming vary within the Pentecostal tradition, one of the more common views holds to a premillennial theology. Here Christ will return initially to rapture his church, removing Christians from the earth prior to seven years of tribulation in which the world will see the rise of the Antichrist. At the end of the seven years, Christ will return and defeat the

Antichrist, after which he will reign on the earth for a thousand years before the final judgment takes place. This understanding of the End Times places on the Pentecostal significant responsibility that patterns lifestyle and determines various actions. First, although Pentecostals believe that the rapture is imminent, the Bible teaches that no one knows the exact time it will occur. In accordance with Scripture it is the believer's responsibility to ensure that they are ready at all times and living in obedience to Christ. Second, Pentecostals are mission oriented in that they believe they are called to preach the salvation message to all people so that as many as possible are saved and ready to be taken up with Christ on the day of the rapture.

Life in the Spirit

Pentecostals hold that the spiritual life is also a supernatural one and that God can be experienced in feeling as well as in intellect. The miracles performed by Jesus and his disciples recorded in the Gospels and the book of Acts were displays of God's supernatural power and such miraculous happenings, it is believed, are still prevalent in the church today. Praying for those with physical, emotional, and spiritual problems constitutes a significant ritualistic component within Pentecostal gatherings. Usually, times of prayer for those in need are highly charged and emotional and many give testimony to the healing power of God.

Less extreme, but none the less experiential, is the interaction with the Holy Spirit, who guides and directs the believer throughout his or her day. Pentecostals often speak of being prompted by the Holy Spirit to carry out some particular task, to pray for an individual or a situation, to read a particular passage from the Bible, or to share a spiritual word of encouragement with someone. Pentecostals stress the intimacy of their relationship with God.

Pentecostalism and Symbolic Ritual

Pentecostal practice is often thought to be lacking in structure and form; the spontaneous expression of praise and worship and the reliance upon the Holy Spirit to intervene and to guide the collective worship experience reinforces this presupposition. Nils Bloch-Hoell suggests that the Pentecostal movement has always been, "opposed to regularity and orderliness" (Bloch-Hoell 1964, 5). The account of the initial outpouring of the Spirit in the book of Acts also suggests a level of informality that led some witnesses of the event to conclude that the eleven apostles were drunk: "All were amazed and perplexed, saying to one another, 'What does this mean?' But others sneered and said, 'They are filled with new wine.'" (Acts 2:12–13). Whereas much emphasis is placed upon freedom and spontaneity within Pentecostalism, a level of structure does exist and in some Pentecostal groups tensions can arise as members negotiate the appropriate balance between form and discomposure.

Water baptism features prominently in Pentecostal ritual. The act is regarded as a symbol of the transition that takes place in a person's life upon conversion. Accounts of baptism in the Bible suggest that the ceremony is only for those who are old enough to consciously choose repentance and to follow Christ. Pentecostals, therefore, reject the practice of infant baptism as conversion is regarded as a reasoned act of the will. Although strongly advocated, baptism is not considered an absolute requisite to salvation; the act itself does not determine one's eternal status, and true salvation is ultimately an internal, spiritual happening. Pentecostals believe that total immersion in water is the true biblical method of baptism, as opposed to the sprinkling of water or the sign of the cross on the forehead, which are the preferred methods of baptism in some other religious traditions. Total immersion highlights the strong symbolism in the ritual. The baptism ceremony is often used as a means of evangelism to illustrate the changed life of the new convert. Onlookers witness the individual descending into the waters of baptism and a "new creation" coming forth from them; the old self giving way to the new self as a believer.

Another symbolic ritual practiced by Pentecostals is that of Communion or breaking of bread. Taken from the injunction of Christ during the Last Supper, this practice entails the distribution of the emblems amongst the congregation. The emblems consist of bread and wine (often a nonalcoholic substitute is used), which are representative of the body and the blood of Christ.

Pentecostalism in the Twenty-First Century

Pentecostalism is not a static movement; its reliance on the free flow of the Holy Spirit inspires considerable innovation, adaptation, and change. It is believed by some that the Holy Spirit, even during the Pentecostal movement's short history, has at different times and places brought religious revivals that have both regenerated believers and brought many nonbelievers to salvation. Sometimes referred to as a "fresh anointing" or "wave" of the Holy Spirit, the Pentecostal influence has also permeated the spiritual experience of many believers traditionally outside of the Pentecostal movement. According to Mary Jo Neitz (1987), Catholic charismatic renewal first emerged in 1967 after two Duquesne University (Pittsburgh, Pennsylvania) faculty members were baptized in the Holy Spirit and began to speak in tongues. This Pentecostal strand within the Catholic Church originated amongst Catholic students and then spread to many Catholic congregations. The same exercising of the charismatic gifts of the Holy Spirit has been present throughout a number of Protestant mainline denominations also.

Although the traditional Pentecostals established spontaneity and reliance upon the Holy Spirit within their gatherings, the extent to which some of the charismatics take this practice has far surpassed the extemporaneous experiences of a generation ago. Indeed, a possible rift may be emerging between the "classical" Pentecostals and the newer charismatic Christians or "neo-Pentecostals." Although great emphasis has always been placed upon the leading of the Holy Spirit within Pentecostalism, classical Pentecostals have generally stressed and maintained the importance of Scripture within their spiritual practice. Each experience correlates to a particular verse or passage in the Bible, thereby grounding the experience in the Word of God. Many of the neo-Pentecostals come from religious denominations that could be considered liberal in theological outlook. Although the newer charismatic Christians are Spirit-baptized, classical Pentecostals are often wary of the lack of biblical stringency they measure their experiences against. The criticism often leveled at neo-Pentecostals by classical Pentecostals is that the supposed displays of the Spirit do not have a scriptural base and are far too excessive. Even given this area of potentially escalating conflict between the classical Pentecostals and the neo-Pentecostals, continued vitality in the movement seems certain. According to Woodhead and Heelas (2000), research suggests that those religions that allow high levels of self-expression and participation tend to attract more people than those religious traditions that maintain a high level of formality.

Malcolm Gold

See also Ecstatic Worship; Glossolalia

Further Reading

Bebbington, D. W. (1989). *Evangelicalism in modern Britain: A history from the 1730's to the 1980's*. London: Routledge.

Bloch-Hoell, N. (1964). *The Pentecostal movement: Its origin, development, and distinctive character*. Oslo, Norway: Scandinavian University Books.

Blumhofer, E. L. (1985). *The Assemblies of God: A popular history*. Springfield, MO: Gospel Publishing House.

Blumhofer, E. L. (1993). *Restoring the faith: The Assemblies of God, Pentecostalism, and American culture*. Chicago: University of Illinois Press.

Blumhofer, E. L., Spittler, R. P., & Wacker, G. A. (Eds.). (1999). *Pentecostal currents in American Protestantism*. Chicago: University of Illinois Press.

Cerillo, A. (1999). The beginnings of American Pentecostalism: A historiographical overview. In Blumhofer, E. L., Spittler, R. P., & Wacker, G. A. (Eds.), *Pentecostal currents in American Protestantism* (pp 229–260). Chicago: University of Illinois Press.

Coleman, S. (2000). *The globalisation of charismatic Christianity: Spreading the gospel of prosperity*. Cambridge, UK: Cambridge University Press.

Cox, H. (1995). *Fire from heaven: The rise of Pentecostal spirituality and the reshaping of religion in the twenty-first century*. Reading, MA: Perseus Books.

Evans, E. (1969). *The Welsh revival of 1904*. London: Evangelical Press.

Hollenweger, W. J. (1972). *The Pentecostals*. Minneapolis: Augsburg Publishing House.

Kay, W. K. (1990). *Inside story: A history of British Assemblies of God*. Mattersey, UK: Mattersey Hall Publishing.

Martin, D. (2002). *Pentecostalism: The world their parish*. Oxford, UK: Blackwell Publishers.

Neitz, M. J. (1987). *Charisma and community*. New Brunswick, NJ: Transaction Books.

Orr, J. E. (1949). *The second evangelical awakening in Britain*. London: Marshall, Morgan & Scott.

Petts, D. (1991). *You'd better believe it*! Nottingham, UK: Life Stream Publications.

Spittler, R. P. (2002). *The new international dictionary of Pentecostal and charismatic movements*. Grand Rapids, MI: Zondervan.

Synan, V. (1997). *The Holiness-Pentecostal tradition: Charismatic movements in the twentieth century*. Grand Rapids, MI: William B. Eerdmans Publishing Co.

Vidler, A. R. (1971). *The church in an age of revolution*. Middlesex, UK: Penguin Books Ltd.

Whittaker, C. (1983). *Seven Pentecostal pioneers.* Basingstoke, UK: Marshall Paperbacks.

Woodhead, L., & Heelas, P. (Eds.). (2000). *Religion in modern times: An interpretive anthology.* Oxford, UK: Blackwell.

Performance, Ritual of

The concept of the ritual of performance is based on the idea that most human performances embody elements similar to those found in traditional ritual. Although theorists disagree over the degree of similarity, most agree that people tend to structure their social interactions in ritualistic ways. Performances—in which people act out through speech and movement the symbolic forms of their culture—are manifestations of people's need to express to other people and to themselves the nature of their thoughts and experiences. Through the process of performance people come to understand themselves and each other and to engage their world.

A performance occurs whenever a person goes from merely carrying out an action to trying to show others what he or she is doing. Such semiotic (relating to the use of signs and symbols) behavior is an essential aspect of the communicative process and, until recently, has been studied primarily in terms of cultural meanings and models of behavior. The anthropologist Victor Turner (1920–1983), whose basically interpretive work forms the foundation for the study of ritual of performance, observed that all performance has at its core a ritual action. Prior to the 1970s functionalist (focusing on the purpose rituals serve in their societies), structuralist (searching for the deep and innate structures of the human mind that undergird such concepts as myth and ritual), and interpretive (stressing the nature of ritual as symbolic manifestations of cultural world views) approaches to ritual tended to restrict analysis to religious ritual. Since then, however, interest in the anthropology of practice has led to studying ritual and ritual-like performances as they are performed and experienced by participants. Seeking theoretical constructs to bridge the gap between theory and practice, theorists use approaches from performance, play, and practice theories. Like Turner, they find ritual in all performances and interpret it more dynamically, seeing it as more flexible and interactive, and they focus less on the cognitive and more on the sensory and physical aspects of ritual activity. Other theorists use performance along with integrative and interpretive approaches from ritual to study a wide variety of performances. These ideas represent a major shift in the understanding of ritual and all other performance genres.

Ritual Elements in Performance

Performance theorists tend to define *performance* as including an assortment of activities, such as theater, film, recitals, sports, lectures, play, and public spectacles. They see similarities between performance and ritual in structure, framing, audience, scripting, and even effect. Both ritual and other types of performance are structured according to specific rules within defined temporal and physical boundaries that set them apart from the ordinary and allow the rules of everyday life to be temporarily suspended. Both operate within a cognitive infrastructure or *frame,* in which certain acts or messages set up an interpretive framework for understanding subsequent acts or messages. In some situations, the frame may be as blatant as a processional and recessional or the raising and lowering of a curtain, whereas in other situations it may be as subtle as the speaking style of the performers, who may switch to archaic or ceremonial speech forms, stylized rhythms, repetitions, and so forth.

Theorists disagree over the role of the audience and its relationship to the proceedings in ritual and other genres of performance. Ritual theorists tend to see the audience in a performance as passively receiving the symbolic package put before it and rarely being spiritually or socially transformed by it. The theorist R. A. Rappaport (1999), for example, notes that passivity as the distinguishing difference between ritual and other types of performance. Performance theorists, on the other hand, see *every* performance, whatever the genre, as a creation of the audience and the performers. Performance is emergent, created anew with each offering and dependent on the interplay of context, performer ability, and audience. Many theorists believe that, if the performance is successful, the audience is transformed by it. Traditional ritual theorists disagree, noting that few performances actually transform their audiences and that, unlike theater, failure rarely occurs in ritual, because ritual is based on the commitment of the participants to fulfill a cultural requirement and is not dependent on the skill of individual performers or the need to engage the audience.

Performance theorist Richard Schechner (1990) believes that all performance is based on restored behavior. Most performance genres are composed of a script of nonvarying sequences of acts and utterances. This script is perceived by the culture, which performs it as having an existence independent from the culture, the script and its parts merely waiting for the performers to restore them to life. Some theorists do not extend the concept of restored behavior to all performance. They note that many performance genres strive for freshness or novelty as they attempt to attract and capture the attention of the audience. The goal of performance art, for example, is to be deliberately and completely unprecedented. Ritual participants, on the other hand, risk social disapproval if they attempt novelty. For example, in a wedding ceremony, the minister who waxes too long or too comedically in administering the vows will likely find that hogging attention is not condoned.

The three phases in the ritual process are separation, marginality (or liminality—relating to a sensory threshold), and reaggregation. They were first proposed by the French ethnologist Arnold Van Gennep, extended by Turner, and have been embraced by performance theorists with little variation. Those scholars who see performance as a vehicle for social and political change particularly focus on Turner's elaboration of the creative aspects and the intense feeling of community spirit and equality, or communitas of liminality and on his theory of social drama.

Turner's Analysis of Social Drama

Turner's analysis of the ritual of performance centers on his concept of the structure of social conflict, or social drama, which he saw as a universal ritual form. He defined *social drama* as a sequence of conflicting social interactions that is processually structured, from a break in relations to reconciliation. In the first phase of social drama, the breach, a conflict or violation of a cultural norm that expresses an underlying conflict occurs within a group. The crisis, the second phase, is reached when the conflict becomes apparent to the group, participants choose sides, factions are formed, and the breach is widened to include all members of the group. In this phase, many of the ambiguous and creative aspects of liminality arise to challenge the group. During the third phase, redress, procedures to mitigate the situation are put into play. Remedies may include rites of purification and sacrifice in an attempt to remove the polluting factor that caused the breach. The final phase is an outcome of either reintegration or schism, the point at which the group members either reunite or accept an irreparable division.

At critical times within the phases of social drama performance, skills are most needed to convey symbolic messages. Purification, for example, depends upon the ability of the group to discover the pollutant and to justify performing the ritual on that person or object. Turner thus contended that the major genres of cultural performance not only originate in social drama but also continue to be influenced by it. Many performances are based on the tension that arises during the crisis phase, when participants are suspended from normal life and must rely on antistructural improvisation (strategies never before considered and possibly counter-cultural in nature).

Like stage drama, social drama involves social reflection as participants grapple with the uncertainty and anxiety of crisis and choose allegiances between conflicting groups. Allowed to play out to its conclusion, Turner believed, social drama ends with a restoration of peace. During the crisis phase participants must play around with a variety of ideas and solutions, and these occasionally lead to innovations, which are often practical and political. Participants may seek reassurance and guidance from the past and begin to idealize a mythical golden age, or they may imagine new, more radical ideas. The social drama becomes a time of both looking back and thinking ahead as participants seek to discover what has worked in the past and what might work in the future. Thus, just as ritual embodies the past, present, and future and provides a space and mechanism for reflection and exploration, so, too, does social drama. Social dramas are invariably political in nature and, rather than directly symbolizing social structure, become part of the dialectical relationship, that struggle between interacting and competing forces in evolving sociocultural and political systems.

Although Turner's theories of phases of ritual and social drama have laid the groundwork for study of the ritual of performance, not all theorists agree. R. Grimes (1990), for example, argues that most cultural performances are complicated and far too contradictory to be to considered a mere dialectical system of cultural symbols. Ritual performance incorporates such a wide assortment of symbols that no coherent system can be created to order it. To Grimes, who formulated a theory of criticism of ritual, societies use performance to deal with cultural symbols while avoiding contradictions. Although Turner points out that cultural performances are processual and generate opposing symbols to present possibility for change, he and Grimes are basically conservative in that they see ritualized performance as a tool to reconcile, support, or conceal the prevailing social and political structure. Performance theorists, on the other hand, have tended to focus on the dynamic aspects of culture rather than on coherent systems. As with the closely aligned practice theorists, performance theorists are ultimately interested in the efficacy of performance and see cultural performances as having potential to effect real social and political change.

Cultural Performances

Cultural performances are a broad category of large-scale, public events, such as carnivals, concerts, sporting events, festivals, and public spectacles. Theorist Milton Singer (1972), who coined the term, believed that cultural performances are expressions of the more abstract and hidden structures of the cultural system. Other theorists see cultural performances, particularly theater and film, in more activist terms as reinterpreting traditional concepts and serving as mediums for social change. Still other theorists see cultural performances as the very form in which culture as a system actually exists and is reproduced.

Since the late 1970s ethnic and minority groups in multicultural societies have used festivals to communicate their identity and to challenge dominant constructions of culture. Similar cultural performances have also been used by the majority to reinforce the hegemonic (relating to influence) constructions of colonial and national identities. These cultural performances often take the form of folk festivals that reflect the concerns of the community by providing a backdrop for expressing particular social and political goals. As festivals have done for centuries, these performances conform to ritual structure, serving as rites of both reintegration and rebellion and strengthening the identity of the group and its power to act in its own interest. However, they also serve as vehicles for social change through the creation of an out-of-the-ordinary experience, which provides opportunities for the articulation of social issues and exploration and negotiation of relationships.

In J. J. MacAloon's (1984) analysis of the Olympic games, he observes that public spectacles are composed of several genres of performance. The Olympics spectacle itself is clearly organized according to Van Gennep's phases of ritual, with heavy emphasis on the liminal phase. The opening ceremonies and lighting of the Olympic flame are the rites of separation that initiate the liminal phase, which is replete with communitas as the games stress the shared humanity of people of all nations. MacAloon points out that the games have also been the forum for international conflicts as nations or groups use them as a forum to protest dominant constructions of group identity or to assert political rights. More remarkably, MacAloon observes that the games have become the focus of a worldwide debate over the purpose of public ritual.

Critics point out that applying ritual concepts to other performances does not further understanding of how cultures draw distinctions between ritual and other activities. Proponents point out that performance theory's emphasis on the physical expression of ritual has, in fact, enhanced understanding of these distinctions. Moreover, performance theory has extended ritual study well beyond the original focus on meaning, and its attention to secular and new forms of ritualistic activity offers a better means of analysis of ritual and performance in secular and pluralistic societies. Most importantly, the active imagery of performance has provided a vocabulary to use to talk about the nonintellectual dimensions of what ritual does—the emotive, physical, and even sensuous aspects of ritual participation.

Jaclyn L. Jeffrey

See also Clothing and Rituals; Haircutting Rituals; Identity Rituals; Marriage Rituals; Puberty Rites; Vision Quest

Further Reading

Beeman, W. (2002). Performance theory in an anthropology program. In C. Wimmer & N. Stucky (Eds.), *Teaching performance studies*. Carbondale: University of Southern Illinois Press.

Bell, C. (1997). *Ritual: Perspectives and dimensions*. New York: Oxford University Press.

Goffman, E. (1974). *Frame analysis*. Cambridge, MA: Harvard University Press.

Grimes, R. (1990). *Ritual criticism: Case studies in its practice, essays on its theory*. New York: Columbia University Press.

MacAloon, J. J. (1984). *Rite, drama, festival, spectacle: Rehearsals toward a theory of cultural performance.*

Philadelphia: Institute for the Study of Human Issues.
Rappaport, R. A. (1999). *Ritual and religion in the making of humanity*. Cambridge, UK: Cambridge University Press.
Schechner, R., & Appel, W. (1990). *By means of performance*. New York: Cambridge University Press.
Singer, M. (1972). *When a great tradition modernizes*. New York: Praeger.
Turner, V. (1986). *The anthropology of performance*. New York: PAJ Publications.
Turner, V. (1992). *From ritual to theatre: The human seriousness of play*. New York: PAJ Publications.
Van Gennep, A. (1960). *The rites of passage* (M. B. Vizedom & G. L. Caffee, Trans.). Chicago: University of Chicago Press.

Personal Rituals

Personal rituals are idiosyncratic rites created and performed by an individual, alone or with the participation of the individual's social group. Some personal rituals are deliberate and highly spiritual and others are not at all. They often deal with issues that society ignores or does not condone, such as celebrating a divorce or performing a pagan renewal ritual. These types of rituals evolve out of a need to give outward form to feelings, beliefs, and experiences that are not acknowledged by society. Although ritual is most often assumed to have a supernatural or religious dimension, recent studies acknowledge that the patterned performances of everyday life, such as the series of activities one does before going to bed or upon waking, may be considered rituals because they share the function of rituals.

Rituals of Everyday Life

Rituals help to reconcile opposing forces in life and impose a sense of order on the world. Thus, the morning routine of waking, heading straight to the kitchen to make coffee, and sitting at the kitchen table to drink it before starting the day constitutes a ritual. Whether it is coffee or a brisk run or a hot shower, individuals discover, mostly by trial and error, a pattern that eases their transition from the sleep state to wakefulness. Likewise, upon going to bed, a person may wash the face, brush teeth, put the dog out, and check the locks on the doors. If any part of that routine is left undone, they find that they are unable to go to sleep. Each small ritual is practiced countless numbers of times, without variation, and often without conscious thought, but the pattern of actions transforms the actor. The ritual, a series of deliberate actions performed in sequence, allows the individual to shift their consciousness and energy from one state to another, and it establishes a sense of order for the day or night.

Is it personal ritual or is it obsessive neurotic behavior to be unable to sleep without checking that the outside doors are locked? Sigmund Freud (1856–1939) saw only a fine line between the obsessive behavior of neurotics and the ritual behavior of the pious. Although he focused on more religious forms of personal ritual, such as prayers and invocations, he noted three similarities: (1) practitioners have qualms of conscience if they neglect their rituals; (2) they prefer complete isolation from other activity while engaged in their ritual, which can be demonstrated by the fact that most do not wish to be interrupted; and (3) every detail of their ritual is carried out with precision and conscientiousness. Some scholars would argue that a ritual ceremony is symbolic and significant, while obsessive behavior is disconnected from reason or values, but Freud noted that neurotics, too, engage in complex symbolic behavior. However, Freud believed that both religious and obsessive behaviors were rooted in repression and displacement, sexual for neurotics and antisocial for the pious.

In a somewhat similar vein, Mary Douglas shows how many personal rituals are attempts to order the world by dealing with the disorder, or impurities, in it. Impurities, dirt, pollution, or things taboo are not inherently unclean; they merely represent elements in a society that are antisocial and antistructural. Eating or not eating certain foods, touching or not touching certain objects helps to create order, but it is not possible to separate oneself entirely from impurities. Therefore, societies have learned to tame or control impurities through ritual, a creative effort to relate form to function. Douglas notes that impurities exist in the eye of the beholder, so rituals are also created to conform to individual need.

Erik Erikson (1902–1994) believed that ritual could be defined as a special form of everyday behavior that begins in infancy. Each morning a mother wakes up and greets her baby in the same manner, and the baby learns to respond to its mother in a consistent way. Erikson observed that humans appear to be born with the need for mutual affirmation on a regular basis, right up to death, and that everyday ritual governs these interactions all along the way. Some rituals are personally motivated but take place in a communal situation. Goffman calls these corrective rituals, because they involve the repair of relationships with others. For example, in his studies of a pedestrian walking down the street, he notes that if the pedestrian sees two people engaged in a conversation, the accepted ritual would be to walk around them rather than in between them, which would disrupt their conversation. If the pedestrian violates this ritual and walks in between them, she is expected to apologize or excuse herself. This personal gesture constitutes a corrective ritual on the part of the individual who understands that society has certain rules of behavior to follow.

In a famous spoof published in 1956, anthropologist Horace Miner ridiculed the everyday rituals of Americans and their obsessive concern with personal grooming and hygiene. Referring to them as the "Nacirema," Miner called attention to their "body rites," beginning with the morning ritual where the natives stood each day before the white porcelain "altar" in the small "shrine" room in their homes to perform specific rites to face, teeth, and hair. He pointed out how strict observance of elaborate daily routines were ritualistic because they were highly repetitive and unvarying and because the practitioners were fixated on accomplishing their actions and unwilling to proceed with daily life until they were completed.

Catherine Bell, on the other hand, considers at least certain mindfulness—if not religion per se—to be necessary in order for everyday routines to be labeled ritual. The scrubbing rituals of Miner's Nacirema, she says, lack deliberation, the close attention to perfection of movement and detail that characterize true ritual action. She suggests that a better example of the nature of personal ritual would be the invariance of routine of monastic life and the attention paid to performing even the humblest of acts. Within a monastery, the mindful ritualization of everyday activities is considered part of religious service, and ritual is not meant to be separated from daily life. Bell also points out that the invariance of routine and control of the body found in Alcoholics Anonymous and Zen monasteries are considered necessary to the reshaping of the individual. The discipline, inspired by control of the physical self, subordinates the desires of the body in favor of mental growth. Meditation, which also focuses on body discipline for spiritual growth, has spread beyond its Hindu and Buddhist origins into the popular culture. Bell notes that meditation is considered by many traditional Buddhist and modern Zen scholars to be an explicit *rejection* of ritual. They argue that meditation does not include mediation or the use of symbols but is meant to be *direct* experience. Other scholars see meditation as a personal ritual, even without symbols or mediation, because it is concerned with the soul, it imposes temporary order on the practitioner's world, and it consciously and deliberately moves the practitioner out of one state and into another.

Personal Rituals and Superstition

Some personal rituals are distinct, intentional, and carefully planned to deal with some area of life that needs to be reconciled or put in order. These types are as varied as the range of human behavior. Some deal with the supernatural and others do not. In his famous study of ritual magic among the Trobriand Islanders, the functionalist anthropologist Bronislaw Malinowski (1884–1942) pointed out that humans rely more on magic when they are operating in an area where they have little control and need more luck. He observed the Trobriand fishermen, who resorted to magic rituals whenever they had to fish on the open sea while virtually ignoring ritual when they fished in the much safer lagoon. Even in the postindustrial world, where superstition is often superseded by scientific technology, ritual can become an important element in risky situations or occupations, where humans attempt to control fate.

Major surgery, for example, is a highly ritualized event. The surgeons themselves often become ritual specialists, determining the staging of the event in minute detail—the time, dramatis personae, sequence of events, and organization of the ritual space, from the order in which the surgical instruments are laid out to the choice of background music. The rest of the surgical team must conform to the wishes of the surgeon—even though these details may be meaningful only to the surgeon—or risk being ejected. Thus, surgery becomes the personal ritual of the person who bears the heaviest burden in seeing that it is performed successfully. Surgeons operate in arenas that rely both on skill and luck. Although they see their work as dealing with science, not magic, ritual provides surgeons with the opportunity to use what resources they have to control their luck. It is not about magic, but it is about imposing order. An alternative view of surgical ritual proposed by Pearl Katz suggests that surgical ritual is used to accentuate the boundaries between the worlds of medicine and culture. Ritual helps to avoid confusion that arises as participants try to separate cultural values from medical science.

George Gmelch, in his observations of ritual among American baseball players, points out that most rituals among athletes evolve out of superstition and the need to control luck. Baseball rituals are highly personal rather than being team centered. Gmelch, himself a former professional baseball player, observes that these superstitious rituals grow out of good performances. When he plays particularly well, a player looks for particular explanations, because he knows that his personal skills don't vary much from game to game. Very often he decides to repeat exactly what he did during the period immediately preceding his good game. He will wear the same clothes, eat the same food, and leave for the stadium at precisely the same time. This often leads, of course, to some unusual and amusing rituals. For example, Gmelch notes that one man always played with a cheese sandwich in his back pocket; another shaved his arms before every game because he once hit three homers with a shaved arm. Batters often spend valuable time performing rituals before addressing the ball, such as tugging their caps, crossing themselves, and tapping or swinging the warm-up bat a prescribed number of times. There is little question that their performances are rituals because players even admit that they don't "feel right" unless they perform their ritual. Gmelch attributes the tendency of ballplayers to acquire personal rituals to the tendency of animals and humans to associate a particular action with the reward that follows it.

Trends in Personal Rituals

In Western society during the 1960s, there developed a marked trend toward rejecting traditional rituals of all kinds. This was partly due to the countercultural movement of the sixties but also the result of increasing mobility, urbanization, and modernization. As family, religious, and ethnic groups commingled or dispersed, many traditional rituals were abandoned. At the same time, many important personal experiences have been deliberately ignored or forgotten in Western society—menarche, returning soldiers, divorce, menopause, retirement. A number of ritual advocates fear the debilitating effects on society of the loss of ritual. Many psychologists and religious advisers encourage people to create their own rituals to commemorate their own experiences or to celebrate their move to a new position in the social order.

Since the sixties it appears that many traditional, communal rituals have been replaced with a wide variety of personal rituals and the improvisation of rituals that represent new cultural groups and values. The ancient pagan, or Wiccan, religion has been resurrected and is gaining a following throughout the Western world. Followers often perform their rituals in private or even individually if they lack available people to participate or if they prefer solitude. The pattern suggests that ritual itself is not dying out, but the trend is individualistic, moving toward small-group or personal rather than collective rituals.

Jaclyn L. Jeffrey

Further Reading

Bell, C. (1997). *Ritual: Perspectives and dimensions.* New York: Oxford University Press.

Douglas, M. (1966). *Purity and danger: An analysis of conceptions of pollution and taboo.* New York: Praeger Press.

Erikson, E. (1968). The development of ritualization. In D. R. Cutler (Ed.), *The religious situation 1968* (pp.711–733). Boston: Beacon Press.

Freud, S. (1907). Zeitschrift fur religion psychologie [Obsessive action and religious practices]. In L. Stratchey (Ed.), & J. Riviere (Trans,) *The collected papers of Sigmund Freud: Vol. 9.* London: Hogarth Press.

Gmelch, G. G. (1992). Superstition and ritual in American baseball. *Elysian Fields Quarterly 11*(3), 25–36.

Goffman, E. (1959). *The presentation of self in everyday life.* Garden City, NY: Doubleday.

Goffman, E. (1967). *Interaction ritual: Essays on face-to-face behavior.* New York: Pantheon Books.

Katz, P. (1981). Ritual in the operating room. *Ethnology* (20), 254–264.

Leach, E. (1999). Ritual. In D. Hicks (Ed.), *Ritual and belief: Readings in the anthropology of religion* (pp. 176–183). Boston: McGraw-Hill College.

Malinowski, B. (1978). The role of magic and religion. In W. A. Lessa and E. Z. Vogt (Eds.), *Reader in comparative religion: An anthropological approach* (4th ed., pp. 37–46). New York: Harper and Row.

Miner, H. (1956). Body ritual among the Nacirema. *American Anthropologist 58*, 503–507.

Pilgrimage

Pilgrims undertake pilgrimages to reach a state that embodies sacred or deeply valued ideals. Pilgrimage is a journey, and the word *pilgrimage* itself is derived from the Latin words *per ager,* meaning "through" and "field." Pilgrimage occurs throughout the world and is not restricted to religions.

On a pilgrimage a person might visit a shrine or a holy person. Alternatively a person might set out on a pilgrimage with no destination. The Japanese haiku (an unrhymed verse form of Japanese origin) poet Matsuo Bashō (1644–1694) is an example of a wandering pilgrim. He practiced Zen (relating to a Japanese sect of Mahayana Buddhism) meditation. After the death of his mother he undertook a series of major wandering pilgrimages, which helped him to cast aside all earthly attachments. He began his first travel anthology with the comment that he followed the example of the Chinese priest Kōmon (Kuang-wên) of the Nansung dynasty (1127–1279), "who is said to have travelled thousands of miles caring naught for his provisions and attaining the state of sheer ecstasy under the pure beams of the moon" (Bashō 1966, 51). In a later travel anthology, *The Records of a Travel-Worn Satchel,* he included the following poem:

> From this day forth
> I shall be called a wanderer,
> Leaving on a journey
> Thus among the early showers.
>
> You will again sleep night after night
> Nestled among the flowers of sasanqua *[Camellia sasanqua].*
> (Bashō 1966, 72)

Pilgrimage might also be conceived of as a spiritual journey, such as experienced by Islamic ascetic (practicing strict self-denial as a measure of spiritual discipline) mystics known as "Sufis." They use spiritual exercises and contemplation in order to reach God rather than make a physical pilgrimage to Mecca in Saudi Arabia to walk seven times around a seventh-century building called the "Kaaba," the earthly house of Allah. An eleventh-century Sufi poet, 'Abdallah al-Ansari, wrote:

> Know that God Most High has built an outward
> Ka'ba out of mud and stone,
> And fashioned an inward Ka'ba of heart and soul alone.
>
> The outward Ka'ba, Abraham did build
> The inward Ka'ba was as the Lord Almighty willed.
> (Coleman & Elsner 1995, 72)

The concept of making a spiritual journey was known in ancient Egypt. Funerary texts of the Middle and New Kingdoms (c. 2040–1069 BCE) relate that the deceased person visited the cult center of Osiris at either Abydos in Upper Egypt or Busiris in the Nile delta of Lower Egypt. Osiris was the deity of the blessed dead, who were people who had been given a good burial and had been mummified. The post-mortem journey to the Osiris cult centers, which presumably took place on a spiritual plane, is known as an "Osirian pilgrimage."

Anthropological Studies of Pilgrimage

Only since the 1970s has a sustained interest in pilgrimage appeared in anthropological literature. Earlier publications include William Robertson Smith's *The Religion of the Semites,* based on lectures given in 1888–1889, and a sociological study by Robert Hertz (1913), who undertook fieldwork at a shrine to Saint Besse in the Italian Alps. The French sociologist Émile Durkheim did not make a direct study of pilgrimage in *The Elementary Forms of the Religious Life* (1915), but his notion of "collective effervescence," which he saw as performing a social function in reinforcing social cohesiveness, has been applied to pilgrimage. In this vein the social anthropologist Eric Wolf published a short article in 1958 on the Virgin of Guadalupe as a Mexican national symbol. Emanuel Marx, social anthropologist, examined Bedouin (nomadic Arab) pilgrimage in Sinai as a communal reunion.

Anthropological interest in pilgrimage became more mainstream with the work of Victor Turner and Edith Turner. Victor Turner developed a theory of ritual inspired by the work of the French sociologist Arnold van Gennep on rites of passage, which are rituals of transition. Van Gennep proposed that such rituals (often associated with initiation) have a threefold organization: (1) separation from the participant's

Pilgrims often flock to the "Cross of Our Lord Jesus" in Pampa, Texas, shown here in 1999. COURTESY OF STEPHEN G. DONALDSON PHOTOGRAPHY.

previous condition, (2) a transitional "liminal" (relating to a sensory threshold) stage, and (3) incorporation into the social group with his or her condition transformed. Victor Turner compared the journey of pilgrimage with the liminal stage of rites of passage because pilgrims are separated from normal society and experience a transitional period of "communitas" when they form a group that is united in a shared purpose. In this theory pilgrimage is antistructural (breaking down fundamental social principles) because the communitas experience can bring together people who in normal life are kept separate by their ethnicity or status. However, Victor Turner recognized that pilgrimages "are still ultimately bound by the structure of the religious systems within which they are generated and persist" (Turner 1974, 205–206).

Anthropologists have tested Turner's theory (Werbner 1977; Morinis 1984; Sallnow 1987) against ethnographic (description based on fieldwork) settings in different parts of the world (see Eade & Sallnow 1991, 4–5). Although aspects of communitas might be found in some pilgrimages, research demonstrates that pilgrimages also maintain and even reinforce social distinctions. Eade and Sallnow point out that approaches derived from Durkheim or Turner rest on structuralist principles (fundamental principles associated with binary oppositions) in that pilgrimage is seen either to support or to subvert the social order. They see the pilgrimage phenomenon as not just "a field of social relations but also as a realm of competing discourses" and believe that Turner's view might serve as an empirical description of aspects of it "which might well co-exist or compete with alternative discourses" (Eade & Sallnow 1991, 5).

In a similar fashion the anthropologist Alan Morinis has observed that Durkheim's "collective effervescence" and Turner's communitas both suffer from imposing uniformity on phenomena that are greatly varied in content. However, Morinis recognizes that Turner has drawn anthropological attention to the individual experiences of pilgrims and says that it is important to emphasize "the complementarity of structure and experience" (Morinis 1984) in the study of pilgrimage.

Types of Pilgrimages

Morinis has devised what he calls "a typology of sacred journeys" (Morinis 1992, 10–14). Rather than focus on the destination, his typology (system of classification) of six types of pilgrimage is based on the journey and the motivation of pilgrims: (1) The devotional pilgrimage is based on an encounter with, and veneration of, a shrine divinity, holy person, or symbols. Buddhist pilgrimages to the shrines where Buddha was present, Hindu pilgrimages in honor of Krishna (a deified hero of Hinduism worshiped as an incarnation of the god Vishnu), and Christian pilgrimages to the Holy Land all belong to this type. (2) On an instrumental pilgrimage pilgrims travel to a shrine for a specific reason. Commonly, childless women seek to conceive, and, in general, people seek cures for illness. Other reasons that pilgrims give concern success in examinations and in business. (3) Normative pilgrimages are undertaken as part of calendrical rituals or as part of the life cycle of the pilgrim. Hindus undertake pilgrimages at various stages of their life, whereas annual community pilgrimages take place in Islamic, Buddhist, and Latin American Catholic traditions. (4) Obligatory

Tourists visiting the home of novelist Jane Austen in Surrey, England in 2003. Although a secular site, the house has become a shrine to Austen and her literary achievements.
COURTESY OF KAREN CHRISTENSEN.

pilgrimages include the hajj, the fifth pillar of Islam, which enjoins all able-bodied Muslims to make a pilgrimage to Mecca at least once in their lifetime. In medieval Europe Christian ecclesiastical and secular authorities imposed obligatory pilgrimages as a form of punishment; convicted criminals frequently made a penitential pilgrimage to Santiago de Compostela in northern Spain. (5) A wandering pilgrimage does not have a geographic destination. The pilgrim sets out, as did Bashō, to obtain visions of eternity in nature or, as did early Christian pilgrims who went into voluntary exile, to die to this world and inherit heaven. (6) Initiatory pilgrimages, according to Morinis, include those that are intended to transform the status or state of the pilgrim. The Huichol people of Mexico undertake journeys in search of a hallucinogenic cactus. The visions that are induced by eating the cactus awaken a higher level of consciousness in the individual and constitute an initiation. Hindu life-cycle initiations *(samskaras)* that are incorporated into pilgrimages also belong to this type, as does the hajj to Mecca because on return the pilgrim occupies a new social rank.

Morinis says many people undertake pilgrimages both to change their social status and to transform their personal state because pilgrimage is intimately tied up with "the pursuit of ideals and salvation within the human condition" (Morinis 1992, 14). Hence, his typology is not exhaustive, and the types are not mutually exclusive. It is possible to detect different types within one religious tradition and also to detect similar practices in cross-cultural contexts.

Pilgrimage in Latin America

Present-day Latin American pilgrimages draw on multiple traditions, including native pre-Hispanic, European Christian, African slave, and other religious roots. In the Morinis typology these pilgrimages display features of the devotional, instrumental, normative, and initiatory types. The normative features are seen in the Yucatec Maya in Mesoamerica, one of whose terms for a pilgrim is *u ximbal ek'ob,* meaning "passage and course of the stars" which, as the anthropologist Herman Konrad observes, emphasizes the cyclical process of pilgrimage. Because a sacred goal appears in all reported cases, wandering does not seem to characterize Latin American pilgrimage.

Morinis and Crumrine argue that the distinctiveness of Latin American pilgrimage is due precisely to the diverse religious traditions that form the background in which it takes place. One of the aspects of pre-Hispanic pilgrimage was an emphasis on feasting. This aspect has continued to the present. Feasting and intoxication, combined with music and dancing, provide "the pilgrim with extraordinary peaks of sensation.... [A]ll of these intense experiences serve to mark off the pilgrim's behavior as exceptional and so make it appropriate for the extraordinary time and place of the pilgrimage" (Morinis & Crumrine 1991, 15).

In *Pilgrims of the Andes* Michael Sallnow points out the importance of pre-Hispanic traditions of pilgrimage in the Andes for understanding pilgrimage today. Archeologists have for a long time regarded certain archeological sites as having served as pilgrimage centers, including Pacatnamú in northern Peru, with its extremely dense concentration of ceremonial architecture, and Pachakamaq/Pachacamac, an important oracle in the Lurín Valley, immediately south of Lima. Pachakamaq grew to its largest extent between 1200 and 1470 CE, and in the late fifteenth century it was controlled by the Inca empire.

The archaeologist Helaine Silverman's study of the Nasca period (which ended about 600 CE) site of Cahuachi in the south of Peru concluded that it was a pilgrimage center on the basis of archeological patterning, comparison with Pachakamaq, and ethnographic analogy with an annual pilgrimage to the regional shrine of the Virgin of the Rosary of Yauca, east of Ica, on the first Sunday in October. There is a lack of evidence for sustained habitation at Cahuachi. Few pottery vessels suitable for food storage were encountered in excavations. In contrast, there is abundant evidence for ceramic panpipes (wind instruments) and elaborate pottery. After the site declined as a ceremonial center, it continued to be used as a burial place, which Silverman finds to be consistent with her pilgrimage hypothesis. Some of the geoglyphs (lines marked on the desert floor south of Cahuachi) point directly to some of the main architectural complexes built on natural hills. Silverman argues that the pampa (plain) was not regarded as just an empty desert but rather that pilgrims walking over the routes to Cahuachi were crossing it in order to enter a "liminal phase that transformed them from the ordinary people they were to the ritual social beings they would become" (Silverman 1993, 308). She argued that Cahuachi pilgrimages confirmed the hierarchical structuring and reordering of the social groups who maintained the ceremonial complexes.

Pachakamaq was not the only important shrine to come under Inca control. Two islands dedicated to the Inca divinities of the sun and moon in the Bolivian sector of Lake Titicaca increasingly acquired religious and political significance as the empire expanded. The archaeologists Brian Bauer and Charles Stanish detected evidence for the emergence of a hierarchical elite and ceremonial centers on the islands shortly before the islands became incorporated into the Tiwanaku state (400–1100 CE). After the collapse of Tiwanaku, the importance of the ceremonial centers on the islands seems to have waned until the arrival of the Incas. Under Inca control people were resettled from other parts of the empire, and elaborate shrine complexes were constructed. Pilgrimage from the mainland to the Sacred Rock, which was believed to be the birthplace of the sun and moon, would have been tightly controlled; apparently nonelite pilgrims gained access only to a viewing platform from where they might observe the rock. Bauer and Stanish argue that the Incas manipulated the pilgrimage within a hegemonic (relating to influence) ideology. They do not consider a suggestion made by Victor Turner that pilgrimages gain in importance at times of rapid social change, which surely would have applied to the forced resettlements that occurred under the Incas.

The contraction and expansion of the shrines on the islands in Lake Titicaca are connected with the development of hierarchies and the waning and waxing of the cult of the sun and moon. Comparable phenomena are known in other parts of the world, as discussed by Richard Werbner, social anthropologist, in the context of African cults. Waxing and waning of enthusiasm for the cult of particular saints also characterized medieval western European pilgrimage. The historian Barbara Abou-El-Haj observed that the medieval cult of saints did not "unfold as a continuous history" (Abou-El-Haj 1994, 1). In her study of pictorial hagiographies (biographies of saints) dating from the eleventh century to the thirteenth century she points out that there were gaps of up to five hundred years between the writing of the first lives of the saints and later versions.

Pilgrimage into the Twenty-First Century

The social anthropologist Coleman and classicist/medievalist Elsner point out that English tourist agent Thomas Cook, the person who instigated leisure travel on a wide scale, was a Baptist minister and social reformer whose intention was to arrange tours that were morally enriching. He included itineraries to the Holy Land, which contributed to the increasingly blurred line between pilgrimage and tourism. Deeply held values of pilgrims are not always, strictly speaking, religious. The grave of Elvis Presley and his home at Graceland, Tennessee, have become the focus of visits by devotees who hold a candlelit vigil at his grave on the anniversary of his death on 16 August 1977. This demonstrates that pilgrimage is a meaningful but also a changing activity.

In 1962 a former Jain (relating to a religion founded in India and based on the ideals of nonviolence, discipline, purity, and enlightenment) monk, Satish Kumar, and a travel companion set out on a walking pilgrimage from Indian nationalist Mohandas Gandhi's grave in India to John F. Kennedy's grave in the United States via Moscow, capital of what was then the Soviet Union. Jain monks walk silently and slowly, in recognition of Mahāvīra, a leader who undertook an ascetic, wandering life and achieved nirvana (the final beatitude that transcends suffering and is sought through the extinction of desire and consciousness) as he walked along the bank of a river in 477 BCE. However, Kumar also walked for a political purpose. He and his companion were peace pilgrims. Under the influence of Gandhi's example of peaceful, passive resistance, they wished to add their voice to the calls for nuclear disarmament.

Pilgrims journey from the familiar, often imperfect world of everyday life through the ideal and sometimes miraculous plane of pilgrimage. They undertake physically arduous and spiritual journeys for personal, religious, and political reasons. As an activity, pilgrimage will be very much part of life in the twenty-first century.

Penelope Dransart

See also Australian Aboriginal; Hajj; Islam; Liminoid; Passage, Rites of

Further Reading

Abou-El-Haj, B. F. (1994). *The medieval cult of saints: Formations and transformations.* Cambridge, UK: Cambridge University Press.

Bashō. (1966). *The narrow road to the deep north and other travel sketches* (N. Yuasa, Trans.). Harmondsworth, UK: Penguin Books.

Bauer, B. S., & Stanish, C. (2001). *Ritual and pilgrimage in the ancient Andes: The islands of the sun and moon.* Austin: University of Texas Press.

Coleman, S., & Elsner, J. (1995). *Pilgrimage: Past and present: Sacred travel and sacred space in the world religions.* London: British Museum Press.

Eade, J., & Sallnow, M. J. (Eds.). (1991). *Contesting the sacred: The anthropology of Christian pilgrimage.* New York: Routledge.

Hertz, R. (1983). St. Besse: A study of an alpine cult. In S. Wilson (Ed.), *Saints and their cults* (pp. 55–100). Cambridge, UK: Cambridge University Press. (Work originally published 1913)

Konrad, H. W. (1991). Pilgrimage as cyclical process: The unending pilgrimage of the holy cross of the Qintana Roo Maya. In N. R. Crumrine & A. Morinis (Eds.), *Pilgrimage in Latin America* (pp. 123–137). New York: Greenwood Press.

Kumar, S. (1978). *No destination.* Llandeilo, Wales: Mochyn Du/Black Pig Press.

Marx, E. (1977). Communal and individual pilgrimage: The region of saints' tombs in south Sinai. In R. P. Werbner (Ed.), *Regional cults* (pp. 29–51). New York: Academic Press.

Morinis, A. (1984). *Pilgrimage in the Hindu tradition: A case study of west Bengal.* Delhi, India: Oxford University Press.

Morinis, A. (Ed.). (1992). *Sacred journeys: The anthropology of pilgrimage.* Westport, CT: Greenwood Press.

Morinis, A., & Crumrine, N. R. (1991). La peregrinación: The Latin American pilgrimage. In N. R. Crumrine & A. Morinis (Eds.), *Pilgrimage in Latin America* (pp. 1–17). New York: Greenwood Press.

Quirke, S. (1992). *Ancient Egyptian religion.* London: British Museum Press.

Robertson Smith, W. (1901). *Lectures on the religion of the Semites: First series; the fundamental institutions.* London: Adam and Charles Black.

Sallnow, M. J. (1987). *Pilgrims of the Andes: Regional cults in Cusco.* Washington, DC: Smithsonian Institution Press.

Silverman, H. (1993). *Cahuachi in the ancient Nasca world.* Iowa City: University of Iowa Press.

Turner, V. (1974). Pilgrimages as social processes. In *Dramas, fields, and metaphors: Symbolic action in human society* (pp. 166–230). Ithaca, NY: Cornell University Press.

Turner, V., & Turner, E. L. B. (1978). *Image and pilgrimage in Christian culture.* New York: Columbia University Press.

Werbner, R. P. (Ed). (1977). *Regional cults.* New York: Academic Press.

Wolf, E. (1958). The virgin of Guadalupe: A Mexican national symbol. *Journal of American Folklore, 71*(1), 34–39.

Polynesia

See Hawai'i

Possession and Trance

The phenomena of possession and trance cover a variety of altered states of consciousness found in almost every culture. The two phenomena are related, although social scientists make distinctions. Within a spiritually defined context, *trance* connotes a dissociated mental state that produces nonordinary awareness and behavior. *Possession* connotes a state of being taken over by another being or consciousness, either benign or malevolent. Not all trances are dependent

THE BORI CULT OF THE HAUSA OF NIGERIA

The Bori cult of the Hausa people of Nigeria is one of the best described of the many possession cults found in religions around the world. The following text describes how one becomes a member of the cult.

A male member of the cult is known as a "son of bori" and a female member as "daughter of the bori," though women predominate to a marked degree in the membership of the cult. The relation of the spirit to the one possessed is expressed in the metaphor of a horse and rider. The possessed one is, according to sex, the "horse" or "mare" of the spirit. The beginning of possession is a process of the spirit "mounting" (haw) his disciple, the end of it "dismounting" (sawka). The fact that the spirit has departed is marked by the devotee's sneezing or coughing.

A person becomes a member of the bori cult in two principal ways. One method is by inheritance, where the spirits that were "on the head" of the parent come to one child. To facilitate this transfer, a figure of the following shape sewn in red leather is worn about the neck by the child of an initiate. It is said to be the throwing-stick of Nakada. When the parent dies, Nakada shows the stick to all the spirits to indicate that the child is a true "child of the bori" and can practice bori without initiation. This device is not always employed; indeed, in the majority of cases in which bori was inherited, it was found that an initiation ceremony had been performed.

The other way in which a person joins the bori cult is as a result of an illness caused by the spirits. After all kinds of remedies have been tried, it is customary to consult the "children of the bori." A "child of the bori" under possession tells the sick person that his only hope of recovery is initiation into the bori cult, since one particular spirit has caused the illness to indicate his desire for the victim as his "mount." The prescribed initiation rite is then carried out as soon as possible, because, as the natives phrased it in the case of one "daughter of the bori," "she has the spirits on her head but she doesn't know their work."

The ceremony of initiation is known as girka, "boiling." The person to be initiated goes to some one who is already a member of the cult and can teach him how to be possessed by the spirit troubling him. This person is known according to sex as the `uban girka, "father of the boiling," or `uwar girka, "mother of the boiling." The initiate is taught to be possessed not only by the one who has caused his sickness, but by a whole repertory of spirits, who will thereafter possess him when summoned.

***Source*: Greenberg, Joseph H. *The Influence of Islam on a Sudanese Religion.* (1946). Monographs of the American Ethnological Society, Vol. 10. New York: J.J. Augustin, pp. 49–50.**

on possession, but all possessions are a form of trance. Possession and trance involve the perceived help of supernatural beings or a mystical dimension of existence. Altered states of consciousness such as hypnosis, self-hypnosis, and meditation appear to be related to trance and spirit possession, but they are not necessarily defined as trance. Trance implies a markedly different cognitive and behavioral break with normatively conscious expression. People who are in a trance can display extraordinary body movements, endure pain, and communicate messages or sounds from supposedly nonhuman powers. They may experience amnesia, not remembering what took place during the trance.

Depending on the culture and belief system, possession and trance are associated with a variety of conditions that can induce shifts of consciousness, such as: (1) suggestion, social pressure, or willingness to conform to group beliefs, (2) sensory deprivation through isolation, sleep deprivation, and/or fasting, (3) infliction of pain, for instance, flagellation or piercing of the flesh, (4) ingestion of alcohol, stimulants, narcotics, or hallucinogens, and (5) repetitive rituals such as dancing, drumming, chanting, singing, or monotonous exercises. One or more of these conditions may be present. Because groups differ in their practices and come from diverse environments, techniques vary widely in content and form.

Societies that accept possession as a physical reality usually give the possessed integrated social roles to play in magical or religious ceremonies. Societies that believe in demonic possession usually view the condition as detrimental. These societies take steps to cure the possessed or to expel them. The Bible claims that Jesus Christ cast out demons, and exorcism is still accepted in some Christian practices, as well as in other cultural contexts such as folk religion. In some cases religions worship negative spirits or gods in order to appease them or to receive information and power from them.

Modern medicine—especially psychiatry—tends to view the physical symptoms of possession as indications of mental illness, mass hysteria, drug-induced psychosis, or a fantasy-prone personality. Sociologists and anthropologists stress the functional nature that beliefs in possession play in creating social roles and social cohesion within a group. In rituals people give themselves to the collective enactment of the group's internal reality. When people appear to be spirit possessed, they are believed to be a conduit for special communications from the supernatural. Similarly, an accomplished enactment of spirit possession or trance indicates that the group's ritual is working properly; thus the social contract between the visible physical world and the invisible spiritual world remains intact.

Possession

Two phases characterize possession: a phase of giving over to the spirit and a subsequent phase of altered consciousness, expressed by excitation or redirected focus. The possessed person usually feels a presence above the head. Some cultures describe the experience as that of a spirit "mounting" a horse. Spirit possession may be accompanied by twisting, dancing, writhing, and glossolalia (ecstatic utterance accompanying religious excitation). Possession can render a person's speech incomprehensible, whereas in other cases a spirit mediumship may occur. Mediumship implies that a spirit is speaking through an individual. Messages from such a spirit will explain the metaphysical causes for physical conditions, such as sickness, discord, or misfortune. Some messages will interpret the past and future. Depending on the culture, the possessed person may act as a kind of folk therapist, relaying helpful messages from the spirit world. Folk healers and shamans sometimes use this kind of altered consciousness to minister to their patients.

Possession occurs in Haitian Vodou (voodoo or hoodoo) rituals where frenzied dancing accompanies animal sacrifice. With the help of a priest people create a *veve,* which is a pattern of cornmeal or flour dedicated to the Loa (spirits). Participants make music with drums and rattles while chanting and singing. As the fervor mounts, someone will drop to the ground because the Loa have possessed him or her. Everyone defers to the possessed person because he or she holds the spirit guests within. They may feed the blood from the sacrifice to the possessed person in order to appease the Loa. Vodou priests *(houngan)* or priestesses *(mambo)* have personal Loa spirits that they use in ceremonies to heal the sick. The avant-garde filmmaker Maya Deren documented Haitian ceremonies from 1947 to 1951 in a film entitled *Divine Horsemen: The Living Gods of Haiti.* Ironically, she experienced possession by the Loa, and she was initiated into the religion. Her film recorded the rhythmic drumming and other compelling features of the rituals.

The Hausa cultures of western Africa support the *bori*-spirit possession cult. In eastern Africa the cult phenomenon is known as *zar.* Over two hundred deities, called *bori,* make up a hierarchical cosmology of good and bad spirits. Certain *bori* cause certain illnesses or misfortunes, whereas others bless social life. The *bori*-spirit possession cult attracts mostly women, although there are a few exceptions, such as in some regions where homosexuals join. Through trance possession, women seek advice about their husbands and other matters of daily life. The women call themselves the "Mares of God" because the spirits supposedly mount them like a horse. Some researchers suggest that the *bori*-spirit possession cult allows the women to process their feelings of oppression in their male-dominated societies.

Although traditional Christianity condemns spirit possession as the work of the devil, it also contains similar themes, such as being "filled with the Holy Spirit." Christians celebrate the holiday of Pentecost, when the Holy Ghost descended upon the apostles. Some Christian sects in the United States, believing that they are filled with the Holy Ghost, handle venomous snakes in their ecstatic religious meetings, based on the belief that spiritual grace protects them. Some Christian revivalists claim that charismatic evangelists can heal the sick during euphoric mass meetings because they are using the power of the Holy Spirit. Whether this can be defined as spirit possession is open to debate, but this type of phenomena illustrates the widespread use of trance in religion.

Trance

From prehistory to modern times the usage of trance endured through the cultural diffusion of magical ideas. Presumably, some prehistoric people used trance in cave rituals while under the influence of psychotropic (acting on the mind) plants, as evidenced by discarded blowpipes found in archeological sites. Ancient Greece employed oracles, the most famous being the Delphic oracle, named the "Pythia," whose prophecy sprang from pharmacologically induced states and the belief that the god Apollo straddled the back of her neck. In the ancient Greek cult of Dionysus women freely drank wine as they engaged in the frantic revelry of dancing, sexual license, and emotional excess. These women, called"maenads" or "Bacchae," believed themselves to be possessed by their fertility god. The earliest Dionysian festivals provided ecstatic ceremonies in which female revelers tore live animals apart for sacrifice. By the middle of the third century BCE men joined the festivities as the cult started to spread to Rome, where it came to symbolize decadent behavior.

In the Hindu festival Thaipusam, dedicated to the deity Lord Muruga, the celebrants engage in activities aimed at both penance and piety. Devoted Hindus fast to prepare themselves for days of sacrifice that cleanse their souls of sins. One devotional action associated with the festival involves penitents piercing their skins while in a trance state. While supposedly feeling no pain and suffering no bleeding, people impale their bodies with skewers or hooks. Some devotees wear a metal apparatus, called a *kavadi,* which displays decorations and offerings. They fasten the *kavadi* to their bare flesh while also piercing their tongues or cheeks. The participants take part in a procession of chanting and wild dancing that leads to temples where offerings are given. Modern medicine believes that such ritual pain causes the release of endorphins, which are natural painkillers akin to morphine.

Anthropologists know the Indonesian island of Bali as a place where trance permeates domestic and public life. The anthropologist Jane Belo (1960) identifies seven types of trancers in Bali: (1) trance doctors, (2) ceremonial mediums, (3) impersonators of Rangda and the Barong (mythical characters), (4) occasional trancers, (5) child trance dancers, (6) folk trancers, and (7) fighting or self-stabbing dancers. The Balinese employ trance doctors, similar to shamans, to diagnose the spiritual causes of illness. Trance doctors visit homes to dispense their folk healing remedies. Ceremonial mediums serve temples, where people consult them about matters of illness or other aspects of life. While listening to a medium, who sometimes conducts séances to communicate with the dead, believers can fall into trances themselves. In some instances, individuals will lose consciousness and collapse at group meetings because they have entered a trance. People can become entranced at ceremonies; they are called "occasional trancers." In the traditional, highly stylized world of Balinese dancers, trance plays a big part in public performances. Some dancers, such as child trance dancers, fall unconscious at various points in their performances. The so-called kris (dagger) dancers perform with knives or swords that are used to cut themselves during the ecstatic reenactment of myths about good fighting evil. When dancers impersonate mythical figures such as Rangda and the Barong, they dance wildly, believing that they have been taken over by the spirits of the gods they represent.

Shamanism

Shamans, who can be either male or female depending on the culture, use trance as part of their spiritual repertoires. Shamans are found throughout the world in most folk traditions, characteristically in Native America, Africa, and Asia. The anthropologist Piers Vitebsky (2001) contends that shamans—sometimes called "medicine men" or "witch doctors"—act as healers, mystics, and even social workers for their communities. Ordinarily, shamans rely on spirit guides, which take many forms contingent on the belief system, as they communicate with the spirit world. Some shamans tell the future for supplicants through their dreams or through the help of their spirit guides during a trance. Typically in hunting or herding cultures, shamans converse with animals in other dimensions of reality, whereas in societies with ancestor worship shamans receive messages from the dead or their other-worldly caretakers. Various kinds of shamans say they turn into animals, and most will describe out-of-body experiences facilitated by trance and ritual. Because they serve as spiritual guardians for their communities, some shamans enter other mystical worlds to combat evil spirits on behalf of their people.

Vitebsky (2001) describes dozens of shamanic practices. The *Vegetalistas* of the Peruvian Amazon practice their type of shamanism by ingesting various hallucinogenic plants to generate visions and to produce a healing form of mucus from their bodies. Amazonian shamans take hallucinogens during elaborate rituals with the intention of becoming jaguars with magical powers. In New Guinea the Baruyan shaman fires enchanted poison darts at an enemy village in order to cause it sickness. Among the San Bushmen of Southern Africa a shamanic healer enters a trance in which he flies to the sky to obtain information about a person's sickness. The Sora shamans of India preside at funerals, and they also provide grief counseling for families. Using traditional regalia and musical instruments, many shamans supply entertainment for communities, such as the Siberian shamans who call the spirits with drums. Shamans can dispense herbal remedies for sickness based on the native plants of their regions, and they may also suggest a magical cure that can involve a sacrificial offering or other requests based on communication with the spirits.

Channeling

Although phenomena associated with possession and trance are usually linked with so-called primitive cultures and magical beliefs, modern technological societies contain subcultures that utilize these forms of expression. Beginning in the 1850s the United States fostered a long tradition of spiritualism that influenced subsequent occult practices. Today spiritualists maintain their own followings but share their place in a modern occult milieu. Since the 1980s and growth of the New Age movement, the custom of channeling has drawn a large following in the United States and in Europe. Channeling entails a trancelike state in which a disincarnate entity or supernatural being supposedly speaks through the voice of a practitioner. For example, the popular channeler J. Z. Knight attracted a significant following as Ramtha, the voice of a thirty-five-thousand-year-old warrior. Ruth Norman, co-founder of Unarius (a flying-saucer religion based in Southern California), voiced the communiqués from the millenarian (relating to the millennium of Christian prophecy) Space Brothers, who maintained that flying saucers would land in 2001. These are a small sample of modern-day trance mediums. Although many groups channel alleged messages from the great beyond, their styles of channeling differ from quiet relaxed messages to animated dramatic deliveries, depending on the practitioner's technique.

The Magical Process

Possession and trance represent probably the oldest forms of spiritual expression that are still found around the world today in both primitive and modern settings. Possession and trance communicate cultural mythologies. They are used to heal the sick and to communicate with the supernatural. Experts describe the process as one of folk psychiatry and as a way for groups to employ cathartic symbolism and emotion. For those who believe that illness and misfortune have supernatural causes, rather than physical causes, possession and trance play therapeutic roles in folk healing. As vehicles for articulating the invisible worlds of the supernatural, possession and trance will survive as long as humans continue to maintain and to invent rituals that explain the irrational, magical side of consciousness and experience.

Diana Tumminia

See also Altered States of Consciousness; Ecstatic Worship; Exorcism; Shakers; Shamanism; Vision Quest; Vodun

Further Reading

Adams, R. B. (Ed.). (1989). *Spirit summonings*. Alexandria, VA: Time-Life Books.

Belo, J. (1960). *Trance in Bali*. New York: Columbia University Press.

Besmer, F. (1983). *Horses, musicians, & gods: The Hausa cult of possession-trance*. South Hadley, MA: Bergin & Garvey.

Bourguignon, E. (1991). *Possession*. Prospect Heights, IL: Waveland Press.

Brandon, R. (1983). *The spiritualists: The passion for the occult in the nineteenth and twentieth centuries*. London: Weidenfeld and Nicolson.

Brown. M. F. (1997). The *channeling zone: American spirituality in an anxious age*. Cambridge, MA: Harvard University Press.

Clottes, J., & Lewis-Williams, D. (1998). *The shamans of prehistory: Trance and magic in the painted caves*. New York: Harry N. Abrams.

Deren, M. (1985). *Divine horsemen: The living gods of Haiti*. New York: Mystic Fire Video.

Dobbin, J. (1986). *The Jombee dance of Montserrat: A study of trance ritual in the West Indies*. Columbus: Ohio State University Press.

Kiev, A. (1964). *Magic, faith, and healing: Studies in primitive psychiatry today*. New York: Free Press.

Laing, R. D. (1967). *The politics of experience*. New York: Ballantine Books.

Lewis, I. M. (1971). *Ecstatic religion: An anthropological study of spirit possession and shamanism*. Harmondsworth, UK: Penguin Books.

Lewis, J. R. (Ed.). (1995). *The gods have landed: New religions from other worlds*. Albany: State University of New York Press.

Rouget, G. (1985). *Music and trance: A theory of the relations between music and possession*. Chicago: University of Chicago Press.

Vitebsky, P. (2001). *Shamanism*. Norman: University of Oklahoma Press.

Wavel, S., Butts, A., & Epton, N. (1967). *Trances*. New York: E. P. Dutton.

Zaretsky, I., & Shambaugh, C. (1978). *Spirit possession and spirit mediumship in Africa and Afro-America: An annotated bibliography*. New York: Garland Publishing.

Prayer

Prayer has most consistently been defined as "communication between humans and God." This definition has been challenged and expanded primarily through fields such as liturgics (the study of formal public worship), hermeneutics (the study of the methodological principles of interpretation), linguistics, and theology, as well as sociology, psychology, and anthropology. In the past thirty years significant developments in philosophical theology, ritual studies, and feminist theology have contributed to a deeper understanding of prayer as a multidimensional activity. Ethnographies (studies of cultures) and comparative religion have yielded insight into the multiplicity of forms that prayer can take globally and its general characteristics.

Concepts of Prayer

Prayers most often involve invocation, praise or petition, and benediction but also can involve meditation, intercession, supplication, dedication, litany (a prayer consisting of a series of invocations and supplications by the leader with alternate responses by the congregation), Beatitude (any of the declarations made in Christ's Sermon on the Mount beginning with "Blessed are"), or penitence. Prayer formulas tend to derive from the actions and words instituted by the founders and prophets of religions. Sacred texts usually contain prayers, and prayers are often drawn from the language of such texts. Much of the framework for explaining prayer academically has its source in Christian hermeneutics—interpretation of the biblical text. Starting in the nineteenth century, great effort was taken to encourage deeper understanding of the ritual life of the Church as it arose from biblical roots. In the mid-nineteenth century liturgics emerged as Christian scholars attempted to develop common discourse about such concepts as prayer. With the birth of the "science" of religions under scholars Edward B. Tylor, Friedrich Max Müller, and James George Frazer in the nineteenth century, secular understanding of concepts such as prayer borrowed heavily from these Christian hermeneutical and liturgical activities. Later work in hermeneutics, such as that by the theologians Hans-Georg Gadamer and Paul Ricoeur, noted that actions may be thought of as text insofar as the meaning of the actions can be detached from the original event—in other words, actions themselves are open to the hermeneutical process. So early Christian prayer is in constant need of reinterpretation in each social context. Ricoeur's work hints at the role that linguistics has played in understanding prayer for academics such as Roy A. Rappaport, Fritz Staal, and Stanley Tambiah. If prayer is thought of as communication, and the interpretation of prayer is socially bound, then at its core prayer is fundamentally meaningless unless syntax is supplied. In this sense prayer can be thought of as pure ritualized activity, the meaning of which is assigned in its performance. There is thus a tension between form and content, between the semantic and the pragmatic, and between the cultural and the universal. Theology has supplied deeper meaning to the concepts of prayer. In *Man's Quest for God,* the Jewish theologian Abraham Heschel wrote, "The issue of prayer is not prayer; the issue is God" (Heschel 1954, 87). This is similar to the French sociologist Emile Durkheim's assertion that ritual is half of the religious whole; the other half is belief. In this way of thinking prayer is less communication and more reflection on—and living in light of—the nature of the divine.

The German sociologist Max Weber argued that prayer is half of "divine worship"; the other half being sacrifice. He argued that prayer is a fluid relationship between "magical formula" and supplication. Prayer is a powerful coercive force designed to control other-worldly forces and to order this-worldly

THE LORD'S PRAYER (MATTHEW 6: 9–13, KJV)

Our Father which art in heaven, Hallowed be thy name.
Thy kingdom come. Thy will be done in earth, as it is in heaven.
Give us this day our daily bread.
And forgive us our debts, as we forgive our debtors.
And lead us not into temptation, but deliver us from evil: For thine is the kingdom, and the power, and the glory, for ever. Amen.

activities. Prayer is a potent sifter of society, enabling religious specialists to rise to the top. The Austrian psychologist Sigmund Freud further explored the realization that in prayer one is involved in a realm that is extraordinary. Freud noted great similarities between the obsessive actions of neurotics and religious observances. Prayer, then, involves repression, displacement, and coping and is best thought of as a universal social neurosis. Prayer is a clue or a marker that leads back to repression, fear, and projection (transference of neuroses onto another's personality). The anthropologist Clifford Geertz gave a more positive assessment of ritual and religion, describing them as a constructive cultural system. Prayer is reflective of—and a symbolic participation in—a wider system of values and order of existence. Following the Spanish-American poet and philosopher George Santayana, Geertz argued that ritual elements are models of reality as it is and expressions of reality as it should be. Geertz's arguments echo the Christian hermeneutical approach in seeing culture as an ensemble of texts, requiring constant reinterpretation. Performing a prayer, for Geertz, involves a symbolic fusion of ethos (distinguishing character, sentiment, moral nature, or guiding beliefs) and worldview. At its core prayer is participation in the "really real."

For the last thirty years philosophical theologians have been examining prayer in light of the concepts of the nature of the divine as it has been conceived within Judeo-Islamic-Christian traditions. The efficacy of prayers of petition, supplication, invocation, or intercession is brought into question in light of the doctrines of omniscience (God's total knowledge) and benevolence (God's total goodness). How can an omniscient and omnibenevolent god be informed of new information or requests at all? Most scholars, however, are not ready to abandon the efficacy of prayer in light of philosophical conceptions of the divine attributes. Following the philosophers Ludwig Wittgenstein and D. Z. Phillips, the scholar Dan R. Stiver argues that religious language as act can be thought of as literal (meaning actual petition, supplication, etc.) but also as metaphorical (as noncognitive, that is, pre-rational; nonpropositional language, replete with social, pragmatic, and orientative, or relational, concerns). Stiver has called this a "speech-act" theory of religious language. Other scholars have gone with a more processive model (a model that emphasizes God's unfolding plan for the universe). William Hasker, following Alvin Plantinga and others, has questioned the validity of asserting God's "middle knowledge" or "foreknowledge" (that is, God's awareness of an action as it happens or before it happens), thus leaving room for the efficacy of prayer, although he points out the inherent difficulty in the human ability to ascertain the *answers to prayers*. Parallel to the developments in philosophical theology, over the last thirty years the field of ritual studies has emerged with some of the most significant developments in the understanding of prayer. The anthropologist Victor Turner analyzed ritual behavior as existence "betwixt and between" emerging realities, creative of *communitas* (modalities of social relations in which there is a communion of relatively equal individuals who submit to the authority of acknowledged ritual specialists). Prayer, then, does much more than merely communicate; it creates "essential" and "generic" human bonds. Drawing on the embodiment theories of Turner (for example, where he defines community as having an existential quality, involving the whole person in relation to there persons), and akin to those of the French philosopher

Michel Foucault and the Italian politician Antonio Gramsci, the ritual theorist Catherine Bell has emphasized how identity can be negotiated and how bodily participation in ritual serves as a primary arena. She has noted how ritual participation, such as collective repetition of prayers, is creative of new self-identity. The older frameworks of religious communities being modeled on heavenly ordained worship have given way to new models based on inner wholeness and a willingness to change aspects of ritual such as prayer. In *Ritual: Perspectives and Dimensions,* Bell has written, "ritual is approached as a means to create and renew community, transform human identity, and remake our most existential sense of being in the cosmos" (Bell 1997, 264). Prayer is evocative language, imbued with its own creative power. Bell (and many other ritual theorists) emphasizes looking beyond traditional patriarchal and occidental (Western) models of ritual activity, instead favoring more universal models that also take account of individual experience. In the last thirty years the feminist movements have begun rethinking the politics of language used in religion and ritual. Prayer and the language of prayer, especially in the West, are thought to create and perpetuate patriarchal community structures. Under the guidance of thinkers such as Mary Daly, Phyllis Trible, and Rosemary Radford Ruether, the language of prayer is being reconceived to include feminine aspects. One example of the trend of looking beyond Western models is the Subaltern Studies Project, loosely based in the Indian subcontinent. This collective of scholars has found inspiration in the embodiment theories of Foucault and Gramsci and has applied them within a historical methodology designed to give voice to the oppressed and powerless. Prayer may here be conceived as the language of resistance, lamentation, and the desire to create new community and reforge identity.

Forms of Prayer

Drawing on a growing body of ethnographic literature, explanations of prayer—having been traditionally cast in Judeo-Christian categories—are emerging as truly cross-cultural concepts. Comparative religionists have also contributed to greater awareness of the multiplicity of forms of prayer globally, even while arguing for certain universal characteristics. Not only have definitions of prayer emerged beyond that of "communication with the divine," but also greater care has been taken to recognize that within the major religions of the world there is tremendous variety in the daily practice of individual followers. Any attempt, therefore, to give an account of the prayer life of the followers of a particular religion is at best impartial and circumspect.

Generally, modern Jewish prayer is considered an effective substitute for most Deutero-Levitical (Hebrew law books) sacrifices. Prayers are usually based on Torah (the body of wisdom and law contained in Jewish Scripture and other sacred literature and oral tradition) reading, usually collective in nature, and occur most often in synagogues or homes. Jewish prayer follows a cycle based loosely on that of the ancient temple of Jerusalem. One of the most important Jewish prayers, the Shema (the Jewish confession of faith) (Deuteronomy 6:4–9, NRSV, is recited morning and evening and during services. The Amidah (a prayer usually containing eighteen or nineteen petitions) serves as the basis for the morning, afternoon, and evening daily services. There are additional prayers each Sabbath and each holiday. Other Jewish prayers include the kaddish (a prayer recited in the daily ritual of the synagogue and by mourners at public services after the death of a close relative), the kiddush (a blessing pronounced over wine or bread in a home or synagogue on a holy day), the Kol Nidre (a formula for the annulment of private vows chanted in the synagogue on the eve of Yom Kippur), the Selihot (prayers of pardon), and the Haggadah (ancient lore forming especially the nonlegal part of the Talmud—the authoritative body of Jewish tradition).

Early Christianity inherited the diasporic (relating to the settling of scattered colonies of Jews outside Palestine after the Babylonian exile) Jewish modes of prayer. The most important Christian prayer is the Lord's Prayer (Matthew 6:9–13, NRSV). Early Christians observed the Jewish hours of prayer, but this practice continued only within monastic communities through the Middle Ages. Christian prayer remained mostly a group activity, but individual contemplative prayer also emerged in the first few centuries CE. Among Catholics the Ave Maria (Hail Mary, a Roman Catholic prayer to the Virgin Mary), coupled with the use of a rosary, remains important. Christian liturgy (rite prescribed for public worship)—standardized after about the fifth century CE—often involves the prayer of the *divine offices,* sacramental prayers, the *kyrie eleison* (Lord have mercy), and the *agnus dei* (O Lamb of God), as well as other invocations, supplications, and the like. Since the

Reformation (a sixteenth-century religious movement marked ultimately by rejection or modification of some Roman Catholic doctrine and practice and establishment of the Protestant churches) prayers have diverged into multiple forms, some continuing to follow high-liturgical standards and others quite spontaneous and free-form.

Islamic prayer has from the seventh century CE remained highly formalized and consistent. As an orthopraxic religion (where correct practice is emphasized over correct belief), Islam places great emphasis on proper performance and participation, especially on Friday. Performed five times daily, *salât* (prayer) involves preparation in the form of answering the *adhan* (call to prayer), performing an ablution, covering the body, and facing the *qibla* (niche facing Mecca). Two cycles *(rak'a)* are performed in which verses from the Qur'an (the book of sacred writings accepted by Muslims as revelations made to Muhammad by Allah) and other prayers are recited while bowing and prostrating. In addition to *salât,* there are other types of prayers, such as petitions *(du'â),* festival *('îd)* prayers, and supererogatory (beyond what is required) *(nawâfil)* prayers.

Hindu prayer has little uniformity, but generally it derives from Sanskritic literature, especially the Vedas (the Hindu sacred writings). Recitation is thought to embody the very language of the gods. The words themselves, especially contained in mantras-sanskrit hymns of power, evoke and imbue the power of the divine presence. Hindu practice generally involves either sacrifice (*yajña,* almost always performed in a temple) or worship (*pûjâ,* performed in a temple, outdoors, or in a home). During either *yajña* or *pûjâ,* various verses are recited or mantras are employed. Prayers can also involve recitation of sacred books during festivals or can involve devotional singing *(kîrtans).*

Buddhist prayers are often based on the mantra (a mystical formula of invocation or incantation) system, especially among the Mahayana sects. In China and Japan these prayers have also become mixed with various Daoist/Confucian elements. In Chinese and Japanese Pure Land Buddhism, prayer has become an important part of devotional life where repeating the name of Amida Buddha is viewed as extremely efficacious. In Tibet prayer can involve hand gestures (mudras), mandalas (Hindu or Buddhist graphic symbols of the universe), and spinning prayer wheels. Prayers are often taught through initiation and given from teacher to disciple.

Few exhaustive works have been written on prayer beyond devotional works designed for the practitioner. Traditional definitions of prayer as "communication with the divine" have only recently been superceded by scholarly developments. Work within fields such as linguistics, hermeneutics, and theology as well as within other human sciences has brought welcome subtlety and complexity to the understanding of prayer. Recent developments within philosophical theology and ritual studies have added great understanding to concepts such as prayer but have also shown that further work must be done, especially along ethnographic and comparative lines.

Eric J. Rothgery

See also Sacrifice and Offerings

Further Reading

Appleton, G. (Ed.). (1985). *The Oxford book of prayer*. New York: Oxford University Press.

Bell, C. (1992). *Ritual theory: Ritual practice*. New York: Oxford University Press.

Bell, C. (1997). *Ritual: Perspectives and dimensions*. New York: Oxford University Press.

Geertz, C. (1973). *The interpretation of cultures*. New York: Basic Books.

Grimes, R. L. (Ed.). (1996). *Readings in ritual studies*. Upper Saddle River, NJ: Prentice Hall.

Heschel, A. (1954). *Man's quest for God*. New York: Harper.

Hitchcock, H. H. (1992). *The politics of prayer: Feminist language and the worship of God*. San Francisco: Ignatius Press.

Stiver, D. R. (1996). *The philosophy of religious language: Sign, symbol & story*. Cambridge, UK: Blackwell.

Turner, V. (1969). *The ritual process: Structure and anti-structure*. New York: Aldine de Gruyter.

Weber, M. (1922). *The sociology of religion*. Boston: Beacon Press.

Protestantism

Protestants make preaching and reading from the Bible central to their devotional life. They often emphasize the didactic function of ritual and its capacity to foster a personal relationship to the faith. Frequently this didactic activity is carried out through

This sign, posted on the wall outside St. Giles's Anglican Church in Shipbourne, Kent, England announces the monthly ritual calendar. COURTESY OF KAREN CHRISTENSEN.

the spoken word, rather than through ritual action. Certain more "liturgical" traditions do emphasize action, as do Pentecostals. Music is central to Protestant rituals and highly valued by participants. Protestants lay great emphasis on the creation of community through their ritual, producing a "horizontal" direction of worship (where the main audience is other community members) rather than "vertical" (where the main audience is the divine).

Historical Overview of Protestant Ritual Practices

The Protestant Reformation constituted a drastic reshaping of the ritual practice of Western Christendom. For the Reformers, ritual was valuable insofar as it aroused faith in the participants. Many medieval Roman Catholic practices were abandoned as useless or idolatrous. The sacraments were reduced to two (baptism and the Eucharist). All the Reformers rejected the medieval understanding of the Eucharist (or "Lord's Supper") as a sacrifice offered to God in which the bread and wine actually became Christ's body. For Luther, Christ's body and blood were truly present in, with, and under the bread and wine. Other Protestants (the "Reformed") took a less literal view, emphasizing Christ's presence in the action of the Supper and in the congregation rather than in the elements. All the Reformers agreed that the Supper could only be celebrated if the congregation received Communion. Since infrequent Communion (one to three times a year) was the norm in the late Middle Ages, and since receiving Communion without being spiritually prepared was seen as dangerous, few were willing to partake frequently. Thus, a service of prayer and preaching became the weekly norm, with Communion monthly, yearly, or somewhere in between. For the Reformed, the Scriptures were a guide not only to doctrine, but also to ritual. Reformed ritual thus was deliberately stripped down to the minimum. The often didactic nature of Protestantism was particularly evident in the Reformed tradition, with a strong emphasis on preaching. While the Lutherans used choirs and organs, the Reformed practiced only unaccompanied congregational singing, primarily using the Psalms.

The English Reformation was strongly influenced by Continental Reformed models, but was more conservative liturgically. With the final establishment of Protestantism in England under Elizabeth I in the sixteenth century, the Book of Common Prayer (which underwent several revisions between 1549 and 1662) was adopted as the sole ritual text in the Church of England. The Book of Common Prayer retained the basic structure of the Mass, and also contained offices of Morning and Evening Prayer, adaptations of the monastic daily prayer service. These services became the backbone of Anglican piety.

The most radical changes in ritual occurred in "Anabaptist" communities, which rejected infant baptism in favor of "believers' baptism," usually administered by pouring. Anabaptists shared the Reformed simplification of ritual, and regarded the two sacraments (or "ordinances") as memorials and signs of faith rather than as means of grace.

The late sixteenth and seventeenth centuries saw the development of various movements fostering a more intense piety, with an increasing emphasis on personal conversion. In England, the Puritan movement attempted to reduce the elements of medieval Catholicism remaining in the established church, and when this attempt failed the Puritans established separate "nonconformist" churches. These churches developed a ritual style based on extempore ministerial prayer, lengthy sermons, and increasingly the use of vernacular hymns, which did not catch on in Anglicanism until a century later.

Some Puritans abandoned the attempt to reform the Church of England long before the newly adopted form of the Book of Common Prayer in 1662. This was done as part of the Restoration of the English monarchy, after the days of Cromwell, and Puritans found this version of the Prayer Book unacceptable and left the Church of England in large number, never to return. Some of these rejected infant baptism and adopted believers' baptism by immersion as the only valid form, becoming known as "Baptists." An even more radical expression of English Protestantism was the Society of Friends (Quakers). Quakers rejected all clerical hierarchies, church buildings, sacraments, and formal rituals. Rather, they turned silence itself into a ritual practice, waiting patiently until the Spirit moved someone to pray or sing or exhort.

In late-seventeenth-century Germany, many Lutherans became dissatisfied with what they saw as the insufficient commitment of most Christians to piety and morality. These "Pietists" formed small groups within the local congregation, dedicated to the study of Scripture. Pietists influenced preaching to become less doctrinal and more emotional, and they also fostered the further development of the rich Lutheran hymn-writing tradition.

The eighteenth century saw an increasing rationalism among all Protestant churches, emphasizing moral behavior rather than doctrine or sacraments. At the same time, Pietist ideals (combined with the Puritan legacy) bore fruit in England and the American colonies in the form of the "evangelical revival" or (in America) "Great Awakening." This explosion of piety focused on personal conversion and the importance of a disciplined life. The most significant ritual expressions of the revival occurred in the Methodist societies, founded by John Wesley in the course of his long evangelistic career. In Wesley's lifetime, British Methodists did not celebrate the sacraments themselves but depended on their local Church of England parish. They developed a parallel set of rituals, meeting on Sunday evenings so as not to conflict with the morning and afternoon services of Anglicanism. Methodist worship featured impassioned lay preaching and the singing of hymns that quickly became classics among English-speaking Protestants. Methodist societies were divided into smaller "bands" and "classes," which met for sessions of mutual confession and exhortation, giving Methodism a tightly knit structure of accountability. Methodists also adopted the practice of the "love feast," a revival of the early Christian agape meal, celebrated with bread and water. This did not replace the Eucharist, which could only be celebrated by Anglican clergy. After Wesley's death, British Methodism formally separated from Anglicanism, developing Sunday-morning services of worship and celebrating the sacraments in their own right.

The major ritual development of nineteenth-century Anglicanism was the Anglo-Catholic movement, which attempted to revive pre-Reformation beliefs and practices, particularly affecting ritual. The Anglo-Catholics, or "Ritualists," reinstituted daily Eucharist, incense, devotions to the saints, prayer for the dead, sacramental private confession, and other practices abandoned at the Reformation. In spite of considerable opposition, they maintained their position as a wing of Anglicanism, and some of their practices have become the Anglican norm. Continental Protestantism saw similar high-church movements, although on a more modest scale.

Return to the early church was a common theme in nineteenth-century ritual developments, but it took widely different forms. Some movements attempted to recapture New Testament worship by adopting an egalitarian form of worship in which any (usually male) believer could participate. Typically such groups practiced the "breaking of bread" (Lord's Supper) weekly as a memorial of Christ's death. This "primitivist" impulse was particularly active in American Christianity.

The History of Protestant Religious Ritual in America

Early American Protestant religious rituals varied greatly. In the early 1800s, what became known as the "camp meeting" tradition had its beginning, mainly among Methodists and Baptists. Drawing on the theological notion that God's salvation was available to all but required a choice from the potential believer, this tradition encouraged people to make a public declaration of their conversion to Christianity or to higher stages of Christian life. Frequently held outside, early camp meetings featured singing, multiple preaching services, a "mourner's bench" where potential converts could pray and be prayed for, "altar calls" that asked for those dedicating themselves to the faith to come forward, and sometimes a climactic celebration of the Eucharist. Aspects of this tradition were often incorporated into services in church buildings.

After mid-century, most large denominations began to distance themselves from revival-style rituals. As members gained money, education, and social status, they reintroduced practices previously associated with European worship. By the late 1800s robes, choirs, churches in Gothic architecture, and printed orders of worship became more common among mainline churches. These developments continued into the twentieth century. Some churches, particularly Episcopalian and Lutheran, never fully participated in revivalism.

The Sunday school or Christian education movement was also a huge influence on American ritual. Sunday schools were at their peak from 1850 to 1950, and were frequently organized into multiple departments by age. These departments often held their own worship activities as well as assembling for "opening exercises" in which the whole Sunday school participated in singing and hearing a moral lesson. Music and ritual practices that began in the Sunday School hour often found their way into Sunday-morning sanctuary rituals.

Many Protestants rejected the increasing respectability and formality of the mainline churches, forming small denominations and independent congregations (a trend that continues today). In the Methodist tradition, most such groups were known as "holiness" churches due to their belief in a climactic experience of consecration to Christ resulting in the "baptism with the Holy Spirit" and freedom from sin (an experience often reached through coming forward for prayer in a camp meeting). Around 1900, certain members of the holiness movement began to preach that anyone who had received the "baptism with the Holy Spirit" would be able to speak in unknown tongues and should demonstrate this in a public ritual setting. This new movement became known as Pentecostalism. Pentecostals emphasized not only speaking in tongues but also the general use of bodily expression in worship. Many of their ritual acts centered around prayers for divine healing. Both holiness and Pentecostal churches still claim many adherents today.

Initiation Rituals

Christian initiation usually takes one of two patterns among Protestants. Anglican, Lutheran, Reformed, and Methodist traditions baptize the children of Christians in infancy, although of course adult converts are baptized also. The candidate may be immersed in water, or water may be poured or sprinkled on the candidate's head. Sprinkling is the most common traditional practice among paedobaptist (infant-baptizing) Protestants, although immersion is returning to favor as the norm for adult baptisms, and a few churches imitate the Orthodox by immersing infants. Infant baptism is accompanied by a profession of faith by the parents or sponsors on behalf of the child. Baptism may be regarded as a means of grace (Anglicans, Lutherans, some Methodists) or as a pledge that the child will be raised in the Christian faith (most Reformed, many Methodists). Christian initiation in paedobaptist churches is not complete until the rite of confirmation in early adolescence, when children undergo a period of training and then profess their allegiance to the Christian faith in front of the assembly. In recent years, some traditions have questioned this structure and have begun giving Communion to infants, regarding initiation as complete at baptism.

The free churches—Anabaptists, Mennonites, Church of the Brethren, Brethren in Christ, Baptists, Pentecostals, Restorationists, and most nondenominational and fundamentalist churches—baptize only those old enough to make a public profession of faith for themselves, although among many Baptists this can be as young as six. Infant baptism is replaced by a rite of dedication to God, which resembles infant baptism except that it does not involve water and is not regarded as a sacrament. Most "believers' baptism" churches recognize immersion as the only valid means of baptism and will rebaptize new members who have been baptized in infancy or by a means other than immersion.

Annual Cycle

Protestant churches vary in their annual cycle of rituals according to their place on the liturgical spectrum. However, almost all Protestant groups recognize the winter festival of the birth of Christ at Christmas and the spring festival of his death and resurrection during Holy Week and Easter as the two focal points of the year. More "liturgical" churches such as Anglicans and Lutherans pay close attention in their annual cycle of ritual to what is known as the "Christian" or "church" year, with periods of preparation before Christmas and Easter (Advent and Lent, respectively) and various feasts celebrating Christ's life and sometimes the lives of biblical saints. Many Protestant churches celebrate civic holidays such as Mothers'

Day, Memorial Day, Father's Day, July 4th, and Thanksgiving.

In practice, the overarching structure of ritual in Protestant denominations often becomes the school year, a fact emphasized by the existence of Christian education programs which operate on the same calendar as the secular school year. Programs and celebrations of the church are "kicked off" by a "Rally Day," usually in early September, which inaugurates the Sunday School program for another year. Some sort of graduation or acknowledgement is celebrated in May or June at the same time as secular commencements, followed by reducing programs and rituals of the church to a more limited, casual summer schedule.

Weekly Ritual Practices

The main focus of ritual practice for Protestants is Sunday morning worship, often accompanied by a less formal evening service. "Liturgical" denominations are usually tied heavily to an order of service that is repeated every week with minor variations. Frequently these churches administer the Eucharist weekly, have music that is more classical in style, and use traditional hymns. Preaching is done from a printed manuscript or extensive notes and attempts to be thought-provoking and intellectual. Four readings from the Bible are normally used in the service. Clergy and other worship participants are robed in "vestments," liturgical clothing appropriate for their particular activity in the service. The use of objects in worship is particularly strong in this tradition.

Middle-of-the-road Protestant churches (Methodists, Reformed, some Baptists) have printed orders of service but allow for considerable variation from week to week, and balance written with extempore prayers. Most of these churches still do not celebrate the Eucharist weekly, and use the biblical lectionary more loosely, or only in part. Clergy are frequently but not uniformly robed, and other worship participants usually do not wear vestments. The music of these churches is sometimes classical, but in the past thirty years has begun to swing more and more toward music written in a popular idiom known as "contemporary Christian." Often, other aspects of a more "low church" form of worship are introduced in conjunction with contemporary music, such as conversational preaching, casual dress, and openness to congregational verbal and physical response. Many mainline churches in this middle tradition are experiencing severe conflicts over these conflicting styles of worship and music.

"Low church" services (e.g., Baptists, holiness, nondenominational, "Churches of Christ") focus more explicitly on preaching that is conversational in style, emphasizes practical application, uses minimal notes, and is delivered with more outward emotion and rhetorical flourish. Sermons are usually longer than in the other two traditions and make more explicit reference to the Bible. There is usually one reading from the Bible directly before the sermon. The order of worship is frequently not printed and is theoretically open to huge variation, although in practice this is not usually the case. Clergy generally dress in suits or more casual attire rather than in liturgical robes. Many low-church congregations continue to worship in traditional Reformed or revivalistic styles. An increasing number, however, worship in a "contemporary" style, with music influenced by rock, country, gospel, and jazz traditions, accompanied by a guitar or by a band using electronic and percussion instruments. In such congregations, worship songs are more likely to be taught aurally or from visual projection than to be read from a hymnbook. Traditionally, "low" churches have fostered spontaneous congregational response through such activities as shouting, clapping, saying "Amen," and raising hands. In Pentecostal contexts this response may also include speaking in tongues.

Additional weekly services may be observed during the week on days other than Sunday. In Anglicanism and other high-church traditions, this may include daily services of morning or evening prayer as given in the church's prayer book, possibly with administration of the Eucharist at one of these services. In middle-to-lower church traditions, a midweek worship service is frequently held on Wednesday evenings, which combines elements of the Sunday morning ritual with a stronger focus on prayer and study of the Scriptures. Sunday evening and Wednesday night services are becoming less common in many churches. Instead, an increasing number of congregations have small groups that meet weekly for Bible study or prayer. Many churches also have special weekly services for men, women, young people, or other specific groups within the congregation.

Daily Rituals

For the most part, daily worship in Protestantism is focused on the home. Evangelical traditions in particular place great emphasis on family devotions, usually involving prayer, Scripture reading, and the religious instruction of children. Devout Protestants also set aside time daily, usually in the morning, for individually reading the Bible and engaging in extemporaneous or silent prayer. Members of higher-church traditions will sometimes read the rites of morning and evening prayer provided in their tradition as a form of private devotions. Some also engage in silent meditation, and more liberal Protestants may incorporate Eastern practices such as yoga into their devotional life. Protestants generally say a prayer of thanksgiving before meals, although the more evangelical traditions place particular importance on this.

Current Trends in Protestant Religious Ritual

The reforms in Roman Catholic worship that resulted from the Second Vatican Council also affected Protestant worship. The resulting changes included orders of worship drawn from early church rather than medieval or nineteenth-century models; a renewed emphasis on weekly celebration of the Eucharist and connecting baptism to a structure of educating in Christian faith; efforts to read more Scripture in worship; the use of ritual action to complement or replace the spoken word; use of art in the ritual space; and changes in vestments and church furnishings. This renewal movement gathered many followers in the 1960s and has influenced most of the recent hymnal and ritual book publications of the mainline denominations, particularly in America. It has also sparked the writing of many new hymns and pieces of ritual music designed specifically for these types of service.

At the same time, as business and corporate models were applied to church management in the 1980s, a different kind of renewal movement took shape. Known as the church-growth movement, it emphasized the creation of large churches that provided many social and cultural services, divided their members explicitly into small groups for spiritual nurture and Bible study, marketed themselves toward middle-class families, and revolved around dynamic, personality-driven pastoral leadership. The ritual style of these churches emphasizes popular music; casual and friendly public conduct of worship; culture-specific references; practical preaching; spontaneous congregational response; the use of art, dance, and drama; and a cultivated informality.

In non-European and North American contexts, one of the fastest-growing ritual trends is the explosion of worldwide Pentecostalism, particularly in Latin America and Africa. Many countries that were formerly Catholic have experienced large amounts of conversions to Pentecostal churches. As in early American Pentecostalism, this tradition emphasizes the use of tongues and bodily movements in worship, highly emotional interactions with the divine, and prayers and rituals aimed at spiritual and physical healing.

Jennifer Woodruff Tait and Edwin Woodruff Tait

Further Reading

Anderson, W. K. (1969). *Protestantism: A symposium*. Freeport, NY: Books for Libraries.

Brilioth, Y. (1953). *Eucharistic faith and practice: Evangelical and Catholic*. London: Society for Promoting Christian Knowledge.

Byars, R. P. (2002). *The future of Protestant worship: Beyond the worship wars*. Louisville, KY: Westminster John Knox.

Davies, H. (1996). *Worship and theology in England* (Vols. 1–3). Grand Rapids, MI: W. B. Eerdmans.

Elford, H. J. (1963). *A layman's guide to Protestant worship*. New York: Abingdon.

Etherington, C. L. (1962). *Protestant worship music: Its history and practice*. New York: Holt, Rinehart & Winston.

Fiddes, V. H. (1961). *The architectural requirements of Protestant worship*. Toronto, Ontario, Canada: Ryerson.

Karant-Nunn, S. (1997). *The reformation of ritual: An interpretation of early modern Germany*. London; New York: Routledge.

Kilde, J. H. (2002). *When church becomes theatre: The transformation of evangelical architecture and worship in nineteenth-century America*. New York: Oxford University Press.

Lovelace, A. C., & Lovelace, W. C. (1987). *Music and worship in the church*. Nashville, TN: Abingdon.

Phifer, K. G. (1965). *A Protestant case for liturgical renewal*. Philadelphia: Westminster.

Steere, D. (1960). *Music in Protestant worship*. Richmond, VA: John Knox.

Skoglund, J. E. (1965). *Worship in the free churches*. Valley Forge, PA: Judson.

Vajta, V. (1958). *Luther on worship: An interpretation*. Philadelphia: Muhlenberg.

White, C. E. (1942). *Worship in the Protestant church.* Roanoke, IN: Roanoke Review.

White, J. F. (1976). *Christian worship in transition.* Nashville, TN: Abingdon.

White, J. F. (1989). *Protestant worship: Traditions in transition.* Louisville, KY: Westminster/John Knox.

White, J. F. (1997). *Christian worship in North America: A retrospective, 1955–1995.* Collegeville, MN: Liturgical.

Puberty Rites

Puberty rites are performed to celebrate coming of age by girls and boys. Accompanied by physical maturity, these rites are associated with the time when a girl or a boy is first considered to be capable of biological reproduction. Puberty rites are celebrated most prominently among the traditional peoples of Africa, Melanesia (islands of the southwest Pacific Ocean), and Native America as meaningful events in the human life cycle (birth, naming, puberty, marriage, and death), which the anthropologist Victor Turner and the sociologist Arnold van Gennep identified as the critical passages that are marked with intense symbolic ritual activities termed "rites of passage."

General Characteristics

Puberty rites are culture bound. Puberty represents for most traditional cultures the survival of a tribe or family with the declaration that its young women or young men have moved into the age of reproduction. Physiological changes, including development of breasts and menarche (onset of menstruation), often provide a background for puberty rites for girls, whereas there are no precise definitions for boys' puberty rites. However, the physical growth of a boy and demonstration of certain physical abilities sometimes determine the period of ritual celebration. A boy may also tell his father that he is ready to receive the marks that identify him as an adult, as is the case among the Nuer people of Africa.

Puberty rites formally introduce the initiate into her or his sex life, ushering a girl into womanhood and motherhood and a boy into manhood. The essence of puberty rites, therefore, is to induce a change and endow the lives of the young women or young men with a sense of meaning and dignity through the symbols of power that are often manipulated and invoked. The rites, however, take a variety of forms because their emphasis differs for girls and boys.

Using the anthropologist Victor Turner's framework, puberty rites have three stages: separation, liminality (relating to a sensory threshold), and incorporation. The importance of the rites lies in the ritual activities that produce a moment of transformation, an ontological (relating to existence) change of the initiate's spiritual, social, biological, and political status. The initiation thus compels the initiate to know intimately her or his "real self" because the rites involve human bodily treatment, decoration, adornment, scarification, and clitoridectomy (surgical removal of the clitoris), most of which are performed by ritual specialists. These activities signify "death" of the former state of existence and "rebirth," a relatively more productive, qualitative, and responsible state in the human life cycle.

Puberty rites involve a period of seclusion when instructions are given. Among some ethnic groups of Sierra Leone in Africa, the Poro (for male) and Sande (for female) societies give such instructions. The instructions are structured around mythic heroines or heroes, sexual activities, and customs and taboos of the community. Such knowledge is important in the adulthood into which the initiate is being incorporated. The rites allow the initiate to continue in the positive flow of life. The process that transforms the initiate into a "new" status involves community feasting with drumming, singing, and dancing.

In Judaism boys—and since the 1960s girls—are expected to have completed a study of important aspects of the Torah (the body of wisdom and law contained in Jewish scripture and other sacred literature and oral tradition) and Talmud (the authoritative body of Jewish tradition) at the age of thirteen. He or she is thus sanctified by the bar mitzvah (son of the commandment) or bat mitzvah (daughter of the commandment) ritual, respectively. After this ritual the boy or girl can be called to recite blessings and lead part of the service in the synagogue.

The Role of the Body

The cultivation of the body of the initiate is central to puberty rites because the body provides access to the sacred and the new status. That is, the body serves as the locus through which the transition, the impartation of knowledge and skills, is made possible. In puberty rites, therefore, the body expresses the ways

PUBERTY RITES IN WEST AFRICA

The following report on puberty rites practiced by the Hausa people of West Africa describes a situation that is fairly common around the world—rites for boys but none for girls.

> **A boy is allowed to play at will until he is seven to nine years of age, when he is circumcised. At this time, as has been indicated, he receives a hut and field of his own. The operation, which marks his entry into the community as a functioning member, is of considerable importance since it is a prerequisite for marriage or any sexual activity, and an uncircumcised boy who dared court a girl would be laughed at. The operation itself is carried out by a Mohammedan barber, and its details are exactly the same for Moslems and for pagans.**
>
> **No ceremony marks the attainment of puberty by a young woman; the occurrence of her first menstruation marks her as no longer a *yarinya*, "girl," but a *budurwa*, "maiden." A period of free dalliance follows for her, ended by marriage which for girls occurs about the age of eighteen, for the boys at about twenty-one. During the earlier period no objections are raised by the parents when sweethearts sleep together. Pregnancy is said to result only rarely; when it does, the boy is subjected to pressure by his own parents to marry the girl.**

***Source*: Greenberg, Joseph H. (1946).**
The Influence of Islam on a Sudanese Religion.
Monographs of the American Ethnological Society, Vol. 10. New York: J.J. Augustin, pp. 23–24.

by which a community's cultural and spiritual values are extolled, understood, and transmitted.

However, puberty rites for both genders revolve around rigorous training that is often expressed in symbolic ritual behavior. For boys activities focus on physical challenges such as being beaten with sticks, fasting, eating dry or disgusting foods, undergoing trials of pain, swimming, dancing wildly, and running.

Body mutilation and scarification—which involve tattooing, scratching or cutting the skin to create a pattern of scars, and circumcision—typify girls' preparation for their transition to adulthood, whereas circumcision typifies preparation for boys. Mutilation of the labia is performed in most parts of Africa, especially among the peoples of Kikuyu in Kenya, Sotho in Lesotho, and Tswana in Botswana and among the Yoruba, Igbo, Ibibio, and Tiv people of Nigeria. Painting with ritual paint and wearing special clothing typify bodily ritual decoration. Girls—and in some cultures boys—paint their bodies with paint, white clay, and sweet-smelling herbs and oils. Among the Akan and Ga people of Ghana the hair of the armpits and pubic area of girls is shaved. The symbolic ritual treatments of the body identify the girl or boy with a particular mythic heroine or hero and represent a cosmic journey, producing in her or him liminality, a state of betwixt and between. The bodies are spiritually, physically, and psychologically prepared for the status that they will soon assume.

Performance

Puberty rites are performed by members of the community or family. In some cultures puberty rites are performed on initiates collectively. In such cases all the initiates in the community are collected and secluded in special houses, female and male separately, for a time. In these houses the remaking of the young women and men takes place to prepare them for their new statuses and new roles in life. In these houses young women and young men receive formal instructions and guidance. In these houses initiates are exposed to culture-bound taboos and break certain taboos that are associated with prepuberty, particularly the taboos about sex. Elderly women initiate young women; elderly men initiate young men. However, certain roles are assigned to opposite-sex elders at some stages in the rites.

In general, the initiatory training includes instructions in the sacred laws of the community, daily life,

PUBERTY RITUALS AND FAMILY TIES

Puberty rituals are a public and often very dramatic mechanism for beginning the process of transforming boys and girls into men and women. But, they are only one part of a complicated process that redefines family and social relations as indicated by this text describing adolescence as experienced by the Mbuti of Central Africa.

> **Only when children approach the age of puberty does the very close family solidarity begin to weaken. Girls fall more under the influence of their mothers; boys, under that of their lineage. At this age also, the sexes are segregated for the first time. Young boys of different families cease following their mothers and sisters and group themselves to organize hunts for rats, mice, and other small slow game in the neighborhood of the camp. Tree climbing is also a favorite sport among the boys. But while the boys become more alienated from their mothers, the young girls continue to be as closely attached to them as ever, though, like the boys, they tend to group together with others of the same age (and older). During this period there is no formal training (Schebesta, 1948, 415 ff.), but boys and girls alike learn all there is to be learned by simple emulation and by assisting their parents and elders in various tasks.**
>
> **At puberty the boys break completely away from their mothers who have no more to do with them, writes Schebesta (1948, 424), than cook their meals. The adolescent girls develop their flirtatious ways, the boys develop their ability as hunters, and thus both prepare themselves for married life.**

***Source*: Turnbull, Colin M. (1965). *The Mbuti Pygmies: An Ethnographic Survey.* American Museum of Natural History, Anthropological Papers *50*, 139—282. New York: American Museum of Natural History, p. 179.**

tribal myths and legends, and human values, including honor, loyalty, respect, and chastity at marriage. The period of training has two stages: the liminal stage, when the initiates are put into seclusion to acquire adult mysteries and ritual dialects; and the incorporation stage, when the initiates make an "outing," a sort of public show. The initiates appear in new clothing to feast and dance with members of their families. They are all reincorporated into the wider community with new personality and identity. Every initiate is given a new name.

Girls' Puberty Rites

As noted, physiological changes, particularly the development of the breasts and menarche, provide some basis for girls' puberty rites in most cultures. The process and elements that are used at initiation carry with them a variety of symbolic meanings, signifying certain physiological facts and processes. A good example are those of the Apaches of North America, whose rites take four days. Planning and rehearsals precede the rites, and a huge amount of food is prepared for the hundreds of people who attend. Also, ritual costumes that the girl will wear—including a wooden staff, decorated and painted in yellow, and a pendant of abalone shell—are prepared. She ties the shell to her hair as a symbol of identity with Changing Woman, the creatress of the Apache community; she keeps the decorated staff all her life.

The rites, which demonstrate a connection between human, spiritual, and natural beings, begin on the first morning at sunrise. As the rites prepare the initiate for marriage and a fruitful life, they evoke the presence and the creative and healing powers of Changing Woman and invoke her blessings on the Apache community, thus renewing it. Dressed in the ritual costume and carrying the wooden staff or sacred cane (she could use either a wooden staff or cane now consecrated to become sacred), the girl is ushered into the dancing ground with songs while facing the rising sun. The songs tell the story of Changing Woman as the girl prays for peace and long life in the name of Changing Woman. Another set of songs recalls the impregnation of Changing Woman by the sun, the process through which the Slayer of Monsters, the foremost western Apache culture hero, was born. The girl then kneels facing the sun and, raising her hands, sways from side to side to receive the fertilizing rays of the sun, personifying the Changing Woman. While the girl lies on a buckskin, her sponsor massages her body, symbolically putting her into the shape of a woman, the shape to which she continues to grow. The girl runs westward and eastward, four times, encircling the wooden staff or sacred cane and invoking health and long life through the stages of life. The rites imbue the girl with the spiritual powers of Changing Woman and transform her from a girl into a woman.

A variety of puberty rites exists among the peoples of Africa. As the Ndembu people of northwestern Zambia initiate a girl into womanhood, Turner notes, the milk tree is the focal symbol of the girl's puberty rites. This tree signifies important aspects of female body imagery such as milk, suckling, breasts and girlish slenderness, and conception because it exudes a white substance. The virtues embedded in the normative aspects of womanhood, motherhood, and the mother-child bond are expected to be acquired by the "novice," who is secluded for several months. The use of the milk tree in the initiation, therefore, symbolizes the girl's future roles, most importantly, as a prospective mother.

Among the Ibibio, Igbo, and Tiv people of Nigeria "fattening houses" are built for girls, who go into seclusion for months. In these houses, they are fed fatty foods, and their bodies are anointed with oil so that they become plump. After their seclusion and a public feasting, the girls paint their bodies with dyes or indigo, and many of them file their teeth. In the fattening houses girls learn about sexual functions and motherhood and the dignity of virginity and chastity at marriage. They also learn songs, dances, the customs of the community, and its myth of origin.

Among the BaMbuti Pygmies of Zaire in Africa, the aborigines in Australia, and the Ulithians in Micronesia, girls undergo instruction in the rudiments of growing up by a female relative, a married member of the community. In some cases female initiates dance for eligible bachelors, announcing their readiness for marriage.

Boys' Puberty Rites

Puberty rites for boys vary from culture to culture. Generally, among African peoples, such rites are conducted when boys are seven to fifteen years old. Circumcision is common, and it is considered a principal element of puberty rites. The operation is performed by the circumciser, who is supported by close family members of the initiate. In some cultures puberty rites are performed collectively, whereas in others rites are performed individually. An initiate is expected to demonstrate a great deal of confidence and endurance in the face of the painful removal of the foreskin of the penis. Circumcision is performed during the wet season, as the dry season is considered harsh on the wound and the heat often causes bleeding of the wound since the circumcision is done without western medical treatment, to reduce pain and bleeding. Adrenaline, found in snail slime which is supposedly recommended by spiritual beings, is applied. In other cases the ritual specialist, circumciser, impersonates ancestral spirits by putting on masks while performing the operation.

Among the Ndembu people, when a group of boys from a cluster of villages approaches puberty, the leaders of the villages hold a rite of circumcision in a camp that is set up for the purpose, and circumcisers are invited. The parents of the boys live in the camp, where a fire is lit and will continue burning for the length of the rites. On this fire the mothers of the boys prepare food for the boys during their seclusion. On the night before the circumcisions people beat drums and dance wildly, led by the circumcisers. The boys are carried from the camp in such a way that they do not touch the ground. The next morning each mother feeds her son a big meal by hand. The boys are grabbed by their fathers and guardians and stripped of their clothes. The boys dash off into the woods, down a newly cut path to the circumcision place, known as "the place of dying." The mothers, chased back into the camp, begin to wail at the announcement of a death. After the operations and some herbal medical treatment, the boys are fed by men and are given beer.

The boys then are secluded in a lodge until their circumcision wounds are healed. During their seclusion they are taught lessons relating to adulthood. Masked dancers beat them with sticks. They are taken to a stream and washed and then sent into the bush to trap animals. Then they return to their parents' camp in painted bodies, disguised in such a manner that their identities are not easily known. The boys return to their villages and participate in adult life.

In other places boys are introduced into secret societies in which they undergo special rites, learn certain secrets, and pass bravery tests. For example, among the Mende people (in Africa), boys are initiated into the Poro society, whereas among the Igbo people, they are initiated into the Mmuo society. Among Hindus the *upanayana* is a ritual introduction to a boy's Vedic (relating to the Hindu sacred writings) guru (teacher).

Recent Attitudes to Puberty Rites

Some practices associated with puberty rites have given way to modernity. Nevertheless, they have not been eliminated because indigenous culture and religiosity have come to mediate life of most indigenous communities. Many practices have been challenged on grounds of cruelty. In recent years religious festivals have replaced elements of puberty rites. The imposition of values and prejudices has also affected practices such as female circumcision, which some people refer to as "female genital mutilation." Nevertheless, puberty rites remain essential elements of many cultures and will continue to have meaning for some time to come.

David Ogungbile

See also Iban; Liminoid; Passage, Rites of; Performance, Ritual of; Purity and Pollution; Ritual as Communication

Further Reading

Awolalu, J. O., & Dopamu, P. A. (1979). *West African traditional religion.* Ibadan, Nigeria: Onibonoje Press.

Basso, K. (1966). The gift of changing woman. *Bulletin of the Bureau of American Ethnology, 196*(76).

Bettelheim, B. (1962). *Symbolic wounds: Puberty rites and the envious male.* New York: Collier.

Brown, J. K. (1963). A cross-cultural study of female initiation rites. *American Anthropologist, 65,* 837–853.

Cohen, Y. A. (1964). *The transition from childhood to adolescence.* Chicago: Aldine.

Cox, J. L. (Ed.). (1998). *Rites of passage in contemporary Africa.* Cardiff, UK: Cardiff Academic Press.

Douglas, M. (1966). *Purity and danger.* New York: Frederick A. Praeger.

Driver, H. E. (1974). Culture element distribution: 16 girls' puberty rites in western North America. In J. G. Jorgenson (Ed.), *Comparative studies by Harold Driver and essays in his honor* (pp. 149–161). New Haven, CT: HRAF Press.

Evans-Pritchard, E. E. (1956). *Nuer religion.* Oxford, UK: Clarendon Press.

Farrer, C. R. (1980). Singing for life: The Mescalero Apache girl's ceremony. In B. Second (Ed.), *Southwestern Indian ritual drama* (pp. 125–159). Albuquerque: University of New Mexico Press.

Frisbie, C. J. (1967). *Kinaaldá: A study of the Navaho girl's puberty ceremony.* Middletown, CT: Wesleyan University Press.

Hoijer, H. (1937). *Mescalero and Chiricahua Apache texts.* Chicago: University of Chicago Press.

Idowu, E. B. (1991). *African traditional religion.* Ibadan, Nigeria: Fountain Publications.

La Fontaine, J. S. (1972). Ritualization of women's life-crises in Bugisu. In J. S. La Fontaine (Ed.), *The interpretation of ritual: Essays in honour of A. I. Richards* (pp. 159–186). London: Tavistock.

Lincoln, B. (1975). The religious significance of women's scarification among the Tiv. *Africa, 45,* 316–326.

Lincoln, B. (1991). *Emerging from the chrysalis: Rituals of women's initiation.* New York: Oxford University Press.

Luckert, K. W. (1977). *Navajo mountain and Rainbow Bridge religion.* Flagstaff: Museum of Northern Arizona.

Ludwig, T. M. (1989). *The sacred paths.* New York: Macmillan.

Olupona, J. K. (Ed.). (1991). *African traditional religions in contemporary society.* St. Paul, MN: Paragon House.

Parrinder, G. E. (1974). *African traditional religion.* London: Sheldon Press.

Sullivan, L. E. (1988). *Icanchu's drum: An orientation to meaning in South American religions.* New York: Macmillan.

Sullivan, L. E. (Ed.). (1989). *Native American religions: North America.* New York: Macmillan.

Sullivan, L. E. (Ed.). (2000). *Native religions and cultures of North America: Anthropology of the sacred.* New York: Continuum International Publishing Group.

Talamantez, I. (2000). In the space between Earth and sky: Contemporary Mescalero Apache ceremonialism. In L. E. Sullivan (Ed.), *Native religions and cultures of North America* (pp. 142–159). New York: Continuum.

Turner, V. W. (1967). *Forest of symbols: Aspects of Ndembu ritual.* Ithaca, NY: Cornell University Press.

Turner, V. W. (1969). *The ritual process.* Chicago: Aldine.

Turner, V. W. (1989). Symbols in African ritual. In A. C. Lehmann & J. E. Myers (Eds.), *Magic, witchcraft and religion: An anthropological study of the supernatural* (pp. 55–63). Mountain View, CA: Mayfield.

Van Gennep, A. (1960). *Rites of passage.* Chicago: University of Chicago Press.

Zuesse, E. M. (1979). *Ritual cosmos: The sanctification of life in African religions.* Athens: Ohio University Press.

Purity and Pollution

Dirt is matter that is out of place, according to anthropologist Mary Douglas. Every society manages matter and assigns values to persons, actions, places, objects, and substances, determining those that are pure and those that are defiling. Frequently societies associate these values with a transcendental or sacred plane of existence, formulating religious proscriptions against certain matter, that is, taboos, and prescriptions to remedy pollution, namely, rituals of purification.

Varieties of Pollution

Every society maintains complex, usually unwritten, rules to denote which persons, actions, places, objects, and substances are understood to be defiling or polluting. Examples from Western society may demonstrate how precisely and tacitly people define pollution. Lovers come into contact with bodily fluids of their beloved. Saliva, for instance, is exchanged in kissing; however, one lover would not spit into a cup and expect the other lover to drink it. This fluid is not necessarily understood to be defiling in itself, but the action or manner of its exchange is. Another instance is tears and clear nasal discharge; both are roughly the same liquid, but the origins of one makes it more acceptable to touch, whereas the origins of the other make it not acceptable to touch. A third instance involves the activity of blowing one's nose. In the Western world people deposit nasal discharge into a piece of paper or cloth and carry it around with them. This seems as peculiar to other societies as it would to Westerners if they encountered a community whose members kept in their pockets other bodily discharges or excrements. Because purity and pollution taboos are socially constructed, one society's pollution can be another's purity, or vice versa.

Indian Hinduism maintains rules about pollution that apply to persons as well as things. The complex social hierarchy, believed to be one's unchangeable lot in life *(dharma)*—with the Brahman caste at the top and the untouchable Dalit caste at the bottom—is related to things that pollute. The Dalits are employed in burying the dead, slaughtering animals, and cleaning toilets and refuse, thus rendering them in a perpetual state of pollution by their coming into contact with polluting things. Brahmans are forbidden to have physical contact with the untouchables, which precludes intermarriage between castes or even a Brahman's receiving cooked food from Dalits.

In varying degrees the so-called People of the Book (adherents of Judaism, Christianity, and Islam) maintain notions of purity and pollution that they have inherited from each other. Proscriptions and prescriptions originated, through a process of historical development, in Judaism. Developed over centuries, Jewish purity laws have two concerns: (1) distinguishing the southern Hebrew kingdom of Judah from the pagan world (primarily through the laws of the book of Deuteronomy that developed after the Assyrian invasion of the northern kingdom of Israel in the eighth century BCE) and (2) preventing another catastrophic disruption of Judah such as had occurred during the invasion of Judah by the Mesopotamian King Nebuchadnezzar, whose forced exile of the Hebrews is known as the Babylonian Captivity (primarily through the priestly laws of the book of Leviticus that developed in the sixth century BCE and after). When Judah came under the imperial regime (in quick succession) of Babylon, Persia, Greece, and, finally, Roman, the Jews were preoccupied with managing to maintain their religious identity and to preserve some degree of political integrity. These laws include moral proscriptions (e.g., controlling sexual relations and diet) and prescriptions (e.g., pertaining to sin offerings) as well as ritual purity laws (e.g., pertaining to definitions of ritual purity, identification of polluting matter, and rituals for restoring purity). By the time of the Jews' subjugation under the Roman Empire, some Jews felt that the religious establishment in Jerusalem was not sufficiently scrupulous about adhering to these laws. The Pharisees (members of a Jewish sect noted for strict observance of rites), for instance, felt that the laws applied with equal vigor to all Jews, not just to the scribes and priests. Even more radical, the Essenes (the community that produced the Dead Sea Scrolls) physically separated themselves from the Jerusalem religious establishment, isolated themselves in the wilderness, practiced sexual segregation and perhaps celibacy, maintained a strict set of purity laws, rejected any member who violated the laws, and practiced ritual

PURITY AND POLLUTION IN CHINESE POPULAR RELIGION

The extract of ethnographic text below describing Chinese popular religion on Taiwan shows how the beliefs about purity and pollution influence ritual behavior.

Probably the major theme which runs throughout the folk religion is the ritual separation of elements which are believed to be pure or polluting; between those which are life oriented and those which are concerned with death; between yang and yin. The systematic nature of beliefs relating to this dichotimization bears on many aspects of belief and activity, and exhibits a remarkable conformity, and an unusually persuasive or even coercive character.

These considerations not only order the religious world, but determine the kinds of ritual service that may be offered by different temples. Because of the separation of pure and polluting elements in theory, rituals directed to yin and yang beings are separated in temple life. In practice, this results in a distinctiveness of temple types, with each type specializing in certain kinds of services. It is this fact, rather than the religious affiliation of the temple, which determines the kinds of ritual services that the temple will offer. It is the pervasiveness of this dichotimization, cutting across each of the major religions, which proves the existence of an underlying stratum of ideology and belief in the folk religion. Temples everywhere are subject to the restrictions imposed by the community of believers and as a result no temples can offer a full and complete set of services for the community. As a result, each temple type is dependent upon the others rather than competing with them, and may be seen as forming one component in a total system of belief.

The distinction between yin and yang, pure and polluted, is as important for understanding the religious picture, as is the separation between private and public, family and community interests; it is not altogether congruent with them, however, and deserves separate treatment. A thorough examination of life and death parameters will not only assist in an understanding of temple types, but also in a classification of spirits, rituals and priests as well.

***Source*: Chesley, Philip *B. Religion in a Chinese Town.* (1975). Taipei, Taiwan: Chinese Association for Folklore, pp. 136–137.**

baths. It is speculated that John the Baptist may have been an Essene or influenced by them and that his ritual immersion in the Jordan River was derived from their purification rites.

Christianity in one sense distinguished itself from Judaism by rejecting the Levitical laws and many of the Deuteronomic laws. Jesus of Nazareth himself differentiated between divine moral law and human ritual law. In his famous parable of the Good Samaritan, all of the conventionally religious people avoided the injured traveler because they were on their way to Jerusalem and did not want to risk becoming ritually impure by contact with his body or his blood. It is the pariah Samaritan who behaves compassionately and thus deserves to be called "neighbor." Within the early Christian community conflicts arose between Judaizers (those who believed that disciples of Christ must also be observant Jews) and Hellenizers (those who believed that Christian discipleship is separate from Jewish religion). Nonetheless, Christianity developed its own set of purity concerns. Married clergy were enjoined to abstain from sexual intercourse at certain times, and all Christians were prohibited from illicit sexual relations. Clerical and monastic celibacy represents anxiety about sexual defilement. Misogynist (relating to a hatred of women) writings and practices viewed women as perennially defiling; for example, women had to be purified before they returned to church after giving birth, and their physical presence in sacred spaces was carefully regulated.

Islamic religious law *(shari'a)*, based on the Qur'an (the book of sacred writings accepted by Muslims as revelations made to Muhammad by Allah) and oral

Hindu men participate in ritual bathing to purify themselves in the Ganges River in Varanasi, India in 1996. COURTESY OF STEPHEN G. DONALDSON PHOTOGRAPHY.

Worshippers replace their everyday footwear with clean slippers before entering a Buddhist temple in Shanghai, China, in 2002. COURTESY OF KAREN CHRISTENSEN.

tradition codified in custom *(hadith)*, maintains dietary and purity proscriptions. Muslims are prohibited from eating the blood of animals, pork, animals that have not been slain with the invocation of the name of Allah, animals that have been killed by strangling, by a violent blow or by an accident, or that use their paws to kill and consume other animals. (Exceptions are made if no other food is available in order to sustain life.) Similarly, intoxicants are forbidden. Sexual intercourse, menstruation, and childbirth constitute polluting activities and substances *(najas)* that require purification.

Rituals of Purification

Although specific rituals differ among societies, there are many common forms of ritual purification, including washing, abjection or expulsion, fire, ingestion, and prayer.

Muslims are to prepare for daily prayer by washing their faces and hands and arms up to the elbow, washing their heads and their feet up to the ankles *(wudu)*, and, if ritually impure, bathing their whole bodies *(ghusl)*. Just as accommodations are made to dietary laws (small amounts of unclean food may be eaten when clean food is not available), so, too, ritual law: In the absence of water (such as in the desert), sand will suffice. Indian Hindus periodically bathe in the Ganges River to cleanse ritual impurity. The preeminent Christian sacrament, baptism, is a ritual designed to cleanse the believer from the most primal pollution, the ontological (relating to existence) impurity of original sin.

Acts of violence or forceful repelling characterize common purification rituals. Ritual sacrifices that entail slaying of a sacrificial animal constitute many purification rites, as do fasting from food, abstaining from certain kinds of food (e.g., consuming only bread and water), performing penitential acts (e.g., committing self-flagellation), and exiling offending members of a community. The ritual scapegoat employs this logic in that an animal is burdened with the sins of the community and cast out of the community's presence. Criminal executions are another form of purification that until modern times was performed quite publicly in a spectacle of communal abjection.

Sacrifices that are consumed by fire represent another element in the economy of purification. Fire can be used as well to eliminate dangerous or polluting substances and persons. The ancient practice of burning witches or heretics and the modern practice of protesters' burning an effigy, a flag, or other such symbol are instances of this ritual.

Some rituals of purification include ingestion of substances held to be sacred, such as a sacred herb or plant. The Jewish Passover meal and its Christian descendant, the Lord's Supper or Holy Communion, are rituals designed to impart holiness onto those who consume the sacred elements.

Although no ritual is performed without some intentional prayer, prayer by itself can constitute a purification rite. This is particularly the case in Western Christianity, with its emphasis on sacred texts and literacy and, in its Protestant forms, a suspicion of ritual. The Catholic sacrament of confession entails verbal confession of sins and a prayer of repentance (followed by the priest's prescription of penitential acts or prayers as reparation). During the Middle Ages, before battle knights were permitted to confess to their horses if no priest was available because warriors needed to be purified of sin before a fight that they might not survive.

Theories of Pollution and Purification

Although pollution proscriptions and purity prescriptions differ among cultures, some similarities exist. Generally speaking, in most cultures purity is not viewed as "contagious," although pollution is. A pure person can become polluted by contact with the impure but cannot restore purity simply by contact with any pure person or substance. Although cultures differ on what precisely constitutes the impure and what ritual measures can restore purity, most seem to have concepts of purity and pollution. As an observable fact, therefore, what is the meaning of pollution and purification rituals? Their phenomenology (the philosophical study of all appearances of a phenomenon) has received considerable attention from philosophers, scholars of religion, and anthropologists.

For Mircea Eliade (1907–1986, the Romanian-born historian of religion whose later career at the University of Chicago initiated a new era of religious studies in the United States) all religious discourses are an attempt to recapture the purity of creation's origins, with religious rituals recovering that original moment, what Eliade called "*in illo tempore*" (that is, "in that time" when the gods created the world). Analyzing ancient Persian new year's practices, he concluded that the last day of the year represented a kind of end of time, with the new year a symbolic beginning of time. He pointed out that end-of-year rituals in the ancient world included temporary social chaos (such as the Saturnalia festival in which servants became masters for a day) that symbolized the chaotic decline of the old world. These were sometimes accompanied by discarding or extinguishing (burning fuel, putting out old fires, consuming harvests) as a symbolic rejection of the old.

In a phenomenological study of the symbolism of evil Paul Ricoeur (Eliade's philosopher colleague at the University of Chicago) analyzed religious symbols more broadly. For example, pollution is the primary symbol of evil; it is typically symbolized as stain, and it represents a dread of divine vengeance as punishment for the violation of a taboo. Primordial taboos are sexual, but sexual transgressions are also related to violence and murder because they both entail penetration, bodily fluids, and frenzy. Sex and violence are disruptions in the normal order of things and require ritual absolution to restore that order. Ricoeur asserts that in most societies taboos are not understood as sins as much as they are understood as representing concentrations of sacred power. Thus incest is taboo, not because it is inherently sinful, but, rather, because it entails proximity to sacred power that is too dangerous for most mortals (thus explaining why royalty in the ancient world were permitted incestuous marriages: members of royalty were already gods). The association of moral transgression (sin) with taboo is characteristic of Judaism, for which transgressions offend God rather than rival him.

Critical theorist Georges Bataille undertook to deconstruct (that is, show the inherent contradictions and ideological foundations of) Western religion's polar oppositions of the sacred and the profane by revealing the economic and political dimensions of that opposition. In his phenomenological analysis, Bataille observed that humans are the only animals who hide the evidence of nature, particularly in their sexual discharges (such as semen or menstrual blood) and digestive excretion (urine and feces). He rejected the distinction between "civilized" modern societies and "primitive" tribal societies because they both share a disgust for the natural condition. Bataille discerned the social dimensions of purity laws and rituals by noting that those people in a society who protect themselves most vigorously from pollution are usually those who have the greatest prestige in a society and the resources to maintain their ritual purity (i.e., it is easier for the wealthy and powerful to maintain or to restore purity). Purity and pollution construct social classes, such as those of the Hindu caste system, and these classes are self-perpetuating.

In an anthropological analysis Mary Douglas similarly emphasized the social capital inherent in systems of purity, pollution, and purification. She has asserted that proscriptions and prescriptions denote a person's status and preserve social order by defining anything "disorderly" as "dirty" (matter that is out of place). For Douglas, physical pollution is a threat because it transgresses the margins of the body; because societies often understand themselves, by analogy, as a body, this threat is not only to the individual but also to the whole "body politic." Douglas distinguishes four kinds of pollutions: those that threaten external boundaries, those that threaten the system internally, those that threaten from the margins of a society, and those whose internal contradictions are threatening. Societies manage these threats in two apparently contradictory ways: either by permitting transgression under regulated conditions (e.g., Saturnalia, Mardi Gras, carnival) or by avoiding transgression under any circumstances (e.g., Hindu caste system, Jewish dietary laws, Islamic Taharah, purity, codes).

For the contemporary French critical theorist Julia Kristeva the Self is defined by selecting and abjecting (or expelling) a *not-Self,* a psychosocial process by which individuals and groups establish who they are (by expelling who they are not). Ambiguity, confused or transgressed rules, and hybrids are psychically intolerable and therefore rendered "impure."

Bruce Lincoln, professor of humanities and religious studies at the University of Minnesota, provides a semiotic (relating to a general philosophical theory of signs and symbols that deals with their function in both artificially constructed and natural languages) analysis of millennial antinomianism. Antinomianism (meaning literally "against law") is the belief that one has transcended secular or religious laws, either because one is a special case (e.g., the saved or the elect) or because one is living at a time of dispensation from those laws, such as the End Times known as The Millennium. Examining a point in the Spanish Civil War during the 1930s when republican Loyalists desecrated Roman Catholic churches and religious artifacts, Lincoln contends that such antinomianism is a threshold moment during which "no law" replaces "old law" as a preparation for imminent "new law." Such direct opposition between an old order and a new order entails "rituals of collective obscenity," deliberately defiling and polluting activities.

Research Directions

Scholarly study of purity and pollution is likely to move away from a strict "hermeneutics [the study of the methodological principles of interpretation] of suspicion" model that dominated religious studies in the twentieth century (in which every religious behavior is considered a form of social control) to a model that attempts to understand these phenomena on their own terms. In addition, the tendency to distinguish between "primitive" and "modern" societies is likely to become even less useful because both demonstrate analogous behaviors. Similarly, the distinction between "sacred" and "profane" becomes less clear, and purity rules will be seen as more complex.

Thomas L. Long

See also Birth Rituals

Further Reading

Bashford, A. (1998). *Purity and pollution: Gender, embodiment, and Victorian medicine.* New York: Palgrave.

Choksy, J. (1989). *Purity and pollution in Zoroastrianism: Triumph over evil.* Austin: University of Texas Press.

Crocker, C. (1973). Ritual and the development of social structure: Liminality and inversion. In J. D. Shaughnessy (Ed.), *The roots of ritual* (pp. 47–86). Grand Rapids, MI: William B. Eerdmans.

Douglas, M. (1966). *Purity and danger: An analysis of the concepts of pollution and taboo.* London: Routledge.

Durkheim, E. (1995). *The elementary forms of religious life* (K. E. Fields, Trans.). New York: Free Press.

Eliade, M. (1959). *Cosmos and history: The myth of the eternal return* (W. R. Trask, Trans.). New York: Harper.

Eliade, M. (1959). *The sacred and the profane: The nature of religion* (W. R. Trask, Trans.). New York: Harcourt, Brace, and World.

Frazier, J. G. (1950). *The golden bough: A study in magic and religion.* New York: Macmillan.

Kristeva, J. (1982). *Powers of horror: An essay on abjection* (L. S. Roudiez, Trans.). New York: Columbia University Press.

Lincoln, B. (1989). *Discourse and the construction of society: Comparative studies of myth, ritual, and classification.* Oxford, UK: Oxford University Press.

Long, T. (2000). Defilement. In R. Landes (Ed.), *Encyclopedia of millennialism and millennial movements.* New York: Routledge.

Ricoeur, P. (1967). *The symbolism of evil* (E. Buchanan, Trans.). Boston: Beacon Press.

R

Ramadan

The rituals of the Islamic month of Ramadan are regulated by Islamic law (shari'a), which jurists *(fuqaha')* base on the Qur'an (the book of sacred writings accepted by Muslims as revelations made to the Prophet Muhammad by God), Hadith (a narrative record of the sayings or customs of the Prophet Muhammad and his companions), tradition (what the Prophet Muhammad said and did), and *ijma'*(general consensus of the early Islamic community).

In the Islamic calendar Ramadan is considered to be the most sacred and blessed month. It is the only month mentioned in the Qur'an (Chapter 2:18). This is the month when the Qur'an was revealed to the Prophet Muhammad and when God's graces are easily accessible. Some poets have called it metaphorically the "king of all months" and the "rose flower." Ramadan is the ninth month of the Islamic calendar. The word *Ramadan* comes from the root *r-m-d* meaning "great heat," which suggests in what season the month used to fall in the solar calendar. In pre-Islamic times it was considered a month of truce. Fighting was prohibited during this month. This tradition was retained in the religion of Islam.

In order to be a Muslim, one must observe five pillars of Islam. Fasting (*sawm* or *siyam*) in the month of Ramadan constitutes the fourth pillar and is obligatory to every Muslim who has reached puberty *(baligh)* and is capable of making rational judgments *('aqil)*. Children, old people, and those who are sick and physically weak are exempt from this obligation. Travelers who undertake journeys lasting more than three days and pregnant women are also exempt from fasting during Ramadan, although they must make up the lost days later in the year. Those Muslims who do not observe fasting without having a legitimate excuse must pay penance *(kaffara)* by feeding thirty poor people for each day of fasting.

The month of Ramadan begins with the appearance of the new moon. Islamic jurists maintain that the moon must have been seen with the naked eye by a Muslim of a good and truthful character *('adl)*. If the moon is not sighted on the twenty-eighth day of the month of Sh'aban, which is the month before Ramadan, the month of Sh 'aban' may be extended to twenty-nine or thirty days.

Fasting consists of not eating, drinking, or smoking from sunrise to sunset. During fasting one is not supposed to commit any sins. A man is allowed to visit his wife only at night. A person must begin his or her fast by saying a formula that expresses the intention of fasting. Early in the morning before sunrise, he or she eats a meal *(sahur, sahri)* and breaks the fast *(iftar)* with something small to eat, usually dates, as the Prophet Muhammad did.

Several days in the month of Ramadan elevate its importance. The sixth day is the birthday of Husayn bin 'Ali, the grandson of the Prophet Muhammad; the tenth day is the day of death of Khadija, the first wife of the Prophet Muhammad. On the seventh day Muslims fought the Battle of Badr against Meccan unbelievers in Saudi Arabia. On the nineteenth day Muslims were finally able to conquer Mecca, and the twentieth day is the anniversary of the death of 'Ali, the cousin and son-in-law of the Prophet Muhammad and also the fourth caliph of the Islamic community.

RAMADAN IN NIGERIA

The following ethnographic account describes how Ramadan was celebrated in a Muslim village of the Kanuri people of northern Nigeria.

> The month of Ramadan (April 2 to May 1, in 1957) is spent in fasting. During that time neither food nor water is taken into the mouth from sunrise to sunset. All Kanuri above the age of fifteen or sixteen keep the fast. For several years before that boys and girls keep a modified fast, in which three days of fasting are followed by nine days in which the fast is not observed. In Geidam all Kanuri outwardly keep the fast, although it was admitted that there were Kanuri who drank water in secret. In Maiduguri there are Kanuri who eat openly in the market-place during Ramadan, but Geidam is too small a town for anyone to violate religious custom so blatantly. As Ramadan in 1957 fell in the hottest and most uncomfortable time of the year, fasting, and in particular abstaining from drinking, is very demanding. Most people radically alter their schedules. During Ramadan they customarily rise at 3 A.M. at the call of a waker, pray and drink something and then remain up doing their work until sunrise (6 A.M.). They then work for an additional two or three hours until the sun is high in the sky, when they retire to sleep until three or four in the afternoon. From four until sunset (6:45 P.M.) people again work, and the women pound and grind millet. At sunset the Ladan calls to announce the end of the day's fast. People then drink quantities of a porridge made of millet and soured milk (balam). At ten or eleven in the evening people eat the one hearty meal of the day. Activities such as visiting, chatting and strolling continue on into the night. During Ramadan, the entire daily schedule is shifted so that people sleep through the hottest hours of the day, work during the cooler periods at sunrise and at sunset, break the fast with a light meal which is followed by a heavy meal some hours later, and spend much of the night in leisure activities. In actual fact little work is accomplished in this month.
>
> As the sun set on Tuesday, April 30th, everyone looked closely for the new moon which would mark the beginning of the new month and the end of the fast. The sky was slightly cloudy and the sliver of the new moon could not be distinguished. The following day, therefore, would once again be a fast day. However, two boys came to the Alkali and swore on the Koran that they had seen the moon. In addition, it was announced over the radio that the moon had been seen in Enugu, so that the fast of Ramadan was in fact ended. Wednesday, instead of a fast day, was the festive Ngumari Ashembe (Ashem means fast), the great festival marking the end of Ramadan.

Source: Rosman, Abraham. (1966).
Social Structure and Acculturation among the Kanuri of Northern Nigeria.
Ann Arbor, University Microfilms, pp. 188–190.

Most importantly, the Night of Power *(laylat al-qadr)* is considered the sacred night. It is commonly said to fall on the twenty-seventh day of the month, but authorities are not unanimous. "Night of Power" is also the name of the ninety-seventh chapter of the Qur'an, in which it is called a night "better than one thousand months." All Muslims, even those who are not particular in the observance of religious duties, make certain not to miss prayer on that night. Pious Muslims can be seen standing in prayers the whole night and asking forgiveness for their sins.

During Ramadan, prayer is held every night *(salat al-tarawih).* Prayer consists of twenty or thirty-two *raka'at* (the ritual of prayer that includes standing while reciting the chapters of the Qur'an, bowing, prostrating, and sitting). Generally, the imam (prayer leader) who has committed the Qur'an to memory recites its portions in this prayer and makes certain that the whole Qur'an is recited completely by the twenty-seventh or the last night prayer of Ramadan. The silver of the new moon ends the month of Ramadan. The next day, fasting of the month of

Ramadan *('id al-fitr)* is celebrated. Thus, Ramadan is for Muslims the month of fasting, praying, intensive purification, and sole devotion to God.

Husain Kassim

See also Islam

Further Reading

Ali, A. Y. (1989). *The holy Qur'an (text, translation and commentary)*. Brentwood, MD: Amana.

Lane, E. W. (1966). *Manners and customs of the modern Egyptians*. New York: Dutton.

Schimmel, A. (2001). *Das islamische Jahr: Zeiten und Feste* [The Islamic year: Times and celebrations]. Munich, Germany: Beck.

Rastafari

Rastafari has been described as a religion, a subculture, and a social movement. Most adherents of Rastafari prefer the term *livity* to describe the totality of their worldview and cultural practices, contending that Rastafari is a way of life informed by theocratic principles. Many Rastafari reject the term "Rastafarianism," arguing that *-isms* imply doctrines and schisms, whereas the term "Rastafari" implies a living testament. Because "belief" implies doubt to most Rastafari, individuals are encouraged to seek the truth for themselves, reasoning that "to know is to know." Rastafari have various communal and spiritual processes that facilitate knowing who God is. One process is reasoning, another is chanting Nyahbinghi.

Rastafari proclaim Emperor Haile Selassie I of Ethiopia (1892–1975) as the living God, Jah Rastafari. A corollary that words—or sounds—are alive and are charged with energy is expressed in the concept of "word-sound-power," which is also central to Rastafari knowing. How Rastafari work with word-sound-power is part of their ritual expression, although Rastafari themselves do not use the term *ritual* to refer to any of their cultural practices.

Rastafari also proclaim that under Haile Selassie's divine guidance, Africans whose ancestors were forcibly stolen from Africa to be enslaved in Babylon (the oppressive society of the West) have the right of repatriation to Africa. For the Rastafari, Africa in general and Ethiopia in particular is Zion. The true home of all black people and the origin of life and of civilization, Zion is considered the source of power invested with redemptive significance—a meaning that the Rastafari counterpose to Babylon—defined as the postcolonial diaspora of the West and the white power structure which has historically enslaved, oppressed, and brutalized African peoples. *Zion* or *Africa* is thus frequently construed in a less literal way to mean repatriation to one's African identity and African culture, even while living in the Babylonian diaspora. Although Rastafari have developed elaborate ceremonial complexes (large-scale gatherings of community that last for three or seven days and that mark the liminal status of participants as "sojourners" in Babylon) and less complicated ritual forms (greetings and other speech acts that similarly mark the identity of participants), one of the major goals of ritual behavior, whether on an individual or a collective level, is to mediate the dynamic tension between Babylon and Zion.

The theme of repatriation to Africa courses through the history of Africans in the diaspora. Rastafari from its inception has worked to achieve repatriation. As a result Rastafari has always had an international orientation, even though it originated in the early 1930s in Jamaica, where a handful of founding figures took the coronation of Haile Selassie I of Ethiopia on 2 November 1930 to be the fulfillment of prophecy. Ideologically Rastafari built upon the foundations of Ethiopianism, Garveyism, and pan-Africanism. The fact that Ethiopia had never been colonized was central to the philosophy of the Ethiopian Independent Church Movement in Africa, known as Ethiopianism. And, it was through the philosophy of biblically based Ethiopianism, that English-speaking diasporic blacks first encountered dignified and human depictions of themselves as Africans; and through Garveyism and pan-Africanism that they articulated the ideas of "a black god for a black people" and the principle of the unity and common destiny of all black peoples wherever they may be domiciled. Rastafari also exhibits some continuities with the worldview and practices of Jamaican folk society. With respect to Afro-Jamaican traditions, for example, Rastafari was influenced by Kumina, a form of ancestor worship involving drumming, dancing, and singing that was carried to Jamaica by post-Emancipation indentured laborers of Central African origins.

Although Rastafari cultural forms developed locally in Jamaica, since the mid-1970s Rastafari has become a global phenomenon on a scale beyond the impact that Rastafari traveling as individuals could make. This globalization of Rastafari occurred first through the medium of reggae music and second through the organized efforts of Rastafari elders who increasingly traveled internationally to teach about the more orthodox forms of Rastafari cultural expression. A series of international Rastafari gatherings and conferences, beginning in 1982, also facilitated its dissemination. At present Rastafari communities exist throughout the Caribbean and circum-Caribbean, North America, the United Kingdom and other European countries, several countries in South America and Africa, Japan, the Pacific, and New Zealand. In addition, diasporic Rastafari have been steadily repatriating to countries in Africa.

Rastafari, having evolved in the Jamaican social context, has had to adjust to local conditions elsewhere, with different histories, politics, and cultural practices. As a result it is extremely difficult to generalize about the role of ritual in Rastafarian *livity*. Furthermore, Rastafari as a social movement has always been noted for its heterogeneity and decentralization. Within Rastafari are different ideological orientations (Houses), and within each House more than one leader (elder) might speak for the orientation. The Twelve Tribes of Israel, the House of Nyahbinghi, the Ethiopia Africa Black International Congress (also known as the Boboshanti), and the Church of Haile Selassie I are Rastafari organizations with an international presence. Many Rastafari belong to the Ethiopian Orthodox Church as well as the Ethiopian World Federation, both of which have several branches in the diaspora. In addition, there are local and regional Rastafarian organizations. Finally, many Rastafari do not belong to any group at all.

This internal diversity creates difficulties in making assumptions about the homogeneity of Rastafarian ritual. Most Rastafari, however, are familiar with reasoning as a dialogical art form and with chanting Nyahbinghi as an act of collective worship. Moreover, at the 1983 International Rastafari Conference in Jamaica it was resolved by the international Rastafari delegates in attendance that the House of Nyahbinghi would be accepted as the foundational orthodoxy of Rastafari.

Reasoning: Communion of the Herbs and the Chalice

Rastafari has made extensive use of written texts such as the Bible and the writings of Jamaican black nationalist leader Marcus Garvey, other pan-Africanists, and Haile Selassie. Since the mid-1970s, an extensive amount of material generated by Rastafari themselves has become available in the form of recordings, books, newspapers, videos, and many ephemera (things having no lasting value). The early foundational texts of Rastafari (such as *The Holy Piby* and *The Promised Key*), out of print for decades, have been reissued in the past ten years due to the publishing efforts of Rastafari themselves. The speeches of Haile Selassie and his autobiography have similarly become more widely available through reprints. However, although it is far easier today to know about Rastafari, individuals are still encouraged to engage in reasoning and in chanting Nyahbinghi in order to know Rastafari in its fullest sense.

Rastafari assert that theirs is an inborn conception, meaning that because one is Rastafari from birth this self-knowledge simply needs to be awakened in one. Thus, meditation (an individual act) and reasoning (a collective act) can be used for revelatory purposes. Although reasoning can incorporate textual knowledge, it is based on the social dynamics of oral culture and facilitates the development of experiential knowledge. Thus, in a sense, reasoning, based on the spoken word, compliments, extends, and especially tests knowledge based on the printed word.

Reasoning is a form of exploratory discourse predicated upon certain assumptions learned only through experience. Participants take as much time to express themselves as they feel is necessary, even if they reason all night. Some Rastafari say that when the pagans sleep, the saints walk, meaning that the night hours have a special significance because one is more easily protected from Babylonian influences, although reasoning can occur at any time of the day or night. One does not interrupt when someone is reasoning, except at certain acknowledged junctures, and then only through stylized interventions (e.g., phrases such as "I pray thee.")

Reasoning by nature is cooperative, not competitive. Participants should reach a consensus on the subject at hand, which could range from an article in the newspaper to the question of Haile Selassie's divinity. Because reasoning is at once disciplined and flexible, participants are encouraged to use inspiration as well as logic to resolve questions.

In the context of wider Caribbean speech acts, reasoning could be considered a highly stylized verbal art form, with experienced participants acquiring a recognized status as inspired interlocutors, Reasoning is not, however, pursued as a secular activity. On the contrary, reasoning activates the concept of word-sound-power, the idea that the power of the Creator is embodied in man through "living sound," while at the same time being central to the Rastafarian sacrament: the use of cannabis or "holy herbs" in a chalice, which is a water pipe, as a form of communion. The ingestion of holy herbs facilitates access to the visionary experience of inspiration, which is so valued in the reasoning process.

There is a whole set of implicit understandings that serves to mediate the boundary between the sacred and the profane, between Zion and Babylon respectively. This includes the specific comportment of the body in terms of appropriate greetings, the style in which one uncovers one's dreadlocks, and the respectful way in which individuals incorporate themselves into the assembly. Coupled with these behaviors, the act of reasoning itself—which includes the ritual preparation, blessing and consumption of herbs—serves to constitute the ground of the sacred. These enactments constitute a process of sanctification that effects the transition from the realm of Babylon to that of Zion.

Depending upon the proclivities of the resident elder or the person who controls the space where communion takes place, there may be some variation within the pattern outlined below. After cleaning, the herbs are carefully cut and kneaded on a special board reserved for that purpose. A decision is made on whether to add tobacco or to be strictly *ital* (natural). The main parts of the chalice, which are the water container, usually made from horn, bamboo, or coconut, and the *cuchi* (clay bowl) that holds the herbs are cleaned as well. Water is added. A small stone known as the 'gritty' is placed in the *cuchi* to prevent the herbs that are added to it from falling through while leaving enough space for air to pass. The *cuchi* is inserted into the water bowl, and then the water level is checked by drawing air through a tube that is attached to the chalice. The chalice has now been "set up."

At this point, the resident or ranking elder (or an individual they designate) will undertake to bless the chalice. If the male participants engaged in this act have not already done so, they will doff the knitted caps or "crowns" that cover their locks and allow them to cascade to about their shoulders and torsos. This act communicates the opening up of the physical temple (body) of participants to the inspiration of Jah Rastafari, the Father and Godhead. Just as the holy herbs is seen as sacra that facilitates communication with Zion, so too are the long knotted and matted locks on the "heavens" (head) of the Rastafari seen as "telepathic antennae which facilitate communication from earth to Zion." Depending upon the perceived importance of the moment, those assembled for a reasoning might stand or sit as the chalice is blessed. And this blessing will typically entail an assortment of Psalms and other passages from the Bible. Whatever the specific content of the blessing, it is intended to emphasize the understanding that those present are potentially vessels of divine communication and inspiration. The principle frequently expressed is that "One cannot go to the Father (Jah) except through the Son; nor to the Son except through the Father."

After the chalice has been blessed, one of the participants will tear a piece of paper from the bag containing the herbs, light it and use it as a torch with which to light the chalice. Traditionally, the chalice is "brought up" with a series of quick shallow puffs followed by one long draught, which is deeply inhaled and released. This procedure is repeated based on the proverbial understanding that "a bird cannot fly on one wing." The chalice is then passed clockwise. Several considerations govern the passage of the chalice among the people assembled. Such groups tend to be exclusively male. Because blessing and lighting the chalice are a privilege, some thought goes into choosing a person to do this. Usually the resident elder is chosen. After it is lit, the chalice is passed around, to the left, across the heart. Each person has a characteristic way of taking a draw, to control both the inhalation and release of smoke. Sometimes the draw is so deep that the herbs catch fire and sparks fly off, occasioning comments such as "fire burn Babylon." At other times the user might be enveloped in smoke. The chalice might be emptied and refilled several times during a reasoning. When the reasoning is finished, everything is cleaned and put up in a safe place.

Nyahbinghi: Giving *Ises* and Chanting Down Babylon

The term *Nyahbinghi* derives from a Rwandan anti-colonial religious movement from the second half of the nineteenth century. The concept of Nyahbinghi subsequently was identified with Haile Selassie's resistance in exile during the Italian occupation of Ethiopia in 1935. Rastafari came to understand the term *Nyahbinghi* as meaning "death to black and white oppressors." Inspired by the spirit of

Nyahbinghi resistance, over time Rastafari developed a ritual Nyahbinghi complex in which the term Nyahbinghi has accreted various meanings. In addition to its original meaning related to racial protest, the term Nyahbinghi came to identify the drums made and played by the Rastafari, the music composed on these drums in praise to Jah Rastafari, as well as the form of spiritual dancing done to this music. Nyabinghi also identifies the three or seven day ceremonial complex of island-wide gatherings at which Rastafari brethren and sistren assemble to worship Jah. This complex consists of giving *ise*s (praises) to Jah Rastafari by chanting, spiritual dancing, and testifying, as well as chanting down Babylon through word-sound-power. Chanting down Babylon is intended to generate spiritual energy in the form of earthforce (lightening, thunder, and earthquake), which is seen to cause the downfall of the oppressive forces of Babylon. Dancing Nyahbinghi or chanting Nyahbinghi is generally recognized as a spiritually energizing and purifying practice in Rastafari although not all Rastafari claim an affiliation with the House of Nyahbinghi as a social formation.

Nyahbinghis are complex affairs that involve considerable planning and resources. Nyahbinghi celebrations are organized around Rastafari holy days such as 23 July, the birthday of Emperor Haile Selassie, and 2 November, the coronation of Haile Selassie. They are usually held outside of a city in the hills or on some other rural venue removed from the perceived ambient influences of Babylon. Because the site chosen is considered a refuge from Babylon, a Nyahbinghi ground is a marked site and security measures are taken to protect its perimeter. Entrée to such a compound is typically marked by specially constructed gates or banners as well as a large bonfire (also referred to as a judgment fire) that burns outside the entryway to the tabernacle. People entering the site are expected to conduct themselves accordingly by abstaining from polluting behaviors such as eating flesh.

On the site a circular tabernacle is constructed around a five- or seven-sided altar. Whereas some tabernacles are permanent, others are temporary. The tabernacle, known as the "Rainbow Circle Throne Room of Jah Rastafari," represents the space of Zion. Their celebrants gather to drum, chant, dance, and testify, usually from dusk to dawn. Outside, a ritual fire is maintained for the duration of the assembly. Banners, flags, and Rastafarian devotional objects are used to focus meditation and mark key points of ingress/egress.

Male elders serving as priests, function as ritual specialists. They officiate at the altar and regulate the chanting and drumming, which is interrupted from time to time by testifying or speechifying. Inasmuch as major Nyahbinghi celebrations are held on recognized Rastafari holy days, these gatherings commemorate events of significance to those assembled, the meanings of which are embellished by the speechifying of the elders. This male speechifying thus combines rhetorical skills with intellectual and social abilities to mark the importance of the occasion. Women participate in these activities but do not play central roles. Both men and women may use herbs during this time, but women do not join in the communion of the chalice with the men. During the night the tempo of the Nyahbinghi goes up and down in accordance with the pace of the drumming. Drummers themselves are ritual experts who specialize in playing one of the three types of Nyahbinghi drums: named the *funde,* the repeater, and the bass. Every Nyahbinghi ends or "seals" with the chanting of the Ethiopian National Anthem (an anthem composed for the Garvey movement) and the symbolism of the event, coupled with the physical removal of participants from the routine spaces of Babylon, underscores the liminal status of participants as Africans in exile awaiting redemption/repatriation to the motherland.

John P. Homiak and Carole D. Yawney

Further Reading

Chevannes, B. (1994). *Rastafari roots and ideology.* Syracuse, NY: Syracuse University Press.

Forsythe, D. (1995). *Rastafari for the healing of the nations.* New York: One Drop Books.

Homiak, J. (1995). Dub history: Soundings on Rasta *livity* and language. In B. Chevannes (Ed.), *Rastafari, revival and other African-Caribbean worldviews* (pp. 127–181). London: Macmillan.

Pollard, V. (2000). *Dread talk.* Kingston, Jamaica: Queen's University Press.

Yawney, C. (1979). Dread wasteland: Rastafarian ritual in west Kingston, Jamaica. In R. Crumrine (Ed.), *Ritual symbolism and ceremonialism in the Americas* (University of Northern Colorado Occasional Publications in Anthropology, Ethnology Series No. 33, pp. 154–178). Greeley, CO: Museum of Anthropology, University of Northern Colorado.

Revitalization Rituals *See* Millennialism

Ritual as Communication

A ritual is an ordered system of symbolic activities that is performed by either a person or a group of persons for the purpose of serving some function. As a symbolic event, a ritual expresses a tradition or history while simultaneously reaffirming the importance and place of that history in the future. All rituals contain a unique grammar and a style that secure their status as primary languages. Because all languages are media for the exchange of messages between and among people, all rituals are by nature social resources with a currency determined by the frequency and priority of use.

A ritual may be verbal or nonverbal or both. A verbal ritual is performed through the expression of words that usually contain rich textual significance and are identified through connotation, metaphor, and allusion to thoughts and ideas understood completely only by others who share in the performance. A nonverbal ritual is even more complex, being performed without words by expressing thoughts and ideas through body movements, eye gaze, use of space, foods, smells, and other such channels of communication. It is rare to find a ritual that is purely verbal or purely nonverbal. Instead, rituals typically combine both verbal and nonverbal measures to assure the proper expression and reception of the performance and its meaning.

Children practicing the Devil Dance and wearing animal-devil masks in El Cerro, Querrero. The idea of naqual believe that some people have a double, an animal that shares their destiny. Whatever happens to the person happens to the animal and whatever happens to the animal happens to the person. COURTESY OF BAETRIZ MORALES COZIER.

Although one might be tempted to view all structured response to recurring stimuli as ritual, a ritual is a conscious activity—planned and orchestrated to communicate a desired message to gain a desired response. The driver who consistently honks his or her car horn to either warn or annoy those who cut him or her off in traffic is not necessarily performing a ritual. On the other hand, the driver who repeats a prayer each time before getting into a car to drive is.

Furthermore, all rituals are contextual and localized within a specific time frame and in response to set events. One cannot define a universal human response to general circumstances by the term *ritual*. The literary critic and rhetorician Kenneth Burke has written that human beings are "rotten with perfection." Humans, in his words, are driven by a desire for order in a world of disorder. When failure to achieve this flawless order inevitably occurs, human beings are wrought with guilt. This guilt forces humans to seek redemption for their imperfect nature by choosing self-mortification (self-blame) or victimage (the blaming of others). This "cycle of purification," as Burke called it, is indeed indicative of structured actions performed in response to particular circumstances, but these actions are not unique. This human disposition to resolve inner conflict is neither contingent upon a specific context nor particular to a given time frame. Universal reactions, or basic human nature, cannot be codified as ritualized performance.

Ritual has not always been viewed as a communicative act. The communication professor Edward Fisher has argued that ritual was not always seen as a living, dynamic exercise meant to express thoughts and feelings. It was seen, instead, as a predetermined mold into which all future event were first poured and then placed into the cauldron. Yet, rituals are constantly changing, adjusting to social conditions and audience makeup. Moreover, as Fisher has stated, even the best-planned ritual will ultimately suffer from a poor or sloppy performance, which suggests the intrinsic role that communication plays. Ritual performed only because it is tradition without the attempt to also express an important message is ritual at its worst. In this case, then, ritual, like communication, is truly an audience-centered phenomenon.

Genres of Ritualized Expression

Students of anthropology, sociology, communication, and other kin disciplines have already outlined many types of rituals. Rituals fall into many genres, including those dealing with birth, death, marriage, adulthood, funerals, baptisms, and entertainment. All of these genres are highly charged with symbolic meaning and performed to communicate a message to others. The reading of the poet Homer's *Iliad* and *The Odyssey* in ancient Greece by bards, philosophers, and others was a religious ritual designed to communicate the kinds of values deemed important by the gods to ordinary citizens. These values included honesty, honor, bravery, magnanimity, physical prowess, rhetorical skill, respect for one's elders, and, of course, respect for the gods. Homer's epic stories, in other words, fulfilled an important function in the oral tradition of the ancient Greeks by building a basic social literacy.

New Rituals

New rituals, in particular, are unique phenomena. To develop a new ritual is to develop a new art form. While taking note of the symbolic possibilities, the artist(s) must conceive of the best method of deriving a particular response from a given audience. This is exactly how the ancient Greek philosopher Aristotle imagined the role of the rhetorician, or the one who is trained in the art of persuasion. The artist who crafts a speech that can move the will of an audience cannot be separated in character from the artist who crafts a new ritual. The new family who is enjoying its first Christmas, for example, examines the possibilities from past and present rituals, perhaps those in which the two parents' families took part, and then creates its own unique ways of doing things. These ways may include going to church or not, opening presents the night before or the day of celebration, buying a real or an artificial tree, singing carols in the home, church, or street, purchasing a new special ornament for each year of celebration, and so on. Teachers, furthermore, develop new rituals for each group of students they meet because every class of students is different—the context and personality of the class dramatically change from semester to semester. Teachers have to decide which class rituals will work best given the audience and context. These rituals could consist of taking attendance at the start of each day or not at all, telling an opening joke to begin each lecture or avoiding any informalities, or sitting in a circle for discussions and in a traditional block formation for lectures or one formation for both.

Rituals are an important part of human life. They are living scripts that help people organize experience and guide people to make sense of the world. Rituals communicate a plan and rationale for living and act as a way to inform and persuade others to understand certain life lessons. Without rituals humans would be blind to the rich symbolic and emotional possibilities that culture and religion provide, losing an essential medium of expression.

Todd S. Frobish

See also Performance, Ritual of

Further Reading

Burke, K. (1966). *Language as symbolic action*. Berkeley and Los Angeles: University of California Press.

Fisher, E. (1973). Ritual as communication. In J. Shaughnessy (Ed.), *Roots of ritual* (pp. 161–184). Grand Rapids, MI: Wm. B. Erdmans.

Ritual Control

Ritual control may be defined as "strategies by which societies establish and maintain control of their members." Religious ritual control includes such strategies as they are embedded in religious style and image. Religious systems, whether or not they posit the existence of spirit beings, appeal to believers on the basis of some answer and direction about the nature of life and the world. For this reason all religious systems lay claim to some notion that they offer "the way" of life.

Order among Primates

As members of the primate order, human beings have created and managed societies by the use of ritual control. Decades before the popularity of primate studies, the primatologist M. R. Chance noticed the use of control among baboons. Primatologists believe that there is a significant correlation between level of potential aggression and strategies of control. With a high potential for aggression, human beings require ritual control.

Societies require compromises between individuals and groups in order to exist. One of the ways in which such compromises are achieved—and groups of individuals are formed and are able to exist—is through ritual control.

Rites Make Right

The English word *ritual* derives from the Latin *ritus*, a derivative of the Greek *arithmoi* or "arithmetic", meaning "to count" or "to number." Rituals are characterized by repetition, which is a strategy familiar to all instructors. Those things that matter are repeated. The efficacy of rituals is believed to lie in doing the same thing that is believed to have been successful previously. From the archeological record, the faithful performance of such rituals was one of the reasons for the invention of writing.

Since the late nineteenth century sociologists and anthropologists have recognized that control is gained through the use of rituals. The purpose of such rituals is to induce the submission of individuals to group control. The French sociologist Emile Durkheim analyzed the functions of rituals in mediating the authority of social structures and social philosophies to individuals. The repetitious character of rituals gives them an authenticity and authority by which they become part of a group's "natural system," in contrast to the rituals of other groups. One's participation in one's group's rituals becomes normative and a basis for distinguishing oneself and one's group from others.

Rituals, a Lifelong Process

Ritual control begins during infancy, quite possibly during pregnancy. Many societies have folk beliefs and rituals that influence behavior during pregnancy, birth, and the months immediately after. During the second and third trimesters of pregnancy, the activities of the expectant mother and her husband may be subject to ritual controls. For example, in some societies neither spouse can tie a knot, lest the umbilical cord be wrapped around the fetus's neck. Neither can drive a nail, lest the birth canal be blocked. Neither can eat cuttlefish, lest the infant be born boneless, or shrimp, lest the infant be born with a curved spine. These prohibitions may seem amusing, but prenatal and postnatal food restrictions may have far-reaching consequences on infants. Some cultures limit a nursing mother to a diet of rice and salt, seriously reducing the nutrients needed by both mother and infant in the early months.

Weaning may be gradual or sudden—a ritual process by which infants are introduced to social attitudes and social control. Although infrequent, children may nurse until age five unless replaced by a sibling or reduction of mother's milk.

Ritual control is introduced by parents and other adults in the transformation of hunger into appetite, the lowering of blood sugar levels and the imposition of eating schedules, and degrees of tolerance of emotional expression. Definitions of food, especially staples and delicacies, are culturally constructed. The provision of a staple—rice, manioc, sago—helps condition the infant to what is available and what is culturally approved. In contrast to members of Western societies, with schedules of eating at breakfast, lunch, and dinner, members of some societies eat early and eat often, having as many as half a dozen smaller meals spread throughout the day, whereas others may eat early and late, with little in between, in response to work schedules. Emotional expression may be encouraged or discouraged, with tolerance for frivolity and jocularity or with little tolerance and a calmer, quieter demeanor.

Ritualization in Middle Childhood

The formative years of middle childhood, once thought to be a quiescent period when little of importance occurs, are now recognized as a period of preparation when children learn behaviors and beliefs that floresce, or manifest themselves, during adolescence. As with the mastery of language, so with a grammar of values: Boys and girls learn habits that will carry over into the senior years. Far from being a latent period, the years from seven to eleven are a period of ritualization, of intense cognitive and social expansion. The relationships and rites that children develop are analogous to what psychologists Joseph Stone and Joseph Church (1973) have called "ancient tribal rituals."

The society of children is also given form by structure, various sets of relationships, by processes of social interaction, and cultural content, especially of cosmological (dealing with the nature of the universe) ideas and values transmitted through myth and ritual. One of the contributions of the Swiss psychologist Jean Piaget was his recognition of the middle childhood years as a time of extreme rigidity in relations to rules and fixity in habits. This recognition was part of a broader study of ritual behavior and its development in children. The absolutism (a clear sense of right and wrong) of the child combines with "participation" beliefs and realism so that the child has difficulty differentiating herself or himself from external causality and objects. This difficulty leads to magical beliefs and rituals during these years, which the child uses to modify reality. Piaget provided many accounts of children in the middle years using preventive magic as a defensive gesture against the uncertainties of a potentially hostile environment.

The Instrumental Priority of Ritual

The channelization or focusing and control of behavior that occur in the middle years are critical to later development. The ritualization of behavior confirms the instrumental or effective priority of ritual in the hierarchy of religious features. Ritual is an element of religion and culture that needs to be emphasized, even at the expense of exaggerating its importance, because the opposite error of underestimating its importance is more serious. Yet, ritual is the element most likely to be neglected by Western intellectuals, who are strongly influenced by the ideational (relating to the forming of ideas) elements in culture and life. On this point, the American anthropologist Anthony F. C. Wallace writes:

> The primary phenomenon of religion is ritual. Ritual is religion in action; it is the cutting edge of the tool. Belief, although its recitation may be a part of the ritual, or a ritual in its own right, serves to explain, to rationalize, to interpret and direct the energy of the ritual performance. It is not a question of priority in time … in observed human behavior the two go together; few if any rituals are any longer instituted before a mythic base is invented to account for them. The primacy is instrumental: just as the blade of the knife has instrumental priority over the handle, and the barrel of a gun over the stock, so does the ritual have an instrumental priority over myth. It is ritual which accomplishes what religion sets out to do. (Wallace 1966, 102)

Rites of Passage

The passage from middle childhood to adolescence is marked by hundreds of societies with some rite of passage. When couched in a religious context, ritual control may be effective in bringing about behaviors of submission. Bar mitzvah (the initiatory ceremony recognizing a boy as having reached the age of Jewish religious duty and responsibility), bas mitzvah (the initiatory ceremony recognizing a girl as having reached the age of Jewish religious duty and responsibility), and confirmation (a Christian rite conferring the gift of the Holy Spirit and, among Protestants, full church membership) are such rites with which readers may be familiar. Each has the same purpose, that is, submission of the young to the old, of the individual believer to the community of faith. A similar purpose lay in the initiate's journey—a three month or three year experience undertaken by young men who must live off the land and by their wits—among the Ibans, the largest pre-state society on the island of Borneo, and in the ritual of subincision, which seems to outsiders an exotic if not horrific rite of passage. Subincision was a secondary initiation rite, following circumcision, and involved the incising of the underside of the penis and, in some instances, the insertion of small pieces of stone. No one is quite sure why the rite was observed, other than to secure the submission of adolescent males to older men.

Subincision was a rite also practiced by Australian aborigines and described by various authors, among them the anthropologist W. Lloyd Warner. In Warner's study of the Murngin, he describes one clan and the mythic background that gave support to the ritual. Two clan sisters committed incest—with two clan brothers—and were forced to leave their community. As they wandered in the outback, they gathered and named plants and animals. Coming to a well, a familiar symbol of life, they cooked the plants and animals, whose souls fled the fire into the well. Below the water lay a python, a symbol of uncontrolled life force. Awakened by the thrashing of the plant and animal souls, the python arose and saw the two sisters and their infants. Terrified by the python, the women tried to control him by dancing, but the python bit their noses and then swallowed the sisters and their infants. The blood from the bites flowed into a small depression in the ground, and later, when the clan brothers came looking for the sisters, they saw the blood and dreamed about their sisters. The sisters told them that all men must produce blood, first by circumcision, then by subincision, and finally, on ritual occasions, by piercing a vein in the arm and collecting the blood in a magical container for use as an adhesive in the application of charcoal and plant down. The mythic account was reinforced among aborigines by the well-nigh universal belief in sorcery. Sorcerers, it was taught, lurked just outside the camp, waiting to capture the unwary man or woman who left the safety of society. Once snared by a sorcerer, the victim was penetrated by a killing stick, and the life blood was drained off. Using an ointment made by mashing together a mass of ants, the sorcerer revived the victim, who returned to camp, only to die within a few days. The sorcerer, aborigines said, made the victim "live to die." By contrast, the rites of circumcision, subincision, and blood-letting provided protection and made each person "die to live."

Other Rituals of Control

Subincision has its parallels in other societies. Among the Nuer and other Nilotic people of east Africa, adolescent men were required to undergo scarification, in which a ritual specialist gave marks by incising the head from ear to ear. Whereas dark-skinned people have practiced scarification, light-skinned people have used tattooing to impose marks indicating physical maturity and passage to manhood or womanhood. Tattooing was common throughout the insular Pacific and, in the case of the Iban, permitted a man who had distinguished himself by acquiring a skull or head trophy to have the backs of his hands tattooed, indicating to all that he was a brave man and to be respected.

Functions of Rituals

An obvious function of ritual is control of the members of a society or, in the case of religious rituals, a community of believers. Ritual also integrates individuals into society by symbolically articulating social patterns and relationships. Ritual provides a bridge between seen and unseen worlds, relating the human world to the world of divine forces and powers, thus validating beliefs that are commonly held. "The family that prays together stays together" because, in order to pray together, the family members must stay together. Ritual helps resolve personal and social dilemmas, often by bringing together persons who previously have been adversaries. Also, ritual may perform a heuristic (aiding in learning) function by giving purpose and focus to actions. Individuals may employ ritual control in focusing their otherwise diffuse physical and psychic energies to accomplish tasks that they regard as worthwhile, especially within a religious context.

Benefits of Ritual Control

Athletes practice ritual control regularly. Such ritual control is synonymous with psychocybernetics, the purposeful employment of feedback to achieve some goal, a strategy prescribed by trainers for athletes. Few athletes have more at stake than do professional baseball, basketball, football, and soccer players. Also, to minimize elements of risk and randomness, all have common and personal myths and rituals. No one knows "how the ball will bounce" or when one may suffer an injury. Baseball players, for example, never step on a foul line or cross bats. Bad luck. Similar rituals exist for other sports. Of all the athletes studied, players in the U.S. National Football League have by far the most complicated rituals. This may be explained by the much more complex schemes and more rigid responsibilities that each player has to his team. In a study of NFL players Pat Takach, former secretary of the Players Union, surveyed both offensive and defensive players. She found a dramatic difference between rituals of the offensive linemen, who reported almost twice as many rituals as did the defensive players. Dennis Harrison, who played in the NFL for ten years as a defensive end, offered this explanation for the difference:

> (Offensive linemen) have a big responsibility. If a defensive guy gets past them, the quarterback can get hurt, he's out of the game. Now your whole offensive may change. Your chance of winning may change. Defensive linemen, if he's messing up, you can replace him, you can do defensive covering, and you have people backing you up, linebackers and things. For the offensive lineman, if he has a bad game, he can get a running back hurt or a quarterback hurt. (Takach 1989, 7)

Whether in lifelong processes of socialization or, more narrowly, in rites of passage, rituals serve to maintain order within human societies. The negative and constraining effects of such rituals are often exaggerated because without some degree of focus, illustrated in the training of athletes, humans would founder, with no sense of goals, meaning, or purpose.

Vinson Sutlive

See also Ritual Specialists

Further Reading

Bossard, J. H. S., & Boll, E. S. (1966). *The sociology of child development.* New York: Harper & Row.

Piaget, J. (1969). *The child's conception of the world.* Totowa, NJ: Littlefield, Adams.

Stone, L. J., & Church, J. (1973). *Childhood and adolescence.* New York: Random House.

Takach, P. (1989). *Form to content: An analysis of pre-game rituals of NFL players.* Williamsburg, VA.

Wallace, A. F. C. (1966). *Religion: An anthropological approach.* New York: Random House.

Ritual Specialists

Ritual specialists are men and women who assume positions of leadership in the performance of rites on behalf of their communities. In most communities, these positions are ad hoc or limited to a short-term need. Such specialists generally are intellectual individuals, whether they are in major religious systems or in prestate (traditional or tribal) societies. They serve at the pleasure of the community and are dependent upon community support and participation to function effectively.

Categories of Specialists

The broadest categories into which ritual specialists are commonly grouped are shamans, mediums, and priests. For most, if not all, specialists there exists a "ministry of mutuality" between themselves and the community. That is, within this system of exchanges, many ritual specialists move into the positions and play the roles associated with those positions through a process of self-selection. The society creates and affirms positions that are taken up by ritual specialists. This is one of the forms of transactional analysis, in which members of society say to such leaders, "I'm not okay, and you're not okay, but that's okay." Specialists may have some personal need that is met in the role, which then provides fulfillment and personal satisfaction. From the community's perspective there is some advantage in having such specialists available as needed. For example, the anthropologist Julian Steward describes the role of the shaman among the Western Shoshone of California. The shaman was the only specialist among the Western Shoshone and, in addition to being a part-time healer, was also mediator whenever disputes arose within the community.

Shamans

Shamans are practitioners of what were the earliest religious and healing traditions. Shamanism is particularly important in societies extending from Siberia through southern and southeastern Asia into eastern Asia and into the New World among Native American societies. The term *shaman* is borrowed from the Siberian Tungus term, *šaman,* meaning "healer." Shamans have been of particular interest to explorers, missionaries, and anthropologists because of their remarkable intellects and their roles as psychotherapists. Shamans have been described as specialists of the soul, seeing things that other people do not see. In many, if not all, of the societies in which shamans are found, people believe in the existence of multiple souls in each individual or in the capacity of the soul to leave the body for a time. Belief in "soul loss" is one of the most common explanations for illness (along with beliefs in possession, breach of taboo or other violations, or a curse) and is the principal reason why a shaman may be summoned to perform a healing ritual.

Most studies of shamans analyze the techniques that the shamans employ, and few analyze how shamans take on the role. This author's 1976 study and the anthropologist Clifford Sather's *Seeds of Play, Words of Power* (2001) are exceptions, each describing the conflicted role of the Iban shaman. The Iban, numbering more than 600,000, are the largest pre-state society on the island of Borneo. These studies confirm the anthropologist Walder Bogoras's study of the Siberian Chukchee shaman and M. A. Czaplicka's study of a Siberian shaman, which concluded that the vocation was not one of choice but rather of coercion by spirits or other forces.

The largest conference of shamans ever held met in Kapit, Sarawak, Malaysia, in 1995. Thirty-eight shamans and fifteen bardic (relating to a tribal poet-singer) priests participated in the three-day conference on the vocation and techniques of healers. Of

A TAOIST PRIEST ON TAIWAN

The ritual of religious Taoism is esoteric; that is, it is not meant to be directly understood and witnessed by all the faithful. The esoteric meaning of Taoist ritual and magic is concealed from all but the initiated; only after many years of training and a gradual introduction to religious secrets is the disciple deemed worthy of elevation to the rank of master and full knowledge of the esoteric meanings of religious ritual. For this reason the aspirant disciple tries to join the entourage of a famous master, so he can learn the formulas for ritual performance and gradually gain access to the bidden aspects of ritual Taoism.

The expertise of a Taoist priest is judged by several criteria, the first one being his external performance of ritual. Learning to sing well, to dance the various ritual steps, perform the mudras or band symbols, memorize the several hundred ceremonial texts and innumerable accompanying formulas, is of course the primary goal of the young disciple in attaching himself to a famous master. Most of the Taoists in Taiwan never go beyond this stage, simply because the ability to perform the standard repertoire of rituals will enable a priest to attract a large enough following among the pious faithful to earn an excellent livelihood. If he can write a stylish fu talisman to cure illness, exorcise evil spirits with sword and oxhorn trumpet, perform ritual dances and acrobatic tumbling, climb a blade-side-up sword ladder, and win a reputation for being a powerful magician, the demands for his services will be almost endless. Most disciples therefore study with a master just long enough to learn the external rituals and enough of the esoteric doctrines to lend credence to their ritual performance.

The second criterion for judging a Taoist, which determines his rank at ordination, is his knowledge of the esoteric secrets of the religion, including the ability to perform the meditations and breath-control techniques of internal alchemy (*nei-tan*), and to recite the classical orthodox lists of spirits' names and apparel and the mantric summons found in the Taoist Canon.

***Source*: Saso, Michael. (1974). "Orthodoxy and Heterodoxy in Taoist Ritual." In Arthur P. Wolf (Ed.), *Religion and Ritual in Chinese Society.* Stanford, CA: Stanford University Press, pp. 325–326.**

interest here is the fact that in the introductory statements of participants, two-thirds stated that if they had been able not to take on the role, they would have chosen not to become healers. Most were relatively small in stature, although admittedly many were of ordinary size.

This author's study describes the experiences of Iban shamans in the Rejang Valley of northwestern Borneo. The shamans whom he knew and interviewed were diminutive and said that in childhood and early adolescence they had felt themselves different from their peers. They did not compete in play, and, when their mates set off on initiate's journeys—a three month or three year experience undertaken by young men who must live off the land and by their wits—among the Ibans, the largest pre-state society on the island of Borneo, they stayed home. Resolution of their conflict came in a dream experience in which each claimed to have seen a spirit who invited him to take up the role of shaman. Supported by his family, each underwent a six-month apprenticeship, at the end of which he was initiated by a group of seven master shamans. Training involves the learning of sleight of hand, manipulation of objects, and, most important, the dramatic performance of the healing chants *(pelian)*, which are the focal points of the therapist. The performance includes trance induction, in which state the *manang* (shaman) is instructed by the familiar, a spirit guide, and while the soul is out of the body, is able to search out the soul of patients. In preparation for his initiation, the apprentice has to go door to door in his own community—and in nearby longhouses if there are any—and collect uncooked rice to be used during the initiation. The significance of this collection is twofold: First, donors indicate their support of the apprentice by contributing rice. Second, the rice will become a mound under which the apprentice will be "buried" to rise a new person. Further, some shamans claim that, having collected rice through such a request, they are thereby enabled to "follow the trail of rice" as they seek the capture and return of souls of that family.

The shamanic initiation ceremony is colorful and elaborate. The ceremony involves not only the ranking shaman of the region, but also the several longhouse communities represented by the healers who participate in the ceremony. Responsibility thus is shared among members of the community and, beyond the host longhouse, by other nearby communities. In addition to the gift of rice, women prepare food and items to be used in offerings. Men prepare the equipment that will be employed in the initiation ceremony, that is, a treadmill, betel palm blossoms, blankets, coconuts, and bamboo staffs.

The initiation ceremony begins early in the morning. Upon arriving at the longhouse, the officiating shamans, all of whom have brought their medical kits, including a collection of charms, amulets, and other paraphernalia, gather in one of the family rooms. Young women, usually unmarried and wearing woven skirts and silver bands that encircle the waist, arrange offerings. The offerings include the items required for such activities: cooked rice, popped rice, rice wine, rice cakes, salt, eggs, tobacco, betel nuts, and betel leaves.

After the offerings have been arranged, each shaman brings out his medical kit and, after extracting the pieces of equipment, ritually bathes by rubbing himself with them to protect against any spirits that may be encountered during the initiation. After the ritual bathing the shamans pair off and begin to whip each other with the palm blossoms. They move up and down the longhouse veranda, returning to circle the ritual center. (This center has been transformed in some communities into a form of gift tree, onto which are attached bottles of beer and soft drinks, fruits, and plastic goods.) Eventually all of the shamans fall into a trance. While they are in a trance, a drum is beaten lest they lose their way, and each is covered with a blanket. Trances last for several minutes, and after the last shaman has revived, they share among themselves the visions they have seen and gifts they received from their familiars.

The shamans then move into a family room from which they climb to the ridgepole of the longhouse. New offerings are arranged and are hung from the ridgepole. The shamans resume whipping each other and again fall into a trance. After they recover consciousness, a chicken is sacrificed, and a feather is used to wipe the blood across the forehead of each shaman. More gifts may be received while in a trance, and these are shared within the group of shamans.

The party of shamans returns to the open porch beyond the veranda, where a pig is killed, and its liver is removed. The veins in the liver are carefully examined. If they are straight and not twisted around each other, this augurs well for the initiate. If, on the other hand, the veins are twisted, a second pig may be sacrificed and so on until a sign of success is obtained.

Afterward rewards are given to the officiating shaman, and a schedule of charges is fixed for the initiate. Charges vary according to the treatment required. For a minor ailment that may be treated with palpation in the family room, a shaman may receive two plates, a knife, and rice. For a more serious, and extensive, treatment on the veranda, a shaman may receive a blanket as well as a knife, a plate, and rice. Payments are subject to negotiation, but there is little evidence that patients or their families have been reluctant to pay for services rendered. The payment was (and possibly still is) regarded as providing "protection for the soul."

The shaman is given a new name, indicating a change of status, and this nameis announced to all present. The name identifies the relationship of the shaman to his familiar. For example, "Manang Landak" means "Shaman Whose Familiar Is the Porcupine Spirit."

The Iban recognize three levels of shaman. The first level is the newly initiated shaman, who is referred to colorfully as a "raw shaman" *(manang mata')*. After seven or more years the raw shaman may advance to the second level, becoming a "cooked [or ripe] shaman" *(manang mansau)*. The third level is that of transvestite, literally, "transformed shaman" *(manang bali')*. This author is unaware of any such shaman during the past century.

Mediums

Mediums are persons who are believed to have a gift to mediate between the seen and unseen worlds. European and North American societies have been influenced by ancient Greek philosophy, particularly by distinctions that ancient Greeks made between monist and dualist interpretations of the world.

Monists, or materialists, believe in a singular dimension of existence: "What you see is what you have." Dualists, on the other hand, believe in the coexistence of material and immaterial domains: "There's more to it than meets the eye." Approximately 80 percent of the sixty-two hundred autonymic or self-naming societies in the world have beliefs that are quite different from European and North American beliefs, and in such societies, mediums are important links between the living and the dead, the visible and the invisible.

Priests

In major religions priests are usually full-time specialists who have undertaken education and training necessary for the performance of their activities. Brahmans (Hindus of the highest caste traditionally assigned to the priesthood) function in Vedic (relating to the Hindu sacred writings) religions to interpret sacred texts, to make food offerings, and, equally important, to help maintain the ritual purity of the twice-born—their own class and that of Kshatriyas (Hindus of an upper caste traditionally assigned to governing and military occupations) and Vaisyas (Hindus of an upper caste traditionally assigned to commercial and agricultural occupations). In the Roman Catholic Church priests are believed to be descendants of a line that can be traced back to Saint Peter, the first bishop of Rome. In Protestant churches, by contrast, many believers regard each believer as "priest," that is, as having unimpeded access to God, independent of a line of descent. Priests or ministers are regarded as persons who have been called by God and confirmed by the community of faith. In traditional societies priests may be part-time specialists who have gone through an extended period of apprenticeship in order to learn the texts that they will chant and the rites that they will perform. In these societies many specialists are able to commit to memory large amounts of texts, which they edit and embellish, customizing them as necessary in different contexts.

Bardic Priests

The Iban *lemambang* (bardic priest) illustrates the alternate role of priests. These men are also known, from their activities during the expansion of the Iban into new territories, as "spirit warriors," believed to be able to magically attack enemies through the chants they performed.

The enduring role of the *lemambang* has been dependent upon Iban beliefs in the self-authenticating word and effectiveness of a curse. Ibans have believed in the ability of spoken words to achieve the intention and spirit of the speaker. Dr. James Masing, the first Iban anthropologist, writes: "To the Iban spoken words are fully capable of determining the course of events. It is believed that what a man first utters will, sooner or later, become a reality" (Masing 1997, 81). Thus, in the Iban Festival of the Ancestors, the chants of the bardic priests bring the dead back to the longhouse to attend the festival held in their honor. In festivals commemorating the bravery of warriors, the bardic priests summon the god of war and his retinue, who are believed to attend and bring charms for future use.

The pacification of peoples once engaged in warfare for land has changed but not eliminated bardic priests. Repositories of knowledge and performers without peer, modern bardic priests are still able to astound their fellow Ibans with their "vast repertoires, not only of *timang* (chants) but also of other traditions" (Masing 1997, 84). Even now it is common for bardic priests to be invited to open government-sponsored programs with chants composed for the specific theme of the program.

The role of bardic priest has been open to any Iban, man or woman. As Iban shamans, many, although not all, such bardic priests experienced a culture-pattern dream through which they took up the role. Masing reports that his informants pursued the role after having a dream in which they performed as a bard:

> In my dream I was assuming the role of a leading *lemambang* … In my dream I was chanting the *timang* invocation …
>
> Long ago Pangiran was dreaming of chanting a *timang for a gawai* ritual … (Masing 1997, 90–91)

After having such a dream, persons interested in becoming a bardic priest approach an experienced priest who agrees to teach them. After the students have been accepted, an offering is made, and the bard's charm ("medicine of memory") is shared with the students. Students learn "portions" of chants by memory. The portions are comprised not so much of the actual words as of the objects or scenes to be recalled in the chants. These portions are represented on the priest's "memory board," which is a piece of wood about two meters in length on which are carved blocks measuring 5 centimeters by 6.3 centimeters and depicting in sequence the episodes to be reviewed in the chant.

Students train with a priest for a period of three days to two weeks. For this training they pay a small amount of cash—usually a few Malaysian ringgit—and the objects of symbolic value that must be paid to a priest. Students learn initially from a single priest, but more interested ones undertake studies with other priests. Students become members of a three-person chorus who responds to a bard's lead and takes opportunities prior to bards' performances to learn from different singers.

The objects of symbolic value are part of the total payment to a priest and his assistants for their performance at a major festival. These objects, and the symbolic importance of each, include a jar to provide a sanctuary for the soul, a piece of iron to strengthen the soul, a knife to clear away obstacles, a plate and a bowl to serve as a "boat" and "bailer" by messengers who summon the gods, a chicken to drive away evil with the fluttering of its wings and to become a sacrifice, and a piece of white cloth that is used as a mantle to protect from all dangers.

Another ritual specialist among the Iban must be noted. The Lemambang Sabak are women who are gifted in singing the richly detailed dirges that accompany the soul of a deceased person as it goes on its journey back to the places from whence the Iban originated. Beyond the three major categories of ritual specialists of shamans, mediums, and priests already discussed, there are additional categories of specialists who do not fit into these three groupings. We now consider ten of these other specialists.

Prophets

Prophets are men or women who have perceived some truth or insight that they feel obliged to share with their community. Strictly speaking, prophecy has little to do with telling the future. Rather, it has to do with a ritual specialist who challenges her or his community to return to a traditional way of life or move on to a new and better way of life. Early prophets in the Jewish tradition were characterized by bizarre behavior, usually manifested as an ecstatic state with temporary loss of awareness of surroundings or circumstance. Beginning with Amos, a prophet of the mid-eighth-century BCE, the role of prophet was transformed into that of one who spoke for God.

Rabbis

Rabbis are persons knowledgeable in the Hebrew Bible and thus well suited to give guidance to Jewish believers. Rabbis emerged as leaders during what is described as the reconstitution of Judaism at Jamnia in ancient Judea.

Singers and chanters (cantors) are persons who have a gift for re-creating events of the past and involving modern believers in them. From Native American singers to Jewish cantors, such specialists recall the mighty acts of God or some other deity and, through the texts that they chant, contemporize the past so that hearers can share in those great moments. Singing and chanting are important ritual acts not only emotionally and psychically but also physiologically.

Imams, Muezzins, and Ayatollahs

Imams and muezzins are ritual specialists unique to Islam. Some imams avoid the honorific term "leader," preferring to identify themselves simply as persons who call others to and join with others in worship. A muezzin is a "crier"—one who calls the faithful to prayer. Five times daily the chant of a muezzin may be heard from a minaret in areas where Muslims live and worship. Ayatollahs are religious leaders among Shi'a Muslims. In contrast with the majority (90 percent) Sunni Muslims, Shi'a Muslims believe that Allah continues to speak to some persons such as ayatollahs. These persons give guidance and instruction that is beyond the Qur'an (the book of sacred writings accepted by Muslims as revelations made to Muhammad by Allah) and its interpretations.

Monks, Nuns, and Ascetics

Monks, nuns, and ascetics are persons who choose an alternate style of life that is often characterized by poverty or a rejection of the materialism of their society. In Buddhism men take on the role of monk for months or years and subsist on gifts of food from other members of their societies. In Christianity some people experience a call to ministry, either in prayer or service, and choose that call as a lifelong commitment. Ascetics are persons who fast and, in some cases, afflict the physical condition for the benefit of the spiritual condition.

Sorcerers and Witches

All of the ritual specialists who have been considered thus far are believed to have positive effects on their communities. Two kinds of specialists who may have both positive and negative effects are sorcerers and witches. Unfortunately, most introductory textbooks in both anthropology and religion perpetuate the simplistic notion that sorcerers work through the manipulation of objects, whereas witches suffer some defect of being by which they are unable to resist a tendency to do evil. The anthropologist Helen Rountree (1966) has compared these two kinds of ritual specialists as reported in eighty-seven societies and has found that the distinctions between the two are much more complex. Sorcerers are believed to have special powers for good or evil. These powers have been acquired through instruction. Witches are believed to have received special powers, more often for evil, from some animal or spiritual agency. Informants and ethnographers (those who study human culture) both have an undeniable gender bias in their distinctions: Witches are predominantly female, may practice cannibalism, dress indecently—when at all—have their own societies, are never professionals, are thought to be immoral, and are always regarded as perverted. Sorcerers are predominantly male, never practice cannibalism, dress like ordinary people, work as professionals, are thought to be illegal, and never are regarded as perverted.

There is a large literature on witches, but two of the most extensive studies of witches are Sir E. E. Evans-Pritchard's *Witchcraft, Oracles, and Magic among the Azande* and Clyde Kluckhohn's *Navaho Witchcraft*. Each study emphasizes ways in which witchcraft is socially conditioned, that is, accusations of witchcraft focus on stressful relationships. Kluckhohn notes that no outsider ever saw the practice of witchcraft and asserts that it is probable that neither did any Navaho. But belief in the practice of witchcraft is important as a means of social control. There is no doubt that persons have died as a result of their faith in the powers of both sorcerers and witches.

Ritual specialists are of many more types than the shaman, medium, and priest commonly presented in introductory textbooks. In the evolution of human societies, the needs of both individuals and groups have been partially met by the creation of religious positions and by the assumption of these positions by persons who felt personal satisfaction in filling them.

Vinson H. Sutlive, Jr.

See also Asceticism; Exorcism; Iban; Shamanism; Sorcery; Witchcraft

Further Reading

Adams, C., Baird, R.D., Bloom, A.,Comstock, W. R., O'Dea, J., & O'Dea, T. (Eds). (1971). *Religion and man: An introduction*. New York: Harper & Row.

Leaf, M. (1979). *Man, mind, and science*. New York: Columbia University Press.

Masing, J. J. (1997). *The coming of the gods*. Canberra, Australia: Department of Anthropology, Research School of Pacific and Asian Studies, Australian National University.

Rountree, H. (1966). *A cross-cultural delineation of the role of the witch and the sorcerer.* Unpublished honors thesis, College of William and Mary, Williamsburg, VA.

Sather, C. (2001). *Seeds of play, words of power: An ethnographic account of Iban shamanism.* Kuching, Malaysia: Tun Jugah Foundation.

Sutlive, V. (1976). The Iban *manang:* An alternate route to normality. In G. N. Appell (Ed.), *Studies in Borneo societies: Social process and anthropological explanation* (pp. 64–71). DeKalb: Center for Southeast Asian Studies, Northern Illinois University.

Rituals of Rebellion

The South African anthropologist Max Gluckman coined the term *rituals of rebellion* to refer to situations in which there is a conflict between individual roles in society and society's overall organization. Rituals of rebellion allow the organization to be challenged in such a manner that its overall order is reaffirmed and reestablished. Rituals of rebellion allow problems to be solved without forcing suppression of those people with grievances because the rituals are a structurally approved way of bringing grievances to public attention.

Rituals of rebellion call attention to conflicts within the social order, and the authority of the social order is reaffirmed in the process of resolving the conflicts. Order's authority over individual gratification restrains everyone, including the rulers themselves.

Rituals of rebellion operate in systems in which there is stable authority and internal cohesion. Otherwise, the systems would be put under intolerable strain.

A Halloween display in a New York village suggests the "universal" nature of the ritual. COURTESY OF DAVID LEVINSON.

Swazi people use these rituals to focus on individual people and challenged the manner in which they failed to perform their roles according to established rules. The rules themselves went unchallenged. For example, the people whom Gluckman studied criticized and rebelled against particular authorities and other people, but they did not question the system of institutions. Zulu women of Africa, for instance, often suffered by being under social subordination and by having their male relatives transfer them to strangers for marriage. However, they desired to be married, have children, and be normal Zulu women. Their frustration was allowed to vent through the Nomkubulwana ritual. During this ritual they became lewd shrews, enlisting their daughters as warlike herders. However, they did not seek to carry that ritual to the point of seeking to replace the system.

Gluckman was careful to note the difference between rebels and revolutionaries. Rebels accepted the existing social order, although they might not have accepted the person in power at the time. There was an acceptance by rebels of the established order as proper, and that, in turn, allowed rituals of rebellion, which the established order kept within bounds. The very license to act out social conflicts, by direct means or by rituals of inversion (those which change the normal order), attests to the social cohesion in which the rituals of inversion are established. As Gluckman stated, the problems are solved.

> not by alterations in the order of offices, but by changes in the persons occupying those offices. The passage of time with its growth and change of population produces over long periods realignments, but not radical change of pattern. And as the social order always contains a division of rights and duties, and of privileges and powers as against liabilities, the ceremonial enactment of this order states the nature of the order in all its rightness. The ceremony states that in virtue of their social position princes and people hate the king, but nevertheless they support him. Indeed, they support him in virtue of, and despite, the conflicts between them. The critically important point is that even if Swazi princes do not actually hate the king, their social position may rally malcontents to them. Indeed, in a comparatively small-scale society princes by their very existence have power, which threatens the king. Hence in their prescribed, compelled, ritual behavior they exhibit opposition to as well as support for the king, but mainly support for the kingship. This is the social setting for rituals of rebellion. (Gluckman 1963)

Extensions

The concept of rituals of rebellion has been extended to religious holidays. Shrove Tuesday (Mardi Gras, Fat Tuesday) is an example. Shrove Tuesday is the final day of Carnival, which is the festival before the Christian penitential season of Lent, which begins the next day on Ash Wednesday. Mardi Gras is a time to say "goodbye" to meat, and a time of license when people are encouraged to do the wrong thing. By doing the wrong thing, engaging in a reversal of established order, they help maintain the established order and stability in society. These rituals help people vent those "forbidden" impulses that following the rules frustrates. Under ritual guidance a catharsis takes place, and people can again start conforming to the norms of society on Ash Wednesday, cleansed of their evil impulses.

As do so many Christian customs Carnival stems from pre-Christian fertility rituals dealing with rebirth and crops. The word *shrove* comes from the infinitive *to shrive,* meaning "to make confession." However, one might think that confessions would need to be made after Carnival as the practice developed.

Carnival is truly a rite of subversion (related to inversion, seeks to overthrow the established order by showing that things are arbitrary), an ambivalent

Indigenous people in Kalimantan, Indonesia reenact a tribal battle at the Erau Festival in September 1996. COURTESY OF STEPHEN G. DONALDSON PHOTOGRAPHY.

occasion. Carnival falls somewhere between genuine opposition to established order and a safety valve to let off steam. It is a kind of joking relationship between those in authority and others who are not in authority that allows the truth to be told and conflict to be expressed. Unlike most commercial festivals, Carnival features real opposition. Carnival springs from the grassroots and is communal and egalitarian. People do not participate in it for profit, and it is not under media control. Carnival is independent of state support and is participatory. All people are encouraged to take part. Moreover, Carnival is largely a safe event in which feelings and opinions can be expressed openly.

Purim is an example of a Jewish ritual of rebellion. People are encouraged to chime in and act up when the story of Esther is repeated by elders.

Many secular holidays are rituals of rebellion. New Year's Eve is an example. The drunkenness and license bid goodbye to the old year and hello to the New Year, when decorum and order return. Halloween, once primarily for the young but now being observed more by older people, is another example of regulated license in which masquerade and regulated rituals of inversion are encouraged.

Play

Scholars who study play have used the related concepts of rituals of rebellion and rituals of reversal. Playing by its nature is breaking rules of ordinary behavior. It is a process of toying with structure and entering a new liminal (relating to a sensory threshold) field. Much ceremony resembles play in these characteristics. Participants often change gender, scare other people, disrespect their superiors, and in many ways flout the rules of their culture. Boundary crossing marks these ceremonies.

The bachelorette party, in which otherwise proper young women cross sexual boundaries, acting like typical males, is an example of the phenomena of play, rituals of rebellion, and rituals of reversal. A bachelorette party is given for a bride-to-be. It begins with a gift-giving session followed by a night of drinking and watching male strippers. Its participants usually state that the bachelorette party is a liberating and feminist experience. It allows them to express their sexuality during a rite of passage—separation, transition, and incorporation, moving the future bride from a single to married state.

"Through exaggerated 'femaleness' expressed by dressing the bride in suggestive clothing, the women acknowledge (male) cultural constructions of their sexuality but not in a way that necessarily indicates acceptance or agreement" (Tye & Powers 1998, 556). The future bride appears to agree to male definitions of her sexuality by allowing the male stripper to take liberties with her body during his performance. By participating in the objectification of her sexuality, she is making a statement that contradicts that objectification.

Gluckman indicates that license can be permitted only when people know the limits and agree to them. He states: "The acceptance of the established order as right and good, and even sacred, seems to allow" (Gluckman 1963, 8) challenges to be made to those who hold positions of power and grievances to be expressed.

Rituals of rebellion generally enact and present social conflicts. The anthropologist Victor Turner developed the social drama approach to emphasize Gluckman's insight that conflicts within societies have a dynamic trajectory. Conflicts enable people to view social structure in action, to reach an understanding of process. Turner viewed social life as dynamic, ever-changing, not static. Rituals allow for safe rebellion that does not threaten the system of government.

Rituals of rebellion also strengthen stable social systems by providing a means for people to channel grievances into directions that resolve conflicts by upholding the social order. Rather than lead to civil war, these grievances focus on individuals who are alleged to be failing to live up to the obligations of the system.

Gluckman notes that although leaders struggle for the kingship and its power, they do not struggle for independence. Thus, battles between contestants for power center on controlling the government, not overthrowing the system of government. These battles keep people focused on the legitimacy of the government even as discontent with particular leaders may surface.

Turner and others emphasize the implications of the processual, ever-changing nature of social life itself. Rituals of rebellion are inherently related to rituals of reversal. Thus, Carnival, Halloween, Purim, and many other religious and secular festivals carry with them the ambivalent and ambiguous relationships that people have to established systems, the double-edged power of affirmation and rebellion, reflecting the complexity of social life.

Frank A. Salamone

See also Inversion, Rites of; Mardi Gras; New Year's Celebrations

Further Reading

Beidelman, T. O. (1982). *Colonial evangelism: A socio-historical study of an East African mission at the grass-roots*. Bloomington: Indiana University Press.

Berghe, P. L. V. (Ed.). (1965). *Africa: Social problems of change and conflict*. San Francisco: Chandler.

Gluckman, M. (1955). *Custom and conflict in Africa*. Oxford, UK: Blackwell.

Gluckman, M. (1963). *Order and rebellion in tribal Africa: Collected essays, with an autobiographical introduction*. New York: Free Press of Glencoe.

Guenther, M. (1999). African ritual. In S. D. Glazier (Ed.), *Anthropology of religion: A handbook* (pp. 181–190). Westport, CT: Praeger.

Hsu, F. L. K. (Ed.). (1961). *Psychological anthropology: Approaches to culture and personality*. Homewood, IL: Dorsey Press.

Humphrey, C., & Laidlaw, J. (1994). *The archetypal actions of ritual: A theory of ritual illustrated by the Jain rite of worship*. Oxford, UK: Oxford University Press.

Parkin, D., Caplan, L., & Fisher, H. (Eds.). (1996). *The politics of cultural performance*. Providence, RI: Berghahn Books.

Plotnicov, L. (Ed.). (1990). *American culture: Essays on the familiar and unfamiliar*. Pittsburgh, PA: University of Pittsburgh Press.

Tye, D., & Powers, A. (1998). Gender, resistance and play: Bachelorette parties in Atlantic Canada. *Women's Studies International Forum*, 21(5), 551–562.

S

Sacred Places

Sacred places are places where holiness or the divine is more directly and fully present than elsewhere. This sometimes means that holiness or the divine can be approached and experienced by humans there more than elsewhere; conversely, the greater presence of holiness may render such places unapproachable by profane human beings, or both: The ark of the covenant in the Hebrew Bible brings the Israelites victory but also kills even Israelites who stray too close to it; and the grove sacred to the Eumenides in the ancient Greek dramatist Sophocles' *Oedipus at Colonus* is the place of Oedipus' final vindication and apotheosis (elevation to divine status), but its holiness demands that he beg for forgiveness for profaning it with his presence. Sacred places are not ordinary places, so they are places of extraordinary events, such as communication with the divine; but not being ordinary, sacred places may also threaten or destroy ordinary, physical life.

The kinds of sacred places vary greatly within and across religious traditions. They can be places in nature, such as a mountain, river, or grove, or they can be a human structure, such as a temple, shrine, sacred pillar, or altar. There are practically no limits on the size, from the sacredness of the whole Earth in most religious traditions, all the way down to the small shrines *(butsudans)* that are a sacred place in many Buddhist homes, and the even smaller mezuzah (small parchment scrolls displayed on doorposts as a reminder of the Jewish faith) on traditional Jewish homes. Many traditions also speak of a holy land (e.g., Israel in Judaism or Japan in Shinto), a holy city (e.g., Jerusalem in Judaism, Christianity, and Islam; Benares [Varanasi] and many other cities in Hinduism), a holy temple, and a holiest spot within a place of worship (e.g., the altar in a Catholic church or the ark where Torah [the body of wisdom and law contained in Jewish Scripture and other sacred literature and oral tradition] scrolls are kept in a synagogue). Within these places is a sense of concentric circles of increasingly concentrated holiness as one moves inward or of dissipating holiness as one moves outward into the increasingly profane world. Considering the different sizes of sacred places helps people to understand two opposite aspects of them because the idea of concentrating holiness helps make sense of how the divine can be present everywhere, while at the same time a sacred place is localized or specified: One cannot flee or escape from the holy because it is everywhere, but there are places where it is more concentrated, and these are called "sacred places."

A related paradox of a sacred place is the sense in which its holiness is eternal, intrinsic, and objective, while it is also somehow constructed in time, chosen from out of other places, and proclaimed such by people. A sacred place must not be arbitrary. Humans cannot make a place sacred: They recognize, revere, celebrate, and fear a holiness that was there before and beyond any of their actions. Obviously, human hands create the temples and altars that mark some sacred places, and they perform the rituals that periodically purify or rededicate these places, but these structures are there only to remind humans of the holiness present there and to direct their thoughts and actions toward them in ways that are recognized and approved by their communities.

SACRED PLACES IN ABORIGINAL AUSTRALIA

Among the Wik-munkan [an aboriginal people of Australia] the *pulwaiya* (ancestor) has a sacred place of origin, its *auwa*, where it resides and whence it issues forth. These *auwa*, or totem centers, are sometimes the nests and breeding places of the birds, animals, and plants concerned and are always situated on the hunting grounds of the clan to which they belong, where the totemic species is abundant. Each *auwa* has its own peculiar characteristics. Trees, bushes, rocks, naturally or artificially arranged, ant beds or holes in the ground in the vicinity of the *auwa*, are sacred to the totems. There is always water nearby in the shape of river, creek, lagoon, waterhole or swamp, or well, at the bottom of which the *pulwaiya* resides and into which the dead of the clan are believed to go. They are said to play about the vicinity of the *auwa* in the form of their totem. This is perhaps why plants or animals are protected near the *auwa* of their representative totem and why the killing of an animal or the injuring of a plant near its *auwa* is not only strictly forbidden but believed to be attended by grave consequences.

***Source:* Roheim, Geza. (1945).**
The Eternal Ones of the Dream: A Psychoanalytic Interpretation of Australian Myth and Ritual.
New York: International Universities Press, p. 152.

Experiences and Roles

Besides differences in kind and size, sacred places offer different experiences of holiness and fill different roles in their religious traditions. None of these experiences or roles is exclusive, and almost any sacred place embraces several of the categories that follow.

Boundary or Gateway

Sacred places are often thought of as being located at the boundary between the profane world and the holy and divine world. They are windows through which people can look at another reality far superior and different from theirs and have it look back at them; they are even doorways through which people can step into holiness or have it invade and sanctify the profane world. As such, sacred places are often celebrated as the preeminent and most efficacious places at which to communicate with the divine through prayers, chants, and sacrifices. The effectiveness and direction of such communication can even connect different sacred places, as well as the people within them. In Islam mosques are sacred places, and they orient all of the people within them toward the more sacred place, Mecca; so, during weekly prayer services, all Muslims are united in prayer in their various mosques, all facing the holy city of Mecca and directing their prayers to it. In what is perhaps the most communally oriented sense of sacred place, profane space is bridged and overcome, and people, communities, and places are united by connecting to the holy.

Center or Axis

A sacred place is often considered the center of the Earth and its inhabitants. Earth is the first place the gods or God created, or it is where the gods or God set a particular people apart for service to them. The physical and social aspects of cosmogony (the creation of the world) usually overlap. This is seen in the Kaaba (a stone building in the court of the Great Mosque at Mecca) of Islam, believed to have been built by the first man, Adam, with the help of the angel Gabriel; but it is also where Muhammad began to build the *umma*, the Islamic community, and it is now the focus of the hajj, the yearly pilgrimage that unites Muslims while obliterating all social and racial distinctions among them. The divine order and rule of this sacred place overshadow the profane social order of the rest of the world and time.

As the center of the Earth, the sacred place is often called "the axis of the earth," and a common symbol therefore associated with it is the sacred pole or pillar. In this symbol, too, the physical centeredness and social centeredness overlap: The sacred poles of some Native American tribes and aboriginal Australians are associated with the creation of the world or with a

The Temple of Heaven in Beijing in August 2002. COURTESY OF KAREN CHRISTENSEN.

story of how the tribe came to live where it now does, a land that its members believe is specially designated by the gods as sacred. Similarly, the Hebrew Bible repeats images of God parting the waters that connect this action to creation and to setting Israel aside for God: first to create the inhabitable world, then to save the Israelites from the Egyptians, then to let the Israelites enter the Holy Land. To create the world was a sanctifying act, redeeming it from chaos and nonbeing, and to give a special part of it to a chosen people further sanctified that part and that people, redeeming them from profane space and time.

Besides cosmic and social order, the centeredness and order of a sacred place may be seen as reflecting the order, beauty, and sacredness of the human body, which is itself a kind of sacred place (a "temple of the Holy Spirit" in some Christian parlance). This is seen graphically in the *purusha* myth of Hinduism, where the body parts of the primal being create, order, and legitimate the parts of the physical world and the social castes of the human world. The sacred place is sometimes called "the navel of the Earth," recalling cosmogony and the connectedness of the world to its Creator. Sacred places can show this kind of order by their parts corresponding to parts of the human body and by their symmetry, beauty, and tendency to draw the gaze of worshipers upward. This sense of sacred place is perhaps the most mysterious, taking believers back to the beginning of time as it directs them to look inward at their own imperfect but divinely created bodies, outward to the social realities that correspond to them, and upward to the mysterious, macrocosmic reflection of them.

Dwelling

Sometimes the sacred place is even more closely connected to the divine than as a doorway that allows

Church in Port Maresby, Papua New Guinea featuring traditional cult house designs. COURTESY OF PAUL SILLITOE.

communication, becoming the divinity's dwelling place that allows one to be in the divine presence. Ancient Greek and Near Eastern temples all included this idea, usually made concrete in a statue of the divinity. For the monotheistic faiths for whom this idea may be too anthropomorphic (having human form) or iconic, the more indirect image that God makes God's "name" dwell in a certain place may be substituted. Being in a dwelling place of a god gives more direct and tangible access than communication, and this can be manifested as healing, miracles, or salvation. The Catholic theology of sacraments shows this kind of idea of dwelling: Christ, the Lord of the Supper (something usually enacted in a home), is really and fully present in the sacraments (usually administered in a sacred place, a church), not as a memory or an idea, but rather as a living and life-changing presence.

Related to the idea of a sacred place as the divinity's home is the common practice of purification before entering it and of purity of spirit and body while in it. This practice is shown in rituals such as dipping one's fingers into holy water and making the sign of the cross upon entering a Catholic church,

Roman Catholic relics on display in Florence, Italy. COURTESY OF CATHLEEN FRACASSE.

removing shoes before entering a Buddhist temple, and the more extensive ritual ablutions before entering a mosque. Such rituals are similar to those practiced upon entering a human dwelling because a human home is also sacred, a place of safety and loving presence, and not equivalent to the dangers and profanity encountered outside it. The similarity runs both ways as well, and human homes often include rituals and objects that recognize and establish their sacredness in ways quite similar to houses of worship: *butsudans* in Buddhist homes, mezuzah in Jewish homes, icons in Orthodox homes, or the even more general idea of the hearth as a special center of the home that gives warmth and light to the family. This is probably the simplest but most pervasive sense of sacred place, as humans constantly surround themselves with rituals and objects to sanctify their world, to recognize it as sacred place; thereby they show their discontent and dissatisfaction with the profane world.

Memorial

When a sacred place is considered sacred because of some event other than cosmogony, then the place is a memorial, commemorating some definitive event or holy person. Even nonreligious persons or communities recognize this kind of sacred place: A grave is usually sacred to the deceased person's family members, even if they are not religious, and most Americans would feel a sense of awe at Gettysburg or the site of the World Trade Center without necessarily thinking of or believing in God. The place can be beautiful and salvific (having the power or intent to save), such as the place of Buddha's first sermon, commemorated with a stupa (Buddhist shrine) that believers walk around, or it can be catastrophic, such as the Wailing Wall in Jerusalem. Whenever the event or person is definitive to people, when they make the event or person what they are, then the place associated with that event or person is sacred to them.

Connected with the idea of memorials are relics, which are items associated with holy people. The places where relics are found are recognized as sacred by the believers who revere the holy people from whom the relics come. Again, for a painful and nonreligious example, consider the enormous efforts taken to sift through the wreckage and recover every possibly identifiable item from the people who died in the World Trade Center attack. Relics make the sacred place portable and even result in places not directly connected to the person now being considered holy because of them: One of the Buddha's fingers was recently moved from China to Taiwan with great fanfare, and the remains of the Three Magi reside in the cathedral in Cologne, Germany—places that none of these holy men ever visited.

Being in a sacred place that is a memorial connects the present to the events and people of the past while expanding a person's outlook toward eternity. As the idea of sacred place as boundary and place of communication brings communities together despite intervening profane space, a sacred place that is a memorial connects the community to all who have gone before and asserts the ultimate holiness of time.

Kim Paffenroth

See also Liminoid

Further Reading

Brereton, J. P. (1987). Sacred space. In M. Eliade (Ed.), *The encyclopedia of religion*. New York: Macmillan.

Bolle, K. W. (1969). Speaking of a place. In J. M. Kitagawa & C. H. Long (Eds.), *Myths and symbols: Studies in honor of Mircea Eliade* (pp. 127–139). Chicago: University of Chicago Press.

Caillois, R. (1959). *Man and the sacred* (M. Barash, Trans.). Chicago: University of Illinois Press.

Eliade, M. (1959). *The sacred and the profane: The nature of religion*. New York: Harper & Row.

Smith, J. Z. (1978). *Map is not territory: Studies in the history of religions*. Chicago: University of Chicago Press.

Sacrifice and Offerings

Sacrifice and offerings are rituals found in virtually every religious system, including all major religions. They are among the most ubiquitous of religious rituals, conducted for a wide variety of reasons and displaying much diversity not only across but also within cultures. Rituals of sacrifice and offering are conducted to remove sin, assuage guilt, win favors, avoid punishment, bond with gods and spirits, give gods or spirits what is theirs, maintain the order of the universe, avoid conflict, resolve disputes, and celebrate events of personal, family, community, or religious significance.

At their core sacrifice and offerings address the relationships between humans and their supernatural worlds. The animals sacrificed and the goods offered are meant to please a supernatural force, whether it be a god, spirit, ghost, or so forth, and to maintain or reestablish the bonds between the believers and their supernatural world. The basic difference between sacrifice and offering is that in sacrifice an animal is killed, whereas in offering a plant, foodstuff, or inanimate object is destroyed or consumed. In all cultures what is sacrificed or consumed is of economic importance and is often a staple food or source of food. However, the sacrificial item has no spiritual essence of its own; it derives this spiritual essence from being sacrificed or offered. Sacrifice is usually an organized ritual conducted in public by ritual specialists. Rules governing ritual sacrifice are usually quite specific, and following them is required if the sacrifice is to have its desired effect. Offerings are more likely to be either public or private and can be more informal than is sacrifice. Sociological explanations for sacrifice stress the bonds created between the human and supernatural worlds and the bonds created among members of the community participating in the sacrifice. Sacrifice is a mechanism that directs people to unite for communal interests rather than individual ones.

The Kélé-ritual at its climax: The high-priest Etienne Wells Joseph (in 1985) is supervising the beheading of the sacrificial ram with one single stroke of the cutlass, releasing the divine power of Ashe which is charging the Shango-stones with its healing energy. COURTESY OF MANFRED KREMSER.

Although sacrifice, or the concept of sacrifice, continues to play a role in major religions, sacrifice as a ritual is far less elaborated than in the past. Sacrifice was especially important in the early centuries of Judaism and ancient Hinduism. For ancient Hebrews ritual sacrifice was the primary ritual activity, and the Hebrew word *qorban* means "to bring God and humans close." Offerings were made each day in the Temple in Jerusalem, livestock (usually sheep or goats) were sacrificed in the Temple each week, and sacrifice marked other events. The Bible's Book of Leviticus provides detailed instructions for conducting sacrifices. With the destruction of the Temple by the Romans in 70 CE and the dispersal of the Jewish community, sacrifice ended and was replaced by prayer services in the daily and weekly calendar of observance. Ritual sacrifice continues to be of symbolic importance in Orthodox Judaism but has little meaning in progressive forms of Judaism.

In Christianity the meaning of sacrifice is attached to the death of Christ, which in the early years of Christianity was seen by some interpreters as having superseded traditional Jewish sacrifice. Eventually Christ's death, seen as voluntary and of value to humanity, came to be seen in many denominations as the ultimate sacrifice and the Eucharist (communion) as a ritual reflection of the centrality of that event.

The exavation of the ancient altar of high sacrifice at Petra, Jordan in 1996. COURTESY OF STEPHEN G. DONALDSON PHOTOGRAPHY.

In Islam the major sacrifice is conducted during Id al-Kabir, the Great Feast, and marks Abraham's sacrifice of a ram in place of his son. As with many other peoples, Muslims see sacrifice as a way of becoming closer to God, and sacrifice often marks a birth.

Perhaps among all religions sacrifice is most important in Hinduism and especially in ancient Hinduism, dating back twenty-five hundred years. During the first centuries of Hinduism, sacrifice and offerings were largely personal matters carried out in the home to win the gods' favors in calendrical and life-cycle events. As Hinduism became more complex and institutionalized during the Vedic (relating to the Hindu sacred writings) period, sacrifice took on a central role and came to be seen as essential to maintenance of the cosmic order and to human control of the gods. Much literature was written on sacrifice, and priests became experts at conducting sacrificial rituals. These rituals gave priests and Brahmans (the priestly caste) much power and also made sacrifices expensive. The expense made sacrifices unsustainable on a broad scale, and they eventually largely disappeared, replaced by rituals in which handfuls of rice were given to people.

In the contemporary world sacrifice has drawn most attention as a religious freedom issue in the United States as regards the animal sacrifice rituals of adherents of Santeria and Vodun (voodoo). Although local jurisdictions have passed laws to ban animal sacrifices, courts have generally allowed them under constitutional protections of religious freedom.

David Levinson

See also Agricultural Rituals; Blood Rituals; Cannibalism; Hunting Rituals; Santeria; Vodun

Further Reading

Bourdillon, M. F. C., & Fortes, M. (1980). *Sacrifice*. New York: Academic Press.

Hubert, H., & Mauss, M. (1964). *Sacrifice: Its nature and function*. London: Cohen & West.

Morris, B. (1987). *Anthropological studies of religion*. Cambridge, UK: Cambridge University Press.

Santeria

Santeria, the "way of the saints," has its origins in Cuba and other parts of the Caribbean. It has been found in the United States from the beginning of Cuban immigration. However, it began to gain popularity among African-Americans as well as Hispanic Americans during the period of Black Power during the 1960s. It provides a form of syncretism essential to popular religion, blending African elements with Christian traditions. Catholic ceremonies, for example, are followed and the Catholic saints are prayed to by the people, but the worshipers direct some elements of the ceremony to indigenous African or Mesoamerican gods.

The use of animal sacrifice in Santeria, as in a number of other African-based syncretic religions, leads to a great deal of criticism and opposition. For example, Miami with its large Cuban population has been the scene of a number of trials against Santeria members who have conducted animal sacrifices. Rigoberto Zamora, the Cuban-born Santeria high priest, found himself in trouble for televising his animal sacrifices. Zamora came to the United States in the late 1970s in the Mariel boatlift and has had no need to learn English. He provides a reason for not needing to learn English, stressing the continuity of Miami's Cuban culture with that of Cuba. "People can rebuild their own cultures in Miami," he states. "So we're getting people not only from Cuba and Latin America, but from Chicago and Union City, New Jersey." (Sell 1997, 23–32)

The large Cuban population and the popularity of Santeria helps explain Miami's "Voodoo Squad," which is responsible for picking up offerings of dead animals and trinkets left to appease the Orishas, the Yoruba spirits behind the Santeria deities. Santeria combines Christian saints with Yoruba deities. The syncretism has been successful and has spread from Nigeria through Cuba, Brazil, and Haiti to middle-class suburbs.

The United States Supreme Court, however, has ruled that followers of Santeria have the right to include ritual sacrifice in their religious practice. The 100,000-plus followers of the religion in south Florida held a giant celebration in 1993 to rejoice in this decision. It was the televising of this celebration, in which Zamora twisted off the head of a live goat on television, that got him in trouble. Zamora pled no contest when he discovered that a more polished high priest would testify against him in court. In fact, the witness was Ernesto Pichardo, the man behind the Supreme Court case. The internal struggle over the meaning of Santeria is an interesting development, the sign of a growing religion adapting to a new setting.

Origins

Santeria has a number of designations. It is sometimes referred to as the Rule of the Orishas and the Order of Lucumi (a religion found mainly in Brazil and based on Yoruba religious themes). The religion came to Cuba from areas of what is now Nigeria and Benin. It is related to the traditional religion of the Yoruba. Yoruba slaves hid their Orishas, spirit icons, behind carvings of Catholic saints. But one did not replace the other. It is a matter of "both at once" rather than "either-or," a fundamental characteristic of Yoruba culture.

The basic purpose of Santeria is to develop a personal tie to one of the Orishas and to perform rituals associated with that spirit. The major saints are Saint Peter, identified by Elgua, who is the gatekeeper to the gods, and Saint Barbara, associated with Shango, the god of iron and the personification of justice. The Orishas offer great returns to devotees: protection, wisdom, and success. Devotees turn to a Babalawo, a "father of the Orishas," to aid them in seeking the help of the spirits. The spirits have possessed these practitioners. This possession enables them to practice divination, throwing bones or shells as in Yoruba Ifa divination. The divination helps reveal the root of the problem. In return the devotees offer food and perform animal sacrifices, cementing their relationship with the Orishas.

The divination ceremonies, called *Bembes,* are dramatic and significant rituals. There is elaborate drumming and communal dancing. Intricate African rhythms fill the air. Orishas mount many of the bodies of the celebrants. Those mounted offer advice to other participants.

The religion spread to Puerto Rico and other Caribbean islands, to Venezuela, and to the United States after the 1959 Cuban Revolution. Although Roman Catholicism is the religion of four-fifths of Panamanians, there are a large number of Santeria followers in Panama, who combine Catholic and West Indian religious customs. Many of the Cuban refugees were members of the Santeria religion and brought the religion to hundreds of thousands of other people. The Black Power Movement of the 1960s and the spread of the movement among musicians did much to popularize the African based religion.

Santeria Beliefs

There are many internal differences in Santeria beliefs. However, there is a certain consensus on some of the beliefs. God is the "owner of heaven" and followers refer to him as Olorun, or Oludamare, the 'owner of heaven." God created the universe and is the supreme deity. He also created the Orishas, the lesser guardians. Each orisha is associated with a Christian saint. Each is associated with a basic principle, number, color, food, emblem, and even a certain type of dance posture. The Orishas are not immortal and require food, animal sacrifice, as well as prepared dishes and human worship to be effective.

Ritual Sacrifice is an essential feature of Santeria rituals. The Babalawo presents the collected blood to the Orisha. Chickens, goats, and other small animals are used in the sacrifice. The successful sacrifice brings forgiveness of sins, purification, and good luck. Possession is another characteristic of Santeria ritual. The rhythmic sounds and dancing aid in achieving possession by an Orisha. The Orisha speaks through the possessed person to the celebrants.

Although ancestors are not Orishas, they are revered and people call on them for help. They are called Ara Oru, People of Heaven, and worshipers look to them for guidance in moral issues and as exemplars for action. At each family ceremony people recite the names of their ancestors.

More so than Judaism, Christianity, or Islam, Santeria is a religion preserved by oral tradition. It has no sacred books of its own. Santeria rituals typically begin with the invocation of Olorun. Drums play a prominent role in this process, using African rhythms. Changes in the *oru* or rhythm are associated with a specific Orisha. Sacrifice and dancing are significant parts of rituals.

Orisha priests are termed Santeros or Babalochas or Babalawos. There are also priestesses and they are called Santeras or Iyalochas. The gender-neutral term

Olorisha refers to either a priest or a priestess. These practitioners receive many years of training in the faith's oral tradition. Before their initiation, they spend a period of time in isolation, meditating on their responsibilities. A good part of their training is the learning of songs, dance, and healing.

There are a number of *botanicas* throughout the United States. These stores provide Santeria adherents with appropriate charms, spices, potions, musical instruments, and other needed materials.

Conflicts over Santeria

The Santeros and other Americans have clashed over the issue of animal rights. The sacrifice of small animals strikes many Americans as cruel and even barbaric. The Santeros counter that they slaughter the animals humanely and then eat them. They do so, they say, in a more humane way than many of the commercial slaughterhouses. Moreover, the ancient Israelis sacrificed animals until the destruction of the temple in Jerusalem. Many other religions also carried out the practice. The U.S. Supreme Court has upheld the right of animal sacrifice, an integral part of the religion, one the justices say is required by the Orishas, who must be fed.

More serious was the Matamoros Incident, which took place in early 1989. The bodies of more than a dozen murdered men were found in Matamoros, Mexico, close to the Texas border. The media played the story up in a spectacular manner, blaming the killing on Satanists, witches, voodoo priests, or Santeros. The murders were the result of drug dealers' actions. Some of the murderers hired by the dealer were members of the Santeria group but others belonged to various other religions, including Catholicism.

Music and Santeria

An important aspect of Santeria has been its influence on music. Until its growth through the spread of Cuban refugees, those who knew about Santeria did so because of its influence on music and musicians, such as Prez Prado and Chano Pozo. The rumba, for example, has always been closely associated with Santeria.

There are families known as *rumbero* families. These families seek to become formally initiated into the Santeria. They undergo a process of learning the appropriate chants and rhythms, serving an apprenticeship under other *rumberos*. Initiation guarantees them steady work at rituals. Most *rumberos* also work in Abukaua song, dance, and drumming rituals, a form of worship related to Santeria. The rumba music has spread to more secular settings, influencing Cuban and Afro-Cuban music among other forms. The *rumberos* are celebrated as outstanding drummers. They are great virtuosos and have enormous creativity. Moreover, their spur-of-the-moment improvisations are remarkable, filled with animation, excitement, group interplay. The *rumberos* employ a drum trio, claves, the *madruga* or shaker, and the *cascara* or *cata*, a cylindrical bamboo instrument played with sticks. Drummers generally place shakers on their wrists and use the *madruga* to keep a basic pulse or ground beat. In rumba, shakers are often used on the wrists of the drummers (*muñecas*, wrist shakers), but the *madruga* is the tin or metallic shaker that keeps a steady basic pulse.

There is a strong connection between rumba and Santeria. There is an interesting syncretization involved in that the major improvisation takes place in the highest register, as in European music, rather than the lowest, as in African music. Many Orisha chants are sung to rumba music and the dancing is often a copy of Santeria dancing.

Frank A. Salamone

Further Reading

Baer, H. A., Singer, M., & Susser, I. (1997). *Medical anthropology and the world system: A critical perspective*. Westport, CT: Bergin & Garvey.

Bailey, E. J. (2000). *Medical anthropology and African American health*. Westport, CT: Bergin & Garvey.

Bell, C. (1997). *Ritual: Perspectives and dimensions*. New York: Oxford University Press.

Brettell, C. B. (Ed.). (1996). *When they read what we write: The politics of ethnography*. Westport, CT: Bergin & Garvey.

Daniel, Y. (1995). *Rumba: Dance and social change in contemporary Cuba*. Bloomington, IN: Indiana University Press.

Evans-Pritchard, E. E. (1963). *Essays in social anthropology*. New York: Free Press of Glencoe.

Glazier, S. D. (Ed.). (1999). *Anthropology of religion: A handbook*. Westport, CT: Praeger.

Gonzalez-Pando, M. E. (Ed.). (1998). *The Cuban Americans*. Westport, CT: Greenwood Press.

Gossen, G. H. (Ed.). (1993). *South and Meso-American native spirituality: From the cult of the feathered serpent to the theology of liberation.* New York: Crossroad.

Harris, J. E. (Ed.). (1993). *Global dimensions of the African diaspora.* 2d ed. Washington, DC: Howard University.

Heinze, R. (Ed.). (2000). *The nature and function of rituals: Fire from heaven.* Westport, CT: Bergin & Garvey.

Karp, I., & Bird, C. S. (Eds.). (1980). *Explorations in African systems of thought.* Bloomington, IN: Indiana University Press.

Kramer, E. M., & Mickunas, A. (1992). *Consciousness and culture: An introduction to the thought of Jean Gebser* (E. M. Kramer, Ed.). Westport, CT: Greenwood Press.

Lippy, C. H. (1994). *Being religious, American style: A history of popular religiosity in the United States.* Westport, CT: Praeger.

Naylor, L. L. (Ed.). (1997). *Cultural diversity in the United States.* Westport, CT: Bergin & Garvey.

Noblitt, J. R., & Perkins, S., P. (2000). *Cult and ritual abuse: Its history, anthropology, and recent discovery in contemporary America* (rev. ed.). Westport, CT: Praeger.

Sargent, C. F., & Johnson, T. M (Eds.). (1996). *Medical anthropology: Contemporary theory and method.* Westport, CT: Praeger Paperback.

Sell, M. (1997). Inside Miami: A letter. *New England Review, 18*(1), 23–40.

Van Ness, P. H. (Ed.). (1996). *Spirituality and the secular quest.* New York: Crossroad Publishing.

Winthrop, R. H. (1991). *Dictionary of concepts in cultural anthropology* (R. G. McInnis, Ed.). New York: Greenwood Press.

Satanic Rituals

Understanding Satanic rituals entails sorting fact from fiction. Much of what is attributed as fact about the subject is false because rumor and myth have created so much misinformation. Contemporary Satanists are a subculture of the modern neo-pagan religious counterculture that is often confused with Wiccan witchcraft. Satanists generally disavow Wiccans and vice versa. Present-day witches, in particular Wiccans, maintain that they do not worship the devil but instead use images connected with nature (i.e., the horned god, a nature symbol like a stag) or images of goddesses. Because some Satanists call themselves "witches," the confusion about these different mystical religions tends to persist. Defining who is a Satanist is further complicated by the variety of levels of involvement. Self-proclaimed Satanists can vary from committed group members who perform rituals to loosely identified dabblers who may experiment with solitary rituals or may not practice any rituals at all. Satanism as a subculture runs the gamut from free-floating opportunism to the established black magic enclaves of the occult.

The Historic Devil, the Black Mass, and the Witch Scares

The concept of the devil slightly predated Christianity with influence of Persian Zoroastrianism on Jewish sects such as the Essenes (the sect that produced the Dead Sea Scrolls). These sects adopted the idea of a God of Light and a Prince of Darkness who engaged in cosmic struggle, an idea eventually incorporated into Christian metaphors. Christian symbolism maintained that the color white signifies good, whereas black signifies evil. Personal and societal problems became identified as the work of the devil and dark magical arts. Christians believed in the reality of the devil, or Satan, an assumption that spawned much fear and retribution. During the fourteenth century Europe periodically erupted with witch scares, which lasted until the seventeenth century. Clerics held trials after they had tortured accused prisoners to extract confessions about witchcraft, and hundreds of accused perished as hysteria swept across scores of communities. Probably the most famous witch scare occurred in 1692 at Salem, Massachusetts, when neighbors turned upon one another with accusations of witchcraft.

According to the cultural belief, witches worshiped the devil in clandestine rituals such as the Black Sabbath. Witches supposedly flew on broomsticks, and they also consorted with the devil during secret rituals, which never actually took place. Those people under social pressure during the witch persecutions confessed with all types of fanciful tales as a result of torture or as a way to avoid further punishment. Many of the accused accommodated their inquisitors with hysterical stories of devil worship. Some scholars assert that the label "witch" served as a scapegoat mechanism aimed at those less privileged in society, such as women and Jews, or those who practiced folk medicine. Furthermore, accusations of witchcraft provided a rationale for some people to persecute religious and political rivals.

The quintessential Satanic ritual, the Black Mass, became part of folklore before there was a religion called "Satanism." Although there are differing

EXTRACT FROM *THE SATANIC BIBLE*, BOOK OF BELIAL: 1.

Ritual magic consists of the performance of a formal ceremony, taking place, at least in part, within the confines of an area set aside for such purposes and at a specific time. Its main function is to isolate the otherwise dissipated adrenal and other emotionally induced energy, and convert it into a dynamically transmittable force. It is purely an emotional, rather than intellectual, act. Any and all intellectual activity must take place before the ceremony, not during it. This type of magic is sometimes known as "GREATER MAGIC."

accounts of when the ritual originated and of what occurred during the ritual, the Black Mass is generally considered an evil parody of the Catholic Mass conducted with profane variations. Legends say that witches or a defrocked priest conducted a Black Mass by saying a Catholic Mass backward with a naked female virgin draped across the altar. The devil himself or a designated male allegedly fornicated with the young woman, who represented a corrupted symbol of the Virgin Mary. People of the time believed that worshipers used a black Eucharist (communion water), or possibly a rotten black turnip, and that they wore black hooded robes as they sacrificed children. The celebrants were said to defecate and urinate on a chalice and to take part in a lustful orgy with the devil.

Academics dispute the origin of the actual term *Black Mass,* which is believed to be of later coinage than the term *Black Sabbath*. The first recorded Black Mass may have occurred in the seventh century, when the Church Council of Toledo, Spain, condemned a so-called Mass of the Dead, which supposedly prayed for a man's death. Heretics and rebels used distorted masses to protest the Catholic Church's power, and at different times those who wished to cast magical spells also usurped the ritual of the *Black Mass* for sinister purposes. These rituals did not necessarily resemble the Black Mass with a naked woman draped across an altar; the term *Black Mass* does not represent a singular coherent phenomenon but rather any purposeful desecration. The modern notion of a Black Mass may have originated during the reign of King Louis XV of France, who commissioned a secret investigative agency whose members wore black robes and held court in a room draped with black curtains.

Throughout the nineteenth and early twentieth century interest in the occult and ritual magic grew in Europe and the United States. This growth led to the influence of a proto-Satanic philosophy espoused by such people as the infamous occult magician Aleister Crowley (1875–1947). Modern Satanism invented itself without relying on a lengthy inherited tradition, despite assumptions to the contrary. Scholars contend that contemporary Satanists borrowed and reinvented their rituals from such traditions and groups as voodoo and legendary witchcraft, Masonic tradition, Order of the Golden Dawn, Ordo Templi Orientis (OTO), and Crowley's Thelema.

Modern Satanists

Capitalizing on the growing interest in the occult in California at the time, Anton LaVey (1930–1997) founded the Church of Satan in 1966. His church faced years of controversy from the outside and schisms from within, but LaVey's publications, in particular *The Satanic Bible* (1969), and his basic tenets of the Church of Satan set the basis for modern Satanism. The Church of Satan instituted the "grotto system," which set up satellite congregations that were allied with the central organization. Grottoes were authorized to do group rituals according to church handbooks and guidelines. The grotto system was supposedly dissolved in the 1970s, but its remnants remain. By 1973 splinter groups had instituted their own organizations, most of which were short-lived, but in 1975 Michael Aquino founded the Church of Set, which still exists. Affiliated Satanists of the twenty-first century represent a diffusion of communities throughout the world. Branches of the Church of Satan, as well as autonomous Satanist organizations and independent practitioners who often publish their personal rituals online, can be found on the Internet.

Rituals

LaVey described his rituals in his many books, such as *The Satanic Bible* and *The Satanic Rituals* (1972). Using a supposedly ancient language, he published Enochian (an ancient mythical language) chants to be used with certain rituals. In 1969 film director Ray Laurent filmed LaVey and his followers performing rituals in the documentary *Satanis: The Devil's Mass*. Counter to the stereotype, LeVeyian Satanism forbids conducting illegal activity, conducting animal or human sacrifice, committing suicide, and allowing underaged members to take part in rituals. Grotto handbooks warn against performing rituals under the influence of alcohol or other drugs. Ideally, rituals rejoice in the pleasures of the flesh and the experience of self-indulgence. Satanic rituals celebrate the individual self, the individual's will, and individual's power over the world. A Satanist's birthday constitutes the most elevated of all celebratory days. Other celebrations include Halloween, the solstices, and the equinoxes. Groups often participate in Friday night rituals of fellowship and gatherings on nights of the full moon and dark moon. In addition, they congregate on Walpurgisnacht (30 April or 1 May eve), an ancient fertility holiday.

Practitioners use the symbol of Satanism, the Sigil of Baphomet (a circle containing an inverted pentagram embellished with a goat's head), in most rituals. The Sigil of Baphomet is the official trademark of the Church of Satan. Outsiders usually stereotype Satanists as devil worshipers by using the Christian connotation. LaVey's version of Satanism is militantly atheistic, but what Satan represents depends on the Satanist. Satan can represent nature, carnality, and hedonism. Some Satanists conceptualize Satan as a symbol of the self or a psychological archetype; others conceptualize Satan as a focus on an impersonal force. Fewer practitioners conceptualize Satan as an actual supernatural being.

Contemporary affiliated Satanists do not generally perform the Black Mass (a naked woman draped across an altar) but rather concentrate on group rituals connected with sex magic (any variety of rituals which involve a sex act), healing/happiness rites, and destructive magic. Other rituals, such as initiations, weddings, funerals, and baptisms, are also practiced. LaVey made a distinction between greater and lesser magic. Greater magic involves group rituals. Lesser magic involves solitary rituals oriented around individual wish fulfillment. A typical group ritual uses black robes, black candles, a silver chalice, a ritual dagger or sword, and a bell, which is rung at the opening and close of the rituals. Rituals are supposed to tap into feelings and bodily sensations, not the intellect; they provide a release from stress and anger or other pent-up emotions. Created originally as psychodramas, Satanic rituals tend to entail iconoclastic activities, which can involve masturbating or directing anger toward a targeted person. Because Satanism does not believe in forgiveness and because "evil" people should be punished, a group may perform a destructive ritual against a designated person. Solitary practitioners also report putting curses on people. In fact, Zeena LaVey, Anton LaVey's youngest daughter, contends that she put on her father a curse that precipitated his death.

Estimates of the number of Satanists run as high as ten thousand. Satanism does not require group membership; therefore, many adherents today practice their beliefs without a commitment to a ritual community. They are referred to as "dabblers," "dilettantes," or "solitaries" (solitary practitioners). Researcher James R. Lewis found that a substantial number of Satanists relate to the Internet as a way to learn and to communicate about their beliefs. The largest proportion of his respondents (48 percent) had no group involvement.

Satanic Ritual Abuse

By the 1980s the public had become alarmed by reports of widespread Satanic ritual abuse (SRA). Today reputable researchers and courts of law have refuted the notion of a Satanic international conspiracy that routinely abused and sacrificed children. Several factors contributed to this notion: the growth of the anticult movement, heavy metal music and its imagery, therapeutic mythmaking, and media sensationalism. The 1970s brought a marked increase in the dissemination of occult literature and the growth of alternative religious movements. Literature on Satanism could be attained easily through bookstores and peer group networks. In addition, alienated teens acquired such literature, some of which was marketed to them in the form of heavy metal music symbolism. With the reestablishment of a more conservative discourse during the Ronald Reagan years, Fundamentalist Christianity acquired prominence, and the related anticult movement concept of "brainwashing" gained a foothold in the public imagination. Adolescent experimentation with Satanic symbols drew a noticeable audience of concerned parents and educators who feared mind-control tactics from demonic forces. As a result, Satanism became one of the scapegoats for the ills of society in part because of the media's focus on the issue. Sociologists identify this as a rumor-panic effect, or a moral crusade phenomenon.

In Michelle Smith's book *Michelle Remembers* (1980), the author told of recovery from cultic ritual abuse that was uncovered with the help of a psychiatrist. In reaction to this book and the belief of some therapists in SRA, many patients told of similar experiences, called "recovered memories." This therapeutic anomaly is now called "false-memory syndrome." Talk shows and the print media championed the cause of recovered memory, unwittingly sparking the spread of further rumors and the continuation of the spurious diagnosis by therapists. Rumors contended that a conspiracy of Satanists held rituals in which they abused and sacrificed children or sustained so-called breeder colonies, producing succeeding generations of victims. So-called experts also accused this Satanic underground of abducting children, performing human sacrifice, and committing cannibalism. Depression, multiple personality disorder, and other psychological ailments were supposedly indicators that SRA had taken place.

Most police agencies developed a task force called "cult cops" who monitored occult crimes. Although a few crimes have been undisputedly linked to Satanist dabblers, such as serial killer Richard Ramirez, most crimes presumed to have a Satanic connection had none, for example, the Matamoras murders. In April 1989 in Matamoras, Mexico, police discovered thirteen mutilated bodies. Early reports attributed the murders to Satanic activity, but further investigation and evidence showed that this was not the case. In retrospect, some of the people accused in child-molestation cases, such as the acquitted defendants in the McMartin preschool case [the best known of the Multi-Victim Multi Offender (MVMO) child abuse cases, lasting six years and resulting in acquittal], were probably victims of a rumor hysteria.

Putting Satanic Rituals in Perspective

By looking back in history, one can see that ancient religions created an image of the devil. In the Western world the devil serves as a psychological boogeyman, an image that becomes frightening real in the mind of society at times of stress and uncertainty. Few subjects are more misinterpreted than those with a "Satanic" label. Satanic rituals remain defiant and rebellious even in this uncertain world of religious mutability, and their contemporary place will ultimately rest with the ability of their practitioners to remain viable in a world that generally fears them.

Diana G. Tumminia

See also Exorcism; Paganism and Neo-Paganism; Wicca; Witchcraft

Further Reading

Bainbridge, W. S. (1972). *Satan's power: A deviant psychotherapy cult*. Berkeley and Los Angeles: University of California Press.

Barton, B. (1990). *The church of Satan: A history of the world's most notorious religion*. New York: Hell's Kitchen.

Baskin, W. (1972). *Dictionary of Satanism*. New York: Philosophy Library.

Bottoms, B. L., & Davies, S. L. (1997). The creation of Satanic ritual abuse. *Journal of Social and Clinical Psychology, 16*(2), 112–132.

Ellis, B. (2000). *Raising the devil: Satanism, new religions, and the media*. Lexington: University Press of Kentucky.

Freedland, N. (1972). *The occult explosion: From magic to ESP, the people who made the new occultism*. New York: G. P. Putnam's Sons.

Kahaner, L. (1988). *Cults that kill: Probing the underworld of occult crime*. New York: Warner Books.

LaVey, A. S. (1969). *The Satanic Bible*. New York: Avon.

LaVey, A. S. (1971). *The compleat witch*. New York: Lancer Books.

LaVey, A. S. (1972). *The Satanic rituals*. Secaucus, NJ: University Books.

Lewis, J. R. (2001). Who serves Satan?: A demographic and ideological profile. *Marburg Journal of Religion, 6*(2), 1–12.

Loftus, E., & Kecham, K. (1996). *Myth of repressed memory: False memories and allegations of sexual abuse*. New York: St. Martin's Press.

Lyons, A. (1988). *Satan wants you: The cult of devil worship in America*. New York: Mysterious Press.

Nathan, D., & Snedeker, M. (1995). *Satan's silence: Ritual abuse and the making of a modern American witch hunt*. New York: Basic Books.

Pendergrast, M., & Gavigan, M. (1996). *Victims of memory: Sex abuse accusations and shattered lives*. Hinesburg, VT: Upper Access Book Publishers.

Richardson, J. T., Best, J., & Bromley, D. G. (Eds.). (1991). *The Satanism scare*. New York: Walter de Gruyter.

Smith, M., & Pazder, L. (1980). *Michelle remembers*. New York: Congdon & Lattes.

Terry, M. (1987). *The ultimate evil*. Garden City, NY: Doubleday.

Tractenberg, J. S. (1983). *The devil and the Jews*. New Haven, CT: Yale University Press.

Victor, J. B. (1993). *Satanic panic: The creation of a contemporary legend*. Chicago: Open Court.

Zaretsky, I., & Leone, M. P. (Eds.). (1974). *Religious movements in contemporary America*. Princeton, NJ: Princeton University Press.

Zellner, W. W. (1995). *Countercultures*. New York: St. Martin's Press.

Scatological Rituals

In general, scatological rituals involve human or animal excreta. In the most restrictive sense *scatological* refers exclusively to the excretory, especially feces. In the psychological and anthropological literature, however, rituals involving urine, pus, mucus, saliva, blood, and other bodily substances are characterized as scatological.

In the West, religious rituals involving human excreta have been misunderstood as the hallmark of "primitive," "barbarian," and "uncivilized" cultures, owing in large part to the arguments first deployed by the Scottish anthropologist James George Frazer (1890) in his influential compendium of rituals and religious practices, *The Golden Bough*, and to the characterizations of rituals employing "exrementitious remedial agents" (1994, 3) by anthropologist John G. Bourke (1891) in his lengthy *Scatologic Rites of All Nations*. During the past century these works have come under attack for their cultural imperialism, social Darwinism, and their dubious reliability. Nevertheless, much of what people know about the history of scatological rituals begins with these works.

The Relativity of Taboo

The anthropologist Mary Douglas challenged Frazer's assertion that "primitive cultures" confuse the sacred and the unclean. Defining religion broadly as the ritual attempt to make sense of the world, in her work *Purity and Danger: An Analysis of Pollution and Taboo* (1966) Douglas argues that what is considered dirty and defiling varies from one culture to the next. Further, although rules concerning that which is clean and sacred help to unify a culture (indeed, hygienics in this sense is the essence of religion for Douglas), they also create dangerous, ritual moments for transgressing and encountering the dirty.

The negative connotations of scatology seem stronger in the West. In many parts of the world human excrement and animal excrement are not necessarily dirty or unclean. Among some Hindus, for example, one can atone for sins by eating cow dung or by drinking *panchakaryam* ["a mixture of purifying substances from the cow, including milk, ghee or clarified butter, curd, dung, and urine" (Spinrad 1999, 87)]. Bourke reported the ritual consumption of large amounts of human excrement in the Urine Dance of the Zuñis, which was performed by the Nehue-Cue (order of medicine men) to "insure the stomachs of members to any kind of food," presumably poisons used in their doctoring (Bourke 1994, 24). Many polytheistic religions of the past also worshiped gods of excrement, such as Crepitus, the Roman god of flatulence, and Cloacina, the Roman goddess of sewers. In other words, it is not difficult to locate religious practice involving the scatological. Considered broadly, one might describe the ritual consumption of the flesh and blood of Christ during the Eucharist as a scatological rite.

Old Testament Prohibition

Some experts have argued that the current widespread taboo of excrement can be traced to the Old Testament, a foundational text of Judaism, Christianity, and Islam. Paul Spinrad and others have suggested that one way in which the radical monotheism of the Israelites established itself as distinct from the surrounding polytheistic practices, such as the worship of the "dung god" Baal-Peor, was by rigorously forbidding the scatological. The Old Testament explicitly denigrates the excremental in numerous places, such as in Malachi 2:1–3 NSRV: "And now, O priests, this command is for you. If you will not listen, if you will not lay it to heart to give glory to my name, says the Lord of hosts, then… I will rebuke your offspring, and spread dung on your faces, the dung of your offerings, and I will put you out of my presence."

The Symbolic Power of the Scatological

Whatever the source of the taboo against excrement in the West, the rigorous policing of the excremental and its gradual movement from the public to the private sphere have increased its transgressive potency. The Black Mass, a mythic parody of the Catholic Mass in which participants are said to ritually kiss the anus of Satan embodied as a goat, eat feces, and drink urine, is a clear example of the association of excrement with evil and the powerfully negative connotations that the scatological has assumed in the West in the last few centuries.

The policing of human excrement plays an important role in psychoanalysis, which has developed numerous theories to explain the significance of excrement in religious and secular contexts. The Austrian neurologist Sigmund Freud's observation that "excreta arouse no disgust in children" led him to propose that children who do not adjust well to toilet training may either develop an "anal personality" (fixated on the control of self and others and, for Freud, later obsessed with money) or later come to fetishize excreta (Freud 1961, 54). The fetish character of excreta as either evil or filthy helps to explain why some people find the ritual use of excreta, particularly in sexual contexts, arousing.

Scatological Ritual of Everyday Life

Finally, it is important to note that the necessity of regular elimination in daily life could be characterized as a religious, scatological ritual. In almost every culture patterned or ritual gestures have developed that regulate how one defecates and urinates. In some cultures, particularly those located in Africa, India, and the Middle East, the use of the left hand in the process of defecation requires the right hand to dominate in more traditional religious practices. For some groups it is inappropriate to talk to others while using the restroom. In some cultures one squats over a hole in the floor, whereas in other cultures one sits on a toilet. In the United States the practice of elimination has led to an unstudied gender myth: At home women tend to complete their "business" procedurally, whereas men tend to use the opportunity to read and meditate, deliberately extending the excretory process longer than necessary.

Joshua Gunn

See also Divination; Magic; Shamanism; Wicca; Witchcraft

Further Reading

Bourke, J. G. (1968). *Scatologic rites of all nations.* New York: Johnson Reprint Corporation. (Original work published 1891)

Bourke, J. G. (1994). The urine dance of the Zunis (pp. 21–26). In L. P. Kaplan (Ed.), *The portable scatalog: Excerpts from scatologic rites of all nations.* New York: William Morrow.

Brown, N. O. (1959). *Life against death.* New York: Vintage Books.

Corbin, A. (1986). *The foul and the fragrant.* Cambridge, MA: Harvard University Press.

Douglas, M. (1966). *Purity and danger: An analysis of concepts of pollution and taboo.* New York: Routledge.

Dundes, A. (1984). *Life is like a chicken coop ladder.* New York: Columbia University Press.

Frazer, J. G. (1996). *The golden bough.* New York: Touchstone Books. (Original work published 1890)

Freud, S. (1961). *Civilization and its discontents* (J. Strachey, Trans.). New York: W. W. Norton.

Laporte, D. (2000). *History of shit* (N. Benabid & R. el-Khoury, Trans.). Cambridge, MA: MIT Press.

Medway, G. J. (2001). *Lure of the sinister: The unnatural history of Satanism.* New York: New York University Press.

Reynolds, R. (1943). *Cleanliness and godliness.* London: Allen & Unwin.

Spinrad, P. (1999). *The RE/Search guide to bodily fluids.* New York: Juno Books.

Scientific Skepticism and Religious Rituals

Many religious rituals, including rituals of technology (e.g., rituals of divination and protection) and rituals of therapy (e.g., rituals of witchcraft and curing), are intended by their practitioners to invoke supernatural causes to generate natural effects. This presents a basic and obvious question for scholarly inquiry: Do religious rituals actually work? In other words, is there, in fact, a causal link between alleged paranormal forces and observed normal effects? (The terms *paranormal* and *supernatural* are essentially synonymous, although they may have slightly different connotations—both refer to phenomena that purport to be exceptions to the natural laws revealed by scientific inquiry.)

Many scholars involved in the study of religious rituals dismiss the question of whether religious rituals actually work because they consider the question to be unanswerable. In *Theories of Primitive Religion,* the anthropologist E. E. Evans-Pritchard offers a classic formulation of the argument in support of this position: "He [the anthropologist] is not concerned,

FIREWALKING

Walking across a bed of hot coals in bare feet is both a religious and secular ritual. In both cases, it is done to enhance the individual's sense of personal control and to instill a sense of community among participants in the ritual. Although it is an important religious ritual in northern Greece, it has drawn most attention since the 1980s as a ritual associated with the New Age and personal growth movements in the United States. In the past, and to some extent, today, advocates of fire walking believe that walkers are not burned or only blister slightly because they enter an altered state of consciousness as they participate in the ritual. Experiments conducted in the 1930s by the University of London Council for Psychical Research showed that participants were not burned because their feet touched the coals only briefly and because wood coals covered by ash have low thermal conductivity. Thus physics, rather than religion, explains firewalking.

David Levinson

qua anthropologist, with the truth or falsity of religious thought. As I understand the matter, there is no possibility of his *knowing* whether the spiritual beings of primitive religions or of any others have any existence or not, and since that is the case he cannot take the question into consideration" (Evans-Pritchard 1965, 17).

Within cultural anthropology, the discipline that is most concerned with the cross-cultural, comparative study of religious rituals, it is probably fair to say that most contemporary scholars are sympathetic to Evans-Pritchard's point of view. Indeed, the notion that the supernatural realm falls beyond the bounds of scientific investigation is widely embraced outside anthropology as well. The evolutionary biologist Stephen Jay Gould (1942–2002), for example, argues that science and religion constitute "nonoverlapping magisteria" or domains of teaching authority. According to Gould, "The net of science covers the empirical realm: what is the universe made of (fact) and why does it work this way (theory). The net of religion extends over questions of moral meaning and value" (Gould 1999a, 58).

The Skeptical Alternative

Although Gould's argument is popular, it is not universally accepted. Those scholars who identify themselves as scientific skeptics maintain instead that science and religion *do* overlap to a considerable extent, and these scholars maintain that the principles of scientific inquiry *can* be applied to supernatural claims. The evolutionary zoologist Richard Dawkins (b. 1941) is a prominent proponent of these views. Dawkins contends that religions make many claims about the existence of various beings and forces and that those claims are clearly amenable to scientific scrutiny. The virgin birth of Jesus, the bodily assumption of the Blessed Virgin Mary, and the resurrection of Jesus are all factual claims, however ambiguous the historical evidence might be. "A universe with a supernatural presence," Dawkins observes, "would be a fundamentally and qualitatively different kind of universe from one without. The difference is, inescapably, a scientific difference" (Dawkins 1999, 64).

For scientific skeptics such as Dawkins the question of whether religious rituals *actually* work is an essential question that must be resolved before any satisfactory explanation of religious rituals could be developed. An anthropologist who wanted to explain why a particular group engages in rain dances, for example, would need to know first whether or not the rain dances were actually effective. The explanation of why people engage in rain dances that had actual meteorological effects would be very different from the explanation of why people engage in rain dances that had no actual meteorological effects. (Among other things, the explanation of why people *believe* in the efficacy of rain dances would be very different in the two cases.) The question then becomes whether it is possible, using the principles of scientific inquiry, to determine if paranormal causality is operative in religious rituals. Scientific skeptics answer in the affirmative.

Scientific Skepticism Defined

In the traditional philosophical sense of the term, *skepticism* refers to the contention that reliable knowledge is impossible. Those contemporary scholars and investigators who identify themselves as scientific skeptics reject this total, negative meaning of *skepticism* and embrace instead a selective, positive meaning of *skepticism*. Scientific skeptics regard skepticism as a methodological principle of inquiry. They affirm that reliable knowledge is possible, but they believe that the only claims to knowledge that are warranted are those that are supported by compelling evidence. They believe that the epistemology (the study of knowledge) of science provides the best means for obtaining factual information about the universe and everything in it, and they reject the contention that supernatural claims fall beyond the purview of rational investigation.

Principles of Scientific Skepticism

In the investigation of any paranormal or supernatural claim (which would include claims for the efficacy of religious rituals of technology and therapy), scientific skeptics would apply the following five principles to the evaluation of the claim:

1. The claim must be testable. The fundamental principle of the skeptical approach to knowledge is that claims should be accepted when they are supported by compelling evidence and rejected when the evidence is insufficient or contradictory. Many religious claims, however, are framed in a manner that makes them immune to testing against the evidence. When rain dances fail to produce rain, for example, the ritual practitioners rarely abandon belief in the efficacy of their rituals. Instead, they typically assert that rain failed to fall because the gods were angry or the dancers' hearts were impure. Whether rain falls or not, the ritual practitioners will cling to their belief in the efficacy of their ritual. In contrast, scientific skeptics insist that factual claims must be vulnerable to the possibility of refutation by contradictory evidence.
2. Arguments offered in support of the claim must be logically consistent. The fundamental rules of logical reasoning are an essential element of the epistemology of science. Thus, scientific skeptics demand that arguments be sound, and scientific skeptics are alert to common errors in logical reasoning, such as begging the question, posing a false dilemma, or appealing to authority, ignorance, or fear. The arguments offered by religious believers in support of the efficacy of religious rituals typically contain logical fallacies.
3. There must be a comprehensive examination of all evidence relevant to the claim. It would obviously be unreasonable to consider only the evidence that appears to support a claim while ignoring the evidence that contradicts it. The fact that religious rituals of technology and therapy *sometimes* achieve their intended effects, for example, is not evidence for the causal efficacy of paranormal forces because religious rituals also frequently fail to achieve their intended effects. Scientific skeptics would seek a consistent explanation of religious rituals that accounts for *all* observed effects.
4. The burden of proof for any claim falls upon the claimant. Religious believers sometimes attempt to justify their beliefs by claiming that their critics have not disproved those beliefs. There is a logical flaw in that reasoning, however: The absence of disconfirming evidence is not the same as the presence of confirming evidence. If it were, anything that could be imagined could be "proved." The intellectual obligations rest with the proponent of any claim to either offer the evidence confirming the claim or to withdraw the claim.
5. Extraordinary claims demand extraordinary evidence. Paranormal claims are inherently improbable by their nature because they purport to be exceptions to well-established scientific knowledge. Thus the evidence presented to overthrow established scientific knowledge would have to be proportional to the certainty attached to that knowledge. In the investigation of paranormal claims, scientific skeptics maintain that appeals to authority and appeals to testimony can never be sufficient in themselves to justify belief in paranormal claims because the probability of human error is always greater than the probability that a well-established scientific law has been violated.

Skeptical Organizations

The goals and assumptions of contemporary scientific skepticism are clearly evident in the various skeptical organizations that have been founded since the fourth quarter of the twentieth century. Prominent among those organizations are the Committee for the Scientific Investigation of Claims of the Paranormal, the Council for Secular Humanism, and the Skeptics Society. These organizations provide an excellent starting point for further inquiry into the nature of contemporary scientific skepticism.

The Committee for the Scientific Investigation of Claims of the Paranormal (CSICOP) was founded in 1976 by the philosopher Paul Kurtz (b. 1925), who also founded Prometheus Books, the leading publisher of skeptical books. Kurtz continues to serve as chairman of CSICOP, which counts among its fellows a number of prominent scholars and other professionals from a wide variety of fields.

CSICOP's mission is to promote science and scientific inquiry, critical thinking, science education, and the use of reason in examining important issues. The organization encourages the critical investigation of paranormal and fringe-science claims from a responsible, scientific point of view and disseminates factual information about the results of such inquiry to the scientific community, the media, and the public. CSICOP publishes a bimonthly journal, *Skeptical Inquirer,* and maintains a website at www.csicop.org.

The Council for Secular Humanism, like CSICOP, is a nonprofit educational organization devoted to the promotion of reason in human life; Paul Kurtz is its founder and chair. The council's fundamental convictions are expressed in a document entitled "The Affirmations of Humanism: A Statement of Principles," which includes the following declarations: "We are committed to the application of reason and science to the understanding of the universe and to the solving of human problems. We deplore efforts to denigrate human intelligence, to seek to explain the world in supernatural terms, and to look outside nature for salvation. We are skeptical of untested claims to knowledge, and we are open to novel ideas and seek new departures in our thinking." (Free Inquiry) The Skeptics Society, like CSICOP, conducts investigations and research into controversial claims and provides information to the media and the public on paranormal topics. As envisioned by the society, the "key to skepticism is to continuously and vigorously apply the methods of science to navigate the treacherous straits between 'know-nothing' skepticism and 'anything goes' credulity." (Skeptic)

Critical Scrutiny

From the point of view of scientific skeptics, no paranormal claim in the history of the world has ever withstood critical scrutiny under the epistemological guidelines outlined in the preceding section on the principles of scientific skepticism. After applying those principles to all available evidence collected to date, scientific skeptics conclude that there is no supernatural component to the universe. This conclusion has fundamental implications for the study of religion and religious rituals.

If the supernatural realm were real, then a host of other questions requiring explanation would be raised, such as why different groups of humans perceive the supernatural realm so differently, and why no human group has figured out how to use supernatural forces to produce the desired natural effects on a consistent basis. On the other hand, if the supernatural realm is an illusion, then the universality of religion becomes the fundamental question that needs to be explained (which is what Pascal Boyer and Steven Pinker attempt to do in their books *Religion Explained* and *How the Mind Works* when they argue that humans are susceptible to religious belief because of certain adapted features of the human mind).

Because any explanation founded upon the assumption that the supernatural realm is real would have profoundly different implications from an explanation founded upon the assumption that the supernatural realm is an illusion, scientific skeptics maintain that any satisfactory explanation of religious rituals must begin with a determination of whether the rituals actually work. That determination would not preclude the investigation of other aspects of religious rituals (including their social, psychological, and ecological functions) but would instead provide the necessary foundation for those investigations.

James Lett

See also Performance, Ritual of; Ritual Control; Ritual Specialists

Further Reading

Boyer, P. (2001). *Religion explained: The evolutionary origins of religious thought*. New York: Basic Books.

Dawkins, R. (1998). *Unweaving the rainbow: Science, delusion, and the appetite for wonder*. Boston: Houghton Mifflin.

Dawkins, R. (1999). *You can't have it both ways: Irreconcilable differences? Skeptical Inquirer*, 23(4), 62–64.

Evans-Pritchard, E. E. (1965). *Theories of primitive religion*. London: Oxford University Press.

Gould, S. J. (1999a). Nonoverlapping magisteria. *Skeptical Inquirer*, 23(4), 55–61.

Gould, S. J. (1999b). *Rocks of ages: Science and religion in the fullness of life*. New York: Ballantine.

Guthrie, S. (1993). *Faces in the clouds: A new theory of religion*. New York: Oxford University Press.

Kurtz, P. (1983). *In defense of secular humanism*. Buffalo, NY: Prometheus Books.

Kurtz, P. (1986). *The transcendental temptation: A critique of religion and the paranormal*. Buffalo, NY: Prometheus Books.

Kurtz, P. (2001). *Skepticism and humanism: The new paradigm*. New Brunswick, NJ: Transaction Books.

Kuznar, L. A. (1997). *Reclaiming a scientific anthropology*. Walnut Creek, CA: AltaMira Press.

Lett, J. (1991). A field guide to critical thinking. In K. Frazier (Ed.), *The hundredth monkey and other paradigms of the paranormal* (pp. 31–39). Buffalo, NY: Prometheus Books.

Lett, J. (1997). *Science, reason, and anthropology*. Lanham, MD: Rowman & Littlefield.

Lett, J. (1997). Science, religion, and anthropology. In S. D. Glazier (Ed.), *Anthropology of religion: A handbook* (pp. 103–120). Westport, CT: Greenwood Press.

Pinker, S. (1997). *How the mind works*. New York: W. W. Norton.

Sagan, C. (1997). *The demon-haunted world: Science as a candle in the dark*. New York: Ballantine.

Free Inquiry. (n.d.). Retrieved June 18, 2003, from http://www.secularhumanism.org/fi

Skeptic. (n.d.). Retrieved June 18, 2003, from http://www.skeptic.com

Schick, T., Jr., & Vaughn, L. (1995). *How to think about weird things: Critical thinking for a new age*. Mountain View, CA: Mayfield.

Shermer, M. (2000). *How we believe: The search for God in an age of science*. New York: W. H. Freeman.

Sperber, D. (1996). *Explaining culture: A naturalistic approach*. Malden, MA: Blackwell.

Wallace, A. F. C. (1966). *Religion: An anthropological view*. New York: Random House.

Wilson, E. O. (1999). *Consilience: The unity of knowledge*. New York: Vintage Books.

Shakers

The Shakers (officially, the United Society of Believers in Christ's Second Appearing) were formed in 1736 in Manchester, England, by Mother Ann Lee (1736–1784), and the Shaker movement grew directly out of her life experiences. First, she was attracted to a small sect founded and led by James and Jane Wardley, which like the Quakers eschewed formal ritual and sacraments in favor of individual surrender to a life in the Spirit. During their worship, members would speak in tongues, shout, and shake. The Wardleys also called members to repent of sin in light of the near approach of the end of the world. The Shakers would emerge as a millennial group with informal and spirited worship. Second, Lee married and bore four children, all of whom died in early childhood. She took their death as a word from God on her own life of lust and concupiscence. She became convinced that purification of the soul required a mortification of the flesh, beginning with an acceptance of chastity and celibacy.

Foundation and Growth

Lee then began to have visions, the first in 1770, from which followers began to gather around her. In 1772, one such vision led the small band of nine to move to America (1774) and settle in northern New York (1775). Communal living began as a necessity for survival. However, the community began to grow. Lee was succeeded by James Whitaker (1751–1787), who established a second center of activity at New Lebanon, New York, and built the first Shaker meetinghouse. He would also place the concept of communal living on a firm theoretical basis.

Baptist minister Joseph Meacham, Jr. (1742–1796), who succeeded Whitaker, called Lucy Wright (1760–1821) as his partner in leadership, thus institutionalizing the group's commitment to gender equality. Meacham also institutionalized the group's orientation on charismatic leadership. The guidance of anointed leaders who brought forth revelations was to be followed. Meacham and Wright moved the group away from the more chaotic worship that had continued from the Wardleys' time and introduced a more ordered activity termed laboring, built around Shaker music and dancing. Shaker life subsequently developed two foci of large laboring meetings and small gatherings that built intimacy and closeness among the members. With Meacham articulating a vision of gathered communities separated from the world, in the early 1790s the movement spread rapidly and nine Shaker communities modeled on New Lebanon were founded.

The communities were highly structured with men and women sharing management equally, though all activity was divided so as to keep men and women from intimate associations. This division would come to be part of every aspect of life, even to buildings that would have separate entrances and stairways for the use of the two sexes. Given the celibate life lived by members, membership increases occurred by the addition of converts and the taking in of orphans, a measurable number of whom went on to join the movement as adults. Literature, including Meacham's popular text, *The Testimony of Christ's Second Appearing*, was printed and distributed to alert prospective members to the community's existence and lifestyle.

Much of Shaker life was spent in productive labor, and Shakers produced a number of products for sale to the outside world—the basis of their prosperity. They taught themselves architecture and constructed a variety of functional communal dwellings. However, the religious life of the community was built around their music and meetings for dancing. The Shakers created thousands of pieces of music. Lyrics were consciously composed by some with poetic tendencies; others were received during trances and ecstatic states. Texts varied from short choruses to lengthy didactic poems. Some songs sounded like speaking-in-unknown-tongues set to a melody. During the times of revival, the number of songs received rather than composed would grow dramatically.

Music was borrowed from the surrounding culture or composed in house, and through the nineteenth century, there was noticeable development in the music's complexity. Toward the end of the century, organ music and four-part harmony became the norm in worship. The most popular tunes were those that could be adapted to dance steps and some of the words to the songs reference the fact of the movements accompanying the singing of them. For example, with the most famous of Quaker songs, "A Gift to Be Simple," one can easily imagine the group moving around the meeting hall as they sang:

> When true simplicity is gain'd
> To bow and to bend we shan't be asham'd,
> To turn, turn will be our delight
> Till by turning, turning we come round right.

The Shakers as a whole prospered through the first half of the nineteenth century, though beset with problems of members unable to live up to the demands of celibacy and defections of members wanting to make a life in the world with the various skills they had mastered from farming to furniture making. Peaking in the decades immediately prior to the American Civil War, the community was periodically hit with times of revival. However, after the war the society began a sharp decline, going from a peak of 3,500 members to less than 1,000 by the end of the century. By 1875, all nineteen communities could no longer be sustained, and they began to close.

Decline

The twentieth century was a time of steady decline for the movement. Heralding the future, in 1904 the last major publication, a book on the meaning of Shakerism, was published. One by one, the remaining communities were closed, and membership consolidated. In 1961, the last Quaker elder died and in 1965, the remaining leadership closed the group to further outsiders joining it (the presence of an elder being a traditionally essential part of the induction process). By this time, only two active Shaker communities remained.

Interestingly, just as the Shakers shut off the possibility of further growth, a new interest in communalism in general and the Shakers in particular emerged. As would-be communalists and scholars focused attention on the Shaker heritage, observers have watched the community decline. The last resident at Canterbury, New Hampshire, died in 1992 and less than a dozen members, all elderly females residing at Sabbathday Lake, lived into the new century.

The new wave of Shaker scholarship at the end of the twentieth century lauded the community as the most successful of the many nineteenth-century American communal experiments and has sought to find the reasons for its spread and longevity, and in that endeavor has explored the Shaker culture of simplicity, worship, and craftsmanship. Meanwhile, those interested in the Shakers' material culture have made original Shaker furniture highly valued and have inspired numerous modern reproductions.

J. Gordon Melton

Further Reading

Andrews, E. D. (1962). *The gift to be simple.* New York: Dover Publications.

Morse, F. (1987). *The Shakers and the world's people.* Hanover, NH: University Press of New England.

Sprigg, J., & Larkin, D. (1987). *Shaker: Life, work, & art.* New York: Stewart Tabori & Chang.

Stein, S. J. (1992). *The Shaker experience in America.* New Haven, CT: Yale University Press.

Shamanism

A shaman is a religious functionary generally associated with tribal religions who has the ability to interact and consult with the gods and spirits recognized by a particular group. The term "shaman" is an anglicized version of the Tungus (people of eastern Siberia) term *saman* that (roughly) refers to an individual who is in a "raised" or ecstatic state and has the ability to "see" into the spiritual world. Some have suggested that perhaps even the Tungus term itself is a derivative of the Pali (the language of Theravada Buddhism) term *samana,* which refers to a Buddhist monk. Whatever its etymology, the term is used today in a generic sense to refer to any number of religious specialists one generally associates with tribal cultures. Thus, the term may be used, especially in popular literature, interchangeably with "medicine man," "sorcerer," "witch," and similar terms. While it is true that a shaman may be inclined to perform the various duties associated with these terms, what distinguishes the shaman from the medicine man or the sorcerer is his or her ability to travel to or access in some way metaphysical realms or alternate realities that stand apart from the mundane, tangible world that we inhabit and, while in these preternatural dimensions, interact with the spirits who reside there.

The eastern Siberian provenance of the term "shaman" notwithstanding, shamanism is a universal practice, although the mechanisms whereby contact might be made with the spirit world vary from place to place. For example, many circumpolar shamans are thought to be possessed by spirits, while the shamans of other areas are thought to leave their body (which remains inert and apparently lifeless for the duration) completely or to have the ability to converse with spirits without actually leaving their body and without spirit-possession. Given both the Old and New World presence of shamanism, it appears as though this practice addresses and accommodates needs that are, perhaps, inherent to our species; in other words, the cultural ubiquity of the practice seems to suggest independent creation rather than diffusion.

While this ability to access the spirit world is, perhaps, the only necessary component of any definition of the term, a shaman, being generally the only religious functionary in many tribal societies, will perform any number of duties. He or she may be called on to play the role of the physician, diagnosing and healing various maladies using both natural and spiritual means; while it is true that many sicknesses may be attributed to soul-loss or possession by a malevolent spirit, diagnoses that require the shaman to work with the spirit world in some capacity, other maladies may be diagnosed as simply "natural" or "biological," requiring the use of herbal medicines. The shaman may also serve as a psychopomp, escorting the souls of the dead to the spirit world to ensure that they do, in fact, depart this world. The shaman may also be expected to fill the roles of a prophet, diviner, priest, teacher, and myth-teller as well.

Initiation

One recurring motif of shamanistic initiation cross-culturally is the usually violent and traumatic rite of passage that an individual must undergo before assuming the title and position of shaman. Often, such experiences may be in the form of a serious and debilitating sickness that is attributed to "being called" by the spirit world. It is commonly noted that potential shamans are eviscerated and pulled apart by the spirits during their ordeal; apparently, not all individuals survive the experience. In some cultures, the initiate is expected to undergo a long period of fasting and isolation, during which time he or she may be overcome by frightening hallucinations and delirium. Yet in other cultures, there may be a very trying and sometimes painful initiation ceremony. Malidoma Patrice Some (1994), a West African shaman, describes a six-week ordeal involving a number of traumatic visits to alternate realities.

The shock and trauma of the initiation experience serves to destroy the former identity of the initiate as a rank-and-file member of his or her group. By virtue of their struggle and ultimate survival of their experiences in the spirit world, they are transformed into a being that is no longer considered to be strictly human or strictly spirit, an ideal disposition, of course, for one who is expected to cross between the real world and the spirit world. Not incidentally, many shamans note that upon their return from their initiatory ordeal, their perception of this world is sharper and deeper, a fact that also seems to indicate

THE INITIATION OF A YAKUT SHAMAN

Shamans undergo a period of training and a formal rite publicly identifying them as shaman. The following are some of the magical formulas repeated by new Yakut shaman at their initiation.

I promise to be a protector of the unhappy, a father of the miserable, and a mother of the orphans. I shall honor the demons who live on the tops of the high mountains, and swear that I shall serve them with all my strength. I shall honor, bow to, and serve the highest and most powerful of them, the demon who commands all demons, the master of the three demon sibs who live on the tops of the mountains, him whom the shamans call Sostuganach Ulu-Toen (the frightful, terrible one); his elder son Ujgul-Toen (the insane one), his wife Ujgul-Chotun (the insane woman), his younger son Kjakja-Curan-Toen (the loudly speaking one), his wife Kjakja-Curan-Chotun, and their numerous family and servants, through whom they send the people diseases, accidents, breakings of legs, and the podagra. I vow to save those who have been affected by these diseases, by sacrificing a cream-colored mare.

I shall profess and worship, bow to, and serve Ulu Toen's younger brother, the demon Chara-Surun-Toen (the black raven), his son Alban-Buran-Toen (the resourceful venturer), his daughter Kys-Salisaj (the virgin who walks), who prompts people to commit manslaughter, suicide, and calumny. I promise to help rid these people of their passions by offering the said demons a black horse.

I shall profess, worship, and bow to the demon Altan-Sobiraj-Toen (the brazen basin), his wife Altan-Sobiraj-Chotun (the one with the bigger brazen arrow), their daughters Timir-Kuturuk (iron tail) and Kejulgan-Darchan (the important, great, lopping woman), who send mankind chronical abscesses. I shall help free the sick by sacrificing some (Arago) liquor, and offering the demons a motley searnew, as a gift of honor.

I shall profess and worship, and bow to the ancestor of these demons who is known as Kjun-Zelerjuma-Sakryl-Chotun (the horrible foe of the sun) who has 52 tables full of holes, and 52 servants. She sends the people the passion of game and drinking, of robbery, plundering, abject deeds, and suicide. I shall try to heal those who are obsessed with these vices. I shall kill a red-spotted young mare who is an ambler, and twist heart and liver of the mare round my neck; I shall perform shaman magic to propitiate the goddess.

I shall profess and honor the demon above the demons of the six sibs who live in the place where the sinners' souls are sent to; I will bow to the one who is known among the shamans as Talirdach-Tan-Taraly-Toen (he who drags into ruin), his daughters Sorocha-Chotun (the wind-driven female beauty, and San-Chotun, and his countless servants who send men and cattle epidemic diseases. To propitiate them I shall offer them a sorrell-spotted mare.

***Source*: Krauss, Friedrich S. (1888) *Das Schamanentum der Jakuten* [Yakut Shamanism]. MIttheilungen der Anthropologischen Gesellschaft in Wien, Vol. XVIII. Wien, Germany: Alfred Holder, p. 170.**

that they are no longer strictly of this world, possessing now some of the attributes associated with spiritual beings.

Shamanistic Trance

Various terms have been used at one time or another to identify the altered states of consciousness associated with shamanism around the world including possession, ecstasy, trance, mediumship, and others. These terms, of course, cover a broad range of activities and ideologies that run the gamut from the largely passive reception of spiritual beings (mediumship and possession) to the active intrusion into the spirit world itself during trance rituals of various sorts. Nevertheless, it is, in fact, the latter that distinguishes the activities of the shaman from that of the medium and other religious functionaries. Whereas the activities of the priest or medium seek to facilitate the manifestation of spiritual beings into this world (consider, for example, the Brahmin priest of Hinduism encouraging one of the many manifestations of the Brahman to breathe its essence into a statue or a Spiritualist medium who serves as a conduit for an entity that has moved on to another sphere of spiritual reality), the shaman departs this world completely and visits one of the many spiritual dimensions that lie beyond in the realm of the supernatural. In simple terms, the activities of priests and mediums involve the intrusion of the divine into the mundane and the activities of the shaman involve intrusion of the mundane into the divine.

Travel to the world of the spirits is accomplished using any number of techniques but the most common are drumming, singing, clapping, dancing, and, on occasion, hallucinogenic substances; in some cases, all of these mechanisms may be used to some extent, in others perhaps only one or two. Thus, while it is true that the use of psychoactive or pharmacological agents may be popular in some areas, it is by no means ubiquitous. It should also be noted that the soul travel–inducing mechanisms listed above serve only as catalysts, i.e., they may be necessary but they are certainly not sufficient. The shamanistic experience, if you will, is the result of a number of factors working together, including the knowledge and abilities of the shaman, the various "catalysts" noted above, and the expectations of the group on whose behalf the shaman is working. The shamanistic experience, in other words, is a synergistic one that consists of much more than simply the consumption of a hallucinogenic powder or the beating of a drum. It is as if those peoples that embrace shamanism are aware that it takes much more than a simple arithmetic combination of worldly practices or ideologies to move one beyond the world we inhabit—entrance into the "otherworldly" realm of the spirits calls for the "world-transcending" synergy of the shamanistic complex.

In preparation for his or her travels to the spirit world, the shaman typically follows a strict regimen of fasting and social isolation. In short, those various activities that define the individual as a social being, for example, sharing meals, working together in a group context, sexual relations, the bonds of friendship, the duties of family and kin, etc., are, for the time being, suspended. This practice is clearly symbolic of the fact that the shaman will soon leave this world for another, a world inhabited not by human beings but spiritual beings. This feat is beyond the capabilities of "normal" or social human beings and can only be accomplished by someone who is, to a great extent, socially ambiguous. The antisocial or asocial behavior of the shaman can be interpreted as an attempt on the part of everyone involved to facilitate the drastic ontological shift that is called for if the shaman is to successfully enter the spirit world. It should be noted here that many shamans suffer from some sort of physical or psychological disability that, again, is simply another symbolic marker of their ambiguous ontological status.

If we combine the rather fluid social status of the shaman as perceived by the group of which he or she is part and the highly subjective nature of shamanistic experiences, it is not difficult to understand how and why many shamans often act as agents of social change. To a greater or lesser extent, the shaman is beyond the control of the society of which he or she is part and their sphere of activity falls far outside the purview of "proper" culture; this is especially true in those cases where society grows more and more complex and the shaman becomes marginalized.

Cosmology

Characteristic of the shamanic universe is the existence of a multilayered cosmos, arranged roughly as parallel layers all connected by a "centering" conduit of some sort; this conduit is sometimes considered to be a special place (having one unique location) or object (which may be anywhere—a special type of tree, for example) or even, in some cases, the shaman himself or herself, who has the ability to access these other layers of reality at will. In many cases, the earth is described as being in an intermediary position and shamans speak of "upper" worlds and "lower" worlds. One must be careful here, however, lest he or she is tempted to analogously invoke the Judeo-Christian notion of heaven and hell; it is not necessarily the case that the spirits of the "upper" worlds are benevolent and those of the "lower" worlds malevolent. In fact, perhaps most "lower" world spirits who reside at the bottoms of seas and rivers are considered friendly and helpful or at least amoral and indifferent.

Shamanic cosmology will typically look back to a mythic past that serves as the grounding and foundation of the present universe. In fact, it can be said that only two "times" are recognized, a mythical past and the present. These two periods are often linked by transformative processes that acted to bring forth the present order out of the world of the gods and spirits. In other words, it is thought that the difference between the real world and spirit world is a matter of degree rather than kind, a belief that accommodates the notion that a human being (the shaman) can actually contact and interact with the gods and spirits of another world.

Some Examples

The Kung people of the Kalahari Desert in southern Africa, researched extensively by Richard Katz (1982), recognize special healers that have the ability to cure sickness and access the spirit world. The Kung claim that *num*, a special healing power available to all Kung, can become excited or agitated (in their words, "boil"), and in such a state the healer will enter *kia*, an alternate spiritual reality. It is thought that all individuals possess *num* but only a few are actually recognized as healers. It should be noted that in this egalitarian and classless society, both males and females are recognized as healers.

Once a healer enters *kia*, he or she has the ability to "see" not only the sickness but its cause as well. Since sickness is dealt with almost exclusively during the healing dances and ceremonies, it is assumed that the etiology is spiritual. In fact, the Kung speak of ancestors and other spirits who attempt to "steal" the souls of the living, thus requiring the healer to "fight" the spirits to regain control of the individual's soul. According to the Kung, a capable healer can actually "see" which ancestors are acting against them and, thus, will be able to figure out who among the living is in danger. Thus, the healing dances are not only curative but preventative as well.

The shaman has long been a vital part of religious life in Korea. Here, the shaman can function as a ritual specialist, a medical doctor, or a medium, and is thought to have the ability to access the spirit world on behalf of his or her patients. There are basically two mechanisms whereby an individual might become a shaman. Some inherit their abilities from their parents, who train them until they are deemed ready to assume the role of healer themselves. Others begin their training as a result of some serious and debilitating illness. In this case, another shaman will attribute the sickness to a particular spirit and teach the young person how to work with and control the spirit so that it can be invoked and utilized to heal others. This type of shaman will sometimes do their healing work while possessed by this spirit, although possession is not a necessary part of healing. Perhaps the most interesting aspect of Korean shamanism is the notion that the healer can invoke a spirit and "work" with it in this world, communicate with the spiritual abode without leaving this world, or, finally, travel to the realm of the spirit. The particular malady or sickness in question and the manner in which it has manifested itself in the patient are included in the factors that determine which form of spirit work will be the most efficacious.

Shamanism in Mexico usually involves the consumption of psychoactive, particularly hallucinogenic, substances that serve as a catalyst for spiritual travel. The various plants used by shamans in this area include the peyote cactus, the *Psilocybe mexicana* mushroom, and a flowering vine known commonly as morning glory. For example, the Mazatecs use the *Psilocybe* mushroom to access the world of the "mushroom spirits." While it is true, of course, that anyone might consume the mushrooms, only certain individuals have the training and the family background that predisposes them, if you will, for a legitimate spiritual experience. The Mazatec shaman will typically venture to the alternate world of the mushroom spirits, where they will be given esoteric knowledge of the world in general and assistance with special cases of sickness that the shaman is attempting to heal.

The Yanomamo, found in the border region of Brazil and Venezuela, contact the spirit world by ingesting a powdered substance made primarily from the bark of the *ebene* tree. A village-mate will blow the powder through a bamboo tube into the nasal passage of the recipient. The Yanomamo claim that consumption of the powder allows them to contact the *hekura*, tiny spiritual, humanoid beings that must be entreated and eventually subdued if the patient is to be restored to health. As was the case above with the Mazatecs, anyone can theoretically consume the hallucinogenic powder, although its use appears to be restricted to males. Napolean Chagnon (1977), the principle ethnographer of the Yanomamo, does write, however, that around half of the Yanomamo males are considered to be shamans. In fact, the Yanomamo believe that any male can at least potentially contact the *hekura*, although they clearly recognize the fact that some are more skilled and experienced at this activity than others.

James Houk

See also Altered States of Consciousness; Healing and Rituals; Native American: Artic; Possession and Trance

Further Reading

Atkinson, J. M. (1992). Shamanism today. *Annual review of anthropology, 21*, 307–330.

Balzer, M. M. (Ed.). (1990). *Shamanism: Soviet studies of traditional religion in Siberia and Central Asia.* Armonk, NY: M. E. Sharpe.

Chagnon, N. A. (1977). *Yanomamo: The fierce people.* New York: Holt, Rinehart and Winston.

Eliade, M. (1964). *Shamanism: Archaic techniques of ecstasy.* Princeton, NJ: Princeton University Press.

Grim, J. A. (1983). *The Shaman: Patterns of Siberian and Ojibway healing.* Norman, OK: University of Oklahoma Press.

Halifax, J. (1979). *Shamanic voices: A survey of visionary narratives.* New York: E. P. Dutton.

Harner, M. J. (Ed.). (1973). *Hallucinogens and Shamanism.* London: Oxford University Press.

Hoppal, M., & von Sadovszky, O. J. (Eds.). (1989). *Shamanism: Past and present.* Budapest, Hungary: ISTOR Books.

Katz, R. (1982). *Boiling energy: Community healing among the Kalahari Kung.* Cambridge, MA: Harvard University Press.

Lewis, I. M. (1989). *Ecstatic religion: An anthropological study of spirit possession and shamanism.* London: Routledge.

Rapinsky-Naxon, M. (1993). *The nature of shamanism: Substance and function of a religious metaphor.* Albany, NY: State University of New York Press.

Reichel-Dolmatoff, G. (1975). *The shaman and the jaguar: A study of narcotic drugs among the Indians of Colombia.* Philadelphia: Temple University Press.

Siikala, A. L., & Hoppal, M. (1992). *Studies on shamanism.* Helsinki, Finland: Finnish Anthropological Society.

Some, M. P. (1994). *Of water and spirit: Ritual, magic, and initiaition in the life of an African shaman.* New York: G. P. Putnam's Sons.

Wilbert, J. (1987). *Tobacco and shamanism in South America.* New Haven, CT: Yale University Press.

Shinto

Broadly speaking, the Japanese religious tradition known as "Shinto" emphasizes rituals of control and revitalization for a community's relationship with powerful deities *(kami)*. Shinto rituals aim to enhance those divine forces which imbue conditions beneficial to society—productivity, fertility, safety, and stability to name a few—as well as to exorcise influences thought to be harmful or defiling. The *kami* can be anything mysterious, marvelous, uncontrolled, strange, or simply having the power to defy human comprehension. As in any human relationship characterized by moods and situations, Shinto rituals to the *kami* likewise employ strategies aimed at influencing and controlling the temperament and degree of influence of these volatile deities. When successful, these rituals were thought to help maintain a reciprocal balance between human, phenomenal, and transhuman worlds, enabling human life and society to prosper.

Before proceeding much further, it is necessary to point out the term "Shinto" is rarely used by the common person to describe this ancient and complex tradition. John Breen and Mark Teeuwen have argued that the term implies the "ideological agenda" (2000, 3) of shrine priests and administrators, which began in the late nineteenth and early twentieth century and continues today, that is rooted in reverence for the imperial institution of the emperor. For most Japanese today, the tradition we call "Shinto" is represented not by this specialized term but through ritualized encounters such as visiting shrines at certain times of year or at certain stages of the life cycle, participating in periodic festivals, or "turning to the deities in times of trouble." Still, for the rest of this discussion, I'll use the term as a kind of catch-all—similar to other world religions such as Buddhism or Christianity, which appear in the singular but are diverse and pluralistic traditions—for a wide range of practices, histories, and ideologies.

Historical Structurings of Shinto Ritual

Ritual in Japanese life, whether Shinto, Buddhist, or a synthesis of the two, helps to create and maintain a sanctified context for social, political, and cultural activities. Ritual can legitimate common origins and interests, empower select individuals (including people historically without much power, such as women), and negate or deny threats (including death) that challenge the legitimacy or survival of the individual or group.

Two of the earliest documented examples of ritual in Japan come from the current era. We know from archaeological evidence that religious rituals occupied a central role in the lives of Jomon (10,000 to 300 BCE) and Yayoi (300 BCE to 300 CE) cultures, but the first written account—concerning the "black magic" used by a female ruler to control her subjects—comes from

Chinese envoys in the third century CE. Another account is found in the early–eighth century mythological and genealogical narratives, the *Kojiki* and *Engi Shiki* texts. Both sources indicate that the earliest rituals were those done in recognition of and gratitude to a simultaneously vague and yet powerfully immediate sense of the sacred specific to local peoples.

As Buddhism made inroads among the administrative elite in the sixth and seventh centuries, considerable amalgamation occurred as Buddhist divinities were worshiped in Shinto rituals, and the *kami* venerated in Buddhist ones. Priests specializing in *kami* worship wanted not only to protect their status as ritual specialists but also to ensure a greater efficacy of communication directed to the deities. Competing with a continental-style liturgical "magic" based on texts, chanting, and prolonged prayer-petitioning before statues representing various Buddhas, bodhisattvas, and ancestral figures, the local *kami* tradition had to innovate in order to retain its powerful patrons. Although historical records are limited for this period (roughly 530 to 900 CE), archaeological evidence indicates that considerable interaction and exchange between *kami* and Buddhist ritual traditions was the norm rather than the exception. This syncretism, more than anything else, also characterizes religious practice for most of Japan's social history. Only in 1868, when the Tokugawa shogunate—representing the dying gasps of feudalism—finally ended in a revolution, did a heightened awareness of Shinto and Buddhism as distinct religious traditions begin to be institutionalized and enforced, with sometimes destructive results.

It was at this time that the new central government became quite active in promoting a kind of "civic" Shinto as the ideological heart of their modernization program, an ideology that later became the obligation of every Japanese to observe. The government's "shrine merger" program, lasting from 1906 to 1912, tried to single out one shrine per village so as to better maintain the correspondence between local and national ritual activities aimed at preserving the nation-state. Scholars are still trying to ascertain the dramatic shifts in ritual practices during this period, as local observances came under scrutiny and management by administrators from distant yet powerful centers of political influence associated with the Meiji government. Rituals at shrines nationwide underwent a process of systematization so as to conform with recently instituted liturgical guidelines issued from Tokyo. In the service of the state, this obscured centuries of ritual complexity and tradition at the local level. This is not to say that shrines and priests willingly and without dissent adopted these practices. Obviously there was resistance to and subversion of authoritative intentions coming from the central government. But since there were often financial rewards and patronage attached to compliance with the national standards, local priests and their institutions often acquiesced to the new standards as much for financial reasons as for civic or patriotic ones.

Ritual Formats

Shinto shrines, through the in-house and highly public rituals *(matsuri)* they stage, provide millions of people yearly a direct experience about the historical, spiritual, and national significance of the tradition and how it interacts with the local community. From *kami* to priest and priest to individuals, businesses, and local governmental representatives, hierarchical positionings put motivated parties directly in line for legitimation and sanctification through rituals.

Sonoda Minoru has proposed two concepts for encompassing both the "old" and "new" aspects of *matsuri*. The first, *saigi*, is the ritual aspect of *matsuri* marked by reverence and solemnity towards an invoked presence of the sacred. The second aspect of *matsuri* evokes an attentiveness to the sudden manifestation of the *kami* into a ritually prepared space and time. During Shinto's golden age in the early and mid-Heian period (794–1192 CE), it was thought efficacious to conduct rituals at night, when the *kami* were believed to move about more freely, unhindered by the profane activities of human affairs. Kyoto's Kamigamo Shrine's *miare-sai* and Iwashimizu-Hachimangu Shrine's 15 September *taisai* festival are among the many that continue this tradition.

Much of what one reads or hears about Shinto rituals from a Japanese perspective often reflects the education, training, and experience of individuals who are intimately involved with shrine affairs, either as priests or as scholars (many of whom also serve as priests). From this vantage point, a "generic" Shinto ritual has three parts, all of which are centered around a phenomenology of the *kami*.

A ritual is said to not really begin until the *kami-oroshi* or "descent of the *kami*" is enacted by the priests. This is only possible, however, after the ritual participants and priests have purified themselves outside the time and space of the main event. Once the *kami* has been summoned and is considered present, each action, offering, or word resonates with sacred significance. With humans and *kami* sharing the same moment and place, the "host" then acknowledges the invited "guest" in the ritual's second stage, the *kami-asobi*. While the word *asobu* commonly means "to play," here it signifies an activity that placates as well as entertains. This second stage covers everything that goes on while the *kami* is present—the food offerings, the invocational prayer *(norito)*, the dance of the shrine female attendants (*urayasu-no-mai*, though not all shrines adopt this practice), and the worship of priests and public participants alike.

It is frequently the case that those in attendance rise to present offerings, bow, and clap twice. Leafy sprigs from the *sakaki* tree (called *tamagushi*) are distributed as emblems that are said to link the individual heart/mind to that of the *kami*. Each designated person (often one represents an entire group) follows the example of the head priest in the *tamagushi hoten*, slowly coming forward, bowing, and then presenting the little branch on a small table so that its stem, pointed first to the center of the individual's body, is now turned to point towards the inner sanctuary. Kneeling in some shrines and standing in others, the participants then bow twice before enacting the two hand-claps of the *kashiwade*, followed by a final, single bow.

The third part of the ritual is the return or "sending back" of the deity (*kami-okuri*, also called *kami-age*). Just as entertaining guests at one's home requires vigilance, resources, and etiquette, so too having the *kami* in one's presence for a sustained period of time is exhausting and fraught with consequences if the inviting party does not maintain ritual propriety. The *kami* are simply too volatile and powerful to entertain for long, and so the "sending off" provides closure to the ritual as well as a bit of healthy distance between the ritual participants and the *kami*.

The final but by no means unimportant aspect of participation occurs after the ritual has formally ended. In many shrines, the lay participants receive a sip of sanctified rice wine *(omiki)* upon leaving the hall of worship. Invited guests and the head and senior priests may then reassemble in an adjacent building's special banquet hall to partake of more substantial fare. Originally, only the same food offerings made to the *kami* were consumed. But current practice usually supplements the offerings with a simple meal prepared in the shrine's kitchen or with catered box lunches. Whatever the style, the postritual gathering serves as a transition between what has been a space and time of intense mediation by symbolic values and structures to a more secular and relaxed state. Called *naorai*, the eating and drinking are also thought to be efficacious means of incorporating the *kami* (which has permeated these offerings with its essence) into one's physical body.

Ritual Calendars

Because of the wide geographical variation and relative autonomy of most shrines, each has its own yearly ritual calendar, or *nenju gyoji*. A shrine's rituals mirror closely the concerns of its surrounding communities, especially emphasizing successful livelihoods and family continuity. However, because of the changes implemented in the early Meiji period (1868–1890) as well as after the Second World War, a majority of shrines now observe the following rituals on the same day and in the same mood and manner. This orthodoxy is due to the training priests receive at two major universities specializing in producing Shinto priests and scholars, as well as the administrative oversight of the Central Association of Shinto Shrines in Tokyo (*Jinja Honcho*).

1 January: *Saiten-sai* (First Offerings of the New Year): These offerings (rice, water, salt, sake, vegetables, fish, and fruit) are usually made in the first hours of the new year, always before the sunrise.

15 January: *Seijin-shiki* (Coming-of-Age Festival for Young Adults): What began as part of samurai culture has become a postwar, mainstream activity for municipal governments and local shrines.

17 January: *Shojo-sai* (Ritual Burning of New Year Talismans and Decorations): Talismans lose their efficacious value over time and must be disposed of in proper, which is to say *ritualized*, ways. Thus, visitors to the shrine during the *hatsumode* period or in the succeeding days frequently bring to the shrine their old talismans and purchase new ones.

11 February: *Kenkoku-kinen-bi* (Founding of the Nation Day): No one really knows when the nation of Japan was created, but conservative leaders have succeeded in implementing this holiday based on mythological accounts. Since Shinto shrines likewise venerate many of these ancient myths, they are supportive of the holiday and hold simple rituals to acknowledge and venerate the founding of the nation.

22 March: *Mitama-matsuri* (Festival for the Ancestral Spirits): Shrines have usually seen death

and dying as defilements to be avoided at all costs. However, these new rituals have developed in recent years as a formal way to acknowledge the individuals and families who have helped to sustain the institution of the shrine.

10 June: *Taue-sai* (Ritual for Rice Planting): This date changes according to the climate of the region under consideration, but the ritual evokes early divinations to ascertain the best time for rice planting. Other rituals closely associated with the livelihood of regional economies (forestry, fishing, and so forth) are also an important part of the yearly ritual calendar.

30 June: *Nagoshi-barae* (Great Purification of Summer): Summer is a time fraught with anxieties about the growing rice, weather, insects, and health. This purification helps to manage those anxieties and enlists the *kami* to help protect against disasters.

3 November: *Shichi-go-san:* Literally "seven-five-three," or the ages at which girls (seven, three) and boys (five) put on formal attire and come to the shrine to petition the *kami* for health and prosperity in their lives.

13 November: *Aiiname-sai* or *niiname-sai* (First Fruits Festival): Farmers in Japan as well as the world over acknowledge and thank the deities for helping provide another successful harvest.

31 December: *Oharae* (Great Purification at Year's End): Ending the year by exorcising its negative consequences in a great purification is observed in the emperor's palace as well as at shrines all across the nation. Together with the *niiname-sai* and the *taue-sai,* the purification rituals are among those continuously performed since the very beginnings of the Japanese state.

31 December to 5 January: *Hatsumode* (First shrine visit of the new year): Shrines throughout Japan welcome large crowds of people for a variety of both public and private rituals to ensure health, success, and prosperity for the coming year. This is part of *Oshogatsu* (New Year's celebrations), one of Japan's two major holidays. The other major holiday is *Obon,* observed in either July or August to acknowledge and welcome the return of ancestral spirits.

Future Developments

An opportunity to loosen the bonds of workplace or social and familial obligations and experience a brief, well-bounded, but nevertheless liminal stage of social existence via ritual and festival is welcomed within modern Japanese urban environments. Festivals of all kinds regularly draw huge crowds of people. Similarly, rural communities suffering demographic change have tried to revitalize old festivals (or create new ones, such as Fukushima's Belly Button Festival), hoping to stimulate local economies with a boost from tourism.

Depending on the situation, there is, to foreign observers, a careless swinging by many Japanese people from Shinto to Buddhist rituals with little regard for the content of these traditions. What matters most, however, is the spiritual and pragmatic benefits *(riyaku)* to be gained via the rituals of both traditions. The more devout parishioners of shrines and temples have altars in their homes (with 45 per cent of a 1994 survey's respondents reporting they had *both* Shinto and Buddhist altars in their homes), where they can make carry out simple rituals on a periodic basis.

If the nearly 80 percent of the Japanese population visiting shrines on or soon after New Year's is any indication, it is likely there is far more substance and reassurance in these activities than participants either know or would ever admit. For those who participate in shrine rituals throughout the year, we can assume a complex interplay of associations and meanings that, at the very least, reinforce cultural identity and historical continuity, empower the individual or group in a variety of ways, and resonate with possibilities for renewal with and realignment to what it means to be human within Japanese society and culture.

John K. Nelson

Further Readings

Ashkenazi, M. (1993). *Matsuri*. Honolulu: University of Hawaii Press.

Bock, F. (1970). *The Engi-shiki: Books 1–12 in two volumes.* Tokyo: Sophia University.

Breen, J., & Teeuwen, M. (Eds.). (2000). *Shinto in history.* Honolulu: University of Hawaii Press.

Nelson, J. K. (1996). *A year in the life of a Shinto shrine.* Seattle: University of Washington Press.

Nelson, J. K. (2000). *Enduring identities: The guise of Shinto in contemporary Japan.* Honolulu: University of Hawaii Press.

Philippi, D. L. (1968). *Kojiki.* Tokyo: University of Tokyo Press.

Plutschow, H. (1996). *Matsuri: The festivals of Japan.* Surrey, UK: The Japan Library.
Schnell, S. (1999). *The rousing drum: Ritual practice in a Japanese community.* Honolulu: University of Hawaii Press.
Smyers, K. (1993). *The fox and the jewel: A study of shared and private meanings in Japanese Inari worship.* Honolulu: University of Hawaii Press.
Sonoda, M. (1988). Festival and sacred transgression. In *Matsuri: Festival and rite in Japanese life.* Tokyo: Institute for Japanese Culture and Classics.

Sikhism

Sikhism is a tradition that was born in 1469 CE in Punjab, northern India, with the birth of Guru Nanak (1469–1539). Nanak was born into a high caste Hindu family, but was also well versed in Islam, the other prevailing tradition in north India. His exquisite hymns of praise to the divine were never dismissive of Hindu or Muslim thought, but he sought a different path; his hymns make it clear that he was dissatisfied with any formalism within orthodox Islam or conventional Hinduism that separated the seeker from deeper truths. Most particularly, the mystic Nanak deplored rituals that obscured religious truths, truths that could only be found within.

Guru Nanak and the subsequent nine gurus were visionaries; their message of liberation extended to all, regardless of caste, religion, and gender. The earlier gurus consistently preached a radical message of interior devotion to the divine, a devotion that was to transcend and even oppose all exterior manifestations of religiosity. During the guru period (1469–1708), the Sikh community increased and its traditions developed, according to both the community's needs and the characters of these ten gurus. Institutionalization, which took the form of the compilation of the sacred songs of the gurus (which in time became sacred scripture), pilgrimage sites, missionary activities to spread the message of the gurus, and specific festivals, changed the character of the developing community. But it became most pronounced with the tenth guru, Guru Gobind Singh (1666–1708); a novel Sikh ideal came into being with the creation of the Khalsa brotherhood in 1699. The new ideal was now to be that of the warrior-saint. The community was thus transformed into a military brotherhood, complete with external military signifiers.

The Khalsa Code and Initiation Ritual

Many of the central Sikh rituals stem from this watershed event in Sikh history. Certainly a rite of initiation for devotees had been present since the time of the earliest gurus, namely, the ritual known as *charan di pahul* (foot initiation), which consisted of the devotee drinking water in which the guru's toe or that of his deputy had been dipped. This rite was a token of the devotee's submission and was open to all, regardless of gender, caste, or previous religious persuasion. The ritual was indicative of the central message of all the gurus: liberation was open to anyone that sought to bring their spirit into harmony with divine nature and order. It was this ritual, above all else, that was transformed with the creation of the Khalsa. The new initiation rite into the brotherhood was now to be known as *khande di pahul* (initiation by the sword) and what was central to it was the close association of initiated devotees with steel. For Guru Gobind Singh, the sword represented the divine and was to be held in great reverence. An iron bowl filled with water and soluble sweets was to be stirred with a double-edged sword *(khanda)*; this mixture was then to be poured over hands, sprinkled into eyes and hair, and finally drunk by the initiates. The water was to be stirred, all the while, with the double-edged sword. Five weapons were also associated with this initiation, which in time developed into what are known today as the Five K's *(panj kakar)*, "K" being the initial letter of each external symbol. The Five K's are uncut hair *(kes)*, comb *(kangha)*, sword *(kirpan)*, breeches that are not to come below the knee *(kachh)*, and an iron or steel bangle *(kara)*. Male members of the Khalsa were also to take on the new surname Singh meaning 'lion', a name common to the Rajputs who were known for their martial abilities. These prescriptions were said to have been delivered by Gobind Singh in a sermon and soon thereafter transmitted into a written code of conduct known as the *Rahit* (the Khalsa code of conduct and belief).

It was thus that the Sikhs were not only prescribed a new uniform and new nomenclature, but the community was also bequeathed a new code by which to conduct their lives. From a fluid religious identity that did little to indicate a complete separation of Sikhism from the numerous reform movements in north India, this new breed of Sikh was to be clearly distinguished from their coreligionists through novel external signifiers and a unifying form of naming. This ritual and code, the latter becoming more multifaceted and complex as a result of later developments and needs and propounded in numerous versions, is known today as the *Sikh Rahit Maryada* and is to be observed today by all who are initiated into the Khalsa.

It would appear that women were initially not included in this militarized ideal. Yet according to early accounts, women were active members within the fledgling Sikh community *(panth)*. However, with increased institutionalization, particularly with the inauguration of the warrior-saint ideal, women's roles within the community as full-fledged participants decreased. As well, not all Sikhs heeded the guru's invitation into the Khalsa; many chose instead to stay with the ideal of the earlier gurus, which stressed the centrality of interior devotion to the divine above and beyond any external manifestations of religiosity. The latter, Guru Nanak had maintained, were simply impediments to true religious aspirations.

It was, however, the Khalsa ideal that became increasingly hegemonic, due in part to large numbers of low caste Jat Sikhs joining the Khalsa order. The earliest followers of the gurus were Khatris, a high ranking trading and merchant caste in the Punjab, the caste of all the Sikh gurus. Important early leadership positions within the community were also filled by Khatris. Jat Sikhs, however, were displacing Khatris within the *panth* in terms of their numbers and influence; it is entirely plausible that the shift in emphasis toward militancy that came to the fore during the time of Guru Gobind Singh, itself came about due to the differing aspirations and militant leanings of the increasingly large numbers of Jat Sikhs coming into the growing Sikh community.

As noted earlier, the Sikh code of conduct has gone through numerous developments. An important revision took place with the rise of a reform movement in the late 1800s and early 1900s known as the Singh Sabha movement. By and large, the core of the Singh Sabha reform movement was educated males who had risen in Punjab's social hierarchy through the educational schemes of the British in India. Given their opportunities for education, these individuals wasted little time in becoming the new transmitters of Sikh tradition, history, and ideals. One important aspect of British influence on these reformers had to do with the "women's question," an issue that reform movements of all stripes were addressing in India during colonial rule. Sikh history, as promulgated by these reformers, was replete with examples of women's full equality with men, particularly during the golden era of the guru period. Accordingly, Sikhs codes of conduct that did not embody this equality needed to be rewritten. The current *Sikh Rahit Maryada* reflects these concerns. Today, both women and men are to be initiated into the Khalsa in precisely the same manner. Whereas male Sikhs are to take on the name Singh, women according to this code of conduct are to take on the name Kaur, meaning "princess," to distinguish them as Sikhs.

The Khalsa rite of initiation is a central aspect of Sikhism. Yet, many Sikhs, both historically and in present times, consider themselves full-fledged Sikhs without being initiated into the Khalsa order. At present there are numerous debates taking place about Sikh identity. Individuals who have been initiated into the order of the Khalsa are known as *Amrit-dhari* (Khalsa-initiated) Sikhs. For many orthodox Sikhs, it is only *Amrit-dharis*, given their initiation into the Khalsa and their observance of the *Rahit*, that are part of the Khalsa order. However, another variety, known as *Kes-dhari* Sikhs, do not cut their hair and are conspicuously recognizable as Sikhs given their strict obedience to the wearing of the Five K's and their observance of the essential *Rahit*. What distinguishes *Kes-dhari*s from *Amrit-dhari*s is that the former have not undergone formal initiation into the Khalsa. By and large, however, given their outward appearances, they are considered to be within the Khalsa fold.

Another category is known as *Sahaj-dhari* Sikhs. The term in its inception referred to the followers of Guru Nanak, who were on the path of liberation toward *sahaj*, the goal of eternal bliss in absolute union with the ivine. The meaning of *Sahaj-dhari* has changed considerably in common and modern parlance. The term is generally utilized to refer to "slow adopters," namely, Sikhs who do not follow the complete *Rahit*, nor do they observe all of the Five K's, including uncut hair, but who, it is optimistically believed, will some day recognize the Khalsa form as the ideal and follow the injunctions of the *Rahit* as stipulated by Guru Gobind Singh, the tenth and last living guru of the Sikhs.

Other Rituals

Another important rite that plays an even more central and unifying role in Sikh religious life is that of the marriage ritual. As noted earlier, many devoted Sikhs are not initiated into the Khalsa order; the marriage rite, however, is upheld by the vast majority of Sikhs. Until the early twentieth century, Sikhs generally followed conventional Hindu marriage rituals. In

1909, under the aegis of the Singh Sabha reformers, a Sikh marriage act was passed, known as Anand Karaj. The sacred scripture of the Sikhs, the *Guru Granth Sahib* or *Adi Granth*, which is honored as the "living guru" by the Sikhs, is the focal point of Anand Karaj (wedding ritual). Guests and the bridal couple will first pay obeisance to the Guru Granth Sahib, and then take their place in front of the scripture. The individual conducting the rite asks the couple and their parents to stand, as the congregation is led in prayer to invoke the blessing of the divine on the occasion. A scripture passage is read, the couple is reminded of their duties to one another, and they are asked if they will fulfill those obligations faithfully. If they agree, the end of the groom's scarf *(pulla)*, which is draped around his neck, is placed in the bride's right hand. The first verse of the wedding hymn, known as *Lavan* (encircling), is sung by the officiant (individual conducting the ceremony); then the couple circles the scripture in a clockwise direction, the groom leading while the bride holds the end of the groom's *pulla*. This takes place four times, after each verse of the wedding hymn is sung. Every time, the bride and groom prostrate themselves before the scripture. Six more appointed stanzas follow, sacramental food *(Karah Prasad)* is handed to everyone present, and the couple is then officially married.

The naming ritual that occurs soon after a child's birth is another central Sikh rite. The baby is taken to the *gurdwara*, the Sikh house of worship, along with either homemade *Karah Prasad* or funds for the making of *Karah Prasad*. Thanksgiving hymns are then read for the birth of the child, and the *Guru Granth Sahib* is then consulted by being opened at random to aid in finding the name of the baby. The first word of the left-hand page is read to the parents, who will then decide on the child's name beginning with this initial. The officiant will then publicly announce the name, adding the appellation Kaur for a girl or Singh for a boy. More appointed hymns are read, prayer is offered, and the *Karah Prasad* is shared, signifying the end of the naming ritual.

Sikhs generally cremate their dead. The death rituals are very much family focused. Members of the family will wash and clothe the body, ensuring that the deceased is wearing the five symbols of Sikhism. In India, the body is then taken to the cremation grounds in a solemn procession by male members of the family, while hymns are sung by the mourners. Women do not enter the cremation ground. The funeral pyre is lit by a close male relative of the deceased, and prescribed evening hymns are sung during the cremation. Prayers are offered and then the mourners return home. A complete reading of the *Guru Granth Sahib* then begins, to be finished within ten days. If the deceased is a family head, a ritual called *pagari* (turban) is performed. The eldest son of the deceased is given a turban from a maternal uncle, signifying his new role as head of the family. For Sikhs in the Diaspora, death rituals have been adapted to local customs; hymns are sung either at the home of the deceased or at the *gurdwara*. The body is placed in a coffin and transported in a hearse to a crematorium. The chief male mourner then pushes the button that delivers the coffin and body to the furnace.

Many of the rituals noted above, with the exception of the Sikh initiation rite, were either introduced or gained currency with the reforms initiated by the Singh Sabha movement. Previous to this time, Sikh generally utilized common Hindu rituals, particularly during times of marriage and death. But the prevailing goal of the Singh Sabha was to conclusively separate Sikhs from their Hindu and Muslim counterparts. It was thus that appropriate *Sikh* rites of passage were developed. These have prevailed to the present time.

Doris R. Jakobsh

See also Hinduism

Further Reading

Barrier, N. D., & Dusenbery, V. A. (Eds.). (1989). *The Sikh diaspora: Migration and the experience beyond Punjab*. Delhi, India: Chanakya Publications. Cole, O. W., & Sambhi, P. S. (1995). *The Sikhs: Their religious beliefs and practices*. Brighton, UK: Sussex Academic Press.

Cole, W. O. (1998). *Teach yourself Sikhism*. London: Hodder & Stoughton. Fox, R. G. (1990). *Lions of the Punjab: Culture in the making*. Delhi, India: Low Price Publications.

Grewal, J. S. (1979). *Guru Nanak in history*. Chandigarh, India: Publication Bureau, Panjab University.

Grewal, J. S. (1990). *The Sikhs of Punjab*. Cambridge, UK: Cambridge University Press.

Grewal, J. S., & Bal, S. S. (1987). *Guru Gobind Singh: A biographical study*. Chandigarh, India: Roxana Printers.

Hawley, J. S., & Mann, G. S. (Eds.). (1993). *Studying the Sikhs: Issues for North America*. Albany: State University of New York Press.

Jakobsh, D. R. (2003). *Relocating gender in Sikh history: Transformation, meaning, and identity*. Delhi, India: Oxford University Press.

Juergensmeyer, M., & Barrier, N. G. (1979). *Sikh studies: Comparative perspectives on a changing tradition*. Berkeley, CA: Graduate Theological Union.

Kapur, R. A. (1987). *Sikh separatism: The politics of faith*. Sahibabad, India: Vikas Publishing House.

McLeod, H. (1997). *Sikhism*. London: Penguin Books.

McLeod, W. H. (1995). *Historical dictionary of Sikhism*. London: The Scarecrow Press, Inc.

McLeod, W. H. (2003). *Sikhs of the Khalsa: A history of the Khalsa Rahit*. Delhi, India: Oxford University Press.

Oberoi, H. (1992). Popular saints, goddesses, and village sacred sites: Rereading Sikh experience in the nineteenth century. *History of Religions, 31*(4) 363–384.

Oberoi, H. (1994). *The construction of religious boundaries: Culture, identity, and diversity in the Sikh tradition*. Delhi, India: Oxford University Press.

O'Connell, J. T., Israel, M., McLeod, W. H., & Grewal, J. S. (Eds.). (1990). *Sikh history and religion in the twentieth century*. Toronto, Canada: University of Toronto.

Singh, M. (Ed.). (2000). *Sikh forms and symbols*. Delhi, India: Manohar.

Singh, P., & Barrier, N. G. (1996). *The transmission of Sikh heritage in the diaspora*. Delhi, India: Manohar.

Singh, P., & Barrier, N. G. (1999). *Sikh identity: Continuity and change*. Delhi, India: Manohar.

Snake Handling

People have thought that snakes have supernatural qualities and powers and have worshiped snakes in a number of religions, including those of ancient Egypt, Greece, and Rome as well as in Gnostic Christianity (relating to early Christian cults distinguished by the conviction that matter is evil), and Hinduism. Hindu snake "charming," in which a man playing a flute apparently induces a cobra to rise out of a basket and spread its hood in an "aggressive" posture, has drawn much attention. In actuality, the cobra does not hear the music, but rather rising up and spreading its hood are normal responses to being confined in a basket and facing a human being. The charmer is at minimal personal risk because cobras can strike only a short distance and strike downward. Snake handling, as practiced since the early twentieth century in some Holiness (a perfectionist movement arising in U.S. Protestantism in the late nineteenth century) churches in the southern United States, is a different matter. It is a serious religious ritual sanctioned by a literal interpretation of the Bible and dangerous. It is also controversial and has been banned in several states, with courts supporting the ban on the grounds that the state has a greater interest in protecting life than in protecting the religious freedom of snake handlers. Nonetheless, experts estimate that members of snake-handling churches in the United States number between two thousand and five thousand, although not all members actually handle snakes. Some handlers are bitten by rattlesnakes, copperheads, and cottonmouths, and an unknown number of snakes die each year.

Although snake handling has always attracted only a small number of followers, it is a fairly well-described ritual, with a number of ethnographic accounts in print. Snake handling emerged as part of the Pentecostal-Holiness movement in the United States in the first two decades of the twentieth century. The first practitioner is thought to have been George Went Hensley (c. 1880–1955), a bootlegger and itinerant preacher in Tennessee who began handling snakes as part of the worship service sometime between 1908 and 1910. He died from a snakebite in 1955. From Tennessee the ritual spread to Virginia, Kentucky, and North Carolina and eventually to West Virginia, southern Ohio, Florida, and Texas. Snake handling evidently began independently in Alabama in 1912 and spread from there to Georgia. Snake-handling churches, which number in the hundreds in the U.S. South, are categorized collectively as the Church of God with Signs Following, although there is no central organization, and members of one church often participate in snake handling at other churches. As with other Holiness churches, members are socially and politically conservative, believe in salvation, sanctification, and baptism of the Holy Ghost, and speak in tongues during worship. A unique practice is the Holy Kiss, in which members of the same sex greet one another by kissing on the lips.

Snake handling as part of the worship service is based on a literal interpretation of the Bible:

> 15 And he said unto them, Go ye into all the world, and preach the gospel to every creature.
> 16 He that believeth and is baptized shall be saved; but he that believeth not shall be damned.
> 17 And these signs shall follow them that believe; In my name shall they cast out devils; they shall speak with new tongues;

18 They shall take up serpents; and if they drink any deadly thing, it shall not hurt them; they shall lay hands on the sick, and they shall recover.
19 So then after the Lord had spoken unto them, he was received up into heaven, and sat on the right hand of God.
20 And they went forth, and preached everywhere, the Lord working with them, and confirming the word with signs following. Amen. (Mark 16:15–20 [KJV])

The worship service consists of singing and preaching followed by the handling of snakes brought by members, usually in the front of the church. Rattlesnakes, copperheads, cottonmouths, and cobras are preferred. Handlers often handle more than one snake at a time, allowing the snakes to crawl over their upstretched hands and arms while the handlers twirl about and speak in tongues. Being bitten is subject to interpretation, from being a sign that the handler is not free of sin to being a sign that the handler lacks faith or has healing powers. In some churches handlers also drink poison (usually strychnine) in accord with Mark 16:18.

David Levinson

Further Reading

Burton, T. (1993). *Serpent handling believers*. Knoxville: University of Tennessee Press.

Covington, D. (1995). *Salvation on Sand Mountain: Snake handling and religion in southern Appalachia*. New York: Penguin Books.

Kane, S. M. (1986). *Snake handlers of southern Appalachia*. Ann Arbor, MI: University Microfilms International.

Kimborough, D. L. (1995). *Taking up serpents: Snake handling believers of eastern Kentucky*. Chapel Hill: University of North Carolina Press.

LeBarre, W. (1969). *They take up serpents*. New York: Shocken Books.

Pelton, R. W., & Carden, K. W. (1974). *Snake handlers: God fearers or fanatics?* Nashville, TN: Thomas Nelson.

Sorcery

The word *sorcery* apparently comes from the Latin *sors* or *sort-* meaning, "to determine by lots." The word has many meanings today. It can refer to any or all of various practices forbidden by God:

No one shall be found among you who… practices divination, or is a soothsayer, or an augur, or a sorcerer, or one who casts spells, or who consults ghosts or spirits, or who seeks oracles from the dead. For whoever does these things is abhorrent to the Lord; it is because of such abhorrent practices that the Lord your God is driving them out before you. (Deuteronomy 18:10–12, NRSV)

Sorcery can also mean the possession and use of extraordinary powers to transform or create things from nothing, a meaning found mainly in literature and myth. *Sorcery* has three broad cultural meanings, which are invariably negative: the invocation and command of evil spirits, evil witchcraft, and negative magic. All three meanings accord with popular meanings of the term *occult:* not only hidden and hence mysterious, but also sinister and dangerous and universally forbidden; most societies have at some time enacted laws against all three. The term sorcery may occasionally refer to the performance of ordinary sympathetic magic, but by calling such magic "sorcery" the user regards it as at least potentially dangerous and perhaps forbidden by religious tenet. The historian of witchcraft Jeffrey Burton Russell uses the term *sorcery* to mean both spirit invocation and sympathetic magic to distinguish them from diabolical witchcraft. The reader must be careful to ascertain how terms are used.

Sorcery is generally regarded as a learned practice that can be performed by anyone, regardless of status in society. Because sorcery is clandestine and universally feared, it is however difficult to obtain reliable documentation of its actual practice. Fantastic claims can be made of sorcerers and their alleged abilities, and certainly sorcery is more imagined than real. But the fear of sorcery can have important social and political functions.

Sorcery as Spirit Invocation

In the most common definition sorcerers are conjurers of evil spirits. According to the model developed by anthropologist Phillips Stevens, all religious systems have two conceptual dimensions of supernatural agencies. Organized along a vertical dimension are specialized divinities—gods, who receive their power from and are often links to the Supreme Being and with whom people establish personal alliances; and a number of lesser supernaturals, such as saints and ancestors. Organized along a horizontal dimension,

UNDOING SORCERY

One of the primary roles of shamans and sorcerers is to undo the evil of sorcerers or witches. The following text is the account of a dream of a Tarahumara shaman in Mexico which tells of one way in which shaman undo the evil of sorcery.

> **(Animals have sickened. The shaman looks for the cause.) He dreams that a shooting star (korimaka traveling across the sky) carried off the hearts (souls) of the animals. When the sorcerer flew off with the hearts, they dripped blood all along the route to the deep pool (whirlpool) where he keeps the souls. There is a large door of pure iron. When the sorcerer reaches the door, the water rises like steam. There are many sorcerers standing like soldados (assistants of the capitan) in the pool. The shaman (who is dreaming) follows the drops of blood to the pool and there he throws a big rock against the door to open it. There he collects the blood and carries it back to the house of the owner of the animals. Then the animals get better.**

***Source*: Fried, Jacob. (1952). *Ideal Norms and Social Control in Tarahumara Society.* Doctoral Dissertation. New Haven: Yale University, p. 116.**

on the same level as human society, are spirits, including ghosts and nature spirits, and the forces of nature that can be manipulated by people in magic. There may be categories of spirits, according to their habitats and their dispositions: beneficent, neutral, or evil (demons). People generally believe that those spirits of human origin—ancestors and ghosts—have human traits; the spirits who were never human are less predictable, and the evil spirits are especially dangerous. Some supernatural agencies can be summoned and commanded by specially trained people—gods by priests, demons by sorcerers. In most cultures the invocation of any spiritual being is risky, primarily because being in the presence of supernatural power is dangerous to people, but also because spiritual beings can be ornery. People may believe that demons cannot resist the summons of a skilled sorcerer, but that after having arrived, demons may choose not to obey the sorcerer and may instead wreak havoc and destruction. In European history sorcery was largely defined within a Christian context; evil spirits were agents of Satan, and trafficking with them was punishable by death, as by biblical decree (Exodus 22:18). The skilled sorcerer is presumed to have learned precautions and defenses against harm to himself—such as the "magic circle" of late medieval occult lore—the sorcerer performed his conjuring inside a circle drawn on the ground, with powerful protective words or signs inscribed around it—but the fact that he deals directly with the spirit world tends to isolate him from ordinary people.

Because of their special esoteric knowledge and ability to deal safely with spirits, priests might be suspected of practicing sorcery. In poverty-stricken Haiti people are certain that occasionally a *houngan* (priest) or *mambo* (priestess) of the religion Vodou (*Voodoo*) will succumb to temptation and sell his or her knowledge to a paying client with evil or selfish intentions, thereby becoming a *bokor* (sorcerer). Among the presumed skills of this sorcerer is the awful ability to create and command zombies, which are formless souls or animated soulless corpses of the dead. The Haitian religion is African in origin, and zombies are sometimes presumed to be employed today in Africa by successful people whose wealth in the midst of hardship is not easily explained.

Shamans can be sorcerers, too. Shamans are religious practitioners distinct from priests who have the gift of ecstasy, which is the ability to project their souls outward from their bodies into the spirit world. Found exclusively in Asia, the extreme northern latitudes, and the Americas, shamans are professionals, either men or women, who negotiate with spirits on behalf of clients. They may obtain from spirits special herbal knowledge and skills in curing disease. However, their motives and ends may not be always honorable; as anthropologists Michael Harner, Michael Fobes Brown, and others have shown, the South American shaman may send his spirit helpers, perhaps in animal form, to torment people, or he may send invisible "spirit darts" into people, causing illness—which he might then be called on to cure. And even when curing or otherwise doing good, he may be called a "sorcerer," as in the anthropologist Claude Lévi-Strauss's article, "The Sorcerer and his Magic."

Sorcery as Witchcraft

Sorcerer and *witch* are often synonymous in popular usage, although some people use the former term for men and the latter term for women; the term *witchcraft* can have all of the meanings of sorcery discussed here, and others. Considered here are only the negative meanings of the term *witchcraft;* not considered here are the forms of modern paganism such as Wicca, whose members profess to do only good, but many members refer to their practice as "witchcraft" and to themselves as "witches." In the historical and cultural senses the English term *witchcraft* refers to a belief in an evil power that develops in certain adults. The power enables its owner—female or male—to change form, to fly, and to do terrible things. At least twelve antisocial, supernatural, and abhorrent practices are ascribed to witches: social subversion; preferentially nocturnal activity; the ability to change themselves into any form or to become invisible; the ability to fly; the sharing of their power with a pet animal or spirit, the "familiar" of European lore; a periodic meeting with all other witches in the community, the Sabbat in medieval Europe; the spread of disease; the abduction of children; illicit sexual behavior; ritual murder of their human captives; cannibalism and vampirism; and an intimate association with death. Belief in witches existed in all of the world's settled societies at all stages of recorded history; such a belief was lacking only in some new composite cultures, such as those resulting from the Atlantic slave trade, and in nomadic societies whose members could move away from the sources of social tension that seem invariably to be associated with suspicion of witchcraft.

The words *sorcery* and *witchcraft* are erroneously applied to African-based religions such as Vodou in Haiti (the origin of *voodoo* and *hoodoo,* which are systems of magical beliefs in the U.S. South), Santería in Cuba and Puerto Rico, and numerous others in the Caribbean and South America, especially those in whose rituals spirit possession and live animal sacrifice are central. These are fully developed religions, with priesthoods, congregations, liturgies (rites prescribed for public worship), and established places of worship; as in all religions, their adherents are allied with specialized divinities organized under a supreme being. By their faith the adherents are protected from any evil, especially sorcery.

The witch or sorcerer, motivated by negative emotions, especially anger and envy, may be presumed guilty of causing a wide range of natural and social problems and misfortunes, including causing livestock to sicken or provisions to rot, stirring up devastating storms, and causing terrible epidemics such as the Black Death in fourteenth-century Europe or AIDS in Africa today. Some maladies blamed on sorcerers are psychosomatic hysterias, such as the "soul-stealing" scare in China in 1768, or the "penis-snatching" fears in late medieval Europe, and in West African cities in the 1990s.

Sorcery as Magic

The sorcerer also is a magician. The word *magic* also has many meanings—mystical, spiritual, miraculous—from all of the meanings of *sorcery* discussed earlier to the universal meaning of the learned use of words and objects to directly affect processes in nature. This definition of the word *sorcery* is the one most generally meant by social scientists and scholars of religion. Magic depends on five components: (1) belief in supernatural power that exists in varying degrees in all things, (2) the idea of dynamic natural forces that activate everything in nature, (3) a coherent universe in which everything—past, present, and future—is connected, (4) symbols, objects, or actions that substitute for others and that take on the power of the things they represent, and (5) nineteenth century folklorist James George Frazer's dual principles of sympathetic magic: similarity and contact. Sympathetic magic works by the belief that things or actions that in any way resemble—or that have been in direct physical contact or close association with—other things or actions have causal relationships with each other. Magic in this sense does not involve spirits; it is direct human manipulation of natural processes by symbolic means.

Magical acts based on these concepts, especially the principle of similarity, are universal and operate at all levels of society. Among the most powerful symbols are words, which are activated and empowered by the speaker's intent and carried on his breath; speech is used magically everywhere. Words of good will are blessing—good magic; but words of ill will or condemnation are curse—sorcery. Curse may be accompanied by finger pointing, which universally is considered rude and in many cultures is a method used by sorcerers to project their malignities at their victims. Finger pointing is enhanced in various places, including early Europe and aboriginal Australia by bone pointing, which is the act of holding a magically treated bone alongside the index finger.

The most common magical method of sorcery is negative image magic, which is manifested in the misnamed "voodoo doll." An image of the intended victim is damaged, and similar harm should befall the victim; if the image contains something that has been in intimate contact with the victim, such as hair or bodily waste or a piece of unwashed underwear, the magic is more powerful. Other methods of sorcery—feared throughout history and widespread in the modern developing world—involve beliefs in concentrated powers in certain animal or human body parts, specifically brains, eyes, breasts, genitals, and hands. Believers in sorcery, however, hold that any culturally avoided object can be an effective vehicle for an evil spell that is placed on it by a sorcerer and deposited where the victim will encounter it.

Considering the social meaning of *sorcery,* two cultural ideas should be recognized. First, underlying many traditional belief systems is what anthropologists have called the concept of "limited good": Things necessary for success in life are sufficient for all but are finite in quantity. If some people have more than they need, others will have less. Magic may be performed to enhance one's holdings or position in life; but if magic deprives someone else it is antisocial—sorcery. Therefore, whether an act is good magic or sorcery may depend on where one stands. Second, people generally believe that the natural order of things is good and that, if left alone, the forces of nature will do what they were programmed to do at the Creation. Good magic can be learned and performed anywhere by anyone, but sorcery is dangerous because it is motivated by negative or selfish intent and pushes the forces in contrary directions—away from their accustomed paths—and can cause unforeseen trouble. Stevens describes a case of sorcery used by a Nigerian boy to help his school table-tennis team win a championship match against a team from another school. The boy purchased some magical materials, and instructions for their use, in the village market: an iron padlock covered in hyena fur and tied with a red silk ribbon and a large iron staple. The meaning of an utterance would be locked into place when the staple was driven into the ground and the padlock closed over it. The symbolic power of the padlock was enhanced by the fur of the hyena, which is a treacherous nocturnal animal associated with witchcraft beliefs, and by the red color (blood, vitality) and expensive material of the ribbon. The boy performed this little rite, wishing for the defeat of the opposing team, in full view of all. Hisaction, which would affect whatever outcome was already determined in the natural cosmic program, terrified the students of both schools, who chased him with intent to somehow nullify whatever forces he might have set in motion—even if that meant beating him senseless, possibly killing him.

Affliction and Cure

Sorcery "works" by causing victims to have a psychosomatic reaction to their suspicion that evil is being perpetrated against them or to their ascription of some real misfortune to such a cause. Reports from all over the world attest to the real power of sorcery, which is manifested most dramatically in the phenomenon of "voodoo death." In this phenomenon victims of sorcery (or taboo violation) believe so strongly that they are doomed—and their beliefs are supported by the behaviors of their friends and relatives, who may shun them and even begin preparations for their funerals—that they may weaken, refuse food and drink, and possibly die unless intervention is made.

By the same mechanisms, with rapid intervention, the patient may undergo dramatic recovery. Wherever there is sorcery there will be culturally sanctioned cures, applied by a priest or shaman or professional healer who plays the role of witch doctor. This person may invoke the assistance of a spirit whose power is believed stronger than that of the spirit who caused the trouble; or the person may perform countermagic to deflect or nullify the sorcery or to return it to its sender. Both processes—succumbing to sorcery and recovering from it—are explained today by better understanding of the neurobiology of the placebo effect (improvement in the condition of a sick person that occurs in response to treatment but cannot be considered to have been caused by the treatment used). Sometimes the "poison" that the sorcerer has used is not only symbolic but also actually toxic, in which cases cures are problematic. In many cases, however, the application of cultural "medicines"—that include ritual as well as substances and perhaps a ritual of divination to ascertain the success of the curing ritual—will satisfy the patient and his or her support group that the sorcery is removed, and complete recovery may occur.

Removal of a sorcerer's hex from person and property is a form of exorcism. People widely believe that evil, like spiritual power, is contagious and that sometimes a ritual cleansing of the immediate surroundings should follow the curing of an afflicted person. Sometimes divination reveals that evil is still present, and repeated applications of the witch doctor/exorcist's methods might be deemed necessary.

Sorcery and Society

Scholars frequently distinguish between sorcery and witchcraft in noting that the sorcerer uses learned means to project evil influence over a distance, whereas the witch is innately endowed with an evil power and goes directly to its target and works on it. However, for people at the receiving end of either form of human supernatural evil, the means may not matter; what matters is the effect on society. No matter its content or method, sorcery is negative and antisocial; and yet it has been shown to have positive social functions. Probably the most-cited function of sorcery and witchcraft is that they satisfy the universal human need for a scapegoat—some other person to blame for a problem. Thus, displacing the burden of guilt provides temporary psychological relief; but, of course, such displacement can increase anxiety for the suspected. In settled societies where people must live in close proximity, social tensions are inevitable; suspicions that some people are using supernatural means to get revenge or to thwart others' ambitions are likely. People know the kinds of situations in which suspicions of sorcery arise, and because social esteem and cooperation are essential, people will take care to behave properly lest they themselves are suspected. People tend to mind their language lest emotion or carelessness prompt them to utter what might be taken as a curse; and children are taught not to point fingers because that may be a method that sorcerers use to send their malignities to their victims. Thus sorcery encourages social conformity. Also, fears of sorcery reinforce authority structures: people with political or economic ambitions in traditional societies may encourage the popular belief that they have sorcery working for them, which will surely give pause to their rivals.

Sorcery is human-instigated evil. It is a social problem. Traditional beliefs in sorcery emerge in situations of conflict in traditional societies today. Mob lynchings of suspected sorcerers have reached alarming numbers in areas undergoing rapid socio-political change: in South Africa in the early 1990s after the end of apartheid and in Indonesia in 1998. African federal and rebel soldiers commonly count "charms" among their armaments; organizers of the African Nations Cup soccer contest in 2002 officially banned sorcerers—who were called "team advisers" and "wise men;" and many African cities are today experiencing fears of "ritual murder" for a trade in human body parts, which are believed to be valuable for life-enhancing rituals. In modern situations, when beliefs in demon invocation, witchcraft, or evil magic may wane, people nevertheless will suspect others of harboring ill will and hatching conspiracies, especially during times of social anxiety. Such fears appear to be socially inevitable and fundamentally human.

Phillips Stevens Jr.

See also Divination; Exorcism; Magic; Shamanism; Witchcraft

Further Reading

Brown, M. F. (1989). Dark side of the shaman. *Natural History, 98*(11), 8–10.

Eastwell, H. D. (1982). Voodoo death and the mechanism for dispatch of the dying in East Arnhem, Australia. *American Anthropologist, 84*(1), 5–17.

Geschiere, P. (1997). *The modernity of witchcraft: Politics of the occult in postcolonial Africa*. Charlottesville: University of Virginia Press.

Harner, M. (1968). The sound of rushing water. *Natural History, 77*(6), 28–33.

Kuhn, P. A. (1990). *Soulstealers: The Chinese sorcery scare of 1768*. Cambridge, MA: Harvard University Press.

Lévi-Strauss, C. (1963). The sorcerer and his magic. In *Structural anthropology*. New York: Basic Books.

Russell, J. B. (1980). *A history of witchcraft: Sorcerers, heretics and pagans*. London: Thames and Hudson.

Stevens, P., Jr. (1988, Summer). Table tennis and sorcery in West Africa. *Play & Culture, 1*(2), 138–145.

Stevens, P., Jr. (1996). Black magic. In G. Stein (Ed.), *The encyclopedia of the paranormal*. Amherst, NY: Prometheus Books.

Stevens, P., Jr. (1996). Sorcery and witchcraft. In D. Levinson & M. Ember (Eds.), *Encyclopedia of cultural anthropology*. New York: Henry Holt.

Stevens, P., Jr. (1996). Zombies. In G. Stein (Ed.), *The encyclopedia of the paranormal*. Amherst, NY: Prometheus Books.

South America: Highland

The highland area of South America—the Andes Mountains—stretches from Colombia in the North to Argentina and Chile in the South, covering almost the entire length of the continent. The central region of the highland area includes Ecuador, Peru, and Bolivia, which are inhabited by Quechua-, Quichua-, and Aymara-speaking Andeans, referred to as "Indians" or "indigenous people."

Social and Economic Organization and Andean Religion

Religious ritual in the Andes is closely associated with rural economic activities and social organization. Andean indigenous economies are oriented toward agricultural production and pastoralism. Primary agricultural products include a variety of potatoes and other tubers, corn, and coca leaves; llamas and alpacas and guinea pigs (*cuyes*) are among the most important domesticated animals. After the Spanish conquest new domesticated animals, including cattle and sheep, were introduced to the Andean landscape and have achieved substantial economic importance, but llamas, alpacas, and guinea pigs remain most central to indigenous religious ritual.

Andean social organization is built around the complex concept of the *ayllu*. The *ayllu* is formally thought of in terms of an endogamous lineage (meaning that one marries within one's own lineage) whose members claim descent from the same mythical ancestor. In practice the *ayllu* is much more flexible and allows less rigid patterns of marriage, often resulting in the union of people hailing from different *ayllus*. According to Andean myth, the ancestors (*huacas*) were godlike and had a tremendous amount of power and control over daily events, weather patterns, crop and animal fertility, and sickness and death.

Over time, and after the *huacas'* duties on Earth were complete, myth suggests that the *huacas* turned to stone; they are now embodied in prominent mountain peaks, anthropomorphic (having human characteristics) rock outcroppings, underground water sources, or other unique features of the landscape. As a result, the Andean landscape itself is sacred. Rituals for the *huacas* typically entailed short pilgrimages to the resting place of the *huacas*, be it a mountain peak or a stone outcropping and so forth, and offerings would be made in the form of food: guinea pigs and llama and alpaca meat, corn beer, and coca leaves. These ritual offerings were thought to appease the *huacas*, resulting in bountiful harvests, ample rainfall, healthy animals, and protection from disease and misfortune.

The Earth, in general, is thought to possess a spiritual energy, and this energy is embodied in the deity *pachamama* (Earth mother). *Pachamama* is the most comprehensive of the Andean deities and is recognized in numerous Andean rituals and even in aspects of everyday life. For example, when people gather to drink corn beer or the slightly sweet sugarcane alcohol commonly referred to as *trago*, it is customary to make an offering to *pachamama* by pouring a few drops onto the ground. Because many native Andeans make their living through agriculture, *pachamama* is central to their very survival, and offerings made to her are partly thought to ensure that she is fertile and that crops will grow.

Other important deities comprising the Andean landscape are certain prominent mountain peaks, sometimes referred to as "*wamanis*" or "*apus*." The sun, *inti*, is also a central figure in Andean cosmology (a branch of metaphysics that deals with the nature of the universe). The sun and the mountain peaks are

Dancers in traditional native American costume open the Roman Catholic Festival of the Virgin in Copacabana, Bolivia in May, 1996. COURTESY OF STEPHEN G. DONALDSON PHOTOGRAPHY.

often represented as masculine, whereas *pachamama* is represented as feminine, a reflection of the gender complementarity and equality in Andean cosmology. In some regions the thunder god Illapa is also an important religious figure.

The Andean Ritual Cycle

The Andean ritual cycle corresponds closely with the agricultural cycle. Different moments on the agricultural calendar (sowing, weeding, irrigating, harvesting) require detailed rituals with deep religious elements. These rituals consist of making offerings to the important deities with the hope that they will contribute to the successful completion of each stage of the agricultural calendar.

One such ritual is performed for the maintenance of irrigation canals each year before people irrigate a community's fields for the first time. Many regions of the Andes suffer from the risk of severe water shortages. Intricate irrigation systems have been created to help mediate water shortages and ensure that all fields receive the necessary quantity of water, but the effective functioning of irrigation systems, and in some cases the mere existence of irrigation canals at all, is linked to Andean spirits. According to early colonial Andean myth, Paria Caca was a great and powerful *huaca*. In addition to being powerful beings *huacas* also often had insatiable sexual appetites, and Paria Caca had his eyes on a beautiful virgin from a rural Andean community. As a sign of gratitude to the community for allowing him to sleep with this virgin, he built an intricate irrigation canal system for the community, helping to rectify the community's chronic water shortage.

Every year before the first irrigation of the fields, the canals need to be cleaned and maintained. Men exchange and chew coca leaves and smoke cigarettes while cleaning and repairing the canals. Meanwhile, offerings of coca leaves and corn beer are made to each of the water sources, thought to correspond to different *wamanis* (spirits of the mountain peaks). An offering of corn beer is also made to *pachamama* by pouring the beer on the different agricultural fields. The combination of these rituals is thought to ensure abundant water to irrigate the fields and the fertility of the fields themselves. In fact, the entirety of the ritual is often treated as joining the male mountain spirits with the female Earth mother in a union not unlike marriage. The water, as it leaves its mountain source and enters the agricultural fields, is representative of the male seed, whose contact with the dormant fields makes them fertile and eventually leads to a successful crop.

Another ritual common throughout the region is the Pukllay Festival. This is a celebration of fertility, procreation, and new life. Again, in this ritual offerings are made to the Earth mother and the mountain deities, and respect for ancestors is central. An important element of this and most other rituals is coca leaves, which have been sacred to indigenous peoples since before the Inca. Although now infamous for their processing into cocaine, unprocessed coca leaves are not narcotic, and, in fact, chewing them is thought to be beneficial to one's health. Coca leaves are commonly chewed in rituals and are thought to possess many important qualities, including acting as mediators between people and the gods. Used in rituals such as the Pukllay Festivals, coca leaves are offered to all the important deities in groups of three, commonly referred to as *k'intus*.

Spanish Conquest and Repression of Andean Religion

Andean religious ritual has been deeply transformed by the Spanish conquest and colonization and more than 450 years of Christian missionizing. Even in the most remote of Andean regions, ritual practice has been transformed by influences of Spanish colonization and the introduction of Catholicism. These influences date to the earliest colonial days, when the abolition of non-Christian religious practices was among the goals of the Spanish.

After the conquest of the Inca Empire by the Spanish, which began when Francisco Pizarro landed on the coast of Peru in 1532, the Spanish colonial government attempted to abolish the practice of Andean religions and to accomplish the mass conversion of Indians to the Christian faith. These attempts were fueled by developments in Spain, where there was great religious fervor and where the Spanish Inquisition (which persecuted suspected devil-worshipers, witches, and idolaters) was in full force. Colonial authorities visited rural Andean communities hoping to identify and punish those people worshiping *huacas*, who were considered idolaters by the Catholic church, and to destroy the physical form of the *huacas*.

Although the Spanish were successful at converting many people to Christianity, destroying many physical representations of *huacas* and punishing some worshipers of the native religion, private worship of *huacas* continued to prosper. Such worship continued largely because Andean religion is flexible and open to the inclusion of different deities in its cosmology. The Christian "gods"—saints, the Virgin Mary, Jesus, and other important religious figures—were incorporated into the pantheon of Andean belief. Therefore, Christianity did not replace Andean religion but instead was frequently viewed as complementary to existing Andean beliefs and rituals.

Taki Onqoy

The conquest and suppression of Andean religion did, however, put considerable strain on indigenous social and religious systems. Many *huacas* were destroyed, many people were accused of devil worship and punished for their beliefs, and numerous communities were resettled, often breaking the association between Andean communities and their deities, which were inscribed in the landscape. These challenges led to a variety of revivalist religious practices, the cult of Taki Onqoy being one. Followers of Taki Onqoy, also known as the "dancing sickness" because those afflicted by it tended to twitch and convulse, predicted that the *huacas* would enjoy a resurgence and that the *huacas* would bring vengeance on the Spanish colonizers of the Andes. The dancing sickness was also thought to be a symptom of Andeans' neglect of their *huacas*, and those afflicted by the dancing sickness were generally cured by making extensive offerings to their *huacas* in the form of corn beer, meat, and coca leaves. This movement also illustrated the ability of Indians to incorporate diverse religious traditions into their cosmology as some of the movement's members adopted the personas of Catholic saints (such as Saint Mary or Saint Mary Magdalene) to capture the power of Christian "deities" but to use them for their own purposes.

Over time Catholic and Andean religious rituals have become interwoven in countless ways. For example, in many parts of the Andes, *kurakas* (native leaders) carry staffs, called "*kinsa rey*," that are passed from father to son. The name of the staffs, in the Quechua language, means "three kings," and some people who carry them have made direct references to the Three Kings of Bethlehem, despite archeological evidence that indicates that these staffs long predate the arrival of Spaniards. The staffs are not only representative of a *kuraka*'s authority, but also are thought to possess a spiritual power themselves and must be appeased with rituals and offerings made to the staffs by those who possess them. The staffs obtain this power by hearing Catholic mass and being blessed Catholic mass by Catholic priests. The power is maintained by the kurakas performing animal sacrifice and bathing the staffs in blood. This is one illustration of the co-existence of Catholic and non-Catholic traditions.

Conversion and the Future of Andean Religious Beliefs

People have offered a variety of explanations for the continued co-existence of Catholic and native religious elements in Andean ritualization and religious practice. On the one hand, some people have argued that the religious practices of indigenous Andeans are experiencing a gradual change whereby elements of native religious practice are slowing giving way to Christian practices. Other people have argued that the flexibility of the native cosmology (which allows Indians to accommodate a variety of beliefs and practices within the Andean religious framework) has allowed Indians to incorporate elements of Christianity into a predominantly Andean framework. Scholars studying colonial religious beliefs question if Indian converts to Christianity fully comprehended Christian doctrine or if the practice of Catholicism only masked the maintenance of pre-Columbian worship in private. Other scholars have argued that Andean religion is syncretic, combining elements of both Andean and Christian beliefs and creating something new in the process. Regardless of how one views the relationship between Christian and Andean religion and ritual, it seems likely that pre-Columbian influences will continue to be important in Indian communities in the Andes for a long time.

Patrick C. Wilson

See also Agricultural Rites; Catholicism; South America: Savanna and Tropical Forest

Further Reading

Abercrombie, T. (1998). *Pathways of memory and power: Ethnography and history among an Andean people.* Madison: University of Wisconsin Press.

Allen, C. J. (1988). *The hold life has: Coca and cultural identity in an Andean community.* Washington, DC: Smithsonian Institution Press.

Bolin, I. (1998). *Rituals of respect: The secret of survival in the high Peruvian Andes.* Austin: University of Texas Press.

Gose, P. (1994). *Deathly waters and hungry mountains: Agrarian ritual and class formation in an Andean town.* Toronto, Canada: University of Toronto Press.

Griffiths, N. (1996). *The cross and the serpent: Religious repression and resurgence in colonial Peru.* Norman: University of Oklahoma Press.

Henman, A. (1980). *Mama coca.* Bogota, Colombia: El Ancora Editores.

Isbell, B. J. (1985). *To defend ourselves: Ecology and ritual in an Andean village.* Prospect Heights, IL: Waveland Press.

Mills, K. (1997)., *Idolatry and its enemies: Colonial Andean religion and extirpation, 1640–1750.* Princeton, NJ: Princeton University Press.

Rasnake, R. N. (1988). *Domination and cultural resistance: Authority and power among an Andean people.* Durham, NC: Duke University Press.

Sallnow, M. J. (1987). *Pilgrims of the Andes: Regional cults in Cuzco.* Washington, DC: Smithsonian Institution Press.

Silverblatt, I. (1987). *Moon, sun, and witches: Gender ideologies and class in Inca and colonial Peru.* Princeton, NJ: Princeton University Press.

Stern, S. (1982). *Peru's Indian peoples and the challenge of the Spanish conquest: Huamanga to 1640.* Madison: University of Wisconsin Press.

South America: Savanna and Tropical Forest

Before the arrival of Europeans in South America the number of Amerindians living there was estimated at 39 million. Today there are 15 million people, most of whom live in Peru (91 percent). The others live in Ecuador, Bolivia, Colombia, Venezuela, Brazil, Guyana and Paraguay. Three thousand languages were spoken prior the European contact; only four hundred languages remain. The Amerindians of South America have complex sociocultural system. They still practice many traditions, such as hunting small mammals, fishing, and farming with the slash-and-burn method.

Savanna

The South American savanna covers 250 million hectares located near the equator between the Tropic of Cancer and the Tropic of Capricorn, the countries of Brazil, Colombia, and Venezuela. The climate varies from tropical wet to dry. The savanna soils are usually low in nutrients and porous, covered with a top thin layer of nutrient humus, which favor the growth of grasses and small trees, shrubs and a ground layer of grasses.

Vegetation in this region grows rapidly once the area has been cleared by using slash and burn techniques. This technique increases the activity of root systems, causing more nutrient uptake from the soil. Nancy Flores points out that Amerindians took much care of their gardens that, "after planting their clearings, most of the villagers went on trek until harvest time, leaving only two ritual guardians to watch over and perform ceremonies to promote the growth of the crops" (Roosevelt 1994, 252)

The tobacco is commonly used among the Amerindians of the savanna. Tobacco originated in the New World where there were several varieties of different species. Nowadays, *Nicotiana tabacum and Nicotiana rustica* are mostly cultivated. *Nicotina rustica* contains a higher concentration of nicotine, which became very significant to the shamans during the practice of ritual smoking. Shamans or healers are common among the Amerindians. Their primary responsibility is to provide a feeling of well being for others. Shamans use tobacco in combination with other hallucinogen plants to connect to the supernatural world. Shamans from the Manasi and Mojo tribes use tobacco for many purposes. They blow tobacco across a river to ask their ancestors to bring good luck to fishermen. The people of Waiwai, Guiana, grow the cassava plant as one of their main sustainable crops. Thus, shamans blow tobacco smoke on the claws of an armadillo when cassava is being planted to ensure that the plants acquire good roots. Tobacco is used not only as a means to connect to the supernatural world, but also as an insecticide and medicine. The Amerindians of Guiana apply tobacco juice to their bodies to remove mosquito larvae.

Myths help the people of the South American savanna understand their history, religious beliefs and practices. Written languages have not been found among these people, and it is through stories and myths they share their stories of creation and stories reflecting their daily life. Their stories are told during ceremonies or in groups. Myths consist of themes, tale types, motifs, a cast of characters, and historical frames (Bierhorst 1998, 11). The basic stories involve heroes such as the Sun and the Moon, the Bird Nester and the Jaguar, and the Star Woman and the Corn Tree.

Tropical Forest

The tropical forest of South America is the largest rain forest in the world, covering 518 million hectares. It includes the tropics of Venezuela, the Guianas, and the Amazon River basin. The average temperature is above 23°C. Rainfall ranges from 152 to 1,000 centimeters a year. The rain forest is made up of four environments: emergent, canopy, understory, and forest floor; each environment contains animals and plants that have adapted to its unique conditions. In the tropical forest people's primary food crop is manioc, which people supplement by hunting and fishing. The French anthropologist Claude Lévi-Strauss listed several palm species and other types of trees that the people use as food, beverages, dyes, medicine, weapons, housing materials, string, baskets, hammocks, and other products.

Gender determines the labor of the people who live in the rain forest. Men hunt, fish, warfare, clear gardens, make baskets, canoes, and rafts, and perform woodwork. Women cook, garden, weave, make pottery, rear children, and care for the animals.

In the rain forest a village is formed of six or more large family houses, arranged in square or circle. Women cook in several small huts. In the center is a small hut for men. These villages are semi permanent. After a few years the palm thatch of the houses begins to decompose, and if the gardens are growing old, the villagers move to a new location.

The people of the rain forest do not believe in a single god; instead they believe in a number of spirits called "tricksters." Tricksters are celestial mythological beings such as the Sun, the Moon, the Stars, the Thunder, and the Rain. Other beings, such as the spirits of the mountains, rocks, and springs, help the people understand their origins and nature. Most of the cultural groups in the rain forest believe that an invisible spirit (soul) lives in each person's body. When a person dies the spirit wanders about the forest in an invisible form or in the form of an animal. The Nukak people believe that men and women physically cannot eat deer, tapir, and jaguar flesh. They believe that in the bodies of deer, tapir, and jaguar live the spirits of those who have died and have gone to a lower world to dominate the nighttime. These spirits come out at night to collect food, but before they come out they put on the skins of deer, tapir, and jaguar.

The rain forest people do not have idols or public ceremonial places to honor their gods or have religious activities to summarize their everyday life. On the contrary, nature and their way of life are connected, and shamans play an important role in a village. Shamans, with the help of the supernatural, cure the sick. Plants from the rain forest or from their shamanic gardens are commonly used during the curing ceremony. Every shaman has their own practice, for example some would collect several bunches of plants from the garden and shake them all over the sick body while chanting. Others would blow *mapucho* or tobacco smoke over the body of the sick, then the shaman would suck out the invisible objects out of the dolorous area that spirits have blown into their bodies. Shamans also practice divination and magic.

The savanna and the tropical forest cultures of South America have undergone a progressive degeneration. Some of their natural resources are being exploited by the outside world. Many of the cultural groups have moved to reservations, and many others work as servants and laborers. Even so, they have retained or adapted their religious beliefs and rituals. Specifically, shamans have been able to understand Western cultures and to adapt some aspects to Amerindian culture.

Mara L. Cosillo-Star

Further Reading

Biehorst, J. (1998). *The mythology of South America.* New York: William Morrow.

Hill, J. D. (1988). *Rethinking history and myth: Indigenous South American perspectives on the past.* Urbana: University of Illinois.

Lévi-Strauss, C. (1966). *From honey to ashes: Introduction to a science of mythology.* New York: Harper & Row.

Matteson Langdon, E. J., & Baer, G. (1997). *Portals of power: Shamanism in South America.* Albuquerque: University of New Mexico Press.

Osburne, H. (1968). *South American mythology.* Verona, Italy: Hamlyn Publisher Group.

Roosevelt, A. (Ed.). (1994). *Amazonian Indians from prehistory to the present: Anthropological perspectives.* Tucson: Arizona Press.

Salazano, F. M., & Callegari-Jacques, S. M. (1988). *South American Indians: A case study in evolution.* Oxford, UK: Clarendon Press.

Wilbert, J. (1987). *Tobacco and shamanism in South America.* New Haven, CT: Yale University Press.

Wilson, D. J. (1999). *Indigenous South America of the past and present and ecological perspective.* Boulder, CO: Westview Press.

Sport and Ritual

In Europe and the United States during the second half of the nineteenth century, the shaping of modernity was related to normative standards of appearance, health, bodily and moral care. There were two competing models of bodily and moral care: the Germanic model, based on gymnastics, and the Euro-American model, based on games and team sport. The rapid expansion of sport practices consolidated a civil society anchored in private clubs and associations and created in the margins of the state and created a national space of sport competition. Sport institutions were relatively autonomous and regulated by their own rules and moral systems. Since the first modern Olympic Games in 1896 a global space for sport competition was a fundamental dimension of modernity because it created stereotypes of performances and symbolic schemes that are still functioning. Sport was a creator of mirrors, human myths, and powerful images open to any nation and its citizens. Sport was a successful avenue for social and symbolic integration into the realms of modernity and nation building. In this direction processes of nation building through sport were checked in time and place by class origins, gendered identities, and regional historical developments. Sports such as tennis, golf, cricket, basketball, rugby, boxing, soccer, football, and baseball conditioned a variety of practices and adoptions. If soccer was spread by the British, becoming an almost universal sport, then baseball was carried abroad by U.S. educators, missionaries, and businessmen who introduced the game wherever they went. Some nations adopted it, others did not. Baseball is less universal than soccer.

The historian Allen Gutmann has argued that baseball's special attraction among team games, all of which combine individualism and cooperation, lies in its primitive-pastoral elements, in its extraordinary modernity, in its closeness to the seasonal rhythms of nature and in the rarified realm of numbers. It has been speculated that Japan has translocated baseball representation from the cornfields of Iowa to a rice paddy outside Hiroshima. This process undoubtedly reflects not only the popularity of baseball but also a Japanese fascination with key elements of U.S. pastoral culture. On the other hand, the universal acceptance of British soccer is strictly associated with the domination of the industrial world, with the culture of the factory, the big city and the life of the local pub or bar (discussing the match and celebrating the victories). The diffusion of soccer can be seen as a central point of attraction for the laboring population of a factory, a district, or a big industrial city.

Rituals in Modern Society

Sport and games have the capacity to produce an asymmetry of winners and losers and, consequently, are expected to flourish in and be a characteristic only of highly competitive industrial societies. The reverse should be true in nonmodern societies where traditional rituals dominate. For some social scientists, in traditional rituals asymmetry is postulated in advance—initiated and uninitiated or profane and sacred—and the "game" consists in making all the participants pass to the winning side by means of ritual participation. In the historical macrosociological approach of the sociologist Norbert Elias, sport was defined as a generalized ritual and a key area in the development of the civilizing process of modern societies. The civilizing process was characterized by continuous state control of the legitimate use of force, the

Ritual behavior by spectators at international sports events often involve nationalistic symbols. At a Women's World Cup soccer match in Foxboro, Massachusetts in 1999, supporters of the U.S. team display American flags. COURTESY OF KAREN CHRISTENSEN.

development of social organizations to reduce open conflict among social groups, and the elaboration of codes for social behavior oriented toward the exercise of individual self-control.

Sport became a typical ritual activity of leisure that, historically, fulfilled some of the required functions for the consolidation of the civilizing process. The exercise of individual self-control is central to sport. For Elias one of the essential problems of many sports is how to reconcile two contradictory functions: the pleasurable decontrolling of human feelings and the full evocation of enjoyable excitement on the one hand and the maintenance of a set of checks to keep the pleasantly decontrolled feelings under control on the other hand. Modern sport is regulated by clear rules that assure equality among the players, make possible the maximization of inner pleasures and the relaxation of individual tensions, and contain the possible exercise of physical violence. Through Elias the minor theme of sport was transformed into a major theme and becomes a privileged field for the analysis of individual and social tensions in modern societies. According to him, a civilizing process may be followed or even accompanied by a retreat in the opposite direction, by a decivilizing process. Elias's followers, convinced of the importance of the dialectics (discussion and reasoning by dialogue as a method of intellectual investigation) of civilizing and decivilizing processes in modern societies, devoted much of their research to an understanding of British soccer hooliganism. Thus, sport can divide as much as it can unite. Elias's model based on ritual harmony, emotional control, and social discipline can be difficult to realize.

The remains of the entrance way to the stadium in Olympia, Greece, the site of the ancient Olympics. During the Greek period, the Olympics were organized in honor of the Greek god Zeus, with a major temple on the site built in his honor. COURTESY OF KAREN CHRISTENSEN.

Participation in Ritual

Sport is regarded as an important field of analysis for achieving a better understanding of the appropriate or contradictory functioning of modern societies. In the arena of sport individual self-fulfillment is related to games producing winners and losers, to exalted nationalism in an age of increasing international competition, and, in some cases, to an abnormal quest for excitement and violence. No one will deny that sport is associated with these practices and values, but sport is much more. One can assume that sport is a ritual and a game at the same time and that it is, as such, a cultural construction that makes symbolic communication among its participants possible. The content of the communication may vary according to degree of formality, rigidity, concentration of meaning, and redundancy. In every ritual, types of participants can be distinguished: the experts in knowledge, the central participants or players, and the peripheral participants or audience. This approximation permits the consideration of a range of discourse and identities produced by the various kinds of participants. In this sense, journalists can produce a written or verbal ideology and morality, and sport fans can verbalize their "obsessions" and their sentimental concerns in the stadiums. A proper historical analysis of the impact of sport can situate these narratives within specific periods of time and place and, consequently, enable people to follow their transformation. The successful narratives of sport have historically been produced by

Shobu Aikido dojo showing the kamiza (altar) to which students bow at the beginning and end of class (also showing founder).
COURTESY OF KAREN CHRISTENSEN.

journalists and have centered on the history of playing styles, clubs, national teams, and players. In the last two decades, coaches have joined journalists in the ideological construction and interpretation of the meanings of sport. Coaches now write books and participate in television programs as experts in rituals, interpreting the development of the game.

Social scientists have commented on the importance of specific rituals in the creation of a certain license to distance one's self from particular dominant values in society. Carnival in its many variants is said to be a type of ritual in which it is possible to suspend particular hierarchies and accordingly to question some of the dominant values. The behavior of hooligans in British soccer can be understood as a questioning of the key values of emotional self-control and public discipline. This approach indicates the importance of considering the types of transgressions that arise in the ritual being analyzed. The ritualization of sport allows for the convergence of tragic and comic elements combined in various types. Such a perspective transforms violence into a dramatic form, latent in rituals, in which central values can be suspended. Thus, violence—symbolic or real—and the lack of violence are not only deviations from a civilizing process but also are the key features in the development of the ritual.

Generally, the symbolic effect of a ritual is charged not only with the presence of tragic and comic elements but also with the content of the ritual itself. This dimension, which one can call "cosmological" (dealing with the nature of the universe), alludes to the ways of classifying social relationships among men and between men and women and allows for a reflection on the national—that sport has produced in the international global landscape of the last century. The chants of soccer supporters in Europe and Latin America are a world full of explicit and implicit meanings. It is a world in which symbolic frontiers appear clearly, starting from thoughts about a set of important social relations: father-son, child-adult and "real men"-homosexuals. The authentic supporters are adult, responsible, and heterosexual men.

Classification

The fans, in their constant activity—creating anthems, inventing nicknames, making ironic comments on the comic situations created in the game, waving their banners, and creating an endless series of chants—dedicate themselves to one central ritual activity: that of classifying and evaluating objects and actions. This classification not only refers to a moral order, to what ought to be done and what ought not to be done, but also expresses a type of knowledge of why things are as they are. In every ritual the moral order, whether subverted or not, temporal or transitory, lends itself to a sort of evaluation of the value of autonomy, of dependency, of control, of freedom, of dignity, of self-esteem, and of loyalty to commitment. In this sense the two orders that have been mentioned—the comic and the tragic—are at the center of soccer as a ritual. This means that for the actors committed to it, the unfolding of the rite allows the experience of a certain totality that characterizes every culturally significant human experience. The comic relates to the transgression of rules of etiquette; the tragic allows reflection on transgressions of a deeper order where what is at stake are major existential (relating to existence) problems—a symbolization of the dramas of life constituted by the alternations of victories and defeats, of promotions and relegations, the intervention of good luck and bad luck and the arbitration of a justice that is sometimes favorable, sometimes unfavorable. In religious ceremonies the comic is customarily absent, just as the tragic is customarily absent from carnival. Soccer thus becomes, among modern rituals, a privileged locus for analyzing the tension between those elements.

The question of mythical heroes in the ritual of sport is of crucial importance. The complex mingling of individuality, gender (masculinity), and nationhood is an integral part of the historical construction of sport. A sports hero is an idol and icon who exists within a separate dimension of time, the time of heroes. The time of heroes, as opposed to the time that encapsulates daily routines or scheduled rituals, represents a glorious, dreamlike time in the minds of the adoring public during which the mediocrity of daily life is suddenly transcended. Sport enables people to ponder the dynamics of culture in a way that other rituals do not. The cult of sports heroes unites the admiration of their performances with the moral and social impact of their lives on followers. The history of real individuals provides a social model to perceive paradoxes and dramas in society and to recognize and question some values. In the real moral evaluation of these heroes, the ultimate criterion is the creative use of their bodies. Explicitly, the great joy given by the outstanding players is more important than any consistent moral evaluation. Thus, freedom of creativity and irresponsibility in inventing the unexpected are a guarantee of admiration. Adoring fans have a kind of emotional contract of joy with their heroes that transcends standard morality and the logic of order of nation-states.

The relation of sport and ritual is a constitutive part of contemporary society. Ritual is a means of social transgression and resistance but also the expression of the life histories of various types of participants and the articulation and representation of sociability and community. Religion and religious experiences appear as the shadow of sport. Players performed prescribed motions in which the perplexing human predicaments interpreted by religion are in play: chance, destiny, providence, defeat, victory, the struggle against evil, human weakness, bodily sacrifices, and physical limitations. Modern societies have in many ways sublimated this sacredness into nationalism and other non-religious identities.

Eduardo P. Archetti

See also Body and Rituals

Further Reading

Archetti, E. P. (1992). Argentinian football: A ritual of violence? *The International journal of the history of sport, 9*(2), 209–235.

Dyck, N. (Ed.). (2000). *Games, sports and cultures*. Oxford, UK: Berg.

Dyck, N., & Archetti, E. P. (Eds.). (2003). *Sport, dance and embodied identities*. Oxford, UK: Berg.

Gutmann, A. (1978). *From ritual to record: The nature of modern sports*. New York: Columbia University Press.

Elias, N., & Dunning, E. (1986). Quest for excitement: Sport and leisure in the civilising process. Oxford, UK: Blackwell.

Star Trek Conventions

Star Trek conventions are the ultimate ritual expression of *Star Trek* fans. Fans who travel to conventions experience a sense of unity much akin to that experienced by pilgrims who travel in religious contexts. Thus, *Star Trek* conventions are the secular inheritors of religious pilgrimage in the modern, leisure-oriented world.

The *Star Trek* Phenomenon

Star Trek conventions are celebrations of both the *Star Trek* franchise and the phenomenon of *Star Trek* fandom. The franchise encompasses five science-fiction television series and ten motion pictures to date. Many fans believe that Gene Roddenberry (1921–1991), the creator and executive producer of *Star Trek,* imbued the show with his optimistic vision of humanity. The original series ran from 1966 to 1969 with seventy-nine episodes. The first *Star Trek* film, *Star Trek: The Motion Picture,* was released in 1979. *Star Trek* returned to television in 1987 with *Star Trek: The Next Generation*. One or more television incarnations of *Star Trek* have been in continuous production since that time.

A sense of *Star Trek* fan identity emerged as early as 1968, when fans of the original *Star Trek* show successfully mounted a letter-writing campaign to prevent cancellation of the show after its second season. Fans also mounted a successful campaign to name NASA's prototype space shuttle *"Enterprise."* The first fan club emerged in 1972, and many more clubs now exist. The Official *Star Trek* Fan Club has over forty thousand members, and more than 100,000 copies of its fan magazine are sold annually. According to a public opinion poll conducted in 1991, 53 percent of Americans considered themselves to be *Star Trek* fans.

The Convention Context

The first *Star Trek* convention was held in New York City in 1972. Organizers expected only a few hundred participants; more than three thousand attended.

Today *Star Trek* conventions are held somewhere in the United States every weekend of the year and on a regular basis internationally in countries such as Canada, Australia, England, Germany, and Brazil. Small conventions draw only a few hundred people; large conventions draw upward of twenty thousand people. Many *Star Trek* fans attend more than one convention per year; some attend as many conventions as their time and budget allow.

Star Trek conventions can be fan based or professionally organized. Fan-based conventions include discussion panels on *Star Trek*-related topics, costume competitions, writing workshops for amateur authors, showings of favorite *Star Trek* episodes, guest appearances by *Star Trek* actors and others connected to the show, autograph-signing opportunities, "filk" singing sessions in which folk songs with *Star Trek*-inspired lyrics are sung, and the sale of *Star Trek*-related merchandise. Professionally organized conventions include costume competitions and costume balls, merchandise rooms, many more guest appearances than fan-based conventions have, autograph-signing opportunities, charity auctions, and insider information on upcoming *Star Trek* films and television shows. Additionally, at both fan-based and professionally organized conventions, fans organize room parties (for a specific group, such as a fan club, held in a private hotel room) and private functions (fan-sponsored events, such as the launch of a new fan club branch or fundraising events) to coincide with the official conventions.

Star Trek Conventions as Pilgrimage

Star Trek convention attendance meets the criteria for pilgrimage outlined by the anthropologist Victor Turner (1920–1983). Turner characterizes pilgrimage as a ritual journey that temporarily frees participants from their everyday social roles and allows them to experience a sense of communal fellowship with their fellow pilgrims. This sense of communal fellowship *(communitas)* can take three forms: existential, normative, and ideological. All three forms are evident in the *Star Trek* convention context.

Existentially, fans idealize the model of futuristic relationships found in the *Star Trek* television series and hold *Star Trek*'s vision of the future as a role model for how social relations should be governed: namely, unfettered by race, gender, or class distinctions. This idealization of futuristic relationships parallels the idealization of mythical or historical models for human behavior found in religious pilgrimage contexts.

Normatively, fans conceptualize their own relationships in the convention context as embodying the ideal model of human relationships portrayed in *Star Trek*. Within the convention context, fans see themselves as unfettered by social distinctions and relate to one another solely on the basis of their shared fan identities. The experience of egalitarian fellowship among pilgrims that transcends social structural distinctions is also what governs normative *communitas* in religious pilgrimage contexts.

Ideologically, fans posit their own egalitarian relationships in the convention context, as modeled on the social relations depicted in *Star Trek*, as signs of what human social relations might one day become if *Star Trek*'s optimistic vision of the future should be actualized. Ideological *communitas* of this kind is implicitly critical of the social order in that *Star Trek*'s utopian model is juxtaposed against the perceived inequities of contemporary North American society. Ideological *communitas* in religious contexts is equally critical of the status quo and can lead to a commitment on the part of pilgrims to bring about the utopian world that their *communitas* experience has shown them is possible. Many *Star Trek* fans similarly dedicate themselves to making the world a more tolerant and egalitarian place as modeled upon that depicted in the *Star Trek* television series.

Fandom, Conventions, and Pilgrimage

Most fans list "fun" as the main reason for attending a *Star Trek* convention. *Star Trek* convention attendance clearly is a fun, leisure pursuit, but it also meets the criteria for pilgrimage. Fans step outside the social constraints of everyday life while attending a convention; they experience a sense of *communitas* there that is unattainable at home; they are inspired to work toward a world in which such egalitarian social relationships are possible. Although *Star Trek* is just a television show, *Star Trek* convention attendance is the secular inheritor of religious pilgrimage.

Jennifer E. Porter

See also Pilgrimage

Further Reading

Gerrold, D. (1973). *The world of Star Trek*. New York: Ballantine Books.

Jindra, M. (1994). *Star Trek* fandom as a religious phenomenon. *Sociology of Religion, 55*(1), 27–51.
Lichtenberg, J., Marshak, S., & Winston, J. (1975). *Star Trek lives!* New York: Bantam Books.
Porter, J. E., & McLaren, D. L. (1999). *Star Trek and sacred ground: Explorations of Star Trek, religion and American culture.* Albany: State University of New York Press.
Tulloch, J., & Jenkins, H. (1995). *Science fiction audiences: Watching Doctor Who and Star Trek.* New York: Routledge.
Turner, V. (1969). *The ritual process: Structure and anti-structure.* Ithaca, NY: Cornell University Press.
Turner, V., & Turner, E. (1978). *Image and pilgrimage in Christian culture.* New York: Columbia University Press.
Wagner, J., & Lundeen, J. (1998). *Deep space and sacred time: Star Trek in the American mythos.* Westport, CT: Praeger.
Winston, J. (1979). *The making of the Trek conventions.* Chicago: Playboy Press.

Sufism

The word "Sufi" appears in the literature in the eighth century, most likely as a reference to the rough wool (Arabic: *suf*) worn by ascetics. Sufism has many meanings but generally refers to Islamic mysticism, including the subjective inner life of Muslims. In a very real sense, Sufism is the essence of Islam, something outsiders can but imagine. What can be described are the rituals and descriptions of Sufi behavior and explanations.

Sufism is concerned with Islamic spirituality and its transmission from one generation to another. At first this transmission was carried on through oral and written teachings from one generation to another via individual masters to their disciples. After four or five centuries, however, individual masters began to found religious brotherhoods centered on rules, forms of meditation, and set forms of behavior. These brotherhoods spread rapidly all over the Islamic world. Each stressed the truth of the unity of God and had a method for attaining that truth, based on litanies of divine names and the gaining of virtues. These virtues allowed one to attain goodness and understand the depths of one's soul.

Each of the Sufi orders stressed a particular element of the path to truth while adapting itself to a specific ethnic group and psychological reality. While maintaining adherence to the orthodox teaching of Islam, each brotherhood incorporated aspect of various artistic forms, from music and poetry to the sacred dance. These adaptations generated an incredibly rich diversity of worship within Islam, enabling people of vastly different backgrounds and temperaments to partake of Sufism's teachings. In turn, the ability of Sufism to adapt so well ensured its perpetuation and that of its teachings, initiations, and recruitment of new members.

Characteristics of the Orders

Over the nine hundred or so years during which Sufi orders or brotherhoods have existed, there have been numerous such organizations in the Islamic world. They vary in size and duration as well as influence. There are some orders that have remained in existence and have exerted influence since the beginning of Sufism. Some of these still teach the way of the path (a series of religious exercises, including isolation and solitude, good works, and prayers) while others offer only Sufism's grace. New masters appear in old orders and revive dying orders. It is also possible to see new masters arise and found new Sufi orders. The tradition of divine revelation to individual mystics is an enduring one in Islam.

Indeed, Sufism has borrowed elements found in Christian monasticism, Gnosticism, as well as Indian mysticism. It basic roots, however, come from the earliest days of Islam when there were groups of penitents found throughout Arabia. Sufism appropriated these figures as its own, including 'Ali ar-Rida, the eighth imam of Twelver Shi'a (c. 768–818), al-Hasan al-Basri, (642–728), and Rabi'ah al-'Adawiyah (713–801). Rabi'ah was a woman from Basra in present-day Iraq who believed that love of God, not fear of punishment or hope of reward, is the only valid reason for worship.

No matter how else they differ, Sufi orders agree on the central tenets of Sufism. These are the concepts of *tawakkul* (all foreign words in this article are Arabic), the total reliance on God, and *dhikr*, the perpetual remembrance of God. Some early Sufi masters were deemed unorthodox by the Muslim religious scholars *(ulama)*; however, in the twelfth century al-Ghazali (1058–1111) urged a reconciliation between Sufism and orthodoxy, a reconciliation that the emergence of Sufi orders helped bring about.

The orders installed a multifaceted system of initiation and progression toward the divine. At the same time literary Sufism developed with the aid of Persian writings and the mystic poetry of Turkish and Urdu poets as well as Persian masters. These aspects of Sufism as well as their ability to assimilate indigenous religious practices enabled the orders to spread Islam, especially in sub-Saharan Africa and central and Southeast Asia.

The Qadiriyya, founded by 'Abd al-Qadir al-Jilani (1077 or 1078–1166) in Baghdad, is the oldest of the extant Sufi orders. There are a number of other important and long-lived Sufi orders, including the Ahmadiyya, especially important in Egypt as well as sub-Saharan Africa; the Naqshbandiyya, significant in central Asia; the Nimatullahiyya in Iran; the Rifaiyya in Egypt; the Southwest Asia), the Shadhiliyya in North Africa and Arabia; the Suhrawardiyya and the Chishtiyya in south and central Asia; and the Tijaniyya in north and west Africa.

Sufism has influenced Islam in a number of ways. It has led to the spread of Islam, the development of calligraphy and literature in Islamic areas, and the assimilation of non-Arabic peoples into the Islamic world. However, many conservative and reformist Muslims have attacked Sufism for its saint veneration, tomb visitation, and use of non-Islamic customs. The tolerance of Sufism and the beauty of its rituals enrage fundamentalists just as Calvinists were enraged by the liturgy and inclusiveness of late medieval Catholicism.

Sufi Rituals

The defining Sufi ritual, often referred to as *the* Sufi ritual, is that of *dhikr*. This ritual consists of the repetition of the name of God in a litany format. The names of God are repeated by Sufis until a trancelike state emerges. In Islamic mysticism, the *dhikr* has become the focal point of their ritual, the heart of the practice of Sufi orders. Sufis have made the expansion of techniques of meditation that use the divine names a specialty.

Dhikr translates into English from the Arabic as "a pronouncement or temperance ritual." It generally includes singing, dance, instrumental music, and, of course, the recitation of God's names. The goal is to enter into a meditative ecstasy and trance. Incense and the use of costumes work toward that goal. During ecstatic trance God's presence is felt. This *hadra*, or presence of God, marks the end of the ritual.

The ceremony is always held on a fixed day of the week that may vary from region to region. Followers of the Sufi order assemble in the mosque or another religious space for the *dhikr* ceremony. The *muqri'* (reader) recites a passage (sura) from the Qur'an. At the end of his recital, he repeats the names of God. There are various rhythmic body movements that help bring on a trance state. These movements accompany and aid accelerated breathing. The ritual ends with a hymn.

The use of music in the *dhikr* is highly controversial within Islam. This fact is especially true concerning instrumental music since only chanting or reciting is found in orthodox practice. Also controversial is the Sufi desire to experience union with God during the *dhikr*. Orthodox Muslims argue that humans are not part of the divine light of God but mere creatures of God. Only adherence to the prescriptions of the Qur'an can move people closer to God, not any mystical practices. Moreover, these mystical practices and beliefs are strongly influenced by Zoroastrianism from Iran, St. John's Gospel, Gnostic concepts, and mystical Judaism—any one of which stirs opposition in conservative Muslims.

However, Sufis point to Qur'anic verses that urge faithful believers to "remember God with increasing remembrance and extol His limitless glory from morn to evening" (Qu'ran 33:41). The Sufi expands on this verse and argues that remembering God entails the forgetting of self. This emphasis on asceticism and detachment resembles that found in numerous religions that have ascetics, including Christianity, Buddhism, and Hinduism. The downgrading of the here and now elevates the mystical sphere of the next life.

The movement from stage to stage of the Sufi path also consists of rituals. Membership in Sufi orders is nonexclusive. Members may belong to a number of orders simultaneously. However, in reality a person tends to become attached to one order and one leader. The leader should have deep spiritual knowledge and an understanding of Muslim law. The most important element is that of worship. Sheikhs are generally more filled with religious faith and fervor than with intellectual attributes. They are painfully honest, freely admitting their shortcomings in understanding Sufi doctrines when that is the case.

The leader is important in bringing new members into the order. The first step in the movement through the order is that of spiritual training, which precedes initiation. This is a severe process, available only to males in Sufi Islam. There are a number of trials to test the seeker's ability to withstand tribulations and to test his willingness to obey the sheikh. Adherence to prescribed religious duties and practices often include things such as periodic retirements to solitude. This solitude requires meditation and remembrance of God, including the recitation of the divine names. Periods of fasting to discipline the body are also required of the seeker. Successful completion of the tests leads to initiation. The ceremony consists of giving an oath of allegiance. The initiate is thus attached to the sheikh and his entire spiritual chain of succession. The ceremony may be held in the community or simply in the presence of the sheikh. The sheikh supervises the initiate's progress along the spiritual path, adding duties and obligations.

There are many other ceremonies. One of the more important ones concerns the yearly celebration of the founding of the Sufi order. Each order has its members meet to celebrate. During the meeting, the excellencies of the founder are recited. A party is held at which singing and dancing takes place, as well as the recitation of the ninety-nine names of God.

Implications

The tradition of Sufism has been one of inclusion and assimilation. Its tolerance and ability to reconcile new customs with the core of Islamic teaching has periodically made it an object of repression from more conservative and fundamentalist segments of Islam. Its emphasis on mystical experience has also attracted and repelled various segments of Islam. However, there is a long tradition within Islam making way for personal mystical experiences and the teachings that emerge from these experiences.

The master who shares these experiences with disciples is a revered figure. The teachings in brotherhoods or orders have long been transmitted from generation to generation by various brotherhoods. Moreover, much of the spread of Islam is due to the Sufi orders, which have adapted to local customs and ways of worship. The spread of Islam into sub-Saharan Africa and various parts of Asia has been largely due to the work of the brotherhoods. The celebrated tolerance of Islam for much of its history as well as its literature, dance, and music incorporated in various rituals have been the result of the work of the Sufi orders.

Frank A. Salamone

Further Reading

Allen, R. (1995). *The Arabic novel: An historical and critical introduction* (2d ed.). Syracuse, NY: Syracuse University Press.

Arkoun, M. (1994). *Rethinking Islam: Common questions, uncommon answers.* (R. D. Lee, Ed. & Trans.). Boulder, CO: Westview Press.

Bulliet, R. W. (2002, Winter). The crisis within Islam. *The Wilson Quarterly, 26*(1) 11–27.

Cook, B. (2001). The 2001 Fez Festival of World Sacred Music: An annual musical event in Morocco embodies and reflects sufi traditions and spirit. *International Journal of Humanities and Peace 17*(1), 54ff.

Dean, M. (1997, February 2). Dervishes' spiritual spins: Sufi dancers bring their sacred whirling to Lisner. *The Washington Times,* p. 3.

Ernst, C. W., & Schimmel, A. (1992). *Eternal garden: Mysticism, history, and politics at a South Asian Sufi Center*. Albany: State University of New York Press.

Geels, A. (1996). A note on the psychology of Dhikr: The Halveti-Jerrahi order of dervishes in Istanbul. *International Journal for the Psychology of Religion 6*(4), 229–251.

Hourani, A. H. (1991). *A history of the Arab peoples.* Cambridge, MA: Belknap Press of Harvard University Press.

Johansen, J. (1996). *Sufism and Islamic reform in Egypt: The battle for Islamic tradition.* Oxford, UK: Oxford University Press.

Johns, A. H. (1995). Sufism in Southeast Asia: Reflections and reconsiderations. *Journal of Southeast Asian Studies 26*(1), 169ff.

Knapp, B. L. (1984). *A Jungian approach to literature.* Carbondale: Southern Illinois University Press.

Nasr, S. H. (Ed.). (1987). *Islamic spirituality: Foundations.* New York: Crossroad.

Ruthven, M. (2000). *Islam in the world*. New York: Oxford University Press.

Shaw-Eagle, J. (2000, January 1). A mystical touch to art. *The Washington Times,* p. 1.

Smith, G. (2000, April 15). Radical Islam conflicts with tradition. *The Washington Times,* p. 6.

Voll, J. O. (1994). *Islam, continuity, and change in the modern world* (2d ed.). Syracuse, NY: Syracuse University Press.

Werbner, P. (2002). The place which is diaspora: Citizenship, religion, and gender in the making of chaordic transnationalism. *Journal of Ethnic and Migration Studies 28*(1) 119–134.

Symbol and Ritual

People disagree over the meaning of the word *symbol*, which comes from the ancient Greek word *symbolon*. A *symbolon* was a piece of slate. In ancient Greece, a group would break pieces of slate from a burned vase and give a piece to each member. When the group members reunited each member fit his piece into the whole, proving his membership. Thus, each member's piece of slate represented the group.

Those people who follow a strict interpretation of the meaning of *symbol* argue that a symbol is intimately part of the group it represents, whereas a sign merely points to something outside itself. The Golden Arches of McDonald's are a sign, whereas a fraternity key at one time was a real symbol that opened a real door for members only. Loose interpretations merge sign and symbol as anything that stands for something else. Thus, a holly wreath symbolizes Christmas and a street sign a street. This latter interpretation, the one that merges sign and symbol, is generally followed here.

Rituals consist of ceremonial acts that a group performs because its tradition or religion requires the performance. Rituals are specific to situations. They are also observable. All known societies have rituals. Additionally, any ritual consists of acts that are symbolic and, like verbal language, based on subjective rules. Therefore, symbol and ritual have an intrinsic relationship.

Ritual paraphernalia at a temporary altar of the ancestral Kélé-tradition of St. Lucia in the Caribbean. The calabash in the center is representing the divine messenger Eshu, the stone-axes near the yam are representing the thunder god Shango, and the iron implements are representing Ogun, the Orisha of civilization and technology. COURTESY OF MANFRED KREMSER.

Some Approaches to Symbol and Ritual

The French sociologist Emile Durkheim and the scholars whom he influenced view rituals as part of a broader system. For them rituals are dynamic aspects of a symbolic system that has three aspects. The individual is the first aspect. The community itself under the guise of a moral order is the second aspect. This moral order consists of the sacred nature of the community, that is, its values or ideology. The symbol is the third aspect. The symbol represents the sacred and mediates between the community and the individual. The symbol makes the abstract sacred community concrete. Adherence to the symbolic representation of the sacred community and its values represents the willingness of the individual to follow the rules that bind a community.

People have made many applications of this type of analysis to secular rituals. Sociologists and anthropologists, for example, have examined types of community commemorative rituals, such as centennial celebrations. The coronation of British Queen Elizabeth II provided an excellent application of Durkheimian understanding of ritual. People also have applied this type of analysis to the French Revolution, modern political civic rituals, and the assassination of President Abraham Lincoln.

Other scholars, such as phenomenologists (who study the development of human consciousness and self-awareness), view myth and symbol as more important than ritual. Mircea Eliade does not dismiss ritual but does believe that myth and symbol give a clearer picture of social life and the sacred than ritual does. For Eliade ritual is basically a reworking of myth and symbol. Phenomenologists argue that myth is far more stable than ritual. Ritual, moreover, can never explain symbol. For Eliade, myth always is about creation, the beginning. It explains ritual. Ritual does not explain myth.

The anthropologist Victor Turner had another approach to the relationship between symbols and rituals. He sought to make clear exactly what a ritual does by studying symbols. He focused on the complex ritual symbols of the Ndembu people of Zambia in Africa. Turner looked at how the Ndembu use rituals, their dynamic and processual nature. Their symbols change over time; they can have many meanings; their purpose is to keep social ties viable. Each symbol is part of a system of symbols and can change its meaning in relationship to other symbols. Turner's analysis of the milk tree illustrates his meaning. When the milk tree is part of an Ndembu girl's initiation, it is scratched and exudes a milky substance, associated with breastfeeding. However, the tree also symbolizes the importance of matrilineal (relating to descent through the maternal lineage) descent and thus tribal values and unity. At other times the milk tree symbolizes can represent the problems that women have with one another.

For Turner, then, symbols are not passive; they are active vehicles that generate meaning and structure social action. Turner argued that the human body is the source of human symbols and the systems that they generate. People, by understanding their body and letting it represent the social world, create that world and come to understand and manipulate it.

Symbolists

Another major approach to the relationship between symbols and ritual is that of the symbolists, also called "culturalists" or "symbolic culturalists." Symbolists see ties between ritual, symbols, and social relationships as inherently weak. They emphasize the similarity between language and symbol systems. For them, rituals, comprised and built upon symbol systems, are modes of communication. They stress what rituals communicate rather than what social systems they maintain or represent. Thus, "culture" becomes the primary focus of their studies and communicates meanings, values, and attitudes. In turn, these meanings, values, and attitudes influence the creation of social organization. Symbolists view culture as being prior to social organization and independent of it.

People view the relationship between symbols and rituals in many other ways. The structuralist school of the French anthropologist Claude Levi-Strauss and variations on it such as that of the English anthropologist Edmond Leach looked for either universal meanings of symbols as they are wired into human brains or culture-specific meanings in each social system.

Whether universal or specific, these symbols took their meanings from their position in a system of symbols. In some way, universally or specifically, they expressed something about human social relationships and found their way into ritual.

Whatever their differences, scholars agree that human symbols, whether distinguished from signs or identified with them, are part of rituals. Rituals express something, or perhaps many things, about human culture and/or relationships. Symbols and rituals are related to myths, which express something about human origins. For many scholars rituals can help influence human behavior. Whatever their differences, scholars agree that symbols and rituals are vital to the understanding of human culture.

Frank A. Salamone

See also Communitas; Liminoid; Naven Ceremony

Further Reading

Adler, R. (1993, January–February). In your blood, live: Re-visions of a theology of purity. *Tikkun 8*(1), 38–65.

Anderson, H., & Foley, E. (1997, November). Experiences in need of ritual. *The Christian Century 114*(31), 1002–1037.

Andrews, D. (2000, June). The rousing drum: Ritual practice in a Japanese community. *Asian Folklore Studies, 59*(2), 326.

Bell, C. (1992). *Ritual theory, ritual practice*. New York: Oxford University Press.

Bell, C. (1997). *Ritual: Perspectives and dimensions*. New York: Oxford University Press.

Birrell, S. (1981). Sport as ritual: Interpretations from Durkheim to Goffman. *Social Forces, 60*(2), 354–376.

Driver, T. F. (1998). *Liberating rites: Understanding the transformative power of ritual*. Boulder, CO: Westview Press.

Erndl, K. M. (1993). *Victory to the mother: The Hindu goddess of northwest India in myth, ritual, and symbol*. New York: Oxford University Press.

Hooke, S. H. (Ed.). (1958). *Myth, ritual, and kingship: Essays on the theory and practice of kingship in the ancient Near East and in Israel*. Oxford, UK: Clarendon Press.

Humphrey, C., & Laidlaw, J. (1994). *The archetypal actions of ritual: A theory of ritual illustrated by the Jain rite of worship*. Oxford, UK: Oxford University Press.

Lada-Richards, I. (1999). *Initiating Dionysus: Ritual and theatre in Aristophanes' Frogs*. Oxford, UK: Oxford University Press.

Noblitt, J. R., & Perskin, P. S. (2000). *Cult and ritual abuse: Its history, anthropology, and recent discovery in contemporary America* (Rev. ed.). Westport, CT: Praeger.

Schwartz, B. (1991). Mourning and the making of a sacred symbol: Durkheim and the Lincoln assassination. *Social Forces*, 70(2), 343–364.

T

Taboo

A taboo is an identity, substance, or practice that people forbid. Taboos are forbidden partly because people find them disgusting and reprehensible or even unspeakable and unimaginable. However, taboos involve more than simple disgust. They lie beyond science and nature and often carry supernatural explanations and sanctions. They are absolutely binding for one's whole life, and they are often self-punishing because violating them brings not only shame but also guilt.

Taboos are dense codes for expressing who people are because they bound or insulate members of a group from others who practice different taboos and communicate effectively the identity of a people. Taboos illuminate the intersection of a people's material life and symbolic life. They often involve ambiguity or anomaly. They fall into the blurry areas between categories of beings that humans like to keep separate. They join the blessed and the cursed in an unlikely alliance. Thus the *aghori* ascetics (persons who practice strict self-denial as a measure of spiritual discipline) of India live in graveyards, have sex with diseased prostitutes, drink from human skulls, sleep on corpses, and hurl feces at their devotees to cure and bless them. By wallowing in pollution they dissolve the boundaries skewering the pure and impure and become holy religious practitioners.

Yet, taboos also create, legitimate, and reproduce relations of power. To study taboos is to plumb the depths of people's humanity and the breadths of human diversity and creativity because nothing is perhaps as interesting as those practices that so frighten and repel people that they try to forbid them, manage them, and redefine them. The best way to understand taboos is through examples that illustrate these features. One way to understand taboo is through a case study that illuminates the complex relationship between taboos, religious rituals, and everyday social life.

Taboos and the Fabric of Life

In his novel *Things Fall Apart,* Chinua Achebe writes movingly of the disintegration of a Nigerian ethnic group, the Igbo, whose way of life was transformed by their colonial encounter with the British. His novel is filled with taboos, which most Igbo obey, some question, and the missionaries violate in order to demonstrate the superiority of the Christian God. The Earth goddess Ani is the most important supreme being among the Igbo, and the plot of the novel follows violations of the taboos that ensure the people's balance with the Earth goddess and thus the Earth. The hero, Okwonko, in a rage beats his wife during the Week of Peace, which is dedicated to Ani to ensure a successful harvest. He later murders a boy who calls him "Father" and then inadvertently shoots another young clansman. Because the clan is as one, violating this taboo also offends the Earth and is punished by exile. The Igbo are paralyzed by this taboo because they cannot fight their own clansmen who have converted to Christianity. More and more desperate Okwonko hangs himself, so violating the Earth that his kin cannot take him down, and the clan has truly fallen apart.

The Igbo reflect throughout the novel on the importance and seeming arbitrariness of a people's

TABOO IN FIJI

When the native code of etiquette deals with the sacredness of chieftainship it is upheld by the tabu system. The tabu system serves to protect the sacred "mana" of the ancestor gods and their direct descendants, the chiefs. High Lauan chiefs are still surrounded by strict tabus which regulate their contact with the world to the minutest detail. For instance, in the presence of the high chief, even today, no native of lower rank is allowed to stand erect. If possible, a person sits crosslegged, bowed, and silent at some distance from him. If it is necessary to walk, a person bends almost to a right angle and backs out of the chief's presence.

Infringement of the sacred tabus was formerly punished by death. Illness is believed automatically to follow the breaking of less sacred tabus. We have seen that a nursing mother is not allowed to have sexual intercourse, because if she does her child will be unable to walk upright. If a pregnant woman or her husband eats fish which has been cut in small pieces the body of the new born infant will be afflicted with sores.

The native code of etiquette and the tabu system still cover many of the judicial needs of the Lauans. Although a break of the sacred, tabus is no longer punished by death, the tabu system is still upheld to some extent, and public opinion is as strong as ever. The native tabu system, however, does not encompass the new moral code introduced by the missionaries and upheld by the government, nor is it effective as a sanction for government regulations. Although some of these innovations, especially those connected with Christianity, have become a part of the accepted code of behavior and hence are backed by public opinion, there are many which have not been so wholeheartedly endorsed by the group.

***Source*: Thompson, Laura. (1940). *Fijian Frontier*. San Francisco: American Council, Institute of Pacific Relations, p. 72.**

taboos. A man who has taken a title cannot climb a palm tree, as he can in other tribes; people cannot unmask the masked ancestral spirits called *"egwugwu,"* nobody can kill or eat the royal python who slithers through houses and beds, and twins must be placed in the evil forest to die. Achebe shows his readers the power that lies in the margins where taboos lurk: As examples, the name of the oracle Agbala also characterizes a reprehensibly effeminate man, and the most powerful *egwugwu* bears the name "Evil Forest," where people with diseases that are abominable to Ani are placed to die.

Thus, among the precolonial Igbo, as among many other peoples, taboos emerge in symbolic areas of anomaly, for example, twins blur the boundary between humans, who do not give plural birth, and animals, which do. Yet, taboos also express power relations—the power of elders over juniors and of men over women. Also, they are woven into the yearly round of an agricultural people who must live closely attuned to the Earth.

Incest Taboo

The incest taboo appears to be universal. Every known culture prohibits sexual relations between members of a designated core of people and explains and sanctions the taboo, often through religious myths and rituals. At the same time the taboo is staggeringly diverse in how strictly it is enforced, how harshly it is punished, and how narrowly or broadly it is extended to cover various categories of people. In some societies the taboo covers cousins, but in other societies cousins are preferred sexual partners. In some societies the taboo covers all descendants of an ancient ancestor. In other societies the taboo covers only brothers, sisters, mothers, fathers, aunts, uncles, and grandparents. Sometimes the supernaturally sanctioned elite violates the taboo to ensure the purity of the royal line. The Egyptian queen Cleopatra was the descendant of eleven generations of brother-sister marriage, and both Incan and Hawaiian royalty practiced sibling marriage.

The French anthropologist Claude Levi-Strauss offered the compelling argument that through the incest taboo, humans try to resolve the opposition between nature and culture by imposing a cultural rule on a biological act. Through the incest taboo people make themselves human by separating themselves from other animals. People create society by forcing themselves to marry out: When people forbid nuclear family members as sexual partners, they forge alliances between other families.

Other explanations for the incest taboo abound, and they range from the Austrian neurologist Sigmund Freud's primal (original) band of brothers through more social role-oriented explanations holding that sex between family members confuses other rights and responsibilities toward members. Most recently anthropologists have called for a theory of the incest taboo that emphasizes power relations and looks more closely at such phenomena as the relatively common practice of abusive, predatory father-daughter incest.

Food Taboos

Taboos most closely associated with religious rituals prescribe special relationships between groups of people and animal totems (things that serve as emblems or revered symbols). A clan, for example, may identify so closely with a particular species of animal that it finds analogues of eating, killing, reproduction, and lineality in that species. Most importantly, such a taboo holds that "this is good to eat, for not me, and obeying that taboo means that one never, ever eats that food" (That is good to eat, but not for me).

Other well-known taboos are those of the ancient Israelites (which are still practiced in somewhat milder form in kosher foodways of modern Jews and in the similar food taboos of Muslims, who also insist on killing an animal in the most painless way possible and never eating pork). Anthropologist Mary Douglas analyzed the detailed and complicated food taboos outlined in the Book of Leviticus and proposed a theoretically elegant model based on the concepts of pollution, anomaly, and disorder. She noted the supreme importance of holiness and blessing to the Israelites and their desire to remind themselves of their relationship to God whenever they ate. Because when people eat they make that which is not them, food uniquely and incorporatively joins nature, culture, the individual, and the sacred. Therefore, Douglas held that foods that were anomalous because they did not live properly in their piece of creation (such as sea creatures without fins and scales) were not true to their class and thus forbidden. Animals that did not chew their cud and had cloven hooves were anomalous on land and thus forbidden. This kind of disorder, or matter out of place, was polluting, and therefore foods that exhibited these qualities were unwhole, or unholy, and violated the overarching principle of the blessing.

Food taboos are sometimes connected to political philosophies, not to religious rituals. For example, many vegetarians do not eat meat because they respect the interconnections of all life or because they decry the excessive consumption of meat-eating societies that take more than their share of the Earth's resources, often ravaging tropical forests or wetlands to do so.

Menstrual Taboos

Anthropologists have not studied menstrual taboos as extensively as they have explored others. When they have, they have often embraced Douglas's theory of pollution and seen menstrual taboos as evidence of the oppression of women. Other scholars have countered that power lies in society's margins and that the pollution ascribed to menstrual blood can empower women, who can threaten to blind men with it or add it to their soup. The most recent research has looked in greater nuance at the multiple values of taboos and the complex ways they are connected to other parts of social life, such as beliefs about fertility and conception. Anthropologist Alma Gottlieb has explored the West African Beng menstrual taboos in great richness. She shows that the taboos against having sex while in the forest or working in the fields while menstruating help to uphold a religious boundary between the fertility ascribed to the village and that ascribed to the Earth. She has also shown that the taboo forbidding a menstruating woman from nearing a corpse speaks to the vulnerability of the woman rather than to the danger that she might pollute the corpse. Gottlieb writes of Beng high cuisine, a delicious, slow-cooked palm oil soup of reddish color that can be prepared only by menstruating women and shared with their friends. Her Beng research sheds interesting cross-cultural light on the premenstrual syndrome held to depress and distract U.S. women, who must keep working at tedious, stressful industrial or domestic tasks during this time. Scholars examining seclusion during a woman's menstrual period or moontime argue that women sometimes synchronize thei periods, seek spiritual guidance, closeness to god, and greater self-understanding during menstruation. These examples demonstrate how the study of taboo can help people understand social problems, social organization, and potential relations between biology, culture, and spirituality.

Death Taboos

Funerals are rich in symbols, rituals, and taboos. Many death taboos attach to the corpse itself as being powerful, dangerous, out of place, and potentially polluting. People in different societies apply different taboos to the dead, ranging from averting the eyes, through practicing menstrual avoidance, to having sacred rules tabooing certain foods, practices, and dress. The anthropologist Maurice Bloch sees two aspects to funerals: the dying, contaminating, dangerous, taboo-riddled stage focused on the corpse and the regenerative, joyful stage when the anomalous dead person is moved into a new social role as ancestor or angel. Bloch argues that in traditional societies ruled by male elders, women are given the tabooed qualities of death, whereas men are associated with the rebirth of social order from the threat posed by death. Bloch thus argues that ideology feeds on death and harnesses it to its own purposes of maintaining power. Funeral taboos are less dramatic and less prevalent today but linger in such forms as a fear of ghosts, who are dead people who won't go away.

The Taboo Problem

Why and how do the forbidden, unspeakable, reprehensible, self-punishing, and ambiguous serve as particularly dense codes for defining who people are and communicating who people are not and for bolstering who has power and who does not? Do taboos express deep archetypal properties of the human mind? Do they help people transform nature into culture? Are they utterly arbitrary constructions? Do people need taboos to protect the innocent, separate themselves from other species, construct a singular social order, or communicate who they are? Do people use taboos to oppress those with discrepant identities, suppress honesty and spontaneity, and support superfluous industries that label, collect, manage, and hide what people fear? When people explore taboos, they enter the world of the forbidden to examine those persons, products, and practices that people surround with such fear and disgust that they try to rule them out. Yet, power and danger, the blessed and the cursed lie in those cultural margins. Entering this world can be difficult, but taboos hold vital clues to people's humanity and to the power relations that shape people's social lives.

Brett Williams

See also Body and Rituals; Haircutting Rituals; Passage, Rites of; Puberty Rites; Purity and Pollution; Sacred Places

Further Reading

Achebe, C. (1959). *Things fall apart*. New York: McDowell.

Bloch, M., & Parry, J. (1982). *Death and the regeneration of life.* New York: Cambridge University Press.

Douglas, M. (1970). *Purity and danger.* Harmondworth, UK: Penguin.

Gottlieb, A., & Buckley, T. (1988). *Blood magic.* Berkeley: University of California Press.

Levi-Strauss, C. (1969). *The elementary structures of kinship.* Boston: Beacon Press.

Meigs, A., & Barlow, K. (2002, March). Beyond the taboo: Imagining incest. *American Anthropologist, 104*(1), 38–49.

Taoism

Taoism consists of a variety of Chinese religious and philosophical teachings that aim to harmonize relations between humans and the natural world.

The word "Tao" means flowing with the way of nature. The philosophical principle behind the religion holds that the universe is a symbiosis of patterns that cannot exist individually. If everything in nature is allowed to proceed without hindrance, then the universe will be in balance since all things will be working together. Reflecting the shamanist background of China, Taoism sees a pervasive spirit world that is both interlocked with and separate from the world of humans.

Taoism is believed to have developed as a religion when Lao-tzu, who may be a historical figure or the name ascribed to a group of anonymous philosophers, assembled all the Tao teachings in the book *Tao Te Ching* ("Canon of the Way and Virtue")

around the sixth century BCE. The book is written in poetic form, making it difficult to clearly grasp its prescriptions for living, but Taoism did clearly offer personal salvation and freedom, making it unique among Chinese faiths of the day. Unlike the followers of Confucius (K'ung Ch'iu; 551–479 BCE), Taoists in this era turned their backs on the worlds of commerce and the court in favor of meditation in remote mountains. This classical period of Taoism lasted only a few centuries before a more popular form emerged. Late in the second century CE, a magical Taoism emerged under the guidance of Chang Tao-ling (Chang Ling; 34–156 CE). Issuing charms and talismans to protect the faithful, this Taoism involved magical healing such as alchemy and spiritual rituals designed to enhance life. Less difficult to practice than its predecessor, it developed a mass following.

To ensure complete physical and spiritual immortality, Taoists espouse a variety of practices to create balance with nature. Aiming for the supreme goal of long life, they once followed the teachings of the legendary Yellow Emperor Huang-Ti (c. 2697–2598 BCE), who associated loss of sperm with loss of primordial force. A notably male-centered faith, Taoism promised men immortality if they slept with as many women as possible without ejaculating. To this end, a number of sex manuals gave guidance on intercourse without emission. Celibacy was not encouraged because balance, the yin and yang, must be maintained. When illness struck, a Taoist priest would exorcise malevolent influences. These rituals for the living, *ch'I-jang chai,* are still popular ways to ensure such desirable occurrences as good fortune, good weather, and the exorcism of pests like locusts. Modern Taoist priests also perform rituals for the dead, *k'ai-tu chai,* since the gates of hell must first be opened to the light of heaven before the souls obstructed in hell can cross over on the bridge of light to paradise.

As Taoism is one of the oldest Chinese religions, its emphasis on working with nature rather than in opposition to it has attracted vast numbers of followers through the ages. In recent years, the Taoist ritual *feng shui,* creating harmony through the placement of buildings, doorways, and furniture and thereby affecting the physical and spiritual life, has become an enormously popular Western trend.

Caryn E. Neumann

See also China: Popular Religion

Further Reading

Chiu, M. M. (1984). *The Tao of Chinese religion.* Lanham, MD: University Press of America.

Clarke, J. J. (2000). *The Tao of the West: Western transformations of Taoist thought.* London: Routledge.

Kohn, L. (Ed.). (1989). *Taoist meditation and longevity techniques.* Ann Arbor: University of Michigan Press.

Kohn, L. (Ed.). (1993). *The Taoist experience: An anthology.* Albany: State University of New York.

Maspero, H. (1981). *Taoism and Chinese religion.* Amherst: University of Massachusetts Press.

Television and Ritual

The first person to bring religion to television was the U.S. Roman Catholic bishop Fulton J. Sheen (1895–1979), an auxiliary bishop of the New York archdiocese. During the 1950s Sheen was a popular author, speaker, and college professor. Catholicism was booming at the time, drawing many converts. Sheen's book *Peace of Soul* (1949) and his radio program paved the way for his entrance into television.

Sheen preceded representatives of Protestant churches in learning how to use the new technology, becoming the first important television preacher in the United States. Sheen discovered the importance of presenting a splendid figure. He wore his full scarlet regalia and bishop's skullcap. He used sparkling wit to put his wisdom across. He was a natural actor and delivered his lines well.

Sheen had parlayed his *Catholic Hour* program from NBC radio (1930–1952) to his *Life Is Worth Living* TV program in 1952. The program moved to ABC from 1955 to 1957, and from 1961 to 1968 he starred in *The Bishop Sheen Program.* Sheen used his scholarship and presence behind a persuasive and quiet voice to present his ideas in a simple and direct manner. He reached out to non-Catholics by not pressing issues that were mainly associated with that religion. He was deeply anti-Communist, but most of his programs went beyond that doctrinaire position. He discussed broad issues, such as the need for belief in a god and the way in which such belief is basic to happiness. For Sheen ethical behavior brought rewards, not necessarily monetary rewards, but rewards nonetheless. In sum, his message was a highly individualized and private one. His audience did not tire of him, but he got into difficulties with his fellow members of the church hierarchy, and his TV career ended.

About the time Sheen left television Protestant televangelism grew in sophistication, and superstars rose among televangelists. Billy Graham, Oral Roberts, Rex Humbard, and Jerry Falwell led that group. Others, such as Jim Bakker and Pat Robertson, were talkers; Jimmy Swaggart was an entertainer, and Richard De Haan and Frank Pollard were teachers. Since the 1950s the number and influence of televangelism programs and other types of religious programs have grown exponentially.

Reasons for Popularity

Many regular viewers of religious programs make instrumental use of TV, seeking information from the programs. They watch religious news programs, panel discussions, and Bible education programs. This viewing behavior can be termed "ritualized television usage." Ritualized television usage includes the habitual use of TV and an association with the medium. In some cases religious TV has replaced church attendance. Watching religious services on television takes the place for some of attending congregational church.

There are also reactionary viewers who watch religious programs as a type of protest against commercial television. Moral support and spiritual guidance replace the stuff of commercial TV. These viewers are selective in their viewing, selecting specific religious programs for specific reasons having to do with seeking salvation, feeling good, and learning how to do both. These viewers are purposeful, selective information seekers.

By the 1980s televangelism, also termed "the electronic church," had become a major force in U.S. culture by capitalizing on the trends of U.S. culture. Televangelism had learned to appeal to people who either could not get to church or preferred not to be involved with a congregation. Televangelists have brought about a kind of revolution in U.S. religion, feeding the rise of personality cults. Televangelists do not usually tell viewers what their connections are to organized religions. They talk instead about a caring God who helps people with their problems.

Televangelists have embraced the fundamentals of popular religion, including the to-the-death battle of good versus evil. Their programs include joyous testimonies of how placing ultimate faith in God makes people happy. God's power is healing and provides psychological and spiritual benefits. He heals divorce woes, worry over children—just about anything. The popular religion of TV is a panacea for whatever monetary, physical, psychological or spiritual ills beset a person.

Power

The Hour of Power, televangelist Robert Schuller's program, most clearly shows the connection between popular religion on TV and power. Schuller tells his viewers that trust in God and self will lead to success, personal fulfillment, and all that one wants and needs in life. Schuller's book *You Can Become the Person You Want to Be* makes the point quite explicitly. As do most televangelists, Schuller plays down the need for religious affiliation. The fine points of doctrine get left behind in his sermons, subservient to the message of fulfilling personal needs.

Jim Bakker founded the PTL (Praise the Lord) Club in Charlotte, North Carolina, in 1974, also delivering a message of power. Bakker had ties to the Heritage Village Church and Missionary Fellowship of Charlotte. He used the developing technology of the computer, fiber optics, and satellite and began building Heritage USA, a Christian theme park and amusement center. Bakker's rise came to an end in 1987 with a sex scandal involving former church secretary Jessica Hahn. His work did not survive his resignation.

In 1960 Pat Robertson established his own TV network, the Christian Broadcasting Network (CBN). He set up the 700 Club, a club comprised of seven hundred viewers who pledged him ten dollars per month. In 1977 Robertson went into the university business, establishing CBN University. The university is accredited and has graduate schools in religion, journalism, and law.

TV Psychics

People in the United States have long had an interest in psychic phenomena. However, until the advent of TV psychics that interest had generally been mostly communal. However, just as with religious programs, people can now follow psychics on TV in their homes.

These people are generally anxious to find a source of certainty in situations of uncertainty. In general these people don't notice failed predictions. A number of studies have followed up on failed predictions. A legal case, *Sanders v. American Broadcasting Companies,* resulted from a 1992 ABC

PrimeTime Live television investigation of the telepsychic industry. Psychic hotlines were quite popular, and late-night TV was filled with thirty-minute psychic programs. A TV reporter, Stacy Lescht, wore a small video camera in her hat and secretly taped psychics hired by the Psychic Marketing Group in Los Angeles. A microphone attached to her bra picked up conversations. She worked undercover for a short time as a telepsychic. About one hundred other employees worked in cubicles in a large room. These employees gave psychic readings over the phone. Lescht talked with the other "psychics" and secretly taped them. An employee named "George Sanders" sued her when the tapes were aired on ABC. The report, aside from legal issues, showed how psychics were generally average people playing a role. Nevertheless, there are psychic superstars, demonstrating that many people may agree that there are frauds in the psychic field but that there may also be genuine psychics.

One reason for the popularity of psychics on television is the interest in Eastern religions, which grew in the 1960s and has continued to the present in New Age movements. Television reflects and feeds that interest, giving scope to its message.

Frank A. Salamone

See also Music; Performance, Ritual of; Ritual as Communication

Further Reading

Caldwell, J. T. (1995). *Televisuality: Style, crisis, and authority in American television*. New Brunswick, NJ: Rutgers University Press.

Calvert, C. (2000). *Voyeur nation: Media, privacy, and peering in modern culture*. Boulder, CO: Westview Press.

Driver, T. F. (1998). *Liberating rites: Understanding the transformative power of ritual*. Boulder, CO: Westview Press.

Duffy, B. K., & Ryan, H. R. (Eds.). (1987). *American orators of the twentieth century: Critical studies and sources*. New York: Greenwood Press.

Ellwood, R. S. (1997). *The fifties spiritual marketplace: American religion in a decade of conflict*. New Brunswick, NJ: Rutgers University Press.

Frank, R. (1987). *Televangelism: The marketing of popular religion*. Carbondale: Southern Illinois University Press.

Gardner, M. (1991). *The new age: Notes of a fringe watcher*. Buffalo, NY: Prometheus Books.

Gossen, G. H. (Ed.). (1993). *South and Meso-American native spirituality: From the cult of the feathered serpent to the theology of liberation*. New York: Crossroad.

Hancock, M. E. (1999). *Womanhood in the making: Domestic ritual and public culture in urban south India*. Boulder, CO: Westview Press.

Himmelstein, H. (1994). *Television myth and the American mind* (2nd ed.). Westport, CT: Praeger.

Hofstadter, D. R. (1985). *Metamagical themas: Questing for the essence of mind and pattern*. New York: Basic Books.

Hunt, N. R. (1999). *A colonial lexicon of birth ritual, medicalization, and mobility in the Congo*. Durham, NC: Duke University Press.

Jorstad, E. (1993). *Popular religion in America: The evangelical voice*. Westport, CT: Greenwood Press.

Kendall, L. (1987). *Shamans, housewives, and other restless spirits: Women in Korean ritual life*. Honolulu: University of Hawaii Press.

Lee, S. (1995). Independent record companies and conflicting models of industrial practice. *Journal of Media Economics, 8*(4), 47–61.

Lowney, K. S. (1999). *Baring our souls: TV talk shows and the religion of recovery*. New York: Aldine De Gruyter.

Marks, D., & Kammann, R. (1980). *The psychology of the psychic*. Buffalo, NY: Prometheus Books.

McDaniel, L. (1998). *The big drum ritual of Carriacou: Praise songs in rememory of flight*. Gainesville: University Press of Florida.

McLuhan, E., & Zingrone, F. (Eds.). (1995). *Essential McLuhan*. New York: Basic Books.

Mio, J. S., & Katz, A. N. (Eds.). (1996). *Metaphor: Implications and applications*. Mahwah, NJ: Lawrence Erlbaum Associates.

Monaco, P. (1998). *Understanding society, culture, and television*. Westport, CT: Praeger.

Moore, R. L. (1995). *Selling God: American religion in the marketplace of culture*. New York: Oxford University Press.

Newman, J. (1996). *Religion vs. television: Competitors in cultural context*. Westport, CT: Praeger.

Nilsen, A. P., & Nilsen, D. L. F. (2000). *Encyclopedia of 20th-century American humor*. Phoenix, AZ: Oryx Press.

Pelling, H. (1960). *Modern Britain, 1885–1955*. Edinburgh, UK: T. Nelson.

Pitts, W. F. (1996). *Old ship of Zion: The Afro-Baptist ritual in the African diaspora*. New York: Oxford University Press.

Schechter, W. (1970). *The history of Negro humor in America*. New York: Fleet Press.

Sherzer, J. (1990). On play, joking, humor, and tricking among the Kuna: The Agouti story. *Journal of Folklore Research, 27*(1–2), 85–114.

Snowman, D. (1977). *Britain and America: An interpretation of their culture, 1945–1975.* New York: New York University Press.

Suman, M. A. (Ed.). (1997). *Religion and prime time television.* Westport, CT: Praeger.

Webster, H. (1948). *Magic, a sociological study.* Stanford, CA: Stanford University Press.

White, M. (1992). *Tele-advising: Therapeutic discourse in American television.* Chapel Hill: University of North Carolina Press.

Ziv, A., & Zajdman, A. (Eds.). (1993). *Semites and stereotypes: Characteristics of Jewish humor.* Westport, CT: Greenwood Press.

V

Vision Quest

The vision quest is a ritual usually performed by young Native American men and women to search for a guardian spirit. Adults in search of power, guidance, or direction in life often repeat the ritual. The vision quest is associated with Plains Native Americans, but it is common among other tribes. The person on a vision quest seeks communication with the spirit world in a series of solitary purifications, offerings, prayers, and fasting during several days and nights at a sacred place. With the exception of the Pueblo people of the U.S. Southwest, dreams and visions have played an integral part in the religious life of Native Americans. Dreams either occur spontaneously, in one's sleep, or are achieved through a ritual. Visions occur during waking hours in the midst of prayer and fasting. Rigorous purification ceremonies and demanding rituals of fasting and making offerings of tobacco or flesh prepare seekers for visions.

The vision quest is probably the most common ritual of Native American religions and makes contact possible between a person and the supernatural. In the past, warriors and hunters sought spiritual assistance through vision quests. Spirits that appeared to members of hunting tribes during vision quests gave power or medicine, taught a sacred song, revealed a dance, showed how to dress, gave instructions for creating a medicine pouch, and told how to obtain guidance.

Dreams and Visions

Dreams and visions are sources of knowledge, contain major revelations, and bring power to the person having the dream or vision. In the past, if an ancestor appeared in a dream, the ancestor might bring a warning, a consolation, or advice about how to act. If the person appearing in a dream was unknown to the dreamer, consultation with the shaman would reveal the meaning of the message carried by the dream. Animals might also appear in dreams. Dreams and visions were valuable channels for obtaining spiritual powers and religious knowledge.

Some of the earliest references to the importance of dreams and visions in Native American religious practices are in the writings of priests in New France during the colonial era. In 1635 Jean de Brebeuf, describing the Huron mission established by French Jesuits, wrote that "Their… feasts, their medicines, their fishing, their hunting, their wars—in short, almost their whole life turns upon this pivot; dreams above all have great credit" (Kenton 1954, 112–113). In 1639 Father Francis du Peron attributed many Huron behaviors to knowledge gained in dreams: "They consider the dream as master of their lives.… It is this which dictates to them their feasts, their hunting, their fishing, their remedies, their dances, their games, their songs" (Kenton 1954, 141–142). A report about Father Jacque Marquette's first visit among the Illinois people described the importance of visions as follows: a Manitou "is a serpent, a bird, or other similar thing, of which they have dreamed while sleeping, and in which they place all their confidence for the success of their war, their fishing, and their hunting" (Kenton 1954, 353). The priests condemned the Native Americans' strong belief in dreams and visions, because they saw it as a barrier to conversion of Indians to Christianity.

Reasons for Vision Quests

In the past Native Americans undertook vision quests for numerous reasons. People sought closeness with the Creator and desired power for living in a world of spirits. When people felt limited and weak, they sought extra spiritual resources to sustain them through dangerous situations. Warriors and war leaders undertook vision quests to gain insight into the success or failure of raids or military forays. Visions helped Native Americans understand problems and revealed a spiritual helper who became a source of power in future times of need. The Iroquois and Huron fasted for many days to achieve a vision that would bring success in hunting, warfare, and healing. Women had dreams and visions that determined their activity in religious rituals.

Vision quests also educated the young. Usually, children learned survival skills, spirituality, and ethical issues from their vision quest experiences. Vision quests were puberty rites for boys and girls. Boys and girls went on vision quests in search of self-understanding and guardian spirits in the transition from childhood to adulthood.

Characteristics of Vision Quests

In preparation for a vision quest the seeker participated in purification rituals in the sweat lodge (dome-shaped structure used for ritual sweat baths to achieve spiritual and physical health.). Typically, the seeker wore only a robe or a breechclout and moccasins. "Hanblecheyapi" is the Lakota lamentation to have a vision or "to call for the voice of the Sacred" (Doll 1994, 156). The seeker went to an elevated wilderness area. In this secluded and sacred place, the seeker cleared a space to stand, sit, or move about as called for in tribal rituals. For Lakota, one sacred place was Okawta (the Gathering Mountain), commonly called "Bear Butte" near the Black Hills of South Dakota. The seeker remained in the place until a vision was obtained or until it became evident that there would be none.

Today an *inipi* (ceremony of purification preparatory to the quest) often precedes the vision quest. The Lakota seeker is then led up Bear Butte to spend several days and nights alone in fasting and prayer. The seeker prays for protection and meditates on his or her purposes. Fasting and thirsting consecrate the seeker's body; prayers to the Great Mystery (the Creator) purify the seeker's mind and spirit. Most people, at least on the Great Plains, carry a pipe, smoking supplies, and a knife. Sioux bring bits of flesh from their forearms and thighs, which are given as a sacrifice to the spirits. A vision is normally submitted for interpretation to the shaman or tribal elders. Some visions are re-created in rituals. Dreamers paint themselves, their gear, tipis, and horses such as those seen in dreams and visions. Some objects revealed in a vision are used to create sacred bundles. Bundle-opening ceremonies follow rituals called for in the vision. Songs prescribed in the vision become an integral part of bundle openings.

Tribal members, having helped the seeker prepare for the quest, often pray for the seeker throughout the ritual. Those seekers who experience visions usually say that they made contact with a spirit helper, typically in the form of an animal, from which they received specific knowledge that would instruct them in calling upon the guardian spirit in the future. Successful seekers conjure up the spirit protector's assistance in times of need.

Scholars have usually recognized that the vision quest is common among many Plains tribes. However, the vision quest has been present in many other Native American cultures. Dreams and visions are considered less important among Native Americans of the U.S. Southwest. This is particularly the case among Pueblos, Navajos, Hopis, Zunis, and Apaches. Among the Pueblo, rituals have greater importance to their spiritual lives than do dreams and visions.

Consequences of Vision Quests

How consequential were vision quests in the lives of Native Americans in the past? Powerful visions elevated some Native Americans to positions of tribal leadership in time of war or peace. Their vision quests became commonly known, and so these people were recognized as having special power. Plenty Coups (1848–1932), a Crow warrior and chief, related in one of his visions that he was informed that he would become a chief, that he learned of the future end of the bison herds, and that he would help preserve the Crow people and their culture. Plenty Coups used the lessons of his vision in leading the Crow from their customary bison-hunting ways to life on a reservation. Sometimes visions came spontaneously, often during illness. Nicholas Black Elk had such an experience in his "Great Vision." "These 'visions without crying' or 'power visions' are usually commissions to a special leadership role" (Young 2002, 200). People regarded persons who had such visions as having full measures of knowledge, wisdom, and skills. Shamans gained reputations as healers because of the power of their visions.

Visions and their meaning became the domain of specialists who served as interpreters of content. During the 1920s Ruth Benedict and other scholars thought that visions and dreams reinforce a group's pattern of culture and that culture determines dream content. Recent studies regard dreams as unique, not stereotypical, and their content as divergent. Native American religious specialists helped diagnose disease, foretell death or a return to health, and predict the outcome of hunting and raiding expeditions. Medicine men and medicine women achieved their positions of healing because of their powerful visions. Sacred dreams or visions usually led to enhanced power for the dreamer, who then had some visible sign of new skills or knowledge in healing, curing, predicting, or interpreting.

Rodger C. Henderson

See also Altered States of Consciousness; Passage, Rites of

Further Reading

Doll, D. (1994). *Vision quest: Men, women, and sacred sites of the Sioux nation*. New York: Crown Publishers.

Dugan, K. M. (1985). *The vision quest of the Plains Indians: Its spiritual significance*. New York: E. Mellen Press.

Hultkrantz, A. (1981). *Belief and worship in native North America*. Syracuse, NY: Syracuse University Press.

Hultkrantz, A. (1987). *Native religions of North America: The power of visions and fertility*. San Francisco: Harper and Row.

Irwin, L. (1994). *The dream-seekers: Native American visionary traditions of the Great Plains*. Norman: University of Oklahoma Press.

Irwin, L. (2000). *Native American spirituality: A critical reader*. Lincoln: University of Nebraska Press.

Kenton, E. (Ed.). (1954). *The Jesuit relations and allied documents*. New York: Vanguard Press.

MacAdams, C., Hunbatz, M., & Bensinger, C. (1991). *Mayan vision quest: Mystical initiation in Mesoamerica*. San Francisco: Harper San Francisco.

Tedlock, B. (1987). *Dreaming: Anthropological and psychological interpretations*. Cambridge, UK: Cambridge University Press.

Young, W. A. (2002). *Quest for harmony: Native American spiritual traditions*. New York: Seven Bridges Press.

Vodun

Vodun designates the religion indigenous to Haiti. It originates in Benin (formerly Dahomey) on Africa's west coast, where *vodu* or *vodun* among the Fon means "deity" or "spirit." As it is used in Haiti, "vodun" names a religion in which its devotees pay homage to spirits or *lwa*s believed to be powerful supernatural forces that manifest themselves in nature and among their devotees. Hence, vodun should not be confused with cannibalism or sorcery as Hollywood and the film industry has portrayed it. It is a religion that, through a complex system of myths and symbols, answers some of the most profound questions of human existence and gives meaning to life. By extension, the word includes a whole assortment of artistic and cultural expressions as well as an elaborate system of folk healing.

Origin and Features

The theology of vodun originated in Africa but took shape on the sugar plantations during the Haitian colonial period (1492–1804). Nearly a million Africans were transported to Haiti as slaves during that period and, despite the hardships that they encountered, they managed to preserve many of their religious traditions. The French colonizers who came to Saint-Domingue (as Haiti was called) regarded vodun as an aberration and worked assiduously to extricate it from colonial life. They enforced a number of laws that criminalized it and tried to convert the slaves to Roman Catholicism. In an effort to prevent the colonizers' officious interference in their clandestine rituals, the slaves learned to mask them by overlaying them with Catholic doctrines and practices. Thus, vodun adopted many symbols of the church, and the saints became identified with the vodun *lwa*s. This religious amalgam gave rise to a system of reinterpretations by which the similarities between the personae and exploits in the lives of the saints in Christian hagiology and those of the gods in African mythology served as the basis for the correspondences between the two.

Vodunists group the *lwas* into pantheons or *nanshons*. There are seventeen *nanshon*s, although vodunists recognize only a few of these. Each *nanshon* has its own characteristic ethos, and the principle that guides the particular choice of *nanshon* to which a *lwa* belongs is based upon his or her mythological persona as envisaged by the devotees. But because a *lwa*

SPIRITS AND ILLNESS

The following anthropological account describes the role of spirits in explanations for illness among adherents of vodun in the Haitian community in New York City.

Several types of illness are believed to be of supernatural origin, caused by angry spirits. Voodoo theology provides a theory to explain the occurrence of such illnesses. Each voodooist family has a spirit protector whose role is to protect its members from the malevolent power of other spirits. When one is initiated into voodoo, one must sign, so to speak, a pact with one's spirit protector. Spirits expect their protégés to offer a ceremony every year in their honor. The annual ceremony is a basic requirement for maintaining a good relationship with one's spirit protector. Individual spirits, however, may add other requirements in accordance with their own wishes and their positions in the spirit hierarchy. Without this kind of recognition, a spirit may be the object of other spirits' mockery, and may lose standing in the spirit hierarchy. To maintain good standing, spirits must show that they have followers, that they are able to protect those followers from other spirits and cure them when they are sick, and that the protégés recognize their power and are afraid of them. Spirits whose protégés demonstrate their respect and fear by offering a ceremonial meal in their honor every year have the respect and fear of other spirits as well.

There is thus a relationship of dependence between spirits and protégés. The protégés depend on the spirits for protection, especially for health, and the spirits depend on their protégés to maintain their status in the spirit hierarchy. The protégés, however, are always subordinate to the spirits.

Illness may occur whenever one gives other spirits an opportunity to make fun of one's spirit protector, as by failing to offer the annual meal. Illness thus becomes a punishment. A spirit may "send an illness" on a protégé or may neglect to intervene if another spirit decides to bother the protégé. Proper propitiation, however, may cause the spirit protector to relent.

Source: Laguerre, Michel S. (1984). ***American Odyssey: Haitians in New York City.*** Ithaca, NY: Cornell University Press, pp. 117–18.

can have several personae, he or she can belong to several *nanshons* simultaneously and bear a different name for each. In effect, a *lwa* is a manifestation of Bondye, the godhead who is the grand master of the universe. In spirit possession, the devotees' behavior reflects the *lwa*s' different personae by turn or simultaneously as creative and destructive, or as terrible and beneficent. But these personae are reconciled by Bondye because the *lwa*s are merely "variations on a theme," or different "faces" of the same cosmic being. As in many African religions, Bondye is too impersonal to be approached directly, but is invoked through less hallowed media.

Spirit possession is an important vehicle through which a religious community encounters the divine directly. It can be defined as a temporary altered state of consciousness in which the self is experienced as disembodied and replaced by that of a *lwa*. During a ritual ceremony in an *ounfò* (vodun temple), the body of a possessed individual is conceived as a "horse" that is "ridden" by a *lwa*. It is manifesting themselves in the body of their devotees that the *lwa*s are given voice with which to impart their wisdom to the community and, conversely, ears with which to listen to their concerns. In short, possession is a quintessential spiritual achievement in a believer's religious life because it is a public commitment to the religion and a testimony to one's faith.

Vodunists use every possible visual and auditory medium to invoke the *lwa*s, and to appeal to them to manifest themselves in the *peristil* (the part of the temple where the public ceremonies are held). Each *lwa* has his or her symbols, names, songs, drum rhythms, and dance movements that are enacted by devotees during the rituals to honor them. The *lwa*s are also said to wear characteristic clothing that depicts their respective personae. These are kept in the temple and are worn by the possessed during the rituals. Moreover each *lwa* has its own *vèvè*, a geometric, cabalalike tracery that symbolizes his or her personae and functions. During a ceremony, the *oungan* (vodun priest) or *mambo* (vodun priestess) or one of their assistants traces the *vèvè*s by using corn flour, which he or she places in a dish held in the left hand. Grasping the flour between the thumb and the forefinger of the right hand, he or she carefully sifts it onto the floor of the *peristil*, meticulously drawing a *vèvè* for each *lwa* to be honored at the ceremony. Vodunists believe that these visual and auditory media summon the *lwa*s to leave their abode and possess their devotees. Vodun ceremonies are held in honor of all the *lwa*s and indirectly to honor Bondye himself, to whom libation is poured at the beginning of each ceremony, but the number of *lwa*s who are invoked directly during each ceremony varies according to the current needs of the community.

Ceremonies

Unlike in Western religions, vodun ceremonies are not weekly occurrences but are held three or four times a year. They can be elaborate affairs that require a great deal of resources including the purchase of ritual paraphernalia, flowers, and foodstuff and beverages tended as offerings to the *lwa*s and consumed by the community. But among all the ceremonies performed in the vodun liturgical year is the pilgrimage at Saut d'Eau, an area near the town of Mirebalais in the central portion of Haiti where the Virgin (and by extension Ezili) is said to have appeared on top of a palm tree near a waterfall. On 16 July, the day dedicated to the Virgin, thousands of devotees attend the celebration of the Mass at the Catholic church in Mirebalais. They also pay homage to Ezili at the waterfall or in the pool of flowing water below it. It is said that those who bathe in these waters will first be possessed and later healed. For these reasons, thousands of pilgrims come to the fall each year, tying blue and pink (the symbolic colors of the Virgin and of Ezili) cloth girdles or ribbons about their waists. They remove them when they reach the falls, ritualistically fastening them around the neighboring trees as protection from whatever defilement might threaten their persons or communities, and ridding themselves of diseases and misfortunes.

All Saints' Day is also an important holy day in vodun's liturgical calendar. Special ceremonies dedicated to Gede (pronounced *Gayday)* are held during the evening before 1 November. Gede is the *lwa* of death and his kingdom is Ginen (from Guinea in Africa), the ancient world of ancestors and the *lwa*s. Ginen is believed to be in Africa, located in the primordial waters under the earth. It is the place in which the ancestral spirits of the "living dead" reside, and from which they arise to "visit" their progeny. Hence, Ginen's portals allow spirits to travel back and forth to the world of the living, and Gede is its gatekeeper. Because ancestral souls can be reclaimed from Ginen and passed on to their living progeny, Gede is also identified with life. He is the lord of death and life; his symbols include the skulls and crossed bones, but also the phallus, which represents life. The rituals to Gede clearly symbolize the unity of the womb and the tomb, the beginning and the end, florescence and decay. Possessed devotees adorn themselves with long black frock coats worn traditionally by undertakers in Haiti and speak in nasal tones that, vodunists say, would be produced by a corpse if it were allowed to speak. They also carry a cane, which is symbolic of the phallus, and the movements of their bodies recall the sexual act.

The cycle of funerary rites entails an elaborate set of observances performed by members of the family that last an entire year after a person's death. Vodunists believe that the body contains a divine spirit with several compartments characterized by their respective functions. The first is the *gwo bon anj* (big good angel), a life-force, the energy source associated with life's vital signs: breathing, the heartbeat, the flow of blood, and the movements of the body. The second compartment is the *ti bon anj* (little good angel); it is the "ego soul" that is identified with one's personality, facial expressions, and general deportment. The third is the *mèt tèt* (master of the head), the guardian spirit who has protected a person from danger throughout his or her life and has been the subject of that person's devotion.

Shortly after death, a special ritual known as *desounen* (literally "the uprooting of life") performed by the *oungan* or *mambo* extracts the parts of the spirits from the body and dispatches them to their respective abodes: the *gwo bon anj* and the *mèt tèt* to Ginen, the *ti bon anj* to heaven (because of the Catholic influence), and the body to the navel of the earth, where it will disintegrate and never rise again.

As in Africa, ancestral spirits exercise authority over the living. That authority derives from a ritual of reclamation performed a year after a person's death.

In this ritual, the soul of the dead is repossessed by the living and placed in a *govi* (clay jar or bottle) that is kept in the *ounfò*. It is from the soul's new shell that an ancestor is said to see the living and guide them in their daily chores. The memory of his or her intelligence and the sacred wisdom acquired in Ginen and from past experiences, is preserved as a valuable legacy for future generations.

The *lwa*s manifest themselves not only in the context of public ceremonies but also privately in times of misfortune. One of such manifestations is seen in the performance of ritual divination. Divination is the art of foretelling the future or ascertaining hidden truths as they are revealed through an object or an event. Divination is one of the most important aspects of life among vodunists. They consult oracles especially in circumstances over which they may or may not have control: a chronic illness, a barren garden, life's sporadic privations, or the uncertain outcomes of momentous decisions. The answers are revealed by the *lwa*s and ancestral spirits, who are believed to disclose the future during divination.

Divination is always performed by a religious specialist who serves as a medium between the spirits and human beings. For theoretical purposes, divination may be divided into two types: *intuitive* and *prognostic.* The first may or may not involve spirit possession, but is an experience in which diviners receive their answers subjectively from the *lwa*s or ancestral spirits through their manipulations of oracular objects. The second is performed in moments in which the unanticipated discovery of certain natural phenomena, the occurrence of an incident such as the sudden rise of a gust of wind, or of an unexpected act such as sneezing, or the appearance of an animal, is believed to be an omen about impending events. These incidents are interpreted in light of conventional wisdom with which the diviner and community are familiar. One distinction between the two forms of divination is that intuitive divination requires the assistance of a diviner, whereas prognostic divination does not. Both forms however, involve the application of certain interpretive schemes based on observable phenomena.

Unfavorable political and economic circumstances in Haiti since the 1970s have forced substantial numbers of Haitians to immigrate into many parts of the world. Living in many of the world's largest cities (namely, New York, Chicago, Québec, Montréal, and Paris), they have established communities where they are performing the vodun rituals abroad and where most of the paraphernalia used in ceremonies are readily available. Even the pilgrimages are reproduced in the diaspora. On Halloween night, vodunists hold ceremonies in honor of Gede in a rented hall in Boston, for instance, and make a pilgrimage in honor of Ezili at the Lady of Mount Carmel Church in New York City or at St. Anne de Beaupré in Québec.

Leslie G. Desmangles

See also Afro-Caribbean; Altered States of Consciousness; Possession and Trance

Further Reading

Bourguignon, E. (1976). *Possession.* Columbus: Ohio State University Press.

Brown, K. M. (1991). *Mama Lola: A vodou priestess in Brooklyn*. Berkeley: University of California Press.

Courlander, H. (1960). *The drum and the hoe: Life and lore of the Haitian people*. Berkeley: University of California Press.

Davis, W. (1988). *Passage of darkness*. Chapel Hill: University of North Carolina Press.

Deren, M. (1972). *Divine horsemen: The living gods of Haiti*. New York: Delta Publishing Company.

Desmangles, L. G. (1993). *The faces of the gods: Vodou and Roman Catholicism in Haiti*. Chapel Hill and London: University of North Carolina Press.

Desmangles, L., and Cardeña, E. (1994). Trance possession and vodou ritual in Haiti. *Jahrbuch fur Transkulturelle Medizin und Psychotherapie, 6,* 297–307.

Hurbon, L. (1993). *Les mystères du vaudou* [The mysteries of voodoo]. Paris: Gallimard.

Kramer, K. (Director and Producer). (1982). *The Legacy of the Spirits* [Motion picture].Watertown, MA: Erzulie Films.

Laguerre, M. (1982). *Urban life in the Caribbean: A study of a Haitian urban community*. Cambridge, MA: Harvard University Press.

Métraux, A. (1978). *Voodoo in Haiti.* New York: Shocken Press.

Rey, Terry. (2000). *Our lady of Class Struggle: The Cult of the Virgin Mary in Haiti*. Trenton, NJ and Asmara, Eritrea: Africa World Press, Inc.

W

Wicca

Wicca, or revival witchcraft, is a religion that traces its ancestry to the works of Gerald B. Gardner (1884–1964) and his followers in mid–twentieth century England. Gardner, a civil servant and amateur folklorist, claimed to have discovered a coven of witches practicing an ancient fertility religion in the outskirts of London in the 1930s. He published his findings in *Witchcraft Today* (1954). Following the writings of other amateur scholars such as Margaret Murray (1863–1963) and Charles Godfrey Leland (1824–1903), Gardner interpreted witchcraft as a pre-Christian European fertility religion that worshipped a goddess of the moon and a horned god of the herds and hunt. According to this theory, medieval witches were persecuted because Christian inquisitors mistook their nature-centered religion for devil-worship. Although there is little historical evidence to support Gardner's claim, his book became very influential, and his version of witchcraft, or Wicca, spread throughout the Western world by the late twentieth century.

The word "Wicca" derives from Old English *wicca,* meaning "wise, knowledgeable." It originally referred only to the religion established by Gardner, but was gradually adopted by other variants of revival witchcraft, eventually becoming a generic term for many modern witchcraft traditions. These differ mostly in ethnic and regional emphasis, and share many practices and beliefs. Today, Wiccans are the largest group within a religious movement known as neopaganism.

Wiccans worship a goddess and often, although not necessarily, a god. They do, however, see sacredness omnipresent in the natural world. Wiccan worldview does not separate humans from nature; therefore human beings also partake of the immanent divine. Goddesses and gods may be identified with particular pantheons; for example, Wiccans with a Celtic emphasis may venerate Brigid, the Irish goddess of smithcraft, poetry, and healing, and Cernunnos, a Gaulish god of the hunt and guardian of the otherworld. More often each specific deity is seen as one manifestation of sacredness that can take many forms. This cosmology allows Wiccans to recognize and worship gods and goddesses from a variety of cultures, historical periods, and pantheons, sometimes in the same ritual.

Wiccans generally worship in covens, groups with between three and thirteen members that meet regularly to perform rituals. Each coven is led by a high priestess, who is in many cases assisted by a high priest. The priestess is often the ultimate authority in the coven, and the priest is in some cases entirely optional. There are also solitary witches who practice individually, without being associated with any particular coven.

Wiccan Rituals: Esbats and Sabbats

Modern Wiccans generally celebrate two types of rituals, "esbats" and "sabbats." Esbats coincide with full moons, and occur more or less monthly. On these occasions, covens meet to worship, study, and conduct business. At these times the coven performs rituals to help those in need, whether within the coven or in the larger community. Individuals may ask for healing, help with business or personal matters, or other kinds of spiritual help, such as divination. New members may be initiated at esbats, especially during the period between 1 February and 21 June. Some covens hold esbats at the new moon in addition to the full moon. The monthly lunar cycle is sacred to Wiccans because it is believed to correspond to the life cycle of the goddess herself, who begins each lunar month in her maiden phase as the new moon, matures into the full moon, and wanes into her crone aspect, the dark moon. This metaphor is often applied to rituals, such that rituals for increase and prosperity are believed to be most successful when done during a waxing moon, while those to banish bad influences, meditate, or divine the future are best performed on the waning moon.

Sabbats are larger rituals that celebrate seasonal shifts in the year cycle, which Wiccans call "the Wheel of the Year." There are eight sabbats, and they coincide with the solstices, the equinoxes, and the cross-quarter days that occur between each solstice and equinox. The eight Wiccan sabbats are:

Samhain	1 November
Winter Solstice or Yule	21 December
Imbolc or Brigid	1 February
Spring Equinox or Eostar	22 March
Beltaine	1 May
Summer Solstice or Litha	21 June
Lammas	1 August
Fall Equinox or Mabon	22 September

While there is no year cycle mythos recognized by all Wiccans, most recognize similar sets of natural symbols associated with each sabbat, and celebrate each sabbat in similar ways. Generally, the cross-quarter days (1 November, 1 February, 1 May, and 1 August) are considered major sabbats, while the solstices and equinoxes are minor feasts; their celebrations may be more muted in nature.

Just as the monthly lunar cycles symbolize the life cycle of the goddess, Wiccans see the Wheel of the Year as symbolizing the solar cycle of the god, who in some Wiccan mythologies is both son and consort to the earth goddess. The god is sometimes said to be conceived at the winter solstice and birthed at Imbolc (1 February). Throughout the spring he matures, until at Beltaine (1 May) he and the goddess join in ecstatic sexual union, which manifests as the flowering and fruiting of vines, trees, and crops on earth as the summer solstice (21 June) approaches. As crops are harvested, the sun begins to wane in the sky and Wiccans celebrate Lammas, the first fruits of the harvest (1 August). The sun god sacrifices himself at the autumn equinox (22 September), so that he can return to the Summerland (the Wiccan otherworld) at Samhain (1 November) for a period of renewal before his rebirth in midwinter. In other Wiccan myths, it is the goddess herself who goes into the otherworld at Samhain to follow her lover, and the spring festivals of Imbolc (1 February) and Eostar (22 March) celebrate her return to the earth and its renewed fruitfulness.

The Wiccan year begins and ends at Samhain, the most important ritual celebration in the Wheel of the Year. During this festival, Wiccans typically honor their beloved dead. Many construct altars in their memory, which they decorate with photographs, flowers, candles, and mementos of their deceased loved ones. Another Samhain tradition is the "dumb supper," a silent dinner at which the souls of dead relatives are invited to commune with their living descendants. The reclaiming tradition of San Francisco, California, stages a Samhain ritual called the Spiral Dance, which can have over 3,000 participants, making it one of the largest Wiccan rituals in the world. The highlight of this spectacular ritual performance, which features a choir, masked dancers, acrobats, and a cast of hundreds, is a visionary journey across the sunless sea of tears to the Summerland, where participants meet and speak with their dead loved ones. This uniformity of experience is achieved through the use of guided meditation, a technique in which a narrator tells a story in which participants can imagine themselves. The ritual ends with a spiral dance during which participants join hands to form a chain that winds around on itself, then out again as participants sing their vows to renew the earth and their own spirits in the year ahead.

Wiccan Rites of Passage

Wiccans have developed a variety of rituals to mark individual rites of passage, such as "Wiccanings" or baby-blessings, "handfastings," or marriages, and funeral services. The most important rites of passage in the lives of Wiccans are initiations. Most Wiccan traditions are initiatory: they require initiation for full membership. Some traditions, such as Gardnerian Wicca, have three degrees of initiation; initiates move through the hierarchy, learning and developing spiritually with each new rite of passage until they become third degree elders, able to lead their own coven.

Initiation rituals are generally "oath-bound," or secret; their contents cannot be revealed to outsiders. However, most initiations share certain features. The initiate is usually asked to master new materials and skills, such as leading rituals or gaining knowledge of a particular tradition. Initiates often face a test or challenge before the initiation: for example, overcoming an irrational fear or gaining deep self-knowledge. New initiates are presented to the gods by the high priestess and high priest, and introduced to the mystical aspects of the religion. They promise to enter the coven "in perfect love and perfect trust," and swear not to reveal the mysteries of the religion to noninitiates. Initiates may also adopt a new name to mark this important spiritual transformation in their lives. Initiation rituals usually end like other esbats with chanting, dancing, and feasting.

Ritual Goals

Whether marking esbats, sabbats, or initiations, the common goal of Wiccan rituals is transformation. Wiccans see transformation as one of nature's most basic forces; it manifests in the individual life cycle, as well as in lunar, solar, and seasonal cycles of life, death, and regeneration. Rituals are thought to help bring about natural transformations; Wiccans believe sabbats help shift the seasonal cycle from one point to another. They also transform consciousness by bringing about alternate states of consciousness and religious ecstasy. The ritual process is key in bringing about personal transformations in the development of the individual—for instance, through initiations. And some witches believe that rituals can also bring about changes in the course of events by directing energy toward specific ends: healing illness, for example, or preventing war. Gerald Gardner's witches claimed to have prevented Hitler's invasion of Britain during World War II through concerted ritual action.

Despite the many popular beliefs that surround the term "witchcraft," Wiccans do not perform ritual to harm others, nor do they worship the devil. Their central ethical principle is "harm none." Since witches perceive divinity as present in all living things, many witches extend this principle to include plants, animals, the earth, the natural environment, and the self. A related ethical precept is the "law of threefold return," according to which all acts return to the sender three times over. Thus good, ethical actions will yield positive results in the long run, while evil or irresponsible actions will bring the actor negative consequences.

Above all, Wiccans strive to remain in balance with the universe and its sacred forces. Illnesses, natural disasters, and painful events are often interpreted as a result of imbalance; ritual transformations are often intended to restore balance in relationships between humans, nature, community, and the gods.

Ritual Structure

Regardless of their purpose, all Wiccan rituals share a common structure rooted in the idea of ritual's transformative process. As they typically take place in private homes, backyards, and gardens, or in some cases in public parks and rented halls (there are no Wiccan temples or churches as such), they all begin by transforming ordinary space into sacred space. This is done by "casting a circle." Coven members stand in a circular formation while the high priestess (or another participant) salutes each of the four cardinal directions (east, south, west, and north). On the altar, water and salt are mixed, and incense is placed on a bit of burning charcoal; this consecrates the water and incense, and at the same time transforms them chemically as harbingers of the ritual transformations yet to come. The priestess then blesses each participant with the consecrated water and incense. Then she draws an imaginary circle around the participants using a sword or "athame," a special sacred knife. The circle is sprinkled with consecrated salt water and asperged with incense to bless and purify it, and to keep out unwanted spiritual influences.

Once the circle is cast, Wiccans "call the quarters," or formally invoke the guardians of each of the four cardinal directions and their elements. Then the goddess (and, if desired, the god) is called into the circle. In some rituals, the presence of the goddess may be invoked into the body of the high priestess, an act Wiccans call "drawing down the moon." In this state, the high priestess's actions and pronouncements are understood as being those of the goddess. The god may also be invoked into the body of the high priest.

Wiccans believe that ritual works by "raising energy" and sending it out into the world for a particular purpose. Energy is conceived of as a life force that infuses all living beings and natural objects, such as stones, rivers, trees, mountains, and the earth itself. Wiccans draw energy from the earth up into their bodies in a variety of ways, but most commonly by dancing in a circle and chanting during the core of their rituals. During this part of the ritual, some participants may enter into alternate states of consciousness during which they commune with the deities and receive personal messages or divine healing. The dancing reaches a frenzied peak as the energy builds up into a "cone of power," which is imagined as rising from the participants' bodies; as the dancing and chanting reach a climax, the energy is released and the participants "ground," or send leftover energy to the earth by touching the floor with their hands. Grounding is important because raw energy from the ritual is believed to be potentially harmful.

During the final phase of the ritual, the priestess plunges the athame into a cup of wine or juice held by the priest. This action, known as the "Great Rite," symbolizes the sexual union of the goddess and the god, the fundamental creative act that underlies all transformations in the universe. The participants then share a meal of consecrated wine (or juice) and bread before the spirits are thanked for their presence and dismissed, and the circle is opened. The wine and bread also symbolize transformation, in that they have been transformed by the processes of fermentation and leavening.

Origins of Wiccan Ritual

Despite Gardner's theory of Wiccan origins, most Wiccan rituals date no further back than the early twentieth century. Some elements—for example, the importance of the four elements and cardinal directions—can be traced to Greek philosophy in 300 BCE. Others developed during the Renaissance, when Greek and Roman mystical traditions were rediscovered and reinterpreted by Western magicians such as Pico della Mirandola (1463–1494), Giordano Bruno (1548–1600), and Heinrich Cornelius Agrippa von Nettesheim (1486–1535). Their writings were often blended with elements of folk magic in "black books," the private notebooks of magical practitioners. (Modern Wiccans keep records of their rituals in "books of shadows," notebooks that recall these precursors.) It was during this time that elements of Hebrew magic from the cabala were incorporated into the Western magical tradition. The structure of Wiccan initiations owes a great deal to Masonic initiatory rituals; Gardner and several other early founders belonged to these orders and adapted a number of terms and procedures to the religions they were constructing. Wiccan rituals also draw freely from folk customs, which Gardner and other early writers interpreted as preserving vestiges of pre-Christian practice. However, the resulting pastiche must not be viewed as lacking in authenticity. Wiccan ritual combines elements from a number of traditions into new, artistic, and moving performances that give practitioners a sense of community and connection to the sacred.

Sabina Magliocco

See also Paganism and Neo-Paganism; Witchcraft

Further Reading

Adler, M. (1986). *Drawing down the moon: Witches, druids, goddess-worshippers, and other pagans in America today*. Boston: Beacon Press. (Original work published 1979)

Berger, H. (1999). *A community of witches. Contemporary neo-paganism and witchcraft in the United States*. Columbia: University of South Carolina Press.

Gardner, G. B. (1973). *Witchcraft today*. Seacaucus, NJ: Citadel Press. (Original work published 1954)

Hutton, R. (2000). *Triumph of the moon: A history of modern pagan witchcraft*. Oxford, UK: Oxford University Press.

Leland, C. G. (1990). *Aradia, or the gospel of the witches*. Blaine, WA: Phoenix Publishing. (Original work published 1890)

Luhrmann, T. M. (1989). *Persuasions of the witches' craft*. Cambridge, MA: Harvard University Press.

Magliocco, S. (1996). Ritual is my chosen art form: The creation of ritual among contemporary pagans. In R. Lewis (Ed.), *Magical religion and modern witchcraft* (pp. 93–119). Albany, NY: SUNY Press.

Murray, M. (1921). *The witch cult of Western Europe*. Oxford, UK: Oxford University Press.

Orion, L. (1995). *Never again the burning times: Paganism revived*. Prospect Heights, IL: Waveland Press.

Salomonsen, J. (2002). *Enchanted feminism: The reclaiming witches of San Francisco*. New York: Routledge.

Starhawk. (1989). *The spiral dance*. New York: Harper Collins.

Witchcraft

Witchcraft (or sorcery) is ritual activity designed to produce an effect desired by the person performing the activity or by a client. Desired effects can include preventing or curing illness, causing illness or death of an enemy, causing someone to fall in love,

THE PERVASIVENESS OF WITCHCRAFT

In societies, such as the Azande of Central Africa described below, where witchcraft is believed in, efforts to limit and control the work of witches can be found in all aspects of life.

Witchcraft is most obviously the cause of death, but it is also the cause of a Zande's misfortunes and is an ever present and normal accompaniment to his life. If the crops are blighted, or if a seemingly sound granary collapses or a well-made pot cracks in firing, if the chief is unfriendly, or a hunt is unsuccessful—these otherwise inexplicable happenings are diagnosed as being the result of witchcraft. Though disinterested observers may attribute a particular incident to carelessness or a fault, all Azande agree that witchcraft is in general the cause of all disasters since it brings a man into "relation with events in such a way that he sustains injury." For example, when a granary collapsed and injured people who happened to be sitting beneath it, Azande recognized that it collapsed because termites had eaten into, and undermined, the supports, and they also agreed that the people were sitting under it to shelter from the rays of the sun; but they added that witchcraft caused the granary to collapse at exactly the time when the people were sitting beneath it.

Witchcraft links what to us are two independent chains of causation; it explains why misfortune, which is ever present in life, comes into direct contact with the individual at a particular time.

When a Zande believes himself to be bewitched he presents to the poison oracle the names of those whom he suspects, at that particular time, of having malevolent thoughts against him — those who are envious of him, or who have at some time been wronged by him. Azande are only interested in witches when they themselves are bewitched and the fact that a man has been proved a witch is not held against him, even if he has previously bewitched the sufferer. Only those who have been found guilty of two or three murders are likely to be marked men and, because of their reputation as witches, will have their names constantly proffered to the oracles. Normally, a Zande seeks to find someone who would have a motive for bewitching him and who might have wished misfortune on him. Indeed, "witchcraft becomes synonymous with the sentiments that are supposed to cause it." Men bewitch others when they hate them. It is the poison oracle which decides whether or not the man who has a motive for bewitching you is actually doing so.

Though both men and women may be witches, women are not allowed to consult the poison oracle, the use of which is restricted to married men; a woman's husband, or possibly her father or brother, has to consult the oracle on her behalf. People are usually bewitched by persons of the same sex, because in Zande society the sexes, apart from husband and wife and brother and sister, mix very little socially, and there are few opportunities for enmity to arise between them. Kinsmen do not bewitch each other, for if you accuse a kinsman, and he is proved to be a witch, you will be supposed to possess the same inherited characteristic.

***Source*: Baxter, P. T. W., & Butt, Andre. (1953). "The Azande, and Related Peoples of the Anglo-Egyptian Sudan and Belgian Congo." In Daryll Forde (Ed.), *Ethnographic Survey of Africa, East Central Africa, Part IX*. London: International African Institute, p. 81.**

producing wealth or financial harm, producing victory or defeat in battle, ensuring a good harvest or crop failure, and controlling the weather. Other desired effects can include preventing or causing accidents and injuries, applying or removing demonic influences, transforming one substance into another, altering physical shapes, altering social relations, producing good or bad luck, and acquiring supernatural abilities such as the ability to fly through the air, walk on water, see the future, control spirits, and converse with the dead. Rituals for worship of deities and for celebration are also common. Not all persons who perform witchcraft rituals are considered to be "witches." The term "witch," usually carries a connotation of illegitimacy in that it implies a person invoking spiritual forces outside of established authority (see the section on Legitimacy and Social Control below).

Magic

Witchcraft as a ritual activity assumes the existence of magic. A magical worldview is one in which all things are connected to each other on an occult, spiritual, or subtler level of existence. Some systems of magical thought have elaborate cosmologies (branches of metaphysics that deal with the nature of the universe) that describe multiple levels of existence such as the physical, mental, and spiritual levels. Generally, magic is seen as the ability to access and manipulate the mental and spiritual levels of existence through ritual activity and thereby alter or control the shapes, actions, and events occurring to persons, spirits, or objects at a distance. Belief in magic is found in all regions of the world and frequently blends into legitimate religion.

Some cultures believe that magical ability must be learned. Other cultures believe that magical ability is inborn or granted by deities. Still others believe that it can have multiple sources.

A common form of magical ritual is sympathetic magic. Sympathetic magic is a ritual based on the manipulation of a substance that has a physical connection to the person or object that is the target of the ritual. For example, a person's hair or nail clippings are thought to contain not only that person's physical substance, but also his or her mental and spiritual levels of existence. The clippings therefore allow access to occult levels that can be ritually manipulated to make that person fall ill or fall in love or to alter that person's behavior. Similar rituals can be performed utilizing a person's clothing or possessions.

Another common form of magical ritual is imitative magic. Imitative magic is a ritual based on the form of the target. In a kind of platonic idealism (the belief that all objects of a similar form are connected as manifestations of an ideal form of the object existing on a higher plane), ritual objects are thought to have an occult connection with the target person or desired effect because of they share a similar form or resemblance. An example is the infamous "voodoo doll" or any other effigy or photograph of the person who is the target of the ritual. Some rituals use parchment with the name of the target person written on it or call for the practitioner to ritually chant the target person's name. The name is thought to possess a mental and spiritual connection to the person. In some cultures, persons do not use their real names in everyday situations because of fear of witchcraft.

Another example of imitative magic is a ritual that includes sexual intercourse as a symbol of cosmic intercourse involving male and female principles or deities. Typically a high priest and priestess representing supernatural forces ritually merge, ensuring an abundant harvest of crops for that year. The persons in the ritual may be costumed as deities and are thought to possess a spiritual connection to the forces they represent. Deities may also be seen as inhabiting or possessing the persons during the ritual. These rituals are typically performed at specific times of the year, for example, at the beginning of the planting season.

Special times and places are also important in witchcraft. The spiritual forces of the universe are thought to coalesce at special times of the year, for example, during solstices and equinoxes, and at certain alignments of the stars and planets. During these times the boundaries between the physical and spiritual levels of existence are thought to become more fluid and permeable, therefore making magic easier and more powerful.

Certain locations are also thought to be centers where the spiritual forces of the Earth coalesce, making those locations powerful for the practice of magic. These locations are numerous and can include mountains (especially volcanoes), valleys (especially at the back end), streams, the confluence of streams, seashores, islands, unusual geological formations (e.g., Ayers Rock in Australia), forests, and any location where hallucinogenic plants grow. Certain human-made structures such as temples, churches, and shrines are also important locations of magical power. These locations are frequently seen as the homes of deities and spirits who can lend their power to the magic through ritual worship, appeasement, petition, possession, or manipulation.

Trance

Rituals designed to produce trance states are frequently used in witchcraft. These rituals can include extensive drumming, dancing, chanting, repetitive recitation, sensory deprivation, fasting, or meditation. All of these activities have in common narrowly focused attention. Trance is the intense focusing of attention on some thought or object. With restricted input the mind creates a spatial and subjective reality based on the object of attention. This object can be a mental object or idea that enlarges and subjectively becomes the totality of subjective experience. In this way the cognition of external reality can be blocked, and the mental object or idea can become subjectively real. This is a psychological mechanism for the subjective experience of magical phenomena by the witch. Some witches also employ hallucinogenic plants in their rituals.

Subjectively, during the ritual the witch experiences a transcendence from the physical level of existence to spiritual levels, which can include conscious contact with spiritual entities and forces. This type of ritual focusing on direct contact with spiritual beings is thought to be the most powerful kind of magic.

Spirit Attack and Possession

Witchcraft is frequently believed to cause attacks by evil spirits and demonic possession. Believers think that witches can manipulate evil spirits and send them to attack or possess their enemies. Two types of attacks are especially common in which victims report nightmares in which they are attacked in their sleep. First, people (especially men) report being strangled or suffocated in their sleep by an evil spirit (e.g., ghost), demon, or witch. Cultural psychiatrists and medical anthropologists have interpreted these experiences as the results of sleep paralysis syndromes.

Second, nightmares of sexual assault by evil spirits are commonly experienced by girls and young women in many parts of the world. Some medical anthropologists have interpreted these in a classical Freudian sense as repression of oedipal guilt. Others have suggested that these nightmares are the symptoms of dissociative disorders. Dissociative disorders usually result from traumatic experiences that can include childhood sexual abuse and can be characterized by nightmares, flashbacks, hallucinations, and a splitting of consciousness such as multiple personalities.

Another type of attack is hauntings by ghosts, demons, and spirits during waking hours. These attacks are experienced by men and women throughout the world. Persons being attacked will usually panic, sometimes running around in a crazed fashion while trying to escape the demons. These attacks are usually interpreted by psychiatrists and anthropologists as symptoms of dissociative or psychotic disorders. All of these types of spirit attack are commonly believed to be evidence of witchcraft by people in premodern cultures.

Witches are also believed to send demons to possess and control the behavior of their enemies. The typical case is a young person (usually female) who suddenly starts having periods of altered consciousness in which her normal personality disappears, and she behaves as an animal, a demon, or some other evil spirit. The possessed person may curse, grunt, froth at the mouth, flail about, or become violent or catatonic. These episodes are usually short lived (a few minutes to a few hours) and recurrent.

Such demonic possessions can also be epidemic, striking several people in a village either in rapid succession or all at once. The epidemic nature of these possessions is usually seen as proof of witchcraft in premodern cultures. The strange illnesses that led to the witch trials in Salem, Massachusetts, in 1692 are an example of this phenomenon. Psychiatrists and anthropologists usually attribute demonic possessions to dissociative disorders and to mass hysteria in epidemic cases.

Exorcism

The usual treatment for demonic possession is exorcism. Exorcisms occur in all cultures where possession by demons and evil spirits is present. If demonic possession is suspected, a witch or shaman (a priest or priestess who uses magic to cure the sick, divine the hidden, and control events) is brought in to exorcize the evil spirits. The witch diagnoses a particular type of demonic possession that requires a particular type of exorcism ritual.

The witch usually induces a state of trance in the victim if the victim is not already in an active state of possession. This is done so that the witch can converse directly with the demon to determine its identity, why it is possessing the victim, and what it wants in exchange for its departure. Negotiations between the witch and the demon then begin. Frequently, the demon refuses to leave, and the witch must threaten the demon with supernatural harm. Usually the witch will be able to call on one or more powerful spirits to do battle with the demon. The witch may call on a succession of increasingly powerful spirit allies in order to banish a particularly difficult demon. Exorcism rituals are primarily aimed at establishing, negotiating, and manipulating the mythological relations between the witch's spirit allies and the possessing demon.

Exorcisms frequently use ritual objects, such as amulets or charmed strings tied around the victim's wrist or neck. Also, a cutting of the victim's hair may be ritually consigned to a sacred container (a cloth or clay pot) and removed from the premises or ritually burned, symbolizing removal of the demon. Offerings and gifts to the demon may also be used as ritual objects. By skillful manipulation of these ritual objects the witch alters the subjective experience of the victim. The victim is usually in a trance and thus may be highly susceptible to hypnotic suggestion. The witch uses this heightened suggestibility to persuade, cajole, and threaten the demon into leaving, thus healing the victim.

Legitimacy and Social Control

The term *witchcraft* commonly has a pejorative meaning associated with evil. Witchcraft is sometimes referred to as "black magic," the implication being that magic used to harm is evil, whereas magic used to help is legitimate and should not be considered witchcraft. However, several scholars have pointed out that magic is not inherently black or white. Throughout the world the use of magic is both an illegal activity as well as a legitimate means of enforcing societal norms. Which it is depends more on who is practicing it rather than on its purpose.

All societies, but especially small-scale, premodern societies, are dependent for their survival on the cooperation of individuals and families for the good of the whole society. Successful social life requires adherence to the moral obligations that structure social interaction in that society. In a society with a magical worldview an effective means of ensuring good behavior is threat of punishment by spiritual forces if moral obligations are broken.

Transgressors can be punished by rituals that cause them to fall ill, have an accident, be attacked by spirits, be shunned (e.g., excommunication), be sentenced to eternal torment by demons (e.g., damnation), or be ritually murdered. However, if these rituals are performed by legitimate authorities to punish immoral or illegal behavior, they are generally not seen as "witchcraft" but rather as an appropriate use of spiritual force. Also, the practitioners are not seen as "witches" but rather as "priests" or other forms of legitimate religious practitioners.

Although the practice of magic is found throughout the premodern world, "witches" or criminal practitioners tend to exist in hierarchical societies. In those societies that have hierarchies of gender, caste, race, class, or ethnicity, control over legitimate magic is typically monopolized as much as possible by the dominant group. This monopoly enhances the dominance of that group. Anyone who is not a member of the dominant group will not be authorized to invoke spiritual forces. If that person does so, he or she is illegitimate and is therefore a "witch" and a criminal. In this sense witchcraft can be defined as invoking spiritual forces outside of established authority.

In some societies the oppressed use illegitimate magic as their only form of resistance. In some modern Western societies, people who perceive themselves to be oppressed by Christian authorities have formed Satanist societies to perform magic in opposition to their Christian enemies. Their rituals mimic Christian rites in many ways but invoke Satan as their primary deity.

This sociopolitical use of magic is probably why witches are most commonly seen as female. Most societies have male dominance. One way for men to maintain their dominance over women is to claim a monopoly over the legitimate use of spiritual forces. Therefore, any woman who invokes spiritual forces in a male-dominant society can be denounced as a witch and be severely punished.

In a society with a magical worldview any negative event such as an illness, an accident, or an unexplained death can be attributed to witchcraft. This provides a pretext for witch hunts and the possible elimination of political enemies.

Similarly, when one society invades and conquers another the conqueror can find it useful for purposes of social control to declare the religion of the conquered people to be a form of witchcraft and therefore illegal. This de-legitimizes the ability of the conquered people to invoke their gods and induces them to accept the religion of the conqueror. This integrates the conquered people into the new social structure at a subordinate level and facilitates control of their behavior. European Christians, for example, commonly used this tactic when conquering non-Christian peoples.

European Witchcraft

Modern-day Christians tend to view witchcraft as something entirely distinct from Christianity. However, from a scholarly perspective, the difference between witchcraft and Christianity is sociopolitical legitimacy, not ritual structure. Both ritually access accepted spiritual entities for practical human benefit and social control.

As the religion historian Keith Thomas has pointed out, the New Testament emphasizes the performance of miracles by Jesus and the Apostles as proof of their control over spiritual forces. Similarly, the Christian scripture *Lives of the Saints* details the activities of Christian holy men who can tell the future, control the weather, provide protection against fire and flood, magically transport heavy objects, and heal the sick. This claim of magical power has been central to the efforts of Christian missionaries in persuading non-Christian peoples to give up their indigenous forms of magic.

The basic Christian ritual utilizes salt and water to bless the person and expel evil spirits. However, there are Christian rituals to bless houses, businesses, food, livestock, crops, ships, tools, wells, travelers, and soldiers in battle and heal the sick, drive away thunder, fight a duel, and cure sterility in people and animals.

The Christian mass has been especially associated with magical power. Masses have been performed for all types of practical needs, such as curing and preventing disease, providing good harvests, and bringing favorable weather. The eucharistic wafer has been used by parishioners as a charm to magically fertilize their crops or cause someone to fall in love. The tradition of placing the wafer directly into the mouths of worshipers began because people were taking it away to utilize its magical power for their own purposes.

The sociopolitical distinction between Christian magic and witchcraft in European culture is illustrated by the witch craze that occurred in Europe and North America between 1450 and 1700 CE. This period was the time of the Renaissance, the Protestant Reformation (a sixteenth-century religious movement marked ultimately by rejection or modification of some Roman Catholic doctrine and practice and establishment of the Protestant churches), and the Counter-Reformation (the reform movement in the Roman Catholic Church after the Reformation). During this time of great social turmoil, perhaps 100,000 people were executed as witches, and hundreds of thousands were persecuted and terrorized by all-male Christian authorities. Anyone could be denounced as a witch, but the vast majority were older single women and political or religious enemies of both the Catholic and Protestant Churches.

By the eighteenth century scientific thinking had produced natural explanations for negative events, and the witch trials ceased. Shortly thereafter, Freemasons and other opponents of Church authority gained enough political strength to lead the American and French Revolutions and guarantee the freedom of religion enjoyed by people in modern democratic societies.

Today in Salem, Massachusetts, anyone can invoke the spiritual forces they believe in without fear of arrest. The practice of magic remains, but the practitioners are no longer criminals. As such, non-Christian forms of magic have proliferated in the United States and other Western countries in what some scholars have termed a "pagan revival." Most of these practitioners, such as Wicca—a form of neo-pagan revivalism involving Nature worship and female deities—do not worship Satan and are not specifically anti-Christian.

Richard J. Castillo

See also Melanesia; Paganism and Neo-Paganism; Performance, Ritual of; Ritual Specialists

Further Reading

Bourguignon, E. (1976). *Possession*. San Francisco: Chandler & Sharp.

Castillo, R. J. (1997). *Culture and mental illness: A client-centered approach*. Pacific Grove, CA: Brooks/Cole.

Castillo, R. J. (Ed.). (1998). *Meanings of madness*. Pacific Grove, CA: Brooks/Cole.

Crapanzano, V., & Garrison, V. (Eds.). (1977). *Case studies in spirit possession*. New York: John Wiley & Sons.

Evans-Pritchard, E. E. (1976). *Witchcraft, oracles and magic among the Azande*. Oxford, UK: Clarendon.

Gaines, A. D. (Ed.). (1992). *Ethnopsychiatry: The cultural construction of professional and folk psychiatries*. Albany: State University of New York Press.

Harwood, A. (1987). *Rx: Spiritist as needed: A study of a Puerto Rican community mental health resource* (2nd ed.). Ithaca, NY: Cornell University Press.

Kendall, L. (1987). *Shamans, housewives, and other restless spirits: Women in Korean ritual life*. Honolulu: University of Hawaii Press.

Kleinman, A. (1980). *Patients and healers in the context of culture: An exploration of the borderland between anthropology, medicine, and psychiatry*. Berkeley and Los Angeles: University of California Press.

Lehmann, A. C., & Myers, J. E. (2001). *Magic, witchcraft, and religion* (5th ed.). Mountain View, CA: Mayfield.

Lewis, I. M. (1989). *Ecstatic religion: A study of shamanism and spirit possession* (2nd ed.). London: Routledge.

McGuire, M. B. (1988). *Ritual healing in suburban America*. New Brunswick, NJ: Rutgers University Press.

McPherson, N. M. (1991). Sorcery and concepts of deviance among the Kabana, West New Britain. *Anthropologica, 33*(2) 127–143.

Metraux, A. (1972). *Voodoo in Haiti*. New York: Schocken.

Orion, L. (1995). *Never again the burning times: Paganism revived*. Prospect Heights, IL: Waveland.

Sakheim, D. K., & Devine, S. E. (Eds.). (1992). *Out of darkness: Exploring Satanism and ritual abuse*. New York: Lexington.

Spiro, M. E. (1967). *Burmese supernaturalism*. Englewood Cliffs, NJ: Prentice Hall.

Stevens, P. (1982). Some implications of urban witchcraft beliefs. *New York Folklore, 8*(1) 29–42.

Stoller, P. (1989). *Fusion of the worlds: An ethnography of possession among the Songhay of Niger*. Chicago: University of Chicago Press.

Thomas, K. (1986). *Religion and the decline of magic*. New York: Charles Scribner's.

Thong, D. (1993). *A psychiatrist in paradise: Treating mental illness in Bali*. Bangkok, Thailand: White Lotus.

Witztum, E., & van der Hart, O. (1993). Possession and persecution by demons: Janet's use of hypnotic techniques in treating hysterical psychosis. In J. M. Goodwin (Ed.), *Rediscovering childhood trauma: Historical casebook and clinical applications* (pp. 65–88). Washington, DC: American Psychiatric Press.

Y

Yom Kippur

Yom Kippur, also known as the "Day of Atonement," is the holiest day of the Jewish year. Observed on the tenth day of the Jewish month of Tishri (which falls in September or October), Yom Kippur is a day of prayer, fasting, and refraining from work.

Ancient Origins

In the ancient world, appeasing the gods was a vital part of religious and civil life. Sacrifices were normally made to pacify offended gods. During high holy days the sacrifice of young children, normally daughters, was part of religious ritual.

As time progressed, most nations moved from the sacrifice of children to the sacrifice of animals. The ancient nation of Israel based its sacrificial system upon divine revelation spelling out how its god was to be appeased. This revelation in recorded in the Torah (the body of wisdom and law contained in Jewish scripture and other sacred literature and oral tradition).

As Israel was constituted as a nation (thirteenth century BCE) through its exodus from Egypt, the Torah records that Moses was told how this new nation was to commune with its god, the Lord. The Torah also tells how the Israelites were to interact with one another. In Moses' first meeting with the Lord, Moses was confronted by the pronouncement that he was to remove his sandals because he was standing on holy ground (Exodus 3:6).

The holiness of the Lord is central to the relationship that Israel has with its god. Holiness is the concept that God or a person is completely pure, righteous, and completely "other" or different from anyone else. Israel was also considered a holy nation because it was to live separately and differently from the surrounding nations. Israelites were to be different, or holy, in their dress, festivals, rituals, and even diet.

Meaning and Purpose

In Jewish scripture all humanity was created in the image of God, but the relationship of God and humans was tainted by sin. Sin is the violation of a covenant between two or more parties. So that people could atone for sin, the Lord set forth in the Torah a series of rituals to be followed. Israel could meet with God by following a detailed set of rules, rituals, and feasts. Yom Kippur became a day of national and personal "affliction of the soul." Historically, if Israel as a nation or any Israelite violated the covenant with God, the violation was regarded as sin. This sin was to be atoned for by the making of sacrifice and sin offerings (Leviticus 16). Personal sin separates God from his people and one person from another. Yom Kippur was given to Israel as a means to bridge the two separated parties: either God and Israel or one person and another.

Chapter sixteen of the Book of Leviticus details the background and procedure of Yom Kippur. The context of this chapter is the recent violation of an aspect of a worship ritual. Two priests were struck dead for not following the ritual precisely. Leviticus details the procedure to be followed to restore the relationship between God and Israel.

Yom Kippur reveals two characteristics about God. First, he is holy and cannot be in the presence of sin of any kind. Second, he desires to have communion with his people. Moses records both characteristics in Exodus 29:45 (NRSV): "I will dwell among the children of Israel, and will be their God." In order for God to dwell there must be a continual process of ritual sacrifices to atone for the sins of the people.

Chapter sixteen of Leviticus shows the elaborate rituals to be performed to accomplish atonement and reconciliation. First, this period was a time of Sabbath when no work was to be done. All attention was to be focused on making atonement. Great preparation was made as this time of atonement approached. Second, highly structured sacrifices were made using goats, rams, and bulls, and personal ritual washings were to take place. Third, prayers were to be made by the priests and the entire people of Israel. Fourth, all of this was to take place in the Tabernacle and eventually in the Temple in Jerusalem.

Historical Developments

The Torah records that when these sacrifices were performed God was pleased with the nation of Israel. But when Israel did not perform the sacrifices wholeheartedly God judged them. As the history of Israel developed the Torah describes how God was no longer satisfied with ritual sacrifices. The passage "For I desire steadfast love and not sacrifice, the knowledge of God rather than burnt offerings" (Hosea 6:6, NRSV) shows the dissatisfaction that God had with empty ritual.

As the first century CE unfolded two major events shifted the focus from Temple ritual sacrifices to other means of atonement. The first event was the movement surrounding Jesus of Nazareth (4 BCE), and the second event was the destruction of the Temple (969–970 BCE) of Israel in Jerusalem by the Roman Empire in 70 CE.

Many first-century Jews began to see that the death of Jesus of Nazareth was in effect a fulfillment of the ritual sacrifices of the Torah. The New Testament focuses on this notion in many places: "For Christ also suffered for sins once for all, the righteous for the unrighteous, in order to bring you to God. He was put to death in the flesh, but made alive in the spirit" (1 Peter 3:18, NRSV).

The construction of the Temple in Jerusalem was attributed to the son of King David (1031 CE), Solomon (1005 BCE). The Temple took the place of the Tabernacle, which was used during the early years of Israel. When the Temple was destroyed there was no longer a place to perform sacrifices for atonement. Yom Kippur then began to take on a new emphasis. The passage "For I desire steadfast love and not sacrifice, the knowledge of God rather than burnt offerings" (Hosea 6:6, NRSV) became an important principle for Israel. The focus was now on the Torah and the knowledge of the Lord and not on animal sacrifice.

Contemporary Observance

Learning the Torah and seeking forgiveness according to the Torah and its interpretations are fundamentally how Yom Kippur is celebrated and understood today. Modern Yom Kippur liturgy (rites prescribed for public worship) is comprised of attending prayer services, reading the Torah, taking vows, confessing sin, and making restitution. The holiday itself begins on the eve of Yom Kippur, when Jews begin their day of fasting by gathering for the Kol Nidre (meaning "all vows" in Aramaic) service. Prayer services resume the next morning and continue through the day. Yom Kippur concludes at nightfall with a long blast of the shofar (ram's horn), followed by a communal or family meal known as the "break fast."

The practices of purifying the soul, growing in knowledge of Torah, and seeking forgiveness and making restitution are at the heart of the modern Yom Kippur observance.

Patrick W. Malone

See also Calendrical Rituals; Judaism; Liminoid; Ramadan

Further Reading

Apsidorf, S. (1997). *Rosh Hashanah Yom Kippur survival kit* (Rev. ed.). Pikesville, MD: Leviathan Press.

Bible, new revised standard version. (1989). New York: National Council of Churches.

Encyclopedia Judaica. (1971). Jerusalem, Israel: Keter Publishing House.

Kline, M. G. (2000). *Kingdom prologue.* Overland Park, KS: Two Age Press.

Menedenhall, G. E. (1954). Covenant form in Israelite tradition. *The Biblical Archaeologist, 27,* 50–76.

Milgrom, J. (Ed.). (1991). *Anchor Bible commentary: Vol. 3. Leviticus.* New York: Doubleday.
Neusner, J. (1984). *Judaism in the beginning of Christianity.* London: Fortress Press.
Noth, M. (Ed.). (1965). *The Old Testament library, Leviticus.* Philadelphia: Westminster Press.

Yoruba

The Yoruba are renowned throughout West Africa and the African diaspora as masters of religious practice and a number of New World religions have their origins in Yoruba practices; among these religions are Santeria, Condombole, and other Afro-Brazilian and Afro-Cuban offshoots. Certainly, the variety of rituals, specialized gods, and types of divination place the Yoruba high on the list of those who are masters of religion.

There is much discussion over whether the Yoruba are, in fact, monotheists with the various *orishas* simply representing different aspects of the Supreme Being or Oludamare. In any event, religion among the Yoruba is not separated from other aspects of life. The spirits, or *orishas*, play an active role in daily life. This fact remains true for those Yoruba who became Christian, or Muslim for that matter. Anthropologists in both the Old and New Worlds have studied the subject of Yoruba syncretism.

Central Concepts

There are two fundamental ideas in the Yoruba religion of the *orishas*. These are "play" and "journey." Yoruba play encapsulates the concepts of spontaneity and ruse. It is personified in the guise of Nala, the trickster. Spontaneity carries with it the idea of improvisation. Improvisation goes with acting on impulse and distinguishes Yoruba ritual from other West African practices.

It is not unusual for a performer to elaborate on his role during the performance of ritual. He may leave the performance area to show up in the audience, playing with people, even fondling them. Then he may hide, popping up behind people to scare them. By violating boundaries, the performer dramatizes the fact that there is no boundary between spectator and performer. Both work together to create the ritual. Play is therefore both a sacred and communal thing, created on the spot through communal collaboration.

The concept of continuous transformation is central to Yoruba ritual. There is a constant reinterpretation of the stories the rituals portray. There is continuity, however, in the midst of change, since the framework remains constant while variations are almost infinite in the manner of performance.

Central to the process of transformation is the idea of the journey. Transformations are journeys from one real of knowledge to a different realm of knowledge. This movement is a fundamental part of Yoruba cosmology. Life is an ontological journey in which a person seeks to gain knowledge and understanding of himself or herself. The individual seeks to understand his or her mind and body. To illustrate this we will use what Drewal calls the ontological journey; the quest for self knowledge. This is a lifelong ritual that, in essence, is focused on understanding one's mind and body.

Rituals

The *Ikose w'aye* ("stepping into the world"), a childbirth ritual, begins the journey. An Ifa (a diety; see below) priest performs Ifa divination to find out what the child's future will be. He lays out a guide for the child to follow for best success in life.

A ritual called "knowing the head" follows when a child is three months old. It is the first step toward "understanding the head" (personality), the *ori inu*. This ritual is a step toward establishing the child's personality. The Yoruba seek to unite the male and female sides of personality, reuniting that which was originally one. There is widespread depiction of this play of gender throughout Yoruba worship, whether it be Sango (god of iron and thunder) worship, Ifa ceremonies, or cross-dressing in the Agemo Festival—a festival of reversal in which women mock men and vice versa through donning the clothes of the other. There is a constant stress on the container, the female, and the contained, the male. The need for compromise and the reintegration and uniting of the two is found throughout Yoruba ritual life.

Divination allows Yoruba people to communicate with Ifa, the deity who received from the sky god Olorun "the power to speak for the gods and communicate with human beings" (Bascom 1969, 80). The *babalawo* is the priest who is the diviner between Ifa and the people. Diviners provide parents with information to guide their children on the path of life, providing medical advice along with moral guidelines.

Death is a time of both sadness and merrymaking. Seven days after death, there is a wake and hymns are sung. There is a viewing of the body. Then there is a procession to the graveyard followed by a party. There is rejoicing in the feats of the person who died and a celebration of his or her passage into the next life.

The market is often used as a metaphor of Yoruba life and religion. It is a place of great contradiction and variety. Quarrels break out. Disputes are settled. Mediation is required. Things change from moment to moment as situations transform themselves in a kaleidoscopic fashion. Males and females seem to come together and part. Compromise and improvisation are the order of the day as one must adapt or fall behind. Play, with its twin characteristics of ruse and improvisation, is essential to survival. Life is both serious and fun, all at the same time.

From birth to death there are rituals to guide the Yoruba. The baby's ritual naming is a community event. The baby is ritually welcomed into the family through ceremonies. The baby is not given a name for seven days because names have meanings and parents and elders study the baby so its names reflect its character and behavior. Throughout life, Yoruba seek to discover character and destiny, using rituals filled with improvisatory transformations to mark the stability and ever-present change inherent in life itself.

Frank A. Salamone

See also Africa, West; Islam

Further Reading

Abimbola, W. (1977). *Ifa: An exposition of Ifa literary corpus*. Ibadan, Nigeria: Oxford University Press.

Abiodun, R. (1983). Identity and the artistic process in Yoruba aesthetic concept of Iwa. *Journal of Cultures and Ideas, 1*, 13–30.

Barrett, S. R. (1977). *The rise and fall of an African utopia: A wealthy theocracy in comparative perspective*. Waterloo, Ontario: Wilfrid Laurier University Press.

Bascom, William. (1969). *Ifa divination: Communication between gods and men in West Africa*. Bloomington, IN: Indiana University Press.

Drewal, H. J. & Drewal, M. T. (1990). *Gelede: Art and female power among the Yoruba*. Bloomington, IN: Indiana University Press.

Drewal, M. T. (1992). *Yoruba ritual: Performers, play, agency*. Bloomington: Indiana University Press.

Gbadegesin, S. (1991). *African philosophy: Traditional Yoruba philosophy and contemporary African realities*. New York: Peter Lang.

Glazier, S. D. (Ed.). (1999). *Anthropology of religion: A handbook*. Westport, CT: Praeger.

Heinze, R. (Ed.). (2000). *The nature and function of rituals: Fire from heaven*. Westport, CT: Bergin & Garvey.

Herskovits, M. J. (1962). *The human factor in changing Africa*. New York: Alfred A. Knopf.

Idowu, E. B. (1963). *Olaodaumarae: God in Yoruba belief*. New York: Praeger.

Lloyd, P. C. (1962). *Yoruba land law*. London: Oxford University Press.

Matibag, E. (1996). *Afro-Cuban religious experience: Cultural reflections in narrative*. Gainesville: University Press of Florida.

Mio, J. S., & Katz, A. N. (Eds.). (1996). *Metaphor: Implications and applications*. Mahwah, NJ: Lawrence Erlbaum Associates.

Olson, J. S. (1996). *The peoples of Africa: An ethnohistorical dictionary*. Westport, CT: Greenwood.

Olupona, J. K. (Ed.). (1991). *African traditional religions in contemporary society*. St. Paul, MN: Paragon House.

Otite, O. (1996). Migrating cultural performances: The Urhobo among the Kale—Yoruba, Ondo State, Nigeria. In D. Parkin, L. Caplan, & H. Fischer (Eds.) *The politics of cultural performance* (pp. 115–124). Providence, RI: Berghahn Books.

Z

Zulu

The Zulu (people of heaven) of South Africa are a people rich in history and culture. Their language is one of the Bantu group of languages and is the root language for understanding many other Bantu and Nguni languages. It is one of the most common languages in South Africa.

The Zulu people live on a reserve of 26,000 square kilometers called "Zululand" (Kwa-Zulu), which lies on the Indian Ocean in Natal Province. The Zulu were traditionally farmers and cattle herders as well as great warriors in the tradition of Shaka, their ancestor, perhaps the most famous African warrior of all times. The warrior role continues as an important aspect of Zulu life for young males.

Patrilineal (based on descent through the paternal lineage) and patriarchal in terms of lineage and power relations, males are highly revered in the family. Polygamy is practiced in the form of polygyny (having more than one wife), based on the number of wives one can afford. Whereas the paternal role can be described as authoritarian, the maternal role is one of nurturance. The Zulu mother passes on Zulu traditions and history orally and socializes children. Traditionally women have also had the primary responsibility for producing and preparing food.

Apartheid (racial segregation) and other elements of colonialism challenged the survival of Zulu culture and religious traditions. However, with the abolition of apartheid, the Zulu have revitalized their traditional culture. A resurgence of pride and culture has been evident in recent years.

Unlike U.S. culture and religious life, in which the separation between religious and nonreligious life is fairly apparent, the bulk of Zulu culture and religious life is highly integrated. Ancestors (*amalozi* or *amakhosi*) are highly venerated in Zulu culture. Believed to reside in the Earth, they are part of every major ritual and constitute a positive presence in life. The quality of life is believed to be shaped by the relationship between the Zulu and their ancestors. If ancestors do not receive their proper respect, the village is left open to negative influences and misfortune.

The God of the Sky also figures prominently in Zulu religious life. He is believed to be the Creator from whom all life flows and from whom Zulus trace their ancestry. The God of the Sky is viewed as the father; his counterpart is Earth, the mother, to whom all Zulus in death return.

Zulu society abounds with rituals. Rituals mark many occasions tied to stages of life and events including birth, death, courtship, marriage, the transition to manhood, induction into an army regimen, new harvest, and the birth of the heir or chief son. Such special occasions are always celebrated with the praising of ancestors and the dressing of the clan or village chief in traditional attire. Ceremonies incorporate music, including song, hand clapping, drums, and stringed instruments; dance of many styles and of many clans; poetry; crafts (especially beadwork); ear piercing; cattle; and animal sacrifice. The wedding ceremony is the most colorful. Elaborate beadwork and dress mark the occasion. The wedding ceremony is punctuated by highly energetic, staccato dancing and drumming. Symbols include spears, shields, skin dress, and beehive-shaped huts.

Young Zulu women participating in a Zulu ritual dance in South Africa. COURTESY OF FRANK SALAMONE.

The Kraal

The structures of a kraal (traditional Zulu village) and Zulu religious culture are intimately tied. The kraal and especially designated hills are sacred places for the Zulu.

The shape and configuration of the kraal are also of significance. The circular cattle kraal is in the center of a circle or semicircle of beehive-shaped homes traditionally constructed of cow dung, with the hut of the chief to the left side of the kraal. Cattle play an important social and religious role in Zulu life. They are a symbol of affluence, are used in sacrifice to the ancestors, and are used as *lobola* (bride price) paid from the prospective son-in-law to the bride's father. Nearly all of the important rituals in Zulu life take place in the cattle kraal. E. Thomas Lawson, perhaps the leading expert on Zulu religious life, says scholars, for this reason, have referred to the cattle kraal as the "temple of the Zulu people" (Lawson 1985, 19). The sacred hills are the other place where important religious rituals are performed.

The Zulu belief system involves a multiplicity of roles. There are six primary leadership and specialist roles.

The *umnumzane* (headman/priest) of each kraal is the chief officer responsible for maintaining Zulu life and ritual. He is the link between the ancestors and his people. He oversees the role of all others in his village and has a place in all major ceremonies.

The diviner is responsible for finding the source of all misfortune that may befall the village or its members. This role requires a special calling and is one most frequently occupied by women. Apprentice training with a mature, experienced diviner is necessary because this role is viewed as highly important.

The herbalist suggests the cure for the problem that the diviner has identified. Although medicine is viewed as an important source of power in Zulu culture and most Zulu have some knowledge of medicine, the herbalist is recognized as having the highest degree of knowledge of medicine. Although his (most herbalists are men) knowledge is largely of traditional medicine, his imperative is to constantly seek out new knowledge and, in turn, cures. Therefore, with exposure to Western medicine, the herbalist incorporates the new with the old.

The heaven-herd role requires a special calling from the God of the Sky. A role occupied by men, the heaven-herd has a special relationship with the God of the Sky, who controls weather. The heaven-herd guides the weather and herds off impending storms much as the cattle herder rounds up and herds off cattle to pasture.

The sorcerer role can be held by any Zulu. The sorcerer exercises power (medicinal and spiritual) to some specific end of revenge, destruction, or evil. The sorcerer often takes his or her direction from knowledge provided by the diviner and the herbalist. A limited knowledge of medicine is all that is required to practice sorcery.

The witch is a person whose identity is usually not known. This is in contrast to the aforementioned five roles, which are all public. The witch, who is usually a woman, uses her powers toward evil ends. She becomes a witch, often unknowingly, through possession. The private nature of witchcraft and its destructive powers provide a challenge to the structured system and roles of Zulu life.

Power is an important element in the Zulu communal drama. Legitimate power comes from the ancestors, the God of the Sky, and medicine. This type of power is positive for the maintenance of Zulu life. Alternatively, illegitimate power, such as that derived from witchcraft, is negative for the maintenance of Zulu life.

Persistence and Change

Although religious systems typically are not static, the Zulu system is particularly adaptive and responsive. Encounters with Western religions have been integrated into Zulu culture. Zulu culture has been adaptive and responsive to the new, and, in some instances the new has further cemented and even advanced some aspects of Zulu culture and religious practice. For example, exposure to Christianity, with its notions of God in heaven, has increased the significance of the God of the Sky for Zulu people. Indeed, although traditional Zulu religious practice persists among the Zulu, including those who practice some form of Christianity, the majority of Zulu today can be classified as Christian.

Other noteworthy adaptations are in medicine. Zulu healers still practice traditional medicine but are gradually combining Western philosophies, medicines, and treatments with it. Thus, Zulu religion and medicine have both survived and evolved.

Perhaps one reason why Zulu traditions have survived is that they are consistent with Shaka's vision that there be solidarity among all Zulus—many clans united into one kingdom. Despite the many attempts to divide and diminish the Zulu people, solidarity among them persists. According to Lawson, "To this very day, the Zulu continue to emphasize such solidarity and to express it in their relationships both with the white people of South African and with the neighboring African groups with traditions of their own" (Lawson 1985, 98).

Oppression under apartheid fostered a pan-African spirit among the oppressed people of South Africa and Africa on the whole. Symbols and traditions of the past have blended with the goal of liberation and *amandla* (power) for Zulus and other Africans in the present and for the future. The strong traditions of the Zulu, a people rich in cultural symbols, ritual, and practice, will continue.

Susan D. Toliver

Further Reading

Campbell, C., & Mare, G. (1995, June). Evidence for an ethnic identity in the life histories of Zulu-speaking Durban Township residents. *Journal of Southern African Studies*, *21*(2), 287–301.

Everett, P. (1990). *Zulus*. Sag Harbor, NY: Permanent Press.

Guy, J. (1979). *The destruction of the Zulu kingdom*. London: Longman.

Lawson, E. T. (1985). *Religions of Africa: Traditions in transition*. Prospect Heights, IL: Waveland Press.

Taldykin, N., & Sris, M. (2003). *Zulu: A traditional South African society*. Retrieved July 10, 2003, from http://www.donmingo.com/zulupeop.html

List of Contributors

Akinade, Akintunde E.
High Point University
Hajj

Angrosino, Michael V.
University of South Florida
Altered States of Consciousness

Archetti, Eduardo P.
University of Oslo
Sport and Ritual

Arthur, Linda
Washington State University
Hawai'i

Beatty, Andrew
Brunel University
Javanese

Bidmead, Julye
California State University, Fresno
New Year's Celebrations

Borer, Michael Ian
Boston University
Inversion, Rites of

Boxberger, Daniel L.
Western Washington University
Native Americans: Northwest Coast

Castillo, Richard J.
University of Hawaii, West Oahu
Witchcraft

Christensen, Karen
Berkshire Publishing Group
Martial Arts

Cosillo-Starr, Mara
Field Museum
Day of the Dead
South America: Savanna and Tropical Forest

Cowan, Douglas
University of Missouri, Kansas City
Online Rites

Crapo, Richley
Utah State University
Catholicism
Hanukkah
Naven Ceremony

Desmangles, Leslie G.
Trinity College
Vodun

Dobbin, Jay
Micronesia

Dransart, Penelope
University of Wales
Death Rituals
Pilgrimage

Dwivedi, Onkar P.
University of Guelph
Hinduism

Eodice, Alexander R.
Iona College
Epiphany
Glossolalia
Greco-Roman
Orthodoxy

Feinberg, Benjamin
Asheville, North Carolina
Passage, Rites of

Ferrero-Paluzzi, Diane
Iona College
Naming Rituals

Frobish, Todd S.
Fayetteville State University
Ritual as Communication

Ghosh, Sujata
McGill University
Buddhism

Gold, Malcolm
Malone College
Pentecostalism

Gossman, Kathleen
Furman University
Clothing and Rituals

Gunn, Joshua
Louisiana State University
Commemorative Rituals
Scatological Rituals

Han, Jin Hee
New York Theological Seminary
Birth Rituals
Food and Rituals

Harlan, Lindsey
Connecticut College
Divali

Hawkins, John P.
Brigham Young University
Mormons

Henderson, Rodger
Pennsylvania State University, Fayette
Native Americans: Pueblo
Vision Quest

Holbrook, Kate
Harvard University
Hunting Rituals

Homiak, John P.
Smithsonian Institution
Rastafari

Hoover, Kara C.
Georgia State University
Liminoid

Hoskins, Janet
University of Southern California
Calendrical Rituals

Houk, James
Louisiana State University
Afro-Brazilian
Cannibalism
Communitas
Shamanism

Irvin, Dale
New York Theological Seminary
Millennialism

Jakobsh, Doris R.
Renison College, University of Waterloo
Sikhism

Jeffrey, Jaclyn
Texas A&M University
Academic Rituals
Camp Meetings
Performance, Ritual of
Personal Rituals

Johnson, Paul C.
University of Missouri, Columbia
Misrecognition and Rituals

Kassim, Husain
University of Central Florida
Islam
Ramadan

Kowalski OSB, Fr. Matthew
Blue Cloud Abbey
Monastic Communities

Kremser, Manfred
University of Vienna
Afro-Caribbean

Lansford, Tom
University of Southern Mississippi
Africa, West
Agricultural Rituals
Asceticism
Australian Aboriginal

Lazich, Michael C.
Buffalo State College
Baha'i

Lett, James
Indian River Community College
Scientific Skepticism and Religious Rituals

Levinson, David
Berkshire Publishing Group
Evil Eye
Healing and Rituals
Sacrifice and Offerings
Snake Handling

Long, Thomas L.
Thomas Nelson Community College
Purity and Pollution

Magliocco, Sabina
California State University, Northridge
Paganism and Neo-Paganism
Wicca

Malone, Patrick W.
Living Hope Presbyterian Church
Passover
Yom Kippur

Melton, J. Gordon
Shakers

Miladinov, Marina
New Europe College
Haircutting Rituals

Neely, Sharlotte
Northern Kentucky University
Native Americans: Northeast
Native Americans: Plains

Nelson, John K.
University of San Francisco
Shinto

Neumann, Caryn E.
Ohio State University
Taoism

Nilsson Stutz, Liv
Lund University
Body and Rituals

Ogungbile, David
Obafemi Awolowo University
Puberty Rites

Paffenroth, Kim
Iona College
Sacred Places

Pollak-Eltz, Angelina
Univeridad Catolica Andres Bello
Ecstatic Worship

Pollock, Kelly
Goleta, California
Gender Rituals

Porter, Jennifer
Memorial University
Star Trek Conventions

Procario-Foley, Elena G.
Iona College
Judaism
Mardi Gras

Rasing, Thera
Leiden University
Africa, Central

Ratsirahonana, Serge
State University of New York, Stonybrook
Madagascar

Rausch, Thomas P.
Loyola Marymount University
Eucharistic Rituals

Richardson, Annette
University of Alberta
Native Americans: Arctic
Oaths and Ordeals

Rothgery, Eric J.
University of Iowa
Prayer

Salamone, Frank A.
Iona College
Azande
Christmas
Easter
Humor and Rituals
Jainism
Music
Nature Worship
Rituals of Rebellion
Santeria
Sufism
Symbol and Ritual
Television and Ritual
Yoruba

Sillitoe, Paul
University of Durham
Melanesia

Simonelli, Jeanne
Wake Forest University
Language, Literacy, and Ritual

Stevens, Jr., Phillips
State University of New York, Buffalo
Divination
Exorcism
Magic
Sorcery

Sutlive, Jr., Vinson H.
College of William and Mary
Iban
Identity Rituals
Ritual Control
Ritual Specialists

Tait, Edwin
Chatham, New York
Protestantism

Terian, Sara Kärkkäinen
Iona College
Crisis Rituals
Marriage Rituals

Toliver, Susan D.
Iona College
African-American Churches
Kwanzaa
Zulu

Tumminia, Diana G.
California State University, Sacramento
Blood Rituals
Possession and Trance
Satanic Rituals

Turner, Edith
University of Virginia
Communitas, Rites of

Williams, Brett
American University
Taboo

Wilson, Patrick C.
University of Lethbridge
South America: Highland

Woodruff, Jennifer Lynn
Drew University
Protestantism

Wright, Patricia
State University of New York at Stony Brook
Madagascar

Wu, Fatima
Loyola Marymount University
China: Popular Religion

Yawney, Carole
York University
Rastafari

Index

Note: Main encyclopedia entries are indicated by **bold** type.

Index

Index